A GRAMMAR OF

MODERN

INDO-EUROPEAN

Third Edition

Part I.	Language and Culture
Part II.	Phonology & Morphology
Part III.	Syntax
Part IV.	Texts & Dictionary Etymology

Carlos Quiles

Fernando López-Menchero

Version 5.20 (October 2012)

INDO-EUROPEAN LANGUAGE ASSOCIATION
Avda. Sta. María de la Cabeza, 3, E-LL, Badajoz 06001, Spain.
Badajoz – Leg. Dep. BA-145-0 (2006) | Sevilla – Leg. Dep. SE -4405-2007 U.E.
ISBN-13: 978-1461022138 | ISBN-10: 1461022134
Information, translations and revisions of this title: <http://indo-european.info/>
Discussion on Modern Indo-European at <http://dnghu.org/forum/>

Printed in the European Union

Published by the *Indo-European Language Association* <http://dnghu.org/>

Images taken or modified from Wikimedia projects are referenced with description and author-date, with usernames (or real names, if available), and links to the websites of origin in the *Bibliography* section, at the end of this book, unless they are in the public domain (PD).

The cover image has been modified from a photo of the *Solvognen* (The Sun Carriage) from the Bronze Age, at display at the National Museum (*Nationalmuseet*) in Denmark (Malene Thyssen 2004). For the epithet 'wheel of the sun', see §10.8.

Table of Contents

TABLE OF CONTENTS **3**

PREFACE **9**

GUIDE TO THE READER 13

ACKNOWLEDGEMENTS 15

CONSIDERATIONS OF METHOD 16

The Three-Dorsal Theory *19*

The Loss of Laryngeals *27*

CONVENTIONS USED IN THIS BOOK 33

Writing System *35*

Modern Indo-European *42*

1. INTRODUCTION **49**

1.1. THE INDO-EUROPEAN LANGUAGE FAMILY 49

1.2. TRADITIONAL VIEWS 51

1.3. THE THEORY OF THE THREE STAGES 53

1.4. THE PROTO-INDO-EUROPEAN *URHEIMAT* 58

1.5. OTHER ARCHAEOLINGUISTIC THEORIES 68

1.6. RELATIONSHIP TO OTHER LANGUAGES 70

1.7. INDO-EUROPEAN DIALECTS 72

Schleicher's Fable: From PIE to Modern English *72*

1.7.1. Northern Indo-European dialects *75*

1.7.2. Southern Indo-European Dialects *107*

1.7.3. Anatolian Languages *126*

2. PHONOLOGY **133**

2.1. CLASSIFICATION OF SOUNDS 133

2.2. PRONUNCIATION 136

2.3. SYLLABLES 138

2.4. PROSODY 141

2.5. ACCENT 142

2.6. VOWEL CHANGE 145

2.7. CONSONANT CHANGE 147

3. WORDS AND THEIR FORMS **151**

3.1. The Parts of Speech ... 151
3.2. Inflection ... 152
3.3. Root and Stem ... 153
3.4. Gender ... 156
3.5. Number ... 159

4. NOUNS ... 161

4.1. Declension of Nouns ... 161
4.2. First Declension ... 166
4.2.1. First Declension Paradigm ... 166
4.2.2. First Declension in Examples ... 167
4.2.3. The Plural in the First Declension ... 168
4.3. Second Declension ... 169
4.3.1. Second Declension Paradigm ... 169
4.3.2. Second Declension in Examples ... 170
4.5.3. The Plural in the Second Declension ... 171
4.4. Third Declension ... 172
4.4.1. Third Declension Paradigm ... 172
4.4.2. In i, u ... 173
4.4.3. In Diphthong ... 175
4.4.4. The Plural in the Third and Fourth Declension ... 176
4.5. Fourth Declension ... 177
4.5.1. Fourth Declension Paradigm ... 177
4.5.2. In Occlusive, m, l ... 178
4.5.3. In r, n, s ... 180
4.5.4. The Plural in the Fourth Declension ... 181
4.6. Variable Nouns ... 181
4.7. Inflection Types ... 182
Excursus: Nominal Accent-Ablaut Patterns ... 184
4.8. Number Developments: The Dual ... 188

5. ADJECTIVES ... 189

5.1. Inflection of Adjectives ... 189
5.2. The Motion ... 189
5.3. Adjective Specialisation ... 191
5.4. Comparison of Adjectives ... 193

5.5. NUMERALS 195
5.5.1. Classification of Numerals *195*
5.5.2. Cardinals and Ordinals *196*
5.5.3. Declension of Cardinals and Ordinals *199*
5.5.4. Distributives *201*
5.5.5. Numeral Adverbs *202*
5.5.6. Multiplicatives *203*

6. PRONOUNS 205
6.1. ABOUT THE PRONOUNS 205
6.2. PERSONAL PRONOUNS 205
6.3. REFLEXIVE PRONOUNS 207
6.4. POSSESSIVE PRONOUNS 208
6.5. ANAPHORIC PRONOUNS 208
6.6. DEMONSTRATIVE PRONOUNS 209
6.7. INTERROGATIVE AND INDEFINITE PRONOUNS 211
6.7.1. Introduction *211*
6.7.2. Compounds *213*
6.7.3. Correlatives *214*
6.8. RELATIVE PRONOUNS 215
6.9. OTHER PRONOUNS 216

7. VERBS 217
7.1. INTRODUCTION 217
7.1.1. Voice, Mood, Tense, Person, Number *217*
7.1.2. Voice *218*
7.1.3. Moods *220*
7.1.4. Aspect *220*
7.1.5. Tenses of the Finite Verb *221*
7.2. FORMS OF THE VERB 221
7.2.1. The Verbal Stems *221*
7.2.2. Verb-Endings *223*
7.2.3. The Thematic Vowel *228*
7.3. THE CONJUGATIONS 229
7.4. THE FOUR STEMS 233
7.4.1. Tense-Stems and Verb Derivation *233*

7.4.2. The Present Stem *235*
7.4.3. The Aorist Stem *246*
7.4.4. The Perfect Stem *249*
7.5. MOOD STEMS 251
7.7. NOUN AND ADJECTIVE FORMS 255
7.8. CONJUGATED EXAMPLES 260
7.8.1. Thematic Verbs *260*
7.8.2. Athematic Inflection *265*
7.8.3. Common PIE Stems *269*
7.9. VERBAL COMPOSITION 271
7.10. THE VERBAL ACCENT 271
8. PARTICLES 273
8.1. PARTICLES 273
8.2. ADVERBS 275
8.3. DERIVATION OF ADVERBS 275
8.4. PREPOSITIONS 277
8.5. CONJUNCTIONS 280
8.6. INTERJECTIONS 282
9. MORPHOSYNTAX 285
9.1. VERBAL MORPHOSYNTAX 285
9.1.1. Person *285*
9.1.2. Tense-Aspect and Mood *285*
9.1.3. Voice *289*
9.2. NOMINAL MORPHOSYNTAX 290
9.2.1. Nominative *290*
9.2.2. Vocative *290*
9.2.3. Accusative *291*
9.2.4. Instrumental *292*
9.2.5. Dative *293*
9.2.6. Ablative *294*
9.2.7. Genitive *294*
9.2.8. Locative *295*
9.2.9. Case Forms: Adverbial Elements *295*
10. SENTENCE SYNTAX 299

10.1. THE SENTENCE 299
10.1.1. Kinds of Sentences *300*
10.1.2. Nominal Sentence *302*
10.1.3. Verbal Sentence *304*
10.2. SENTENCE MODIFIERS 305
10.2.1. Intonation Patterns *305*
10.2.2. Sentence Delimiting Particles *308*
10.3. VERBAL MODIFIERS 309
10.3.1. Declarative Sentences *309*
10.3.2. Interrogative Sentences *310*
10.3.3. Negative Sentences *312*
10.4. NOMINAL MODIFIERS 314
10.4.1. Adjective and Genitive Constructions *314*
10.4.2. Compounds *316*
10.4.3. Determiners in Nominal Phrases *321*
10.4.4. Apposition *322*
10.5. MODIFIED FORMS OF PIE SIMPLE SENTENCES 323
10.5.1. Coordination *323*
10.5.2. Complementation *326*
10.5.3. Subordinate Clauses *328*
10.6. SYNTACTIC CATEGORIES 335
10.6.1. Particles as Syntactic Means of Expression *335*
10.6.2. Marked Order in Sentences *338*
10.6.3. Topicalisation with Reference to Emphasis *338*
10.6.4. Wackernagel's Law and the placement of clitics *341*
10.7. PHRASE AND SENTENCE PROSODY 344
10.8. POETRY 345
10.9. NAMES OF PERSONS 348

APPENDIX I: INDO-EUROPEAN IN USE 353

I.1. KOMTLOQJOM (CONVERSATION) 353
I.2. HORATJOSJO KANMṆ (*HORATII CARMINVM*) 356
I.3. THE NEW TESTAMENT IN INDO-EUROPEAN 358
I.3.1. Pater Nos *(Lord's Prayer)* *358*
I.3.2. *Slwēje Marijā* *(Hail Mary)* *359*
I.3.2. **Kréddhēmi** *(Nicene Creed)* *359*

I.3.3. Noudós Sūnús (Parable of the Prodigal Son) ... *362*

I.3.4. Newom suwéistunjom (New Testament) – Jōhanēs, 1, 1-14 ... *367*

I.4. THE RIGVEDA IN INDO-EUROPEAN ... 369

APPENDIX II: LATE INDO-EUROPEAN LEXICON ... 371

FORMAL ASPECTS ... 371

II.1. ENGLISH – LATE INDO-EUROPEAN ... 373

II.2. LATE INDO-EUROPEAN – ENGLISH ... 411

APPENDIX III: IN-DEPTH ANALYSIS ... 491

III.1. ROOT NOUNS ... 491

III.2. PRONOUNS ... 496

III.2.1. Indefinite Pronouns ... *496*

III.2.2. Demonstrative Pronouns ... *497*

III.2.3. Personal Pronouns ... *498*

III.3. WORD FORMATION: COMMON PIE LENGTHENINGS AND SUFFIXES ... 502

III.4. PHONETIC RECONSTRUCTION ... 509

III.4.1. Consonants ... *509*

III.4.2. Vowels and syllabic consonants ... *510*

BIBLIOGRAPHY AND FURTHER READING ... 513

ONLINE RESOURCES ... 516

Wikipedia ... *516*

Images and maps ... *517*

BIOGRAPHY ... 519

PREFACE

In this newer edition of our Grammar, we follow the first intention of this work, trying not to include personal opinions, but a collection of the latest, most reasoned academic papers on the latest reconstructible PIE, providing everything that might be useful for the teaching and learning of Indo-European as a living language.

With that aim in mind, and with our compromise to follow the scientific method, we have revised the whole text in search for out-dated material and unexplained forms, as well as inconsistencies in reconstructions or conventions. We have also restricted the amount of marginal choices in favour of the general agreement, so that we could offer a clear, sober, and commonly agreed manual to learn Indo-European.

The approach featured in this book for more than half a decade already is similar to the one followed in Gamkrelidze–Ivanov (1994-1995), and especially to that followed by Adrados–Bernabé–Mendoza (1995-1998). Both returned to (and revised) the 'Brugmannian' Indo-European, the historical result of the development of certain isoglosses, both phonetic (loss of laryngeals, with the development of brief and long vowel system) and morphological (polythematic system in noun and verb, innovations in their inflection).

Adrados–Bernabé–Mendoza (1995-1998) distinguished between Late Indo-European and its parent-language *Indo-Hittite* – laryngeal, without distinction in vowel length, monothematic system. We developed that trend further, focussing on a post-Late Indo-European period, in search for a more certain, post-laryngeal IE, to avoid the *merged laryngeal* puzzle of the 'disintegrating Indo-European' of Bomhard (1984), and the conventional notation of a *schwa indogermanicum* (kept in Adrados–Bernabé–Mendoza), most suitable for a description of a complex period of phonetic change – which is possibly behind the *flight* of all other available modern works on PIE to the highly theoretical (but in all other respects clear and straightforward) PIH phonology. Morphology and syntax remain thus nearest to the older IE languages attested, always compared to Anatolian material, but avoiding the temporal inconsistencies that are found throughout the diachronic reconstructions in other, current manuals.

We try to fill the void that Gamkrelidze–Ivanov and Adrados–Bernabé–Mendoza left by following works (Lehmann 1972, Rix 1986, etc.) that already differentiated PIH from Late Indo-European, trying to "see the three-stage theory to the bitter end. Once established the existence of the three-staged IE, a lot must still be done. We have to define the detail, and we must explain the reason for the evolution, which formal elements does PIE deal with, and how they are ascribed to the new functions and categories. These developments shall influence the history of individual languages, which will have to be rewritten. Not only in the field of morphology, but also in phonetics and syntax" (Adrados–Bernabé–Mendoza 1995-1998).

Apart from a trustable reconstruction of the direct ancestors of the older IE languages (North-West Indo-European, Proto-Greek and Proto-Indo-Iranian), this work 'corrupts' the natural language – like any classical language grammar – with the intention to show a living language, and the need to establish some minimal writing conventions to embellish the phonetic notation. The question 'why not learn Indo-European as a living language?' arises from the same moment on when reconstruction is focussed on a (scientifically) conservative approach – an ultimate consequence of the three-stage-theory, and the search for more certain reconstructions –, yielding a reliable language system. A language system free from the need for theoretical artifices, or personal opinions on 'original' forms, that try to fill unending phonetic, morphological and syntactical uncertainties of the current diachronic PIE reconstruction.

As the learned reader might have already inferred, the question of "natural" vs. "artificial" is not easily answered concerning ancient languages. Ancient Greek phonetics, for example, is known through internal as well as external reconstruction, and the actual state of the art is largely based on the body of evidence discussed extensively by linguists and philologists of the nineteenth and twentieth centuries, with lots of questions unsolved. Furthermore, Ancient Greek is not one language; in fact, there are many dialects, each with different periods, and different representations of their sounds, all of which account for what we know with the unitary name *Ancient Greek*. Another example is Sanskrit, retained as different historical linguistic stages and dialects through oral tradition. Its first writings and grammatical rules were laid down centuries after it had ceased to be spoken, and centuries earlier before it became *the* classical Indian language. Latin is indeed not different from the above examples, being systematised in the so-called classical period, while a real, dialectally and temporarily variable Vulgar Latin was used by the different peoples who lived in the Roman Empire, making e.g. some questions over the *proper* pronunciation still debated today.

The interest in the study and use of Indo-European as a living language today is equivalent to the interest in the study and use of these ancient languages as learned languages in the the Byzantine Empire, India and Mediaeval Europe, respectively. With regard to certainty in reconstruction, Late Indo-European early dialects are not *less natural* than these classical languages were in the past. Even modern languages, like English, are to a great extent *learned* languages, in which social trends and linguistic artifices are constantly dividing between *formal* and *colloquial*, *educated* and *uneducated*, often simply *good* or *bad* usage of the language.

About the question of 'dead' vs. 'living' languages, heated debate is e.g. held on the characterisation of Sanskrit, which is not as other dead languages, being spoken, written and read today in India. The notion of the *death* of a language remains thus in an unclear realm between academia and public opinion.

I prefer to copy Michael Coulson's words from the preface of a great introductory work on Sanskrit (from the *Teach Yourself®* series), referring originally to the way Indians used Sanskrit as a learned (and dead) language, far beyond the rules that grammarians had imposed. I think this text should also be valid if we substituted 'Sanskrit' for 'Indo-European'; the 'rules' of 'Sanskrit grammarians' for the 'reconstruction' of 'IE scholars'; and the 'renowned Sanskrit writers' for the 'potential future IE writers':

> «By [the time Kālidāsa, a writer fl. ca. the fifth century AD, lived] Sanskrit was not a mother tongue, but a language to be studied and consciously mastered. This transformation had come about through a gradual process, the beginnings of which are no doubt earlier than Pāṇini [ancient Indian Sanskrit grammarian, fl. fourth century BC] himself. (...) Kālidāsa learnt his Sanskrit from the rules of a grammarian living some 700 years before his time. Such a situation may well strike the Western reader as paradoxical. Our nearest parallel is in the position of Latin in Medieval Europe. There is, however, an important difference. Few would deny Cicero or Vergil a greater importance in Latin literature than any mediaeval author. Conversely, few Sanskritists would deny that the centre of gravity in Sanskrit literature lies somewhere in the first millennium AD, for all that its authors were writing in a so-called 'dead-language'.

On this point it may be useful to make a twofold distinction – between a living and a dead language, and between a natural and a learned one. A language is natural when it is acquired and used instinctively; it is living when people choose to converse and formulate ideas in it in preference to any other. To the modern Western scholar Sanskrit is a dead as well as a learned language. To Kālidāsa or Śaṅkara [ninth century Indian philosopher from a Dravidian-speaking region] it was a learned language but a living one. (The term 'learned is not entirely satisfactory, but the term 'artificial', which is the obvious complementary of 'natural', is normally reserved for application to totally constructed languages such as Esperanto.)

(...) Living languages, whether natural or learned, change and develop. But when a learned language such as literary English is closely tied to, and constantly revitalized by, a natural idiom, its opportunities for independent growth are limited. Sanskrit provides a fascinating example of a language developing in complete freedom from such constraints as an instrument of intellectual and artistic expression. To say that Classical Sanskrit was written in conformity with Pāṇini's rules is true, but in one sense entirely misleading. Pāṇini would have been astounded by the way in which Bāṇā or Bhavabhūti or Abhinavagupta handled the language. It is precisely the fact that Sanskrit writers insisted on using Sanskrit as a living and not as a dead language that has often troubled Western scholars. W. D. Whitney, a great but startlingly arrogant American Sanskritist of the nineteenth century, says of the Classical language: 'Of linguistic history there is next to nothing in it all; but only a history of style, and this for the most part showing a gradual depravation, an increase of artificiality and an intensification of certain more undesirable features of the language – such as the use of passive constructions and of participles instead of verbs, and the substitution of compounds for sentences.' Why such a use of passives, participles and compounds should be undesirable, let alone depraved, is left rather vague, and while there have been considerable advances in linguistic science in the past fifty years there seems to have been nothing which helps to clarify or justify these strictures. Indeed, Whitney's words would not be worth resurrecting if strong echoes of them did not still survive in some quarters.

Acceptance of Pāṇini's rules implied a final stabilization of the phonology of Sanskrit, and also (at least in the negative sense that no form could be used which was not sanctioned by him) of its morphology. But Pāṇini did not fix syntax. To do so explicitly and incontrovertibly would be difficult in any language, given several ways of expressing the same idea and various other ways of expressing closely similar ideas.»

Badajoz, April 2011

GUIDE TO THE READER

A. ABBREVIATIONS

abl.: ablative
acc.: accusative
act.: active
adj.: adjective
adv.: adverb
Alb.: Albanian
Arm.: Armenian
aor.: aorist
aux.: auxiliary
Av: Avestan
BSl.: Balto-Slavic
CA: Common Anatolian
Cel.: Celtic
cf.: *confer* 'compare, contrast'
Cz.: Czech
dat.: dative
Du.: Dutch
e.g.: *exempli gratia* 'for example'
Eng.: English
esp.: especially
f.: feminine
fem.: feminine
gen.: genitive
Gaul.: Gaulish
Gk.: Greek
Gmc.: Proto-Germanic
Goth.: Gothic
Hitt.: Hittite
Hom.: Homeric
IE: Indo-European
IED: Late Indo-European dialects
imp.: imperative
imperf.: imperfect
Ind.-Ira.: Indo-Iranian
ins.: instrumental
int.: interrogative
Ita.: Italic
Lat.: Latin
LIE: Late Indo-European
Lith.: Lithuanian
Ltv.: Latvian
loc.: locative
Luw./Luv.: Luvian
Lyc.: Lycian
m.: masculine
NP: noun phrase
NWIE: North-West Indo-European
O: object
Obj.: object
O.Av.: Old Avestan
O.C.S.: Old Church Slavic
O.E.: Old English
O.Ind.: Old Indian
O.Ir.: Old Irish
O.H.G.: Old High German
O.Hitt.: Old Hittite
O.Lat.: Archaic Latin
O.Lith.: Old Lithuanin
O.N.: Old Norse
O.Pers.: Old Persian
O.Pruss.: Old Prussian
O.Russ.: Old Russian
opt.: optative
Osc.: Oscan
OSV: object-subject-verb order
OV: object-verb order
perf.: perfect
PAn: Proto-Anatolian
PGmc.: Pre-Proto-Germanic
PII: Proto-Indo-Iranian
PGk: Proto-Greek
Phryg: Phrygian
PIE: Proto-Indo-European
PIH: Proto-Indo-Hittite
pl.: plural
pres.: present
pron.: pronoun
Ptc.: particle
Russ.: Russian
sg.: singular
Skt.: Sanskrit
Sla.: Slavic
SOV: subject-object-verb order
subj.: subjunctive
SVO: subject-verb-object order
Toch.: Tocharian
Umb.: Umbrian
Ved.: Vedic
v.i.: *vide infra* 'see below'
VO: verb-object order

masc.: masculine
M.H.G.: Middle High German
mid.: middle-passive voice
MIE: Modern Indo-European
Myc.: Mycenaean
n.: neuter
neu.: neuter
nom.: nominative
voc.: vocative
VP: verb phrase
v.s.: *vide supra* 'see above'
VSO: verb-subject-object order
1st: first person
2nd: second person
3rd: third person

B. SYMBOLS

*	denotes a reconstructed form, not preserved in any written documents
**	denotes a reconstructed form through internal reconstruction
<	"comes from" or "is derived from"
→	"turns into" or "becomes"
-	indicates morpheme boundary, or separates off that part of a word that the reader should focus on
( )	encloses part of a word that is not relevant to the discussion, or that is an optional part
Ø	"zero desinence" or "zero-grade"
×	denotes a wrong formation

C. SPELLING CONVENTIONS

All linguistic forms are written in *italics*. The only exceptions are reconstructed IED forms, that are given in **boldface**; and in ***italics*** if morphemes or dialectal forms (from PII, PGk, or from East or West European). We use a non-phonetic writing for IEDs, following the conventions in *Writing System* (see below).

When representing word schemes:

C = consonant
R = resonant (r, l, m, n)
T = dental
K = occlusive
J = glide (j, w)
H = any laryngeal or merged laryngeal

V = vowel
V̄ = long vowel
I = i, u
° = *epenthetic* or *auxiliary* vowel
(conventionally, the symbol ° under the vocalic resonants is placed before it in these cases)
= syllabic limit

Citation: parenthetical referencing of author-date is used for frequently cited books (referenced in the Bibliography), and author-title for articles and other books.

ACKNOWLEDGEMENTS

I owe special and personal gratitude to my best friend and now fiancée Mayte, whose many lovely qualities do not include knowledge of or an interest in historical linguistics. But without her this never would have been written.

I have been extremely fortunate to benefit from Fernando López-Menchero's interest and from his innumerable contributions, revisions, and corrections. Without his deep knowledge of Ancient Greek and Latin, as well as his interest in the most recent research in IE studies, this grammar would have been unthinkable.

I have received the invaluable support of many colleagues and friends from the University of Extremadura (UEx), since we began publishing this book half a decade ago. The University has been crucial to this enterprise: first in 2005 when prof. Antonio Muñoz PhD, Vice-Dean of the Faculty of Library Science, expert in Business Information, as well as other signatories – doctors in Economics and English Philology –, supported this language revival project before the competition committee and afterwards; in 2006, when representatives of the Dean's office, of the Regional Government of Extremadura, and of the Mayor's office of Caceres, recognised our work awarding our project a prize in the "Entrepreneurship Competition in Imagination Society", organising and subsidising a *business trip* to Barcelona's most innovative projects; and in 2007, when we received the unconditional support of the Department of Classical Antiquity of the UEx.

Over the years I have also received feed-back from informed end-users, as well as from friends and members of the Indo-European Language Association, who were in the best position to judge such matters as the intelligibility and consistency of the whole. I am also indebted to Manuel Romero from *Imcrea Diseño Editorial*, for his help with the design and editorial management of the first printed edition.

The influence of the work of many recent scholars is evident on these pages. Those who are most often cited include (in alphabetical order): D.Q. Adams, F.R. Adrados David Anthony, R.S.P. Beekes, Emile Benveniste, Alberto Bernabé, Thomas Burrow, George Cardona, James Clackson, B.W. Fortson, Matthias Fritz, T.V. Gamkrelidze, Marija Gimbutas, Eric Hamp, V.V. Ivanov, Jay Jasanoff, Paul Kiparsky, Alwin Kloekhorst, F.H.H. Kortlandt, Jerzy Kuryłowicz, W.P. Lehmann, J.P. Mallory, Manfred Mayrhofer, Wolfgang Meid, Michael Meier-Brügger, Torsten Meissner, Craig Melchert, Julia Mendoza, Anna Morpurgo Davies, Norbert Oettinger, Edgar Polomé, C.J. Ruijgh, Paolo Ramat, Donald Ringe, Helmut Rix, A.L. Sihler, Sergei Starostin, J.L. Szemerényi, Francisco Villar, Calvert Watkins, M.L. West.

CONSIDERATIONS OF METHOD

This work is intended for language learners, and is not conceived as a defence of personal research. Excerpts of texts from many different sources have been copied literally, especially regarding controversial or untreated aspects. We feel that, whereas the field of Indo-European studies is indeed mature, and knowledge is out there to be grasped, we lack a comprehensive summary of the available consensual theories, scattered over innumerable specialised personal books and articles.

We must begin this work by clearly exposing our intended working method in selecting and summing up the current available theories: it is basically, as it is commonly accepted today for PIE reconstruction, the comparative method, with the help of internal reconstruction.

NOTE. Adrados–Bernabé–Mendoza (1995-1998): "We think (...) that a linguist should follow, to establish relations among languages, linguistic methods. If then the results are coincident, or compatible, or might be perfected with those obtained by archaeologists, so much the better. But a mixed method creates all types of chain mistakes and arbitrary results. We have seen that many times. And a purely archaeological method like the one supported lately by Renfrew 1987 or, in certain moments, the same Gimbutas 1985, clashes with the results of Linguistics.

The method has to rely on [the comparative method and internal reconstruction]. We have already expressed our mistrust in the results based on typological comparisons with remote languages (glottalic theory, ergative, etc.). Now they are more frequent in books like Gamkelidze-Ivanov 1994-1995.

And fundamentally lexical comparisons should not be the first argument in comparisons, either. We do not doubt their interest in certain moments, e.g. to illuminate the history of Germanic in relation with Finnish. And they could have interest in different comparisons: with Uralo-Altaic languages, Semitic, Caucasic, Summerian, etc."

The guidelines that should be followed, as summarised by Beekes (1995):

1. "See what information is generated by internal reconstruction.
2. Collect all material that is relevant to the problem.
3. Try to look at the problem in the widest possible contact, thus in relation to everything else that may be connected with it. (...)
4. Assume that corresponding forms, that is to say, forms whose meaning (probably) and whose structures (probably) seem to be alike, all derive from one common ancestor.
5. The question of how deviant forms should be evaluated is a difficult one to answer. When such a form can be seen as an innovation within a particular language (or group of languages), the solution is that the form in question is

young and as such cannot be important for the reconstruction of the original form. Whenever a deviant form resists explanation it becomes necessary to consider the possibility that the very form in question may be one that preserves the original. (...)

6. For every solution the assumed (new) sound-laws must be phonetically probable, and the analogies must be plausible.
7. The reconstructed system must be probable (typological probability). If one should reconstruct a system which is found nowhere else in any of the known languages, there will always be, to say the least, reasons for doubt. On the other hand, every language is unique, and there is thus always the possibility that something entirely unknown must be reconstructed."

There are two main aspects of the comparative method as is usually applied that strikes the 'pure scientific' reader, though, always obsessed with adopting a *conservative* approach to research, in the sense of *security* or *reliability*. We shall take words from Claude Bernard's major discourse on scientific method, *An Introduction to the Study of Experimental Medicine (1865)*, to illustrate our point:

1. *Authority vs. Observation.* It is through observation that science is carried forward — not through uncritically accepting the authority of academic or scholastic sources. Observable reality is our only authority. "When we meet a fact which contradicts a prevailing theory, we must accept the fact and abandon the theory, even when the theory is supported by great names and generally accepted".

NOTE. Authority is certainly a commonly used, strong and generally sound basis to keep working on comparative grammar, though, because it this is a field based on 'pyramidal' reasoning and not experimental research. But authority should be questioned whenever it is needed. Authority – be it the view of the majority, or the opinion of a renowned linguist or linguistic school – do not mean anything, and ideas are not to be respected because of who supports (or supported) them.

2. *Verification and Disproof.* "Theories are only hypotheses, verified by more or less numerous facts. Those verified by the most facts are the best, but even then they are never final, never to be absolutely believed". What is rationally true is the only authority.

On hypothesis testing in science, decisions are usually made using a statistical *null-hypothesis test* approach. Regarding linguistics and its comparative method, sometimes authority is placed as null hypothesis or H_0 (as in many non-experimental sciences), while counter-arguments must take the H_1 position, and are therefore at disadvantage against the authority view.

If two theories show a strong argument against the basic H_0 ("nothing demonstrated"), and are therefore accepted as alternative explanations for an observed fact, then the most reasonable one must be selected as the new H_0, on the grounds of the *lex parsimoniae* (or the so-called *Ockham's razor*), whereby H_0 should be the competing hypothesis that makes the fewest new assumptions, when the hypotheses are equal in other respects (e.g. both sufficiently explain available data in the first place).

NOTE. The principle is often incorrectly summarised as "the simplest explanation is most likely the correct one". This summary is misleading, however, since the principle is actually focussed on shifting the burden of proof in discussions. That is, the Razor is a principle that suggests we should tend towards simpler theories until we can trade some simplicity for increased explanatory power. Contrary to the popular summary, the simplest available theory is sometimes a less accurate explanation. Philosophers also add that the exact meaning of "simplest" can be nuanced in the first place.

As an example of the applicability of the scientific method, we will take two difficult aspects of PIE reconstructions: the series of velars and the loss of laryngeals.

The problem with these particular reconstructions might be summarised by the words found in Clackson (2007): "It is often a fault of Indo-Europeanists to over-reconstruct, and to explain every development of the daughter languages through reconstruction of a richer system in the parent language."

THE THREE-DORSAL THEORY

PIE phonetic reconstruction is tied to the past: acceptance of three series of velars in PIE is still widespread today. We followed the reconstruction of 'palatovelars', according to general authority and convention, but we have changed minds since the first edition of this grammar.

Direct comparison in early IE studies, informed by the *centum-satem* isogloss, yielded the reconstruction of three rows of dorsal consonants in Late Indo-European by Bezzenberger (*Die indogermanischer Gutturalreihen*, 1890), a theory which became classic after Brugmann included it in the 2nd Edition of his *Grundriss*. It was based on vocabulary comparison: so e.g. from PIE **kṃtóm* 'hundred', there are so-called *satem* (*cf.* O.Ind. *śatám*, Av. *satəm*, Lith. *šimtas*, O.C.S. *sto*) and *centum* languages (*cf.* Gk. *-katón*, Lat. *centum*, Goth. *hund*, O.Ir. *cet*).

The palatovelars $*k^j$, $*g^j$, and $*g^{jh}$ were supposedly [k]- or [g]-like sounds which underwent a characteristic phonetic change in the *satemised* languages – three original "velar rows" had then become two in all Indo-European dialects attested. After that original belief, then, the centum group of languages merged the palatovelars $*k^j$, $*g^j$, and $*g^{jh}$ with the plain velars $*k$, $*g$, and $*g^h$, while the satem group of languages merged the labiovelars $*k^w$, $*g^w$, and $*g^{wh}$ with the plain velars $*k$,$*g$, and $*g^h$.

The reasoning for reconstructing three series was very *simple*: an easy and straightforward solution for the parent PIE language *must be* that it had *all* three rows found in the proto-languages, which would have merged into two rows depending on their dialectal (centum vs. satem) situation – even if no single IE dialect shows three series of velars. Also, for a long time this division was identified with an old dialectal division within IE, especially because both groups appeared not to overlap geographically: the centum branches were to the west of satem languages. Such an initial answer should be considered unsound today, at least as a starting-point to obtain a better explanation for this 'phonological puzzle' (Bernabé).

Many Indo-Europeanists still keep a distinction of three distinct series of velars for Late Indo-European (and also for Indo-Hittite), although research tend to show that the palatovelar series were a late phonetic development of certain satem dialects, later extended to others. This belief was originally formulated by Antoine Meillet (*De quelques difficulties de la théorie des gutturals indoeuropéennes*,

1893), and has been followed by linguists like Hirt (*Zur Lösung der Gutturalfrage im Indogermanischen*, 1899; *Indogermanische Grammatik, BD III, Das Nomen* 1927), Lehmann (*Proto-Indo-European Phonology*, 1952), Georgiev (*Introduzione allo studio delle lingue indoeuropee*, 1966), Bernabé (*"Aportaciones al studio fonológico de las guturales indoeuropeas", Em. 39*, 1971), Steensland (*Die Distribution der urindogermanischen sogenannten Guttrale*, 1973), Miller (*"Pure velars and palatals in Indo-European: a rejoinder to Magnusson", Linguistics 178*, 1976), Allen (*"The PIE velar series: Neogrammarian and other solutions in the light of attested parallels", TPhS*, 1978), Kortlandt (*"H2 and oH2", LPosn*, 1980), Shields (*"A new look at the centum/satem Isogloss", KZ* 95, 1981), etc.

NOTE. There is a general trend to reconstruct labiovelars and plain velars, so that the hypothesis of two series of velars is usually identified with this theory. Among those who support two series of velars there is, however, a minority who consider the labiovelars a secondary development from the pure velars, and reconstruct only velars and palatovelars (Kuryłowicz), already criticised by Bernabé, Steensland, Miller and Allen. Still less acceptance had the proposal to reconstruct only a labiovelar and a palatal series (Magnusson).

Arguments in favour of only two series of velars include:

1. In most circumstances palatovelars appear to be allophones resulting from the neutralisation of the other two series in particular phonetic circumstances. Their dialectal articulation was probably constrained, either to an especial phonetic environment (as Romance evolution of Latin *k* before *e* and *i*), either to the analogy of alternating phonetic forms.

NOTE. However, it is difficult to pinpoint exactly what the circumstances of the allophony are, although it is generally accepted that neutralisation occurred after *s* and *u*, and often before *r* or *a*; also apparently before *m* and *n* in some Baltic dialects. The original allophonic distinction was disturbed when the labiovelars were merged with the plain velars. This produced a new phonemic distinction between palatal and plain velars, with an unpredictable alternation between palatal and plain in related forms of some roots (those from original plain velars) but not others (those from original labiovelars). Subsequent analogical processes generalised either the plain or palatal consonant in all forms of a particular root. Those roots where the plain consonant was generalised are those traditionally reconstructed as having plain velars in the parent language, in contrast to palatovelars.

2. The reconstructed palatovelars and plain velars appear mostly in complementary distributions, what supports their explanation as allophones of the same phonemes. Meillet (*Introduction à l'étude comparative des langues indo-européennes*, 1903) established the contexts in which there are only velars: before

a, *r*, and after *s*, *u*; while Georgiev (1966) clarified that the palatalisation of velars had been produced before *e*, *i*, *j*, and before liquid or nasal or *w* + *e*, *i*, offering statistical data supporting his conclusions. The presence of palatalised velar before *o* is then produced because of analogy with roots in which (due to the ablaut) the velar phoneme is found before *e* and *o*, so the alternation **kʲe/*ko* would be levelled as **kʲe/*kʲo*.

3. There is residual evidence of various sorts in satem languages of a former distinction between velar and labiovelar consonants:

- In Sanskrit and Balto-Slavic, in some environments, resonants become *iR* after plain velars but *uR* after labiovelars.
- In Armenian, some linguists assert that k^w is distinguishable from *k* before front vowels.
- In Albanian, some linguists assert that k^w and g^w are distinguishable from *k* and *g* before front vowels.

NOTE. This evidence shows that the labiovelar series was distinct from the plain velar series in LIE, and could not have been a secondary development in the centum languages. However, it says nothing about the palatovelar vs. plain velar series. When this debate initially arose, the concept of a phoneme and its historical emergence was not clearly understood, however, and as a result it was often claimed (and sometimes is still claimed) that evidence of three-way velar distinction in the history of a particular IE language indicates that this distinction must be reconstructed for the parent language. This is theoretically unsound, as it overlooks the possibility of a secondary origin for a distinction.

4. The palatovelar hypothesis would support an evolution $k^j \rightarrow k$ of centum dialects, i.e. a move of palatovelars to back consonants, what is clearly against the general tendency of velars to move forward its articulation and palatalise in these environments. A trend of this kind is unparallelled and therefore typologically *a priori* unlikely (although not impossible), and needs that other assumptions be made.

5. The plain velar series is statistically rarer than the other two in a PIE lexicon reconstructed with three series; it appears in words entirely absent from affixes, and most of them are of a phonetic shape that could have inhibited palatalisation.

NOTE. Common examples are:

- **yug-óm* 'yoke': Hitt. *iukan*, Gk. *zdugón*, Skt. *yugá-*, Lat. *iugum*, O.C.S. *igo*, Goth. *juk*.
- **gʰosti-* 'guest, stranger': Lat. *hostis*, Goth. *gasts*, O.C.S. *gostĭ*.

"The paradigm of the word for 'yoke' could have shown a palatalizing environment only in the vocative **yug*-e, which is unlikely ever to have been in common usage, and the word for 'stranger' *ghosti-* only ever appears with the vocalism *o*". (Clackson 2007).

6. Alternations between plain velars and palatals are common in a number of roots across different satem languages, where the same root appears with a palatal in some languages but a plain velar in others.

NOTE. This is consistent with the analogical generalisation of one or another consonant in an originally alternating paradigm, but difficult to explain otherwise:

- **ak-/ok-* 'sharp', *cf.* Lith. *akúotas*, O.C.S. *ostrŭ*, O.Ind. *asrís*, Arm. *aseln*, but Lith. *asrùs*.
- **akmon-* 'stone', *cf.* Lith. *akmuõ*, O.C.S. *kamy*, O.Ind. *áśma*, but Lith. *âsmens*.
- **keu-* 'shine', *cf.* Lith. *kiáune*, Russ. *kuna*, O.Ind. *svas*, Arm. *sukh*.
- **bʰleg-* 'shine', *cf.* O.Ind. *bhárgas*, Lith. *balgans*, O.C.S. *blagŭ*, but Ltv. *blâzt*.
- **gʰerdʰ-* 'enclose', O.Ind. *gṛhá*, Av. *gərəda*, Lith. *gardas*, O.C.S. *gradu*, Lith. *zardas*, Ltv. *zârdas*.
- **swekros* 'father-in-law', *cf.* O.Sla. *svekry*, O.Ind. *śvaśru*.
- **peku-* 'stock animal'; *cf.* O.Lith. *pẽkus*, Skt. *paśu-*, Av. *pasu-*.
- **kleus-* 'hear'; *cf.* Skt. *śrus*, O.C.S. *slušatĭ*, Lith. *kláusiu*.

A rather weak argument in favour of palatovelars rejecting these finds is found in Clackson (2007): "Such forms could be taken to reflect the fact that Baltic is geographically peripheral to the satem languages and consequently did not participate in the palatalization to the same degree as other languages".

7. There are different pairs of *satemised* and *non-satemised* velars found within the same language.

NOTE. The old argument proposed by Brugmann (and later copied by many dictionaries) about "*centum loans*" is not tenable today. For more on this, see Szemerény (1978, review from Adrados–Bernabé–Mendoza 1995-1998), Mayrhofer *("Das Guttrualproblem un das indogermanische Wort für Hase", Studien zu indogermanische Grundsprache,* 1952), Bernabé (1971). Examples include:

- **selg-* 'throw', *cf.* O.Ind. *srjáti, sargas*
- **kau/keu-* 'shout', *cf.* Lith. *kaukti*, O.C.S. *kujati*, Russ. *sova* (as Gk. *kauax*); O.Ind. *kauti, suka-*.
- **kleu-* 'hear', Lith. *klausýti, slove*, O.C.S. *slovo*; O.Ind. *karnas, sruti, srósati, śrnóti, sravas*.
- **leuk-*, O.Ind. *rokás, ruśant-*.

8. The number and periods of satemisation trends reconstructed for the different branches are not coincident.

NOTE. So for example Old Indian shows two stages,

- PIE **k* → O.Ind. *s*
- PIE *$k^{w}e$, *$k^{w}i$ → O.Ind. *ke, ki*; PIE **ske*, **ski* > O.Ind. *c* (*cf. cim, candra*, etc.)

In Slavic, three stages are found,

- PIE **k*→*s*
- PIE *$k^{w}e$, *$k^{w}i$→*č* (*čto, čelobek*)
- PIE *$k^{w}oi$→**koi*→**ke* gives *ts* (as Sla. *tsená*)

9. In most attested languages which present aspirates as a result of the so-called palatovelars, the palatalisation of other phonemes is also attested (e.g. palatalisation of labiovelars before *e, i*), what may indicate that there is an old trend to palatalise all possible sounds, of which the palatalisation of velars is the oldest attested result.

NOTE. It is generally believed that satemisation could have started as a late dialectal 'wave', which eventually affected almost all PIE dialectal groups. The origin is probably to be found in velars followed by *e, i*, even though alternating forms like **gen/gon* caused natural analogycal corrections within each dialect, which obscures still more the original situation. Thus, non-satemised forms in so-called satem languages would be non-satemised remains of the original situation, just as Spanish has *feliz* and not ×*heliz*, or *fácil* and not ×*hácil*, or French *facile* and *nature*, and not ×*fêle* or ×*nûre* as one should expect from its phonetic evolution.

10. The existence of satem languages like Armenian in the Balkans, a centum territory, and the presence of Tocharian, a centum dialect, in Central Asia, being probably a northern IE dialect.

NOTE. The traditional explanation of a three-way dorsal split requires that all centum languages share a common innovation that eliminated the palatovelar series, due to the a priori unlikely move of palatovelars to back consonants (see above). Unlike for the satem languages, however, there is no evidence of any areal connection among the centum languages, and in fact there is evidence against such a connection – the centum languages are geographically noncontiguous. Furthermore, if such an areal innovation happened, we would expect to see some dialect differences in its implementation (*cf.* the above differences between Balto-Slavic and Indo-Iranian), and residual evidence of a distinct palatalised series. In fact, however, neither type of evidence exists, suggesting that there was never a palatovelar series in the centum languages. (Evidence does exist for a distinct labiovelar series in the satem languages, though; see above.)

11. A system of two gutturals, velars and labiovelars, is a linguistic anomaly, isolated in the IE occlusive subsystem – there are no parallel oppositions b^{w}-*b*, p^{w}-*p*, t^{w}-*t*, d^{w}-*d*, etc. Only one feature, their pronunciation with an accompanying rounding of the lips, helps distinguish them from each other. Such a system has

been attested in some older IE languages. A system of three gutturals – palatovelars, velars and labiovelars –, with a threefold distinction isolated in the occlusive system, is still less likely.

NOTE. In the two-dorsal system, labiovelars turn velars before *-u*, and there are some neutralisation positions which help identify labiovelars and velars; also, in some contexts (e.g. before *-i*, *-e*) velars tend to move forward its articulation and eventually palatalise. Both trends led eventually to centum and satem dialectalisation.

Those who support the model of the threefold distinction in PIE cite evidence from Albanian (Pedersen) and Armenian (Pisani), that they seem to treat plain velars differently from the labiovelars in at least some circumstances, as well as the fact that Luwian could have had distinct reflexes of all three series.

NOTE 1. It is disputed whether Albanian shows remains of two or three series (*cf.* Ölberg *"Zwei oder drei Gutturaldreihen? Vom Albanischen aus gesehen" Scritti...Bonfante* 1976; Kortlandt 1980; Pänzer *"Ist das Französische eine Satem-Sprache? Zu den Palatalisierung im Ur-Indogermanischen und in den indogermanischen Einzelsprachen", Festschrift für J. Hübschmidt,* 1982), although the fact that only the worst and one of the most recently attested (and neither isolated nor remote) IE dialect could be the only one to show some remains of the oldest phonetic system is indeed very unlikely. Clackson (2007), supporting the three series: "Albanian and Armenian are sometimes brought forward as examples of the maintenance of three separate dorsal series. However, Albanian and Armenian are both satem languages, and, since the $*k^j$ series has been palatalised in both, the existence of three separate series need not disprove the two-dorsal theory for PIE; they might merely show a failure to merge the unpalatalised velars with the original labio-velars."

NOTE 2. Supporters of the palatovelars cite evidence from Luwian, an Anatolian language, which supposedly shows a three-way velar distinction $*k^j \rightarrow z$ (probably [ts]); $*k \rightarrow k$; $*k^w \rightarrow ku$ (probably [k^w]), as defended by Melchert (*"Reflexes of $*h_3$ in Anatolian", Sprache 38* 1987). So, the strongest argument in favour of the traditional three-way system is that the the distinction supposedly derived from Luwian findings must be reconstructed for the parent language. However, the underlying evidence "hinges upon especially difficult or vague or otherwise dubious etymologies" (see Sihler 1995); and, even if those findings are supported by other evidence in the future, it is obvious that Luwian might also have been in contact with *satemisation* trends of other Late IE dialects, that it might have developed its own satemisation trend, or that maybe the whole system was remade within the Anatolian branch. Clackson (2007), supporting the three series, states: "This is strong independent evidence for three separate dorsal series, but the number of examples in support of the change is small, and we still have a far from perfect understanding of many aspects of Anatolian historical phonology."

Also, one of the most difficult problems which subsists in the interpretation of the satemisation as a phonetic wave is that, even though in most cases the variation $*k^j/k$ may be attributed either to a phonetic environment or to the analogy of alternating apophonic forms, there are some cases in which neither one nor the other may be applied, i.e. it is possible to find words with velars in the same environments as words with palatals.

NOTE. Compare for example **ok*ʲ*tō(u)*, eight, which presents k before an occlusive in a form which shows no change (to suppose a syncope of an older **ok*ʲ*itō*, as does Szemerényi, is an explanation *ad hoc*). Other examples in which the palatalisation cannot be explained by the next phoneme nor by analogy are **swekru-* 'husband's mother', **akmōn* 'stone', **peku* 'cattle', which are among those not shared by all satem languages. Such unexplained exceptions, however, are not sufficient to consider the existence of a third row of 'later palatalised' velars (see Bernabé 1971; Cheng & Wang *"Sound change: actuation and implementation", Lg. 51,* 1975), although there are still scholars who come back to the support of the hypothesis of three velars. So e.g. Tischler 1990 (reviewed in Meier-Brügger 2003): "The centum-satem isogloss is not to be equated with a division of Indo-European, but rather represents simply one isogloss among many...examples of 'centum-like aspects' in satem languages and of 'satem-like aspects' in centum languages that may be evaluated as relics of the original three-part plosive system, which otherwise was reduced everywhere to a two-part system."

Newer trends to support the old assumptions include e.g. Huld (1997, reviewed in Clackson 2007), in which the old palatal **k*ʲ is reconstructed as a true velar, and **k* as a uvular stop, so that the problem of the *a priori* unlikely and unparallelled merger of palatal with velar in centum languages is theoretically solved.

As it is clear from the development of the dorsal reconstruction, the theory that made the fewest assumptions was that an original Proto-Indo-European had two series of velars. These facts should have therefore shifted the burden of proof, already by the time Meillet (1893) rejected the proposal of three series; but the authority of Neogrammarians and well-established works of the last century, as well as traditional conventions, probably weighted (and still weight) more than reasons.

NOTE. More than half century ago we had already a similar opinion on the most reasonable reconstruction, that still today is not followed, as American Sanskritist Burrow (1955) shows: "The difficulty that arises from postulating a third series in the parent language, is that no more than two series (...) are found in any of the existing languages. In view of this it is exceedingly doubtful whether three distinct series existed in Indo-European. The assumption of the third series has been a convenience for the theoreticians, but it is unlikely to correspond to historical fact. Furthermore, on examination, this assumption does not turn out to be as convenient as would be wished. While it accounts in a way for correspondences like the above which otherwise would appear irregular, it still leaves over a considerable number of forms in the satem-languages which do not fit into the framework (...) Examples of this kind are particularly common in the Balto-Slavonic languages (...). Clearly a theory which leaves almost as many irregularities as it clears away is not very soundly established, and since these cases have to be explained as examples of dialect mixture in early Indo-European, it would appear simplest to apply the same theory to the rest. The case for this is particularly strong when we remember that when false etymologies are removed, when allowance is made for suffix alternation, and when the possibility of loss of labialization in the vicinity of the vowel u is considered (e.g. *kravíṣ-*, *ugrá-*), not many examples remain for the foundation of the theory."

Of course, we cannot (and we will probably never) actually *know* if there were two or three series of velars in LIE, or PIH, and because of that the *comparative method* should be preferred over *gut intuition*, historical authority, or convention, obstacles to the progress in a dynamic field like IE studies.

As Adrados (2005) puts it with bitterness: "Indo-Europeanists keep working on a unitary and flat PIE, that of Brugmann's reconstruction. A reconstruction prior to the decipherment of Hittite and the study of Anatolian! This is but other proof of the terrible conservatism that has seized the scientific discipline that is or must be Indo-European linguistics: it moves forward in the study of individual languages, but the general theory is paralised".

THE LOSS OF LARYNGEALS

Today, the reconstruction of consonantal sounds to explain what was reconstructed before as uncertain vocalic *schwa indogermanicum* or *schwa primum* is firmly accepted in IE studies in general, and there is a general agreement on where laryngeals should be reconstructed. Even the number and quality of those laryngeals is today a field of common agreement, although alternative number of laryngeals and proposals for their actual phonemic value do actually exist.

However, as Clackson (2007) sums up: "Particularly puzzling is the paradox that laryngeals are lost nearly everywhere, in ways that are strikingly similar, yet apparently unique to each language branch. We can of course assume some common developments already within PIE, such as the effect of the laryngeals *h_2 and *h_3 to change a neighbouring **e* to **a* or **o*, but the actual loss of laryngeals must be assumed to have taken place separately after the break-up of the parent language (...) it would have seemed a plausible assumption that the retention of *h_2, and possibly also *h_1 and *h_3, is an archaism of Anatolian, and the loss of the laryngeals was made in common by the other languages."

In the vocalic inventory of current Late Indo-European reconstruction, the following evolution paradigm is widespread, following Beekes (1995), Meier-Brügger (2003) and Ringe (2005):

PIH	pre-LIE	post-LIE	NWIE	PGk	PII	PIH	pre-LIE	post-LIE	NWIE	PGk	PII
**iHC*	**iHC*	**ī*	**ī**	***ī***	***ī***	**Hi*	**Hi*	**i*	**i**	***i***	***i***
**uHC*	**uHC*	**ū*	**ū**	***ū***	***ū***	**Hu*	**Hu*	**u*	**u**	***u***	***u***
**oH*	**oH*	**ō*	**ō**	***ō***	***ā***	**Ho*	**Ho*	**o*	**o**	***o***	***a***
*eh_1	**eH*	**ē*	**ē**	***ē***	***ā***	*h_1e	**He*	**e*	**e**	***e***	***a***
*eh_2	**aH*	**ā*	**ā**	***ā***	***ā***	*h_2e	**Ha*	**a*	**a**	***a***	***a***
*eh_3	**oH*	**ō*	**ō**	***ō***	***ā***	*h_3e	**Ho*	**o*	**o**	***o***	***a***

PIH	*Ch_1C	*Ch_2C	*Ch_3C	*h_1C-	*h_2C-	*h_3C-	**VHV*	**CRHC*
pre-LIE	*h_1°	*h_2°	*h_3°	*$H(H^{\circ})$	*$H(H^{\circ})$	*$H(H^{\circ})$	**VHV*	*$R^{\circ}H$
post-LIE	**ə*	**ə*	**ə*	-	-	-	**VʔV*	*$^{(o)}R^{\circ}H$
NWIE	**a**	**a**	**a**	-	-	-	**V̄**	$^{(o)}$**R**^{ə}**ʔ**
PGk	***e***	***a***	***o***	***e***	***a***	***o***	***V̄***	***RV̄***
PII	***i***	***i***	***i***	-	-	-	***V(ʔ)V***	***(R)Vʔ***

NOTE 1. A differentiation between *early* or *pre*-LIE and *late* or *post*-LIE has to be made. An auxiliary vowel was firstly inserted in the evolution PIH → pre-LIE in a certain position, known because it is found in all dialects alike: *Ch_1C → *$Ch_1{}^{\circ}C$, *Ch_2C → *$Ch_2{}^{\circ}C$, *Ch_3C → *$Ch_3{}^{\circ}C$. By post-LIE we assume a period of a Northern-Southern dialectal division and Southern dialectal split, in which the whole community remains still in contact, allowing the spread of innovations like a generalised vocalisation of the auxiliary vowel (during the first migrations in the Kurgan framework, the assumed end of the LIE community). During that period, the evolution pre-LIE → post-LIE would have been as follows: *$Ch_1{}^{\circ}C$ → *Ch_1*əC*→**CHəC*→**CəC*. That evolution reached IEDs differently: whereas in South-West IE (Greek, Armenian, Phrygian, Ancient Macedonian) the pre-LIE laryngeal probably colourised the vocalic output from *Ch_1*əC* as in the general scheme (into ***e***, ***a***, ***o***), in NWIE and PII the late LIE the **ə* from **CəC* was assimilated to another vowel: generally to **a** in NWIE, and to ***i*** in PII. Word-initially, only South-West IE dialects appear to have had an output **H°*→ **Hə*→ ***e***, ***a***, ***o***, while the other dialects lost them **H*→ Ø.

NOTE 2. The following developments should also be added:

- In South-West IE there are no cases of known **Hj-* → **Vj-*. It has been assumed that this group produced in Greek a *z*.
- It seems that some evidence of word-initial laryngeals comes from Indo-Iranian, where some compound words show lengthening of the final vowel before a root presumed to have had an initial laryngeal.
- The *-*i*h_2 group in auslaut had an alternative form *-*j°*h_2, LIE *-*ī/-jə*, which could produce IED **-ī**, **-ja** (alternating forms are found even within the same dialect).
- Apparently a reflect of consonantal laryngeals is found between nonhigh vowels as *hiatuses* (or *glottal stops*) in the oldest Indo-Iranian languages – Vedic Sanskrit and Old Avestan, as well as in Homeric Greek (Lindeman *Introduction to the 'Laryngeal Theory'*, 1987). For a discussion on its remains in Proto-Germanic, see Connolly (*"'Grammatischer Wechsel' and the laryngeal theory", IF 85* 1980).
- Contentious is also the so-called Osthoff's Law (which affected all IE branches but for Tocharian and Indo-Iranian), which possibly shows a general trend of post-LIE date.
- When **H* is in a post-plosive, prevocalic position, the consonantal nature of the laryngeal values is further shown *CHVC → *C^hVC; that is more frequent in PII, *cf.* **pl̥t*h_2*ú-* → Ved. *pr̥t*^{h}*ú-*; it appears also in the perfect endings, *cf.* Gk. *oistha*.
- The group *CR̥HC is explained differently for the individual dialects without a general paradigm; so e.g. Beekes (1995) or Meier-Brügger (2003) distinguish the different dialectal outputs as: Tocharian (**r̥HC*→**r°HC*), Germanic (**r̥H*→**r̥*) and to some extent Balto-Slavic (distinction by accentuation), Italo-Celtic (**r̥H*→**r°H*), while in Greek the laryngeal determined the vowel: e.g. **r̥*h_1→**r̥°*h_1→**r̥eH*.

  There are multiple examples which do not fit in any dialectal scheme, though; changes of outputs from PIH reconstructed forms with resonants are found even within the same dialects. The explanation in Adrados–Bernabé–Mendoza (1995-1998) is probably nearer to the actual situation, in going back to the pronunciation of the common (pre-

LIE) group: "the different solutions in this case depend solely on two factors: a) if there are one or two auxiliary vowels to facilitate the pronunciation of this group; b) the place where they appear." So e.g. a group *CR̥HC could be pronounced in LIE with one vowel (*CR°HC or *C°RHC) or with two (*C°R°HC, *C°RH°C, or *CR°H°C). That solution accounts for all LIE variants found in the different branches, and within them.

- The laryngeal of *RHC- in anlaut was vocalised in most languages, while the resonant was consonantal (*R̥HC- became *RVC-).
- In the group *CR̥HV, a vowel generally appears before the resonant and the laryngeal disappears; that vowel is usually coincident with the vocalic output that a resonant alone would usually give in the different dialects, so it can be assumed that generally *CR̥HV→C(V)R̥V, although exceptions can indeed be found. A common example of parallel treatment within the same dialect is Greek *pros/paros* < **pros/p°ros*.
- Accounting for some irregularities in the outcome of laryngeals (especially with *-h_2, but not limited to it) is the so-called "Saussure effect", whereby LIE dialects do not show an usual reflection of the inherited sequences #HRo- and -oRHC-. According to Nussbaum (*Sound law and analogy: papers in honor of Robert S.P. Beekes on the occasion of his 60th birthday*, Alexander Lubotsky, 1997), this effect "reflects something that happened, or failed to happen, already in the proto-language".

Hence, for the moment, we could assume that a South-East and a South-West IE dialects were already separated, but still closely related through a common (Northern) IE core, because the loss (or, more exactly, the vocalic evolution) of laryngeals of Northern IE did in fact reach Graeco-Aryan dialects similarly and in a complementary distribution. That is supported by modern linguistic Northern-Southern separation model (*v.i.* §§1.3, 1.4, 1.7): "(...) today it is thought that most innovations of Greek took place outside Greece; no doubt, within the Indo-Greek group, but in a moment in which certain eastern isoglosses didn't reach it." Adrados–Bernabé–Mendoza (1995-1998).

Apart from those fictions or artifices that help linguists keep on with their work on individual dialects from a *secure* starting point (conventional PIH phonetics), there is no reason to doubt that the most (scientifically) conservative starting point for PIE evolution is that LIE had lost most laryngeals but for one merged **H* – of the "Disintegrating Indo-European" of Bomhard (*Toward Proto-Nostratic: A New Approach to the Comparison of Proto-Indo-European and Proto-Afroasiatic*, 1984) – into the known timeline and groupings, and that a late *post*-LIE vocalisation of interconsonantal **H* into **Hə* and later **ə* did eventually substitute the original forms, albeit at a different pace, arriving probably somehow late and incompletely to the earliest dialects to split up, which completed independently the laryngeal loss.

Some individual finds seem to support a different treatment of laryngeals in certain dialects and environments, though.

NOTE. Examples are the contentious Cogwill's Law ("such shortening is fairly common cross-linguistically, and the IE examples may have each arisen independently", Fortson 2004), or other peculiar sound changes recently found in Latin and Balto-Slavic, all of them attested in late IE dialects that had already undergone different vocalic evolutions.

Meier-Brügger (2003) mentions 3 non-Anatolian *testimonies* of laryngeals:

1) Indo-Iranian: "the Vedic phrase *devyètu*, i.e. *devì etu* – *v* is best understandable if we suppose that *devī́* 'goddess' still contained the laryngeal form **dewíH* (with **-iH<*-ih*$_2$) at the time of the formulation fo the verse in question. In the phase **-íH* it was possible for the laryngeal simply to disappear before a vowel". Other common example used is **wr̥kiH*. It is not justified, though, that it must represent a sort of unwritten laryngeal, and not an effect of it, i.e. a *laryngeal hiatus* or glottal stop, from older two-word sandhis that behave as a single compound word, see §2.4.3. Interesting is also that they are in fact from words alternating in pre-LIE **-iH/*-j°H* (or post-LIE **-ī/*-jə*) which according to Fortson (2004) reflect different syllabification in Indo-Iranian vs. Greek and Tocharian, whilst "[t]he source of the difference is not fully understood". In line with this problem is that the expected case of **-aH* stems is missing, what makes it less likely that Indo-Iranian examples come from a common hypothetic PII stage in which a word-final **-H* had not still disappeared, and more likely that it was a frozen remain (probably of a glottal stop) in certain formal expressions. In fact, it has long been recognised that the treatment of word-final laryngeals shows a strong tendency to disappear (so e.g. in Hittite), and most of the time it appears associated with morphological elements (Adrados–Bernabé–Mendoza 1995-1998). They should then be considered – like the hiatuses or glottal stops found in Hom. Gk. and Germanic compositions – probable ancient reminiscences of a frozen formal language.
2) The sandhi variant in **-aH* is found, according to Meier-Brügger (2003) and Ringe (2006), in Greek and Old Church Slavonic. In both "clear traces are missing that would confirm a PIE ablaut with full grade **-eh*$_2$*-* and zero grade **-h*$_2$*-* (...) That is why it appears as if the differentiation between the nominative and vocative singular in this case could be traced to sandhi-influenced double forms that were common at a time when the stems were still composed of **-ah*$_2$, and the contraction **-ah*$_2$*-* >**-ā-* had not yet occurred". Szemerény (1999) among others already rejected it: "The shortening of the original IE ending *-ā* to *-ă* is regular, as the voc., if used at the beginning of a sentence or alone, was accented on the first syllable but was otherwise enclitic and unaccented; a derivation from *-ah* with the assumption of a prevocalic sandhi variant in *-a* fails therefore to explain the shortening."
3) The latest example given by Meier-Brügger is found in the unstable *CRHC model (see above), which is explained with PIE **gn̥h*$_1$*-tó-* 'created, born': so in Vedic *jātá-* < PII ***ǵātó-*** < **ǵaHtó-* < **g*^{j}*n̥h*$_1$*tó-*, which would mean that the laryngeal merged after the

evolution LIE **n̥* → PII ***a***. The other irregular dialectal reconstructions shown are easily explained following the model of epenthetic vowel plus merged laryngeal (or glottal stop?) in **gn*^{ə}*h*$_{1}$*tó-*; *cf.* for the same intermediate grade PGk ***gnētó-*** (< post-LIE **gn*^{e}*Htó-*), pre-NWIE ***g***$^{(o)}$***n***^{a}***ʔtó-*** (<post-LIE **gn*^{ə}*Htó-*) into Ita., Cel. **gnātó-*, PGmc. **kunʔda-*, Bal.-Sla. **ginətó-*. Such dialectal late loss of the merged laryngeal **H* (or glottal stop) is therefore limited to the groups including a sonorant, and the finds support a vocalisation of LIE **n̥*, **m̥* → PII ***a*** earlier than the loss of laryngeal (or glottal stop) in that environment. That same glottal stop is possibly behind the other examples in Meier-Brügger: O.Av. *va.ata-*< PII ***waʔata-***, or Ved. **ca-kar-ʔa* (the *ʔ* still preserved in the period of the activity of Brugmann's law), or Ved. *náus* < **naʔus*.

In Lubotsky (1997) different outputs are proposed for *CRH groups before certain vowels: "It is clear that the "short" reflexes are due to laryngeal loss in an unaccented position, but the chronology of this loss is not easy to determine. If the laryngeal loss had already occurred in PIIr., we have to assume that PIIr. *CruV subsequently yielded CurvV in Sanskrit. The major problem we face is that the evidence for the phonetically regular outcome of *CriV and *CruV in Indo-Iranian is meager and partly conflicting." Again, the conflict is solved assuming a late loss of the laryngeal; however, the attestation of remains of glottal stops, coupled with the auxiliary vowel solution of Adrados–Bernabé–Mendoza (1995-1998) solves the irregularities without making new assumptions and dialectal sound laws that in turn need their own further exceptions.

Kortlandt seems to derive the loss of laryngeals from Early Slavic (see below §1.7.1.I.D), a sister language of West and East Baltic languages, according to his view. Also, on Italo-Celtic (2007): "If my view is correct, the loss of the laryngeals after a vocalic resonant is posterior to the shortening of pretonic long vowels in Italic and Celtic. The specific development of the vocalic liquids, which is posterior to the common shortening of pretonic long vowels, which is in its turn posterior to the development of *ē*, *ā*, *ō* from short vowel plus laryngeal, supports the hypothesis of Italo-Celtic linguistic unity." Hence the problematic environments with sonorants are explained with a quite late laryngeal loss precisely in those groups.

The most probable assumption then, if some of those peculiar developments are remnants of previous laryngeals, as it seems, is that the final evolution of the merged **H* was coincident with LIE disintegration, and might have reached its end in the different early prehistoric communities, while still in contact with each other (in order to allow for the spread of the common trends); the irregular vocalic changes would have then arisen from unstable syllables (mainly those which included a resonant), alternating even within the same branches, and even in the same phonetic environments without laryngeals (*v.i.* §2.3).

While there are reasons to support a late evolution of the *pre*-LIE merged laryngeal, there seems to be no strong argument for the survival of LIE merged **H* into the later periods of NWIE, PGk or PII dialects, still less into later proto-languages (as Germanic, Slavic, Indo-Aryan, etc.). However, for some linguists, the complete loss of the LIE laryngeal (or even *laryngeals*) *must* have happened independently in each dialectal branch attested; so e.g. Meier-Brügger (2003): "As a rule, the laryngeals were disposed of only after the Proto-Indo-European era"; Clackson (2007): "But the current picture of laryngeal reconstruction necessitates repeated loss of laryngeals in each language branch".

NOTE. The question is then brought by Clackson into the Maltese and Modern Hebrew examples, languages isolated from Semitic into an Indo-European environment for centuries. That is indeed a *possible* explanation: that all IE branches, after having split up from the LIE common language, would have become independently isolated, and then kept in close contact with (or, following the Maltese example, *surrounded by*) non-IE languages without laryngeals. Then, every change in all branches could be explained by way of *diachronic* and *irregular* developments of vowel quality. In Clackson's words: "(...) the comparative method does not rely on absolute regularity, and the PIE laryngeals may provide an example of where reconstruction is possible without the assumption of rigid sound-laws."

Even accepting that typologically both models of (a common, post-LIE *vs.* an independent, dialectal) laryngeal loss were equally likely, given that all languages had lost the merged laryngeal before being attested, all with similar outputs, and that even the final evolution (*laryngeal hiatuses* or glottal stops) must have been shared in an early period – since they are found only in frozen remains in old and distant dialects –, an early IED loss of laryngeals fits into a coherent timeline within the known dialectal evolution. With that *a priori* assumption, we limit the need for unending *ad hoc* 'sound-laws' for each dialectal difference involving a sonorant, which would in turn need their own exceptions. Therefore, we dispense with unnecessary hypotheses, offering the most conservative approach to the problem.

CONVENTIONS USED IN THIS BOOK

1. We try to keep a consistent nomenclature throughout the book, when referring to the different reconstructible stages of Proto-Indo-European (PIE). From Pre-PIH, highly hypothetical stage, only reconstructible through internal reconstruction, to the most conservative reconstruction of early LIE dialects (IEDs). We do so by using the following schema of frequent terms and dates:

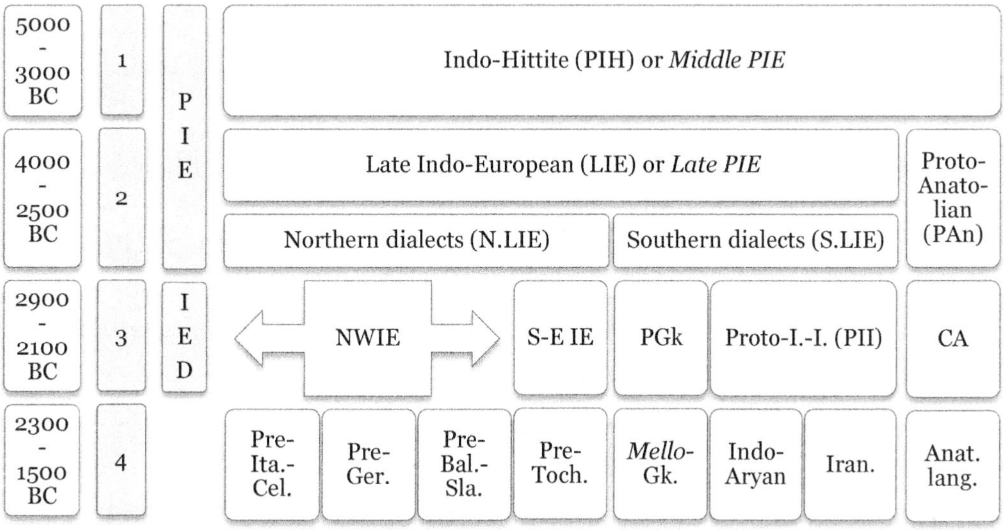

NOTE. This is just a simplified summary to understand the following sections. The full actual nomenclature and archaeological dates are discussed in detail in §§1.3, 1.4, and 1.7.

The dates include an archaeological *terminus post quem*, and a linguistic *terminus ante quem*. In such a huge time span we could differentiate between language periods. However, these (linguistic and archaeological) limits are usually difficult to define, and their differentiation hardly necessary in this grammar. Similarly, the terms Hittite, Sanskrit, Ancient Greek, Latin, etc. (as well as modern languages) might refer in the broadest sense to a time span of over 1,000 years in each case, and they are still considered a single language; a selection is made of the prestigious dialect and age for each one, though, as it is done in this grammar, where the prestigious language is Late Indo-European, while phonetics remains nearer to the middle-late period of IEDs, whose post-laryngeal output is more certain.

2. The above graphic is intended to show stemmatic, as well as synchronic levels. The reconstruction of North-West Indo-European is based on secondary materials: it is a level 3 proto-language, reconstructed on the basis of level 5 proto-languages (of ca. 1000 BC), i.e. primary Proto-Celtic, Proto-Italic, secondary Proto-Balto-Slavic (through Proto-Slavic and Proto-Baltic) and secondary Pre-Proto-Germanic (through internal reconstruction), see §1.7.1.

NOTE. Coeval level 3 dialects Proto-Greek (from level 5 Mycenaean and level 6 Ancient Greek primary materials) and Proto-Indo-Iranian (from level 5 Old Indian and level 6 Iranian materials) could be considered reconstructions based on primary as well as secondary materials. All of them, as well as data from other dialects (Tocharian A and B, Armenian, Albanian), conform the secondary and tertiary materials used to reconstruct a level 2 Late Indo-European. Proto-Anatolian is a level 2 internal reconstruction from level 3 Common Anatolian, in turn from level 4 and level 5 primary materials on Anatolian dialects. Both Late Indo-European and Proto-Anatolian help reconstruct a parent language, Indo-Hittite, which is then a level 1 language.

Each reconstructed parent level is, indeed, more uncertain and inconsistent than the previous one, because the older a material is (even primary texts directly attested), the more uncertain the reconstructed language. And more so because all parent reconstructions are in turn helpful to refine and improve the reconstruction of daughter and sister proto-languages. With that scheme in mind, it is logical to consider more consistent and certain the reconstruction of IEDs, these in turn more than LIE, and this more than PIH.

3. Palatovelars are neither reconstructed for Late Indo-European, nor (consequently) for Indo-Hittite. While not still a settled question (*v.s. Considerations of Method*), we assume that the satem trend began as an areal dialectal development in South-East Indo-European, and spread later (and incompletely) through contact zones – e.g. into Pre-Balto-Slavic.

NOTE. Because West and Central European (Italo-Celtic and Germanic) and Proto-Greek were not affected by that early satemisation trend –although Latin, Greek and Celtic actually show late independent 'satemisations' –, the reconstruction of centum NWIE and PGk, and satem PII (the aim of this book) should be an agreed solution, no matter what the different personal or scholarly positions on LIE and PIH might be.

4. We assume an almost fully vocalic – i.e. post-laryngeal – nature of IEDs since the end of the LIE community (assumed to have happened before ca. 2500 BC, according to archaeological dates), although not a settled question either (*v.s. Considerations of Method*). Whether LIE lost the merged laryngeal **H* sooner or later, etymological roots which include laryngeals will be labelled PIH and follow the general three-laryngeal convention, while some common LIE vocabulary will be shown either with pre-LIE merged **H* or post-LIE vocalic output **ə* (which was assimilated to NWIE **a**, PII **i**), or with the reconstructed post-LIE glottal stop **ʔ*.

NOTE. In this grammar we will show the reconstructed phonetics of a post-LIE period, focussing on NWIE vocalism, while keeping a vocabulary section with a Late Indo-European reconstruction, respecting NWIE/PII dialectal differences; not included are the different vocalic outputs of South-West IE, from word-initial and interconsonantal laryngeals.

WRITING SYSTEM

This table contains common Proto-Indo-European phonemes and their proposed regular corresponding letters in alphabets and Brahmic alphasyllabaries.

CONSONANTS AND CONSONANTAL SOUNDS

Phoneme	Greek	Latin	Perso-Arab	Armenian	Cyrillic	Nāgarī
[p]	Π π	P p	پـ ـپـ ـپ	Պ պ	П п	प
[b]	Β β	B b	بـ ـبـ ـب	Բ բ	Б б	ब
[b^h]	Βη βη	Bh bh	بهـ ـبهـ ـبه	Բh բh	Бх бх	भ
[t]	Τ τ	T t	تـ ـتـ ـت	Տ տ	Т т	त
[t^h]	Θ θ	Th th	تهـ ـتهـ ـته	Թ թ	Тх тх	थ
[d]	Δ δ	D d	د ـد ـد	Դ դ	Д д	द
[d^h]	Δη δη	Dh dh	دهـ ـدهـ ـده	Դh դh	Дх дх	ध
[k]	Κ κ	K k	کـ ـکـ ـک	Կ կ	К к	क
[k^h]	Χ χ	Kh kh	کهـ ـکهـ ـکه	Ք ք	Кх кх	ख
[g]	Γ γ	G g	گـ ـگـ ـگ	Գ գ	Г г	ग
[g^h]	Γη γη	Gh gh	گهـ ـگهـ ـگه	Գh գh	Гх гх	घ
[k^w]	Ϙ ϙ	Q q	قـ ـقـ ـق	Խ խ	Къ къ	क़
[g^w]	Ͱ ͱ	C c	غـ ـغـ ـغ	Ղ ղ	Гъ гъ	ग़
[g^{wh}]	Ͱη ͱη	Ch ch	غهـ ـغهـ ـغه	Ղh ղh	Гъх гъх	ग़ह
[h]	Η η	H h	هـ ـهـ ـه	Հ h	Х х	ह
[ʔ]	’	’	ء	’	’	॰
[j]	J j	J j	پـ ـپـ ـي	Յ յ	Й й	य
[w]	Ϝ ϝ	W w	ۋ ـۋ ـۋ	Ւ ւ	В в	व
[r]	Ρ ρ	R r	ر ـر ـر	Ռ ռ	Р р	र
[l]	Λ λ	L l	لـ ـلـ ـل	Լ լ	Л л	ल
[m]	Μ μ	M m	مـ ـمـ ـم	Մ մ	М м	म
[n]	Ν ν	N n	نـ ـنـ ـن	Ն ն	Н н	न
[s]	Σ σ ς	S s	سـ ـسـ ـس	Ս ս	С с	स

Sounds found in Proto-Greek only

[pʰ]	Φ φ	Ph ph	پھ ـپھـ ـپھ	Փ փ	Пх пх	फ
[kʷʰ]	Ϙη ϙη	Qh qh	قھ ـقھـ ـقھ	Խh խh	Чх чх	क़ह
[t͡s]	Tσ τσ	Ts ts	تسـ ـتسـ ـتس	Ծ ծ	Ц ц	तस
[d͡z]	Δζ δζ	Dz dz	دز ـدز ـدز	Ձ ձ	Дз дз	दष

Sounds found in Proto-Indo-Iranian only

[t͡ɕ]	Tϻ τϻ	Ķ ķ	تژ ـتژ ـتژ	Չ չ	Ч ч	तश
[d͡ʑ]	Δϻ δϻ	Ģ ģ	دژ ـدژ ـدژ	Ց g	Дщ дщ	दष
[d͡ʑʰ]	Δϻη δϻη	Ģh ģh	دژھ ـدژھ	Ցh gh	Дщ дщ	दषह
[t͡ʃ]	Tþ τþ	Ķ ķ	چـ ـچـ ـچ	Ճ ճ	Тш тш	च
[d͡ʒ]	Δþ δþ	Ġ ġ	جـ ـجـ ـج	Ջ ջ	Дж дж	ज
[d͡ʒʰ]	Δþη δþη	Ġh ġh	ھ ـجھـ ـجھ	Ջh ջh	Джх джх	झ
[ʃ]	Þ þ	Š š	ش ـش ـش	Շ շ	Ш ш	श

VOWELS AND VOCALIC ALLOPHONES

Phoneme	Greek	Latin	Perso-Arab	Armenian	Cyrillic	Nāgarī
[a]	Α α	A a	ا ـا ـا	Ա ա	А а	अ
[e]	Ε ε	E e	ـيَـ ـيَ ـیَ	Է է	Е е	ए
[o]	Ο ο	O o	وَ ـوَ ـوَ	Օ օ	О о	ओ
[aː]	Ᾱ ᾱ	Ā ā	اَ ـاَ ـاَ	Աˋ աˋ	Ā ā	आ
[eː]	Ē ε̄	Ē ē	ـيَـ ـيَ ـیَ	Էˋ էˋ	Ē ē	ऐ
[oː]	Ō ō	Ō ō	وَ ـوَ ـوَ	Օˋ օˋ	Ō ō	औ

[i]	Ι ι	I i	ـيـ ـي ی	Ի ի	И и	इ
[iː]	Ῑ ῑ	Ī ī	ـيِـ ـيِ یِ	Իˋ իˋ	Й й	ई
[u]	Υ υ	U u	و ـو ـو	Ո ո	У у	उ
[uː]	Ῡ ῡ	Ū ū	وُ ـوُ ـوُ	Ոˋ ոˋ	Ӯ ӯ	ऊ

[r̥]	Ρ̣ ρ̣	Ṛ ṛ	ر ـر ـر	Ռ ռ	Р̣ р̣	ऋ
[l̥]	Λ̣ λ̣	Ḷ ḷ	لـ ـلـ ـل	Լ լ	Л̣ л̣	ऌ
[m̥]	Μ̣ μ̣	Ṃ ṃ	مـ ـمـ ـم	Մ մ	М̣ м̣	अं
[n̥]	Ν̣ ν̣	Ṇ ṇ	نـ ـنـ ـن	Ն ն	М̣ м̣	अः

This proposal is purely conventional, and it takes into account values such as availability, simplicity (one letter for each sound), transliteration, tradition.

NOTE. We have followed this order of objectives in non-Brahmic scripts:

- Availability: especially of letters in common Latin and Cyrillic keyboards and typography, since they account for most of the current Northern IE world.
- Simplicity: each sound is represented with one letter (or letter plus diacritics). Digraphs used only when necessary: aspirated consonants are represented with the consonant plus the letter for [h], unless there is an independent character for that aspirated consonant.
- Equivalence of letters: a character in one alphabet should be transliterated and read directly in any other to allow an automatic change from the main alphabets into the others without human intervention. The lack of adequate characters to represent PIE phonetics (resonants, semivowels, long vowels) in alphabets conditions the final result.
- Tradition: the historic or modern sound of the letters is to be retained when possible.

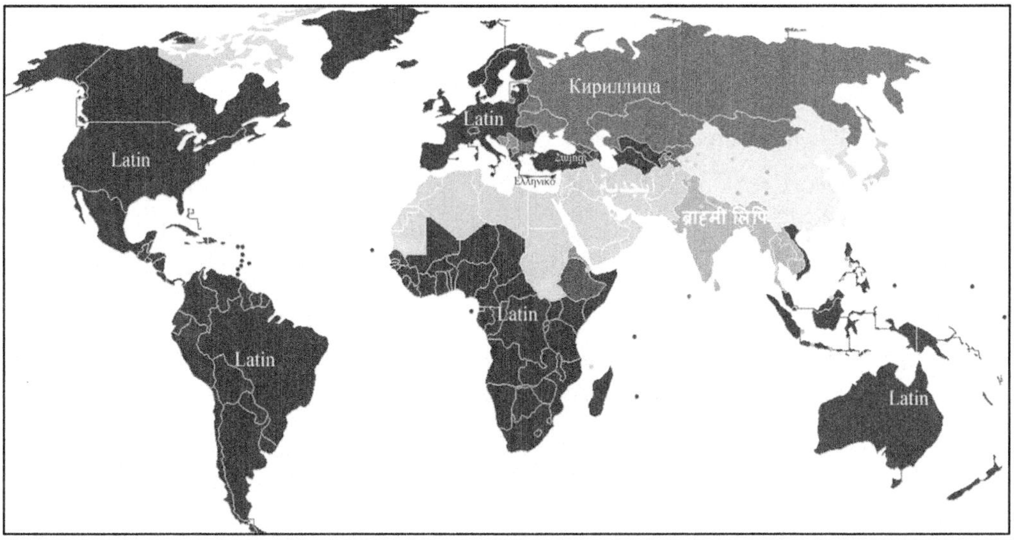

Writing systems of the Indo-European World. (2011, modified from Mirzali Zazaoğlu 2008)

The names of the consonants in Indo-European following the Latin pattern would be – **B**, **be** (pronounced *bay*); **Bh**, **bhe** ($b^{h}ay$); **C**, **ce** ($g^{w}ay$); **Ch**, **che** ($g^{wh}ay$); **D**, **de** (*day*); **Dh**, **dhe** ($d^{h}ay$); **G**, **ge** (*gay*); **Gh**, **ghe** ($g^{h}ay$); **H**, **ha**; **K**, **ka**; **L**, **el**; **M**, **em**; **N**, **en**; **P**, **pe**; **Q**, **qa** ($k^{w}a$); **R**, **er**; **S**, **es**; **T**, **te**; **W**, **wa**.

In Aryan, the letters are named with their sound followed by ***a***, as in Sanskrit – ***ba***, ***bha***, ***ca***, ***cha***, ***da***, ***dha***, ***ga***, ***gha***, and so on.

An acute accent (´) is written over the vowel in the accented syllable, except when accent is on the second to last syllable (or *paenultima*) and in monosyllabic words.

NOTE. Since all non-clitic words of more than one syllable would be marked with one accent, as we have seen, a more elegant convention is not to write *all* accents *always*. The second to last syllable seems to be the most frequent accented syllable, so we can spare unnecessary diacritics if the accent is understood in that position, unless marked in other syllable.

Long vowels are marked with a macron (¯), and vocalic allophones of resonants are marked with a dot below it (̣). Accented long vowels and resonants are represented with special characters that include their diacritics plus an acute accent.

NOTE. It is recommended to write all diacritics if possible, although not necessary. The possibility of omitting the diacritical marks arises from the lack of appropriate fonts in traditional typography, or difficulty typing those marks in common international keyboards. Therefore, alternative writings include **pater/patḗr**, m. *father*, **nmrtos/n̥mr̥tós**, m. *immortal*, **kmtom/km̥tóm**, *hundred*, etc. Such a defective representation of accents and long vowels is common even today in Latin and Greek texts, as well as in most modern languages, which lack a proper representation for sounds. That does not usually hinder an advanced reader from read a text properly.

1. The Modern Greek alphabet lacks letters to represent PIE phonetics properly. Therefore, the Ancient Greek letters and values assigned to them are used instead.

NOTE. The consonant cluster [kʰ] was in Ancient Greece written as X (Chi) in eastern Greek, and Ξ (Xi) in western Greek dialects. In the end, **X** was standardised as [kʰ] ([x] in modern Greek), while **Ξ** represented [ks]. In the Greek alphabet used for IE, **X** represents [kʰ], while **Ξ** represents [kʷʰ], necessary for the representation of a Proto-Greek voiceless aspirate. As in Ancient Greek, **Φ** stands for [pʰ], and **Θ** for [tʰ].

The Greek alphabet lacks a proper representation for long vowels, so they are all marked (as in the other alphabets) with diacritics. **H** is used to represent the sound [h], as it was originally used in most Ancient Greek dialects; it is also used to mark (voiced) aspirated phonemes. **Ē** represents [eː] and **Ō** stands for [oː] in the Greek alphabet for IE. For more on the problem of historical Eta and its representation in the Modern Greek alphabet, see <http://www.tlg.uci.edu/~opoudjis/unicode/unicode_aitch.html>.

While not a practical solution (in relation to the available Modern Greek keyboards), we keep a traditional Ancient Greek script, assuming that it will enjoy the transliteration of texts mainly written in Latin or Cyrillic letters; so e.g. Archaic koppa **Ϙ** stood for [k] before back vowels (e.g. Ϙόρινθος, *Korinthos*), hence its IE value [kʷ]. Archaic digamma **F** represented [w], a sound lost already in Classical Greek. Additions to the IE alphabet are new letter koppa ϟ for [gʷ], based on the alternative Unicode shapes of the archaic koppa, and the 'more traditional' inverted iota ℩ for [j], preferred over Latin yot – although the lack of capital letter for inverted iota makes the use of (at least) a capital **J** necessary to distinguish [j] from [i]. See <http://www.tlg.uci.edu/~opoudjis/unicode/yot.html>.

2. The Latin alphabet used to write Indo-European is similar to the English, which is in turn borrowed from the Late Latin *abecedarium*. Because of the role of this alphabet as model for other ones, simplicity and availability of the characters is preferred over tradition and exactitude.

NOTE. The Latin alphabet was borrowed in very early times from the Greek alphabet and did not at first contain the letter G. The letters Y and Z were introduced still later, about 50 BC. The Latin character **C** originally meant [g], a value always retained in the abbreviations *C.* (for *Gaius*) and *Cn.* (for *Gnaeus*). That was probably due to Etruscan influence, which copied it from Greek **Γ**, *Gamma*, just as later Cyrillic **Г**, *Ge*. In early Latin script C came also to be used for [k], and K disappeared except before in a few words, as Kal. (Kalendae), Karthago. Thus there was no distinction in writing between the sounds [g] and [k]. This defect was later remedied by forming (from C, the original [g]-letter) a new character G. In Modern Indo-European, unambiguous **K** stands for [k], and **G** for [g], so **C** is left without value, being used (taking its oldest value [g]) to represent the labiovelar [g^w].

V originally denoted the vowel sound [u] (Eng. oo), and F stood for the sound of consonant [w] (from Gk. ϝ, called *digamma*). When F acquired the value of our [f], V came to be used for consonant [w] as well as for the vowel [u]. The Latin [w] semivowel developed into Romance [v]; therefore V no longer adequately represented [u] or [w], and the Latin alphabet had to develop alternative letters. The Germanic [w] phoneme was therefore written as VV (a doubled V or U) by the seventh or eighth century by the earliest writers of Old English and Old High German. During the late Middle Ages, two forms of V developed, which were both used for its ancestor U and modern V. The pointed form V was written at the beginning of a word, while a rounded form U was used in the middle or end, regardless of sound. The more recent letters **U** and Germanic **W** probably represent the consonantal sounds [u] and [w] respectively more unambiguously than Latin V.

The letter **I** stood for the vowel [i], and was also used in Latin (as in Modern Greek) for its consonant sound [j]. **J** was originally developed as a swash character to end some Roman numerals in place of I; both I and J represented [i], [iː], and [j]. In IE, **J** represents the semivowel [j], an old Latin value current in most Germanic and Slavic languages. **Y** is used to represent the vowel [y] in foreign words. That [j] value is retained in English J only in foreign words, as *Hallelujah* or *Jehovah*. Because Romance languages developed new sounds (from former [j] and [g]) that came to be represented as I and J, English J (from French J), as well as Spanish, Portuguese or Italian J have sound values quite different from [j]. The romanisation of the sound [j] from different writing systems (like Devanagari) as Y – which originally represented in Latin script the Greek vowel [y] – is due to its modern value in English and French, and has spread a common representation of [j] as Y in Indo-European studies, while J is used to represent other sounds.

A different use of the Latin alphabet to represent PIE, following the Classical Latin tradition, is available at <http://verger1.narod.ru/lang1.htm>.

3. The Perso-Arabic script has been adapted to the needs of a fully differentiated PIE alphabet, following Persian, Urdu and Kurdish examples.

NOTE. The Perso-Arabic script is a writing system that is originally based on the Arabic alphabet. Originally used exclusively for the Arabic language, the Arabic script was modified to match the Persian language, adding four letters: پ [p], چ [tʃ], ژ [ʒ], and گ [g]. Many languages which use the Perso-Arabic script add other letters. Besides the Persian alphabet itself, the Perso-Arabic script has been applied to the Urdu or Kurdish Soraní alphabet.

Unlike the standard Arabic alphabet, which is an abjad (each symbol represents a consonant, the vowels being more or less defective), the IE perso-arabic script is a true alphabet, in which vowels are mandatory, making the script easy to read.

Among the most difficult decisions is the use of letters to represent vowels – as in modern alphabets like Kurdish or Berber – instead of diacritics – as in the traditional Arabic or Urdu scripts. Following tradition, hamza (originally a glottal stop) should probably be placed on the short vowels and resonants, instead of the long ones (especially above 'alif), but automatic equivalence with the other alphabets make the opposite selection more practical.

Because waw و and yodh ي could represent short and long vowels u and i, and consonantal w and j, a conventional selection of current variants has been made: Arabic letter Ve, sometimes used to represent the sound [v] when transliterating foreign words in Arabic, and also used in writing languages with that sound (like Kurdish) is an obvious selection for consonantal [w] because of its availability. The three-dotted yodh becomes then a consequent selection for consonantal yodh. Hamza distinguishes then the long vowel from the short ones, which is represented with the original symbols.

4. Armenian characters, similarly to Greek, need to be adapted to a language with a different series of short and long vowels and aspirated phonemes.

NOTE. Because of that, a tentative selection is made, which needs not be final – as with any other script. Because Armenian lacks a proper character for [u], and because it has not different characters to represent long vowels other than [eː] or [oː], the more practical choice is to imitate the other alphabets to allow for equivalence. The characters that represent short vowels also represent different sounds; as, Ե for [ɛ] and word initially [jɛ], and Ո for [o] and word initially [vo], so a less ambiguous choice would be Է for [e] and Օ for [o]. Hence the letter Ո historically used to write [o] and [u] (in digraphs) stands for [u].

The conventional selection of one-character representation of aspirated voiceless consonants follows Armenian tradition and equivalence with Greek, a closely related language, as we have already seen; i.e. Proto-Greek is probably the nearest branch to the one Pre-Armenian actually belonged to, and it is therefore practical to retain equivalence between both scripts.

Armenian diacritics (like the abbreviation mark proposed for long vowels) are defined as 'modifier letters', not as 'combining diacritical marks' in Unicode, so they do not combine as true superscript. Some fonts do combine them, as Everson Mono Ա՟ ա՟ Է՟ է՟ Օ՟ օ՟ Ի՟ ի՟ Ո՟ ո՟.

6. The Cyrillic script is used following its modern trends, taking on account that Russian is the model for most modern keyboards and available typography.

NOTE. Non-Russian characters have been avoided, and we have followed the principle of one letter for each sound: While Й is commonly used to represent [j], Cyrillic scripts usually lack a character to represent consonantal [w], given that usually [v] (written B) replaces it. While У is generally used in Cyrillic for foreign words, a 'one character, one sound' policy requires the use of a character complementary to Й, which is logically found in Ў – a sound lacking in Indo-European.

In Slavistic transcription *jer* Ъ and front *jer* Ь were used to denote Proto-Slavic extra-short sounds [ŭ] and [ĭ] respectively (e.g. *slověnьskъ* adj. 'slavonic'). Today they are used with other values in the different languages that still use them, but the need for traditional 'labial' [ʷ] and 'palatal' [ʲ] signs available in most Cyrillic keyboards made them the most logical selection to mark a change of value in the characters representing stops.

7. The Brahmic or Indic scripts are a family of abugida (alphabetic-syllabary) writing systems, historically used within their communities – from Pakistan to Indochina – to represent Sanskrit, whose phonology is similar to the parent PIE language. Devanāgarī has come to be the most commonly used Brahmic script to represent Sanskrit, hence our proposal of its character values for the rest of them.

NOTE. The characters and accents are generally used following their traditional phonetic value. Exceptions are the lack of vocalic characters to properly represent [m̥] and [n̥]. Hence anusvara अं, which represents [ṃ], is used to represent [m̥]. Also, visarga अः, which stands for [ḥ] (allophonic with word-final r and s) is proposed for [n̥].

Automatic transliteration between many Brahmic scripts is usually possible, and highly available within scripts used in India.

NOTE. That happens e.g. with the InScript keyboard: because all Brahmic scripts share the same order, any person who knows InScript typing in one script can type in any other Indic script using dictation even without knowledge of that script.

However, due to the lack of characters in western alphabets to represent resonants and long vowels, diacritics are used. These diacritics are not commonly available (but for the Arabic hamza), and therefore if they are not written, transliteration into Brahmic scripts becomes defective. That problem does not exist in the other direction i.e. from Brahmic scripts into the other alphabets.

MODERN INDO-EUROPEAN

1. Modern Indo-European (MIE) is therefore a set of conventions or 'rules' applied to systematise the reconstructed North-West Indo-European dialect of Late Indo-European – see below §§ 1.3, 1.7.1. Such conventions refer to its writing system, morphology and syntax, and are conceived to facilitate the transition of the reconstructed language into a learned and living one.

2. Because proto-languages were spoken by prehistoric societies, no genuine sample texts are available, and thus comparative linguistics is not in the position to reconstruct exactly how the language was, but more or less certain approximations, whose statistical confidence decrease as we get further back in time. The hypothesised language will then be always somewhat controversial.

NOTE 1. Mallory–Adams (2007): "How real are our reconstructions? This question has divided linguists on philosophical grounds. There are those who argue that we are not really engaged in 'reconstructing' a past language but rather creating abstract formulas that describe the systematic relationship between sounds in the daughter languages. Others argue that our reconstructions are vague approximations of the proto-language; they can never be exact because the proto-language itself should have had different dialects (yet we reconstruct only single proto-forms) and our reconstructions are not set to any specific time. Finally, there are those who have expressed some statistical confidence in the method of reconstruction. Robert Hall, for example, claimed that when examining a test control case, reconstructing proto-Romance from the Romance languages (and obviously knowing beforehand what its ancestor, Latin, looked like), he could reconstruct the phonology at 95% confidence, and the grammar at 80%. Obviously, with the much greater time depth of Proto-Indo-European, we might well wonder how much our confidence is likely to decrease. Most historical linguists today would probably argue that reconstruction results in approximations. A time traveller, armed with this book and seeking to make him- or herself understood would probably engender frequent moments of puzzlement, not a little laughter, but occasional instances of lucidity."

On the same question, Fortson (2004): "How complete is our picture of PIE? We know there are gaps in our knowledge that come not only from the inevitable loss and replacement of a percentage of words and grammatical forms over time, but also from the nature of our preserved texts. Both the representative genres and external features such as writing systems impose limits on what we can ascertain about the linguistic systems of both PIE and the ancient IE languages (...)

In spite of all the scholarly disagreements that enliven the pages of technical books and journals, all specialists would concur that enormous progress has been made since the earliest pioneering work in this field, with consensus having been reached on many substantial issues. The Proto-Indo-Europeans lived before the dawn of recorded human history, and it is a testament to the power of the comparative method that we know as much about them as we do."

NOTE 2. The Hebrew language revival is comparable to our proposal of speaking Indo-European as a living language. We have already said that 'living' and 'dead', 'natural' and 'learned', are not easily applicable to ancient or classical languages. It is important to note that, even though there is a general belief that Modern Hebrew and Ancient Hebrew are the same languages, among Israeli scholars there have been calls for the "Modern Hebrew" language to be called "Israeli Hebrew" or just "Israeli", due to the strong divergences that exist – and further develop with its use – between the modern language spoken in Israel and its theoretical basis, the Ancient Hebrew from the Tanakh. The old language system, with its temporary and dialectal variations spanned over previous centuries of oral tradition, was compiled probably between 450-200 BC, i.e when the language was already being substituted by Aramaic. On that interesting question, prof. Ghil'ad Zuckermann considers that "Israelis are brainwashed to believe they speak the same language as the prophet Isaiah, a purely Semitic language, but this is false. It's time we acknowledge that Israeli is very different from the Hebrew of the past". He points out to the abiding influence of modern Indo-European dialects – especially Yiddish, Russian and Polish –, in vocabulary, syntax and phonetics, as imported by Israel's founders.

3. Features of Late Indo-European that are common to IEDs (North-West Indo-European, Proto-Greek and Proto-Indo-Iranian), like most of the nominal and verbal inflection, morphology, and syntax, make it possible for LIE to be proposed as *Dachsprache* for the living languages.

NOTE 1. Because North-West Indo-European had other sister dialects that were spoken by coeval prehistoric communities, languages like Modern Hellenic (a revived Proto-Greek) and Modern Aryan (a revived Proto-Indo-Iranian) can also be used in the regions where their surviving dialects are currently spoken. These proto-languages are not more different from North-West Indo-European than are today English from Dutch, Czech from Slovenian, Spanish from Italian. They might also serve as *linguae francae* for closely related languages or neighbouring regions; especially interesting would be to have a uniting Aryan language for today's religiously divided South and West Asia.

NOTE 2. The terms *Ausbausprache-Abstandsprache-Dachsprache* were coined by Heinz Kloss (1967), and they are designed to capture the idea that there are two separate and largely independent sets of criteria and arguments for calling a variety an independent "language" rather than a "dialect": the one based on its social functions, and the other based on its objective structural properties. A variety is called an *ausbau language* if it is used autonomously with respect to other related languages.

Dachsprache means a language form that serves as standard language for different dialects, even though these dialects may be so different that mutual intelligibility is not possible on the basilectal level between all dialects, particularly those separated by significant geographical distance. So e.g. the *Rumantsch Grischun* developed as such a Dachsprache for a number of quite different Romansh language forms spoken in parts of

Switzerland; or the *Euskara Batua*, "Standard Basque", and the Southern Quechua literary standard, both developed as standard languages for dialect continua that had historically been thought of as discrete languages with many dialects and no "official" dialect. Standard German and standard Italian to some extent function (or functioned) in the same way. Perhaps the most widely used Dachsprache is Modern Standard Arabic, which links together the speakers of many different, often mutually unintelligible Arabic dialects.

The *standard Indo-European* looked for in this grammar takes Late Indo-European reconstruction as the wide Dachsprache necessary to encompass (i.e. to serve as linguistic umbrella for) the modern usage of IEDs, whose – phonetic, morphological, syntactical – peculiarities are also respected.

4. Modern Indo-European words to complete the lexicon of North-West Indo-European, in case that no common vocabulary is found in Late Indo-European, are to be loan-translated from present-day Northwestern IE languages. Common loan words from sister dialects can also be loan-translated or borrowed as loan words.

NOTE. Even though the vocabulary reconstructible for IEDs is indeed wider than the common Proto-Indo-European lexicon, a remark of Mallory–Adams (2007) regarding reconstructible PIE words is interesting, in that it shows another difficulty of trying to speak a common LIE or PIH:

"To what extent does the reconstructed vocabulary mirror the scope of the original PIE language? The first thing we should dismiss is the notion that the language (any language) spoken in later prehistory was somehow primitive and restricted with respect to vocabulary. Counting how many words a language has is not an easy task because linguists (and dictionaries) are inconsistent in their definition or arrangement of data. If one were simply to count the headwords of those dictionaries that have been produced to deal with nonliterate languages in Oceania, for example, the order of magnitude is somewhere on the order of 15,000–20,000 'words'. The actual lexical units are greater because a single form might have a variety of different meanings, each of which a speaker must come to learn, e.g. the English verb take can mean 'to seize', 'to capture', 'to kill', 'to win in a game', 'to draw a breath', 'imbibe a drink', 'to accept', 'to accommodate' to name just a few of the standard dictionary meanings. Hence, we might expect that a language spoken c. 4000 BC would behave very much like one spoken today and have a vocabulary on the order of 30,000–50,000 lexical units. If we apply fairly strict procedures to distinguishing PIE lexical items to the roots and words listed in Mallory and Adams's Encyclopedia or Calvert Watkins's The American Heritage Dictionary of Indo-European Roots (1985) we have less than 1,500 items. The range of meanings associated with a single lexeme is simply unknown although we occasionally get a hint, e.g. **bher-* indicates both 'carry (a load)' and 'bear (a child)'. So the PIE vocabulary that we reconstruct may well provide the basis for a much larger lexicon given the variety of derivational features in PIE."

Examples of loan translations from modern NWIE languages are e.g. from Latin *aquaeduct* (Lat. *aquaeductus* → MIE **aqāsduktos**) or *universe* (Lat.

*uniuersus<*oin(i)-uors-o-<*oino-wr̥t-to-* → MIE **oinowr̥stós** 'turned into one'); from English, like *software* (from Gmc. *samþu-, warō* → MIE **somtúworā**); from French, like *ambassador* (from Cel. *amb(i)actos* → MIE **ambhíagtos** 'public servant'); or *chamber* (from O.Lat. *camera*, from PGk. *kamárā, 'vault'* → MIE **kamarā**); from Russian, like *bolshevik* (MIE **belijówikos**); etc.

NOTE. Loan words from sister IE dialects can be either loan-translated or directly taken as loan-words; as e.g. 'photo', which should be taken directly as loan-word o-stem ***pháwotos***, from Gk ***phawots***, gen. ***phawotós***, as Gk. φῶς (<φάϝος), φωτός, in compound **phawotogr̥phjā**, *photography*, derived from IE root **bhā-**, *shine*, which could be loan-translated as MIE ˣ***bháwots***, from ˣ***bhawotogr̥bhjā***, but without having a meaning for extended ***bha-wes-***, still less for ***bha-wot-***, in North-West Indo-European or even Proto-Indo-European, as it is only found in Ancient Greek dialects. Or MIE **skholā́**, from Lat. *schola*, taken from Gk. σχολή (<PGk. ***skholā́***) 'spare time, leisure, tranquility', borrowed from Greek with the meaning 'school', which was in O.Gk. σχολεῖον (*scholeíon*), translated as PGk. ***skholehjom*** <**-esjo-m*, from IE root **segh-**, which could also be loan-translated as MIE ˣ***sgholā́*** or even more purely (and artificially) ˣ***sgholesjom***, none of them being Proto-Indo-European or common Indo-European terms. Examples from Indo-Iranian include **wasāk̥áranas**, *bazaar*, from O.Ira. *vahacarana* 'sale-traffic, bazaar', which could also be translated as proper MIE ˣ***wesāqólenos***, from PIE roots **wes-** and **qel-**; or **k̥atúrangam**, *chess*, from Skt. *caturaŋgam* (which entered Europe from Pers. *shatranj*) a *bahuvrihi* compound, meaning 'having four limbs or parts', which in epic poetry often means 'army', possibly shortened from **k̥aturangabalam**, Skt. *caturaŋgabalam*, lit. 'four-member force', 'an army comprising of four parts', could be loan-translated as MIE ˣ***qaturangom*** and ˣ***qaturangobelom***, from roots **qetur-**, **ang-** and **bel-**.

Loan words and loan translations might also coexist in specialised terms; as, from **h₁rudʰrós, red*, PGk ***eruthrós***, in loan ***eruthrókutos***, *erythrocyte*, proper MIE **rudhrós**, in **rudhrā́ (ésenos) kētjā**, *red (blood) cell*; *cf.* also MIE **mūs**, **musós**, *mouse, muscle*, PGk ***mūs***, ***muhós***, in loan ***muhokutos***, *myocyte*, for **muskosjo kētjā**, *muscle cell.*

1.8.5. The name of the Modern Indo-European is **eurōpājóm**, or **eurōpājā́ dn̥ghwā**, *European language*, from adj. **eurōpājós**, m. *European*, in turn from the Greek noun **Eurōpā**.

NOTE. Gk. *Eurōpā* is from unknown origin, even though it was linked with Homer's epithet for Zeus *euruopā*, from **hurú-oqeh₂* 'far-seeing, broad', or **h₁urú-woqeh₂* 'far-sounding' (Heath, 2005). Latinate adj. *europaeus*, which was borrowed by most European languages, comes from Gk. adj. *eurōpaíos*, in turn from PGk ***eurōpai-jós*** < PIE **eurōpeh₂-jós* → MIE **eurōpā-jós**. For the evolution PIH **-eh₂jo-* → PGk **-aijo-*, *cf.* adjective formation in Gk. *agorā́-agoraíos*, Ruigh (1967).

In the old IE languages, those which had an independent name for languages used the neuter. Compare Gk. n.pl. Ἑλληνικά (*hellēniká*), Skt. n.sg. संस्कृतम् (*saṃskṛtam*), O.H.G. *diutisc*, O.Prus. *prūsiskan*, etc.; *cf.* also in Tacitus Lat. *uōcābulum latīnum*. In most IE languages, the language is also referred to as 'language' defined by an adjective, whose gender follows the general rule of concordance; *cf.* Skt. *saṃskṛtā vāk* 'refined speech', Gk. ελληνική γλώσσα, Lat. *latīna lingua*, O.H.G. *diutiska sprāhha* (Ger. *Deutsche Sprache*), O.Prus. *prūsiskai bilā*, O.C.S. словѣньскыи ѩзыкъ (*slověnĭskyi językŭ*), etc.

Common scholar terms would include **sindhueurōpājóm**, *Indo-European*, **prāmosindhueurōpājóm**, *Proto-Indo-European*, **ópitjom sindhueurōpājóm**, *Modern Indo-European*,etc.

PART I

LANGUAGE & CULTURE

Collection of texts and images adapted and organised by Carlos Quiles, with contributions by Fernando López-Menchero

1. INTRODUCTION

1.1. THE INDO-EUROPEAN LANGUAGE FAMILY

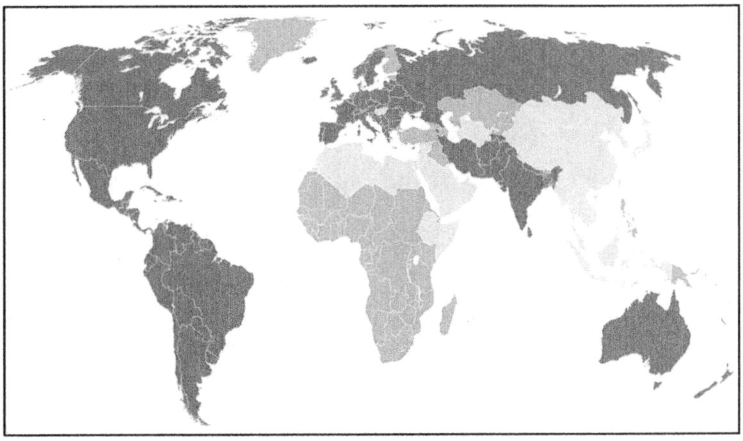

Countries with a majority (dark colour) and minority or official status (light) of Indo-European language speakers. (2011, modified from Brianski 2007)

1.1.1. The IE languages are a family of several hundred modern languages and dialects, including most of the major languages of Europe, as well as many in Asia. Contemporary languages in this family include English, German, French, Spanish, Portuguese, Hindustani (i.e., Hindi and Urdu among other modern dialects), Persian and Russian. It is the largest family of languages in the world today, being spoken by approximately half the world's population as mother tongue. Furthermore, the majority of the other half speaks at least one of them as second language.

1.1.2. Romans didn't perceive similarities between Latin and Celtic dialects, but they found obvious correspondences with Greek. After grammarian Sextus Pompeius Festus:

"Suppum antiqui dicebant, quem nunc supinum dicimus ex Graeco, videlicet pro adspiratione ponentes <s> litteram, ut idem ὕλας dicunt, et nos silvas; item ἕξ sex, et ἑπτά septem"

Such findings are not striking, though, as Rome was believed to have been originally funded by Trojan hero Aeneas and, consequently, Latin was derived from Old Greek.

1.1.3. Florentine merchant Filippo Sassetti travelled to the Indian subcontinent, and was among the first European observers to study the ancient Indian language, Sanskrit. Writing in 1585, he noted some word similarities between Sanskrit and Italian, e.g. *deva/dio* 'God', *sarpa/serpe* 'snake', *sapta/sette* 'seven', *ashta/otto* 'eight', *nava/nove* 'nine'. This observation is today credited to have foreshadowed the later discovery of the Indo-European language family.

1.1.4. The first proposal of the possibility of a common origin for some of these languages came from Dutch linguist and scholar Marcus Zuerius van Boxhorn in 1647. He discovered the similarities among Indo-European languages, and supposed the existence of a primitive common language which he called '*Scythian*'. He included in his hypothesis Dutch, Greek, Latin, Persian, and German, adding later Slavic, Celtic and Baltic languages. He excluded languages such as Hebrew from his hypothesis. However, the suggestions of van Boxhorn did not become widely known and did not stimulate further research.

1.1.5. On 1686, German linguist Andreas Jäger published *De Lingua Vetustissima Europae*, where he identified an remote language, possibly spreading from the Caucasus, from which Latin, Greek, Slavic, 'Scythian' (i.e. Persian) and Celtic (or 'Celto-Germanic') were derived, namely *Scytho-Celtic*.

1.1.6. The hypothesis re-appeared in 1786 when Sir William Jones first lectured on similarities between four of the oldest languages known in his time: Latin, Greek, Sanskrit and Persian:

"The Sanskrit language, whatever be its antiquity, is of a wonderful structure; more perfect than the Greek, more copious than the Latin, and more exquisitely refined than either, yet bearing to both of them a stronger affinity, both in the roots of verbs and the forms of grammar, than could possibly have been produced by accident; so strong indeed, that no philologer could examine them all three, without believing them to have sprung from some common source, which, perhaps, no longer exists: there is a similar reason, though not quite so forcible, for supposing that both the Gothic and the Celtic, though blended with a very different idiom, had the same origin with the Sanskrit; and the old Persian might be added to the same family"

1.1.7. Danish Scholar Rasmus Rask was the first to point out the connection between Old Norwegian and Gothic on the one hand, and Lithuanian, Slavonic, Greek and Latin on the other. Systematic comparison of these and other old languages conducted by the young German linguist Franz Bopp supported the theory, and his *Comparative Grammar*, appearing between 1833 and 1852, counts as the starting-point of Indo-European studies as an academic discipline.

NOTE. The term Indo-European itself now current in English literature, was coined in 1813 by the British scholar Sir Thomas Young, although at that time there was no consensus as to the naming of the recently discovered language family. Among the names suggested were *indo-germanique* (C. Malte-Brun, 1810), *Indoeuropean* (Th. Young, 1813), *japetisk* (Rasmus C. Rask, 1815), *indisch-teutsch* (F. Schmitthenner, 1826), *sanskritisch* (Wilhelm von Humboldt, 1827), *indokeltisch* (A. F. Pott, 1840), *arioeuropeo* (G. I. Ascoli, 1854), Aryan (F. M. Müller, 1861), *aryaque* (H. Chavée, 1867), etc.

In English, Indo-German was used by J. C. Prichard in 1826 although he preferred Indo-European. In French, use of indo-européen was established by A. Pictet (1836). In German literature, *Indo-Europäisch* was used by Franz Bopp since 1835. The term *Indo-Germanisch* had already been introduced by Julius von Klapproth in 1823, intending to include the northernmost and the southernmost of the family's branches, as it was as an abbreviation of the full listing of involved languages that had been common in earlier literature; that opened the doors to ensuing fruitless discussions whether it should not be *Indo-Celtic*, or even *Tocharo-Celtic*.

1.2. TRADITIONAL VIEWS

1.2.1. In the beginnings of the Indo-European studies using the comparative method, Indo-European was reconstructed as a unitary proto-language. For Rask, Bopp and other linguists, it was a search for *the* Indo-European. Such a language was supposedly spoken in a certain region between Europe and Asia and at one point in time.

1.2.2. The *Stammbaumtheorie* or *Genealogical Tree* theory states that languages split up in other languages, each of them in turn split up in others, and so on, like the branches of a tree. For example, a well-known out-dated theory about Indo-European is that, within *the* PIE language, two main groups of dialects known as *centum* and *satem* were formed, a model represented by a clean break-up from the parent language.

NOTE. The *centum* and *satem* isogloss is one of the oldest known phonological differences of IE languages, and is still used by many to classify PIE in two main dialectal groups – postulating the existence of *proto-Centum* and *proto-Satem* languages –, according to their pronunciation of PIE **(d)kmtóm, hundred,* disregarding their relevant morphological and syntactical differences, and usually implicitly accepting a common PIE series of palatovelars.

Tree diagrams remain the most used model for understanding the Indo-European language reconstruction, since it was proposed by A. Schleicher (*Compendium*, 1866). The problem with its simplicity is that "the branching of the different groups is portrayed as a series of clean breaks with no connection between branches after they have split, as if each dialectal group marched away from the rest. Such sharp splits are possible, but assuming that all splits within Proto-Indo-European were like this is not very plausible, and any linguist surveying the current Indo-European languages would note dialectal variations running through some but not all areas, often linking adjacent groups who may belong to different languages" (Mallory–Adams, 2007).

1.2.3. The *Wellentheorie* or Waves Theory, of J. Schmidt, states that one language is created from another by the spread of innovations, the way water waves spread when a stone hits the water surface. The lines that define the extension of the innovations are called isoglosses. The convergence of different isoglosses over a common territory signals the existence of a new language or dialect. Where isoglosses from different languages coincide, transition zones are formed.

NOTE. After Mallory and Adams (2007), "their criteria of inclusion, why we are looking at any particular one, and not another one, are no more solid than those that define family trees. The key element here is what linguistic features actually help determine for us whether two languages are more related or less related to one another."

1.2.4. Because of the difficulties found in the modelling of Proto-Indo-European branches and daughter languages into the traditional, unitary 'Diverging Tree' framework, i.e. a uniform Proto-Indo-European language with its branches, a new model called '*Converging Association of Languages*' was proposed, in which languages that are in contact (not necessarily related to each other) exchange linguistic elements and rules, thus developing and acquiring from each other. Most linguists have rejected it as an implausible explanation of the irregularities found in the old, static concept of PIE.

NOTE. Among the prominent advocates is N.S. Trubetzkoy (*Urheimat*, 1939): "The term 'language family' does not presuppose the common descent of a quantity of languages from a single original language. We consider a 'language family' a group of languages, in which a considerable quantity of lexical and morphological elements exhibit regular equivalences (...) it is not necessary for one to suppose common descent, since such regularity may also originate through borrowings between neighboring unrelated languages (...) It is just as conceivable that the ancestors of the Indo-European language branches were originally different from each other, but though constant contact, mutual influence, and borrowings, approached each other, without however ever becoming identical to one another" (Meier-Brügger, 2003).

Agreeing with Neumann (1996), Meier-Brügger (2003) rejects that *association of languages* in the Proto-Indo-European case by stating: "that the various Indo-European languages have developed from a prior unified language is certain. Questionable is, however, the concrete 'how' of this process of differentiation", and that this "thesis of a 'converging association of languages' may immediately be dismissed, given that all Indo-European languages are based upon the same Proto-Indo-European flexion morphology. As H. Rix makes clear, it is precisely this morphological congruence that speaks against the language association model, and for the diverging tree model."

1.3. THE THEORY OF THE THREE STAGES

1.3.1. Even the first Indo-Europeanists had noted in their works the possibility of reconstructing older stages of the 'Brugmannian' Proto-Indo-European.

NOTE. The development of this theory of three linguistic stages can be traced back to the very origins of Indo-European studies, firstly as a diffused idea of a non-static PIE language, and later widely accepted as a dynamic dialectal evolution, already in the twentieth century, after the decipherment of the Anatolian scripts. Most linguists accept that Proto-Indo-European must be the product of a long historical development, as any 'common language' is being formed gradually, and proto-languages (like languages) have stages, as described by Lehmann (*Introducción a la lingüística histórica, Spa. transl.* 1961). On this question, H. Rix (*Modussystem*, 1986) asserts "[w]hereby comparative reconstruction is based upon a group of similar forms in a number of languages, internal reconstruction takes its point of departure from irregularities or inhomogeneities of the system of a single language (...) The fundamental supposition of language-internal reconstruction is that such an irregularity or inhomogeneity in the grammar of a language is the result of a diachronic process, in which an older pattern, or homogeneity is eclipsed, but not fully suppressed". According to Meier-Brügger (2003), "Rix works back from Late Proto-Indo-European Phase B (reconstructible Proto-Indo-European) using deducible information about an Early Proto-Indo-European Phase A, and gathers in his work related evidence on the Proto-Indo-European verbal system". On that question, see also the "Late Indo-European" differentiation in Gamkrelidze–Ivanov (1994-1995), Adrados–Bernabé–Mendoza (1995-1998); a nomenclature also widespread today stems from G.E. Dunkel's *Early, Middle, Late Indo-European: Doing it My Way* (1997); etc.

1.3.2. Today, a widespread *Three-Stage* theory divides PIE internal language evolution into three main historic layers or stages, including a description of branches and languages either as clean breaks from a common source (e.g. PAn and LIE from Indo-Hittite) or from intermediate *dialect continua* (e.g. Germanic and Balto-Slavic from North-West IE), or classifying similarities into continued linguistic contact (e.g. between Balto-Slavic and Indo-Iranian):

1) *Pre-Proto-Indo-European* (Pre-PIE), more properly following the current nomenclature *Pre-Indo-Hittite* (Pre-PIH), also *Early PIE*, is the hypothetical ancestor of Indo-Hittite, and probably the oldest stage of the language that comparative grammar could help reconstruct using internal reconstruction. There is, however, no common position as to how it was like or when and where it was spoken.

2) The second stage corresponds to a time before the separation of Proto-Anatolian from the common linguistic community where it should have coexisted (as a Pre-Anatolian dialect) with Pre-LIE. That stage of the language is

today commonly called *Indo-Hittite* (PIH), and also Middle PIE, but often simply Proto-Indo-European; it is identified with early kurgan cultures in the Kurgan Hypothesis.

NOTE. On the place of Anatolian among IE languages, the question is whether it separated first as a language branch from PIE, and to what extent was it thus spared developments common to the remaining Proto-Indo-European language group. There is growing consensus in favour of its early split from Indo-European (Heading, among others, 'Indo-Hittite'); see N. Oettinger (*'Indo-Hittite' – Hypothesen und Wortbildung* 1986), A. Lehrman (*Indo-Hittite Revisited*, 1996), H. Craig Melchert (*The Dialectal Position of Anatolian within IE in IE Subgrouping,* 1998), etc.

For Kortlandt (*The Spread of The Indo-Europeans, JIES 18,* 1990): "Since the beginnings of the Yamnaya, Globular Amphora, Corded Ware, and Afanasievo cultures can all be dated between 3600 and 3000 BC, I am inclined to date Proto-Indo-European to the middle of the fourth millennium, and to recognize Proto-Indo-Hittite as a language which may have been spoken a millennium earlier."

For Ringe (2006), "[i]nterestingly, there is by now a general consensus among Indo-Europeanists that the Anatolian subfamily is, in effect, one half of the IE family, all the other subgroups together forming the other half."

On the Anatolian question and its implications on nomenclature, West (2007) states that "[t]here is growing consensus that the Anatolian branch, represented by Hittite and related languages of Asia Minor, was the first to diverge from common Indo-European, which continued to evolve for some time after the split before breaking up further. This raises a problem of nomenclature. It means that with the decipherment of Hittite the 'Indo-European' previously reconstructed acquired a brother in the shape of proto-Anatolian, and the archetype of the family had to be put back a stage. E. H. Sturtevant coined a new term 'Indo-Hittite' (...) The great majority of linguists, however, use 'Indo-European' to include Anatolian, and have done, naturally enough, ever since Hittite was recognized to be 'an Indo-European language'. They will no doubt continue to do so."

3) The common immediate ancestor of most of the reconstructed IE proto-languages is approximately the same *static 'Brugmannian' PIE* searched for since the start of Indo-European studies, before Hittite was deciphered. It is usually called Late Indo-European (LIE) or Late PIE, generally dated some time ca. 3500-2500 BC using linguistic or archaeological models, or both.

NOTE. According to Mallory–Adams (2007): "Generally, we find some form of triangulation based on the earliest attested Indo-European languages, i.e. Hittite, Mycenaean Greek, and Indo-Aryan, each of these positioned somewhere between c. 2000 and 1500 BC. Given the kind of changes linguists know to have occurred in the attested histories of Greek or Indo-Aryan, etc., the linguist compares the difference wrought by such changes with the degree of difference between the earliest attested Hittite, Mycenaean

Greek, and Sanskrit and reconstructed Proto-Indo-European. The order of magnitude for these estimates (or guesstimates) tends to be something on the order of 1,500-2,000 years. In other words, employing some form of gut intuition (based on experience which is often grounded on the known separation of the Romance or Germanic languages), linguists tend to put Proto-Indo-European sometime around 3000 BC plus or minus a millennium (...) the earliest we are going to be able to set Proto-Indo-European is about the fifth millennium BC if we want it to reflect the archaeological reality of Eurasia. We have already seen that individual Indo-European groups are attested by c. 2000 BC. One might then place a notional date of c. 4500-2500 BC on Proto-Indo-European. The linguist will note that the presumed dates for the existence of Proto-Indo-European arrived at by this method are congruent with those established by linguists' 'informed estimation'. The two dating techniques, linguistic and archeological, are at least independent and congruent with one another."

Likewise, in Meier-Brügger (2003), about a common Proto-Indo-European: "No precise statement concerning the exact time period of the Proto-Indo-European linguistic community is possible. One may only state that the ancient Indo-European languages that we know, which date from the 2nd millennium BC, already exhibit characteristics of their respective linguistic groups in their earliest occurrences, thus allowing one to presume the existence of a separate and long pre-history (...) The period of 5000-3000 BC is suggested as a possible timeframe of a Proto-Indo-European language."

However, on the early historic and prehistoric finds, and the assumption of linguistic communities linked with archaeological cultures, Hänsel (*Die Indogermanen und das Pferd*, B. Hänsel, S. Zimmer (eds.), 1994) states that "[l]inguistic development may be described in steps that, although logically comprehensible, are not precisely analyzable without a timescale. The archaeologist pursues certain areas of cultural development, the logic of which (if one exists) remains a mystery to him, or is only accessible in a few aspects of its complex causality. On the other hand, he is provided with concrete ideas with regard to time, as vague as these may be, and works with a concept of culture that the Indo-European linguist cannot attain. For the archaeologist, culture is understood in the sense of a sociological definition (...) The archaeological concept of culture is composed of so many components, that by its very nature its contours must remain blurred. But languages are quite different. Of course there are connections; no one can imagine cultural connections without any possibility of verbal communication. But it is too much to ask that archaeologists equate their concept of culture, which is open and incorporates references on various levels, to the single dimension of linguistic community. Archaeology and linguistics are so fundamentally different that, while points of agreement may be expected, parallels and congruency may not. The advantage of linguistic research is its ability to precisely distinguish between individual languages and the regularity of developments. The strength of archaeology is its precision in developing timelines. What one can do, the other cannot. They could complement each other beautifully, if only there were enough commonality."

1.3.3. Another division has to be made, so that the dialectal evolution is properly understood. Late Indo-European had at least two main *inner* dialectal branches, the *Southern or Graeco-Aryan* (S.LIE) and the *Northern* (N.LIE) ones.

It seems that speakers of *Southern* or *Graeco-Aryan* dialects spread in different directions with the first LIE migrations (ca. 3000-2500 BC in the Kurgan framework), forming at least a South-East (including Pre-Indo-Iranian) and a South-West (including Pre-Greek) group. Meanwhile, speakers of Northern dialects migrated to the North-West (see below), but for speakers of a North-East IE branch (from which Pre-Tocharian developed), who migrated to Asia.

NOTE. Beekes (1995), from an archaeological point of view, on the Yamnaya culture: "This is one of the largest pre-historic complexes in Europe, and scholars have been able to distinguish between different regions within it. It is dated from 3600-2200 B.C. In this culture, the use of copper for the making of various implements is more common. From about 3000 B.C. we begin to find evidence for the presence in this culture of two- and four-wheeled wagons (...) There seems to be no doubt that the Yamnaya culture represents the last phase of an Indo-European linguistic unity, although there were probably already significant dialectal differences within it."

Fortson (2004) similarly suggests: "in the period 3100-2900 BC came a clear and dramatic infusion of Yamna cultural practice, including burials, into eastern Hungary and along the lower Danube. With this we seem able to witness the beginnings of the Indo-Europeanization of Europe. By this point, the members of the Yamna culture had spread out over a very large area and their speech had surely become dialecticaly strongly differentiated."

Meier-Brügger (2003): "Within the group of IE languages, some individual languages are more closely associated with one another owing to morphological or lexical similarities. The cause for this, as a rule, is a prehistoric geographic proximity (perhaps even constituting single linguistic community) or a common preliminary linguistic phase, a middle mother-language phase, which would however then be posterior to the period of the mother language."

About Tocharian, Adrados–Bernabé–Mendoza (1995-1998): "even if archaic in some respects (its *centum* character, subjunctive, etc.) it shares common features with Balto-Slavic, among other languages: they must be old isoglosses, shared before it separated and migrated to the East. It is, therefore, [a N.LIE] language. It shows great innovations, too, something normal in a language that evolved isolated."

On the Southern (*Graeco-Aryan* or *Indo-Greek*) LIE dialect, see Tovar (*Krahes alteuropäische Hydronymie und die west-indogermanischen Sprachen*, 1977; Actas del II *Coloquio sobre lenguas y culturas prerromanas de la Península Ibérica, Salamanca*, 1979), Gamkrelidze–Ivanov (1993-1994), Clackson (*The Linguistic Relationship Between Armenian and Greek,* 1994), Adrados–Bernabé–Mendoza (1995-1998), etc. In Mallory–Adams (2007): "Many have argued that Greek, Armenian, and Indo-Iranian share a number of innovations that suggest that there should have been some form of linguistic *continuum* between their predecessors."

On the Graeco-Aryan community, West (2007) proposes the latest *terminus ante quem* for its split: "We shall see shortly that Graeco-Aryan must already have been differentiated from [LIE] by 2500. We have to allow several centuries for the development of [LIE] after its split from proto-Anatolian and before its further division. (...) The first speakers of Greek – or rather of the language that was to develop into Greek; I will call them *mello-Greeks* – arrived in Greece, on the most widely accepted view, at the beginning of Early Helladic III, that is, around 2300. They came by way of Epirus, probably from somewhere north of the Danube. Recent writers have derived them from Romania or eastern Hungary. (...) we must clearly go back at least to the middle of the millennium for the postulated Graeco-Aryan linguistic unity or community."

1.3.4. The so-called *North-West* Indo-European is considered by some to have formed an early linguistic community already separated from other Northern dialects (which included Pre-Tocharian) before or during the LIE dialectal split, and is generally assumed to have been a later IE *dialect continuum* between different communities in Northern Europe during the centuries on either side of 2500 BC, with a development usually linked to the expansion of the Corded Ware culture.

NOTE. A *dialect continuum*, or dialect area, was defined by Leonard Bloomfield as a range of dialects spoken across some geographical area that differ only slightly between neighbouring areas, but as one travels in any direction, these differences accumulate such that speakers from opposite ends of the *continuum* are no longer mutually intelligible. Examples of *dialect continua* included (now blurred with national languages and administrative borders) the North-Germanic, German, East Slavic, South Slavic, Northern Italian, South French, or West Iberian languages, among others.

A *Sprachbund*, also known as a linguistic area, convergence area, diffusion area or language crossroads – is a group of languages that have become similar in some way because of geographical proximity and language contact. They may be genetically unrelated, or only distantly related. That was probably the case with Balto-Slavic and Indo-Iranian, *v.i.* §1.7.

North-West IE was therefore a language or group of closely related dialects that emerged from a parent (N.LIE) dialect, in close contact for centuries, which allowed them to share linguistic developments.

NOTE. On the so-called *"Nort-West Indo-European" dialect continuum*, see Tovar (1977, 1979), Eric Hamp *("The Indo-European Horse"* in T. Markey and J.Greppin (eds.) *When Worlds Collide: Indo-Europeans and Pre-Indo-Europeans,* 1990), N. Oettinger *Grundsätzliche überlegungen zum Nordwest-Indogermanischen* (1997), and *Zum nordwestindogermanischen Lexikon* (1999); M. E. Huld *Indo-Europeanization of Northern Europe* (1996); Adrados–Bernabé–Mendoza (1995-1998); etc.

Regarding the dating of European proto-languages (of ca. 1500-500 BC) to the same time as Proto-Greek or Proto-Indo-Iranian (of ca. 2500-2000), obviating the time span between them, we might remember Kortlandt's (1990) description of what "seems to be a general tendency to date proto-languages farther back in time than is warranted by the linguistic evidence. When we reconstruct Proto-Romance, we arrive at a linguistic stage which is approximately two centuries later than the language of Caesar and Cicero (*cf.* Agard 1984: 47-60 for the phonological differences). When we start from the extralinguistic evidence and identify the origins of Romance with the beginnings of Rome, we arrive at the eighth century BC, which is almost a millennium too early. The point is that we must identify the formation of Romance with the imperfect learning of Latin by a large number of people during the expansion of the Roman empire."

1.3.4. Apart from the shared phonology and vocabulary, North-Western dialects show other common features, as a trend to reduce the noun inflection system, shared innovations in the verbal system (merge of imperfect, aorist and perfect in a single preterite, although some preterite-presents are found) the ***-r*** endings of the middle or middle-passive voice, a common evolution of laryngeals, etc.

The southern IEDs, which spread in different directions and evolved without forming a *continuum*, show therefore a differentiated phonology and vocabulary, but common older developments like the augment in ***é-***, middle desinences in ***-i***, athematic verbal inflection, pluperfect and perfect forms, and aspectual differentiation between the types **bhére/o-* and **tudé/o-*.

1.4. THE PROTO-INDO-EUROPEAN *URHEIMAT*

The search for the *Urheimat* or 'Homeland' of the prehistoric Proto-Indo-Europeans has developed as an archaeological quest along with the linguistic research looking for the reconstruction of the proto-language.

NOTE. Mallory (*Journal of Indo-European Studies 1*, 1973): "While many have maintained that the search for the PIE homeland is a waste of intellectual effort, or beyond the competence of the methodologies involved, the many scholars who have tackled the problem have ably evinced why they considered it important. The location of the homeland and the description of how the Indo-European languages spread is central to any explanation of how Europe became European. In a larger sense it is a search for the origins of western civilization."

According to A. Scherer's *Die Urheimat der Indogermanen* (1968), summing up the views of various authors from the years 1892-1963, still followed by mainstream Indo-European studies today, "[b]ased upon the localization of later languages such as Greek, Anatolian, and Indo-Iranian, a swathe of land in southern Russia north of the Black Sea is often proposed as the native area of the speakers of Proto-Indo-European".

1.4.1. HISTORICAL LINGUISTICS

In Adrados–Bernabé–Mendoza (1995-1998), a summary of main linguistic facts is made, supported by archaeological finds:

"It is *communis opinio* today that the languages of Europe have developed *in situ* in our continent; although indeed, because of the migrations, they have remained sometimes dislocated, and also extended and fragmented (...) Remember the recent date of the 'crystallisation' of European languages. 'Old European' [=North-West IE], from which they derive, is an already evolved language, with opposition masculine/feminine, and must be located in time ca. 2000 BC or before. Also, one must take into account the following data: the existence of Tocharian, related to [Northern LIE], but far away to the East, in the Chinese Turkestan; the presence of [Southern LIE] languages to the South of the Carpathian Mountains, no doubt already in the third millennium (the ancestors of Thracian, Iranian, Greek speakers); differentiation of Hittite and Luwian, within the Anatolian group, already ca. 2000 BC, in the documents of Kültepe, what means that Common Anatolian must be much older.

NOTE. Without taking on account archaeological theories, linguistic data reveals that:

a) [Northern LIE], located in Europe and in the Chinese Turkestan, must come from an intermediate zone, with expansion into both directions.
b) [Southern LIE], which occupied the space between Greece and the north-west of India, communicating both peninsulas through the languages of the Balkans, Ukraine and Northern Caucasus, the Turkestan and Iran, must also come from some intermediate location. Being a different linguistic group, it cannot come from Europe or the Russian Steppe, where Ural-Altaic languages existed.
c) Both groups have been in contact secondarily, taking on account the different 'recent' isoglosses in the contact zone.
d) The more archaic Anatolian must have been isolated from the more evolved IE; and that in some region with easy communication with Anatolia.

(...) Only the Steppe North of the Caucasus, the Volga river and beyond can combine all possibilities mentioned: there are pathways that go down into

Anatolia and Iran through the Caucasus, through the East of the Caspian Sea, the Gorgan plains, and they can migrate from there to the Chinese Turkestan, or to Europe, where two ways exist: to the North and to the South of the Carpathian mountains.

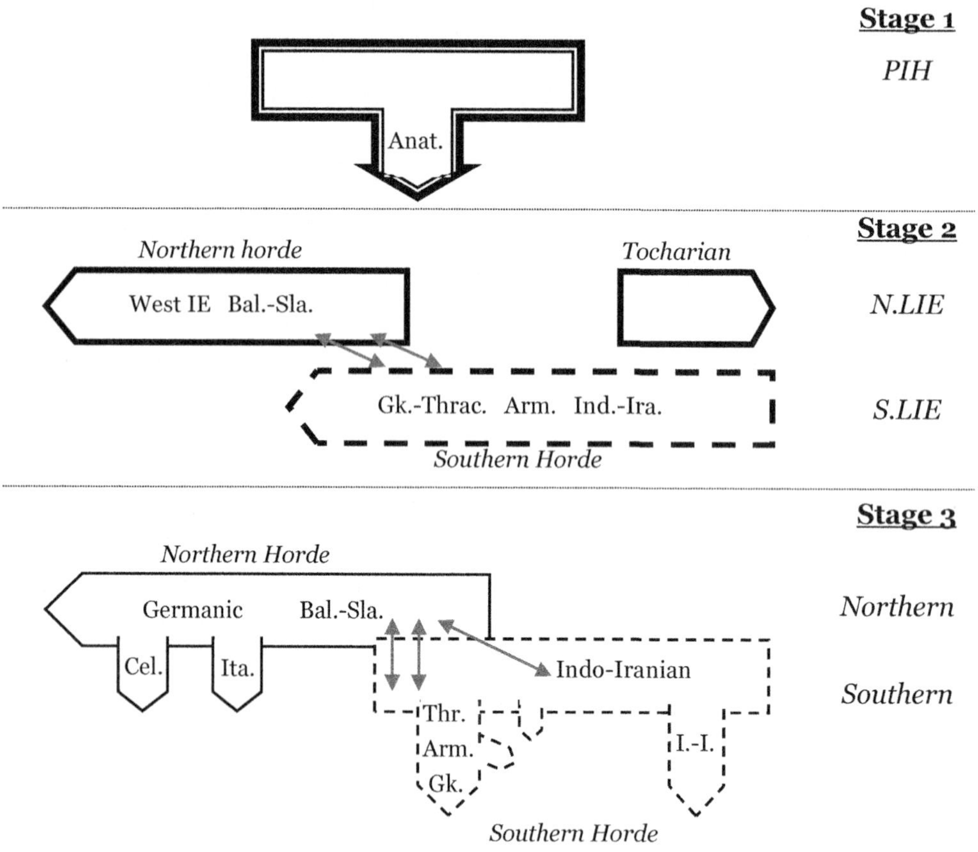

Diagram of the expansion and relationships of IE languages. Adapted from Adrados (1979).

These linguistic data, presented in a diagram, are supported by strong archaeological arguments: they have been defended by Gimbutas 1985 against Gamkrelidze–Ivanov (1994-1995) (...). This diagram proposes three stages. In the first one, [PIH] became isolated, and from it Anatolian emerged, being first relegated to the North of the Caucasus, and then crossing into the South: Common Anatolian must be located there. Note that there is no significant temporal difference with the other groups; it happens also that the first IE wave into Europe was older. It is somewhere to the North of the people that later went to Anatolia that happened the great revolution that developed [LIE], the 'common language'.

The following stages refer to that common language. The first is the one that saw both [N.LIE] (to the North) and [S.LIE] (to the South), the former being fragmented in two groups, one that headed West and one that migrated to the East. That is a proof that somewhere in the European Russia a common language [N.LIE] emerged; to the South, in Ukraine or in the Turkestan [S.LIE].

The second stage continues the movements of both branches, that launched waves to the South, but that were in contact in some moments, arising isoglosses that unite certain languages of the [Southern IE] group (first Greek, later Iranian, etc.) with those of the rearguard of [Northern IE] (especially Baltic and Slavic, also Italic and Germanic)".

NOTE. The assumption of three independent series of velars (*v.s. Considerations of Method*), has logical consequences when trying to arrange a consistent chronological and dialectal evolution from the point of view of historical linguistics. That is necessarily so because phonological change is generally assumed to be easier than morphological evolution for any given language. As a consequence, while morphological change is an agreed way to pinpoint different ancient groups, and lexical equivalences to derive late close contacts and culture (using them we could find agreement in grouping e.g. Balto-Slavic, Italo-Celtic, and Germanic between both groups, as well as an older Graeco-Aryan dialects), phonetics is often used – whether explicitly or not – as key to the groupings and chronology of the final split up of Late Indo-European, which is at the core of the actual archaeological *quest* today.

If we assume that the satem languages were show the most natural trend of leniting palatals from an 'original' system of three series of velars; if we assume that the other, centum languages, had undergone a trend of (unlikely and unparallelled) depalatalisation of the palatovelars; then the picture of the dialectal split must be different, because centum languages must be more closely related to each other in ancient times (due to the improbable happening of depalatalisation in more than one branch independently). That is the scheme followed in some manuals on IE linguistics or archaeology if three series are reconstructed or accepted, as it is commonly the case.

From that point of view, Italic, Celtic and Tocharian must be grouped together, while the satem core can be found in Balto-Slavic and Indo-Iranian. This contradicts the finds on different Northern and Graeco-Aryan dialects, though. As already stated, the Glottalic theory might support that dialectal scheme, by assuming a neater explanation of the natural evolution of glottalic, voiced and voiceless stops, different from the *depalatalisation* proposal. However, the glottalic theory is today mostly rejected (see below §1.5). Huld's (1997) explanation of the three series could also support this scheme (see above).

1.4.2. ARCHAEOLOGY

The *Kurgan hypothesis* was introduced by Marija Gimbutas (*The Prehistory of Eastern Europe, Part 1*, 1956) in order to combine archaeology with linguistics in locating the origins of the Proto-Indo-Europeans. She named the set of cultures in question "Kurgan" after their distinctive burial mounds and traced their diffusion into Eastern and Northern Europe.

NOTE. People were buried with their legs flexed, a position which remained typical for peoples identified with Indo-European speakers for a long time. The burials were covered with a mound, a kurgan (Turkish loanword in Russian for 'tumulus').

According to her hypothesis, PIE speakers were probably a nomadic tribe of the Pontic-Caspian steppe that expanded in successive stages of the Kurgan culture and three successive "waves" of expansion during the third millennium BC:

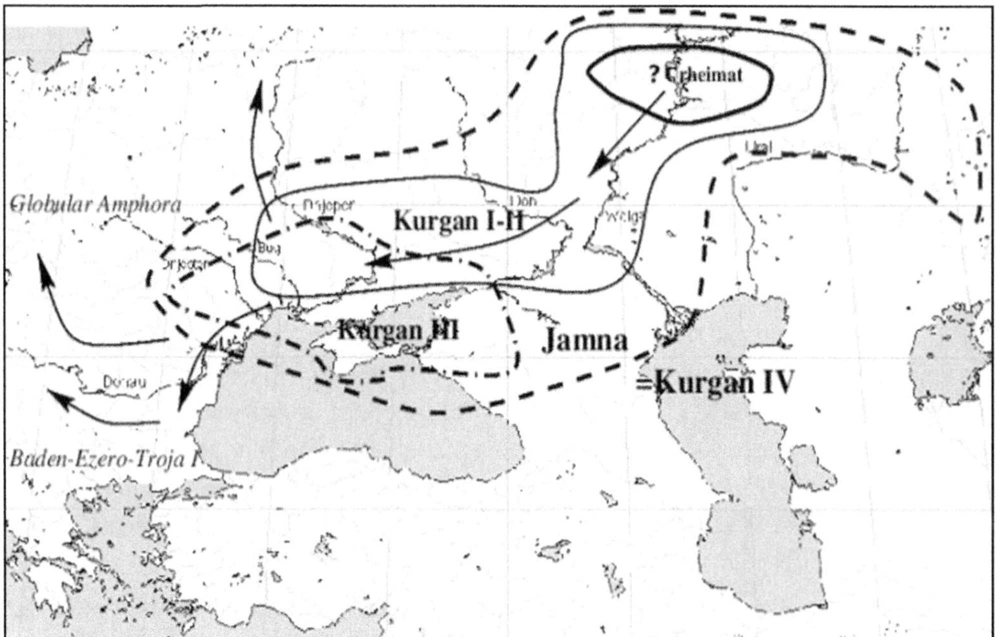

Hypothetical Urheimat (Homeland) of the first PIE speakers, from 4500 BC onwards. The Yamna (Pit Grave) culture lasted from ca. 3600 till 2200 BC. In this time the first wagons appeared. (PD)

- Kurgan I, Dnieper/Volga region, earlier half of the fourth millennium BC. Apparently evolving from cultures of the Volga basin, subgroups include the Samara and Seroglazovo cultures.

- Kurgan II–III, latter half of the fourth millennium BC. Includes the Sredny Stog culture and the Maykop culture of the northern Caucasus. Stone circles, early two-wheeled chariots, anthropomorphic stone *stelae* of deities.

- Kurgan IV or Pit Grave culture, first half of the third millennium BC, encompassing the entire steppe region from the Ural to Romania.

There were proposed to be three successive "waves" of expansion:

- o Wave 1, predating Kurgan I, expansion from the lower Volga to the Dnieper, leading to coexistence of Kurgan I and the Cucuteni culture. Repercussions of the migrations extend as far as the Balkans and along the Danube to the Vinča and Lengyel cultures in Hungary.
- o Wave 2, mid fourth millennium BC, originating in the Maykop culture and resulting in advances of *kurganised* hybrid cultures into northern Europe around 3000 BC – Globular Amphora culture, Baden culture, and ultimately Corded Ware culture.
- o Wave 3, 3000-2800 BC, expansion of the Pit Grave culture beyond the steppes; appearance of characteristic pit graves as far as the areas of modern Romania, Bulgaria and eastern Hungary.

The 'kurganised' Globular Amphora culture in Europe is proposed as a 'secondary Urheimat' of PIE, the culture separating into the Bell-Beaker culture and Corded Ware culture around 2300 BC. This ultimately resulted in the European IE families of Italic, Celtic and Germanic languages, and other, partly extinct, language groups of the Balkans and central Europe, possibly including the proto-Mycenaean invasion of Greece.

1.4.3. QUANTITATIVE ANALYSIS

Glottochronology tries to compare lexical, morphological or phonological traits in order to develop more trustable timelines and dialectal groupings. It hasn't attracted much reliability among linguists, though, in relation with the comparative method, on which the whole IE reconstruction is still based.

NOTE. Most of these glottochronological works are highly controversial, partly owing to issues of accuracy, partly to the question of whether its very basis is sound. Two serious arguments that make this method mostly invalid today are the proof that Swadesh *formulae* would not work on all available material, and that language change arises from socio-historical events which are of course unforeseeable and, therefore, incomputable.

A variation of traditional glottochronology is *phylogenic reconstruction*; in biological systematics, *phylogeny* is a graph intended to represent genetic relationships between biological taxa. Linguists try to transfer these biological models to obtain "subgroupings" of one or the other branch of a language family.

NOTE. Clackson (2007) describes a recent phylogenetic study, by Atkinson et al. (*"From Words to Dates: Water into Wine, Mathemagic or Phylogenetic Inference?", Transactions of the Philological Society 103*, 2005): "The New Zealand team use models which were originally designed to build phylogenies based on DNA and other genetic information, which do not assume a constant rate of change. Instead, their model accepts that the rate of change varies, but it constrains the variation within limits that coincide with attested linguistic sub-groups. For example, it is known that the Romance languages all derive from Latin, and we know that Latin was spoken 2,000 years ago. The rates of lexical change in the Romance family can therefore be calculated in absolute terms. These different possible rates of change are then projected back into prehistory, and the age of the parent can be ascertained within a range of dates depending on the highest and lowest rates of change attested in the daughter languages. More recently (Atkinson et al. 2005), they have used data based not just on lexical characters, but on morphological and phonological information as well."

Their results show a late separation of the Northwestern IE languages, with a last core of Romance-Germanic, earlier Celto-Romano-Germanic, and earlier Celto-Romano-Germano-Balto-Slavic. Previous to that date, Graeco-Armenian would have separated earlier than Indo-Iranian, while Tocharian would have been the earliest to split up from LIE, still within the Kurgan framework, although quite early (ca. 4000-3000 BC). Before that, the Anatolian branch is found to have split quite earlier than the dates usually assumed in linguistics and archaeology (ca. 7000-6000 BC).

Holm proposed to apply a *Separation-Level Recovery* system to PIE. This is made (Holm, 2008) by using the data on the new *Lexikon der indogermanischen Verben*, 2nd ed. (Rix *et al.* 2001), considered a "more modern and linguistic reliable database" than the data traditionally used from Pokorny IEW. The results show a similar grouping to those of Atkinson *et al.* (2005), differentiating between North-West IE (Italo-Celtic, Germanic, Balto-Slavic), and Graeco-Aryan (Graeco-Armenian, Indo-Iranian) groups. However, Anatolian is deemed to have separated quite late compared to linguistic dates, being considered then just another LIE dialect, therefore rejecting the concept of Indo-Hittite altogether. Some of Holm's studies are available at <http://hjholm.de/>.

The most recent quantitative studies then apparently show similar results in the phylogenetic groupings of recent languages, i.e. Late Indo-European dialects, excluding Tocharian. Their dates remain, at best, just approximations for the separation of late and well attested languages, though, while the dating (and even grouping) of ancient languages like Anatolian or Tocharian with modern evolution patterns remains at best questionable.

One of the newest studies published in this field is "Mapping the Origins and Expansion of the Indo-European Language Family", by Remco Bouckaert et al. (2012), published in Science, in an article that included a podcast with an interview, at <http://www.sciencemag.org/content/337/6097/989.2.full>. They have even created a dedicated website with media (including a video) and FAQ / controversies section at <http://language.cs.auckland.ac.nz/>. It seems that 'Bayesian Phylogeography' is in fashion these days.

yamnaya R1a
corded ware R1B

1.4.4. ARCHAEOGENETICS

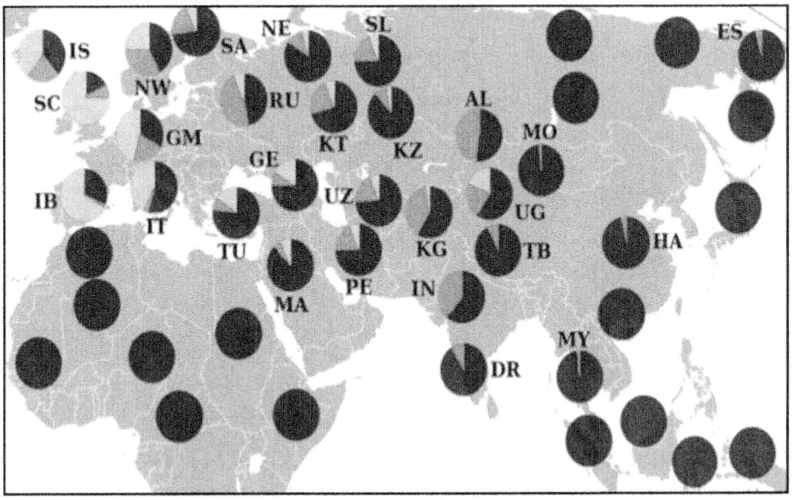

Distribution of haplotypes R1b (light colour) for Eurasiatic Paleolithic and R1a (dark colour) for Yamna expansion; black represents other haplogroups. (2009, modified from Dbachmann 2007)

Cavalli-Sforza and Alberto Piazza argue that Renfrew (*v.i.* §1.5) and Gimbutas reinforce rather than contradict each other, stating that "genetically speaking, peoples of the Kurgan steppe descended at least in part from people of the Middle Eastern Neolithic who immigrated there from Turkey".

NOTE. The genetic record cannot yield any direct information as to the language spoken by these groups. The current interpretation of genetic data suggests a strong genetic continuity in Europe; specifically, studies of mtDNA by Bryan Sykes show that about 80% of the genetic stock of Europeans originated in the Paleolithic.

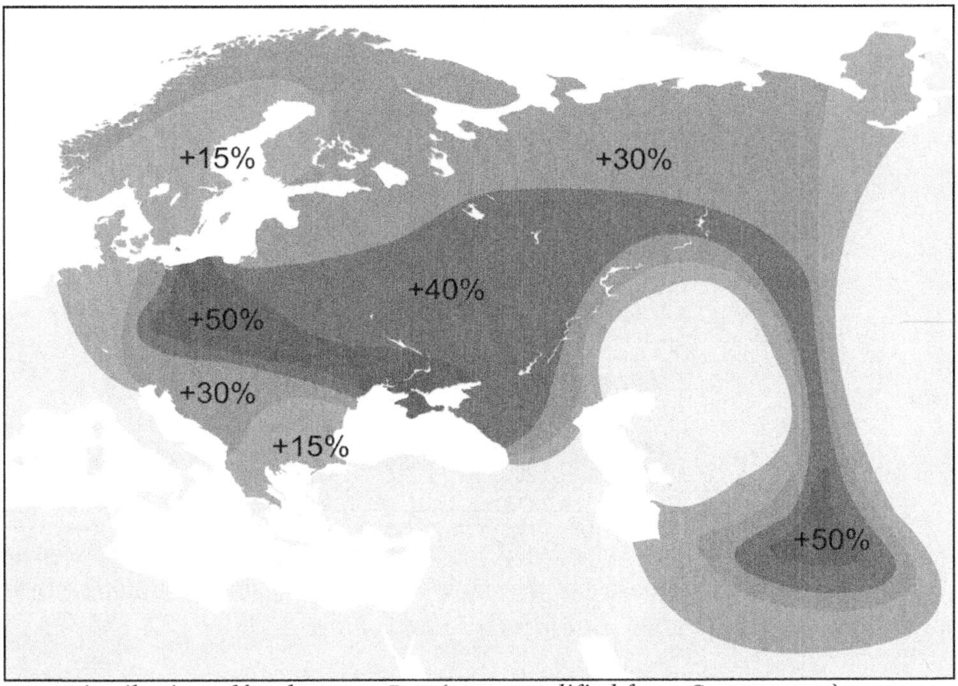

Distribution of haplogroup R1a (2011, modified from Crates 2009)

Spencer Wells suggests that the origin, distribution and age of the R1a1 haplotype points to an ancient migration, possibly corresponding to the spread by the Kurgan people in their expansion across the Eurasian steppe around 3000 BC, stating that "there is nothing to contradict this model, although the genetic patterns do not provide clear support either".

NOTE. R1a1 is most prevalent in Poland, Russia, and Ukraine, and is also observed in Pakistan, India and central Asia. R1a1 is largely confined east of the Vistula gene barrier and drops considerably to the west. The spread of Y-chromosome DNA haplogroup R1a1 has been associated with the spread of the Indo-European languages too. The mutations that characterise haplogroup R1a occurred ~10,000 years bp. Haplogroup R1a1, whose lineage is thought to have originated in the Eurasian Steppes north of the Black and Caspian Seas, is therefore associated with the Kurgan culture, as well as with the postglacial Ahrensburg culture which has been suggested to have spread the gene originally.

The present-day population of R1b haplotype, with extremely high peaks in Western Europe and measured up to the eastern confines of Central Asia, are believed to be the descendants of a refugium in the Iberian peninsula at the Last Glacial Maximum, where the haplogroup may have achieved genetic homogeneity. As conditions eased with the Allerød Oscillation in about 12000 BC, descendants of this group migrated and eventually recolonised all of Western Europe, leading to the dominant position of R1b in variant degrees from Iberia to Scandinavia, so evident in haplogroup maps.

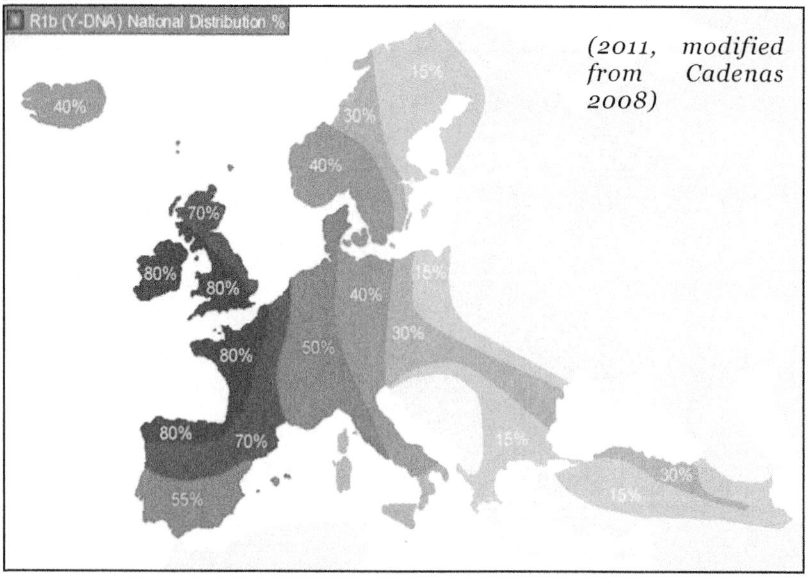

(2011, modified from Cadenas 2008)

NOTE. High concentrations of Mesolithic or late Paleolithic YDNA haplogroups of types R1b (typically well above 35%) and I (up to 25%), are thought to derive ultimately of the robust Eurasiatic Cro Magnoid homo sapiens of the Aurignacian culture, and the subsequent gracile leptodolichomorphous people of the Gravettian culture that entered Europe from the Middle East 20,000 to 25,000 years ago, respectively.

1.4.5. THE KURGAN HYPOTHESIS AND THE THREE-STAGE THEORY

ARCHAEOLOGY (Kurgan Hypothesis)	*LINGUISTICS (Three-Stage Theory)*
ca. 4500-4000 BC. Sredny Stog, Dnieper-Donets and Sarama cultures, domestication of the horse.	*Proto-Indo-Hittite?*
ca. 4000-3500 BC. The Yamna culture, the kurgan builders, emerges in the steppe, and the Maykop culture in northern Caucasus.	*Pre-LIE and Pre-PAn dialects evolve in different communities but presumably still in contact within the same territory.*
ca. 3500-3000 BC. Yamna culture at its peak: stone idols, two-wheeled proto-chariots, animal husbandry, permanent settlements and hillforts, subsisting on agriculture and fishing, along rivers. Contact of the Yamna culture with late Neolithic Europe cultures results in kurganised Globular Amphora and Baden cultures. Maykop culture shows earliest evidence of the beginning Bronze Age.	*Proto-Anatolian becomes isolated (either to the south of the Caucasus or in the Balkans), and has no more contacts with the linguistic innovations of the common Late Indo-European language.* *Late Indo-European evolves in turn into dialects, at least a Southern or Graeco-Aryan and a Northern one.*
ca. 3000-2500 BC. The Yamna culture extends over the entire Pontic steppe. The Corded Ware culture extends from the Rhine to the Volga, corresponding to the latest stage of IE unity. Different cultures disintegrate, still in loose contact, enabling the spread of technology.	*Dialectal communities begin to migrate, remaining still in loose contact, enabling the spread of the last common phonetic and morphological innovations, and loan words. PAn, spoken in Asia Minor, evolves into Common Anatolian.*
ca. 2500-2000 BC. The Bronze Age reaches Central Europe with the Beaker culture of Northern Indo-Europeans. Indo-Iranians settle north of the Caspian in the Sintashta-Petrovka and later the Andronovo culture.	*The breakup of the southern IE dialects is complete. Proto-Greek spoken in the Balkans; Proto-Indo-Iranian in Central Asia; North-West Indo-European in Northern Europe; Common Anatolian dialects in Anatolia.*
ca. 2000-1500 BC. The chariot is invented, leading to the split and rapid spread of Iranians and other peoples from the Andronovo culture and the Bactria-Margiana Complex over much of Central Asia, Northern India, Iran and Eastern Anatolia. Greek Darg Ages and flourishing of the Hittite Empire. Pre-Celtic Unetice culture.	*Indo-Iranian splits up in two main dialects, Indo-Aryan and Iranian. European proto-dialects like Pre-Germanic, Pre-Celtic, Pre-Italic, and Pre-Balto-Slavic differentiate from each other. Anatolian languages like Hittite and Luwian are written down; Indo-Iranian attested through Mitanni; a Greek dialect, Mycenaean, is already spoken.*
ca. 1500-1000 BC. The Nordic Bronze Age sees the rise of the Germanic Urnfield and the Celtic Hallstatt cultures in Central Europe, introducing the Iron Age. Italic peoples move to the Italian Peninsula. Rigveda composed. Decline of Hittite Kingdoms and the Mycenaean civilisation.	*Celtic, Italic, Germanic, Baltic and Slavic are already different proto-languages, developing in turn different dialects. Iranian and other related southern dialects expand through military conquest, and Indo-Aryan spreads in the form of its sacred language, Sanskrit.*
ca. 1000-500 BC. Northern Europe enters the Pre-Roman Iron Age. Early Indo-European Kingdoms and Empires in Eurasia. In Europe, Classical Antiquity begins with the flourishing of the Greek peoples. Foundation of Rome.	*Celtic dialects spread over western Europe, German dialects to the south of Jutland. Italic languages in the Italian Peninsula. Greek and Old Italic alphabets appear. Late Anatolian dialects. Cimmerian, Scythian and Sarmatian in Asia, Palaeo-Balkan languages in the Balkans.*

1.5. OTHER ARCHAEOLINGUISTIC THEORIES

1.5.1. The most known new alternative theory concerning PIE is the Glottalic theory. It assumes that Proto-Indo-European was pronounced more or less like Armenian, i.e. instead of PIE **p*, **b*, *b^h, the pronunciation would have been **p'*, **p*, **b*, and the same with the other two voiceless-voiced-voiced aspirated series of consonants usually reconstructed. The IE *Urheimat* would have been then located in the surroundings of Anatolia, especially near Lake Urmia, in northern Iran, hence the archaism of Anatolian dialects and the glottalics found in Armenian.

NOTE. Those linguistic and archaeological findings are supported by Gamkredlize-Ivanov ("*The early history of Indo-European languages*", *Scientific American*, 1990) where early Indo-European vocabulary deemed "of southern regions" is examined, and similarities with Semitic and Kartvelian languages are also brought to light.

This theory is generally rejected; Beekes (1995) for all: "But this theory is in fact very improbable. The presumed loan-words are difficult to evaluate, because in order to do so the Semitic words and those of other languages would also have to be evaluated. The names of trees are notoriously unreliable as evidence. The words for panther, lion and elephant are probably incorrectly reconstructed as PIE words."

1.5.2. Alternative theories include:

I. The *European Homeland thesis* maintains that the common origin of the IE languages lies in Europe. These hypotheses are often driven by archeological theories. A. Häusler (*Die Indoeuropäisierung Griechenlands, Slovenska Archeológia* 29, 1981; etc.) continues to defend the hypothesis that places Indo-European origins in Europe, stating that all the known differentiation emerged in the *continuum* from the Rhin to the Urals.

NOTE. It has been traditionally located in 1) *Lithuania* and the surrounding areas, by R.G. Latham (1851) and Th. Poesche (*Die Arier. Ein Beitrag zur historischen Anthropologie*, 1878); 2) *Scandinavia*, by K.Penka (*Origines ariacae*, 1883); 3) *Central Europe*, by G. Kossinna ("*Die Indogermanische Frage archäologisch beantwortet*", *Zeitschrift für Ethnologie*, 34, 1902), P.Giles (*The Aryans*, 1922), and by linguist/archaeologist G. Childe (*The Aryans. A Study of Indo-European Origins*, 1926).

a. The *Paleolithic Continuity theory* posits that the advent of IE languages should be linked to the arrival of Homo sapiens in Europe and Asia from Africa in the Upper Paleolithic. The PCT proposes a continued presence of Pre-IE and non-IE peoples and languages in Europe from Paleolithic times, allowing for minor invasions and infiltrations of local scope, mainly during the last three millennia.

NOTE. There are some research papers concerning the PCT available at <http://www.continuitas.com/>. Also, the PCT could in turn be connected with Frederik Kortlandt's Indo-Uralic and Altaic studies <http://kortlandt.nl/publications/>.

On the temporal relationship question, Mallory–Adams (2007): "Although there are still those who propose solutions dating back to the Palaeolithic, these cannot be reconciled with the cultural vocabulary of the Indo-European languages. The later vocabulary of Proto-Indo- European hinges on such items as wheeled vehicles, the plough, wool, which are attested in Proto-Indo-European, including Anatolian. It is unlikely then that words for these items entered the Proto-Indo-European lexicon prior to about 4000 BC."

b. A new theory put forward by Colin Renfrew relates IE expansion to the *Neolithic revolution,* causing the peacefully spreading of an older pre-IE language into Europe from Asia Minor from around 7000 BC, with the advance of farming. It proposes that the dispersal (discontinuity) of Proto-Indo-Europeans originated in Neolithic Anatolia.

NOTE. Reacting to criticism, Renfrew by 1999 revised his proposal to the effect of taking a pronounced Indo-Hittite position. Renfrew's revised views place only Pre-Proto-Indo-European in seventh millennium Anatolia, proposing as the homeland of Proto-Indo-European proper the Balkans around 5000 BC, explicitly identified as the "Old European culture" proposed by Gimbutas.

Mallory–Adams (2007): "(...) in both the nineteenth century and then again in the later twentieth century, it was proposed that Indo-European expansions were associated with the spread of agriculture. The underlying assumption here is that only the expansion of a new more productive economy and attendant population expansion can explain the widespread expansion of a language family the size of the Indo-European. This theory is most closely associated with a model that derives the Indo-Europeans from Anatolia about the seventh millennium BC from whence they spread into south-eastern Europe and then across Europe in a Neolithic 'wave of advance'.

(...) Although the difference between the Wave of Advance and Kurgan theories is quite marked, they both share the same explanation for the expansion of the Indo-Iranians in Asia (and there are no fundamental differences in either of their difficulties in explaining the Tocharians), i.e. the expansion of mobile pastoralists eastwards and then southwards into Iran and India. Moreover, there is recognition by supporters of the Neolithic theory that the 'wave of advance' did not reach the peripheries of Europe (central and western Mediterranean, Atlantic and northern Europe) but that these regions adopted agriculture from their neighbours rather than being replaced by them".

Talking about these new hypotheses, Adrados–Bernabé–Mendoza (1995-1998) discuss the relevance that is given to each new personal archaeological 'revolutionary' theory: "[The hypothesis of Colin Renfrew (1987)] is based on ideas about the diffusion of agriculture from Asia to Europe in [the fifth millennium Neolithic Asia Minor], diffusion that would be united to that of Indo-Europeans; it doesn't pay attention at all to linguistic data. The [hypothesis of Gamkrelidze–Ivanov (1980, etc.)], which places the Homeland in the contact zone between Caucasian and Semitic peoples, south of the Caucasus, is based on real or supposed lexical loans; it disregards morphological data altogether, too. Criticism of these ideas – to which people have paid too much attention – are found, among others, in Meid (1989), Villar (1991), etc."

II. Another hypothesis, contrary to the European ones, also mainly driven today by nationalistic or religious views, traces back the origin of PIE to Vedic Sanskrit, postulating that this is very *pure*, and that the origin of common Proto-Indo-European can thus be traced back to the Indus Valley Civilisation of ca. 3000 BC.

NOTE. Pan-Sanskritism was common among early Indo-Europeanists, as Schlegel, Young, A. Pictet (*Les origines indoeuropéens*, 1877) or Schmidt (who preferred Babylonia), but are now mainly supported by those who consider Sanskrit almost equal to Late Proto-Indo-European. For more on this, see S. Misra (*The Aryan Problem: A Linguistic Approach*, 1992), Elst (*Update on the Aryan Invasion Debate*, 1999), followed up by S.G. Talageri (*The Rigveda: A Historical Analysis*, 2000), both part of "*Indigenous Indo-Aryan*" viewpoint by N. Kazanas, the "*Out of India*" theory, with a framework dating back to the times of the Indus Valley Civilisation.

1.6. RELATIONSHIP TO OTHER LANGUAGES

1.6.1. Many higher-level relationships between PIE and other language families have been proposed, but these speculative connections are highly controversial. Perhaps the most widely accepted proposal is of an Indo-Uralic family, encompassing PIE and Proto-Uralic, a language from which Hungarian, Finnish, Estonian, Saami and a number of other languages belong. The evidence usually cited in favour of this is the proximity of the proposed *Urheimaten* for both of them, the typological similarity between the two languages, and a number of apparent shared morphemes.

NOTE. Other proposals, further back in time (and correspondingly less accepted), model PIE as a branch of Indo-Uralic with a Caucasian substratum; link PIE and Uralic with Altaic and certain other families in Asia, such as Korean, Japanese, Chukotko-Kamchatkan and Eskimo-Aleut (representative proposals are Greenberg's Eurasiatic and its proposed parent-language Nostratic); etc.

1.6.2. Indo-Uralic or Uralo-Indo-European is therefore a hypothetical language family consisting of Indo-European and Uralic (i.e. Finno-Ugric and Samoyedic). Most linguists still consider this theory speculative and its evidence insufficient to conclusively prove genetic affiliation.

NOTE. The problem with lexical evidence is to weed out words due to borrowing, because Uralic languages have been in contact with Indo-European languages for millennia, and consequently borrowed many words from them.

Björn Collinder, author of the path-breaking *Comparative Grammar of the Uralic Languages* (1960), a standard work in the field of Uralic studies, argued for the kinship of Uralic and Indo-European (1934, 1954, 1965).

The most extensive attempt to establish sound correspondences between Indo-European and Uralic to date is that of the late Slovenian linguist Bojan Čop. It was published as a series of articles in various academic journals from 1970 to 1989 under the collective title *Indouralica*. The topics to be covered by each article were sketched out at the beginning of "Indouralica II". Of the projected 18 articles only 11 appeared. These articles have not been collected into a single volume and thereby remain difficult to access.

Dutch linguist Frederik Kortlandt supports a model of Indo-Uralic in which its speakers lived north of the Caspian Sea, and Proto-Indo-Europeans began as a group that branched off westward from there to come into geographic proximity with the Northwest Caucasian languages, absorbing a Northwest Caucasian lexical blending before moving farther westward to a region north of the Black Sea where their language settled into canonical Proto-Indo-European.

1.6.3. The most common arguments in favour of a relationship between PIH and Uralic are based on seemingly common elements of morphology, such as:

Meaning	PIE	Proto-Uralic
'I, me'	**me* 'me' (Acc.), **mene* 'my' (Gen.)	**mun*, **mina* 'I'
'you' (sg)	**tu* (Nom.), **twe* (Acc.), **tewe* 'your' (Gen.)	**tun*, **tina*
1st P. singular	*-*m*	*-*m*
1st P. plural	*-*me*	*-*me*
2nd P. singular	*-*s* (active), *-*tHa* (perfect)	*-*t*
2nd P. plural	*-*te*	*-*te*
Demonstrative	**so* 'this, he/she' (animate nom)	**ša* (3rd person singular)
Interr. pron. (An.)	*k^w*i*- 'who?, what?'; *k^w*o*- 'who?, what?'	**ken* 'who?', **ku*-, 'who?'
Relative pronoun	**jo*-	*-*ja* (nomen agentis)
Accusative	*-*m*	*-*m*
Ablative/partitive	*-*od*	*-*ta*
Nom./Acc. plural	*-*es* (Nom. pl.), *-*m̥-s* (Acc. pl.)	*-*t*
Oblique plural	*-*i* (pronomin. pl., *cf.* **we-i*- 'we', **to-i*- 'those')	*-*i*
Dual	*-H_1	*-*k*
Stative	*-*s*- (aorist); *-*es*-, *-*t* (stative substantive)	*-*ta*
Negative particle	**nei*, **ne*	**ei*- [negative verb] , **ne*

‘to give’	**deh*$_3$-	**toHe-*
‘to wet’,’water’	**wed-* ‘to wet’, **wodr̥-* ‘water’	**weti* ‘water’
‘water’’	**mesg-* ‘dip under water, dive’	**muśke-* ‘wash’
‘to assign’, ‘name’	**nem-* ‘to assign, to allot’, **h*$_1$*nomn̥-* ‘name’	**nimi* ‘name’
‘metal’	**h*$_2$*weseh*$_2$- ‘gold’	**waśke* ‘some metal’
‘trade’	**mei-* ‘exchange’	**miHe-* ‘give, sell’
‘fish’	**(s)k*^{w}*alo-* ‘large fish’	**kala* ‘fish’
‘sister-in-law’	**galou-* ‘husband's sister’	**käl3* ‘sister-in-law’
‘much’	**polu-* ‘much’	**palj3* ‘thick, much’

1.7. INDO-EUROPEAN DIALECTS

SCHLEICHER’S FABLE: FROM PIE TO MODERN ENGLISH

The so-called *Schleicher's fable* is a poem composed in PIE, published by August Schleicher in 1868, originally named “*The Sheep and the Horses*”. It is written here in the different reconstructible IE dialects for comparison.

Translation: « *The Sheep and the Horses. • A sheep that had no wool • saw horses, • one pulling a heavy wagon, • one carrying a big load, • and one carrying a man quickly. • The sheep said to the horses: • “My heart pains me, • seeing a man driving horses”. • The horses said: “Listen, sheep, • our hearts pain us when we see this: • a man, the master, makes the wool of the sheep • into a warm garment for himself. • And the sheep has no wool”. • Having heard this, the sheep fled into the plain.* »

Proto-Indo-Hittite ca. 3500? BC	**Common Anatolian (Proto-Anatolian dialect) , ca. 2500 BC**
$h_2$owis $h_1$ekwōs-k^we.	Howis ekwōs-k^wu.
$h_2$owis (h)josmi wl̥$h_1$neh$_2$ ne-$h_1$est	Howis josmi ulhneh ne est,
$h_1$ekwoms dedorke,	ekwons dedorke,
tom g^wr̥$h_3$úm wog^{h}om wég^{h}ontm̥,	tom g^wurrúm wogom wégontm̥,
tom megeh$_2$m b^{h}orom,	tom megehm borom,
tom d^{h}h$_1$g^{h}monm̥ $h_1$oh$_1$ku b^{h}érontm̥.	tom dgomonm̥ oku bérontm̥.
$h_2$owis $h_1$ékwob^{h}os weuk^{w}ét:	Howis ékwobos wūk^{w}ét:
“kērd $h_2$ég^{h}nutoi $h_1$moí,	“Kr̥di xégnutor moi,
widn̥téi d^{h}h$_1$g^{h}monm̥ $h_1$ekwoms $h_2$égontm̥”.	dgomonm̥ ekwons xégontm̥ widn̥tę”.
$h_1$ekwōs weuk^{w}ónt: “klu $h_2$owi!	Ekwōs wūk^{w}ónt: “Klu, howi!
kērd $h_2$ég^{h}nutoi n̥sméi widn̥tb^{h}ós:	kr̥di hegnutor n̥smę widn̥tbós:
d^{h}h$_1$g^{h}mōn, potis, $h_2$owjom-r̥ wl̥h$_1$neh$_2$m̥	dgomōn, potis, howjom-r̥ ulhnehm̥
sweb^{h}ei g^{wh}ormom westrom k^wr̥neuti.	swebę g^wermom wéstrom k^wr̥nūdi.
$h_2$owjom-k^we wl̥hneh$_2$ ne $h_1$esti”.	Howjomk^wu ulhneh ne esti”.
tod kekluwṓs $h_2$owis $h_2$egrom b^{h}ugét.	Tod kekluwṓs howis hegrom bugét.

North-West IE (Northern Late IE dialect), ca. 2500 BC	Literal English gloss
Owis ekwōs-kʷe.	*(the)sheep (the)horses-and.*
Owis josmi wl̥nā ne est,	*(a)sheep (on)which wool not-is*
ekwons dedorke,	*horses saw,*
tom gʷrawúm wogʰom wégʰontm̥,	*one(of-them) (a) heavy wagon pulling,*
tom megām bʰorom,	*one(of-them) (a)big load,*
tom gʰomonom ōkú bʰérontm̥.	*one(of-them) (a)human quickly carrying.*
Owis ékwobʰos weukʷét:	*(the)sheep (to the)horses said:*
"Kr̥di ágʰnutor moi,	*" (the)heart is-hurt me,*
gʰomonom ekwons ágontm̥ widn̥téi".	*seeing (a)human horses driving".*
Ekwōs weukʷónt: "Kl̥néu, owi!	*(the)horses said: "listen, sheep*
kr̥di ágʰnutor n̥sméi widn̥tbʰós:	*(the)heart pains us seeing:*
gʰomonos, potis, owjos wl̥nām	*(a)man, (the)master, (of)sheep wool*
sebʰei gʷʰormom westrom kʷr̥neuti.	*himself (a)warm garment make.*
Owjomkʷe wl̥nā ne esti".	*(the)sheep-and wool not-has".*
Tod kekluwṓs owis agrom bʰugét.	*this having-heard, (the)sheep (to-the)plain fled*

NOTE. These versions of early Indo-Hittite, Anatolian, and early LIE dialects (NWIE, PII, PGk) fit prof. Biltoo's version of Schleicher's fable, with the vocabulary and expressions that appear in *Prometheus* (2012) and in its deleted scenes and script. As in any other language, there are a dozen ways to say almost the same in PIE, with combinations of synonyms, lexical and verbal periphrases, etc. This is just one of the possible translations of Schleicher's poem.

Proto-Indo-Iranian (Southern Late IE dialect, ca. 2500 BC)	Proto-Greek (Southern Late IE dialect, ca. 2500 BC)
Awis aķwāsķa.	Owis ekʷoi-kʷe.
Awis, jasmi wr̥nā na āst,	Ówis, josmi wlānā ne ēst,
aķwans dadarka,	ekʷons dedorke,
tam gurúm waǵʰam wáǵʰantm̥,	tom kʷarúm wokʰom wekʰontm̥,
tam maǵʰam bʰaram,	tom megām pʰorom,
tam ǵʰámanam āķu bʰarantm̥.	tom kʰtʰómonm̥ ōku pʰérontm̥.
Awis áķwabʰjas áwaukat:	Ówis ékʷopʰos éweukʷet:
"Ķr̥di ágʰnutai mai,	"Kr̥di ákʰnutoi moi,
ǵʰámanam aķwans aǵantam widn̥tái".	kʰtʰómonm̥ ekwons ágontm̥ widn̥téi".
Áķwās áwaukant: "Ķr̥nudʰí avi!	Ékʷoi éweukʷont: "Kl̥nutʰi, owi!
ķr̥d ágʰnutai n̥smái widn̥tbʰjás:	kr̥di ágnutoi n̥sméi widn̥tpʰós:
ǵʰámanas, patis, awjas wr̥nām	kʰtʰómōn, potis, owjos wlānām
swabʰi gʰarmam wastram kr̥nauti.	sepʰei kʷʰermom westrom kʷr̥neuti.
Awjamķa wr̥nā na asti".	Owjom-kʷe wlānā ne esti".
Tat ķaķruwā́s awis aǵram ábʰugat.	Tot kekluwṓs owis agrom épʰuget.

Proto-Celtic (North-West IE dialect, ca. 1000 BC)	Proto-Italic (North-West IE dialect, ca. 1000 BC)
Owis ekʷoikʷe.	Owis ekwoikʷe.
Owis, josmi wlanā ne est,	Owis, josmi wlānā ne est,
ekʷōs dedarke,	ekwōs dedorke,
tom barúm woxom wéxontam,	tom grāwúm woxom wéxontem,
tom megam borom,	tom megam φorom,
tom dxonjom āku berontam.	tom xomonem ōku φerontem.
Owis nu ékʷobos weukʷét:	Owis nu ékwoφos weukʷét:
“Kridi áxnutor mai,	“Kordi áxnutor mei,
ekʷōs ágontom wīróm widantí”.	ekwōs ágontom wīróm widentéi”.
Ekʷoi tu wewkʷónt: “Kalnéu, owi!	Ekwoi tu wewkʷónt: “Kalnéu, owi!
kridi áxnutor ansméi widantbós:	kordi axnutor ensméi widentφós:
neros, φotis, owjom ar wlanām	neros, potis, owjom ar wlānām
sebi gʷormom westrom kʷarneuti.	seφei gʰormom westrom kʷorneuti.
Owjomkʷe wlanā ne esti”.	Owjomkʷe wlānā ne esti”.
Tod kekluwṓs owis agrom bugét.	Tud kekluwṓs owis agrom φugít.

Pre-Proto-Germanic (North-West IE dialect, ca. 1000 BC)	Proto-Balto-Slavic (North-West IE dialect, ca. 1000 BC)
Awiz exwazxʷe.	Awis eḳwōskʲe.
Awiz, jasmi wulnō ne est,	Awis, jasmi wilnā ne est,
exwanz dedurke,	eḳwas dedirke,
þan karún wagan wéganðun,	tan grun waġan wéġantun,
þan mekon baran,	tan megan baran,
þan gúmanan āxu béranðun.	tan ġmanan ōku bérantun
Awiz nu éxwamaz weuxʷéð:	Awis nu eḳwamas wjaukʲét:
“Hurti ágnuðai mei,	“Ḳirdi ágnutei mei,
exwanz ákanðun werán witanðī”.	ekwans ágantun wirán widuntéi”.
Exwaz tu wewxʷant: “Hulnéu, awi!	Eḳwōs tu wjaukunt: “Kludí, awi!
hurti áknuðai unsmí witunðmáz:	ḳirdi ágnutei insméi widūntmás:
neraz, faþiz, awjan ar wulnōn	neras, patis, awjam ar wilnān
sibī warman wesþran hʷurneuþi.	sebi gormom westran kʲirnjautĭ.
Awjanxʷe wulnō ne isti”.	Áwjamkʲe wilnā ne esti”.
Þat hexluwā́z awiz akran bukéþ.	Ta kʲekluwṓs awis agram bugít.

1.7.1. NORTHERN INDO-EUROPEAN DIALECTS

I. NORTH-WEST INDO-EUROPEAN

1. North-West Indo-European was probably spoken in Europe in the centuries on either side of ca. 2500 BC, including Pre-Celtic, Pre-Italic, Pre-Germanic, Pre-Baltic, and Pre-Slavic, among other ancestors of IE languages attested in Europe. Its original common location is usually traced back to "some place to the East of the Rhine, to the North of the Alps and the Carpathian Mountains, to the South of Scandinavia and to the East of the Eastern European Lowlands or Russian Plain, not beyond Moscow" (Adrados–Bernabé–Mendoza 1995-1998).

2. The Corded Ware (also Battle Axe or Single Grave) complex of cultures, traditionally represents for many scholars the arrival of the first speakers of Northern LIE in central Europe, coming from the Yamna culture. The complex dates from about 3200-2300 BC. The Globular Amphorae culture may be slightly earlier, but the relationship between these cultures remains unclear.

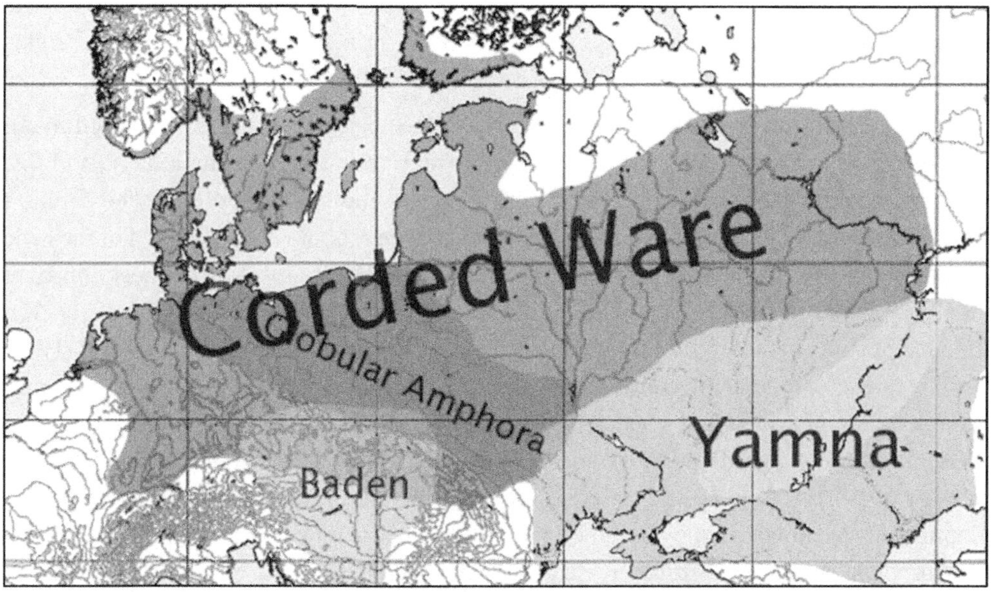

Generalized distribution of all Corded Ware variants (ca. 3200-2300), with adjacent third millennium cultures. Mallory–Adams (1997). The Globular Amphora culture (ca. 3400-2800) overlaps with the early territory of the Corded Ware culture (ca. 3200-2800 BC), which later expanded to east and west. (2011, modified from Dbachmann 2005)

NOTE. From a linguistic-archaeological point of view, Beekes (1995): "The combined use of the horse and the ox-drawn wagon made the Indo-Europeans exceptionally mobile. It is therefore not surprising that they were able to migrate over such a very large area after having first taken possession of the steppes (...). It has long been assumed that the Corded Ware culture (from 3300 to 2300 B.C., in German the 'Schnurkeramiker' of which the

Battle Axe culture, the Single Grave Folk, the East Baltic and the Fatyanovo culture on the upper reaches of the Volga are all variants) from the middle Dniepr region and the upper Volga as far as Scandinavia and Holland, was developed by an Indo-European people. They would seem to have been nomads, their society was warlike, and they introduced both the horse and wagon. We find them in Holland as early as 3000 B.C., where they are clearly immigrants, and it is here that the earliest wheels of western Europe have been found. There is a problem in the fact that this culture is very early indeed when compared to the Yamnaya culture (3600-2200 B.C., although the Yamnaya may be still older), but the central problem is the origin of Corded Ware. The Globular Amphorae culture ('Kugelamphoren' in German) preceded that of the Corded Ware (as of 3500 B.C.) in roughly the same area, though it extended in a more southerly direction and reached as far as the middle Dniepr and the Dniestr. The relation between this culture and the Corded Ware culture is not clear, but it does seem probable that there was a relationship of some kind."

Mallory–Adams (2007): "Many of the language groups of Europe, i.e. Celtic, Germanic, Baltic, and Slavic, may possibly be traced back to the Corded Ware horizon of northern, central, and eastern Europe that flourished c. 3200-2300 BC. Some would say that the Iron Age cultures of Italy might also be derived from this cultural tradition. For this reason the Corded Ware culture is frequently discussed as a prime candidate for early Indo-European."

Anthony (2007) gives a detailed account of archaeological events: "The Corded Ware horizon spread across most of northern Europe, from Ukraine to Belgium, after 3000 BCE, with the initial rapid spread happening mainly between 2900 and 2700 BCE. The defining traits of the Corded Ware horizon were a pastoral, mobile economy that resulted in the near disappearance of settlement sites (much like Yamnaya in the steppes), the almost universal adoption of funeral rituals involving single graves under mounds (like Yamnaya), the diffusion of stone hammer-axes probably derived from Polish TRB [=Funnelbeaker] styles, and the spread of a drinking culture linked to particular kinds of cord-decorated cups and beakers, many of which had local stylistic prototypes in variants of TRB ceramics. The material culture of the Corded Ware horizon was mostly native to northern Europe, but the underlying behaviors were very similar to those of the Yamnaya horizon, the broad adoption of a herding economy based on mobility (using oxdrawn wagons and horses), and a corresponding rise in the ritual prestige and value oflivestock. The economy and political structure of the Corded Ware horizon certainly was influenced by what had emerged earlier in the steppes(...).

The Yamnaya and Corded Ware horizons bordered each other in the hills between Lvov and Ivano-Frankovsk, Ukraine, in the upper Dniester piedmont around 2800-2600 BCE (see figure). At that time early Corded Ware cemeteries were confined to the uppermost headwaters of the Dniester west of Lvov, the same territory that had earlier been occupied by the late TRB communities infiltrated by late Tripolye groups. If Corded Ware societies in this region evolved from local late TRB origins, as many believe, they might already have spoken an Indo-European language. Between 2700 and 2600 BCE Corded Ware and late

Yamnaya herders met each other on the upper Dniester over cups of mead or beer. This meeting was another opportunity for language shift (...). The wide-ranging pattern of interaction that the Corded Ware horizon inaugurated across northern Europe provided an optimal medium for language spread. Late Proto-Indo-European languages penetrated the eastern end of this medium, either through the incorporation of Indo-European dialects in the TRB base population before the Corded Ware horizon evolved, or through Corded Ware-Yamnaya contacts later, or both. Indo-European speech probably was emulated because the chiefs who spoke it had larger herds of cattle and sheep and more horses than could be raised in northern Europe, and they had a politico-religious culture already adapted to territorial expansion."

3. The Corded Ware horizon spans over centuries. Most linguists agree that Northern LIE dialects shared a common origin within the original Yamnaya territory (ca. 3500-2500 BC), and that North-West Indo-European was a close linguistic community, already separated from Pre-Tocharian, during the time of the first Corded Ware migrations (ca. 2900-2500 BC, in the Kurgan framework). After that shared linguistic community, their speakers migrated to the east and west, spreading over a huge territory, which turned into a European *continuum* of different IE dialects in close contact.

4. The general internal linguistic division proposed for North-West Indo-European includes a West European group, with Pre-Italic and Pre-Celtic, and an East European group, comprising Pre-Baltic and Pre-Slavic. Pre-Germanic is usually assumed to have belonged to the West European core, and to have had contacts with East European later in time, into a loose Balto-Slavo-Germanic community.

NOTE 1. Those who divide between Italo-Celto-Germanic and Balto-Slavic include e.g.:

Burrow (1955): "The Western group of Indo-European languages consisting of Italic, Celtic and Germanic, is distinguished by certain common features in grammar and vocabulary, which indicate a fairly close mutual connection in prehistoric times. These ties are particularly close in the case of Italic and Celtic, even though they are not sufficient to justify the theory of common Italo-Celtic."

Kortlandt (1990): "If the speakers of the other *satem* languages can be assigned to the Yamnaya horizon and the western Indo-Europeans to the Corded Ware horizon, it is attractive to assign the ancestors of the Balts and the Slavs to the Middle Dnieper culture [an eastern extension of the Corded Ware culture, of northern Ukraine and Belarus, see below *Indo-Iranian*]."

Beekes (1995): "Probably the Corded Ware people were the predecessors of the Germanic, Celtic and Italic peoples, and, perhaps, of the Balto-Slavic peoples as well."

Adrados–Bernabé–Mendoza (1995-1998): "We think, to sum up, that a language more or less common, between Celtic and Germanic, is plausible. And that in equally gradual terms, but with a unity, if not complete, at least approximate, we should think the same for Baltic and Slavic. Even though it is a theory that has awoken polemic discussions, with Meillet and Senn as main representatives of the separation idea, Stang and Scherer of the unity; *cf.* Untermann 1957, Birnbaum 1975 (...) still more dubious is in relation with Illyrian, Venetic, etc. And models of more unitary 'common languages', like Indo-Iranian (...)."

Those who divide between Italo-Celtic and Balto-Slavo-Germanic:

Gamkrelidze–Ivanov (1993-1994), departing from an Anatolian homeland: "Especially intense contacts at level 5 can be found between the Balto-Slavic-Germanic and Italic-Celtic dialect areas. A long list of cognates can be adduced with lexical isoglosses reflecting close historical interaction between these areas (see Meillet 1922) (...) New arrivals joined earlier settlers to form an intermediate homeland shared by the tribes which later moved on to the more western zones of Europe. This intermediate settlement area thus became a zone of contacts and secondary rapprochements of dialects which had partially differentiated before this. This is where the common lexical and semantic innovations were able to arise. (...) The out-migration of the dialects from this secondary area - a secondary, or intermediate, proto-homeland - to central and western Europe laid the foundation for the gradual rise of the individual Italic, Celtic, Illyrian, Germanic, Baltic, and Slavic languages."

Mallory–Adams (2007), who suppose an early separation of all European dialects independently from the parent language: "A major group presumably created or maintained by contact is labelled the North-West group and comprises Germanic, Baltic, and Slavic (as one chain whose elements may have been in closer contact with one another), and additionally Italic and Celtic. (...) The evidence suggests that this spread occurred at some time before there were marked divisions between these languages so that these words appear to have been 'inherited' from an early period"; also, "[t]here are so many of these words that are confined within these five language groups (Celtic, Italic, Germanic, Baltic, and Slavic) that most linguists would regard cognates found exclusively between any two or among all of these groups as specifically North-West Indo-European and not demonstrably Proto-Indo-European. To accept a series of cognates as reflections of a PIE word requires that the evidence come from further afield than a series of contiguous language groups in Europe"; and, "[t]he North-West European languages (Germanic, Baltic, Slavic, Celtic, Italic) shared a series of common loanwords (probably created among themselves as well as derived from some non-Indo-European source) at some period."

This late *continuum* of closely related Northwestern IE languages has been linked to the Old European (*Alteuropäisch*) of Krahe (*Unsere ältesten Flußnamen*, 1964; *Die Struktur der alteuropäischen Hydronymie*, 1964), the language of the oldest reconstructed stratum of European hydronymy in Central and Western Europe.

NOTE. This "Old European" is not to be confused with the term as used by Marija Gimbutas, who applies it to Neolithic Europe. The character of these river names is Pre-

Germanic and Pre-Celtic, and dated by Krahe to ca. 2000 BC, although according to the recent archaeological and linguistic studies, it should probably be deemed slightly earlier. Old European river names are found in the Baltic and southern Scandinavia, in Central Europe, France, the British Isles, and the Iberian and Italian peninsulas. This area is associated with the spread of the later Western Indo-European dialects, the Celtic, Italic, Germanic, Baltic, Slavic, and Illyrian branches. Notably exempt are the Balkans and Greece. Krahe locates the geographical nucleus of this area as stretching from the Baltic across Western Poland and Germany to the Swiss plateau and the upper Danube north of the Alps, while he considers the Old European river names of southern France, Italy and Spain to be later imports, replacing "Aegean-Pelasgian" and Iberian substrates, corresponding to Italic, Celtic and Illyrian invasions from about 1300 BC.

Tovar (1977, 1979) combines the split of the Graeco-Aryan group with the development of an 'Old European' language in Europe, which evolved into the historical languages attested. Adrados (*Arquelogía y diferenciación del indoeuropeo*, Em. 47, 1979) assume, as we have seen, a North-West Indo-European or Old European language (of ca. 2000 BC or earlier, according to Krahe's account). In his view, the western core (Italo-Celto-Germanic) is still a unitary dialect in the late *dialect continuum*, while the eastern core (Pre-Balto-Slavic) is another, closely related dialect. This grouping has been supported by the latest phylogenetic studies (Atkinson *et al.* 2005, Holm 2008, *v.s.*). According to that view, the late North-West Indo-European community would have been similar e.g. to the German or to the North-Germanic *dialect continua*: a West European core (equivalent to the German and Scandinavian cores), plus a more different East European or Pre-Balto-Slavic territory (equivalent to Dutch, and to Icelandic, respectively).

About the identification of the North-West European dialect *continuum* with the "Old European" concept, Adrados–Bernabé–Mendoza (1995-1998): "The IE languages of Europe are all derived from [Late Indo-European]; most of them are [Northern dialects], Greek (and Thracian, we think) are [Southern] dialects. The first ones "crystallised" late, ca. 1000 BC or even later. But there are marks of earlier IE languages in Europe. Then a hypothesis results, whereby an ancient IE language could have existed in Europe, previous to Baltic, Slavic, Germanic, Latin, etc., a [Late Indo-European], or maybe an [Indo-Hittite] dialect.

This was put forward by the theory defended by Krahe (1964a, 1964b, among many writings), in which the European hydronymy, because of its roots and suffixes, bears witness to the existence of a European language previous to the differentiated languages (Germanic, Celtic, etc.), which would have been born from it in a later date. This is the so-called "Old European" (Alteuropäisch). We would have here a new intermediate language. For a defence of its presence in [the Iberian] Peninsula, *cf.* de Hoz 1963.

We lack otherwise data to decide the dialectal classification of this hypothetical language (the existence of a distinct feminine speaks in favour of a [LIE dialect]). Some names have been proposed: *Drava, Dravos*; *Druna, Dravina, Dravonus*; *Dravan-, Dravantia, Druantia*; *Druta, Drutus*. Or, to put other example, *Sava, Savos*; *Savina*; *Savara, Savira*; *Savintia*; *Savistas*. In cases like these, the roots are clearly IE, the suffixes too. The thesis that it is an IE language previous to the known ones seems correct, if we take into account the huge time span between the arrival of Indo-Europeans to Europe (in the fourth millennium BC) until the "crystallisation" of European languages, much more recent (...)

Therefore, the proposal of Schmid [(*Alteuropäisch und Indogermanisch,* 1968)], that the "Old European" of Krahe is simply IE, cannot be accepted. Apart from the arguments of Tovar in different publications, especially in Tovar 1979 and 1977, we have to add that in our view this IE knew the opposition masc./fem. *-os/-a* (*-yə*), i.e. it [derived from LIE]. We have to add Tovar's corrections: we shouldn't think about a unitary language, impossible without political and administrative unity, but about a series of dialects more or less evolved which clearly shared certain isoglosses. (...)

Indeed, all these discoveries, that took place in the 1950s and later, remain valid today, if we place them within the history of [Late Indo-European]. We still have to broaden its base by setting "Old European" (or more exactly its dialects) to the side of some IE languages whose existence we trace back to Europe in a previous date to the formation of the big linguistic groups that we know. They have left their marks not only in hydronymy (and toponymy and onomastics in general), but also in the vocabulary of the later languages, and even in languages that arrived to the historical age but are too badly attested; and, in any case, they aren't Celtic, nor Illyran, nor Venetic, nor any other historical dialect, but independent and – we believe – older languages.

The investigation of "Old European" began precisely with the study of some toponymies and personal names spread all over Europe, previously considered "Ligurian" (by H. d'Arbois de Jubainville and C. Jullian) or "Illyrian" (by J. Pokorny), with which those linguistic groups – in turn badly known – were given an excessive extension, based only on some lexical coincidences. Today those hypotheses are abandoned, but the concept of "Old European" is not always enough. It is commonly spoken about "Pre-Celtic" languages, because in territories occupied by Celts toponyms and ethnic names have non-Celtic phonetics: especially with initial *p* (*Parisii, Pictones, Pelendones, Palantia*); there are also, in the Latin of those regions, loans of the same kind (so *Paramus* in Hispania).

In [the Iberian] Peninsula, more specifically, it has been proposed that peoples like the Cantabri, Astures, Pellendones, Carpetani and Vettones were possibly of Pre-Celtic language (*cf.* Tovar 1949:12). More closed is the discussion around Lusitanian (...)" (see below).

5. Linguists have pointed out ancient language contacts of Italic with Celtic; Celtic with Germanic; Germanic with Balto-Slavic. Southern dialectal isoglosses affect Balto-Slavic and Tocharian, and only partially Germanic and Latin.

NOTE. According to Adrados–Bernabé–Mendoza (1995-1998): "One has to distinguish, in this huge geographical space, different locations. We have already talked about the situation of Germans to the West, and by their side, Celtic, Latin and Italic speakers; Balts and Slavs to the East, the former to the North of the later. See, among others, works by Bonfante (1983, 1984), about the old location of Baltic and Slavic-speaking communities. Isoglosses of different chronology let us partially reconstruct the language history. Note that the output obtained with phonetics and morphology match up essentially those of Porzig, who worked with lexica."

Celtic too shares isoglosses with Southern dialects, according to Meier-Brügger (2003): "Celtic contacts with eastern Indo-Europe are ancient. Compare the case, among others, of relative pronouns, which in Celtic, contrarily to the Italic $*k^wo$-/$*k^wi$-, is represented by *Hi̯o-, a characteristic that it shares with Greek, Phrygian, Indo-Iranian and Slavic."

Against the inclusion of Pre-Latin IE within West Indo-European, there are some archaeological and linguistic theories (Szemerényi, Colin Renfrew; *v.s.* for J.P. Mallory); Polomé (*"The Dialectal Position of Germanic within West-Indo-European", Proc. of the 13th Int. Congress of Linguists, Tokyo,* 1983) and Schmidt (1984, reviewed in Adrados–Bernabé–Mendoza, 1995-1998) argued that innovations common to Celtic and Germanic came from a time when Latin peoples had already migrated to the Italian peninsula, i.e. later than those common to Celtic, Latin and Germanic.

On the unity of Proto-Italic and Proto-Latin, Adrados–Bernabé–Mendoza (1995-1998): "dubious is the old unity scheme, no doubt only partial, between Latin and Osco-Umbrian, which has been rejected by famous Italian linguists, relating every coincidence to recent contacts. I am not so sure about that, as the common innovations are big; *cf.* Beeler 1966, who doesn't however dispel the doubts. Obviously, according to the decision taken, there are different historical consequences. If one thinks that both linguistic groups come from the North, through the Alps (*cf.* Tovar 1950), from the end of the 2nd millennium, a previous unity can be proposed. But authors like Devoto (1962) or Szemerényi (1962) made Latin peoples come from the East, through Apulia." There has been a continued archaeological and (especially) linguistic support by mainstream IE studies to the derivation of Italic (and Latin) from a West Indo-European core, even after critics to the old Italo-Celtic concept (C. Watkins *Italo-Celtic Revisited*, 1963, K.H. Schmidt *Latein und Keltisch*, 1986); see Porzig (*Die Gliederung des indogermanischen Sprachgebiets*, 1954), Dressler (*"Über die Reknostruktion der idg. Syntax", KZ 85,* 1971), Tovar (1970), Pisani (*Indogermanisch und Europa*, 1974), Bonfante ("Il celtibèrico, il cèltico e l'indoeuropeo" in RALinc., ser. VIII 1983; *"La protopatria degli Slavi", in Accademia Polaca delle Scienze, Conferenze 89,* 1984), Adrados–Bernabé–Mendoza (1995-1998), etc.; on the archaeological question, see Ghirshman (*L'Iran et la migration des indo-aryens et des iraniens*, 1977), Thomas (*"Archaeological Evidence for the Migrations of the Indo-Europeans"*, in Polomé (ed.) 1984), Gimbutas (*"Primary and Secondary homeland of the Indo-Europeans", JIES 13,* 1985), etc.

On Meillet's Italo-Celtic, it appears today that the idea is rejected by a majority of scholars, on the grounds of shared isoglosses which do not conform a community (*cf.* e.g. Watkins 1966). However, some common elections do reflect that both linguistic domains could in ancient times penetrate each other (Adrados–Bernabé–Mendoza 1995-1998). Recent publications (Gamkrelidze–Ivanov 1994-1995, Kortlandt 2007, etc.), as well as quantitative studies (see above §1.4.3) classify Italic and Celtic within the same branch, although sometimes as a West group including a late Italo-Germanic or Celto-Germanic subgroup.

NOTE 3. Today, the contacts between Balto-Slavic and Indo-Iranian are usually classified as from a late 'areal' contact or *Sprachbund*, or some sort of late North-West–East *continuum* (so e.g. in Kortlandt 1990, Mallory 1989, Adrados–Bernabé–Mendoza 1995-1998, West 2007, Anthony 2007); e.g. Mallory–Adams (2007): "The Indo-Iranian and Balto-Slavic languages share both satemisation and the ruki-rule and may have developed as some form of west–east (or northwest–south-east) *continuum* with certain features running through them" (see below *Indo-Iranian*).

6. The Germanic homeland is usually traced back to the Nordic Late Neolithic in Scandinavia, still in contact with the Italo-Celtic homeland in Central Europe (Proto-Únětice?); the Late Corded Ware groups to the east probably represent the Balto-Slavic homeland. Beekes (1995), Adrados–Bernabé–Mendoza (1995-1998), etc.

Eurasian cultures in 2000 BC, after the disintegration of IEDs.

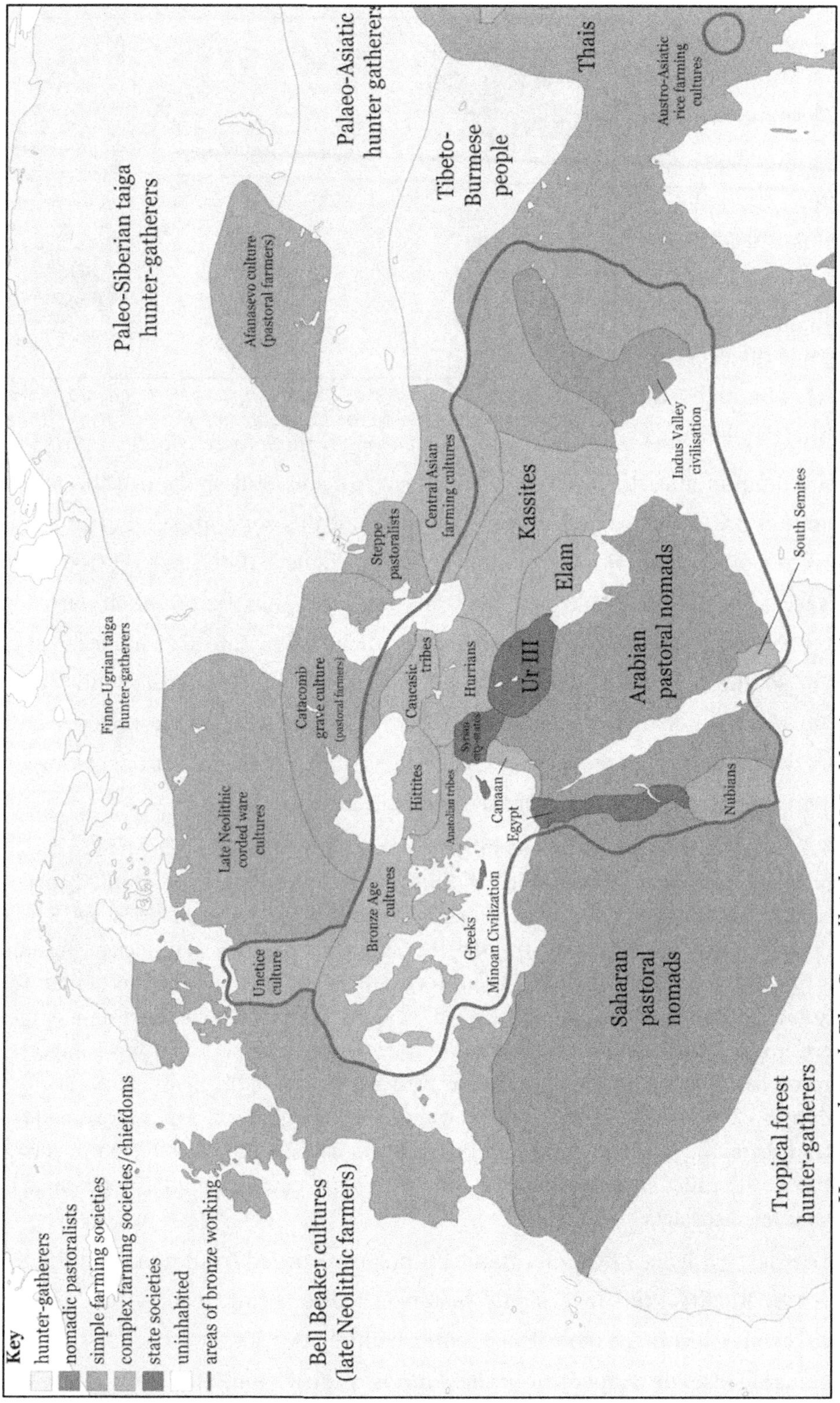

Haywood et al. The Cassell Atlas of World History. (1997) (2011, modified from Briangotts 2009)

A. GERMANIC

The largest Germanic languages are English and German, with ca. 340 and some 120 million native speakers, respectively. Other significant languages include Low Germanic dialects (like Dutch) and the Scandinavian languages.

Germanic languages as first language of the majority (dark colour) or official language of the country (light colour). (2011, modified from Shardz-Hayden 2010)

Their common ancestor is Proto-Germanic, probably still spoken in the mid-1st millennium B.C. in Iron Age Northern Europe, since its separation from an earlier Pre-Proto-Germanic, a Northern Indo-European dialect dated ca. 1500-500 BC. The succession of archaeological horizons suggests that before their language differentiated into the individual Germanic branches the Proto-Germanic speakers lived in southern Scandinavia and along the coast from the Netherlands in the west to the Vistula in the east around 750 BC. Early Germanic dialects enter history with the Germanic peoples who settled in northern Europe along the borders of the Roman Empire from the second century AD.

NOTE. A few surviving inscriptions in a runic script from Scandinavia dated to ca. 200 are thought to represent a later stage of Proto-Norse; according to Bernard Comrie, it represents a *Late Common Germanic* which followed the "Proto-Germanic" stage. Several historical linguists have pointed towards the apparent material and social continuity connecting the cultures of the Nordic Bronze Age (1800-500 BC) and the Pre-Roman Iron Age (500 BC - AD 1) as having implications in regard to the stability and later development of the Germanic language group. Lehmann (1977) writes: "Possibly the most important conclusion based on archeological evidence with relevance for linguistic purposes is the assumption of 'one huge cultural area' which was undisturbed for approximately a thousand years, roughly from 1500-500 BC Such a conclusion in a stable culture permits inferences concerning linguistic stability, which are important for an interpretation of the Germanic linguistic data."

The earliest evidence of the Germanic branch is recorded from names in the first century by Tacitus, and in a single instance in the second century BC, on the *Negau helmet*. From roughly the second century AD, some speakers of early Germanic dialects developed the *Elder Futhark*. Early runic inscriptions are also largely limited to personal names, and difficult to interpret. The Gothic language was written in the Gothic alphabet developed by Bishop Ulfilas for his translation of the Bible in the fourth century. Later, Christian priests and monks who spoke and read Latin in addition to their native Germanic tongue began writing the Germanic languages with slightly modified Latin letters, but in Scandinavia, runic alphabets remained in common use throughout the Viking Age.

The so-called Grimm's law is a set of statements describing the inherited North-West Indo-European stops as they developed in Pre-Proto-Germanic. As it is presently formulated, Grimm's Law consists of three parts, which must be thought of as three consecutive phases in the sense of a chain shift:

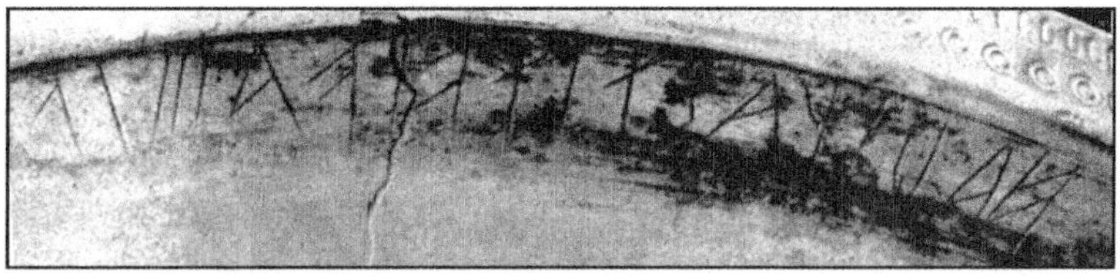

Negau helmet. It reads (from right to left):

harikastiteiva\\\ip, "Harigast the priest". (PD, n.d.)

- Voiceless stops change to PGmc. voiceless fricatives: **p**→**f*, **t**→**θ*, **k**→**x*, **kʷ**→**xʷ*.
- Voiced stops become PGmc. voiceless stops: **b**→**p*, **d**→**t*, **g**→**k*, **gʷ**→**kʷ*.
- Voiced aspirated stops lose their aspiration and change into plain voiced stops: **bʰ**→**b*, **dʰ**→**d*, **gʰ**→**g*, **gʷʰ**→**gʷ*,**g*,**w*.

Verner's Law addresses a category of exceptions, stating that unvoiced fricatives are voiced when preceded by an unaccented syllable: PGmc. **s*→**z*, **f*→**v*, **θ*→**ð*; as, NWIE **bʰrātḗr** → PGmc. **brōþēr* 'brother', but NWIE **mātḗr** → PGmc. **mōðēr* 'mother'.

NOTE 1. W. P. Lehmann (1961) considered that Jacob Grimm's "First Germanic Sound Shift", or Grimm's Law and Verner's Law, which pertained mainly to consonants and were considered for a good many decades to have generated Proto-Germanic, were Pre-Proto-Germanic, and that the "upper boundary" was the fixing of the accent, or stress, on the root syllable of a word, typically the first. Proto-Indo-European had featured a moveable pitch accent comprising "an alternation of high and low tones" as well as stress of position determined by a set of rules based on the lengths of the word's syllables.

The fixation of the stress led to sound changes in unstressed syllables. For Lehmann, the "lower boundary" was the dropping of final -a or -e in unstressed syllables; for example, PIE **woid-á** >, Goth. *wait*, "*knows*" (the > and < signs in linguistics indicate a genetic descent). Antonsen (1965) agreed with Lehmann about the upper boundary but later found runic evidence that the **-a** was not dropped: Gmc. *ékwakraz ... wraita* 'I wakraz ... wrote (this)'. He says: "We must therefore search for a new lower boundary for Proto-Germanic".

NOTE 2. Sometimes the shift produced allophones (consonants that were pronounced differently) depending on the context of the original. With regard to original PIE **k** and **k**^{w}, Trask (2000) says that the resulting PGmc. *x and *x^w were reduced to *h and *h^w in word-initial position. Consonants were lengthened or prolonged under some circumstances, appearing in some daughter languages as geminated graphemes. Kraehenmann (2003) states that Proto-Germanic already had long consonants, but they contrasted with short ones only word-medially. Moreover, they were not very frequent and occurred only intervocally almost exclusively after short vowels. The phonemes *b, *d, *g and *g^w, says Ringe (2006) were stops in some environments and fricatives in others.

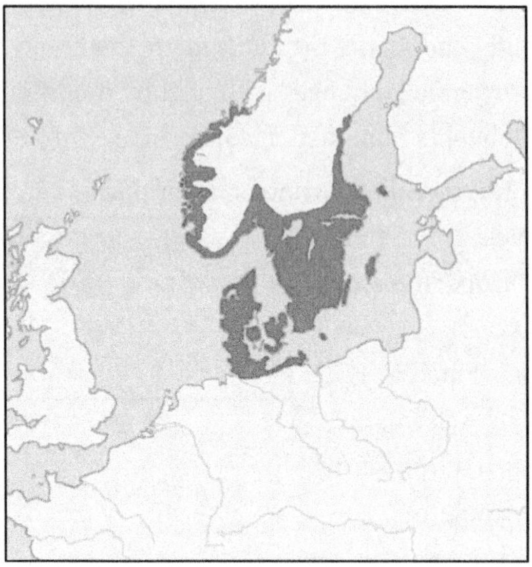

Nordic Bronze Age culture (ca. 1200 BC), Harper Atlas of World History (1993, PD)

Effects of the aforementioned sound laws include the following examples:

- **p**→*f*: **pods,** *foot, cf.* PGmc. *fōts*; *cf.* Goth. *fōtus*, O.N. *fōtr*, O.E. *fōt*, O.H.G. *fuoz*.
- **t**→*þ,ð*: **tritjós**, *third, cf.* PGmc. *þriðjaz*; *cf.* Goth. *þridja*, O.N. *þriðe*, O.E. *þridda*, O.H.G. *dritto*.
- **k**→*x,h*: **kwon**, *dog, cf.* PGmc. *xunðaz*; *cf.* Goth. *hunds*, O.N. *hundr*, O.E. *hund*, O.H.G. *hunt*.
- **k**^{w}→x^w,h^w: **k**^{w}**os**, *what, who, cf.* Gmc. h^woz; *cf.* Goth. *hwas*, O.N. *hverr*, O.S. *hwe*, O.E. *hwā*, O.Fris. *hwa*, O.H.G. *hwër*.
- **b**→*p*: **werbō**, *throw, cf.* Gmc. *werpō*; *cf.* Goth. *wairpan*, O.S. *werpan*, O.N. *verpa*, O.E. *weorpan*, M.L.G., Du. *werpen*, Ger. *werfen*.
- **d**→*t*: **dekm̥**, *ten, cf.* Gmc. *tehun*; *cf.* Goth. *taihun*, O.S. *tehan*, O.N. *tiu*, O.Fris. *tian*, O.Du. *ten*, O.H.G. *zehan*.
- **g**→*k*: **gelu**, *ice, cf.* Gmc. *kaldaz*; *cf.* Goth. *kalds*, O.N. *kaldr*, O.E. *cald*, O.H.G. *kalt*.
- **g**^{w}→*kw*: **g**^{w}**īwós**, *alive, cf.* Gmc. k^w*i(k)waz*; *cf.* Goth. k^w*ius*, O.N. *kvikr*, O.E. *cwic*, O.H.G. *quec*.

- **b^h**→b: **b^hrātēr**, *brother*, *cf.* Gmc. *brōþēr*; *cf.* Goth. *bróþar*, O.N. *brōþir*, O.E. *brōþor*, O.H.G. *bruoder*.
- **d^h**→*d*: **d^hworis**, *door*, *cf.* Gmc. *duriz*; *cf.* Goth. *daúr*, O.N. *dyrr*, O.E *duru*, O.H.G. *turi*.
- **g^h**→*g*: **g^hansis**, *goose*, *cf.* Gmc. *gansiz*; *cf.* Goth *gansus*, O.N. *gās*, O.E. *gōs*, O.H.G. *gans*.
- **g^{wh}**→*gw/g/w*: **g^{wh}ormos**, *warm*, *cf.* Gmc. *warmaz*; *cf.* O.N. *varmr*, O.E. *wearm*, O.H.G. *warm*. For **g^{wh}ondos**, *fight*, *cf.* Gmc. *gandaz*; *cf.* Goth. *gunþs*, O.N. *gandr*, O.E. *gūþ*, O.H.G. *gund*.

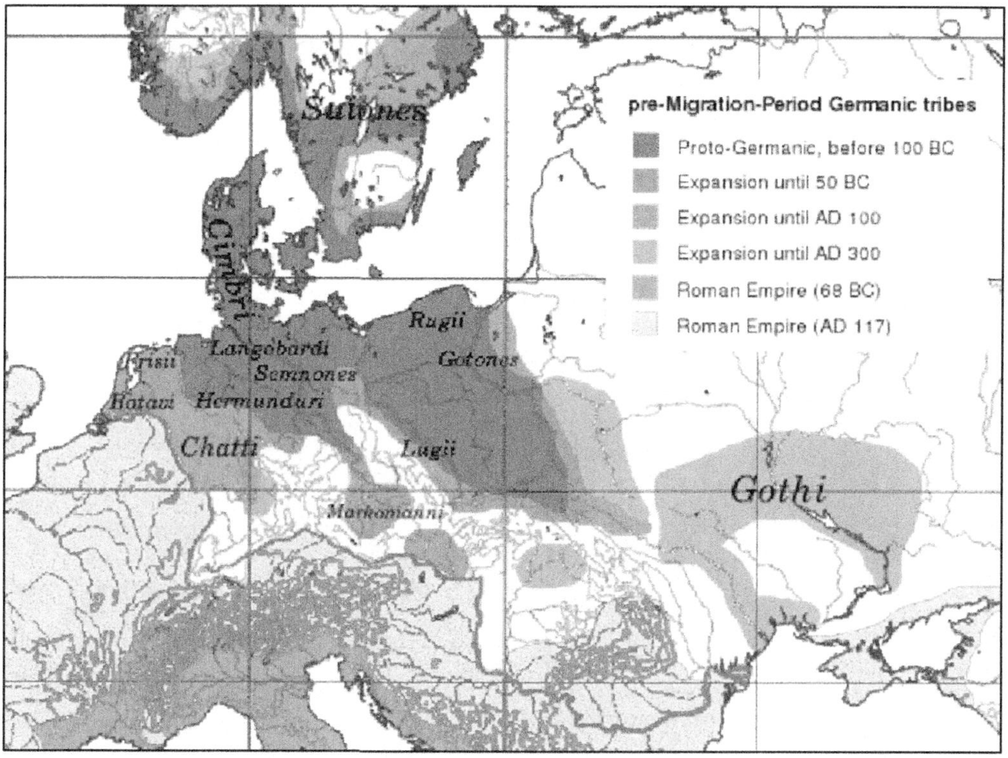

Putzger, Historischer Atlas (1954) (Dbachmann 2005)

A known exception is that the voiceless stops did not become fricatives if they were preceded by PIE ***s***., i.e. **sp**, **st**, **sk**, **sk^w**. Similarly, PIE **t** did not become a fricative if it was preceded by **p**, **k**, or **k^w**. This is sometimes treated separately under the Germanic *spirant law*.

NWIE vowels: **a,o**→**a*; ***ā,ō***→**ō*. PGmc. had then short **i*, **u*, **e*, **a*, and long **ī*, **ū*, **ē*, **ō*, **ǣ*?

NOTE 1. Similar mergers happened in the Slavic languages, but in the opposite direction. At the time of the merge, the vowels probably were [ɒ] and [ɒ:] before their timbres differentiated into maybe [ɑ] and [ɔ:].

NOTE 2. PGmc. **ǣ* and **ē* are also transcribed as $*\bar{e}^1$ and $*\bar{e}^2$; $*\bar{e}^2$ is uncertain as a phoneme, and only reconstructed from a small number of words; it is posited by the comparative method because whereas all probable instances of inherited NWIE **ē** (PGmc. $*\bar{e}^1$) are distributed in Gothic as *ē* and the other Germanic languages as *ā*, all the Germanic languages agree on some occasions of *ē* (e.g. PGmc. $*h\bar{e}^2r$ → Goth.,O.E.,O.N. *hēr*, "*here*"). Krahe treats $*\bar{e}^2$ (secondary *ē) as identical with **ī*. It probably continues NWIE **ei** or **ēi**, and it may have been in the process of transition from a diphthong to a long simple vowel in the Proto-Germanic period. Gothic makes no orthographic and therefore presumably no phonetic distinction between $*\bar{e}^1$ and $*\bar{e}^2$. The existence of two Proto-Germanic [e:]-like phonemes is supported by the existence of two e-like Elder Futhark runes, *Ehwaz* and *Eihwaz*.

B. LATIN

Regions where Romance languages are spoken as official languages (dark), by sizeable minorities or official status (lighter) (2011 modified from PD)

The Romance or Romanic (also Neolatin) languages comprise all languages that descended from Latin, the language of the Roman Empire.

Romance languages have some 800 million native speakers worldwide, mainly in the Americas, Europe, and Africa, as well as in many smaller regions scattered through the world. The largest languages are Spanish and Portuguese, with about 400 and 200 million mother tongue speakers respectively, most of them outside Europe. Within Europe, French (with 80 million) and Italian (70 million) are the largest ones. All Romance languages descend from Vulgar Latin, the language of soldiers, settlers, and slaves of the Roman Empire, which was substantially different from the Classical Latin of the Roman *literati*. Between 200 BC and AD 100, the expansion of the Empire, coupled with administrative and educational policies of Rome, made Vulgar Latin the dominant native language over a wide area spanning from the Iberian Peninsula to the Western coast of the Black Sea. During the Empire's decadence and after its collapse and fragmentation in the fifth century, Vulgar Latin evolved independently within each local area, and eventually diverged into dozens of distinct languages. The oversea empires established by Spain, Portugal and France after the fifteenth century then spread Romance to the other continents — to such an extent that about two thirds of all Romance speakers are now outside Europe.

Latin is usually classified, along with Faliscan, as an Italic dialect. The Italic speakers were not native to Italy, but migrated into the Italian Peninsula in the course of the second millennium BC, and were apparently related to the Celtic tribes that roamed over a large part of Western Europe at the time.

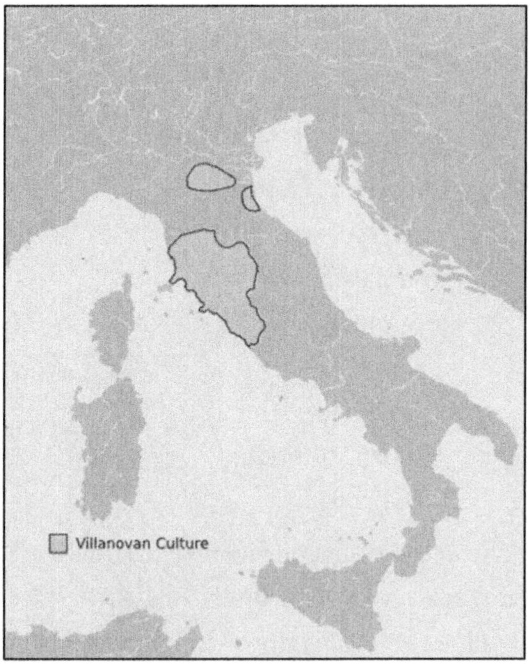

Based on The Harper Atlas of World History 1987 (Zymos 2007)

Archaeologically, the Apennine culture of inhumations enters the Italian Peninsula from ca. 1350 BC, east to west; the Iron Age reaches Italy from ca. 1100 BC, with the Villanovan culture (with the practice of cremation), intruding north to south. The later Osco-Umbrian, Veneti and Lepontii peoples, as well as the Latino-Faliscans, have been associated with this culture. The first settlement on the Palatine hill dates to ca. 750 BC, settlements on the Quirinal to 720 BC, both related to the founding of Rome. As Rome extended its political dominion over Italy, Latin became dominant over the other Italic languages, which ceased to be spoken perhaps sometime in the first c. AD.

Italic is usually divided into:

- Sabellic, including:
    - Oscan, spoken in south-central Italy.
    - Umbrian group:
        - *Umbrian*.

- *Volscian.*
- *Aequian.*
- *Marsian.*
- *South Picene.*

- Latino-Faliscan, including:
  - Faliscan, spoken in the area around *Falerii Veteres*, north of the city of Rome.
  - Latin, spoken in west-central Italy. The Roman conquests eventually spread it throughout the Roman Empire and beyond.

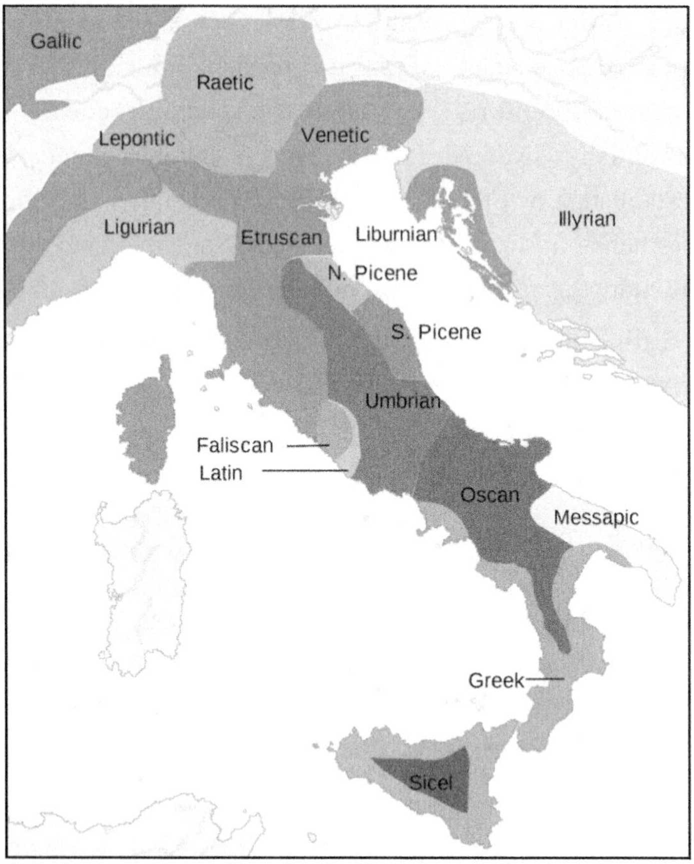

Ethnic groups within the Italian peninsula, ca. 600-500 BC. In central Italy, Italic languages, (2011, modified from Ewan ar Born)

The ancient Venetic language, as revealed by its inscriptions (including complete sentences), was also closely related to the Italic languages and is sometimes even classified as Italic. However, since it also shares similarities with other Western Indo-European branches (particularly Germanic), some linguists prefer to consider it an independent IE language.

Phonetic changes from NWIE to Latin include: $\mathbf{b^h}$→*f/b*, $\mathbf{d^h}$→*f/b*, $\mathbf{g^h}$→*h/f*, $\mathbf{g^w}$→*w/g*, $\mathbf{k^w}$→k^w/k, **p**→p/k^w.

The Italic languages are first attested in writing from Umbrian and Faliscan inscriptions dating to the seventh century BC. The alphabets used are based on the Old Italic alphabet, which is itself based on the Greek alphabet. The Italic languages themselves show minor influence from the Etruscan and somewhat more from the Ancient Greek languages.

Oscan had much in common with Latin, though there are also some differences, and many common word-groups in Latin were represented by different forms; as, Lat. *uolo*, *uelle*, *uolui*, and other such forms from PIE **wel-**, *will*, were represented by words derived from $\mathbf{g^her}$-, *desire*, *cf.* Osc. *herest* 'he wants, desires' as opposed to Lat. *uult* (id.). Lat. *locus* 'place' was absent and represented by Osc. *slaagid*.

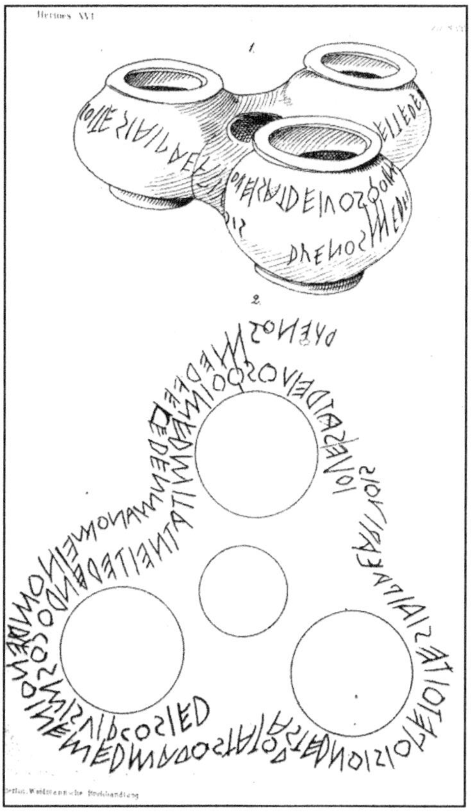

The Duenos (O.Lat. duenus, *Lat.* buenus) *Inscription in Old Latin, sixth century BC. Illustration from Hermes (1881, PD)*

In phonology, Oscan also shows a different evolution, as NWIE $\mathbf{k^w}$→ Osc. *p* instead of Lat. *kw* (*cf.* Osc. *pis*, Lat. *quis*); NWIE $\mathbf{g^w}$ → Osc. *b* instead of Latin *w*; NWIE medial $\mathbf{b^h}$, $\mathbf{d^h}$ → Osc. *f*, in contrast to Lat. *b* or *d* (*cf.* Osc. *mefiai*, Lat. *mediae*); etc.

NOTE. A specimen of Faliscan appears written round the edge of a picture on a patera: *foied vino pipafo, cra carefo*, which in Old Latin would have been *hodie vinom bibabo, cras carebo*, translated as 'today I will drink wine; tomorrow I won't have any' (R. S. Conway, *Italic Dialects*). Among other distinctive features, it shows the retention of medial *f* which became Lat. *b*, and evolution of NWIE $\mathbf{g^h}$→*f* (*fo-*, contrast Lat. *ho-*).

Hence the reconstructed changes of NWIE into Proto-Italic:

- Voiced labiovelars unround or lenite: $\mathbf{g^w}$→**g*/**w*, $\mathbf{g^{wh}}$→*g^h.
- Voiced aspirates become first unvoiced, then fricativise: $\mathbf{b^h}$→*p^h→*ϕ→**f*; $\mathbf{d^h}$→*t^h→*θ; $\mathbf{g^h}$→*k^h→**x*.

NOTE. About intervocalic $\mathbf{g^h}$ → Ita. **x*, linguists (see Joseph & Wallace 1991) generally propose that it evolves as Faliscan *g* or *k*, while in Latin it becomes glottal *h*, without a change of manner of articulation. Picard (1993) rejects that proposal citing abstract phonetic principles, which Chela-Flores (1999) argues citing examples of Spanish phonology.

- NWIE **s** → Ita. *θ before *r* (*cf.* Ita. *kereθrom*, Lat. *cerebrum*); unchanged elsewhere.

Up to 8 cases are found; apart from the 6 cases of Classic Latin (i.e. N-V-A-G-D-Ab), there was a locative (*cf.* Lat. *proxumae viciniae, domī, carthagini*; Osc. *aasai*, Lat. '*in ārā*', etc.) and an instrumental (*cf.* Columna Rostrata Lat. *pugnandod, marid, naualid*, etc; Osc. *cadeis amnud*, Lat. '*inimicitiae causae*'; Osc. *preiuatud*, Lat. '*prīuātō*', etc.). For originally differentiated genitives and datives, compare genitive (Lapis Satricanus:) *Popliosio Valesiosio* (the type in *-ī* is also very old, Segomaros *-ī*), and dative (Praeneste Fibula:) *numasioi*, (Lucius Cornelius Scipio Epitaph:) *quoiei*.

C. CELTIC

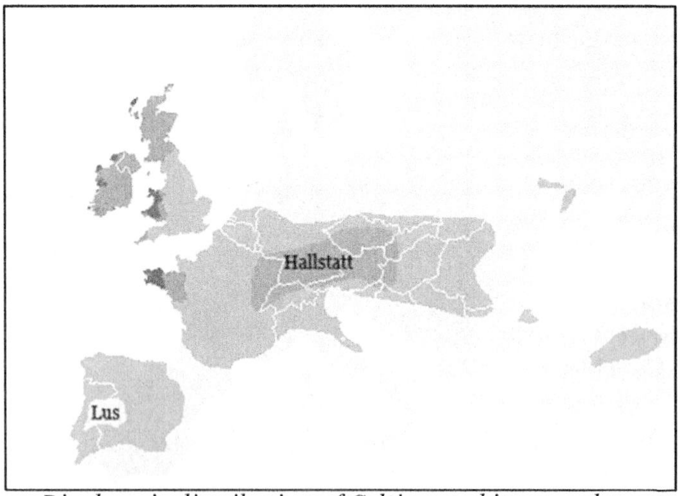

Diachronic distribution of Celtic-speaking peoples: maximal expansion (ca. 200 BC) and modern Celtic-speaking territories. (2011, modified from Dbachmann 2010)

The Celtic languages are the languages descended from Proto-Celtic, or Common Celtic.

During the first millennium BC, especially between 400-100 BC they were spoken across Europe, from the southwest of the Iberian Peninsula and the North Sea, up the Rhine and down the Danube to the Black Sea and the Upper Balkan Peninsula, and into Asia Minor (Galatia). Today, Celtic languages are now limited to a few enclaves in the British Isles and on the peninsula of Brittany in France.

The distinction of Celtic into different sub-families probably occurred about 1000 BC. The early Celts are commonly associated with the archaeological Urnfield culture, the La Tène culture, and the Hallstatt culture.

Some scholars distinguish Continental and Insular Celtic, arguing that the differences between the Goidelic and Brythonic languages arose after these split off from the Continental Celtic languages. Other scholars distinguish P-Celtic from Q-Celtic, putting most of the Continental Celtic languages in the former group – except for Celtiberian, which is Q-Celtic.

NOTE. There are two competing schemata of categorisation. One scheme, argued for by Schmidt (1988) among others, links Gaulish with Brythonic in a P-Celtic node, leaving Goidelic as Q-Celtic. The difference between P and Q languages is the treatment of NWIE **k**ʷ, which became **p* in the P-Celtic languages but **k* in Goidelic. An example is the Cel. verbal root *kʷrin-* 'to buy', which became Welsh *pryn-*, but O.Ir. *cren-*.

The other scheme links Goidelic and Brythonic together as an Insular Celtic branch, while Gaulish and Celtiberian are referred to as Continental Celtic. According to this theory, the 'P-Celtic' sound change of *kʷ* to *p* occurred independently or regionally. The proponents of the Insular Celtic hypothesis point to other shared innovations among Insular Celtic languages, including inflected prepositions, VSO word order, and the lenition of intervocalic *m* to *β*, a nasalised voiced bilabial fricative (an extremely rare sound), etc. There is, however, no assumption that the Continental Celtic languages descend from a common "Proto-Continental Celtic" ancestor. Rather, the Insular/Continental schemata usually consider Celtiberian the first branch to split from Proto-Celtic, and the remaining group would later have split into Gaulish and Insular Celtic.

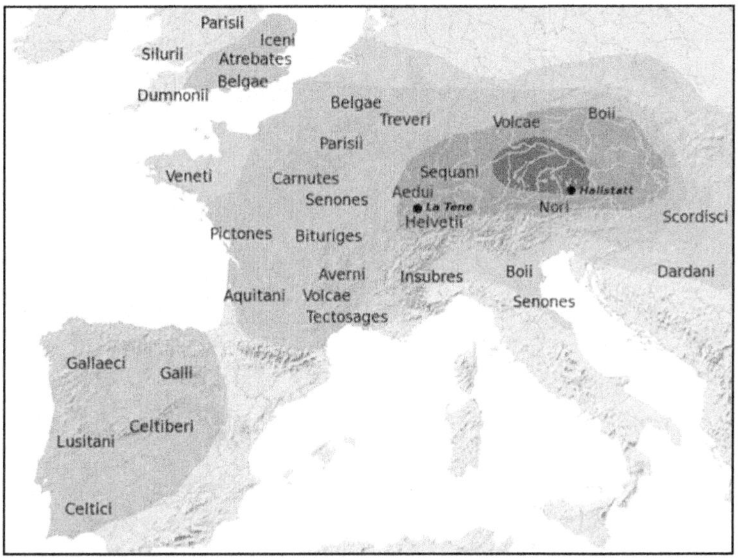

Hallstatt core territory (ca. 800 BC) and its influence (ca. 500 BC); La Tène culture (ca. 450) and its influence (ca. 50 BC). Major Celtic tribes are labelled. (Mod. from Dbachmann 2008)

Known NWIE evolutions into Proto-Celtic include:

- Consonants: **p** →**ɸ*→**h*→∅ in initial and intervocalic positions. Cel. **ɸs*→*xs*, **ɸt*→*xt*

NOTE. LIE **p** was lost in Proto-Celtic, apparently going through the stages *ɸ* (perhaps in Lus. *porcos*) and *h* (perhaps attested by the toponym *Hercynia* if this is of Celtic origin) before being lost completely word-initially and between vowels. NWIE **sp**- became Old Irish *s* and Brythonic *f*; while Schrijver (1995) argues there was an intermediate stage **sɸ*- (in which *ɸ* remained an independent phoneme until after Proto-Insular Celtic had diverged into Goidelic and Brythonic), McCone (1996) finds it more economical to believe that **sp**- remained unchanged in PC, that is, the change **p** to *ϕ did not happen when **s** preceded.

- Aspirated: **d**^{h}→*d*, **b**^{h}→*b*, **g**^{h}→*x*, **g**^{wh}→*g*^{w}; but **g**^{w}→*b*.
- Vowels: **ō** → *ā, ū* (in final syllable); **ē**→*ī*; NWIE ***u-w*** → Cel. *o-w*.
- Diphthongs: ***āi***→*ai*, ***ēi***→*ei*, ***ōi***→*oi*; ***āu***→*au*, ***ēu,ōu***→*ou*.
- Resonants: **l̥**→*la, li* (before stops); **r̥** → *ar, ri* (before stops); **m̥** → *am;* **n̥** → *an*.

Gaulish iscription CΕΓΟΜΑΡΟC ΟΥΙΛΛΟΝΕΟC ΤΟΟΥΤΙΟΥC ΝΑΜΑΥCΑΤΙC ΕΙωΡΟΥ ΒΗΛΗCΑΜΙ CΟCΙΝ ΝΕΜΗΤΟΝ "Segomaros, son of Uillū, citizen (toutious) of Namausos, dedicated this sanctuary to Belesama" (Fabrice Philibert-Caillat 2004)

Italo-Celtic refers to the hypothesis that Italic and Celtic dialects are descended from a common ancestor, Proto-Italo-Celtic, at a stage post-dating Late Indo-European. Since both Proto-Celtic and Proto-Italic date to the early Iron Age (say, the centuries on either side of 1000 BC), a probable time frame for the assumed period of language contact would be the late Bronze Age, the early to mid-second millennium BC. Such grouping was proposed by Meillet (1890), and has been recently supported by Kortlandt (2007), among others (see above).

NOTE. One argument for Italo-Celtic was the thematic genitive in *I* (e.g. *dominus, domini*). Both in Italic (*Popliosio Valesiosio*, Lapis Satricanus) and in Celtic (Lepontic, Celtiberian -*o*), however, traces of PIE genitive ***-osjo*** have been discovered, so that the spread of the *i*-genitive could have occurred in the two groups independently, or by areal diffusion. The community of -*ī* in Italic and Celtic may be then attributable to late contact, rather than to an original unity. The *i*-Genitive has been compared to the so-called Cvi formation in Sanskrit, but that too is probably a comparatively late development.

Other arguments include that both Celtic and Italic have collapsed the PIE Aorist and Perfect into a single past tense, and the *ā*-subjunctive, because both Italic and Celtic have a subjunctive descended from an earlier optative in -*ā*-. Such an optative is not known from other languages, but the suffix occurs in Balto-Slavic and Tocharian past tense formations, and possibly in Hitt. -*ahh*-.

D. SLAVIC

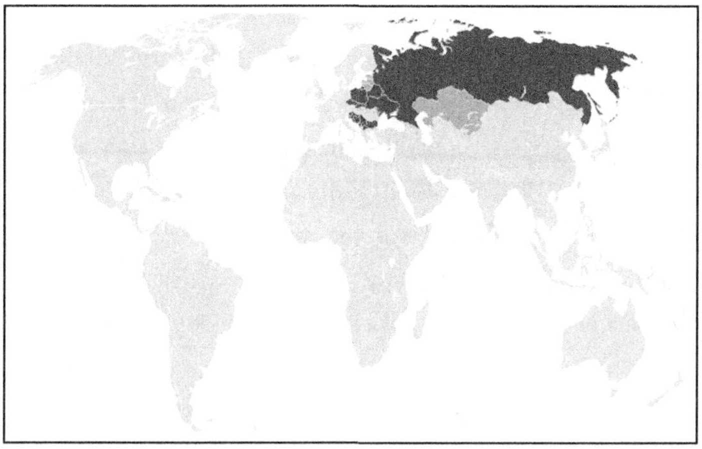

World map of countries with a majority Slavic speakers (dark colour), and a significant minority (light) of more than 10%. (Therexbanner 2010)

The Slavic or Slavonic languages have speakers in most of Eastern Europe, in much of the Balkans, in parts of Central Europe, and in the northern part of Asia. The largest languages are Russian and Polish, with 165 and some 47 million speakers, respectively. The oldest Slavic literary language was Old Church Slavonic, which later evolved into Church Slavonic.

There is much debate on whether Pre-Slavic branched off directly from a Northern LIE dialect, or it passed through a common *Proto-Balto-Slavic* stage, which would have necessarily split apart before 1000 BC in its two main sub-branches.

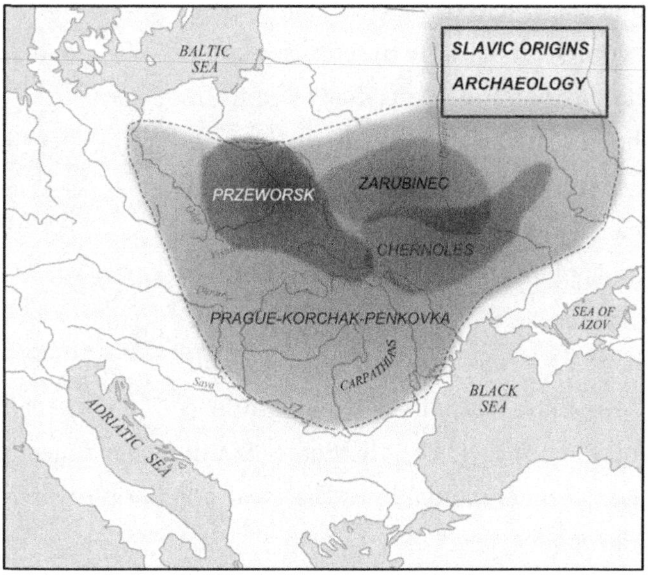

Based on information and maps from Mallory–Adams (1997). (Slovenski Volk 2009)

The original homeland of the speakers of Proto-Slavic remains controversial too. The most ancient recognisably Slavic hydronyms are to be found in northern and western Ukraine and southern Belarus. It has also been noted that Proto-Slavic seemingly lacked a maritime vocabulary.

The Proto-Slavic language secession from a common Proto-Balto-Slavic is estimated on archaeological and glottochronological criteria to have occurred between 1500-1000 BC (see below *Baltic*). Common Slavic is usually reconstructible to around AD 600.

By the seventh century, Common Slavic had broken apart into large dialectal zones. Linguistic differentiation received impetus from the dispersion of the Slavic peoples over a large territory – which in Central Europe exceeded the current extent of Slavic-speaking territories. Written documents of the ninth, tenth and eleventh centuries already show some local linguistic features.

NOTE. For example the Freising monuments show a language which contains some phonetic and lexical elements peculiar to Slovenian dialects (e.g. rhotacism, the word *krilatec*).

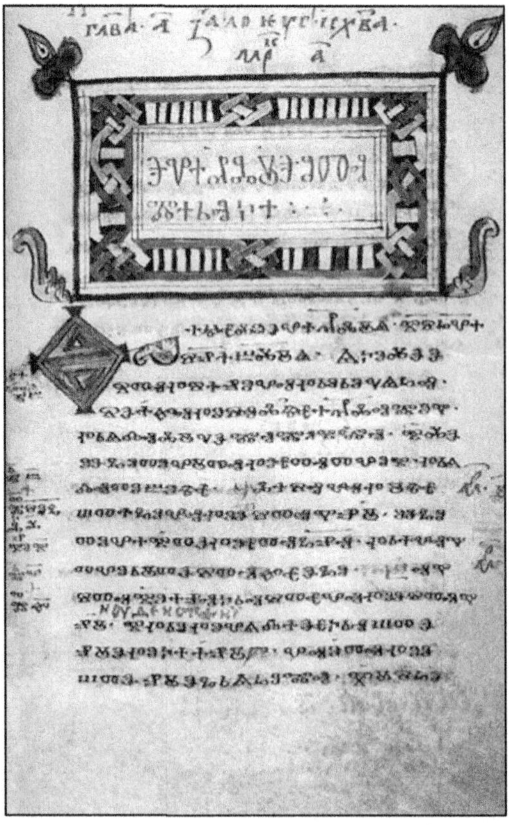

Page from Codex Zographensis *(10th - 11th c. AD) in Old Church Slavonic. (PD)*

In the second half of the ninth century, the dialect spoken north of Thessaloniki became the basis for the first written Slavic language, created by the brothers Cyril and Methodius who translated portions of the Bible and other church books. The language they recorded is known as Old Church Slavonic. Old Church Slavonic is not identical to Proto-Slavic, having been recorded at least two centuries after the breakup of Proto-Slavic, and it shows features that clearly distinguish it from Proto-Slavic. However, it is still reasonably close, and the mutual intelligibility between Old Church Slavonic and other Slavic dialects of those days was proved by Cyril's and Methodius' mission to Great Moravia and Pannonia. There, their early South Slavic dialect used for the translations was clearly understandable to the local population which spoke an early West Slavic dialect.

As part of the preparation for the mission, the Glagolitic alphabet was created in 862 and the most important prayers and liturgical books, including the Aprakos Evangeliar – a Gospel Book lectionary containing only feast-day and Sunday readings –, the Psalter, and Acts of the Apostles, were translated. The language and the alphabet were taught at the Great Moravian Academy (O.C.S. *Veľkomoravské učilište*) and were used for government and religious documents and books. In 885, the use of the O.C.S. in Great Moravia was prohibited by the Pope in favour of Latin. Students of the two apostles, who were expelled from Great Moravia in 886, brought the Glagolitic alphabet and the Old Church Slavonic language to the Bulgarian Empire, where it was taught and Cyrillic alphabet developed in the Preslav Literary School.

Vowel changes from Late Indo-European to Proto-Slavic:

- LIE *ī, *ei → Sla. *i_1; LIE *i →*i → Sla. *ь; LIE *u → *u → Sla. *ъ; LIE ū → Sla. *y.
- LIE *e → Sla. *e; LIE *ē → Sla. *$ě_1$;
- LIE *en, *em → Sla. *ę; LIE *an, *on; *am, *om →*an; *am → Sla. *ǫ.
- LIE *a, *o → *a → Sla. *o; LIE *ā, *ō → *ā → Sla. *a; LIE *ai, *oi → *ai → Sla. *$ě_2$. Reduced *ai (*ăi/*ui) → Sla. *i_2; LIE *au,*ou → *au → Sla. *u.

After Barford (A history of Eastern Europe: crisis and change, 2007). (Slovenski Volk (2009)

NOTE. Apart from these simplified equivalences, other patterns appear (see Kortlandt's article <http://www.kortlandt.nl/publications/art066e.pdf>, *From Proto-Indo-European to Slavic*):

o The vowels *i_2, *$\check{e}_2$ developed later than *i_1, *$\check{e}_1$. In Late Proto-Slavic there were no differences in pronunciation between *i_1 and i_2 as well as between *$\check{e}_1$ and *$\check{e}_2$. They had caused, however, different changes of preceding velars, see below.

o Late Proto-Slavic yers *ь, *ъ < earlier *i, *u developed also from reduced LIE *e, *o respectively. The reduction was probably a morphologic process rather than phonetic.

o We can observe similar reduction of *ā into *ū (and finally *y) in some endings, especially in closed syllables.

o The development of the Sla. *i_2 was also a morphologic phenomenon, originating only in some endings.

o Another source of the Proto-Slavic *y is *ō in Germanic loanwords – the borrowings took place when Proto-Slavic no longer had *ō in native words, as LIE *ō had already changed into *ā.

o LIE *ə disappeared without traces when in a non-initial syllable.

o LIE *eu probably developed into *jau in Early Proto-Slavic (or during the Balto-Slavic epoch), and eventually into Proto-Slavic *ju.

o According to some authors, LIE long diphthongs *ēi, *āi, *ōi, *ēu, *āu, *ōu had twofold development in Early Proto-Slavic, namely they shortened in endings into simple *ei, *ai, *oi, *eu, *au, *ou but they lost their second element elsewhere and changed into *ē, *ā, *ō with further development like above.

Other vocalic changes from Proto-Slavic include *jo, *jъ, *jy changed into *je, *jь, *ji; *o, *ъ, *y also changed into *e, *ь, *i after *c, *ʒ, *s' which developed as the result of the 3rd palatalisation; *e, *ě changed into *o, *a after *č, *ǯ, *š, *ž in some contexts or words; a similar change of *ě into *a after *j seems to have occurred in Proto-Slavic but next it can have been modified by analogy.

On the origin of Proto-Slavic consonants, the following relationships are found:

- LIE *p → Sla. *p; LIE *b, *b^h → Sla. *b.
- LIE *t → Sla. *t; LIE *d, *d^h → Sla. *d.
- LIE *k, *k^w → Sla. k (palatalised *k^j → Sla. s); LIE *g, *g^h, *g^w, *g^{wh} → Sla. *g (palatalised *g^j, *g^{jh} → Sla. *z)
- LIE *s → Sla. *s; before a voiced consonant LIE *z → Sla. *z; before a vowel when after *r, *u, *k, *i, probably also after *l → Sla. *x.
- LIE word-final *m → Sla. *n (<BSl. *n).
- LIE *m̥ → Sla. *im, *um; LIE *n̥ → Sla. *in, *un; LIE *l̥ → Sla. *il, *ul; LIE r̥ → Sla. *ir, *ur.
- LIE *w → Sla. *v (<BSl. *w); LIE *j → Sla. *j.

In some words the Proto-Slavic *x developed from LIE phonemes like *ks, *sk.

E. BALTIC

The Baltic languages were spoken in areas extending east and southeast of the Baltic Sea in Northern Europe.

Adapted from Gimbutas (The Balts, 1963). (Map Master 2007)

The language group is often divided into two sub-groups: Western Baltic, containing only extinct languages as Prussian or Galindan, and Eastern Baltic, containing extinct as well as the two living languages in the group, Lithuanian and Latvian. While related, Lithuanian and Latvian differ substantially from each other and are not mutually intelligible.

The oldest Baltic linguistic record is the Elbinger lexicon of the beginning of the fourteenth century. It contains 802 Old Prussian equivalents of Old Middle German words. The oldest Baltic text is Old Prussian as well; it comes from the middle of the fourteenth century and includes only eleven words. The first Old

Lithuanian and Old Latvian texts come from the sixteenth century and appear already in book form, and were translations of a catechism and the Lord's Prayer.

Baltic and Slavic share so many similarities that many linguists, following the lead of such notable Indo-Europeanists as August Schleicher and Oswald Szemerényi, take these to indicate that the two groups separated from a common ancestor, the Proto-Balto-Slavic language, dated ca. 1500-500 BC, depending on the different guesstimates.

NOTE 1. About Balto-Slavic guesstimates, "Classical glottochronology" conducted by Czech Slavist M. Čejka in 1974 dates the Balto-Slavic split to -910±340 BC, Sergei Starostin in 1994 dates it to 1210 BC, and "recalibrated glottochronology" conducted by Novotná & Blažek dates it to 1400-1340 BC. This agrees well with Trziniec-Komarov culture, localised from Silesia to Central Ukraine and dated to the period 1500-1200 BC.

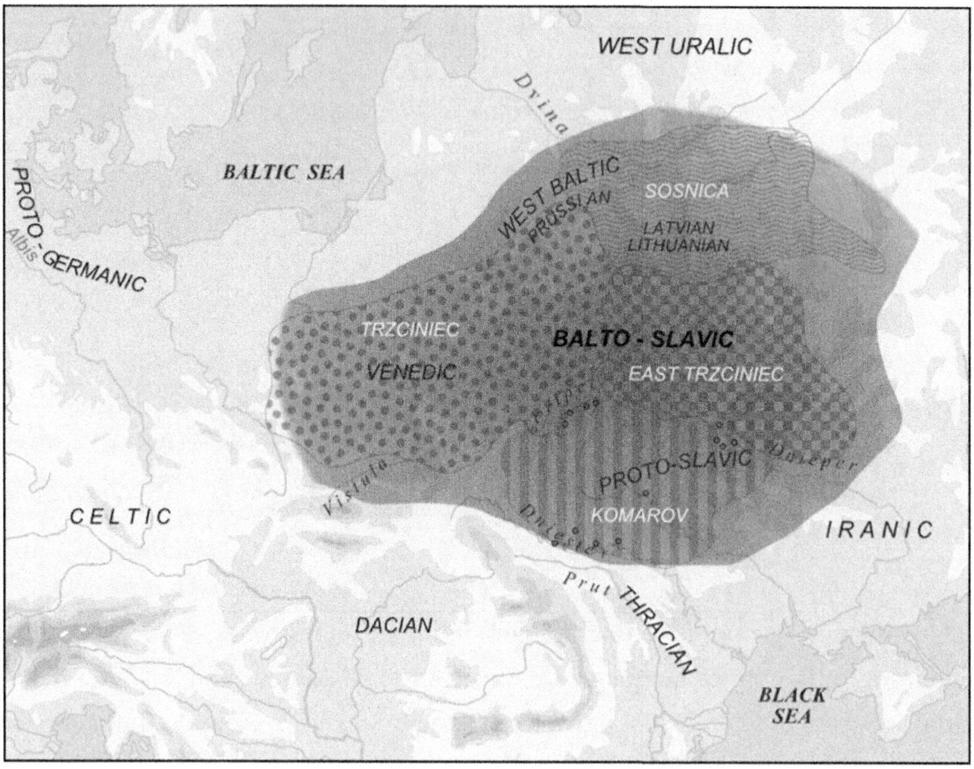

Linguistic area of Balto-Slavic areas, Ramat (1993). (Slovenski Volk 2009)

NOTE 2. Until Meillet's *Dialectes indo-européens* of 1908, Balto-Slavic unity was undisputed among linguists – as he notes at the beginning of the *Le Balto-Slave* chapter, "*L'unité linguistique balto-slave est l'une de celles que personne ne conteste*". Meillet's critique of Balto-Slavic confined itself to the seven characteristics listed by Karl Brugmann in 1903, attempting to show that no single one of these is sufficient to prove genetic unity. Szemerényi in his 1957 re-examination of Meillet's results concludes that the Balts and Slavs did, in fact, share a "*period of common language and life*", and were probably separated due to the incursion of Germanic tribes along the Vistula and the Dnieper roughly at the beginning of the Common Era.

A new theory was proposed in the 1960s by V. Ivanov and V. Toporov: that the Balto-Slavic proto-language split from the start into West Baltic, East Baltic and Proto-Slavic. In their framework, Proto-Slavic is a peripheral and innovative Balto-Slavic dialect which suddenly expanded, due to a conjunction of historical circumstances. Onomastic evidence shows that Baltic languages were once spoken in much wider territory than the one they cover today, and were later replaced by Slavic.

NOTE. The most important of these common Balto-Slavic isoglosses are:

- Winter's law: lengthening of a short vowel before a voiced plosive, usually in a closed syllable.
- Identical reflexes of LIE syllabic resonants, usually developing *i* and *u* before them. Kuryłowicz thought that *uR reflexes arose after LIE velars, and also notable is also older opinion of J.Endzelīns and *R. Trautmann according to whom *uR reflexes are the result of zero-grade of morphemes that had LIE **o* → PBSl. **a* in normal-grade. Matasović (2008) proposes following internal rules after LIE **r̥* → BSl. **ər*: 1) **ə*→**i* in a final syllable; 2) **ə*→**u* after velars and before nasals; 3) **ə*→**i* otherwise.
- Hirt's law: retraction of LIE accent to the preceding syllable closed by a laryngeal.
- Rise of the Balto-Slavic acute before LIE laryngeals in a closed syllable.
- Replacement of LIE genitive singular of thematic nouns with ablative.
- Formation of past tense in *-*ē* (*cf.* Lith. pret. *dãvė*, "he gave", O.C.S. imperfect *bě*, "he was")
- Generalisation of the LIE neuter ***to***- stem to the nominative singular of masculine and feminine demonstratives instead of LIE ***so***- pronoun, **so**, **sā**, **tod** → BSl. **tos, *tā, *tod.*
- Formation of *definite adjectives* with a construction of adjective and relative pronoun; *cf.* Lith. *geràsis*, "the good", vs. *gẽras*, "good"; O.C.S *dobrъjь*, "the good", vs. *dobrъ*, "good".

Common Balto-Slavic innovations include several other prominent, but non-exclusive isoglosses, such as the satemisation, Ruki, change of LIE **o* → BSl. **a* (shared with Germanic, Indo-Iranian and Anatolian) and the loss of labialisation in LIE labiovelars (shared with Indo-Iranian, Armenian and Tocharian). Among Balto-Slavic archaisms notable is the retention of traces of an older LIE pitch accent. 'Ruki' is the term for a sound law which is followed especially in BSl. and Aryan dialects. The name of the term comes from the sounds which cause the phonetic change, i.e. LIE **s* → *š* / *r, u, k, i* (it associates with a Slavic word which means *'hands'* or *'arms'*). A sibilant *s is retracted to **ʃ* after **i*, **u*,* *r*, and after velars (i.e. **k* which may have developed from earlier **k*, **g*, *g^h*). Due to the character of the retraction, it was probably an apical sibilant (as in Spanish), rather than the dorsal of English. The first phase (*s → *š) seems to be universal, the later retroflexion (in Sanskrit and probably in Proto-Slavic as well) is due to levelling of the sibilant system, and so is the third phase - the retraction to velar *x in Slavic and also in some Middle Indian languages, with parallels in e.g. Spanish. This rule was first formulated for IE by Holger Pedersen.

Baltic and Slavic show a remarkable amount of correspondence in vocabulary too; there are at least 100 words exclusive to BSl., either being a common innovation or sharing the same semantic development from a PIE root; as, BSl. *lēipā, "tilia" → Lith. líepa, O.Prus. līpa, Ltv. liẽpa; Sla. *lipa; BSl. *rankā, "hand" → Lith. rankà, O.Prus. rānkan, Ltv. rùoka; Sla. *rǭkà (*cf.* O.C.S. rǫka). BSl. *galwā́, "head" → Lith. galvà, O.Prus. galwo, Ltv. galva; Sla. *golvà (*cf.* O.C.S. glava).

F. FRAGMENTARY DIALECTS

MESSAPIAN

Messapian (also known as *Messapic*) is an extinct language of south-eastern Italy, once spoken in the regions of Apulia and Calabria. It was spoken by the three Iapygian tribes of the region: the Messapians, the Daunii and the Peucetii. The language, a centum dialect, has been preserved in about 260 inscriptions dating from the sixth to the first century BC. It became extinct after the Roman Empire conquered the region and assimilated the inhabitants.

Some have proposed that Messapian was an Illyrian language. The Illyrian languages were spoken mainly on the other side of the Adriatic Sea. The link between Messapian and Illyrian is based mostly on personal names found on tomb inscriptions and on classical references, since hardly any traces of the Illyrian language are left.

NOTE. Some phonetic characteristics of the language may be regarded as quite certain:

- PIE short **o→a*, as in the last syllable of the genitive *kalatoras*.
- PIE final **m→n*, as in *aran*.
- PIE **nj→nn*, as in the Messapian praenomen *Dazohonnes* vs. the Illyrian praenomen *Dazonius*; the Messapian genitive *Dazohonnihi* vs. Illyrian genitive *Dasonii*, etc.
- PIE **tj→tth*, as in the Messapian praenomen *Dazetthes* vs. Illyrian *Dazetius*; the Messapian genitive *Dazetthihi* vs. the Illyrian genitive *Dazetii*; from a *Dazet-* stem common in Illyrian and Messapian.
- PIE **sj→ss*, as in Messapian *Vallasso* for *Vallasio*, a derivative from the shorter name *Valla*.
- The loss of final **-d*, as in *tepise*, and probably of final **-t*, as in *-des*, perhaps meaning 'set', from PIE **dʰe-* 'set, put'.

- The change of voiced aspirates in Proto-Indo-European to plain voiced consonants: PIE *d^h→*d*, as in Messapian *anda* (< PIE *en-d^ha- < PIE *en-* 'in', compare Gk. *entha*); and PIE *b^h→*b*, as in Messapian *beran* (< PIE *b^her- 'to bear').
- PIE **au*→*ā* before (at least some) consonants: *Bāsta*, from *Bausta*.
- The form *penkaheh* – which Torp very probably identifies with the Oscan stem *pompaio* – a derivative of the Proto-Indo-European numeral **penk^{w}e* 'five'.
- If this last identification be correct it would show, that in Messapian (just as in Venetic and Ligurian) the original labiovelars (*k^w,*g^w, *g^{wh}) were retained as gutturals and not converted into labials. The change of *o* to *a* is interesting, being associated with the northern branches of Indo-European such as Gothic, Albanian and Lithuanian, and not appearing in any other southern dialect hitherto known. The Greek *Aphrodite* appears in the form *Aprodita* (Dat. Sg., *fem.*).
- The use of double consonants which has been already pointed out in the Messapian inscriptions has been very acutely connected by Deecke with the tradition that the same practice was introduced at Rome by the poet Ennius who came from the Messapian town Rudiae (Festus, p. 293 M).

VENETIC

Venetic was spoken in the Veneto region of Italy, between the Po River delta and the southern fringe of the Alps. It was a centum language.

The language is attested by over 300 short inscriptions dating between the sixth century BC and first century AD. Its speakers are identified with the ancient people called *Veneti* by the Romans and *Enetoi* by the Greek. The inscriptions use a variety of the Northern Italic alphabet, similar to the Old Italic alphabet. It became extinct around the first century when the local inhabitants were assimilated into the Roman sphere.

NOTE. The exact relationship of Venetic to other Indo-European languages is still being investigated, but the majority of scholars agree that Venetic, aside from Liburnian, was closest to the Italic languages. Venetic may also have been related to the Illyrian languages, though the theory that Illyrian and Venetic were closely related is debated by current scholarship.

Interesting parallels with Germanic have also been noted, especially in pronominal forms:

Ven. *ego* 'I', acc. *mego* 'me'; Goth. *ik*, acc. *mik*; but *cf.* Lat. *ego*, acc. *me*.

Ven. *sselboisselboi* 'to oneself'; O.H.G. *selb selbo*; but *cf.* Lat. *sibi ipsi*.

Venetic had about six or even seven noun cases and four conjugations (similar to Latin). About 60 words are known, but some were borrowed from Latin (*liber.tos.* < *libertus*) or Etruscan. Many of them show a clear Indo-European origin, such as Ven. *vhraterei* (< PIE *b^hreh$_2$terei) 'to the brother'.

In Venetic, PIE stops *b^h→f, *d^h→f, *g^h→h*, in word-initial position (as in Latin and Osco-Umbrian), but to *b^h→b, *d^h→d, *g^h→g*, in word-internal intervocalic position, as in Latin. For Venetic, at least the developments of *b^h and *d^h are clearly attested. Faliscan and Osco-Umbrian preserve internal *b^h→f,* d^h→f, *g^h→h*.

There are also indications of the developments of PIE initial *g^w→w-*, PIE *k^w→kv* and PIE initial *g^{wh}→f* in Venetic, all of which are parallel to Latin, as well as the regressive assimilation of PIE sequence *p...k^w... → k^w...k^w...* (e.g. *penk^{w}e → *k^{w}enk^{w}e*, "*five*", *perk^{w}u → *k^{w}erk^{w}u*, "oak"), a feature also found in Italic and Celtic (Lejeune 1974).

LIGURIAN

The Ligurian language was spoken in pre-Roman times and into the Roman era by an ancient people of north-western Italy and south-eastern France known as the Ligures. Very little is known about this language (mainly place names and personal names remain) which is generally believed to have been Indo-European; it appears to have adopted significantly from other IE languages, primarily Celtic (Gaulish) and Latin.

Strabo states *"As for the Alps... Many tribes (éthnê) occupy these mountains, all Celtic (Keltikà) except the Ligurians; but while these Ligurians belong to a different people (hetero-ethneis), still they are similar to the Celts in their modes of life (bíois)."*

LIBURNIAN

The Liburnian language is an extinct language spoken by the ancient Liburnians in the region of Liburnia (south of the Istrian peninsula) in classical times. It is usually classified as a *centum* language. It appears to have been on the same Indo-European branch as the Venetic language; indeed, the Liburnian tongue may well have been a Venetic dialect.

NOTE. No writings in Liburnian are known, though. The grouping of Liburnian with Venetic is based on the Liburnian onomastics. In particular, Liburnian anthroponyms show strong Venetic affinities, with many common or similar names and a number of common roots, such as *Vols-*, *Volt-*, and *Host-* (<PIE *g^hos-ti-* 'stranger, guest, host'). Liburnian and Venetic names also share suffixes in common, such as *-icus* and *-ocus*.

These features set Liburnian and Venetic apart from the Illyrian onomastic province, though this does not preclude the possibility that Venetic-Liburnian and Illyrian may have been closely related, belonging to the same Indo-European branch. In fact, a number of linguists argue that this is the case, based on similar phonetic features and names in common between Venetic-Liburnian on the one hand and Illyrian on the other.

Liburnia was conquered by the Romans in 35 BC, and its language was eventually replaced by Latin, undergoing language death probably very early in the Common Era.

LUSITANIAN

Lusitanian or Lusatian (so named after the *Lusitani* or Lusitanians) was a Paleohispanic IE language known by only five inscriptions and numerous toponyms and theonyms. The language was spoken before the Roman conquest of Lusitania, in the territory inhabited by Lusitanian tribes, from Douro to the Tagus

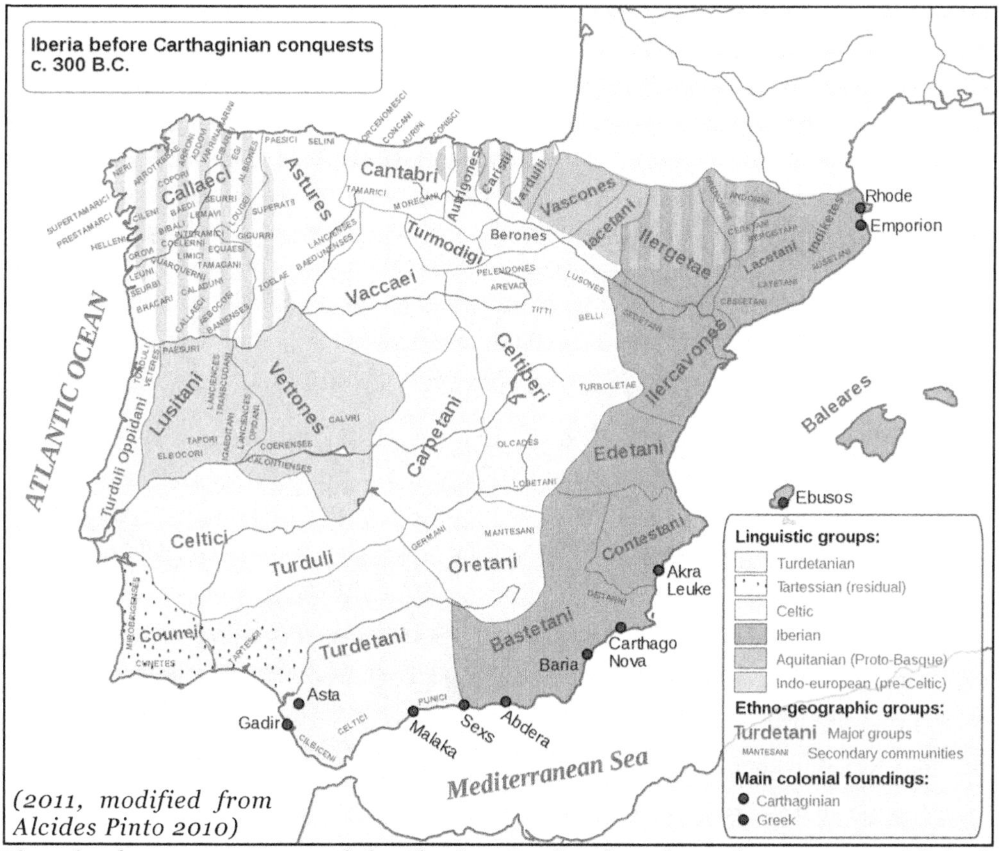

(2011, modified from Alcides Pinto 2010)

River in the western area of the Iberian Peninsula, where they were established already before the sixth century BC.

Their language is usually considered a Pre-Celtic (possibly stemming from a common Italo-Celtic) IE dialect, and it is sometimes associated with the language of the Vettones and with the linguistic substratum of the Gallaeci and Astures, based on archaeological findings and descriptions of ancient historians.

NOTE. The affiliation of the Lusitanian language within a Pre-Celtic IE group is supported by Tovar, Schmidt, Gorrochategui, among others, while Untermann e.g.

considers it a Celtic language.The theory that it was a Celtic language is largely based upon the historical fact that the only Indo-European tribes that are known to have existed in Hispania at that time were Celtic tribes. The apparent Celtic character of most of the lexicon —anthroponyms and toponyms — may also support a Celtic affiliation. There is a substantial problem in the Celtic theory, though: the preservation of PIE initial **p*-, as in Lusitanian *pater* 'father', or *porcom* 'pig'. The Celtic languages had lost that initial PIE **p*- in their evolution; compare Lat. *pater*, Gaul. *ater*, and Lat. *porcum*, O.Ir. *orc*. However, that does not necessarily preclude the possibility of Lusitanian being Celtic, because of the theoretical evolution of LIE initial **p* → **ɸ* → **h* → Cel. ∅, so it might have been an early Proto-Celtic (or Italo-Celtic) dialect that split off before the loss of **p*-, or when **p*- had become **ɸ*- (before shifting to **h*- and then being lost); the letter *p* of the Latin alphabet could have been used to represent either sound.

F. Villar and R. Pedrero relate Lusitanian with the Italic languages. The theory is based on parallels in the names of deities, as Lat. *Consus*, Lus. *Cossue*, Lat. *Seia*, Lus. *Segia*, or Marrucinian *Iovia*, Lus. *Iovea(i)*, etc. and other lexical items, as Umb. *gomia*, Lus. *comaiam*, with some other grammatical elements.

II. NORTHERN INDO-EUROPEAN IN ASIA: TOCHARIAN

Tocharian or Tokharian is one of the most obscure branches of the Northern dialects. The name of the language is taken from people known to the Greek historians (Ptolemy VI, 11, 6) as the Tocharians (Greek Τόχαροι, *Tókharoi*).

NOTE. These are sometimes identified with the Yuezhi and the Kushans, while the term *Tokharistan* usually refers to first millennium Bactria. A Turkic text refers to the Turfanian language (Tocharian A) as *twqry*. F. W. K. Müller has associated this with the name of the Bactrian *Tokharoi*. In Tocharian, the language is referred to as *arish-käna* and the Tocharians as *arya*.

Tocharian consisted of two languages; Tocharian A (Turfanian, Arsi, or East Tocharian) and Tocharian B (Kuchean or West Tocharian). These languages were spoken roughly from the sixth to ninth centuries; before they became extinct, their speakers were absorbed into the expanding Uyghur tribes. Both languages were once spoken in the Tarim Basin in Central Asia, now the Xinjiang Autonomous Region of China.

NOTE. Properly speaking, based on the tentative interpretation of *twqry* as related to *Tokharoi*, only Tocharian A may be referred to as *Tocharian*, while Tocharian B could be called *Kuchean* (its native name may have been *kuśiññe*), but since their grammars are usually treated together in scholarly works, the terms A and B have proven useful.

Tocharian is documented in manuscript fragments, mostly from the eighth century (with a few earlier ones) that were written on palm leaves, wooden tablets and Chinese paper, preserved by the extremely dry climate of the Tarim Basin.

Samples of the language have been discovered at sites in Kucha and Karasahr, including many mural inscriptions.

Tocharian A and B were not intercomprehensible. The common Proto-Tocharian language must have preceded the attested languages by several centuries, probably dating to the first millennium BC.

1.7.2. SOUTHERN INDO-EUROPEAN DIALECTS

I. GREEK

Ancient Greek dialects by 400 BC after R.D. Woodard (2004). (2009, modified from Fut. Perf. 2008)

1. Greek has a documented history of 3500 years. Today, Modern Greek is spoken by 15 million people.

2. The major dialect groups of the Ancient Greek period can be assumed to have developed not later than 1120 BC, at the time of the Dorian invasions, and their first appearances as precise alphabetic writing began in the eighth century BC.

3. Mycenaean is the most ancient attested form of the Greek branch, spoken on mainland Greece and on Crete between 1600-1100 BC, before the Dorian invasion. It is preserved in inscriptions in Linear B, a script invented on Crete before the fourteenth century BC. Most instances of these inscriptions are on clay tablets found in Knossos and in Pylos. The language is named after Mycenae, the first of the palaces to be excavated.

NOTE. The tablets remained long undeciphered, and every conceivable language was suggested for them, until Michael Ventris deciphered the script in 1952 and proved the language to be an early form of Greek. The texts on the tablets are mostly lists and inventories. No prose narrative survives, much less myth or poetry. Still, much may be glimpsed from these records about the people who produced them, and about the Mycenaean period at the eve of the so-called Greek Dark Ages.

5. Unlike later varieties of Greek, Mycenaean probably had seven grammatical cases, the nominative, the genitive, the accusative, the dative, the instrumental, the locative, and the vocative.

The instrumental and the locative however gradually fell out of use.

Mycenaean tablet (MY Oe 106) inscripted in linear B coming from the House of the Oil Merchant (ca. 1250 BC). The tablet registers an amount of wool which is to be dyed. National Archaeological Museum of Athens. (Marsyas 2005)

NOTE. For the locative in *-*ei*, compare *di-da-ka-re*, '*didaskalei*', *e-pi-ko-e*, '*Epikóhei*', etc (in Greek there are syntactic compounds like *puloi-genēs*, '*born in Pylos*'); also, for remains of an ablative case in **-ōd*, compare (months' names) *ka-ra-e-ri-jo-me-no*, *wo-de-wi-jo-me-no*, etc.

6. Proto-Greek (the so-called *Proto-Hellenic*, or *Pre-Greek* in Sihler 1995) was a Southern LIE dialect, spoken in the late third millennium BC, roughly at the same time as North-West Indo-European and Proto-Indo-Iranian, most probably in the Balkans.

NOTE. According to Anthony (2007): "Greek shared traits with Armenian and Phrygian, both of which probably descended from languages spoken in southeastern Europe before 1200 BCE, so Greek shared a common background with some southeastern European languages that might have evolved from the speech of the Yamnaya immigrants in Bulgaria". Proponents of a Proto-Greek homeland in Bulgaria or Romania are found in Sergent (1995), J. Makkay (*Atti e memorie del Secondo Congresso Internazionale di Micenologia*, 1996; *Origins of the Proto-Greeks and Proto-Anatolians from a Common Perspective*, 2003).

7. Proto-Greek (Pre-Greek or Proto-Hellenic) has been posited as a probable ancestor of Phrygian, and a possible ancestor of Thracian, Dacian, and Ancient Macedonian. Armenian has traditionally been regarded as derived from it through Phrygian, although this is disputed today.

NOTE. The *Graeco-Armenian hypothesis* proposed a close relationship to the Greek language – putting both in the larger context of the Paleo-Balkan *Sprachbund* – notably including Phrygian, which is widely accepted particularly close to Greek –, consistent with Herodotus' recording of the Armenians as descending from colonists of the Phrygians. That traditional linguistic theory, proposed by Pedersen (1924), proposed a close relationship between both original communities, Greek and Armenian, departing from a common language. That vision, accepted for a long time, was rejected by Clackson (1994) in *The linguistic relationship between Armenian and Greek*, which, while supporting the *Graeco-Aryan* community, argues that there are not more coincidences between Armenian and Greek than those found in the comparison between any other IE language pair; shared isoglosses would therefore stem from contiguity within the common S.LIE community. Those findings are supported by Kortlandt in *Armeniaca* (2003), in which he proposes an old Central IE *continuum* Daco-Albanian / Graeco-Phrygian / Thraco-Armenian. Adrados (1998), considers an older Southern *continuum* Graeco-[Daco-]Thraco-Phrygian / Armenian / Indo-Iranian. Olteanu (2009) proposes a Graeco-Daco-Thracian language.

8. The unity of Proto-Greek probably ended as Hellenic migrants entered the Greek peninsula around 2300 BC.

NOTE. About the archaeological quest, Anthony (2007): "The people who imported Greek or Proto-Greek to Greece might have moved several times, perhaps by sea, from the western Pontic steppes to southeastern Europe to western Anatolia to Greece, making their trail hard to find. The EHII/III transition about 2400-2200 BCE has long been seen as a time of radical change in Greece when new people might have arrived (...)".

In West's (2007) words, "The first speakers of Greek – or rather of the language that was to develop into Greek; I will call them *mello*-Greeks – arrived in Greece, on the most widely accepted view, at the beginning of Early Helladic III, that is, around 2300. They came by way of Epirus, probably from somewhere north of the Danube".

9. The primary sound changes from PIE to Proto-Greek include:

• Aspiration of PIE intervocalic **s* → PGk ***h***.

NOTE. The loss of PIE prevocalic **s-* was not completed entirely, famously evidenced by the loss of prevocalic *s was not completed entirely, famously evidenced by PGk

sūs (also ***hūs***, *pig*, from PIE *suh_1-); *sun* 'with', sometimes considered contaminated with PIE **kom* (*cf.* Latin *cum*) to Homeric / Old Attic *ksun*, is possibly a consequence of Gk. psi-substrate (Villar).

- De-voicing of PIE voiced aspirates: *b^h→***p^h***, *d^h→***t^h***, *g^h→***k^h***, *g^{wh}→***k^{wh}***.
- Dissimilation of aspirates (Grassmann's law), possibly post-Mycenaean.
- PIE word-initial **j-* (not **Hj-*) is strengthened to PGk ***dj-*** (later Gk. ζ-).
- In the first stage of palatalisation (Sihler 1995), PIE **dj-* was possibly palatalised into PGk ***$d^z(j)$-*** , while PIE **tj-*, *d^hj- probably became PGk ***$t^s(j)$-***.
- Vocalisation of laryngeals between vowels and initially before consonants, i.e. *h_1→***e***, *h_2→***a***, *h_3→***o***; as, from PIE *h_2nēr 'man', PGk. ***anḗr***.

NOTE. That development is common to Greek, Phrygian and Armenian; *cf.* Gk. *anḗr*, Phrygian *anar*, and Armenian *ayr* (from earlier **anir*). In other branches, laryngeals did not vocalise in this position and eventually disappeared. The evolution of Proto-Greek should be considered with the background of an early Palaeo-Balkan *Sprachbund* that makes it difficult to delineate exact boundaries between individual languages. Phrygian and Armenian also share other phonological and morphological peculiarities of Greek.

- The sequence CRHC evolves generally as follows: *CRh_1C → PGk CRēC; PIE *CRh_2C → PGk CRāC; PIE *CRh_3C → PGk CRōC.
- The sequence PIE **CRHV* becomes generally PGk CaRV.

NOTE. It has also been proposed by Sihler (2000) that PIE *Vk^w→***uk^w***; *cf.* PIE *nok^wts 'night' → PGk ***nuk^wts*** → Gk. *nuks/nuxt-*; *cf.* also *k^wek^wlos 'wheel' → PGk ***k^wuk^wlos*** → Gk. *kuklos*; etc. This is related to Cowgill's law, raising **o* to ***u*** between a resonant and a labial.

10. Later sound changes from Proto-Greek into *mello-Greek* (or from *Pre-Greek* into *Proto-Greek* after Sihler 1995), from which Mycenaean was derived, include:

- The second stage of palatalisation, which affected all consonants, including the restored ***t^sj*** and ***d^zj*** sequences (Sihler 1995).
- Loss of final stop consonants; final *m*→*n*.
- Syllabic ***m̥***→*am*, and ***n̥***→*an*, before resonants; otherwise both were nasalised ***m̥/n̥***→*ã*→*a*.
- Loss of ***s*** in consonant clusters, with supplementary lengthening, e.g. *esmi*→*ēmi*.
- Creation of secondary *s* from clusters, ***ntja***→*nsa*. Assibilation ***ti***→*si* only in southern dialects.
- Mycenaean i-vocalism and replacement of double-consonant ***-kw-*** for *-k^wk^w-*.

NOTE. On the problematic case of common Greek ἵππος (*^{h}ippos*), *horse*, derived from PIE and PGk ***ekwos***, Meier-Brügger (2003): "the i-vocalism of which is best understood as an inheritance from the Mycenaean period. At that time, *e* in a particular phonetic situation must have been pronounced in a more closed manner, *cf. di-pa* i.e. *dipas* neuter 'lidded container fror drinking' vs. the later δέπας (since Homer): Risch (1981), O. Panagl (1989). That the i-form extended to the entire Greek region may be explained in that the word, very central during Mycenaean rule of the entire region (second millennium BC), spread and suppressed the e-form that had certainly been present at one time. On the *-pp-*: The original double-consonance *-ku̯-* was likely replaced by -k^wk^w- in the pre-Mycenaean period, and again, in turn by *-pp-* after the disappearance of the labiovelars. Suggestions of an ancient -*k^wk^w*- are already given by the Mycenaean form as *i-qo* (a possible **i-ko-wo* does not appear) and the noted double-consonance in alphabetic Greek. The aspiration of the word at the beginning remains a riddle."

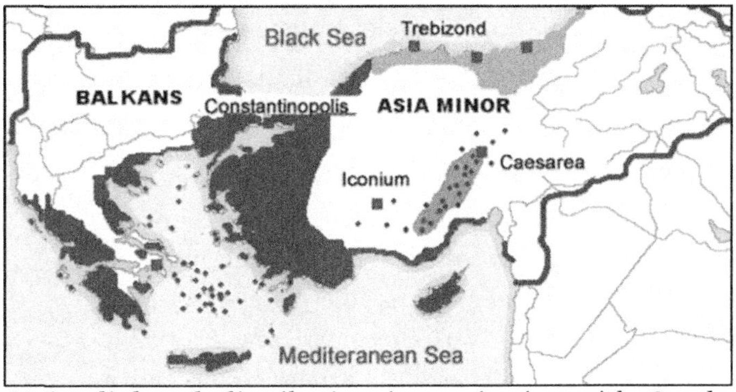

Main dialectal distribution in territories with Greek-speaking majorities (ca. 15th c.): Koiné, Pontic and Cappadocian Greek. The language distribution in Anatolia remained almost unchanged until the expulsion of Greeks (1914-1923) from Turkey. (2011, modified from Ivanchau, Infocan 2008)

Other features common to the earliest Greek dialects include:

- Late *satemisation* trend, evidenced by the post-Mycenaean change of labiovelars into dentals before *e*; as, *k^we* → *te* 'and'.
- PIE dative, instrumental and locative were syncretised into a single dative.
- Dialectal nominative plural in *-oi, -ai* (shared with Latin) fully replaces LIE common **-ōs, *-ās*.
- The superlative *-tatos* (<PIE **-tm̥o-*) becomes productive.
- The peculiar oblique stem *gunaik-* 'women', attested from the Thebes tablets is probably Proto-Greek; it appears, at least as *gunai-* also in Armenian.
- The pronouns *houtos, ekeinos* and *autos* are created. Use of *ho, hā, ton* as articles is post-Mycenaean.
- The first person middle verbal desinences *-mai, -mān* replace *-ai, -a*. The third singular *pherei* is an analogical innovation, replacing the expected PIE **b^héreti*, i.e. Dor. **phereti*, Ion. **pheresi*.
- The future tense is created, including a future passive and an aorist passive.
- The suffix *-ka-* is attached to some perfects and aorists.
- Infinitives in *-ehen, -enai* and *-men* are also common to Greek dialects.

II. ARMENIAN

The earliest testimony of the Armenian language dates to the fifth century AD, the Bible translation of Mesrob Mashtots. The earlier history of the language is unclear and the subject of much speculation. It is clear that Armenian is an Indo-European language, but its development is opaque.

NOTE. Proto-Armenian sound-laws are varied and eccentric, such as IE **dw-* yielding Arm. *k-*, and in many cases still uncertain. In fact, that phonetic development is usually seen as **dw-* to *erk-*, based on PIE numeral **dwo-* 'two', a reconstruction Kortlandt (Armeniaca 2003) dismisses, exposing alternative etymologies for the usual examples.

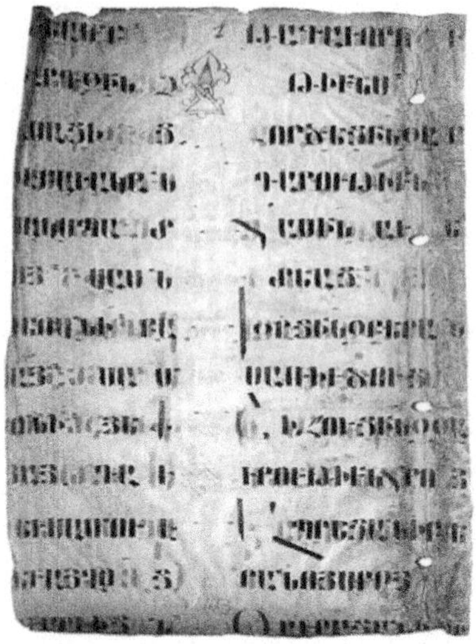

Armenian manuscript, ca. 5th-6th c. AD (PD)

PIE voiceless stops are aspirated in Proto-Armenian.

NOTE. That circumstance gave rise to the Glottalic theory, which postulates that this aspiration may have been sub-phonematic already in Proto-Indo-European. In certain contexts, these aspirated stops are further reduced to *w*, *h* or ∅ in Armenian – so e.g. PIE **p'ots*, into Arm. *otn*, Gk. *pous* 'foot'; PIE **t'reis*, Arm. *erek'*, Gk. *treis* 'three'.

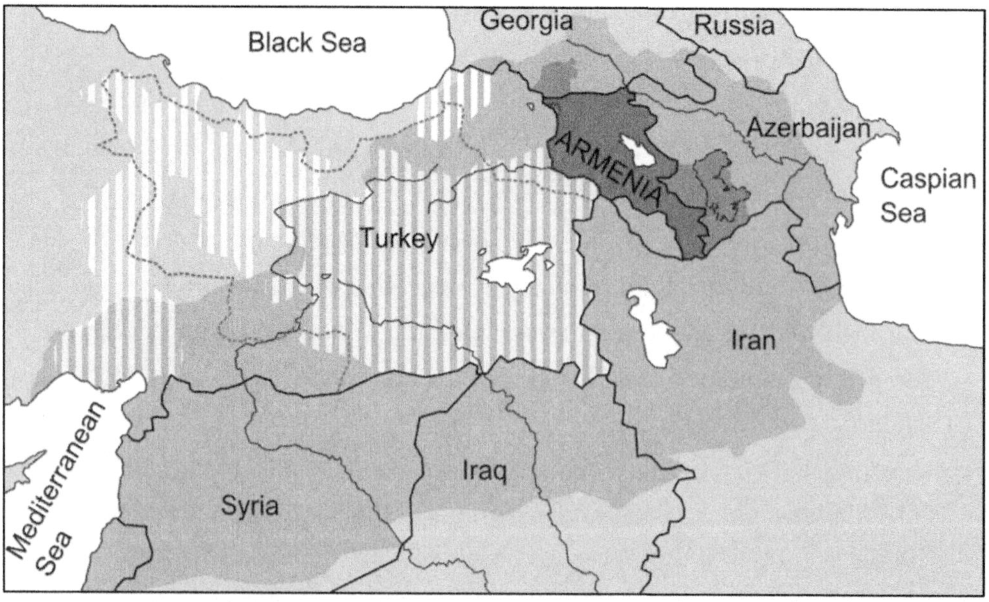

Armenia today (darkest colour), Armenian majorities (dark) and greatest extent of the Kingdom of Armenia (light). Territory of the 6 Armenian Vilayets in the Ottoman Empire (dotted line), and areas with significant Armenian population prior to the Armenian Genocide (stripes). Ivaşca Flavius (2010).

III. INDO-IRANIAN

The Indo-Iranian or Aryan language group consists of two main language subgroups, Indo-Aryan and Iranian. Nuristani has been suggested as a third one, while Dardic is usually classified within Indo-Aryan.

The contemporary Indo-Iranian languages form the second largest sub-branch of Late Indo-European (after North-West Indo-European), with more than one billion speakers in total, stretching from Europe (Romani) and the Caucasus (Ossetian) to East India (Bengali and Assamese). The largest in terms of native speakers are Hindustani (Hindi and Urdu, ca. 540 million), Bengali (ca. 200 million), Punjabi (ca. 100 million), Marathi and Persian (ca. 70 million each), Gujarati (ca. 45 million), Pashto (40 million), Oriya (ca. 30 million), Kurdish and Sindhi (ca. 20 million each).

While the archaeological identification of Pre-Proto-Indo-Iranians and Proto-Indo-Iranians remains unsolved, it is believed that ca. 2500 BC a distinct Proto-Indo-Iranian language must have been spoken in the eastern part of the previous Yamna territory.

NOTE. Parpola (*The formation of the Aryan branch of Indo-European*, 1999) suggests the following identifications:

Date range	Archaeological culture	Suggested by Parpola
2800-2000 BC	Late Catacomb and Poltavka cultures	LIE to Proto-Indo-Iranian.
2000-1800 BC	Srubna and Abashevo cultures	Proto-Iranian
2000-1800 BC	Petrovka-Sintashta	Proto-Indo-Aryan
1900-1700 BC	BMAC	"Proto-Dasa" Indo-Aryans establishing themselves in the existing BMAC settlements, defeated by "Proto-Rigvedic" Indo-Aryans around 1700
1900-1400 BC	Cemetery H	Indian Dasa
1800-1000 BC	Alakul-Fedorovo	Indo-Aryan, including "Proto–Sauma-Aryan" practicing the Soma cult
1700-1400 BC	early Swat culture	Proto-Rigvedic = Proto-Dardic
1700-1500 BC	late BMAC	"Proto–Sauma-Dasa", assimilation of Proto-Dasa and Proto–Sauma-Aryan
1500-1000 BC	Early West Iranian Grey Ware	Mitanni-Aryan (offshoot of "Proto-Sauma-Dasa")
1400-800 BC	late Swat culture and Punjab, Painted Grey Ware	late Rigvedic
1400-1100 BC	Yaz II-III, Seistan	Proto-Avestan
1100-1000 BC	Gurgan Buff Ware, Late West Iranian Buff Ware	Proto-Persian, Proto-Median
1000-400 BC	Iron Age cultures of Xinjang	Proto-Saka

It is generally believed that early Indo-Iranian contacts with the easternmost part of North-West IE (Pre-Balto-Slavic) accounts for their shared linguistic features, such as *satemisation* and *Ruki* sound law. Assuming – as it is commonly done – that both phonetic trends were late developments after the LIE community, an early North-West–South-East *Sprachbund* or *dialect continuum* must have taken place before the Proto-Indo-Iranian migration to the East.

NOTE. From a linguistic point of view, Burrow (1955): "(...) in the case of Sanskrit migrations at a comparatively late date took it to the extreme East of the Indo-European domain. Before this period its ancestor, primitive Indo-Iranian must have held a fairly central position, being directly in contact with the other dialects of the satem-group, and having to the East of it that form of Indo-European which eventually turned into the dialects A and B of Chinese Turkestan. Its position can further be determined by the especially close relations which are found to exist between it and Balto-Slavonic. Since the Balts and the Slavs are not likely to have moved far from the positions in which they are to be found in their earliest recorded history, the original location of Indo-Iranian towards the South-East of this area becomes highly probable."

As we have seen Kortlandt's (1990) interpretation of linguistic contacts according to

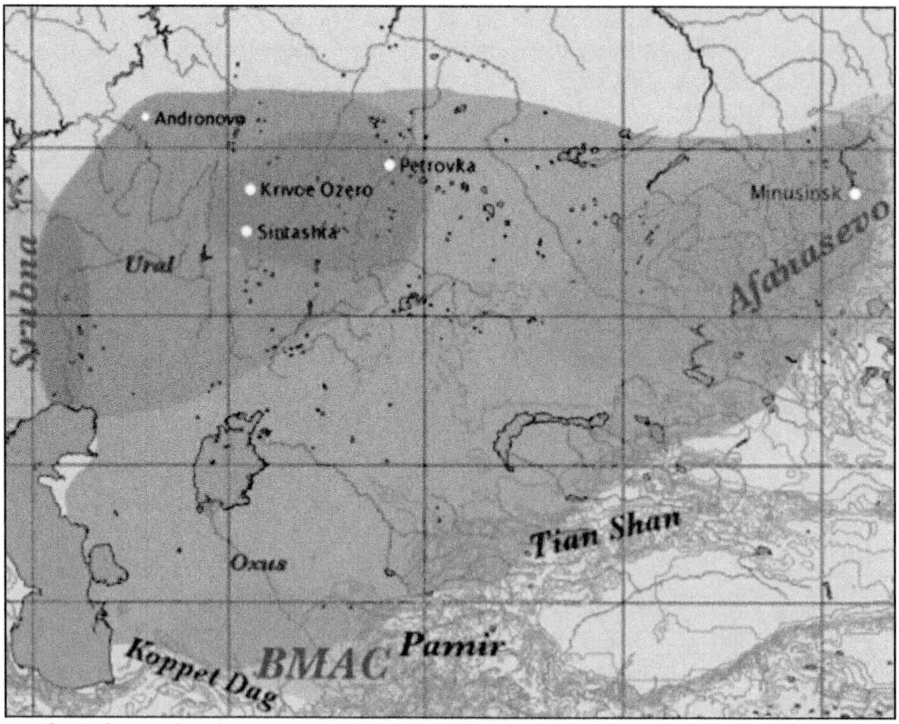

Archaeological cultures associated with late Indo-Iranian migrations. The early phases of the Andronovo culture have often been seen to offer a "staging area" for Indo-Iranian movements. The BMAC offers the Central Asian cultural "filter" through which some argue the Indo-Iranians must have passed southwards to such sites as Mehrgarh and Sibri. Mallory–Adams (1997) (Dbachmann 2005)

Mallory's (1989) account of archaeological events (*v.s.* §1.7.1. *North-West Indo-European*): "If the speakers of the other *satem* languages can be assigned to the Yamnaya horizon and the western Indo-Europeans to the Corded Ware horizon, it is attractive to assign the ancestors of the Balts and the Slavs to the Middle Dnieper culture", an identification also made by Anthony (2007).

Similarly, Adrados–Bernabé–Mendoza (1995-1998), about the dialectal situation of Slavic (from a linguistic point of view): "To a layer of archaisms, shared or not with other languages (...) Slavic added different innovations, some common to Baltic. Some of them are shared with Germanic, as the oblique cases in *-m* and feminine participle; others with Indo-Iranian, so *satemisation*, *Ruki* sound law (more present in Slavic than in Baltic) (...) Most probably, those common characteristics come from a recent time, from secondary contacts between [N.LIE] (whose rearguard was formed by Balto-Slavs) and [S.LIE] (in a time when Greeks were not in contact anymore, they had already migrated to Greece).

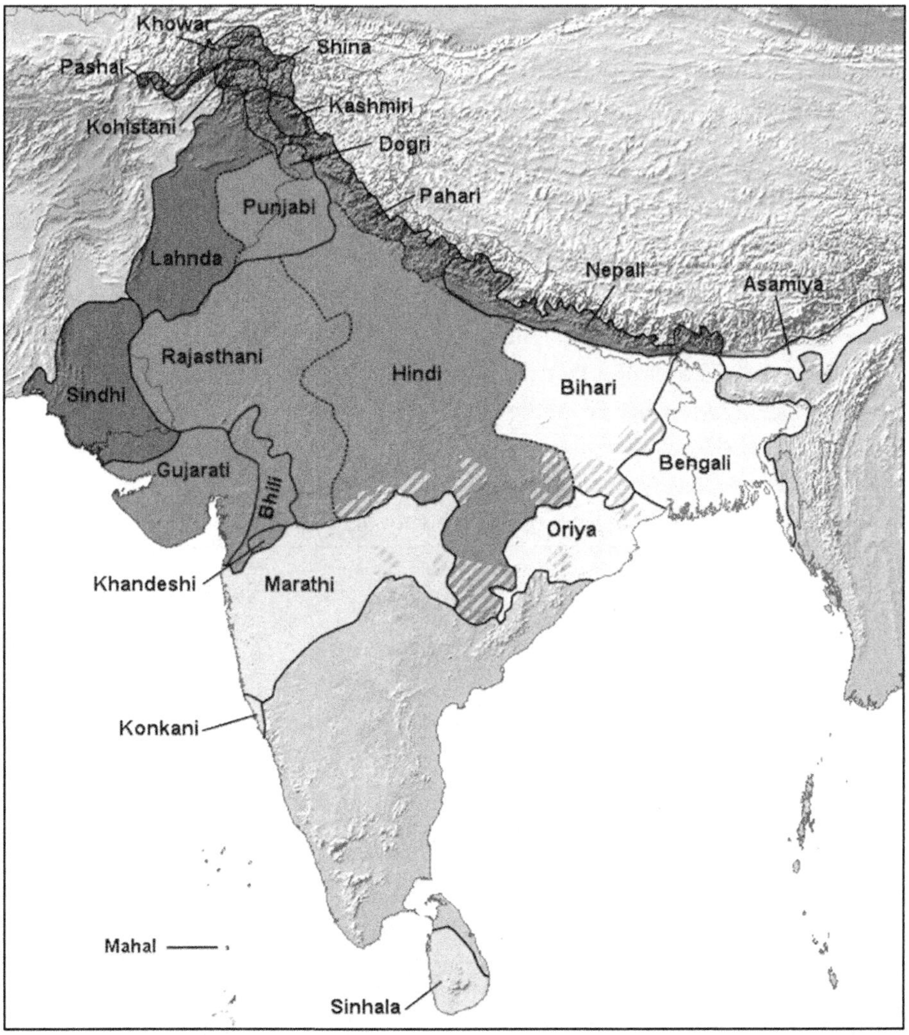

Current distribution of Indo-Aryan languages, A Historical Atlas of South Asia (1992) (Dbachmann 2008)

Because Proto-Indo-Aryan is assumed to have been spoken ca. 2000-1500 BC (preceding Vedic cultures), historical linguists broadly estimate that the *continuum* of Indo-Iranian languages had to diverge ca. 2200-2000 BC, if not earlier. The Aryan expansion before the Indo-Iranian split – for which the *terminus ante quem* is 2000 BC (*cf.* Mallory 1989) –, implies centuries of previous Pre-Indo-Aryan and Pre-Iranian differentiation. This time is commonly identified with the early bearers of the Andronovo culture (Sintashta-Petrovka-Arkaim, in Southern Urals, 2200-1600 BC), who spread over an area of the Eurasian steppe that borders the Ural River on the west, the Tian Shan on the east – where the Indo-Iranians took over the area occupied by the earlier Afanasevo culture –, and Transoxiana and the Hindu Kush on the south.

A Two-wave model of Indo-Iranian expansion has been proposed (Burrow 1973, Parpola 1999), strongly associated with the chariot. Indo-Aryans left linguistic remains in a Hittite horse-training manual written by one "Kikkuli the Mitannian". Other evidence is found in references to the names of Mitanni rulers and the gods they swore by in treaties; these remains are found in the archives of the Mitanni's neighbours, and the time period for this is about 1500 BC.

NOTE. The standard model for the entry of the Indo-European languages into South Asia is that the First Wave went over the Hindu Kush, either into the headwaters of the Indus and later the Ganges. The earliest stratum of Vedic Sanskrit, preserved only in the Rigveda, is assigned to roughly 1500 BC. From the Indus, the Indo-Aryan languages spread from ca. 1500 BC to ca. 500 BC, over the northern and central parts of the subcontinent, sparing the extreme south. The Indo-Aryans in these areas established several powerful kingdoms and principalities in the region, from eastern Afghanistan to the doorstep of Bengal.

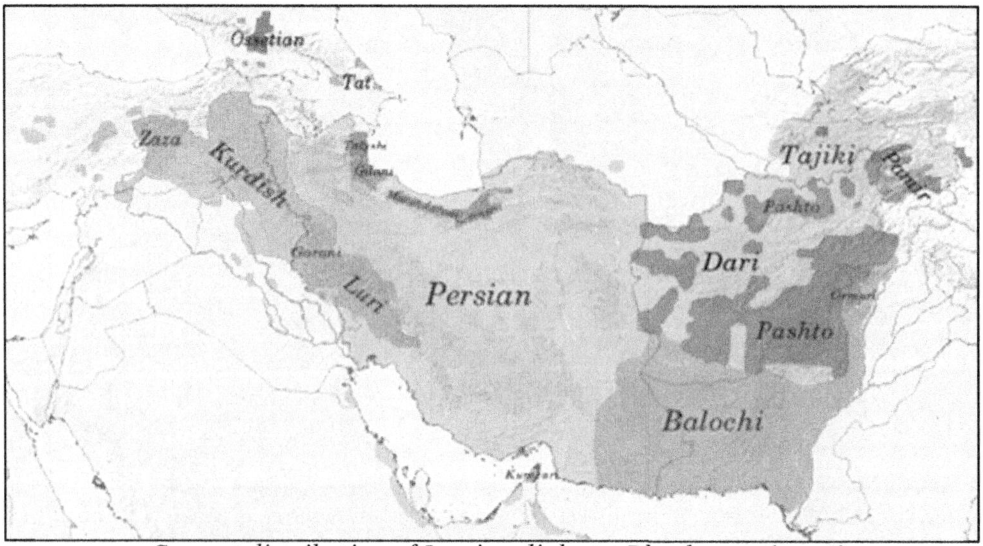

Current distribution of Iranian dialects. Dbachmann(2006)

The Second Wave is interpreted as the Iranian wave. The Iranians would take over all of Central Asia, Iran, and for a considerable period, dominate the European steppe (the modern Ukraine) and intrude north into Russia and west into central and Eastern Europe well into historic times and as late as the Common Era. The first Iranians to reach the Black Sea may have been the Cimmerians in the eighth century BC, although their linguistic affiliation is uncertain. They were followed by the Scythians, who are considered a western branch of the Central Asian Sakas, and the Sarmatian tribes.

The main changes separating Proto-Indo-Iranian from Late Indo-European include (according to Burrow 1955 and Fortson 2004):

- Early *satemisation* trend: The *satem* shift, consisting of two sets of related changes:
  - Palatalisation of LIE velars: **k* →t͡ɕ, **g*→d͡ʑ, **g^h*→d͡ʑ^h; as, **km̥tóm* → ***ḳatám***, **gónu* → ***ǵānu***, **g^{h}éimn̥* → ***ǵ^{h}ima-***.
  - Merge of LIE labiovelars with plain velars: **k^w*→***k*** , **g^w*→***g***, **g^{wh}*→***g^h***; as, **k^{w}o-*→ ***ka-***, **g^{w}ou-* → ***gau-***, **g^{wh}ormó-* → ***g^{h}armá-***.
- These plain velars, when before a front vowel (pre-PII *i or *e) or the glide **j*, were then palatalised to affricates: **k*→t͡ʃ, **g*→d͡ʒ, **g^h*→d͡ʒ^h; as, **k^{w}e* → ***ḳa-***, **g^{w}īwós* → ***ġīwás***, **g^{wh}énti* → ***ġ^{h}anti***.

NOTE. This palatalisation is often called the Law of Palatals. It must have happened before the merge of PIE *e, *o, with *a. An illustrative example is found in weak perfect stem **k^{w}e-k^{w}r-* 'did' → pre-PII **ke-kr-* → **ḳe-kr-* → PII ****ḳa-kr-*** (Ved. *cakr-*, Av. and O.Pers. *caxr-*).

- Before a dental occlusive, *ḳ* → ***š***, *ġ* → ***ž***; *ġ^h*→***ž***, with aspiration of the occlusive; as, **oḳtṓ*→ ***aštā́***, **mr̥ǵt-* → ***mr̥žd-***, **uǵ^{h}tó-* → ***užd^{h}á-***.
- The sequence **ḳs* was simplified to ***šš***; as, **aks-* → ***ášš-***.
- Assimilation of LIE vowels **e*, **o* → ***a***; **ē*, **ō* → ***ā***.
- Interconsonantal and word-final LIE **H*→ PII ***i***, *cf.* **ph$_2$tḗr* → PII ***pitā́r***, *-*med^{h}H* →*-***mad^{h}i***.
- LIE **m̥* **n̥* merge with ***a***; as, **km̥tóm* → ***ḳatám***, **mn̥tó-* → ***matá-***.
- Bartholomae's law: an aspirate immediately followed by a voiceless consonant becomes voiced stop + voiced aspirate. In addition, **d^h+t* → ***dzd^h***; as, **ub^{h}to-* → ***ubd^{h}a-***, **urd^{h}to-* → ***urdzd^{h}a-***, **aug^h-tá-* → ***augd^{h}á-***.
- The Ruki rule: **s* is retracted to ***š*** when immediately following **r* **r̥* **u* **k* or **i*. Its allophone **z* likewise becomes ***ž***; as, **wers-* → ***warš-***, **pr̥sto* → ***pr̥šta-***, **geus-* → ***ǵauš-***, **k^{w}sep-* → ***kšap-***, **wis-* → ***wiš-***, **nisdo-* → ***nižda-***.

- Brugmann's law: **o* in an open syllable lengthens to **ō**; **deh*$_3$*tór-m̥* → Pre-PII **deh*$_3$*tṓr-m̥** → ***dātāram***.
- Resonants are generally stable in PII, but for the confusion *l/*r, which in the oldest Rigveda and in Avestan gives a trend LIE **l̥* → PII **r̥**, as well as **l*→***r***; as, **wĺ̥kʷos* → ***wl̥kas / wr̥kas***.

A synoptic table of Indo-Iranian phonetic system:

		Labials	Coronals		Affricates		Velars	Gutturals
			dental/ alveolar	post- alveolar	alveolo- palatal	post- alveolar		
Plosive	*Voiceless*	**p**	**t**		**ķ**	**ḳ**	**k**	**ʔ**
	Aspirated		$\mathbf{t^h}$				$\mathbf{k^h}$	
	Voiced	**b**	**d**		**ǵ**	**ġ**	**g**	
	Aspirated	$\mathbf{b^h}$	$\mathbf{d^h}$		**ǵ**^{h}	**ġ**^{h}	$\mathbf{g^h}$	
Nasals		**m**	**n**					
Fricatives	*Voiceless*		**s**	**š**				**h**
	Voiced		(**z**)	(**ž**)				
Liquids			**l**	**r**				
Approximant		**w**			**j**			

IV. PALAEO-BALKAN LANGUAGES

A. PHRYGIAN

The Phrygian language was spoken by the Phrygians, a people that settled in Asia Minor during the Bronze Age. It survived probably into the sixth century AD, when it was replaced by Greek.

Phrygian Kingdom ca. 800-700 BC, from "Atlas of the Bible Lands" (1959) (2011 from PD)

Ancient historians and myths sometimes did associate Phrygian with Thracian and maybe even Armenian, on grounds of classical sources. Herodotus recorded the Macedonian account that Phrygians migrated into Asia Minor from Thrace, and stated that the Armenians were colonists of the Phrygians, still considered the same in the time of Xerxes I. The earliest mention of Phrygian in Greek sources, in the *Homeric Hymn to Aphrodite,* depicts it as different from Trojan: in the hymn, Aphrodite, disguising herself as a mortal to seduce the Trojan prince Anchises, tells him:

"*Otreus of famous name is my father, if so be you have heard of him, and he reigns over all Phrygia rich in fortresses. But I know your speech well beside my own, for a Trojan nurse brought me up at home*". Of Trojan, unfortunately, nothing is known.

Phrygian is attested by two corpora, one, Palaeo-Phrygian, from around 800 BC and later, and another after a period of several centuries, Neo-Phrygian, from around the beginning of the Common Era. The Palaeo-Phrygian corpus is further divided geographically into inscriptions of Midas-city, Gordion, Central, Bithynia, Pteria, Tyana, Daskyleion, Bayindir, and "*various*". The Mysian inscriptions show a language classified as a separate Phrygian dialect, written in an alphabet with an additional letter, the "*Mysian s*". We can reconstruct some words with the help of some inscriptions written with a script similar to the Greek one.

Its structure, what can be recovered from it, was typically LIE, with at least three nominal cases, three gender classes and two grammatical numbers, while the verbs were conjugated for tense, voice, mood, person and number.

Phrygian seems to exhibit an augment, like Greek and Armenian, as in Phryg. *eberet,* probably corresponding to PIE **é-b^{h}er-e-t* (*cf.* Gk. *epheret*).

A sizable body of Phrygian words is theoretically known; however, the meaning and etymologies and even correct forms of many Phrygian words (mostly extracted from inscriptions) are still being debated.

Phrygian words with possible PIE origin and Graeco-Armenian cognates include:

- Phryg. *bekos 'bread',* from PIE **b^{h}eh$_3$g-*; *cf.* Gk. *p^{h}ōgō* 'to roast'.
- Phryg. *bedu 'water',* from PIE **wed-*; *cf.* Arm. *get* '*river*'.
- Phryg. *anar* 'husband, man', PIE **h$_2$ner-* 'man'; *cf.* Gk. *aner-* 'man, husband'.
- Phryg. *belte* 'swamp', from PIE root **b^{h}el-* 'to gleam'; *cf.* Gk. *baltos* 'swamp'.
- Phryg. *brater* 'brother', from PIE **b^{h}reh$_2$ter-*; *cf.* Gk. *p^{h}rāter-*.

- Phryg. *ad-daket* 'does, causes', from PIE stem *$d^h\bar{e}$-k-*; *cf.* Gk. *$et^h\bar{e}ka$.*
- Phryg. *germe* 'warm', from PIE *$g^{wh}er$-mo-*; *cf.* Gk. *t^hermos.*
- Phryg. *gdan* 'earth', from PIE *d^hg^hom-*; *cf.* Gk. *$k^ht^h\bar{o}n$.*

NOTE. For more information on similarities between Greek and Phrygian, see Neumann (*Phrygisch und Griechisch*, 1988).

B. ILLYRIAN

The Illyrian languages are a group of Indo-European languages that were spoken in the western part of the Balkans in former times by ethnic groups identified as *Illyrians*: Delmatae, Pannoni, Illyrioi, Autariates, Taulanti.

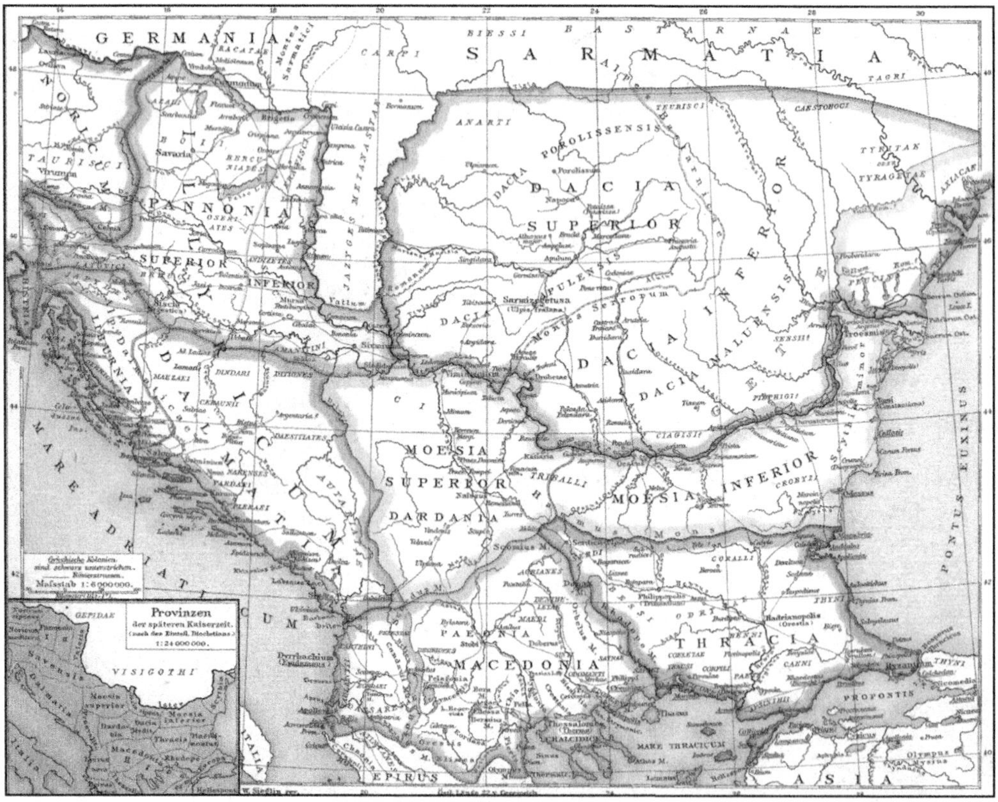

Roman provinces in the Balkans, Droysens Historischem Handatlas (1886)

The main source of authoritative information about the Illyrian language consists of a handful of Illyrian words cited in classical sources, and numerous examples of Illyrian anthroponyms, ethnonyms, toponyms and hydronyms. Some sound-changes and other language features are deduced from what remains of the Illyrian languages, but because no writings in Illyrian are known, there is not sufficient evidence to clarify its place within the Indo-European language family aside from its probable *centum* nature.

NOTE. A grouping of Illyrian with the Messapian language has been proposed for about a century, but remains an unproven hypothesis. The theory is based on classical sources, archaeology, as well as onomastic considerations. Messapian material culture bears a number of similarities to Illyrian material culture. Some Messapian anthroponyms have close Illyrian equivalents. A relation to the Venetic language and Liburnian language, once spoken in northeastern Italy and Liburnia respectively, is also proposed.

B. THRACIAN

Excluding Dacian, whose status as a Thracian language is disputed, Thracian was spoken in what is now southern Bulgaria, parts of Serbia, the Republic of Macedonia, Northern Greece – especially prior to Ancient Macedonian expansion –, throughout Thrace (including European Turkey) and in parts of Bithynia (North-Western Anatolia). Most of the Thracians were eventually Hellenised (in the province of Thrace) or Romanised (in Moesia, Dacia, etc.), with the last remnants surviving in remote areas until the fifth century AD.

NOTE. As an extinct language with only a few short inscriptions attributed to it, there is little known about the Thracian language, but a number of features are agreed upon. A number of probable Thracian words are found in inscriptions – most of them written with Greek script – on buildings, coins, and other artifacts. Some Greek lexical elements may derive from Thracian, such as *balios* 'dappled' (< PIE **b^hel-* 'to shine', Pokorny also cites Illyrian as possible source), *bounos* 'hill, mound', etc.

C. DACIAN

The Dacian language was spoken by the ancient people of Dacia. It is often considered to have been either a northern variant of the Thracian language, or closely related to it.

There are almost no written documents in Dacian. It used to be one of the major languages of South-Eastern Europe, stretching from what is now Eastern Hungary to the Black Sea shore. Based on archaeological findings, the origins of the Dacian culture are believed to be in Moldavia, being identified as an evolution of the Iron Age Basarabi culture.

It is unclear exactly when the Dacian language became extinct, or even whether it has a living descendant. The initial Roman conquest of part of Dacia did not put an end to the language, as free Dacian tribes such as the Carpi may have continued to speak Dacian in Moldavia and adjacent regions as late as the sixth or seventh century AD, still capable of leaving some influences in the forming of Slavic languages.

E. PAIONIAN

The Paionian language is the poorly attested language of the ancient Paionians, whose kingdom once stretched north of Macedon into Dardania and in earlier times into southwestern Thrace.

Classical sources usually considered the Paionians distinct from Thracians or Illyrians, comprising their own ethnicity and language. Athenaeus seemingly connected the Paionian tongue to the Mysian language, itself barely attested. If correct, this could mean that Paionian was an Anatolian language. On the other hand, the Paionians were sometimes regarded as descendants of Phrygians, which may put Paionian on the same linguistic branch as the Phrygian language.

NOTE. Modern linguists are uncertain on the classification of Paionian, due to the extreme scarcity of materials we have on this language. However, it seems that Paionian was an independent IE dialect. It shows a/o distinction and does not appear to have undergone satemisation. The Indo-European voiced aspirates became plain voiced consonants, i.e. $*b^h \rightarrow b$, $*d^h \rightarrow d$, $*g^h \rightarrow g$, $*g^{wh} \rightarrow g^w$; as in Illyrian, Thracian, Macedonian and Phrygian (but unlike Greek).

F. ANCIENT MACEDONIAN

The Ancient Macedonian language was the tongue of the Ancient Macedonians. It was spoken in Macedon during the first millennium BC. Marginalised from the fifth century BC, it was gradually replaced by the common Greek dialect of the Hellenistic Era. It was probably spoken predominantly in the inland regions away from the coast. It is as yet undetermined whether the language was a dialect of Greek, a sibling language to Greek, or an Indo-European language which is a close cousin to Greek and also related to Thracian and Phrygian.

Knowledge of the language is very limited, because there are no surviving texts that are indisputably written in the language. However, a body of authentic Macedonian words has been assembled from ancient sources, mainly from coin inscriptions, and from the fifth century lexicon of Hesychius of Alexandria, amounting to about 150 words and 200 proper names. Most of these are confidently identifiable as Greek, but some of them are not easily reconciled with standard Greek phonology. The 6,000 surviving Macedonian inscriptions are in the Greek Attic dialect.

NOTE. Suggested phylogenetic classifications of Macedonian include: An Indo-European language which is a close cousin to Greek and also related to Thracian and Phrygian languages, suggested by A. Meillet (1913) and I. I. Russu (1938), or part of a *Sprachbund* encompassing Thracian, Illyrian and Greek (Kretschmer 1896, E. Schwyzer 1959). An "Illyrian" dialect mixed with Greek, suggested by K. O. Müller (1825) and by G. Bonfante (1987). Various explicitly "Greek" scenarios: A Greek dialect, part of the North-Western (Locrian, Aetolian, Phocidian, Epirote) variants of Doric Greek, suggested amongst others by N.G.L. Hammond (1989) Olivier Masson (1996) and Michael Meier-Brügger (2003). A northern Greek dialect, related to Aeolic Greek and Thessalian, suggested among others by A.Fick (1874) and O.Hoffmann (1906). A Greek dialect with a non-Indo-European substratal influence, suggested by M. Sakellariou (1983). A sibling language of Greek within Indo-European, Macedonian and Greek forming two subbranches of a Greco-Macedonian subgroup within Indo-European (sometimes called "Hellenic"), suggested by Joseph (2001) and others.

The Pella curse tablet, a text written in a distinct Doric Greek idiom, found in Pella in 1986, dated to between mid to early fourth century BC, has been forwarded as an argument that the Ancient Macedonian language was a dialect of North-Western Greek. Before the discovery it was proposed that the Macedonian dialect was an early form of Greek, spoken alongside Doric proper at that time.

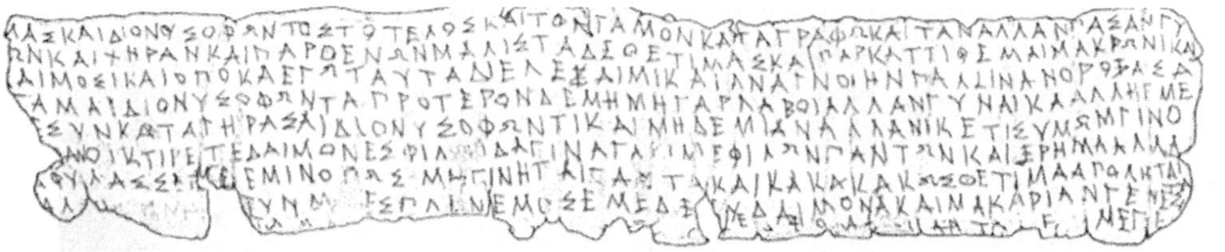

The Pella katadesmos is a katadesmos *(a curse, or magic spell) inscribed on a lead scroll, probably dating to 380-350 BC. It was found in Pella in 1986 (PD)*

NOTE. Olivier Masson thinks that "in contrast with earlier views which made of it an Aeolic dialect (O.Hoffmann compared Thessalian) we must by now think of a link with North-West Greek (Locrian, Aetolian, Phocidian, Epirote). This view is supported by the recent discovery at Pella of a curse tablet which may well be the first 'Macedonian' text attested (...); the text includes an adverb "opoka" which is not Thessalian". Also, James L. O'Neil states that the "curse tablet from Pella shows word forms which are clearly Doric, but a different form of Doric from any of the west Greek dialects of areas adjoining Macedon. Three other, very brief, fourth century inscriptions are also indubitably Doric. These show that a Doric dialect was spoken in Macedon, as we would expect from the West Greek forms of Greek names found in Macedon. And yet later Macedonian inscriptions are in Koine avoiding both Doric forms and the Macedonian voicing of consonants. The native Macedonian dialect had become unsuitable for written documents."

From the few words that survive, a notable sound-law may be ascertained, that PIE voiced aspirates *d^h, *b^h, *g^h, appear as δ (=*d[ʰ]*), β (=*b[ʰ]*), γ (=*g[ʰ]*), in contrast to Greek dialects, which unvoiced them to θ (=t^h), φ (=p^h), χ (=k^h).

NOTE. Since these languages are all known via the Greek alphabet, which has no signs for voiced aspirates, it is unclear whether de-aspiration had really taken place, or whether the supposed voiced stops β, δ, γ were just picked as the closest matches to express voiced aspirates PIE *b^h, *d^h, *g^h. As to Macedonian β, δ, γ = Greek φ, θ, χ, Claude Brixhe (1996) suggests that it may have been a later development: The letters may already have designated not voiced stops, i.e. [b, d, g], but voiced fricatives, i.e. [β, δ, γ], due to a voicing of the voiceless fricatives [φ, θ, x] (= Classical Attic [p^h, t^h, k^h]). Brian Joseph (2001) sums up that "The slender evidence is open to different interpretations, so that no definitive answer is really possible", but cautions that "most likely, Ancient Macedonian was not simply an Ancient Greek dialect on a par with Attic or Aeolic". In this sense, some authors also call it a "deviant Greek dialect".

- PIE *d^h*enh*$_2$- 'to leave', → A.Mac. δανός (*δanós*) 'death'; *cf.* Attic θάνατος (*tʰánatos*). PIE *h_2*aid*^{h}- → A.Mac. ἄδραια (*aδraia*) 'bright weather', Attic αἰθρία (*aitʰría*).
- PIE *b^h*asko-* → A.Mac. βάσκιοι (*βáskioi*) 'fasces'. Compare also for A.Mac. ἀϐροῦτες (*aβroûtes*) or ἀϐροῦϝες (*aβroûwes*), Attic ὀφρῦς (*opʰrûs*) 'eyebrows'; for Mac. Βερενίκη (*Bere-níkē*), Attic Φερενίκη (*Pʰere-níkē*) 'bearing victory'.
  - According to Herodotus (ca. 440 BC), the Macedonians claimed that the *Phryges* were called *Brygoi* (<PIE *b^h*rugo-*) before migrating from Thrace to Anatolia ca. 1200 BC.
  - In Aristophanes' The Birds, the form κεϐλήπυρις (*keβlē-pyris*) 'red-cap (bird)', shows a voiced stop instead of a standard Greek unvoiced aspirate, i.e. Macedonian κεϐ(α)λή (*keβalē*) vs. Greek κεφαλή (*kepʰalē*) 'head'.
- If A.Mac. γοτάν (*γotán*) 'pig', is related to PIE *g^w*ou-* 'cow', this would indicate that the labiovelars were either intact (hence *g^w*otán*), or merged with the velars, unlike the usual Gk. βοῦς (*boûs*). Such deviations, however, are not unknown within Greek dialects; compare Dor. γλεπ- (*glep-*) for common Gk. βλεπ- (*blep-*), as well as Dor. γλάχων (*gláchōn*) and Ion. γλήχων (*glēchōn*) for Gk. βλήχων (*blēchōn*).
- Examples suggest that voiced velar stops were devoiced, especially word-initially: PIE **genu-* → A.Mac. κάναδοι (*kánadoi*) 'jaws'; PIE **gomb*^{h}- → A.Mac. κόμϐους (*kómbous*) 'molars'.
  - Compared to Greek words, there is A.Mac. ἀρκόν (*arkón*) vs. Attic ἀργός (*argós*); the Macedonian toponym *Akesamenai*, from the Pierian name *Akesamenos* – if *Akesa-* is cognate to Greek *agassomai, agamai* 'to astonish'; *cf.* also the Thracian name *Agassamenos*.

V. ALBANIAN

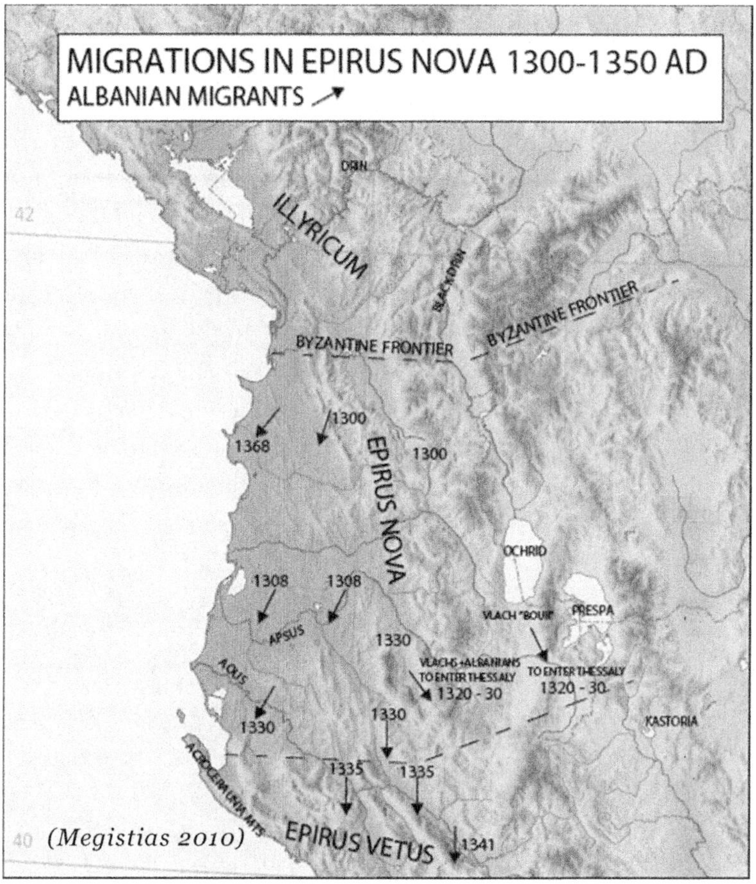

(Megistias 2010)

Albanian is spoken by over 8 million people primarily in Albania, Kosovo, and the Former Yugoslav Republic of Macedonia, but also by smaller numbers of ethnic Albanians in other parts of the Balkans, along the eastern coast of Italy and in Sicily. It has no living close relatives among the modern IE languages. There is no consensus over its origin and dialectal classification.

References to the existence of Albanian survive from the fourteenth century AD, but without recording any specific words. The oldest surviving documents written in Albanian are the *Formula e Pagëzimit* (Baptismal formula), *Unte paghesont premenit Atit et birit et spertit senit* 'I baptise thee in the name of the Father, and the Son, and the Holy Spirit', recorded by Pal Engjelli, Bishop of Durres in 1462 in the Gheg dialect, and some New Testament verses from that period.

1.7.3. ANATOLIAN LANGUAGES

The Anatolian branch is generally considered the earliest to split off from the Proto-Indo-European language, from a stage referred to as *Proto-Indo-Hittite* (PIH). Typically a date ca. 4500-3500 BC is assumed for the separation.

NOTE. A long period of time is necessary for Proto-Anatolian to develop into Common Anatolian. Craig Melchert and Alexander Lehrman agreed that a separation date of about 4000 BCE between Proto-Anatolian and the Proto-Indo-Hittite language community seems reasonable. The millennium or so around 4000 BC, say 4500 to 3500 BC, constitutes the latest window within which Proto-Anatolian is likely to have separated.

Within a Kurgan framework, there are two possibilities of how early Anatolian speakers could have reached Anatolia: from the north via the Caucasus, and from the west, via the Balkans. The archaeological identification of Anatolian speakers remains highly speculative, as it depends on the broad guesstimates that historical linguistics is able to offer. Nevertheless, the Balkans route appears to be somewhat more likely for archaeologists; so e.g. Mallory (1989) and Steiner (1990).

Map of the Hittite Empire at its greatest extent under Suppiluliuma I (ca.1350-1322 BC) and Mursili II (ca. 1321–1295 BC). (Javier Fernandez-Vina 2010).

Attested dialects of the Anatolian branch are:

- Hittite (*nesili*), attested from ca. 1800 BC to 1100 BC, official language of the Hittite Empire.
- Luwian (*luwili*), close relative of Hittite spoken in Arzawa, to the southwest of the core Hittite area.

2000 - FORMATION OF HITTITE EMPIRE

- Palaic, spoken in north-central Anatolia, extinct around the thirteenth century BC, known only fragmentarily from quoted prayers in Hittite texts.
- Lycian, spoken in Lycia in the Iron Age, most likely a descendant of Luwian, became extinct ca. the first century BC. A fragmentary language, it is also a likely candidate for the language spoken by Trojans.
- Lydian, spoken in Lydia, extinct ca. the first century BC, fragmentary, possibly from the same dialect group as Hittite.
- Carian, spoken in Caria, fragmentarily attested from graffiti by Carian mercenaries in Egypt from ca. the seventh century BC, extinct ca. the thirteenth century BC.
- Pisidian and Sidetic (Pamphylian), fragmentary.
- Milyan, known from a single inscription.

Clay tablet in Hittite cuneiform containing the correpondance between the Luwian King of Arzawa and the Pharaoh of Egypt. (PD)

Anatolia was heavily Hellenised following the conquests of Alexander the Great, and it is generally thought that by the first century BC the native languages of the area were extinct.

Hittite proper is known from cuneiform tablets and inscriptions erected by the Hittite kings and written in an adapted form of Old Assyrian cuneiform orthography. Owing to the predominantly syllabic nature of the script, it is difficult to ascertain the precise phonetic qualities of some Hittite sounds.

The Hittite language has traditionally been stratified – partly on linguistic and partly on paleographic grounds – into Old Hittite, Middle Hittite and New or Neo-Hittite, corresponding to the Old, Middle and New Kingdoms of the Hittite Empire, ca. 1750-1500 BC, 1500-1430 BC and 1430-1180 BC, respectively.

Luwian was spoken by population groups in Arzawa, to the west or southwest of the core Hittite area. In the oldest texts, e.g. the Hittite Code, the Luwian-speaking areas including Arzawa and Kizzuwatna were called Luwia. From this homeland, Luwian speakers gradually spread through Anatolia and became a contributing factor to the downfall, after ca. 1180 BC, of the Hittite Empire, where it was already widely spoken. Luwian was also the language spoken in the Neo-Hittite states of Syria, such as Milid and Carchemish, as well as in the central Anatolian kingdom of Tabal that flourished around 900 BC. Luwian has been preserved in two forms, named after the writing systems used: Cuneiform Luwian and Hieroglyphic Luwian.

Luwian language spreading, second to first millennium BC (Hendrik Tammen 2006)

For the most part, the immediate ancestor of the known Anatolian languages, Common Anatolian (a late Proto-Anatolian dialect spoken ca. 3000-2000 BC) has been reconstructed on the basis of Hittite. However, the usage of Hittite cuneiform writing system limits the enterprise of understanding and reconstructing Anatolian phonology, partly due to the deficiency of the adopted Akkadian cuneiform syllabary to represent Hittite sounds, and partly due to the Hittite scribal practices.

NOTE. This especially pertains to what appears to be confusion of voiceless and voiced dental stops, where signs -dV- and -tV- are employed interchangeably different attestations of the same word. Furthermore, in the syllables of the structure VC only the signs with voiceless stops are generally used. Distribution of spellings with single and geminated consonants in the oldest extant monuments indicates that the reflexes of PIE voiceless stops were spelled as double consonants and the reflexes of Proto-Indo-European voiced stops as single consonants.

Known changes from Indo-Hittite into Common Anatolian include:

- Voiced aspirates merged with voiced stops: *d^h→*d, *b^h→*b, *g^h→*g.
- Voiceless stops become voiced after accented long vowel or diphthong: PIH *wēk- → CA *wēg- (*cf.* Hitt. *wēk-* 'ask for'); PIH *d^heh_1ti 'putting' → CA *dǣdi (*cf.* Luw. *taac-* 'votive offering').
- Conditioned allophone PIH **tj-* → CA **tsj-*, as Hittite still shows.
- PIH *h_1 is lost in CA, but for *eh_1→*ǣ, appearing as Hitt., Pal. *ē*, Luw., Lyc., Lyd. *ā*; word-initial *h_2→*x, non-initial *h_2→*h; *h_3→*h.

NOTE 1. Melchert proposes that CA *x (voiceless fricative) is lenited to *h (voiced fricative) under the same conditions as voiceless stops. Also, word-initial *h_3 is assumed by some scholars to have been already lost in CA.

NOTE 2. There is an important assimilation of laryngeals within CA: a sequence *-VRHV- becomes -VRRV-; *cf.* PIH *$sperh_1V$- → Hitt. *isparr-* 'kick flat'; PIH *sun-h_3-V- → Hitt. *sunna-* 'fill', Pal. *sunnuttil-* 'outpouring'; etc.

- PIH resonants are generally stable in CA. Only word-initial *r̥ has been eliminated. Word-initial **je-* shows a trend to become CA **e-*, but the trend is not complete in CA, as Hittite shows.
- Diphthong evolved as PIH **ei* → CA *ę̄; PIH **eu* → CA *ū. PIE **oi*, **ai*, **ou*, **au*, appear also in CA.

NOTE. Common Anatolian preserves PIE vowel system basically intact. Some cite the merger of PIH **o* and (a controversial) **a* as a Common Anatolian innovation, but according to Melchert that merger was secondary shared innovation in Hittite, Palaic and Luwian, but not in Lycian. Also, the lengthening of accented short vowels in open syllables cannot be of Common Anatolian, and neither can lengthening in accented closed syllables.

- The CA nominal system shows an productive declension in **-i*, **-u*, considered an archaic feature retained from PIH.
- There are only two grammatical genders, animate and inanimate; this has usually been interpreted as the original system in PIH.
- Hittite verbs are inflected according to two general verbal classes, the *mi-* and the *hi*-conjugation. They had two voices (active and mediopassive), two moods (indicative and imperative), and two tenses (present and past), two infinitive forms, one verbal substantive, a supine, and a participle.

PART II

PHONOLOGY & MORPHOLOGY

By Carlos Quiles & Fernando López-Menchero

2. PHONOLOGY

2.1. CLASSIFICATION OF SOUNDS

2.1.1. The vowels are short [a], [e], [i], [o], [u], written **a**, **e**, **i**, **o**, **u**, and long [aː], [eː], [iː], [oː], [uː], written **ā**, **ē**, **ī**, **ō**, **ū**, respectively. The other sounds are consonants.

The Indo-European diphthongs proper are [ei̯], [oi̯], [ai̯], written **ei**, **oi**, **ai**, and [eu̯], [ou̯], [au̯], written **eu, ou, au**. Both vowel sounds are heard, one following the other in the same syllable.

NOTE. For the so-called *long diphthongs* [eːi̯], [oːi̯], [aːi̯], written **ēi**, **ōi**, **āi**, and [eːu̯], [oːu̯], [aːu̯], written **ēu**, **ōu**, **āu**, which remained only in Indo-Iranian, Greek and partly in Baltic languages, Schulze (1885) interpreted a regular correspondence of the type **āi/ā/ī**, which came respectively from the full grade of the long diphthong, the full grade before consonant (where the second element was lost), and the zero-grade (a contraction of *schwa* with the semivowel). Martinet (1953) proposed that laryngeals were behind those long diphthongs.

In any case, in the languages in which they are retained, *long diphthongs* have not a longer duration than normal diphthongs; phonologically they are equivalent, as Vedic and Greek metric shows. Adrados–Bernabé–Mendoza (1995-1998): "[t]he difference, therefore, is not the duration of the group, but the relative duration of their components; in other words, e.g. **ei** and **ēi** have the same phonological duration (they are long, as opposed to a brief vowel), but in **ei** both elements have approximately the same duration, whereas in **ēi** the duration of **i** is perceptibly shorter than **e**. Because of that, the name 'long first-element diphthongs' is more appropriate to refer to these phonemes." *Cf.* Allen (*"Long and short diphthongs"*, in Morpurgo Davies and Meid (eds.), 1976) for an analysis of these diphthongs.

Strictly speaking, phoneticians do not consider the so-called rising diphthongs, [i̯e], [i̯o], [i̯a], [i̯eː], [i̯oː], [i̯aː], nor [we], [wo], [wa], [weː], [woː], [waː], as diphthongs proper, but rather sequences of glide and vowel.

The formations usually called triphthongs are [i̯ei̯], [i̯oi̯], [i̯ai̯], [i̯eu̯], [i̯ou̯], [i̯au̯], as well as [wei̯], [woi̯], [wai̯], [weu̯], [wou̯], [wau̯]; and none can be strictly named triphthong, since they are formed by a consonantal sound [j] or [w] followed by a diphthong. The rest of possible formations are made up of a diphthong and a vowel.

NOTE. Whilst most Indo-Europeanists differentiate between sequences of approximant and vowel (rising diphthongs) from true falling diphthongs in their transcriptions, i.e. writing [i̯e] (from [i]+[e]) but [ei] or [ei̯] (from [e]+[i]), some use a different approach, considering all of them combinations of vowel plus glide or glide plus vowel, i.e. writing [je] and [ej], or [i̯e] and [ei̯].

2.1.2. Consonants are either voiced (sonant) or voiceless (surd). Voiced consonants are pronounced with vocal cords vibration, as opposed to voiceless consonants, where the vocal cords are relaxed.

a. The voiced consonants are [b], [d], [g], [g^w], [l], [r] and [ɾ], [m], [n], [z], [j], [w].

b. The voiceless consonants are [p], [t], [k], [k^w], [s].

c. The digraphs **bh** [b^h], **dh** [d^h], **gh** [g^h] and **ch** [g^{wh}] represent the Indo-European voiced aspirates proper whereas **th** [t^h], **kh** [k^h], represent voiceless aspirates.

NOTE. Although written as digraphs, each aspirate is considered a single consonant, not a combination of 'consonant plus aspiration'. The same is valid for labiovelars.

d. The resonants [r], [l], [m], [n], and the semivowels [j] and [w], can function both as consonants and vowels, i.e. they can serve as syllabic border or centre.

NOTE. There is a clear difference between the vocalic allophones of the semivowels and those of the resonants, though: the first, [i] and [u], are very stable as syllabic centre, whereas the resonants ([r̥], [l̥], [m̥], [n̥]) aren't, as they cannot be pronounced more open. Because of that, more dialectal differences are found in their evolution.

2.1.3. The mutes are classified as follows:

	voiceless	*voiced*	*aspirated*
labials	p	b	b^h
dentals	t	d	d^h
velars	k	g	g^h
labiovelars	k^w	g^w	g^{wh}

Labialised velars or Labiovelars **q** [k^w], **c** [g^w], **ch** [g^{wh}], are pronounced like [k], [g], [g^h] respectively, but with rounded lips.

NOTE 1. Labiovelar stops are neutralised adjacent **w**, **u** or **ū**; as in Gk. *bou-kólos* 'cowherd', from **g^wou-kolos*, dissimilated from **g^wou-k^wolos* (which would have given Gk. **bou-pólos*), *cf.* Gk. *ai-pólos* 'goatherd'<**ai(g)-k^wolos* (Fortson 2004). This is related to the question of the actual existence of the groups [kw], [gw], and [g^hw], different from (and similar or identical in their dialectal outputs to) labialised [k^w], [g^w], and [g^{wh}]. A distinction between both is often found, though; as, **kwōn**, *dog*, **ekwos**, *horse*, **ghwer-**, *wild*, **kweidos**, *white*, **kwet-**, *cook* (*cf.* O.Ind. *kwathati*), **tekw-**, *run*, etc. For a defence of such unified forms, see e.g. Halla-aho <http://ethesis.helsinki.fi/julkaisut/hum/slavi/vk/halla-aho/problems.pdf>.

NOTE 2. German Neogrammarians reconstructed a fourth series of phonemes, the voiceless aspirates *p^h, *t^h, *k^h, to explain some irregularities in the outputs of the voiceless row. Most Indo-Europeanists reject this fourth independent row of phonemes, and findings of Indo-Iranian, Armenian and Greek have been explained as 1) expressive in origin, 2) contact of a voiceless with a laryngeal phoneme, and 3) effect of a prior **s**. For support of the fourth row, see e.g. Szemerényi (1985).

2.1.4. The so-called liquids are **l**, which represents the alveolar lateral approximant [l], and **r**, pronounced in PIE and (at least occasionally) in most modern IE languages as alveolar trill [r], today often allophonic with an alveolar tap [ɾ], particularly in unstressed positions. These sounds are voiced.

NOTE. *Cf.* Ban'czerowski (*"indoeuropäisches* r *und* l", *LPosn.* 12/13, 1968).

2.1.5. The nasals are labial [m], written **m**, and dental [n], written **n**. These are voiced. The velar nasal [ŋ] – as *ng* in English *sing* – could have existed in IE as allophone of [n] before velars.

NOTE. Erhart (*Studien zur indoeuropäischen Morphologie*, 1970) reconstructs three nasals, *N, *M1 and *M2, this one a fricative seminasal with which he explains the results of alternating **m** and **w** in some suffixes and roots; as, ***-ment-/-went-***, ***men-/wen-***, etc. He left unexplained, though, under which conditions they would have changed.

2.1.6. The fricatives are voiceless [s] and voiced [z], with **z** being usually the output of **s** before voiced consonants.

NOTE. [z] was already heard in Late Indo-European, as a different pronunciation (allophone) of [s] before voiced stops, as can be clearly seen in LIE **nisdos** [nizdos] *nest*, which comes from PIE roots **ni-**, *down*, and zero-grade ***-sd-*** of **sed-**, *sit*.

2.1.7. The semivowels are usually written **j**, and **w**. These are voiced.

NOTE. Some authors make a distinction between consonantal [j], [w], and vocalic [i], [u]. Actually, however, both appear as CIC and VJV, and never as CJC or VIV (and the same is valid for resonants and their vocalic allophones).

2.1.8. Gemination appears in phonemes whose duration is long enough to be perceived – their implosion and explosion, both audible – as distributed in two syllables. They existed in LIE: in stops, as **appās**, **attās** (and **tātā**), *dad*, **pappājō**, *eat*, or **kakkājō**, *shit*; in nasals, as **annā**, **ammā** (and **mammā**), *mother, mum*; in liquids, as **bōullā**, *buble*; and in the sibilant, as **kussō**, *kiss*.

NOTE. They appear mostly in words of expressive origin, children vocabulary, onomatopoeia, etc., which makes it more likely that PIE inherited gemination mainly as an expressive resource, different from its central phonological system; a resource that was retained for a long time by most IE languages as a recurrent possibility.

A synoptic table of the Indo-European phonetic system:

		Labials	Coronals	Palatal	Velars	Labiovelars	Gutturals
Plosive	*Voiceless*	**p**	**t**		**k**	$\mathbf{k^w}$	**ʔ**
	Aspirated		$\mathbf{t^h}$		$\mathbf{k^h}$		
	Voiced	**b**	**d**		**g**	$\mathbf{g^w}$	
	Aspirated	$\mathbf{b^h}$	$\mathbf{d^h}$		$\mathbf{g^h}$	$\mathbf{g^{wh}}$	
Nasals		**m**	**n**				
Fricatives	*Voiceless*		**s**				**h**
	Voiced		**(z)**				
Liquids			**l, r**				
Approximant		**w**		**j**			

NOTE. The glottal stop **ʔ** is the remain of the unified Late Indo-European laryngeal **H* (*v.s. The Loss of Laryngeals*). Its effect was usually a lengthening of the preceding vowel, although remains might be found in some ancient lexica and frozen expressions, especially accompanying sonorants. It is not usually written in this book, though; *cf.* **gn̥ᵃ'tó-**, written with a late West IE output **gnātó-** for practical reasons; see §5.5.2 for writing conventions in numerals. Examples of its actual pronunciation are found today in Germanic; *cf.* American Eng. *cat* [kʰæʔ(t)], BBC Eng. *button* [b̥ɐʔn̩], Ger. (northern dialects) *Beamter* [bəˈʔamtɐ], (western dialects) *Verwaltung* [ˌfɔʔˈvaltʊŋ], Du. *beamen* [bəʔamən], or Danish *hand* [hɛnʔ].

2.2. PRONUNCIATION

2.2.1 The following pronunciation scheme is substantially that used by Indo-European speakers at the end of the common Late Indo-European period.

2.2.2. Indo-European vowels and examples in English and French:

	English	French
ā	*father*	*tard*
ē	*made* (esp. Welsh)	*été* (but longer)
ī	*meet*	*pire*
ō	*note* (esp. Welsh)	*port*
ū	*boo*	*court*

	English	French
a	*idea*	*partie*
e	*met*	*les*
i	*chip*	*ici*
o	*pot*	*mot*
u	*put*	*tout*

NOTE. Following the mainstream laryngeal theory, Proto-Indo-Hittite knew only two vowels, *e and *o, while the other commonly reconstructed vowels were earlier combinations with laryngeals. Thus, short vowels **a** < *$*h_2e$; **e** < *$*(h_1)e$; **o** < *$*h_3e$, *$*(h_1)o$; long vowels **ā** < *$*eh_2$; **ē** < *$*eh_1$; **ō** < *$*eh_3$, **oh*. Different schools consider **a** or **o** to be the output of *$*h_2o$ in Late Indo-European. Short and long vowels **ĭ**, **ŭ** are variants of the semivowels **j** and **w**.

2.2.3. Falling diphthongs and equivalents in English and French:

ē̆i as in Eng. *vein*, Fr. *Marseille*	**ē̆u** Eng. *e* (*met*) + *u* (*put*), Fr. *Séoul*
ō̆i as in Eng. *oil*, Fr. *coyotes*	**ō̆u** as in Eng. *know*, Fr. *au* + *ou*
ā̆i as in Eng. *Cairo*, Fr. *travail*	**ā̆u** as in Eng. *out*, Fr. *caoutchouc*

NOTE. In long diphthongs, the first component is pronounced longer than the second one, but the duration of the group is the same (see above).

2.2.4. Consonants:

1. **b**, **d**, **h**, **l**, **m**, **n**, are pronounced as in English.

2. **p**, **k**, **t**, are plain as in Romance, Balto-Slavic, Greek or Indo-Iranian languages, and unlike their English or German equivalents, *cf.* Fr. *pôle* vs. Eng. *pain*, Fr. *qui* vs. Eng. *key*, Fr. *tous* vs. Eng. *tongue*.

NOTE. The aspirate or 'h-sound' which follows the English *k* disappears when the *k* is preceded by an *s*, as in *skill*.

3. **t** and **d** are made by striking the edge of the teeth with the tip of the tongue, as in Romance languages, and unlike English, in which it is made with the tongue drawn a little further back, so that the tip strikes against the front of the palate or the teethridge. In other words, the place of articulation is the same as for the English *th* en *thin*.

4. **g** always as in *get*.

NOTE. For Balto-Slavic palatalisation, compare the *g* in *garlic* and *gear*, whispering the two words, and note how before e and i the *g* is sounded farther forward in the mouth (more 'palatal') than before *a* or *o*. That is what we represent as [g^j] when writing a palatalised ***g***. Similarly, we use [k^j] pronounced as *k* in *key* compared to *c* in *cold*.

5. **c** stands for [g^w], which is pronounced similar to [g] but with rounded lips. Compare the initial consonant in *good* with *get* to feel the different articulation. The voiceless **q** (which stands for [k^w]) is similar to [k] but pronounced with rounded lips; as *c* in *cool*, compared to *c* in *car*.

6. The voiceless aspirated **kh**, **th**, are pronounced very nearly like English word-initial *p*, *k*, *t*, as in *pen*, *ten*, *Ken*, but much more aspirated. The extra aspiration might be trained by using English words with combinations of *p+h*, *t+h*, *k+h*, i.e. to the corresponding mutes with a following breath, as in *loop-hole*, *hot-house*, *block-house*, pronouncing them first in two distinct parts and then more rapidly, trying to run the *p*, *k*, *t*, on to the following syllable.

7. The aspiration of voiced **bh, dh, gh, ch**, must be a voiced aspiration, which makes their pronunciation troublesome.

NOTE. "The key to the pronunciation of all these letters is learning to pronounce a voiced *h* instead of the voiceless English *h* (it is true that some English speakers make voiced *h* a rather infrequent allophone of *h* – e.g. in the word *inherent*). Voiced sounds are those made with a vibration of the vocal cords. Some consonants are voiced, others voiceless. All vowels are voiced, unless you whisper them. An extremely easy way to tell whether a sound is voiced or not is to put your hands firmly over your ears: start by making a prolonged sss sound, which is voiceless; then make a zzz sound, which is voiced, and you will hear the vibration of the vocal cords very plainly as a droning in your ears. Lengthen the ordinary English h into a prolonged breathing and it will be quite obviously voiceless. The task now is to modify this breathing until you can hear that it is accompanied by the droning. The sound you are aiming at is similar to the sound children sometimes use when they want to make someone jump. The voiced h, once produced, can easily be combined with g, b, etc., and practice will soon smooth the sound down until you do not seem to be trying to give your listeners a series of heart attacks." Coulson (2003).

8. **j** as the sound of *y* in *yes* (probably more lightly), never the common English [d͡ʒ], as *j* in *join*; **w** as in *will*.

9. Indo-European **r** was probably slightly trilled with the tip of the tongue (still common today in many IE languages), as in Scottish English *curd*. In the majority of IE languages, and thus possibly in PIE, this sound is at least occasionally allophonic with an alveolar tap [ɾ], pronounced like the intervocalic *t* or *d* in American or Australian English, as in *better*.

NOTE. Speakers of Southern or BBC English should be careful always to give r its full value, and should guard against letting it colour their pronunciation of a preceding vowel.

10. **l** is dental, and so even more like a French than an English *l*. It does not have the 'dark' quality which in varying degrees an English *l* may have.

11. **s** is usually voiceless as in English *sin*, but there are situations in which it is voiced (therefore pronounced **z**), when followed by voiced phonemes (see below).

12. Doubled letters, like **ss**, **nn**, etc., should be so pronounced that both members of the combination are distinctly articulated, as *s+s* in English '*less soap*', *n+n* in Eng. *greenness*.

2.3. SYLLABLES

2.3.1. In many modern languages, there are as many syllables in a word as there are separate vowels and diphthongs. Indo-European follows this rule too:

swe-sōr, *sister*, **skrei-bhō**, *write*, **ne-wā**, *new*, **ju-góm**, *yoke*.

NOTE. According to Fortson (2004): "PIE grouped sounds into syllables in much the same way as Greek, Latin, Sanskrit and many other languages. In any given sequence of consonants and vowels, the vowels constituted the syllabic peaks, and were linked to a preceding consonant (if one was available) which formed the onset (beginning) of a syllable. If two or more consonants occurred together in the middle of a word, they were usually split between two syllables. In the abstract, a word of the structure VCCVCVCCVC would have been syllabified VC.CV.CVC.CVC. It is possible that certain consonant clusters could group together in the middle of a word as the onset of a syllable; if so, by a universal phonological principle they would have also been able to form word-initial onsets".

2.3.2. Resonants can also be centre of a syllable. It is possible to hear similar sound sequences in English *interesting* (*'íntṛsting'*), *cattle* (*'cattḷ'*), *bottom* (*'bottṃ'*), or *Brighton* (*'Brightṇ'*), as well as in other modern languages, as in German *Haben* (*'Habṇ'*), Czech *hlt*, Serbian *srpski*, etc. In this kind of syllables, it is the vocalic resonant [r̥], [l̥], [m̥], or [n̥] –constrained allophones of [r], [l], [m], [n] –, the one which functions as syllabic centre, instead of a vowel proper:

kṛ-di, *heart*, **wḷ-qos**, *wolf*, **de-kṃ**, *ten*, **nō-mṇ**, *name*.

NOTE. Words derived from these groups, represented CRC, are unstable and tend to add auxiliary vowels before or after the resonants, i.e. C°RC or CR°C. Because of that, their evolutions differ greatly in modern IE languages. For example, **dṇghwā**, *language*, evolved probably as **d°nghwā*, into PGmc. *tung(w)ō*, and later English *tongue* or German *Zunge*, and into Old Latin *dingwa*, and then the initial *d* became *l* in Classic Latin, written *lingua*, which is in turn the origin of Modern English words "linguistic" and "language". For **wḷqos** (*cf.* Ved. *vṛkas* < PII ***wṛkas***), it evolved either as **w°lkʷos* into PGmc. **wulxʷaz* (*cf.* O.H.G. *wolf*) or BSl. **wilkas* (*cf.* O.C.S. *vьlkъ*), or as **wlᵘkʷos* into Common Greek **wlukʷos* (*cf.* Gk. *lykos*), Ita. **wlupos* (*cf.* Lat. *lupus*).

2.3.3. According to Ringe (2006), each sequence of one or more resonants was syllabified as follows. If the rightmost member of the sequence was adjacent to a syllabic (i.e. a vowel, on the initial application of the rule), it remained nonsyllabic, but if not, it was assigned to a syllable peak. The rule then iterated from right to left, the output of each decision providing input to the next.

NOTE. Ringe (2006): Forms of **kwon-**, *dog*, neatly illustrate the process: The zero grade was basically **kwn-** (since full-grade forms show that the high vocalic was an alternating resonant, not an underlying syllabic high vowel). The genitive singular **kwn-ós**, *dog's, of a dog*, was syllabified as follows: the **n** was adjacent to a vowel and therefore remained nonsyllabic; consequently the **w** was not adjacent to a syllabic, and it therefore surfaced as syllabic **u**, giving **kunós** (*cf.* Skt. *śúnas*, Gk. *kunós*). On the locative plural **kwn-sú**, *among dogs*, was syllabified as follows: the **n** was not adjacent to a vowel and therefore became syllabic **ṇ**; consequently the **w** was adjacent to a syllabic and therefore remained nonsyllabic, giving **kwṇ-sú** (*cf.* Skt *śvásu*). There are some exceptions to this rule, though.

2.3.4. Apart from the common vocalic resonant CRC, another, less stable sequence is found in PIE *C°RV → CVRV/CRV; as, **kerwos**<**k°rwos*, *deer*. Auxiliary vowels were sometimes inserted in difficult *CRC; as, **cemjō**<**g$^{w°}$mjō*, *come*, etc.

NOTE. "Some have proposed a 'reduced IE vowel', the so-called *schwa secundum* (Hirt 1900, Güntert 1916, Sturtevant 1943), although they were probably just auxiliary vowels, mere 'allophonic vocoids' initially necessary to articulate complex groups" (Adrados–Bernabé–Mendoza 1995-1998). It is commonly accepted that LIE dialects did in fact add an auxiliary vowel to this sequence at early times, probably before the first dialectal split: as early Indo-Iranian and Balto-Slavic dialects show, vocalisation of most *CRV groups had already happened when *CRC hadn't still been vocalised, i.e. PIE *C°RV → *CVRV.

The most unstable *CRV sequences found in LIE are possibly those with a resonant or glide as the initial consonant, i.e. *RRV; as, suffix ***-m°no-***, **m°rijar**, *die*, etc. Although *cf.* also adjectival suffix *(**-t/s**)-**°mo-***, ordinal **sépt°mos**, etc.

NOTE. Such *irregular* forms kept their apparent alternating pattern in post-LIE period, hence probably an auxiliary vowel was still inserted in the IEDs. The convention is to write the dot ° before the resonant, but in this grammar we prefer a simpler notation, with the dot below; since compounds of CRV cannot naturally include a resonant in IE, there is no possible confusion. From the examples above, it is written here conventionally ***mn̥o-*** (*v.i.* §7.7.2), **mr̥ijar**, *die* (*cf.* Skt. *mriyate*, Av. *miryeite*, Gk. *emarten*, Lat. *morior*, O.C.S. *mĭrǫ*, *mrěti*, Lith. *mir̃ti*), suffix *-(**t/s**)-**m̥o**-* (*v.i.* §5.4), **séptm̥os**, etc.

Most dialects show a common auxiliary vowel with maximal opening (in [a]) for the resonant, into a general CaRV, even in those dialects that show different outputs (as well as non-vocalisation) for CRC; i.e. ***m(a)rijōr***, *-(**t/s**)-**amo**-*, ***séptamos***, etc. Adrados–Bernabé–Mendoza (1995-1998). As with consonant change, in this grammar the phonetically correct notation is therefore avoided in favour of the phonemically correct notation.

2.3.5. In the division of words into syllables, these rules apply:

a. A single consonant is joined to the following vowel or diphthong; as **lon-dhom**, *land*, **rei-dhō**, *ride*, etc.

b. Combinations of two or more consonants are regularly separated, and the first consonant of the combination is joined to the preceding vowel; as **legh-trom**, *support*, **pen-qe**, *five*, etc.

When a consonant is followed by a resonant or a glide, the consonants are not separated, even in the middle of a word and preceded by a vowel; as, **a-gros**, *field*, **me-dhjos**, middle.

c. In compounds, the parts are usually separated; as **a-pó-sta-tis**, *distance*, from **apo** + **statis**.

2.3.6. The semivowels [j], [w] are more stable than resonants when they are syllable centres, i.e. [i] or [u].

NOTE. Both forms appear – like resonants – in a complementary distribution, i.e. as CIC and VJV, and never as ˣCJC or ˣVIV. Some authors make a distinction between consonantal [j], [w], and vocalic [i], [u]; see Schmitt-Brandt (*Die Entwicklung des Indogermanischen Vokalsystems*, 1967), Szemerényi (1985), or Mayrhofer (*"Lautlehre (Segmentale Phonologie des Indogermanischen)"*, in *Indogermanische Grammatik I*, Cogwill-Mayrhofer 1986).

When they are pronounced *lento*, they give the allophones (or *allosyllables*) **ij**, **uw**. Examples of alternating forms in PIE include **médhijos** (*cf.* Lat. *medius*), and **medhjos** (*cf.* O.Ind. *mádhjas* or Gk. μέσσος); **dwōu**, *two* (*cf.* Goth. *twai*, Gk. δω-), and **duwōu** (*cf.* O.Ind. *duva*, Gk. *dúō* < *dúwō*, Lat. *duo*).

NOTE. The so-called Sievers' Law was behind most of these forms; it explains that the weight of a syllable in LIE affected the pronunciation of following consonant clusters consisting of a consonant plus a glide before a vowel (e.g. ***-tjo-***, ***-two-***): if the syllable before the cluster was heavy (i.e. if it ended in -VCC or - V̄C), the vocalic equivalent of the glide was inserted into the cluster (yielding ***-tijo-***, ***-tuwo-***). One of the conditions is that the rule only applied when the glide began the final syllable of the word.

It is the same rule as Lindeman's Law, whereby monosyllables beginning with consonant plus glide (like **kwōn**, *dog*, or **djēus**, *sky*) had the cluster broken up in the same way as Sievers' Law (**kuwṓn, dijḗus**) if the word followed a word ending in a heavy syllable. Descendants of both alternating forms might be preserved in the same dialect, or be found in different different dialects. Lindeman's Law can be interpreted as the sandhi equivalent to Sievers' Law; the variant **dijḗus** is determined by the final position of the preceding word: on one hand we have **##...V̄#dijḗus ##** and **##...VR#dijḗus##**, on the other **##...C#djēus##**. See Fortson (2004) and Meier-Brügger (2003).

2.4. PROSODY

2.4.1. The Indo-European verse is quantitative: it is based, that is to say (as in Latin, Greek or Sanskrit), on a regular arrangement of long and short syllables and not, as in English, of stressed and unstressed syllables.

Syllables are distinguished according to the length of time required for their pronunciation. Two degrees of quantity are recognised, *long* and *short*.

NOTE. To distinguish long and short syllables more clearly from long and short vowels the former may be referred to as *heavy* and *light* respectively (corresponding to the Sanskrit terms *guru* and *laghu*, IE ***crāwú*** and ***leghú***, respectively).

In syllables, quantity is measured from the beginning of the vowel or diphthong to the end of the syllable. Such distinctions of long and short are not arbitrary and artificial, but are purely natural, a long syllable requiring more time for its pronunciation than a short one.

2.4.2. A syllable is long or *heavy* usually,

a. if it contains a long vowel; as, **mā-tḗr**, *mother*, **kē-lā-jō**, *hide*,

b. if it contains a diphthong; as, **lai-wós**, *left*, **oi-nos**, *one*,

c. if it is followed by two or more consonants (even in another word); as, **dherghs**, *shit*, **korm-nos**, *bleach*.

2.4.3. A syllable is short or *light* usually if it contains a short vowel (or vocalic resonant) followed by a vowel or by a single consonant; as, **dre-pō**, *cut*, or **e-í-mi**, *go*; or **qṛ-mis**, *worm*, **cṃ-tis**, *march*.

NOTE. In old compositions, sometimes final short vowels are found as heavy syllables; as, Skt. *deví etu*, or vocat. *vṛki*, *tanu*, *cf.* Lindeman (1987) or Beekes ("*On laryngeals and pronouns*", *KZ96*, 1982). They are possibly glottal stops, remains of the old merged LIE laryngeal **H*, i.e. **dewíH*, **wr̥kiH*, etc. "The Rig Veda preserves many words that must scan as though a laryngeal or some remnant of a laryngeal (like a glottal stop) were still present between vowels, a phenomenon called *laryngeal hiatus*". For example, Skt. *vā́tas* '*wind*' must sometimes scan trisyllabically as *va'atas*, which comes from earlier pre-PII **weHn̥tos* or PII ***wáʔatas*** < PIE *$h_2$weh$_1$n̥tos → NWIE **wentos**; although for Ringe (2006) from Lat. *ventus*, Welsh *gwynt*, PGmc. **windaz*, only NWIE **wentós** or **wēntos** (*cf.* Proto-Toch. **wʸentë*) could be reconstructed.

2.5. ACCENT

2.5.1. There are accented as well as unaccented words. The last could indicate words that are always enclitic, i.e., they are always bound to the accent of the preceding word, as **-qe**, *and*, **-wĕ**, *or;* while another can be proclitics, like prepositions.

2.5.2. Evidence from Ancient Greek, Vedic Sanskrit and Balto-Slavic accent let us reconstruct a LIE pitch (also *tonic* or *musical*) accent system, with only one, acute accent. Late Indo-European was therefore a stress language in which syllable strength was chiefly a matter of pitch differences: the accented syllable was higher in pitch than the surrounding syllables.

NOTE 1. For Beekes (1995): "There are several indications that Proto-Indo-European was a tone language at some time in its development. The accent-systems of both Sanskrit and Greek already give reason enough to surmise that this may have been the case."

According to Clackson (2007): "Qualitatively our best evidence for PIE accent comes from two of the oldest and most conservative branches: Greek and Vedic Sanskrit. For both languages there is a large body of texts with word-accents marked and adequate metalinguistic descriptions of the nature of the accentual system. The accent of both Greek and Sanskrit was a mobile pitch-accent type, but there were differences between the two systems (...) Since the two *morae* of some of the Greek circumflex nuclei have arisen from contraction of two syllables, it seems reasonable to assume that the syllable-based accent of Sanskrit is original (...)."

We can therefore assume that the attested distinction between acute and circumflex accent in Ancient Greek and Baltic languages does not come from the LIE period, but were late independent dialectal developments. According to this description of events, the Greek and Indic systems were lost: Modern Greek has a pitch produced stress accent, and it was lost entirely from Indic by the time of the Prākrits. Balto-Slavic retained LIE pitch accent, reworking it into the opposition of 'acute' (rising) and 'circumflex' (falling) tone, and which, following a period of extensive accentual innovations, yielded pitch-accent based system that has been retained in modern-day Lithuanian and West South Slavic dialects. Some other modern Indo-European languages have pitch accent systems; as, Swedish and Norwegian, deriving from a stress-based system they inherited from Old Norse, and Punjabi, which developed tone distinctions that maintained lexical distinctions as consonants were conflated.

NOTE 2. A possibility is that PIE (or, more exactly, PIH) was a tonal language, i.e. that it had more than the limited word-tone system usually called pitch-accent. This position was argued by Szemerényi (1985), Lubotsky (*The system of nominal accentuation in Sanskrit and Proto-Indo-European*, 1988) and by Kortlandt (*"The laryngeal theory and Slavic accentuation"* in *Bammesberger* (ed.), 1988). They are mainly based on Sanskrit accentual system and typological considerations, since such a system would account for the old ablauting patterns found in PIE.

2.5.3. The accent is free, but that does not mean anarchy. On the contrary, it means that each non-clitic word has an accent and only one accent, and one has to know – usually by way of practice – where it goes. Its location usually depends on the inflectional type to which a given word belongs.

NOTE. The term free here refers to the position of the accent—its position is (at least partly) unpredictable by phonological rules, i.e. it could stand on any syllable of a word, regardless of its structure. Otherwise homophonous words may differ only by the position of the accent, and it is thus possible to use accent as a grammatical device.

2.5.4. The place of the original accent is difficult to reconstruct, and sometimes different positions are attested. According to Clackson (2007), comparison of Germanic, Baltic, Slavic, Greek and Sanskrit allows us to reconstruct the place of the PIE word accent with confidence, what let us deduce some properties of the accentual system:

a) The accent can fall on any element which functions as a syllabic nucleus.

b) The accent can fall on any syllable of a word.

c) No word has more than one accent.

2.5.5. According to Ringe (2006), thematic nominal (i.e. those ending in the thematic vowel) had the accent on the same syllable throughout the paradigm; thematic verb stems also have generally a fixed accent.

Some athematic verb stems and nominal have fixed accent (mostly on the root), but most had alternating accent; there were different patterns, but in all of them the surface accent was to the left in one group of forms (the nominative and accusative cases of nominal, the active singular of verbs) and to the right in the rest.

Stems and endings can be underlyingly accented or not, and words with no underlying accent are assigned accent on the leftmost syllable by default.

NOTE. According to Lehmann (1974): "The location of the high pitch is determined primarily from our evidence in Vedic; the theory that this was inherited from PIE received important corroboration from Karl Verner's demonstration of its maintenance into Germanic (1875). Thus the often cited correlation between the position of the accent in the Vedic perfect and the differing consonants in Germanic provided decisive evidence for reconstruction of the PIE pitch accent as well as for Verner's law, as in the perfect (preterite) forms of the root **deyk-*, 'show'."

	IE	Vedic	O.E.	O.H.G.
1 sg.	***dedóika***	*didéśa*	*tāh*	*zēh*
1 pl.	***dedikmé***	*didiśimá*	*tigon*	*zigum*

Feminine nouns in a tend to be stressed on the root, while abstracts tend to be accented on the ending, although there are many exceptions.

NOTE. Probert's article in <http://www.ling-phil.ox.ac.uk/files/uploads/OWP2006.pdf> discusses this question, and is probably the best reference for feminine accent. In most reconstructions we follow the most obvious rule in case of doubt, though, *cf.* Gk. *poinḗ*, OCS *cená*; Gk. *skia*, air. *chāyā́-*. Nussbaum also discusses this matter, but without too much detail, in his article about the Saussure effect (Lubotsky 1997).

2.6. VOWEL CHANGE

2.6.1. The vowel grade or *ablaut* is normally the alternation between full, zero or lengthened grade vocalism. Proto-Indo-European had a regular ablaut sequence that contrasted the five usual vowel sounds called *thematic*, i.e. **e/ē/o/ō/∅**. This means that in different forms of the same word, or in different but related words, the basic vowel, a short **e**, could be replaced by a long **ē**, a short **o** or a long **ō**, or it could be omitted (transcribed as ∅).

NOTE. The term *Ablaut* comes from Ger. *Abstufung der Laute*, 'vowel alternation'. In Romance languages, the term apophony is preferred.

In Romance languages, *theme* is used instead of *stem*. Therefore, *theme vowel* and *thematic* refer to the stem endings. In the Indo-European languages, a common conventional nomenclature is that *thematic* stems are those stems that have the common "*theme vowel*", i.e. the **e/o** ending. *Athematic* stems lack that *theme vowel*, and attach their inflections directly to the stem itself.

2.6.2. When a syllable had a short **e**, it is said to be in the *e grade*; when it had no vowel, it is said to be in the *zero grade*, when in **o**, in *o grade*, and they can also be *lengthened*. The e-grade is sometimes called *full grade*.

NOTE. While changes in the length of a vowel (as **e-∅-ē**, **o-∅-ō**) are usually termed *quantitative ablaut*, changes in the quality of a vowel (as **e-o** or **ē-ō**), are termed *qualitative ablaut*. Because qualitative changes are more frequent than lengthened-grades, these forms are usually termed *e-grade* or *o-grade* for convenience (Fortson 2004).

A classic example of the five grades of *ablaut* in a single root is provided by the following different case forms of IE **patḗr**, *father*, and **n̥patōr**, *fatherless*.

Ablaut grade	IE	Greek	(translit.)	Case
e-grade or full grade	**pa-<u>ter</u>-m̥**	πα-τέρ-α	*pa-tér-a*	Accusative
lengthened e-grade	**pa-<u>tḗr</u>**	πα-τήρ	*pa-tḗr*	Nominative
zero-grade	**pa-<u>tr</u>-ós**	πα-τρ-ός	*pa-tr-ós*	Genitive
o-grade	**n̥-pá-<u>tor</u>-m̥**	ἀ-πά-τορ-α	*a-pá-tor-a*	Accusative
lengthened o-grade	**n̥-pa-<u>tōr</u>**	ἀ-πά-τωρ	*a-pá-tōr*	Nominative

NOTE. Another example of the common Ablaut is t-stem **nepot-**, *grandson*, which gives lengthened grade Nominative, **nep-ōts**, full-grade Genitive **nép-ot-os**, and zero-grade feminine **nep-t-is**, *grand-daughter*. The study of declensions and practice with vocabulary should help the reader learn such alternations.

2.6.3. Synoptic table of common examples of different vowel grades (adapted from Adrados–Bernabé–Mendoza 1995-1998):

Vowel Grade	Full (F)	Zero (Ø)	Lengthened (L)
e/o - Ø - ē/ō	***dom-***	***dm-***	***dōm-***
je/jo - i - jē/jō	***djeu-***	***diw-***	***djēu-***
we/wo - u - wē/wō	***kwon-***	***kun-***	***kwōn***
ei/oi/ai - u/i - ēi/ōi/āi	***bheid-***	***bhid-***	***bhēid-***
eu/ou/au - u/i -	***bheud-***	***bhud-***	***bhēud-***
au/ai - u/i - āu/āi	***pau-***	***pu-***	***pāu-***
ā/ē/ō - a - ā/ē/ō	***stā-***	***sta-***	***stā-***
ēi/ōi - ū/ī - ēi/ōi	***pōi***	***pī***	***pōi***

2.6.4. There are also some other possible vowel grade changes, as *a-grade*, *i-grade* and *u-grade*, which usually come from old root endings, rather than from systematised phonetic changes.

NOTE. It seems that the alternation full-grade/zero-grade in PIE was dependent on the accent. Compare **klewos/klutós**, **eimi/imés**, **patérm̥/patrós**, etc., where the unstressed morpheme loses its vowel. This happens only in the oldest formations, though, as Late Indo-European had probably lost this morphological pattern, freezing many older ablauting words and creating a new (more stable) vocabulary without changes in accent or vowel grade.

2.6.5. As we have seen, vowel change was common in Proto-Indo-European. In many words the vowel varies because of old ablauting forms that gave different derivatives.

So for example in o-grade **domos**, *house*, which gives **dómūnos**, *lord*, as Lat. *dominus*, Skt. *dámūnas*; but full grade root **dem-**, which gives **demspóts**, *master, lord* (from older gen. **dems*) as Gk. *δεσπότης* (*despótēs*), Skt. *dampati*, Av. *dəṇg patōiš*, (with *fem.* **demspotnja**).

NOTE. The forms attested in Indo-Iranian (and maybe Greek) come from i-stem **potis**, probably derived from the original Late PIE form **dems-póts**, *cf.* **ghósti-pots**, *guest*, as Lat. *hospēs*, *hospitis*, O.Russ. *gospodь<*-ostьpot-*; compare, for an original PIE ending **-t** in compounds, Lat. *sacerdōs* < *sakro-dhots, O.Ind. *devastút-*, "*who praises the gods*", etc. The compound is formed with **pot-**, *lord, husband*, and **pot-nja**, *mistress, lady*.

2.6.6. Different vocalisations appeared in IE dialects in some phonetic environments, especially between two occlusives in zero-grade; as e.g. **skp-**, which evolved as Lat. *scabo* or Got. *skaban*.

NOTE. According to Fortson (2004): "In word-initial consonant clusters consisting of two stops plus a resonant, a prop vowel was introduced between the two stops to break up the cluster; this vowel was introduced between the two stops to break up the cluster; this vowel is called "schwa secundum" (...) . For example, one of the forms of numeral 'four' was *k^{w}*tu̯or-*, which developed a schwa secundum to become *k^{w}_{e}*tu̯or-* or *$k^{w}_{ə}$*tu̯or-*, yielding Lat. *quattuor* and Homeric Gk. *písures* (as opposed to Gk. *téssares* from a different form, *k^{w}*etu̯or-*)."

Although the dialectal solutions to such consonantal groups aren't unitary, we can find some general PIE timbres. A general **a**; an **i** with a following dental (especially in Gk. and BSl.); or **u**, also considered general, but probably influenced by the context, possibly when in contact with a labial, guttural or labiovelar. Adrados–Bernabé–Mendoza (1995-1998).

2.6.7. Sometimes different reconstructions might account for some vowel differences, most frequently in combinations of *RH or *HR; as, **lawō* for **lowō**, *wash*, **Sm̥os* for **Samos**, *summer*, **kr̥wos* for **kerwos**, *deer*, etc.

NOTE. Different reconstructions might be equally valid, depending on the criteria employed. Sometimes different PIE language stages have to be taken into account; as, for root **neqt-**, *night*, a common PIH **noqts* is reconstructible, which had a genitive in **neqts* according to Hitt. *nekut*; however, pre-LIE shows a generalised non-ablauting pattern; *cf.* O.Gk. *nuks, nuktós*, O.Lat. *nox, noctis*. The newer i-stem **noqtis** was the general post-LIE (and later also PII, NWIE) form, without accent-ablaut changes; *cf.* O.Ind. *nakti*, Gmc. *naxti*, Sla. *notjь*, Bal. *nakti*. See below §4.7 for a discussion on the reconstruction of root nouns.

2.7. CONSONANT CHANGE

2.7.1. Regarding consonant change, different similar reconstructions might appear, too. Some might not fit into a single LIE original word; as, **ghortos**, *garden* (*cf.* Gk. *khortos*, Lat. *hortus*, O.Ir. *gort*), and **ghordhos**, *enclosure* (*cf.* Gk. *khortis*, Lith. *gardas*, O.C.S. *gradu*, Goth. *gards*, Phry. *-gordum*, Alb. *garth*).

NOTE. They have been explained as one original form borrowed with a (dialectal) consonant change into other dialects, but it is more likely that both forms were found in LIE.

2.7.2. The so called s-*mobile* refers to the phenomenon of alternating word pairs, with and without **s** before initial consonants, in roots with similar or identical meaning. This '*moveable*' prefix **s-** is always followed by another consonant. Typical combinations are with voiceless stops **(s)p-**, **(s)t-**, **(s)k-**, with liquids and nasals, **(s)l-**, **(s)m-**, **(s)n-**; and rarely **(s)w-**.

NOTE. Examples include **(s)ten-**, *cf.* with **s-** O.Ind. *stánati*, Gk. *sténō*, O.Eng. *stenan*, Lith. *stenù*, O.Sla. *stenjo*, and without **s-** in O.Ind. *tányati*, Gk. Eol. *ténnei*, Lat. *tonare*, O.H.G. *donar*, Cel. *Tanaros* (name of a river). For **(s)pek-**, *cf.* O.Ind. *spáśati*, Av. *spašta*,

Gk. *skopós* (<*spokós*), Lat. *spektus*, O.H.G. *spehon*, without **s-** in O.Ind. *páśyati*, Alb. *pashë*. For **(s)ker-**, *cf.* O.Ind. *ava-*, *apa-skara-*, Gk. *skéraphos*, O.Ir. *scar(a)im*, O.N. *skera*, Lith. *skiriù*, Illyr. *Scardus*, Alb. *hurdhë* (<*skr̥d-), without **s-** in O.Ind. *kr̥náti*, Av. *kərəntaiti*, Gk. *keíro*, Arm. *kcorem*, Alb. *kjëth*, Lat. *caro*, O.Ir. *cert*, O.N. *horund*, Lith. kkarnà, O.Sla. *korŭcŭ*, Hitt. *kartai-*, and so on. Such pairs with and without **s** are found even within the same branch, as Gk. *(s)tégos*, 'roof', *(s)mikrós*, *'little'*, O.Ind. *(s)tr̥*, *'star'*, and so on.

NOTE. Some scholars posit that it was a prefix in PIE (which would have had a causative value), while others maintain that it is probably caused by assimilations of similar stems – some of them beginning with an **s-**, and some of them without it. It is possible, however, that the original stem actually had an initial **s**, and that it was lost by analogy in some situations, because of phonetic changes, probably due to some word compounds where the last ***-s*** of the first word assimilated to the first ***s-*** of the second one. That helps to explain why both stems (with and without s) are recorded in some languages, and why no regular evolution pattern may be ascertained: so for example in **wl̥qons spekjont**, *they saw wolves*, becoming ***wl̥qons 'pekjont***. Adrados–Bernabé–Mendoza (1995-1998).

2.7.3. In a cluster of two consonants differing in voicing, the voicing of the first is assimilated to that of the second.

Voiceless **s** was assimilated to voiced **z** before a voiced consonant; as, **nisdos** ['niz-dos], *nest*, **misdhom** ['miz-d^{h}om], *meed, salary*, or **osdos** ['oz-dos], *branch*.

Voiced stops become voiceless when followed by a voiceless consonant: e.g. **agtós** [ak-'tos] (*cf.* Gk. ακτος (*aktos*), Lat. *actus*). The same happens with voiced aspirates, as in **leghtrom**, *support* (*cf.* Gk. *lektron*, O.H.G. *Lehter* or from the same root Lat. *lectus*); or **nictós**, *washed* (*cf.* Gk. *a-niptos* <*n̥-niqtos, *'unwashed'*, O.Ir. *necht*).

Voiceless stops become voiced before voiced consonants; as, **ped-** in zero-grade -**pd-**, *cf.* Gk. επιβδα (*epi-bd-a*), Av. *frabda*, 'forefoot'.

Voiced and voiceless stops are pronounced alike in final position; as, **qid** [k^{w}it] (*cf.* O.Ind. *cit*), or **pod**, *foot* (*cf.* voiceless O.Ind. nom. *pāt*, after having lost the final -s).

NOTE. Although the accuracy of some allophones in Late Indo-European is certain, for practical reasons the phonetically correct notation is therefore avoided in favour of the phonemically correct notation. We deem that to write them as a general rule, like writing '*thə*' or '*thi*' for English *the*, or '*dogz*' for *dogs*, while possibly helpful to show the actual pronunciation, would probably be an obstacle to the understanding of the underlying etymology; also, such phonetical variations exist naturally, and don't need to be supported by the orthography.

2.7.4. A sequence of two dentals -TT- (such as ***-tt-***, ***-dt-***, ***-tdh-***, ***-ddh-***, etc.) was eliminated in all Indo-European dialects, but the process of this suppression differed among branches: Vedic Sanskrit shows little change, some others an intermediate -sT- (Iranian, Greek, Balto-Slavic) and others *-ss-* or *-s-* (Italic, Celtic, Germanic). Compounds were not affected by this trend; as, **kréd-dhēmi**, *believe*.

We find a common intermediate stage in Iranian, Proto-Greek (*cf.* Gk. *st, sth*, in *pistis, oistha*), and North-West Indo-European (*cf.* **Hed-ti 'eats'*, in Lat. *est*, Lith. *esti*, OCS *jastŭ*, and afield O.H.G. examples). Therefore, we can assume that PIE **d+t, *t+t, *dh+t* → NWIE, PGk ***st***; PIE **d+d, *t+d, *dh+d* → NWIE, PGk ***sd***; PIE **d+dh, *t+dh, *dh+dh* → NWIE, PGk ***sdh***.

Common examples are found in forms derived from PIE root **weid-**, *know, see*, which gave verb **widējō**, *cf.* Lat. *vidēre*, Goth. *witan*, O.C.S. *viděti*, Lith. *pavydéti*; p.p. **wistós**, *seen*, from ***wid-tó-***, *cf.* O.Ind. *vitta-*, but Av. *vista-*, O.Pruss. *waist*, O.Sla. *věstъ*, or Ger. *ge-wiss*, Lat. *vīsus*, O.Gk. ϝιστος (*wistos*), O.Ir. *rofess*, etc.; noun **wistis**, *sight, vision*, from ***wid-ti-***, *cf.* Goth *wizzi*, Lat. *vīsiō*; Greek **wistōr**, *wise, learned man*, from ***wid-tor***, *cf.* Gk. ἵστωρ (*ʰístōr*)<*ϝίστωρ (*wístōr*), PGk ***wistorjā***, *history*, from Gk. ἱστορία (*ʰistoría*); Imp. ***wisdhi!*** *know!*, from ***wid-dhi***, *cf.* O.Ind. *viddhí*, O.Gk. ϝίσθι (*wístʰi*), O.Lith. *veizdi*, and so on.

NOTE. An older PIE *TT → *TsT has been proposed, i.e. that the cluster of two dental stops had a dental fricative **s** inserted between them (giving *-tst- and *-dzd-). It is based on some findings in Hittite, where cluster *tst* is spelled as *z* (pronounced *tˢ*), as in PIH **h₁ed-te*, '*eat!*' → **h₁ette* → **h₁etˢte* → Old Hitt. *ēzten* (pronounced *étsten*), or Ved. Skt. *attá* (interpreted as from **atstá*, where *s is lost). *Cf.* also for Indo-Iranian imperative **da-d-dhí* 'give!' in L.Av. *dazdi*, O.Ind. *dehí<dazdhi<*dadzdhi* (Mayrhofer *Lautlehre* 1986), instead of the expected O.Ind. **daddhi*. However, confirmation from a common LIE ***-***st***- is found in Indo-Iranian too (which might be interpreted as previous *TsT where the initial *T is lost); as, O.Ind. *mastis*, *"measure"*, from **med-tis*, or Av. *-hasta-*, from **sed-tós*. This LIE evolution TT (→ TsT)? → sT was overshadowed by dialectal developments, *v.s.* §1.7.2.III.

2.7.5. It seems that simplification of geminated PIE **-ss-* occurred already in LIE, as Greek and Indo-Iranian dialects show. However, in this book the written gemination is considered the most conservative approach. Only the attested simplification of gemination is reconstructed; as, **esi** for **es-si**, *you are*.

NOTE. So, from *essi we have O.Ind. *ási*, Av. *ahi*, Gk. *εἶ* <*esi (Hom. and Dor. ἐσσί are obviously analogic forms), etc. That form from **es-** is reconstructed e.g. by Adrados–Bernabé–Mendoza (1995-1998), Fortson (2004), Cardona (2004), Ringe (2006), among others. It is therefore to be pronounced with a simple /-s-/, and written accordingly **-s-**.

This is not the only solution to gemination in PIE, though, as shown by e.g. Lat. *amassō*, *propriassit*, with original IE gemination after Kortlandt. Therefore, the fact that *-ss- is simplified into -s- in some attested words does not confirm that the simplification occurred necessarily and always in LIE (or IED) times, because it could have occurred later, although it shows a clear trend toward simplification.

2.7.6. Consonant clusters *KsK were simplified by loss of the first stop; as, present stem of **prek-**, *ask*, **pr̥k-skṓ-** [pr̥-'sko:] (*cf.* Lat. *poscit*, Skt. *pr̥ccʰáti*).

2.7.7. Word-final **-n** was often lost after **ō**; as, **kwō(n)**, *dog* (*cf.* O.Ir. *cú*); or **dhghomō(n)**, *man* (*cf.* Lat. *homō*); this loss was not generalised, although it seems that it was already common in Late Indo-European.

NOTE. Fortson (2004): PIE forms where the *-n disappeared, like the word for 'dog' above, are written by Indo-Europeanists variously with or without the n, or with n in parentheses:" **kwōn** or **kwō** or **kwō(n)**. We prefer to write them always with **-n** by convention.

3. WORDS AND THEIR FORMS

3.1. THE PARTS OF SPEECH

3.1.1. Words are divided into eight parts of speech: nouns, adjectives (including participles), pronouns, verbs, adverbs, prepositions, conjunctions, and interjections.

3.1.2. A noun is the name of a person, place, thing or idea; as, **Klewopatrā**, *Cleopatra*, **dānus**, *river*, **dhworis**, *door*, **wṛdhom**, *word*.

Names of particular persons and places are called proper nouns; other nouns are called common.

NOTE. An abstract noun is the name of a quality or idea. A collective noun is the name of a group or a class.

3.1.3. An adjective is a word that attributes a quality; as, **patrjóm**, *parental*, **leukós**, *bright*, **kartús**, *hard*, **gṛndhís**, *grown*.

NOTE 1. A participle is a word that attributes quality like an adjective, but, being derived from a verb, retains in some degree the power of the verb to assert.

NOTE 2. Etymologically there is no difference between a noun and an adjective, both being formed alike. So, too, all nouns originally attribute quality, and any common noun can still be so used. Thus, **Aleksanōr Regs**, *King Alexander*, distinguishes this *Alexander* from other *Alexanders*, by the attribute expressed in the noun **regs**, *king*. See §10.9 for names of persons, and §10.4.4 for apposition of titles.

3.1.4. A pronoun is a word used to distinguish a person, place, thing or idea without either naming or describing it: as, **egṓ**, *I*, **twos**, *thine*, **wejes**, *we*.

Nouns and pronouns are often called substantives.

3.1.5. A verb is a word capable of asserting something: as, **bherō**, *I carry, bear*.

NOTE. In English the verb is usually the only word that asserts anything, and a verb is therefore supposed to be necessary to complete an assertion. Strictly, however, any adjective or noun may, by attributing a quality or giving a name, make a complete assertion, see below §10 *Syntax*.

3.1.6. An adverb is a word used to express the time, place, or manner of an assertion or attribute: as, **peri**, *in front*, **epi**, *near*, **antí**, *opposite*.

NOTE. These same functions are often performed in Indo-European by cases of nouns, pronouns and adjectives, and by phrases or sentences.

3.1.7. A preposition is a word which shows the relation between a noun or pronoun and some other word or words in the same sentence; as, e.g., **ad**, *at, to,* **dē**, *from upwards,* **kom**, *with,* **ek(sí)**, *outside,* **upo**, *under,* and so on.

3.1.8. A conjunction is a word which connects words, or groups of words, without affecting their grammatical relations: as, **-qe**, *and,* **-wĕ̄**, *or,* **-ma**, *but,* **-r**, *for.*

3.1.9. Interjections are mere exclamations and are not strictly to be classed as parts of speech; as, **alā!** *hello!,* **ō** *O* (vocative), **wai**, *alas* (grief), **ha ha!** (laughing sound); **ha!** (surprise); etc.

NOTE. Interjections sometimes express an emotion which affects a person or thing mentioned, and so have a grammatical connection like other words.

3.2. INFLECTION

3.2.1. Indo-European is an inflected language. Inflection is a change made in the form of a word to show its grammatical relations.

NOTE. Some modern Indo-European languages, like most Germanic and Romance dialects, have lost partly or completely their earliest attested inflection systems – due to different simplification trends –, in nominal declension as well as in verbal conjugation.

3.2.2. Inflectional changes sometimes take place in the body of a word, or at the beginning, but oftener in its termination:

pods, *the* or *a foot,* **pedós**, *of the foot*; **eimi**, *I go,* **imés**, *we go.*

3.2.3. Terminations of inflection had possibly originally independent meanings which are now obscured. They probably corresponded nearly to the use of prepositions, auxiliaries and personal pronouns in English.

Thus, in **ghórdejos**, *of the barley* (Gen.), the termination is equivalent to "*of the*"; in **deikō**, *I show* (indicative), and **deikom**, *I was showing, I used to show* (imperfect),.

3.2.4. Inflectional changes in the body of a verb usually denote relations of tense or mood, and often correspond to the use of auxiliary verbs in English:

Present **déikesi**, *thou show,* aorist **dikés**, *you showed*; present **(gí)gnṓsketi**, *he knows, recognises, is able,* perfect **gnowa**, *I am able* or *'I am in the state of knowing (having recognised)'*; the change of vowel grade and accent signifies a change in the aspect.

3.2.5. The inflection of nouns, adjectives, pronouns and participles to denote gender, number and case is called declension, and these parts of speech are said to be *declined.*

The inflection of verbs to denote voice, mood, tense, number and person is called conjugation, and the verb is said to be *conjugated*.

NOTE. Adjectives are often said to have inflections of comparison. These are, however, properly stem-formations made by derivations.

3.2.6. Adverbs, prepositions, conjunctions and interjections are not inflected, and together form the group of the so-called particles.

3.3. ROOT AND STEM

3.3.1. The body of a word, to which the terminations are attached, is called the stem. The stem contains the idea of the word without relations; but, except in the first part of compounds (e.g. **somo-patōr**, *"of the same father"*, *sibling*, **mn̥-dōmi**, *commit*), it cannot ordinarily be used without some termination to express them.

Thus the stem **pater-** denotes *father*; **patḗr**, nominative, means *a father* or *the father*, as the subject or agent of an action; **patér** (or **pater**) is the vocative, as in *O father!*; **patérm̥** is the accusative and means *to a father* or *to the father*, as the direct object; **patrós** is the genitive and indicates *of a father* or *of the father*, and so on.

NOTE. In inflected languages like Indo-European, words are built up from roots, which at a very early time were possibly used alone to express ideas. Roots are modified into stems, which, by inflection, become fully formed words. The process by which roots are modified, in the various forms of derivatives and compounds, is called stem-building. The whole of this process is originally one of composition, by which significant endings are added one after another to forms capable of pronunciation and conveying a meaning.

According to Mallory–Adams (2007): "To the root might be added a variety of suffixes to create a stem and then finally the case endings depending on number and perhaps gender. In some cases, the so-called root-nouns, there are no suffixes before the case ending. Using R for 'root', S for 'stem-creating suffix', and E for 'case-number-ending', we might establish the formula for an inflected word in Proto-Indo-European as R-(S)-E."

3.3.2. A root is the simplest form attainable by analysis of a word into its component parts. Such a form contains the main idea of the word in a very general sense, and is common also to other words either in the same language or in kindred languages; *cf.* for **stā-**, *stand*, reduplicated present **sí-stā-mi**, *I stand*, noun **stā-mn̥**, *place for standing*, zero-grade p.p. **sta-tós**, *placed, standing*, or noun **sta-tis**, *erection, standing*.

For example, the root of verb **spekjō**, *look*, is **spek-**, which does not necessarily mean *to look*, or *I look*, or *looking*, but merely expresses vaguely the idea of *looking*, and possibly cannot be used as a part of speech without terminations.

The roots of the reconstructed PIE language are basic morphemes carrying a lexical meaning. By addition of suffixes, they form stems, and by addition of desinences, they form grammatically inflected words (nouns or verbs).

NOTE. Clackson (2007): "The most influential theory of root-structure was put forward by Benveniste, in a chapter of a book concerning nominal formations in IE languages (Benveniste 1935). Benveniste used recent findings from work on the laryngeal theory (...) to present a unified view of the PIE root, and his root theory closely follows earlier work by Cuny and Kuryłowicz (see Szemerényi 1973). According to Benveniste, the basic structure of all PIE roots was *CeC- (C = any consonant), i.e. monosyllabic, with initial and final consonants" and with e as fundamental vowel; as, **sed-**, *sit*, **b^{h}er-**, *carry*.

Fortson (2004) offers a practical summary of complementary information to the theory:

- This template could be modified in certain ways, especially by adding consonants either at the beginning or the end to form consonant clusters. Most commonly, a resonant could occur on either side of the vowel, resulting in roots of the shape *CReC-, *CeRC-, and *CReRC- (remember that both i and u can function as resonants). Examples of them are **dhwer-**, *door*, **derk-**, *see*, or **ghrendh**, *grind*.
- Roots could also have any of the basic structures above preceded by **s**; as, **spek-**, *see*, **sneich-**, *snow*. We have already talked about the *s-mobile*, *v.s.* §2.7.
- Certain classes of consonants rarely or never co-occur within a given PIE root. According to Meillet, impossible PIE combinations are voiceless stop and voiced aspirate (as in **teb^h* or **b^{h}et*), as well as two plain unaspirated voiced stops (as in **ged* or **bed*). The **tebh* type is commonly found if preceded by an *s-, though. The source of these constraints is unknown, although similar constraints are known from other language families.
- A few roots began with a cluster consisting of two stops; as, **tkei-**, *settle*, and **pter**, *wing*, as well as those with word-initial 'thorn' clusters, as **r̥tkos**, *bear*, or **dhghom-**, *earth*.

NOTE 2. For peculiarities of the PIH reconstruction, also from Forston (2004):

The bulk of roots with laryngeals fall into four types: *CeH-, *HeC-, *HReC and *CeRH. In all these cases, the laryngeal was either the first or last consonant of the root. Some roots contained a laryngeal before the final consonant.

Some roots had **a** rather than **e** as the original PIH vowel; as, **nas-**, *nose*, **sal-**, *salt*. For reasons that are debated, initial ***k***- is particularly common in this class of roots; as, **kadh-**, protect, **kamp-**, *bend*, and **kan-**, *sing*.

3.3.3. The reconstructed PIE roots that appear with extra phonetic material (one or two sounds) added on to them, without any discernible change to the meaning of the root, are called *extended roots* (Fortson 2004).

NOTE. Clackson (2007) compares **gheud-**, *pour* (Lat. *fundō*, perf. *fūdī*, Goth. *giutan*), with **ghew-**, *pour* (*cf.* Skt. *juhóti*, Gk. *khéō*, Toch B *kewu*): "The longer form **gheud-* is easily taken to be composed of **ghew-* followed by a 'determinative' **d*. According to Benveniste, every root with a structure more complex than *CeC- was an extended root (he used the term thème to denote what we call here 'extended root'). The root *yeug- can therefore be seen as an extended form of a more basic *yew-, a hypothesis which is supported by the fact that there is actually a root *yew- 'join' reconstructed from Sanskrit *yuváti* 'ties' and Lithuanian *jáuju* 'I mix'."

3.3.4. Most of the reconstructed PIE lexicon is in the form of roots. However, there are some words which apparently belong to a very ancient layer of IE vocabulary, and cannot easily derived from roots; as, **sāwōl**, *sun*, **dhughtēr**, *daughter*, **acnos**, *lamb*, **wortokos**, *quail*.

A few, like **abel-**, *apple*, and **pélekus**, *ax*, have a shape that seems un-Indo-European, and are thought by some to be prehistoric borrowings from non-IE languages. Fortson (2004).

3.3.4. The stem may be the same as the root; as, **dō-**, *give*, **dakru**, *tear*; but it is more frequently formed from the root:

1. By changing or lengthening its vowel; as, from athematic root verb **dā-**, *divide*, common derivative **dai-mai**, *divide up, distribute*.

NOTE. Formally, following Benveniste's theory, the PIE root for the verb is reconstructed as *deh_2(j)-, i.e. from root *deh_2-, and enlargement *-j-, see Rix (2001).

2. By the addition of a simple suffix; as, from root **dā-**, *divide*, derivative **dā-mos**, *people, people's division* (*cf.* Dor. Gk. δημος, O.Ir. *dām*, Hitt. *da-ma-a-iš*).

NOTE. Some suffixes probably conveyed an earlier underlying meaning, e.g. the suffix -**trom** tends to indicate an instrument, as **arā-trom**, *plough*, from a verb **arājō**, *plough*, while kinship names tend to have the suffix ***-er-*** or ***-ter-***, *cf.* **swes-ōr**, *sister*, **bhrā-tēr**, *brother*.

3. By two or more of these methods; from the same root, suffixed derivative **dai-tis**, *time, period*, *cf.* Gmc. *tīþ*, Arm *ti*, as well as Gk. δαιτύς, O.Ind. *dātu-*.

4. By derivation and composition, following the laws of development peculiar to the language, which we will see in the corresponding chapters.

3.3.5. Inflectional terminations are modified differently by combination with the final vowel or consonant of the stem, and the various forms of declension and conjugation are so developed.

3.4. GENDER

3.4.1. The genders distinguished in Late Indo-European are three: masculine, feminine (both are referred to as animate) and neuter or inanimate.

The masculine functions as the negative term in the opposition of animates; i.e. when the gender is not defined when referring to animates, the masculine is used.

NOTE. This is a grammatical utility, one that is only relevant for concordance, and whose development is probably related to the evolution of the language and its inflection. Therefore, the feminine is the positive term of the opposition within the animates, because when we use it we reduce the spectrum of animates to the feminine, while the masculine still serves as the negative (i.e. non-differentiated) term for both animates – masculine and feminine – when used in this sense, i.e. when not differentiating the gender.

Clackson (2007): "Masculine nouns in other IE languages appear as nouns of the common gender in Hittite, but Hittite has no nominal declension corresponding to the feminine stems in **-eh*$_2$ or **-ih*$_2$. The lack of a feminine gender in Hittite has led scholars to ask whether the feminine ever existed in the Anatolian branch."

According to Mallory–Adams (2007): "The fact that Proto-Indo-European also forms collectives in **-h*$_2$*-* (e.g. the Hittite collective *alpa*, '*group of clouds*' from a singular *alpeš*, '*cloud*') has suggested that this was its original use and that it later developed the specifically feminine meaning."

3.4.2. The gender of Indo-European nouns is either *natural* or *grammatical.*

a. Natural gender is distinction as to the sex of the object denoted: **bhrātēr** (m.), *brother*; **cenā** (f.), *woman, wife.*

b. Grammatical gender is a formal distinction as to sex where no actual sex exists in the object. It is shown in the form of the adjective joined with the noun: as **swādús noqtis** (f.), *a pleasant night*; **mr̥ghú kanmn̥** (n.), *brief song*. The gender of the adjective is simply a gender of concordance: it indicates to which noun of a concrete gender the adjective refers to.

NOTE 2. Names of classes or collections of persons may be of any gender. For example, **wolgos** (masc.), *(common) people*, or **teutā** (fem.), *people (of a nationality).*

3.4.3. The neuter or inanimate gender differs from the other two in inflection, not in the theme vowel. The gender of animates, on the contrary, is usually marked by the theme vowel, and sometimes by declension, vocalism and accent.

3.4.4. The neuter does not refer to the lack of sex, but to the lack of liveliness or life. Sometimes, however, animates can be designated as inanimates and *vice versa*.

While the distinction between masculine and feminine is usually straightforward, sometimes the attribution of sex is arbitrary; thus, different words for parts of the body are found feminine, as **nāsis**, *nose*, **kanmā**, *leg*; masculine, as **kolsos**, *neck*, **armos**, *arm, upper arm*; and neuter, as **kaput**, *head*, or **genu**, *knee*.

3.4.5. The animate nouns can have:

a. An oppositive gender, marked:

I. by the lexicon, as in **patḗr/mātḗr**, *father/mother*, **bhrātēr/swesōr**, *brother/sister*, **sūnús/dhugtēr**, *son/daughter*;

II. by the stem ending, as in general **ekwos/ekwā**, *horse/mare*; or infrequent **wlqos/wlqīs**, *wolf/she-wolf*, **deiwos/deiwja**, *god/ goddess*;

III. by both at the same time, as in **swekros/swekrús**, *father-in-law-mother-in-law*, **wīrós/cenā**, *man-woman*, **regs/regeinā**, *king-queen*.

b. An autonomous gender, that does not oppose itself to others, as in **nāus** (f.), *ship*, **pods** (m.), *foot*, **egnis** (m.), *fire*, **owis** (f.), *sheep*, **jewos** (n.) or **legs** (f.), *law*.

c. A common gender, in nouns that are masculine or feminine depending on the context; as, **cōus**, *cow* or *bull*, **deuks**, *leader*, **ghostis**, *foreigner*.

d. An epicene gender, which, although being masculine or feminine, designates both sexes; as, **médodiks**, *doctor*, **nawāgós**, *sailor*, **nemots**, *enemy*, **setis**, *visitor*.

3.4.6. The gender of a noun can thus be marked by the stem vowel (or sometimes by inflection), or has to be learnt: it is a feature of a word like any other. In its context, concordance is a new gender mark; a masculine noun has a masculine adjective, and a feminine noun a feminine adjective. However, not all adjectives differentiate between masculine and feminine, a lot of them (those in ***-i-s***, ***-u-s***, ***-ēs***, ***-ōn***, and some thematic in ***-os***) are masculine and feminine: only the context, i.e. the noun with which they agree, helps to disambiguate them. This happens also in nouns with a common gender.

3.4.7. Most endings do not indicate gender, as in **patḗr** and **mātḗr**. Only by knowing the roots in many cases, or from the context in others, is it possible to determine it.

NOTE. Clackson (2007): "Nouns of all genders can occur in the athematic declension. Non-neuter animate nouns are usually assigned gender through correspondence with the natural sex of the referent, non-neuter inanimate nouns are assigned gender by convention."

Some of the suffixes determine, though, totally or partially if they are masculine or feminine. These are the following:

1. ***-os*** marks masculine when it is opposed to a feminine in ***-ā*** or ***-ī/-ja***, as in **ekwos/ekwā**, **deiwos/deiwja**, *god/goddess*, etc. This happens also in adjectives in the same situation, as in **newos/newā**, or **bheronts/bherontja**, *bearing*.

In isolated nouns, ***-os*** is generally masculine, but some traces of the old indistinctness of gender still remained in LIE, as in the names of trees (among others). In adjectives, when the ending ***-os*** is not opposed to feminine, concordance decides. A common example is **snusós**, *daughter-in-law*, a feminine from the o-declension.

2. ***-ā*** marks the feminine in oppositions of nouns and adjectives. It is usually also feminine in isolated nouns, in the first declension.

NOTE. There seems to be no reconstructible masculines in ***-ā***; so e.g. BSl. **slough*ā́*, *servant* (*cf.* O.Sla. *slŭga*, Lith. *slauga* "*service*", O.Ir. *sluag*, "*army unit*") etc. is probably to be reconstructed as original NWIE **sloughos** (*cf.* Ir. *teg-lach* < **tegoslougo-*).

According to Clackson (2007): "(...) the only one of the three major declension classes to show a restriction to a single gender is the class of feminine nouns formed with the suffix *-eh₂ or *-ih₂. Where IE languages show masculine nouns in this declension class, such as Latin *agricola* 'farmer' or Greek *neānías* 'young man', they can be explained as post-PIE developments. The feminine is only therefore distinguished in one declension type, and it is this same declension that is absent in Hittite. It appears that the category of feminine gender is to be closely associated with the declension class in *-h₂."

3. Endings ***-ā̆*** <**-(e/o)h₂*, ***-ī/-ja*** <**-ih₂*, although generally feminine in LIE, show remains of its old abstract-collective value, as neuter plural. It appears in nouns, adjectives and pronouns

3.5. NUMBER

3.5.1. Nouns, pronouns, adjectives and participles, all are declined in Indo-European in two numbers, singular and plural. The same is found in the PIE verbal conjugations.

NOTE. The same categories of case are found in singular and plural, but with a greater degree of syncretism in the latter, with common ablative-dative endings, and nominative-vocative, see below. According to Meier-Brügger (2003): "Singular and plural are grammatical categories that are common to the verb and the noun. They permit one to indicate by means of congruence the association of the noun with the subject of the action, indicated by the verb form employed. The relationship of singular to plural is a question of syntax."

3.5.2. Late Indo-European shows also traces of a dual number for some nouns and pronouns, but the formation of stable verbal dual forms is only traceable to individual dialects.

NOTE. Clackson (2007): "The dual does not just denote that there are two of something: it can also be used as an associative marker in a construction standardly referred to as the *elliptical dual* in grammars and handbooks." So e.g. Ved. Skt. dual *Mitrā́* refers to Mitra and his companion Varuna; Hom. Gk. dual *Aíante* referred probably to Ajax and his brother Teucer. In languages that do not show dual, however, the plural is used as an associative to denote pairs in Latin *Castorēs*, the plural of the name 'Castor', is used to denote the semi-god Castor and his twin Pollux.

Meier-Brügger (2003) reproduces the words of Matthias Fritz's work on the dual: "The origins of the dual are contained in two word types: On the one hand, the personal pronoun is a starting point of the *numerus* dual; on the other, among nouns, terms for paired body parts are of great importance. While pronouns in the first and second person feature the dual as grammatical category as far back as they can be traced, the dual category initially does not exist among substantives. In the case of the terms for paired body parts the duality is lexically founded. (...) The formation of verbal dual forms based upon the first person personal pronoun takes place where the formation was no longer completed in the Proto-Indo-European period, which then does not take place in the language branches. Thus, the secondary endings may be reconstructed. In the case of syntagmata, using the substantive as a basis, a dual form and the number word for 'two' transferred the dual inflection over to the *numera*, thus echoing the relation of syntagmata to pronouns and adjectives."

Given the scarcity of remains found in West IE languages, it is likely that that LIE did not have a fully developed system for the dual. Also, its use seems to have been optional even in its most common use: body parts.

NOTE. Clackson (2007): "The dual is reconstructed for pronouns, animate nouns and inanimate nouns, but it is likely that its usage was optional at least with words denoting inanimates (that is, the lower end of the 'animacy hierarchy'). Note that in the two early IE languages with a paradigmatic dual, Greek and Sanskrit, pairs of body parts, such as hands, eyes, legs, knees etc., may be denoted either by the plural or by the dual, and the plural is in fact more common for bodypart terms in Homeric Greek."

3.5.3. Verbs which are collocated with non-neuter plural forms of nouns must agree with them in number; that is also the case for most neuter plural forms of nouns.

However, the so-called *collective* neuter plural requires concordance in the singular. Such forms are scarce, and found only in the nominative and accusative; in the other cases, they follow the plural paradigm.

NOTE. Examples are given in Meier-Brügger (2003) and Clackson (2007) from Greek *kúklos* 'wheel, circle' (*kúkloi* 'circles' vs. *kúkla* 'set of wheels'), *mērós* 'thigh' (*mȇroí* 'thigh-pieces' vs. *mēra* 'agglomeration of thigh-meat'), Hitt. *alpas* 'cloud' (*alpes* 'clouds' vs. *alpa* 'cloud-mass'), or Lat. *locus* 'place' (*locī* 'places' vs. *loca* 'places').

4. NOUNS

4.1. DECLENSION OF NOUNS

4.1.1. Declension is made by adding terminations to different stem endings, vowel or consonant.

Adjectives are generally declined like nouns, and are etymologically to be classed with them, but they have some peculiarities of inflection which will be later explained.

4.1.2. There are eight commonly reconstructed cases for Late Indo-European:

I. The nominative is the case of the subject of a sentence and predicate nominative.

II. The vocative is the case of direct address.

III. The accusative is the case of the direct object of a verb. It is used also with many prepositions.

IV. The genitive may generally be translated by the English possessive.

V. The ablative, the source or place from which.

VI. The dative, the case of the indirect object. It also indicates possession, and beneficiary of an action.

VII. The locative, the place *where*.

VIII. The instrumental, the means and the agent.

NOTE. The oblique cases appear in the English pronoun set; these pronouns are often called *objective pronouns*; as in *she loves me* (accusative), *give it to me* (dative) or *that dirt wasn't wiped with me* (instrumental), where me is not inflected differently in any of these uses; it is used for all grammatical relationships except the genitive case of possession, *mine*, and a non-disjunctive nominative case as the subject, *I*.

4.1.3. Nouns and adjectives are inflected in LIE in four regular declensions, distinguished by their final phonemes – characteristic of the stem –, and by the opposition of different forms in irregular nouns. They are numbered following Graeco-Roman tradition: first or a-stem declension, second or o-stem declension, third or i/u-stem declension, fourth or c-stem declension, and the variable nouns.

The stem of a noun may be found, if a consonant stem, by omitting the case-ending; if a vowel stem, by substituting for the case-ending the characteristic vowel.

Decl.	Stem ending	Nominative	Genitive
1.	**ā (ja/ī, ē, ō)**	-∅	***-s***
2.	**e/o** (*Thematic*)	*m., f.*-***s***, *n.*-***m***	***-os/-osjo***
3.	**i, u** and Diphthong	*m., f.*-***s***, *n.*-∅	***-eis, -eus; -jos, -***
4.	Resonants &	***-s***, -∅	***-es/-os***
(5)	*Heteroclites*	-∅, ***-r***	*-(e)**n***

NOTE. Most Indo-Europeanists tend to distinguish at least two major types of declension for the oldest PIE, thematic and athematic. Thematic nominal stems are formed with a suffix ***-o-*** (also ***-e-***), and the stem does not undergo *ablaut*, i.e. there is no ablaut difference between the *strong* and the *weak* cases, and there is no accent change, see below.

Feminine stems in **-ā** < **-eh₂* were originally c-stems with final **-h₂* which, under pressure from the o-stem adjectives, were adapted to the thematic paradigm of the masculine o-stems. It is sometimes separated from the athematic declension into a new class, even if being originally consonantal, because of such peculiarities; so e.g. in Clackson (2007): "In respect of the reconstructed case-endings, the class of feminine nouns in [a-stem declension] shows clear affinities with the athematic class [c-stem declension], and the o-stem declension diverges more radically from both. In the daughter languages, however, there is a general tendency for the o-stem class and the feminine ā-stems to become more closely associated, almost certainly through the combination of the two classes in a number of pronominal and adjectival declensions as masculine and feminine alternatives."

The declension of i/u-stems and c-stems is more complex, as it involves accent-ablaut changes. Fortunately the most productive (thus more frequent) declensions in LIE are mainly o-stems and ā-stems.

NOTE. Stems in consonant, **i**, and **u**, are more archaic, and they are classified further by their ablaut behaviour into different so-called *dynamic* patterns, after the positioning of the early PIE accent in the paradigm. See below §4.7.

The distinction of i-stems and u-stems from c-stems is also traditional, but according to Fortson (2004), to keep that distinction for PIH probably "is both unnecessary and misleading, as it masks the fundamentally identical behavior of both groups over against that of the thematic nouns". In LIE, however, there are pragmatic reasons to distinguish them.

4.1.3. The following are general rules of declension:

a. The nominative singular for animates ends in ***-s*** when the stem endings are **i**, **u**, diphthong, occlusive and thematic (***-os***); in -∅ when the stem ends in **ā**, resonant and **s**; in the plural ***-es*** is general, ***-s*** for those in **ā**, and ***-os*** for the thematic ones.

NOTE. For collectives/feminines in ***-ja/-ī*** <*-*jə*<*-*ih₂* we prefer to use in our texts the ending ***-ja*** for feminines, and ***-ī*** for neuters as a general rule. It is not intended as a 'normative' selection, though, but as a conventional simplification of the otherwise tedious repetition ***-ja/-ī*** that is followed in other books, while at the same time reflecting the natural evolution pattern of such forms in NWIE (see below §§4.2, 4.4.2). So e.g. this convention does not limit the use of feminines in ***-ī;*** as e.g. Lat. *-trīx*, or *coxendīx*.

b. The accusative singular of all masculines and feminines ends in ***-m*** or ***-m̥*** (after consonant), the accusative plural in ***-ns*** or ***-n̥s***.

NOTE. A general accusative plural ending ***-ns*** (***-n̥s*** after consonant) is usually reconstructed for Late Indo-European, because e.g. within the u-stem from PIE *-*u-ns*, early IE languages show *-*uns*, *-*ūns*, *-*ūs*; *cf.* Goth. *sununs*, O.Ind. *sūnū́n*, Gk. *uíuns*, Lith. *sū́nus*, O.C.S. *syny*, Lat. *manūs*. See H. Rix (FS Risch 1986). Most scholars also posit an 'original', older **-*ms* form (a logical accusative singular ***-m-*** plus the plural mark ***-s***), but they usually prefer to reconstruct the attested *-*ns*, thus implicitly suggesting either the theoretical origin of the ending, or a previous PIH *-*ms* → LIE *-***ns***. For a PIH *-*ms*, *cf.* maybe Hitt. *-uš* (Ottinger 1979), but Lyc *-s* (<*-*ns*?). To be consistent with decisions taken elsewhere in this grammar (as e.g. reconstructed PIE *-T(s)T- as NWIE intermediate -sT-, see §2.7), the intermediate, attested ***-ns*** is the conservative choice, whereas **-*ms* is just a probable hypothesis about its actual origin.

c. The vocative singular for animates is always -Ø, and in the plural it is identical to the nominative.

d. The genitive singular is common to animates and inanimates, it is formed with ***-s***: ***-s***, ***-es***, ***-os***. An alternative possibility is extended ***-os-jo***. The genitive plural is formed in ***-ōm***, and in ***-ām*** in a-stems.

NOTE. Case endings in **-e/o-**, **-ē/ō-**, are generally written in this book in **-o-**, **-ō-**, in inflected nouns, given the alternating nature of these forms even within the same dialectal branches, and the unknown nature of the original ablauting forms. Sihler (1995), Fortson (2004), Ringe (2006), reconstruct 'original' forms in ***-es***, while Beekes (1995) deems -(***o***)***s*** the oldest athematic declension. Meier-Brügger (2003) or Adrados–Bernabé–Mendoza reconstruct both as alternating ***-es/-os***. For Sihler (1995), since e-grade is typical of consonant stems, maybe forms in ***-o-*** in o-stems were the 'original' ones, and those in **-e-** were secondary creations; that same argument is found for the genitive of athematic nouns in ***-es***, supposedly substituted by the 'original' thematic ***-os*** (Fortson 2004). In any case, it seems that in Late Indo-European forms in ***-o-*** prevailed, as did the thematic declension; as, **kunós**, over **kunés**, from **kwōn**.

e. The obliques singular end usually in ***-i***: it can be ***-i-***, ***-ei-***, ***-ēi-***, ***-oi-***, ***-ōi-*** or ***-āi-*** , and their extensions. In the plural, there are two series of declensions, instr. -

bhis*/-*mis (from sg. -***bhi***), dat.-abl. -***bhos*/-*mos*** (PII -***bhjas***) as well as (BSl. and PII) loc. in -***su*** (PGk. -***si***).

NOTE. Comparison shows an ins. sg. -***bhi***, (*cf.* Gk. -*pʰi*, Myc. -*pi*, and also *Arm.* ins. *marb*), BSl. -***mi*** (*cf.* Lith. *akmenimì*, O.C.S. *kamenĭmĭ*) and for Northwestern IE dialects a division between Italic+Celtic and Germanic+Balto-Slavic Plural forms: Celtic shows traces of an instrumental -***bhis*** (*cf.* O.Ir. dat.-loc.-ins.-abl. *cridib*, and in Graeco-Aryan, *cf.* O.Ind. *sūnúbhis*, Av. *bāzubīs*, Arm. *srtiwkh*), Italic and Celtic show a dat.-abl. -***bhos*** (*cf.* Celtiberian dat.-loc.-ins.-abl. *arecoraticubos*, Lat. *matribus*, Osc. *luisarifs*), while Balto-Slavic shows Inst. -***mis*** (*cf.* Lith. *sunumìs*, O.C.S. *synumĭ*), dat.-abl. -***mos*** (*cf.* O.C.S. *synŭmŭ*, Lith. *sūnùms*, *sūnùmus*), and Germanic shows a dat.-abl.-ins. -***m***-.

Meier-Brügger (2003) considers that "[e]vidence seems to indicate that while the dative and ablative plural were marked with *-*mos*, the instrumental plural was marked with *-*bʰi* (...) Thus, -*bʰ*- would have established itself in Italic and Indo-Iranian as the sole initial consonant, replacing -*m*-. Conversely, -*m*- would have established itself in Balto-Slavic and Germanic. Indo-Iranian *-*bʰi̯as* can thus be regarded as a cross between the instrumental *-*bʰi* and the dative/ablative *-*mos*". Similarly Mallory–Adams (2007) differentiate for the oldest PIH declension a Dat. *-*mus*, instrumental *-*bhi*, and Abl. *-*bh(j)os*. Kortlandt (1983) and Beekes (1985) reconstruct an original Dat. Pl. *-*mus* and Abl. Pl. *-*jos*, both supposedly substituted later by the ending *-*bh(j)os*.

For an original *-*mus*, the Leiden school revitalised an old claim (Van Helten 1890, Loewe 1918) to explain the lack of Umlaut of -*i* in dat. pl., as e.g. OHG *tagum*, which followed Georgiev's (1963) and Kortlandt's (1983) proposals to explain the ending away by comparing it to O.Lith. -*mus*, thereby suggesting an original *-*u*-. That proposal has been questioned e.g. on the basis that the O.Prus. dat. pl. -*mans*, is generally believed to have resulted from the contamination of dat. Pl. *-*mos* > -*mas*, and acc. Pl. -*ans* (Bemeker 1896, Brugmann 1911, Poljakov 1995). The Leiden position has been questioned on the grounds of the late and dialectal character of BSl. and Gmc. edings among others by Álvarez-Pedrosa (2001) <http://revistas.ucm.es/fll/15781763/articulos/ESLC0101110239A.PDF>, and Halla-aho (2006), see <http://ethesis.helsinki.fi/julkaisut/hum/slavi/vk/halla-aho/problems.pdf>).

Fortson (2004) sums up the problem of reconstructing -***bh***- and -***m***- endings for PIH: " All this taken together suggests that the *-*bh*- and * -*m*- endings developed late, probably after Anatolian split off from the family, and may have originally been postpositions or adverbs ultimately related to Eng. *by* and Germ. *mit* 'with'. (It is cross-linguistically common for postpositions to develop into case-endings.)"

What is certain is that there was a NWIE west/east dialectal differentiation into -***bh***- or -***m***-; i.e. dat.-abl. pl. -***bhos*/-*mos*** (and PII -***bhjas***), ins. sg. -***bhi*/-*mi***, ins. pl. -***bhis*/-*mis***. We generally prefer to write the only the forms in -***bh***- in this grammar, though, given the extension of those forms in all PIE territory, against the forms in -***m***-, limited to Germanic and Balto-Slavic. In any case, when writing these endings, one should keep in mind that they are dialectally distributed in a uniform way, so that forms in -***bh***- are not found in the same branches as those in ***-m-***; i.e., if you use forms in ***-m-*** when writing or speaking IE, don't use forms in ***-bh-***, and *vice versa*.

f. Inanimates have a syncretic form for nom.-acc.-voc. -∅ in athematics, or ***-m*** in thematics. The plural forms end in ***-ā̆***.

NOTE. Inanimates have a nom.-voc.-acc in **-(e/o)h₂*, which evolved as ***-ā*** in Sanskrit and Slavic, and ***-a*** in most other dialects. A convention is therefore followed in this book, using short ***-a*** to distinguish the overlapping neu. pl. nom.-voc.-acc. from the fem. sg. nom.

g. All animates share the same form in the plural for nom.-voc. ***-es***.

4.1.4. The so-called *oblique* cases – opposed to the *straight* ones, nom.-acc.-voc –, are the genitive and the obliques proper, i.e. ablative, dative, locative, and instrumental. Straight cases are generally identified with *strong* cases (those which do not undergo ablaut in athematic declension), while the rest are the *weak* cases.

NOTE. IE languages show an irregular oblique declension system, especially in the plural, due to its syncretic original nature and to late dialectal merging trends. Sanskrit or Avestan had 8 cases. Anatolian and Italic dialects show up to 8 (*cf.* Osc. loc. *aasai for* Lat. '*in ārā*', or ins. *cadeis amnud* for Lat. '*inimicitiae causae*', *preiuatud* for Lat. '*prīuātō*', etc.). Balto-Slavic shows seven, Mycenaean at least six cases, while Koiné Greek and Proto-Germanic had five.

Nominal Desinences (Summary)

	Singular		*Plural*	
	Animates	*Inanimates*	*Animates*	*Inanimates*
NOM.	***-s***, -∅	***-m***, -∅	***-es***	***-ā̆***, -∅
VOC.	***-e***, -∅			
ACC.	***-m***		***-ns***	
GEN.	***-es/-os/-s; -osjo***		***-om***	
ABL.	***-es/-os/-s; -ēd/-ōd/-d***		***-bhos (-mos)***; ***-om***	
DAT.	***-ei***		***-bhos (-mos)***	
LOC.	***-i***		***-su (-si)***	
INS.	***-ē/-ō; -bhi (-mi)***		***-eis***; ***-bhis (-mis)***	

4.2. FIRST DECLENSION

4.2.1. FIRST DECLENSION PARADIGM

1. They are usually animate nouns and end in **ā** (or **jā**), and rarely in **ja/ī**, **ē**, and **ō**. Stems in **ā** are very common, generally feminine in nouns and always in adjectives, and the **ā** ending is used to make feminines in the adjectival motion. Those in **ja/ī** are rare, generally feminine, and etymologically identical to the neuter plural in nom.-acc.-voc. Those in **ō** and **ē** are feminine only in lesser used words.

NOTE. The entire stem could have been reduced to IE **a** (hence a-stem declension), because this is the origin of the whole PIE stem system, the ending **-(e)h₂*.

2. The IE first declension corresponds loosely to the Latin first declension (*cf.* Lat. *rosa*, *rosae*, or *puella*, *puellae*), and to the Ancient Greek alpha declension (*cf.* Gk. χώρᾱ, χώρᾱς, or τῑμή, τῑμῆς).

a-Declension Singular Paradigm

NOM.	-∅
VOC.	-∅ (-ŏ)
ACC.	***-m***
GEN.	***-s***
ABL.	***-d/(-s)***
DAT.	***-i***
LOC.	***-i***
INS.	-∅/***-bhi (-mi)***

NOTE. This declension in **ā**, older **-eh₂*, is usually reconstructed in the singular as older (athematic) PIH nom.-voc. **-eh₂* (voc. *-h₂e?*) acc. **-eh₂m̥*, gen.(-abl.) **-(e)h₂os*, dat. **-(e)h₂ei*, loc. **-eh₂i*, ins. **-(e)h₂eh₁*, abl. **-(e)h₂ed*; as, dat. **h₁ekw(e)h₂ei* → **ekwāi** (see Beekes 1995, Clackson 2007). The ablative sg. was linked to the genitive sg. (-**s**) in the older stages of the language, but as the feminine declension was adapted to the thematic declension in **o/e**, an ablative in -***d*** was generalised already by Late Indo-European. From Beekes (1995), Adrados–Bernabé–Mendoza (1995-1998), Clackson (2007).

3. It is therefore identical to those nouns in **r**, **n**, **s** of the fourth declension, but for some details in vocalism: the gen. has an -***s*** and not -***es***/-***os***; the difference between nom. and voc. can be obtained by nom. -***ā*** vs. voc. -***a*** (as found in Gk. and BSl.). The zero-grade of the nom.-acc.-voc. in **ja/ī** stems is different from the gen. in **jā**.

4.2.2. FIRST DECLENSION IN EXAMPLES

1. Nominative singular in -∅; as, **ekwā**, *mare*, **patrjā**, *fatherland*, adj. **newā**, *new*, **cowijā́**, *bovine*.

NOTE. The representative noun of this paradigm is the word for 'mare' which occurs in Sanskrit *áśvā*, Latin *equa* and (Old) Lithuanian *ašvà*. This word is probably not of common PIE origin, although it is likely a post-LIE word that appeared to differentiate the feminine of the animate 'horse', which was previously used for male and female alike. Clackson (2007).

Examples of **ja/ī** include **potnja/potnī**, *lady*, *mistress*, **deiwja/deiwī**, *goddess*.

NOTE. Stems in **ja/ī** (<*-ih₂) are productive in adjectives of the ***-u-*** and ***-nt-*** form, found generally as **-ī** in Indo-Iranian (*cf.* Skt. *bhárantī*), **-ja** in NWIE (*cf.* O.C.S. *nesǫšti* <*-ontj-) and PGk (*cf. phérousa*<*-ontja), Beekes (1995). Because they were not productive in nouns already in IEDs, the declension of the attested nouns is frozen as an athematic stem from which they derive. So e.g. from nom. ***deiwī***, Skt. *dev-ī́*, Gk. *dī́-a (<*diw-ja), gen.-abl.* ***diwjā́s***, *cf.* Skt. *dev-yā́s*, Gk. *dī́-ās* (<*diw-jās). Clackson (2007).

Those in **ē**, **ō**, also rare, make the nominative in ***-s***; as, ***spekjēs***, *aspect*.

NOTE. These are known from Latin (since Indo-Iranian merged ē with ā especially from the word for 'path'. Like the forms from *-ih₂, these old nouns in *-eH or *-oH retain their c-stem declension paradigm (with *accent-ablaut*); a famous example found in Beekes (1995) or Fortson (2004) includes ***pontēs***, *path*, found in Skt. *pánthās*, Av. *pantå*, and afield in Lat. *vātēs* – although later reinterpreted as i-stem **pontis** in NWIE, *cf.* Lat. *pons*, Russ. *put'*, O.Pruss. *pintis*. Its declension is reconstructed as nom. ***pontēs***, acc. ***pontēm***, gen. ***pn̥tós***, ins. pl. ***pn̥tbhí***.

2. Vocative singular in -∅. It is normally identical to the nominative, but disambiguation could happen with distinct vowel grades, i.e. nom. in ***-ā***, voc. in ***-a***.

NOTE. According to Ringe (2006), the vocative of those in **ja/ī**<*-iH would have been made in *-i, following the example of the 'fall of the laryngeal' in vocatives of those in *-aH.

3. Accusative singular in ***-m***; as, **ekwām**, **patrjām**, **potnjam/potnīm**, **spekjēm**.

4. Genitive singular in ***-s***; as, **ekwās**, **patrjās**, **spekjēs**.

Stems in **ja/ī** produces a genitive singular in ***-ās***; as, **potnjās**.

5. Dative-ablative singular in ***-āi***, **ekwāi**, **patrjāi**.

NOTE. This LIE ***-i*** comes probably from an older PIE general dat. *-ei* ending; as, *h₁ekweh₂-ei → **ekwāi**. A dat.-abl. ending *-ei* is also found for stems in **ē** and in **ja/ī**.

6. Locative singular in ***-āi***; as, **ekwāi**, **patrjāi**.

7. Instrumental singular in -∅, ***-ā-bhi***, ***-ā-mi***; as, **ékwābhi**, **pátrjābhi**.

	f. ***ekwā***	*adj.f.* ***cowijā́***	*f.* ***potnja***	*f.* ***spekjē-***
NOM.	**ekwā**	**cowijā́**	**potnja/potnī**	**spekjēs**
VOC.	**ekwă̄**	**cowijā́**	**potnja/potnī**	**spekjē**
ACC.	**ekwām**	**cowijā́m**	**potnjam/potnīm**	**spekjēm**
GEN.	**ekwās**	**cowijā́s**	**potnjās**	**spekjēs**
ABL.	**ekwād**	**cowijā́d**	**potnjād**	**spekjēd**
DAT.	**ekwāi**	**cowijā́i**	**potnjāi**	**spekjēi**
LOC.	**ekwāi**	**cowijā́i**	**potnjāi**	**spekjēi**
INS.	**ékwābhi**	**cowijā́bhi**	**potnjābhi**	**spekjēbhi**

There is only one example from this declension with a proterodynamic inflection (see §4.7), namely the word for 'woman': nom. **cenā**, gen. **cnās**, *cf.* O.Ir. nom. *ben*, gen. *mná*, Skt. nom. *jánis* (*gnā́*), gen. *gnā́s* (*jányur*). Beekes (1995).

4.2.3. THE PLURAL IN THE FIRST DECLENSION

1. The following table presents the plural paradigm of the *a-stem declension*.

a-Declension Plural Paradigm

NOM.-VOC.	***-s***
ACC.	***-ns***
GEN.	***-m***
DAT.-ABL.	***-bhos (-mos)***
LOC.	***-su (-si)***
INS.	***-bhis (-mis)***

NOTE. The plural is reconstructed as from PIH nom.-vocc. **-eh$_2$(e)s*, Acc. **-eh$_2$n̥s* (<**-*eh$_2$- m̥-s*), gen.(-abl.) **-(e)h$_2$om*, dat.-abl. **-(e)h$_2$bh(j)os or *-(e)h$_2$mus*, loc. **-(e)h$_2$su*, ins. **-(e)h$_2$bhi(s)*; as, **h$_1$ekweh$_2$es* → **ekwās**. From Beekes (1995), Clackson (2007).

2. Nominative-vocative plural in ***-s***: **ekwās**, **patrjās**, **cowijā́s**.

3. Accusative plural in ***-ms***: **ekwāns**, **patrjāns**.

4. Genitive plural in ***-m***: **ekwām**, **patrjām**.

5. Dative and ablative plural in ***-bhos***, ***-mos***, and PII ***-bhjas***; as, **ékwābhos**, **patrjābhos**.

6. Locative plural in ***-su*** (also PGk ***-si***); as, **ékwāsu**, **pátrjāsu**.

6. Instrumental plural in ***-bhis***, ***-mis***; as, **ékwābhis**, **patrjābhis**.

NOTE. The obliques have also special dialectal forms Gk. ***-āisi***, ***-ais***, Lat. ***-ais***; as, Lat. *rosīs<*rosais*.

	f. ekwā	***f. cowijā́***	***f. potnja***
NOM.-VOC.	**ekwās**	**cowijā́s**	**potnjās**
ACC.	**ekwāns**	**cowijā́ns**	**potnjāns**
GEN.	**ekwām**	**cowijā́m**	**potnjā́m**
DAT.-ABL.	**ékwābhos**	**cowijā́bhos**	**pótnjabhos**
LOC.	**ékwāsu**	**cowijā́su**	**pótnjasu**
INS.	**ékwābhis**	**cowijā́bhis**	**pótnjabhis**
ABL.	**ékwābhos**	**cowijā́bhos**	**pótnjabhos**

4.3. SECOND DECLENSION

4.3.1. SECOND DECLENSION PARADIGM

1. Nouns of the second declension have a stem ending in **e/o**, and they are usually called *thematic*. They can be animates and inanimates, as well as adjectives. The inanimates have an ending ***-m*** in nom.-acc.-voc. The animates, with a nominative in ***-s***, are generally masculine in nouns and adjectives, but there are also feminine nouns and animate (i.e. masc.-fem.) adjectives in ***-os***, probably remains of the old indistinctness of animates.

NOTE. The o-stem declension is probably very recent in PIE – even though it happened already in PIH, before the Proto-Anatolian split – and that's why it is homogeneous in most IE dialects. As Mallory–Adams (2007) say, "[t]he o-stems were the most productive form of declension. By this is meant that through time, especially at the end of the Proto-Indo-European period and into the early histories of the individual Indo-European languages, the o-stems appeared to proliferate and replace other stem types. In Vedic Sanskrit, for example, they constitute more than half of all nouns. High productivity is often interpreted as evidence that the o-stems are a later declensional form than many of the other stems. Highly productive forms are ultimately capable of replacing many other forms as they provide the most active model by which speakers might decline a form."

2. The IE second declension is equivalent to the second declension in Latin (*cf.* Lat. *dominus*, *dominī*, or *uinum*, *uinī*), and to the omicron declension in Greek (*cf.* Gk. λόγος, λόγου, or δῶρον, δῶρου).

o-Declension Singular Paradigm

<table>
<tr><th></th><th>Animate</th><th>Inanimate</th></tr>
<tr><td>NOM.</td><td>-os</td><td rowspan="3">-om</td></tr>
<tr><td>VOC.</td><td>-e</td></tr>
<tr><td>ACC.</td><td>-om</td></tr>
<tr><td>GEN.</td><td colspan="2">-os/-osjo/(-oso)/(-ī)</td></tr>
<tr><td>ABL.</td><td colspan="2">-ēd/-ōd</td></tr>
<tr><td>DAT.</td><td colspan="2">-ōi</td></tr>
<tr><td>LOC.</td><td colspan="2">-ei/-oi</td></tr>
<tr><td>INS.</td><td colspan="2">-ē/-ō</td></tr>
</table>

NOTE 1. This model could have been written without the initial vowel ***-o-***; the probable origin of this vowel is the ending of some primitive 'original' stems in **-o**, while other, primitive athematic stems would have then been reinterpreted, and an ***-o*** added to their stems by means of analogy (Adrados–Bernabé–Mendoza 1995-1998). This paradigm could be read from a historical point of view as nom. ***-s***, acc. ***-m***, gen. ***-s***, ***-sjo***, ***-so***, and so on.

NOTE 2. The thematic declension is usually reconstructed in the singular as from older PIH nom. **-os*, voc. **-e*, acc. **-om* (neu. nom.-voc.-acc. **-om*), gen. **-os*, dat. **-ōi* (<***-o-ei*), loc. **-oi*, ins. **-oh$_1$*, abl. **-ōd* (<***-o-ed*); as, dat. **wl̥k^{w}o-ei* → ***wl̥qōi***, abl. **wl̥k^{w}o-ed* → ***wl̥qōd***. Sometimes, the a-stem and o-stem ablative is reconstructed as from PIE **-ot* or **-et*, or even **-h$_2$at* (in Fortson 2004). As we have seen, *-d* and *-t* are pronounced alike at the end of the word, so the difference is mainly an etymological one.

4.3.2. SECOND DECLENSION IN EXAMPLES

1. Nominative singular animate in ***-os***; as in **wl̥qos**, *wolf*, **dómūnos**, *lord*, **wīrós**, *man*, adj. **cīwós**, *alive*.

2. Vocative singular animate in ***-e***; as in **wl̥qe**, **dómūne**, **cīwé**.

3. Accusative singular animate in ***-om***; as in **wl̥qom**, **dómūnom**, **cīwóm**.

4. Nominative-vocative-accusative singular inanimate in ***-om***; as in **jugóm**, *yoke*, adj. **newom**, *new*.

5. Genitive singular in ***-os***, ***-osjo***, also ***-e/oso***, ***-ī***; as in **wl̥qosjo**, **jugós**, **dómūnosjo**.

NOTE. The original genitive form ***-os*** is rare in animates, as the genitive had to be distinguished from the nominative. This disambiguation happens by alternatively lengthening the ending, as ***-os-jo*** (or ***-e/os-o***, probably from the pronominal declension) or changing it altogether, as in Ita.-Cel. ***-ī***. In Hittite, the genitive ***-os*** is found, so it is usually considered the oldest form, as in the athematic declension. A generalised ***-osjo*** is found in Sanskrit, Armenian, Greek and Italic, so this alternative ending must have replaced -***os*** early, still within the LIE community.

6. Ablative singular in -***ōd***, -***ēd***: **wl̥qōd, cīwṓd, jugṓd.**

7. Dative singular in -***ōi***: **wl̥qōi, dómūnōi, newōi, jugṓi.**

8. Locative singular in -***oi***, -***ēi***: **wl̥qoi, dómūnoi, newoi, jugói.**

9. Instrumental singular in -***ō***, -***ē***: **wl̥qō, dómūnō, newō, jugṓ.**

	m. ***wl̥qo-***	*n.* ***jugó-***	*adj.* ***newo-***
NOM.	**wl̥qos**	**jugóm**	**newos**
VOC.	**wl̥qe**	**jugom**	**newe**
ACC.	**wl̥qom**	**jugóm**	**newom**
GEN.	**wĺ̥qosjo**	**jugós**	**newosjo**
ABL.	**wl̥qōd**	**jugṓd**	**newōd**
DAT.	**wl̥qōi**	**jugṓi**	**newōi**
LOC.	**wl̥qoi**	**jugói**	**newoi**
INS.	**wl̥qō**	**jugṓ**	**newō**

4.5.3. THE PLURAL IN THE SECOND DECLENSION

1. The thematic plural system is usually depicted as follows:

o-Declension Plural Paradigm

	Animate	Inanimate
NOM.-VOC.	***-ōs/(-oi)***	***-ă̄***
ACC.	***-ons***	
GEN.	***-ō̆m/-ēm***	
DAT.-ABL.	***-obhos (-omos)***	
LOC.	***-oisu (-oisi)***	
INS.	***-ō̆is***	

NOTE. The animate plural paradigm is reconstructed as PIH nom.-voc. **-ōs* (<**-*o-es*), acc. **-ons* (<**-*o-m-s*), gen.(-abl.) **-ō̆m* (<**-*o-om*), dat.-abl. **-o(i)bh(j)os/-omos*, loc. **-oisu (<**-o-eis-su)*, ins. **-ō̆is* (<**-*o-eis*); as,**wl̥kʷo-es* → **wl̥qōs**. Inanimates have a nom.-voc.-acc in *-*(e/o)*h_2 evolved as -***ā*** in Sanskrit and Slavic, and -***a*** in most dialects. A nom.-voc. (pronominal) ending -***oi*** is also found. See Beekes (1995), Fortson (2004), Clackson (2007).

2. Nominative-vocative animate plural in -***ōs***; as, **wl̥qōs, dómūnōs, wīrṓs.**

3. Accusative animate pural in -*ons*; as, **wl̥qons**, **dómūnons**, **cīwóns**.

4. Nom.-voc.-acc. inanimate plural in -**ā̆**; as, **jugá**, **cīwá**.

5. Genitive plural in -*ōm*; as, **wl̥qōm**, **dómūnōm**, **cīwṓm**, **jugṓm**.

6. Dative and ablative plural in -*obhos*, -*omos*; as, **wl̥qobhos**, **cīwóbhos**.

7. Locative in -*oisu*, PGk. -*oisi*; as, **wīrṓisu**, **dómūnoisu.**

8. Instrumental in -*ō̆is*; **dómūnōis**, **cīwṓis**, **jugṓis**.

	m. ***wlqo-***	*n.* ***jugó-***	*adj.* ***newo-***
NOM.-VOC.	**wl̥qōs**	**jugā́**	**newōs**
ACC.	**wl̥qons**	**jugā́**	**newons**
GEN.	**wl̥qōm**	**jugṓm**	**newōm**
DAT.-ABL.	**wĺ̥qobhos**	**jugóbhos**	**newobhos**
LOC.	**wĺ̥qōisu**	**jugóisu**	**newōisu**
INS.	**wl̥qōis**	**jugṓis**	**newōis**

4.4. THIRD DECLENSION

4.4.1. THIRD DECLENSION PARADIGM

1. Third declension nouns end in **i**, **u** (also **ī**, **ū**) and diphthong. They are found as neuter, masculine or feminine; those in ***ī***, ***ū***, are always feminine.

2. This declension usually corresponds to Latin nouns of the third declension in -*i* (*cf.* Lat. *ciuis*, *ciuis*, or *pars*, *partis*), and of the fourth declension in -*u* (*cf.* Lat. *cornū*, *cornūs*, or *portus*, *portūs*), and to Greek vowel stems in ι, υ, ευ, αυ, ου, ω (*cf.* Gk. ἰχθύς, ἰχθύος, or πόλις, πόλεως).

i/u-Declension Singular Paradigm

	Animate	*Inanimate*
NOM.	-***s***	-∅
VOC.	-∅	
ACC.	-***m***	
GEN.-ABL.	-***s***	
DAT.	-***ei***	
LOC.	-∅/-***i***	
INS.	-ō/-***ē***/-***bhi*** ***(-mi)***	

NOTE. The i/u-stem declension is a variation of the common athematic declension of c-stems. The obliques show weak stems (root ablaut and accent shift) in some nouns.

The proterodynamic paradigm for u-stems is reconstructed in the sg. as nom. **-u-s*, voc. **-eu*, acc. **-u-m*, gen. **-ou-s*, dat. **-eu-i*, loc. **-ēu*, ins. **-u-h₁*; for i-stems nom. **-i-s*, voc. **-ei*, acc. **-i-m*, gen. **-oi-s*, dat. **-ei-i*, loc. **-ēi*, ins. **-i-h₁*. See Beekes (1995).

3. The ***-s*** can indicate nominative and genitive: the distinction is made through the full-grade or extension of the vowel before the declension, see below.

4.4.2. IN I, U

1. Nominative sg. animate in ***-s***; as, **owis**, *sheep*, **noqtis**, *night*, **ghostis**, *guest*, **sūnús**, *son*, **egnis**, *fire*, **pr̥tus**, *ford*, **swē̆dhus**, *custom*; adj. **swādus**, *pleasant.*

2. Vocative singular animate in -Ø, or full grade ***-ei***, ***-eu***; **owi**, **sūnéu/sūneu**, **swēdhu**.

3. Accusative singular animate in ***-m***; as in **owim**, **noqtim**, **ghostim**, **sūnúm**.

4. Nominative-vocative-accusative singular inanimate in -Ø; as in **mari**, *sea*, **kr̥di**, *heart*, **peku**, *cattle*, **deru**, *wood*, **medhu**, *mead*, adj. **swādu**.

5. The genitive singular shows two inflection types:

- Type I genitive singular in ***-eis***, ***-eus***, also ***-ois***, ***-ous***; as, **ghosteis**, **mareis**, **sūnéus**, **swēdheus**, adj. **swādeus**.
- Type II genitive singular in ***-(e)jos***, ***-(e)wos***; as, **owjos**, **noqtjos**, **kr̥dejós**, **swē̆dhewos**, **pékewos**.

NOTE 1. About both types of inflection, a description was made by Wackernagel-Debrunner (*Altindische Grammatik*, 3 vols., 1896/1954), Kuryłowicz (*The inflectional categories of Indo-European*, 1964), Szemerényi (1985), etc. It is so found in Sihler (1995), Adrados–Bernabé–Mendoza (1995-1998).

They are usually said to be derived from a PIH proterodynamic inflection, originally made with a weak form (vowel change and accent shift), from which LIE simplified its root ablaut formation and accentuation; starting from the weak stems, zero grade roots were generalised and accents became static on the root or the suffix (Meier-Brügger, 2003); as, from PIH **pertus, pr̥téus*, remade LIE (without root ablaut) **pr̥tus**, **pr̥tewos**, *v.i.* §4.7.

NOTE 2. Both types are sometimes said to be derived from two 'original' PIH i/u-stem accent-ablaut inflections, later merged into the known paradigms. They would have been a proterokinetic inflection, represented by ***mént-ēi-s*, ***mént-i-m*, ***mn̥t-éi-s*, and an amphikinetic (?) inflection represented by **h₃ew-i-s, ***h₃w-éi-m*, ***h₃w-jo-s*, that gave birth to the LIE types known to us. Sihler (1995): "In any case, the surviving i-stem inflections, which in this view are a sort of Chinese menu selection of items from [proterokinetic] and [amphikinetic], exhibit too much agreement in detail in InIr., Gmc., Ital. and BS to be independent innovations. Accordingly, even if this theory is accepted, the necessary leveling to get to the usual reconstruction must have been complete in the parent language."

A collection of inflected nouns may be found at <http://www.ling.upenn.edu/~rnoyer/courses/51/PIENouns.pdf>; among them, ***noqts*** as consonant stem (p.11), and **mén-ti-s** with gen. **mn̥-téi-s**, which is attested in Goth. *-ti* inflection, Osc. *aiteis* or O.Ind. *mateh*. However, O.Ind. *matyāh* (probably analogic) and Lat. *senatuos* for stems in *-tu* are difficult to explain. It seems that the arguments to consider gen. ***-téis*** and not ***-tjos*** are solid enough.

6. Dative in ***-ei***, usually full ***-ei-ei***, ***-eu-ei***; as, **ghóstejei, pékewei**.

NOTE. For dat. sg. ***-ei***, pure stem or full ending in ***-i***, *cf.* Gk. *-seï* (<**-t-ej-i?*), O.C.S. *kosti*.

7. Locative in ***-ei***, ***-eu***, usually lengthened ***-ēi***, ***-ēu***, ***-ewi***; as, **noqtēi, sunḗu**.

8. Instrumental in ***-ī***, ***-ū*** (<*-h_1), in ***-ē*** (<*-eh_1) following the genitive, or in-***bhi***, -***mi***: **pr̥tū, pr̥téwē**.

NOTE. While the instrumental ending *-h_1 (from Indo-Iranian) follows the athematic declension, the ending ***-mi*** from Balto-Slavic (hence also LIE ***-bhi***) follows the thematic declension, but could have been a later innovation from an old trend to reinterpret athematic as thematic nouns. The older Hitt. *-awet* doesn't clarify the situation.

	Type I			*Type II*		
	f. ***ghosti-***	*m.* ***sūnu-***	*n.****mari-***	*f.* ***noqti-***	*m.* ***pr̥tu-***	*n.* ***peku-***
NOM.	**ghostis**	**sūnús**	**mari**	**noqtis**	**pr̥tus**	**peku**
VOC.	**ghosti**	**sūnéu**	**mari**	**noqtei**	**pr̥tu**	**peku**
ACC.	**ghostim**	**sūnúm**	**mari**	**noqtim**	**pr̥tum**	**peku**
G.-A.	**ghosteis**	**sūnéus**	**mareis**	**noqtjos**	**pr̥téwos**	**pékewos**
DAT.	**ghóstejei**	**sūnéwei**	**márejei**	**nóqtejei**	**pr̥téwei**	**pékewei**
LOC.	**ghostēi**	**sūnḗu**	**marēi**	**noqtēi**	**pr̥tḗu**	**pékewi**
INS.	**ghostī**	**sūnewē**	**marī**	**noqtī**	**pr̥téwē**	**pekū**

NOTE. For information on the alternative reconstruction **mari/mori**, *sea*, see Appendix II *Formal Aspects*.

THE STRONG TYPE

Its inflection is similar to the consonant stems, and they have no alternating vowels before the declension; **ī** and **ū** are substituted before vowel by ***-ij***, ***-uw***. They are always feminine, and they cannot be inanimates nor adjectives. They are mostly PIE roots (in **-iH*, **-uH*), and found mainly in Indo-Iranian.

NOTE. This inflection is usually classified within the i/u-stems, for nouns where an i precedes the final laryngeal, i.e. in **-i(e)H-* (It is not always clear when it comes from *-h_1 and when from *-h_2; they were probably completely parallel in LIE and merged). The old declension shows nom. **-iH*, acc. **-ieH-m*, gen. **-iH-os*: in Sanskrit **-iH* became generalised, showing gen. *-ías*, while Slavic and Germanic show **-jā-** < **-jəH*. The **-uH* stems are completely parallel with those in *-iH; *cf.* for *'tongue'*, a general LIE **dn̥ghwā**, but also found as PII ***dn̥ghūs***. See Beekes (1995), Adrados–Bernabé–Mendoza (1995-1998).

Only NWIE forms and declension is followed here (***wl̥qī-***, *she-wolf*, is apparently found in Celtic, apart from Indo-Iranian).

	f. ***bhrū-***	*f.* ***sū-***	*f.* ***dhī-***	*f.* ***wl̥qī-***
NOM.	**bhrūs**	**sūs**	**dhīs**	**wl̥qīs**
VOC.	**bhrū**	**sū**	**dhī**	**wl̥qī**
ACC.	**bhrūm**	**sūm**	**dhīm**	**wĺ̥qīm**
GEN.-ABL.	**bhruwā́s**	**suwā́s**	**dhijā́s**	**wl̥qijā́s**
DAT.	**bhruwéi**	**suwéi**	**dhijéi**	**wl̥qijéi**
LOC.	**bhruwí**	**suwí**	**dhijí**	**wl̥qijí**
INS.	**bhrūbhí**	**sūbhí**	**dhībhí**	**wl̥qībhí**

4.4.3. IN DIPHTHONG

1. There are long diphthongs **āu**, **ēu**, **ōu**, **ēi**, which sometimes present short vowels.

NOTE. Other stems that follow this declension in the attested dialects, in **ā**, **ē**, **ō**, are probably remains of older diphthongs. Therefore, these can all be classified as diphthong endings, because the original stems were formed as diphthongs in the language history.

Its paradigm is reconstructed for those in *-u* as **-ē/ōus(s)*, acc. **-e/ou-m*, gen. **-u-os*, and for those in *-i* as nom. **-oi*, **-is*, acc. **-oi-m*, gen. **-i-os*. Beekes (1995). It is not a common declension, and IE nouns proper included in it are found inflected as follows: strong forms with nom. **-s*, voc. **-Ø*, acc. **-m*, loc. **-i*; weak forms with gen.-abl. **-és*, dat. **-éi*, ins. **-éh_1*.

	m.f. ***cōu-***	*m.* ***djēu-***	*f.* ***nāu-***
NOM.	**cōus**	**djēus**	**nāus**
VOC.	**cou**	**djeu**	**nāu**
ACC.	**cōm**	**djēm/dijḗm**	**nāum**
GEN.-ABL.	**cous**	**diwós**	**nāwós**
DAT.	**cowéi**	**diwéi**	**nāwéi**
LOC.	**cowi**	**djewi/*diwí***	**nāwí**
INS.	**cowḗ**	**diwḗ**	**nāwḗ**

NOTE. An expected accent-ablaut reconstruction for **nāu**- would be strong **nāu** <**neh$_2$u-*, weak **nau**-<**nh$_2$u-* or rather **n°h$_2$u-*; however, forms in **nāu**- are found in Vedic and Ancient Greek dialects throughout the whole paradigm, possibly indicating older strong **noh$_2$u-* and weak **neh$_2$u-*, respectively. See Meier-Brügger (2003) for more on this question.

In zero-grade genitives there are forms with ***-i-*** or ***-ij-***, ***-u-*** or ***-uw-***.

NOTE 1. Some secondary formations – especially found in Greek – are so declined, in ***-eus***, ***-ewos*** as in Av. *bāzāus*, Arm.,Gk. *Basileus*, possibly from PIE **-āus** (Perpillou, 1973) but Beekes (2007) considers it Pre-Greek.

NOTE 2. Stang's law governs the word-final sequences of a vowel + semivowel ***j*** or ***w*** + nasal, simplified in PIE so that semivowels are dropped, with compensatory lengthening of a preceding vowel, i.e. VJM → V̄M; as, ***djēm***, not **djewm̥*; ***cōm***, not **gʷowm̥*, ***cōns***, not **gʷowns̥*, etc. A similar trend is found with laryngeals, *VJh$_2$m > V̄M; as, ***sūm***, also attested as ***suwm̥***, etc.

4.4.4. THE PLURAL IN THE THIRD AND FOURTH DECLENSION

1. The following table depicts the general plural system of the fourth declension.

i/u- and Consonant-Declension Plural Paradigm

	Animate	*Inanimate*
NOM.-VOC.	***-es***	***-ă̄***
ACC.	***-ns***	
GEN.	***-ŏ̄m/-ēm***	
DAT.-ABL.	***-bhos (-mos)***	
LOC.	***-su (-si)***	
INS.	***-bhis (-mis)***	

NOTE. An older plural paradigm for u-stems is reconstructed as nom.-voc. **-eu-es*, acc. **-u-ns*, gen.-abl. **-eu-om*, dat. **-u-bhos*, **-u-mos* (<***-u-mus?*), loc.* *-u-su*, ins. **-u-bhis*, **-u-mis* (<***-u-bhi?*). See Beekes (1995), Fortson (2004).

2. Unlike in the singular, in which only some nominatives have an ***-s***, in nom.-voc. plural the ***-s*** is general, and there is always one fix-grade vowel, **e**. So, the opposition singular-plural in ***-s/-es*** is actually **∅/e**.

3. The nom.-voc. plural animate is made in ***-es***, in full-grade ***-ei-es*** for **i**, ***-eu-es*** for **u**, and ***-ijes***, ***-uwes***, for **ī**, **ū**; as **ówejes**, **sūnewes**, **pŕtewes**, **bhruwes**.

4. The accusative plural animate is in ***-ns***: **owins**, **sūnúns**, **pr̥tuns**, **cōns**.

5. The nom.-voc. acc. plural inanimate in ***-a***: **pekwa**, **marja**, **swādwa**.

NOTE. The athematic inanimate plural ending commonly represented by -***a*** corresponds to an older *collective* *-h_2, which sometimes lengthened the preceding vowel (**i** or **u**) instead.

6. Gen. pl. in -***om*** (type I usually in full -***ei-om***, -***eu-om***); as, **ghóstejom**, **pr̥twom**.

NOTE. The -***m*** of the acc. sg. animate, nom.-acc.-voc. sg. inanimate and this case could sometimes be confused. It was often disambiguated with the vocalic grade of the genitive, full or lengthened, as the singular is always Ø.

7. For the obliques plural, *cf.* dat.-abl. **ówibhos**, **sūnubhos**, **nóqtibhos**; loc. **sūnusu**, **nóqtisu**, ins. **sūnubhis**, **ówibhis**, **máribhis**.

	Type I		*Type II*		*Diphth.*
	f. ***ghosti-***	*m.* ***sūnu-***	*f.* ***noqti-***	*n.* ***peku-***	*m.* ***cou-***
NOM.-VOC.	**ghóstejes**	**sūnewes**	**nóqtejes**	**pekwa**	**cowes**
ACC.	**ghostins**	**sūnúns**	**noqtins**	**pekwa**	**cōns**
GEN.	**ghóstejom**	**sūnewom**	**noqtjom**	**pekwom**	**cowom**
DAT.-ABL.	**ghóstibhos**	**sūnubhos**	**nóqtibhos**	**pékubhos**	**coubhos**
LOC.	**ghóstisu**	**sūnusu**	**nóqtisu**	**pékusu**	**cousu**
INS.	**ghóstibhis**	**sūnubhis**	**nóqtibhis**	**pékubhis**	**coubhis**

4.5. FOURTH DECLENSION

4.5.1. FOURTH DECLENSION PARADIGM

1. The stem of nouns of the second declension ends in consonant or resonant, i.e. -***n***, -***r***, -***s***, occlusive (especially -***t***), and rarely -***l***, -***m***. The inflection of animates is essentially the same as that of the second or thematic declension.

2. Nouns of the fourth declension correspond to Latin nouns of first declension in *-r* (*cf.* Lat. *magister, magistrī*), and third declension in consonant (*cf.* Lat. *prīnceps, prīncipis, cōnāmen, cōnāminis,* etc.), and to the Ancient Greek consonant stems declension (*cf.* Gk. πατὴρ, πατρὸς, τάπης, τάπητος, ἡγεμών, ἡγεμόνος, etc.).

The nominative ending is -***s*** (with occlusive, -***m***, -***l***), but there is also a nominative sg. with pure stem vowel (desinence -Ø and lengthened ending vowel), so that the full-grade vocative is differentiated. And there is no confusion in nom./gen., as -***s*** has a different vowel grade (nom. -***s***, gen. -***és*** or -***os***).

Consonant-Declension Singular Paradigm

	*Occlusive, **-m, -l***	***-r, -n, -s***
NOM.	***-s***	-∅ *(long vowel)*
ACC.	***-m̥***	
VOC.	-∅	-∅ *(full grade)*
GEN.-	***-es/-os***	
DAT.	***-ei***	
LOC.	***-i/-∅***	
INS.	***-ē/-bhi (-mi)***	

NOTE. The so-called *common, basic* or *athematic* paradigm, the hypothetically oldest attainable PIE noun declension system, is reconstructed in the singular as nom. *-*s*, *-∅, voc. *-∅, acc. *-*m*, gen.-abl. *-*(e/o)s*, dat. *-*ei*, loc. *-*i*, *-∅, ins. *-*(e)h₁*. See Meier-Brügger (2003), Fortson (2004). This paradigm was originally common to the i/u-stems, and it was probably inherited (and innovated) by the first and second declensions.

Besides the usual loc. ending -*i* there was also the bare stem without ending. Such unmarked ('flat') locatives are widely encountered in modern languages (*cf.* Eng. *next door*, *home*), and in PIE they are well-attested in n-stems, but are rare in other consonant stems.

3. Inanimates have pure vowel stems with different vowel grades. In nouns there should be no confusion at all, as they are different words, but neuter adjectives could be mistaken in nominative or vocative animate. Distinction is thus obtained with vocalism, as in animate ***-ōn*** vs. inanimate ***-on***, animate ***-ēs*** vs. inanimate ***-es*** (neuter nouns in **-*s*** show ***-os***).

4.5.2. IN OCCLUSIVE, M, L

1. Nominative sg. animate in -***s***; as, **pods**, *foot*, **regs**, *king*, **preks**, *plea*, **ghjems**, winter, **nepēts**, *grandson*, adj. **bélowents**, *strong*.

NOTE. The nom. of some stems are often reconstructed with a long vowel; as, **pōds*, **rēgs*, **prēks*. Such forms are found in the different languages showing ablaut with lengthened grade; as, *ō/o* in Goth. *fotus*, Gk. *pód-a*, and *ē/e* in Lat. *pēs*, *pedis*. It is usually interpreted that these are levelled forms from an original **o/e** opposition, so the long vowel vs. short vowel becomes unnecessary for the parent language. Also, sometimes it is doubted whether the original nominative had an s, *cf.* **pōd(s)* in Beekes (1995), because all attested languages show a lengthened vowel with either the final occlusive or -*s*, but not with both (*cf.* Skt. *pā́t*, which could derive from **ō*, **ē*, or **o*, Dor. Gk. *pōs*, Lat. *pēs*), what suggests a compensatory lengthening with the loss of a final consonant cluster, that was reinterpreted as the original stem in declension (e.g. to form the accusative in some languages), i.e **pods** → **pōs* → **pōds* (Sihler 1995).

2. Accusative singular animate in ***-m̥***; as, **podm̥, regm̥, ghjemm̥, népētm̥, bélowentm̥**.

NOTE. Forms in **m** make the accusative by lengthening the root vowel, *Vmm > *V̄m, as a consequence of Stang's Law, *v.s.* §4.4.2; as, nom. **doms*, *'house'*, acc. **dōm* (<**dom-m̥*), *cf.* Arm. *tun* or Gk. *δῶ*, or nom. **dhghōm*, *'earth'*, acc. **dhghōm* (<**dhghom-m̥*), *cf.* Skt. *kṣām*. Root nouns like these ones are quite old in the language history, and are therefore rare in LIE, which had replaced them for newer derived nouns; as, **domos**, *house*, or **dhghm̥ós**, *earth*.

3. Vocative singular animate in -Ø; as, **pod, reg, bélowent**.

4. The nom.-voc.-acc. singular inanimate in -Ø; as **sal**, *salt*, part. **bheront**.

5. Genitive singular in ***-os***, ***-es***; as, **pedós, rēgos, bhurghos, ghimós, salós, népotos, bélowentos, bhérontos**.

NOTE. Older root nouns made the genitive-ablative often in ***-s***, ***-é/ós***, i.e. ablaut and accent on stem vowel; as, for strong nom. **doms*, weak gen. **dems* or **dmés/dmós*, for strong nom. **dhghōm*, gen. **dhghmés/*dhghmós* or (possibly already in the proto-language) metathesised **ghdhmés/*ghdhmós*. They appear in IEDs mainly frozen in compounds (*cf.* ***dems-*** in **demspots**), because most of them were reinterpreted. On forms like **dmés* or **pdós*, "[u]nsurprisingly, such forms have been largely eliminated from the attested paradigms." Sihler (1995). For the original lengthened grade ***rēgos/rēges***, see §4.7.

6. Dative singular in ***-ei***: **pedei, rēgei, bhérontei**.

7. Locative singular in ***-i***: **podi, regi, bélowenti**.

	m. ***pod-***	*f.* ***prek-***	*n.* ***bheront-***
NOM.	**pods**	**preks**	**bheront**
VOC.	**pod**	**prek**	**bheront**
ACC.	**podm̥**	**prekm̥**	**bheront**
GEN.-ABL.	**pedós**	**prēkos**	**bhérontos**
DAT.	**pedéi**	**prēkei**	**bhérontei**
LOC.	**pedí**	**preki**	**bhéronti**
INS.	**pedbhí**	**prēkbhi**	**bhérontbhi**

4.5.3. IN R, N, S

1. Nominative singular animate in -Ø with lengthened vowel; as in **mātḗr** (also **mā́tēr**), *mother*, **elōr**, *swan*, **kwōn**, *dog*, **osēn**, *autumn*, **ōs**, *mouth*, **mōs**, *character*, **spēs**, *hope*, adj. **juwōn**, *young*, **n̥mātōr**, *motherless*.

NOTE. The lengthening of the predeclensional vowel in stems in **r**, **n** and **s** stems has been explained (Szemerényi's Law) as a consequence of an older (regular PIE) nom. **-s** ending; as, ***ph₂tér-s→*ph₂tḗr*, ***kwon-s→*kwōn*, etc.

Common s-stems without lengthening include neuter stems (which are not usually marked in the nominative); as, **opos**, *work*, **nebhos**, *cloud*, etc.

Adjectives usually end in **-es**; as, **sugenḗs**, *well-born, of good stock* (*cf.* Gk. *eugenḗs*, O.Ind. *sujanāḥ*).

2. Accusative sg. animate in ***-m***; as in **māterm̥**, **élorm̥**, **kwonm̥**, **óposm̥**, **júwonm̥**.

3. Voc. sg. animate in -Ø with full vowel; as **mātér**, **élor**, **kúon**, **juwon**, **opos**, **sugenés**.

4. The nom.-acc.-voc. singular inanimate in -Ø; as in **nōmn̥**, *name*, **genos**, *kin*.

The adjectives in **-s** have a neuter in ***-es***; as, **sugenés**.

5. Genitive singular in ***-os***, usually with an ***e***, not an ***o***, as the final stem vowel; as, **éleros**, **nómenos**, **bhugenos**, **júwenos**, **nébhesos**, **génesos**, **ópesos**, **ēsos, spēsos**; but *cf.* zero-grade in old stems, as **mātrós**, **kunós**, and also ***o***, as **mosós**.

NOTE. Athematic nouns made the genitive in ***-es***, ***-os***; even though some reconstruct only one gen. ending for an 'original' paradigm, we prefer to write always ***-ós*** for pragmatic reasons; as, **kunós** instead of ***kunés***. Examples of an apparently old, so-called *static* inflection, is found in PII nom. ***mā-tr***, gen. ***mā-tr-s***, acc. pl. ***mā-tr-ns***; remains of this rare paradigm are also found in Gmc. dialects for 'father' in gen. ***patŕs***.

6. Dative singular in ***-ei***, **mātréi**, **élerei**, **kunei**, **júwenei**, **ópesei**, **sugenesei**.

7. Locative singular in ***-i***: **māteri**, **éleri**, **kuni**, **júweni**, **ópesi**, **sugenesi**.

8. Instrumental singular in ***-ē*** or ***-bhi***/***-mi***: **mātr̥bhí**, **élerbhi**, **patr̥bhí**, **kunbhí**, **júwenbhi**, **ópesbhi**, **sugenesbhi**.

	m. ***kwon-***	*f.* ***pater-***	*n.* ***genes-***	*n.* ***nomṇ-***	*adj.****sugenes-***
NOM.	**kwōn**	**patḗr**	**genos**	**nōmṇ**	**sugenḗs**
VOC.	**kwon**	**patér**	**genos**	**nōmṇ**	**sugenés**
ACC.	**kwonṃ**	**paterṃ**	**genos**	**nōmṇ**	**sugenesṃ**
G.-A.	**kunós**	**patrós**	**génesos**	**nómenos**	**sugeneses**
DAT.	**kunéi**	**patréi**	**génesei**	**nómenei**	**sugenesei**
LOC.	**kuní**	**pateri**	**génesi**	**nómēn**	**sugenesi**
INS.	**kwṇbhí**	**patṛbhí**	**génesbhi**	**nómenbhi**	**sugenesbhi**

NOTE. "Where the derivation is transparent, neut. *s*-stem nouns were built to the tonic e-grades of verb roots. The stem had the form **-os* in the (endingless) nom./acc.sg., **-ōs<**-*osH_2 in the nom./acc.pl; the stem of the remaining cases and numbers was an invariant **-es-*". Sihler (1995), who further reconstructs the inflected forms of **genos**, with root accent throughout the paradigm.

4.5.4. THE PLURAL IN THE FOURTH DECLENSION

With a paradigm common to the third declension, here are some inflected examples.

	m. ***pod-***	*f.* ***prek-***	*m.* ***kwon-***	*f.* ***māter-***	*n.* ***genes-***
N.-V.	**podes**	**prekes**	**kwones**	**māteres**	**génesa**
ACC.	**podṇs**	**prekṇs**	**kwonṇs**	**māterṇs**	**génesa**
GEN.	**pedóm**	**prēkom**	**kunóm**	**mātróm**	**génesom**
D.-A.	**pedbhós**	**prēkbhos**	**kwṇbhós**	**mātṛbhós**	**génesbhos**
LOC.	**pedsó**	**prēksu**	**kwṇsú**	**mātṛsú**	**génesu**
INS.	**pedbhí**	**prēkbhi**	**kwṇbhí**	**mātṛbhís**	**génesbhis**

NOTE. The plural of adj. **ṇmātōr**, *motherless*, consists of masc./fem. nom. **ṇmā́tores**, neu. nom-voc.-acc. **ṇmā́tora** gen. **ṇmatróm**, etc.

4.6. VARIABLE NOUNS

4.6.1. Many nouns vary in declension, and they are called *heteroclites.*

4.6.2. Heteroclitic forms are isolated and archaic, given only in inanimates, as remains of an older system, well attested in Anatolian.

4.6.3. They consist of one form to mark the nom.-acc.-voc, and another for the obliques, usually ***r/(e)n***; as, **bhemṛ/bhémenos**, *thigh*, **ghēsṛ/ghésenos**, *hand*, **gutr̥/gútenos**, *throat*, **kowr̥/kówenos**, *cavern*, **ūdhr̥/ū́dhenos**, *udder*, **wedhr̥/wédhenos**, *weapon*, etc.

4.6.4. Different paradigms are also attested:

- Opposition ***r/(e)n-*** (lengthened ending); as, **jeqr̥/jeqóneros**, *liver*,

NOTE. For PIE **jeqr̥**, *cf.* Ved. *yákr̥t*, Gk. *hēpar*, Lat. *iecur*, Av. *yākarə*, and compare its Obl. Skt. *yakn-ás*, Gk. *hḗpat-os<*hēpn̥t-*, Lat. *iecinoris*.

- Alternating with other suffixes; as, **gheimr̥/gheims/ghjems**, *winter*, **skīwr̥/kīwōn/skinōn**, *shinbone*, later *column*, **wēsr̥/wēsn̥tós**, *spring*, **wedr̥/wédenos/wodā**, *water*, **swepr̥/swopnos**, *dream*.
- Formed from the consonant **r** or **n** of the heteroclite; as, **pāwr̥/pūr/puōn**, *fire*, **nomr̥/nómeros/nómenos**, *precision, number*, Gk. *skōr* (gen. *skatos*), Hitt. *šakkar* (gen. *šaknaš*), Lat. *-scerda*, *"shit"*.

4.6.5. The *heteroclites* follow the form of the genitive singular when forming the obliques. That is so in accent-ablaut and in the lengthening before declension.

4.7. INFLECTION TYPES

1. While in o-stems and generally in a-stems there are generally no accent-ablaut changes, within the c-stems it is possible to distinguish different old accent-ablaut patterns, which make this a more complicated declension.

NOTE. Fortson (2004): "To understand athematic nomina inflection, one must distinguish between the so-called strong and weak cases. The strong cases differ from the weak cases typically in where the accent is located and which morpheme is in the full grade; most commonly, the full grade and the accent shift rightward in the weak cases, comparable to the shift seen in most athematic verbs."

Fortunately it is the least productive of all declensions (i.e. it is infrequent in new nouns), and most stems that included accent-ablaut patterns were progressively substituted for other stems in LIE.

NOTE. Fortson (2004): "All athematic nouns consisted of three parts: root, suffix, and ending. (...) As already alluded to, these three morphemes could each show up in different ablaut grades depending principally on the position of the accent, which could fall on any of the three. According to the standard theory, in any given case-form of an athematic noun the unstressed morphemes appeared in the zero-grade, while the stressed morphemes were in a grade "stronger" than zero-grade- that is, one with a vowel, generally *e*, but also *o*."

2. We can distinguish at least two kinds of inflections in PIE, which differ in ablaut and accent. These types are called hysterodynamic (*dynamis* 'accent';

hystero- 'more toward the back') and proterodynamic (*protero-* 'more toward the front). In these types the accent shifts rightward in the weak cases from its position in the strong cases (Beekes 1995).

NOTE. Other inflection pattens are apparently inherited from the parent language – the definition, pattern and the very existence of some of them is still debated –, but they are usually not found in IEDs, if not in frozen remains of the older system. Therefore, it is not interesting to complicate the *regular* athematic system further, and we will treat such remains as irregularities of a common LIE system. For more information, see below.

3. The neuters followed the proterodynamic inflection, and do not have nom. ***-s***, acc. ***-m***. Some of the masculine-feminine nouns follow the proterodynamic inflection too.

4. In hysterodynamic nouns, the suffix is accented in the strong cases, the ending in the weak. So e.g. in the word for 'father', we have strong nom. sg. **pa-tḗr** s, acc. sg. **patér-m̥**, but weak gen. **pa-tr-és**.

NOTE. Fortson (2004): "Root nouns with mobile accent (on the root in the strong cases, on the endings in the weak cases) are often considered as belonging to this type, though the fit is not exact: they have full grade or lengthened grade of the root in the strong cases and full grade of the ending in the weak cases". For pragmatic purposes, we will include nouns formed with only a root and ending among hysterodynamics, too. The most common type has o-grade of the root in strong cases, and e-grade in the weak cases. So e.g. for foot, nom. **pods**, acc. **pedós**.

In the so-called amphikinetic nouns, the root is also accented in the strong cases, the ending in the weak, and the suffix is typically in the lengthened o-grade (rather than the expected zero-grade) in the nominative singular, and ordinary o-grade in the accusative singular. The old word for *dawn* (found in PGk and PII) belongs here; ***áus-ōs*** (c. Gk. *aúōs*), acc. sg. ***áus-os-m̥*** (Ved. *uṣasam*), gen. ***us-s-és*** (Ved. usás).

5. In proterodynamic nouns, the root is in the full grade and accented in the strong cases, and both accent and full grade shift to the suffix in the weak cases.

NOTE. According to Fortson (2004): "Most i- and u-stems in Sanskrit appear to have been proterokinetic, such as Ved. nomin. *matís* 'thought', accus. *matím*, genit. *mates*, from PIE **mén-ti-s*, **mén-ti-m*, **mn̥-téi-s*." Vedic had generalised the zero-grade of the root throughout the paradigm, as the other languages; hence LIE **mn̥tis**, **mn̥téis**. The same could be said of the remodelling of old **pertus*, **pr̥téus*, remade **pr̥tus**, **pr̥tewos**.

As we have seen, some i/u-stems behave in parallel to those athematic nouns, showing zero-grade ending **-i-**, **-u-** in strong cases (as nom. ***-i-s***, ***-u-s***, acc. ***-i-m***, ***-u-m***, and full-grade ***-ei-***, ***-eu-*** in weak cases (nom. ***-ei-s***, ***-ei-os***, ***-eu-s***, ***-eu-os***). By the time of LIE these nouns do not usually show ablaut in their root syllable. Common examples are found of verbal abstract nouns in ***-ti-***, one of the most common groups of i-stems; also common were abstract nouns in ***-tu-***, although this usually appears in post-LIE infinitives.

Remodellings like these led to a new class of proterodynamics that descriptively had o-grade of the root in the strong cases and zero-grade in the weak. Among animate nouns of this type, the best attested is the word for 'dog', nom. **kwōn**, acc. **kwōn-m̥**, gen. **kun-ós** (or **kun-és**).

EXCURSUS: NOMINAL ACCENT-ABLAUT PATTERNS

While nominal accent-ablaut patterns are very interesting for internal reconstruction, they remain a marginal issue for the largely thematic Late Indo-European language, and more so for IEDs. The state of the art about such patterns is summed up in a recent article by Kloekhorst at <http://www.kloekhorst.nl/KloekhorstIENominalAblautPatterns.pdf>.

The author exposes results based on testimonies of Hittite, in which he is a renowned expert. Accent-ablaut paradigms can be reconstructed according to two systems, Leiden and Erlangen, which correspond to two different times, which we could roughly assign to PIH and (early) LIE respectively. He explains the transformations from one system to the other, from which a system of two models (static and dynamic) turns into a system of four (static, proterodynamic, hysterodynamic, and resulting from analogical changes, amphidynamic).

The system of four models of Erlangen is explained by Frazier in the following link, with examples in p. 112: <http://roa.rutgers.edu/files/819-0406/819-FRAZIER-0-0.PDF> and summed up in <http://www.unc.edu/~melfraz/ling/frazier-UCLA-handout.pdf>.

The Erlangen system is therefore nearer to the Late Indo-European system, because the reconstructed patterns are more recent. However, in some cases the reconstructed forms – since they look for a logical agreement with Anatolian – are clearly different from non-Anatolian results; as e.g. the oblique cases of _*nebhos_ – see note 34 in Kloekhorst's article and Clackson (2007, p. 94).

About root nouns of the type Lat. *rex*, *lux*, *pēs*, etc., the problem gets more complicated. *A priori* there are only two possibilities about the distribution of the tone: either static (with columnar accent on the root), or kinetic/dynamic, with accent on the root in the strong forms, and on the ending in the weak forms. However, to make grades and vowel ablaut fit into common patterns is more difficult (see Appendix III.1 for some examples).

Kloekhorst shows some problems in the ablaut models of root nouns. Examples are:

- The word for 'foot', which is usually reconstructed as having a static paradigm, _*pṓd-s_, _*pód-m_, _*péd-s_, seems to be mobile in Hittite: acc.pl. *pāduš* < _*pód-ms_ vs. gen.pl. *patān* < _*pd-óm_.

- Av. *vāxs* shows gen. *vacō*, but Old Indian and Latin show systematically lengthened grade (gen. O.Ind. *vācáh*, Lat. *uōcis*); for example Brugmann's Law, if applicable, should apply to O.Ind. and Av. See <http://www.fas.harvard.edu/~iranian/Avesta/a14_lesson11.pdf>, p.4 for Avestan grammar. Hence it could be that O.Ind. and Av. alternate with different ablauts.
- The inflection of **gʷow* is static in Old Indian, but dynamic in Greek.
- Inflection of **ker(d)* is dynamic in O.Ind., but is the only example of static inflection in Greek, so this could correspond to an older model.
- The position of the accent in weak cases of **kwon* are not coincident in Gk. and O.Ind.
- *suH and **dieH* show alternating forms in O.Ind.
- The reconstruction of **j(e)uH* needs **juHs-* in Sanskrit and Lithuanian, but **jeuHs-* in Slavic (de Vaan).
- Also, Greek has lost the ablaut changes in those monosyllabics (e.g. *χείρ*); Latin has merged diphthongs and has lost the original ablaut patterns; O.Ind. has merged vocalic ablaut **e/o* into *a*; in Hittite, root nouns are limited to some words in transition to other inflection types (*pat*, *gʷau*, *siw-at*, *nekuz*, *karaz*, *tekan*, *kess-ar*, *gim(a)-*, *happar-*, *tuekk-*). Frequently root nouns of one language are only found as derived nouns in others, and because of that coincidences are scarce.

Paul Kiparsky helps clarify the problem with the following recent article <http://www.stanford.edu/~kiparsky/Papers/ucla_IE_09.submitted.new.pdf>, although in p.7 he exposes the difficulties of fitting the attested results with the created models. In section d) p. 12 of this article, Kiparsky resorts to the artifice of 'accented morphemes' to explain the brief **o* of O.Ind. dat. *gáve*. It is possibly derived from weak form **gʷew*.

Clackson (2007) proposes a different alternating paradigm; in p.86 he reconstructs **pods*, gen. **peds.*, while Kloekhorst in the note of p. 3 proposes **pōds/peds*. In Greek and Old Indian, these nouns aren't acrostatic.

About Lat. *rex*, in Latin, Celtic, and Old Indian, the declension of this word shows systematically lengthened grade – in Latin letter *x* is considered as two consonants, so the syllable is in every case long. For results in Celtic, see p. 19 in the article <http://www.univie.ac.at/indogermanistik/download/Stifter/oldcelt2008_1_general.pdf>

Fort he reconstruction of this root noun there are, a priori, at least four possibilities:

a) Nom. sg. **Hregs* / gen. **Hrgós*, as Gk. nom. ἀνήρ <**Hner-s* gen. ἀνδρός<**Hnrós*. It seems that the Vedic (Sharfe) Celtic (*McCone*) words for king and queen point to that form.

b) Nom. sg. **Hregs* / gen. **rēgos*, as Gk. κῆρ, where the weak form is not **Hr̥g*, but **reHg-*.

NOTE. It has been assumed that it is acrostatic, with alternating full/long, based on:

- The attested nominative could be analogical in relation to the weak forms.
- The long vowel appears systematically in the attested languages.
- The derived form in O.Ind. *rājan* has lengthened grade, when long grade was expected (there could be a special form in Gk. *arēgṓn*). *Cf.* Av. bərəzi-*rāz* with Osc. *meddiss* (zero-grade).

c) Nom sg. **rēgs*, gen. **rēgós*, taking as model O.Ind. *vac* (if the long vowel is not derived from Brugmann's Law), or *náuh*.

d) Nom sg. **rēgs*, gen. **regós*, taking as model Av. *vac*, or O.Ind. *ap*. In this case we should have to explain the difference in results within Old Indian as a result of later analogies with *nau*.

It is therefore quite difficult to obtain unequivocal reconstructions for these old athematic root nouns, so the forms reconstructed are usually just one possibility of the alternating patterns.

Unfortunately it often happens that we can demonstrate one form and the opposite at the same time. Fernando López-Menchero has followed these criteria in the reconstruction of the LIE lexicon in Appendix II, according to the available data on LIE dialects:

Acrostatic:

- **gʷow-*, Lat. *Bōs* o/e, maybe o/o
- **knouk-*, Lat. *Nux* o/e
- **pod-*, Lat. *Pēs* o/e
- **woq-*, Lat. *Vox* o/e AK maybe dynamic of the type ō/o – ō/ō (a.i.) or maybe ō/e (Avestan), or o/o (Greek)

Dynamic:

- **djeHw-*, Lat. *Diēs* e/∅
- **(H)reHj-*, Lat. *Rēs* e/∅
- **weik-*, Lat. *Vīcus* e/∅
- **leuk-*, Lat. *Lux* e/∅

- **deuk-*, Lat. *Dūx* e/∅
- **sneich-*, Lat. *Nix* e/∅
- **ghjems-*, Lat. *Hiems* e/∅
- **weis-*, Lat. *Vīs* e/∅ (also **wejos/es*)

Special dynamics:

- **āp/ap-*, ā/a
- **kwon-*, Lat. *Canis* o/∅
- **naHw-*, Lat. *Nāuis* ā/ā
- **dheghom-*, Lat. *Humus* e-o/∅-∅
- **mōs/mosós*, Lat. *Mōs* ō/o (or maybe ō/ō?)

Without reference – these nouns are supposedly full/lengthened within an acrostatic system, hence they are all put into the same group (even though Lat. *prex* is not inflected with a long vowel):

- **leg-* Lat. *Lex*
- **reg-* Lat. *Rex*
- **prek-* Lat. *Prex*
- **pag-* Lat. *Pax*
- **H_3ops* (*ēpos*) – the laryngeal does not colour the following vowel (Eichner's Law)
- **ros*, *rēsos*, Lat. *Rōs* (*H_3ops* and *ros* could be inflected like *mōs* and *vice versa*)
- **jeus* could be inflected on the basis of **jūs*; on the other hand, it is commonly reconstructed meus as **mūs<*muHs*, and **sūs<*suHs*, so the weak forms would have a long **ū* (Kiparsky in p. 16 shows the same paradigm with **séuh-nu-s*, **suh-nú-s*).

Some stems that only appear dialectally as root nouns have been transferred to their general o-stem or i-stem declension:

**kerd-* 'heart', **mems-* 'meat', **meHns-* 'month', **nas* 'nose', **ner* 'man', **noqt-* 'night'; stems in **os/es*, **puwos* 'pus, rottenness' and **bhāos* 'light' and 'speech'. **sal*, **dont* (assimilated to a root noun) and **weis* 'strength' are reconstructed as alternating.

g^wen- has been transferred to the feminine declension. For its consideration as root noun, see

<http://www.people.fas.harvard.edu/~jasanoff/pdf/Old%20Irish%20be_.pdf>, by Jasanoff.

4.8. NUMBER DEVELOPMENTS: THE DUAL

4.7.1. While singular and plural are relatively fixed values, the dual has proven to be unstable; it is found in Ind.-Ira., Gk., BSl. and Cel.

NOTE. Generally speaking, the rise and decline of the dual may be directly investigated in individual IE languages, e.g. in Greek, in which the dual is a fixed component of the language, while it is missing altogether in Ionic and Lesbian. The origins of the dual might be found in two word types: the personal pronoun and terms for paired body parts (as 'ears', 'eyes', 'breasts', etc.). It is uncertain whether the dual was an old category that gradually disappeared, or more likely a recent (Late Indo-European) development that didn't reach all IE dialects. See Meier-Brügger (2003).

4.7.2. The formations vary depending on the stems.

1. The nominative-accusative-vocative is made:

- Stems in **a**: in -***āi*** for **ā**; in -***ī*** for **ja/ī**.
- Stems in **o**: Animates in -***ōu*** (alternating -***ō***/-***ōu***); inanimates in -***oi***.
- Stems in **i**, **u**: Animates and inanimates in -***ī***, -***ū***.
- Consonant stems: in -***e*** (not general).

NOTE. The endings are usually summed up as a common PIE *-$h_1(e)$*, *-$(i)h_1$*. See Fortson (2004).

2. The obliques were still less generalised, the system being reconstructed as follows:

- Genitive in -***ous***,
- Dative-ablative in -***bhos***/-***mos***,
- Locative in -***ou***,
- Instrumental in -***bhis***/-***mis***.

5. ADJECTIVES

5.1. INFLECTION OF ADJECTIVES

5.1.1. In Proto-Indo-European, the noun could be determined in three different ways: with another noun, as in *stone wall*; with a noun in genitive, as in *the father's house*; or with an adjective, as in *paternal love*. The adjective corresponds to the third way, i.e., to that kind of words – possibly derived from older genitives – that are declined to make it agree in case, gender and number with the noun they define.

5.1.2. The adjective is from the older stages like a noun, and even today Indo-European languages have the possibility to make an adjective a noun (as *English*), or a noun an adjective (*stone wall*). Furthermore, some words are nouns and adjectives as well: **wersis**, *male,* can be the subject of a verb (i.e., a noun), and can determine a noun.

Most stems and suffixes are actually indifferent to the opposition noun/adjective. Their inflection is common, too, and differences are usually secondary. This is the reason why we have already studied the adjective declensions; they follow the same inflection as nouns.

5.1.3. However, since the oldest reconstructible PIE language there were nouns different from adjectives, as **wl̥qos**, *wolf,* or **pods**, *foot,* and adjectives different from nouns, as **rudhrós**, *red*, **solwos**, *whole*. Nouns could, in turn, be used as adjectives, and adjectives be nominalised.

NOTE. Noun has a wide sense in PIE, for many nouns may be used both adjectivally and substantivally, and the classification of nouns by inflectional type is independent of whether they are substantives or adjectives. In this book the terms 'noun' and 'nominal' are then to be interpreted in their wider sense.

5.2. THE MOTION

5.2.1. In accordance with their use, adjectives distinguish gender by different forms in the same word, and agree with the nouns they define in gender, number and case. This is the *motion* of the adjective.

5.2.2. We saw in §3.4 that there are cases of motion in the noun. Sometimes the opposition is made between nouns, and this seems to be the older situation; as, **patḗr/mātḗr, bhrātēr/swesōr**.

But an adjective distinguishes between masculine, feminine and neuter, or at least between animate and neuter (or inanimate). This opposition is of two different kinds:

a. Animates are opposed to inanimates by declension, and also vocalism and accent; as, ***-os/-om***, ***-is/-i***, ***-nts/-nt***, ***-ēs/-es***.

b. The masculine is opposed to the feminine, when it happens, by the stem vowel; as, ***-os/-ā***, ***-nts/-ntja***, ***-us/-wja***.

NOTE. From Beekes (1995): Two feminine forms are strongly deviant:

- fem. **potnja**, *mistress* (originally *powerful*), next to masculine **potis**. The feminine may contain the individualising suffix ***-en-***, 'one who is (powerful)'.
- fem. **piwerja**, *fat*, alongside masc. **piwōn**. Here too the forms are originally independent: from **peiHu-ōn* 'one who is fat', and fem. from **peiH-ur* 'fat'.

The general system may be so depicted:

	Animates		*Inanimates*
	Masculine	*Feminine*	*Neuter*
-o-	***-os***	***-ā***	***-om***
-i-	***-is***	***-is***	***-i***
-u-	***-us***	***-wja/-wī***	***-u***
-nt-	***-nts***	***-ntja/-ntī***	***-nt***
-e-	***-ēs***	***-ēs***	***-es***

5.2.3. Compare the following examples:

1. For the so-called *thematic adjectives*, in ***-os***, ***-ā***, ***-om***, *cf.* **somós**, **-ā́**, **-óm**, *equal*, **rudhrós**, **-ā́**, **-óm**, *red*, **wolós**, **-ā́**, **-óm**, *willing*, **kserós**, **-ā́**, **-óm**, *dry*, etc. But note the root accent in **newos**, **-ā**, **-om**, *new*, **solwos**, **-ā**, **-om**, *whole*, **kaikos**, **-ā**, **-om**, *blind*, **lajos**, **-ā**, **-om**, *fat*, etc.

NOTE. Most adjectives have **o**-stem, among them verbal adjectives and compound adjectives, *cf.* **diwós**, *heavenly*, **klutós**, *heard, famous*. The corresponding feminine forms feature **ā**.

2. For adjectives in ***-is***, ***-i***, *cf.* **gr̥dhís**, **-í**, *grown*, **lēnis**, **-i**, *weak*, **moinis**, **-i**, *obliged*, **muttis**, **-i**, *speechless*, **n̥widis**, **-i**, *ignorant*, etc.

3. For adjectives in ***-us***, ***-wja/-wī***, ***-u***, *cf.* **ēsús**, **-ujá**, **-ú**, *good*, **mr̥ghús**, **-ujá**, **-ú**, *short*, **leghús**, **-ujá**, **-ú**, *light*, **ōkús**, **-ujá**, **-ú**, *swift*. With root accent, *cf.* **swādus**, **-uja**, **-u** (Southern IE ***swādús***, ***-ujá***, ***-ú***), *pleasant*, **ml̥dus**, **-uja**, **-u**, *soft*, **tn̥ghus**, **-uja**, **-u**, *fat*, **tanus**, **-uja**, **-u**, *thin*, **tr̥sus**, **-uja**, **-u**, *dry*, **dhr̥sus**, **-uja**, **-u**, *bold*, etc.

NOTE. On the original stress of PIE **swādus*, see the so-called *Erlangen School Ablaut system*, e.g. at <https://openaccess.leidenuniv.nl/bitstream/1887/2667/1/299_021.pdf> from Lubotsky (1987), and Frazier (2006) at <http://roa.rutgers.edu/files/819-0406/819-FRAZIER-0-0.PDF>.

4. Adjectives in ***-nts***, ***-ntja***, ***-nt***, are frequently found in suffixes; as, ***-went-***, *possessing*, *rich in* (masc. nom. ***-wents***, gen. ***-wn̥tós***, neu. ***-wn̥t***, fem. ***-wn̥t-ja***), and especially in present participles in ***-nt-***.

The old athematic declension is reconstructed as hysterodynamic, with nom. -***´nts***, acc. -***´ntm̥***, gen. ***-ntós***.

NOTE. Some participles also show traces of the static inflection that we saw in athematics, especially in PII; they show nom. ***-nt-s***, acc. ***-nt-m̥***, gen. ***-nt-s***. Beekes (1995).

However, **-o/e-nt-** was reinterpreted (probably still within the LIE community) as from the thematic conjugation, where no accent-ablaut patterns are applied, see §7.7.2. Only Sanskrit shows a generalisation of the athematic paradigm.

5. Adjectives in ***-ēs***, ***-es***, are found with possessive semantics formed from neuter s-stems by internal derivation; so e.g. ***-klewḗs***, *-famed*, from **kléwos**, *fame*; -**genḗs**, *-born*, from **genos**, *kin*; or ***-menḗs***, *-minded*, from **menos**, *sense* (*intelligence*).

A special s-stem is perfect participle suffix ***-wos-***, which has an ablauting declension; as, *knowing*, nom. **weid-wṓs** (*cf.* O.Ind. *vidús-*, Av. *vīduuā́*, Gk. *eidós*), acc. **weid-wos-m̥**, zero-grade oblique forms, as gen. **weid-us-os** (*cf.* Skt. *vidúṣas*, Av. *vīdušō*, Gk. *weidwótos*), fem. **wid-us-ja / wid-us-ī** (*cf.* Skt. *vidúsī*, Gk. *widúia*, Myc. *a-ra-ru-ja*), pl. nom. **weid-wos-es**, gen. **weid-us-om**, etc.

NOTE. *Cf.* for the zero-grade further afield Toch. B. acc. *lt-wes*, fem. *lt-usa*, and Lith. fem. *áug-us-i* 'having grown'. For tentative reconstructions of 'original' PIH ablaut-accent nom. **wéid-wos or *wíd-wos*, acc. **weid-wós-* or **wid-wós*, gen. **wid-ús-*, etc. *cf.* Beekes (1995), Sihler (1995), Fortson (2004).

5.3. ADJECTIVE SPECIALISATION

5.3.1. Adjectives could be formed by the addition of suffixes to roots or word-stems. Most adjectives so formed are o-stems.

5.3.2. Common adjectival suffixes for nouns and verbs are (Fortson 2004):

The all-purpose adjectival suffix ***-jo-*** and ***-ijo-***, also used as a compositional suffix (*cf.* Lat. *ēgregius*), and often to form patronymics ('son of...'), *cf.* Hom. Gk. *Telamṓn-ios Aías* 'Aias (Ajax) son of Telamon', Lat. *Seru-ius* 'son of a slave (*seruus*), Servius'.

NOTE 1. For adjectival suffix ***-jo-*** and ***-ijo-***, *cf.* Hitt. *istarniya-* 'central' (<*ištarna 'between'*), Ved. *dámiya-* 'domestic', *gávya-* 'pertaining to cows', Lat. *ēgregius* 'outstanding' (<*ē grege* 'out of the herd') etc. According to one widely held view, locational adjectives like Skt. *dámiya-* (from *dam-* 'home') were originally possessive derivatives formed by adding **-o-** or **-ó-**.

NOTE 2. It is important, in these type of adjectives in ***-jo-***, to remember the so-called Wheeler's law, which refers to the position of the accent in these adjectives, in which the accent is moved to the second-to-last syllable, when the third-to-last syllable is long; cf Gk. *antíos* (Skt. antyas), *plēsíos*, vs. *agios, agrios.*

The suffix ***-ko-*** is most commonly found added to nouns to indicate origin or material composition, *cf.* Gaul. *Are-mori-cī* 'those by the sea, Aremoricans', Goth. *staina-hs* 'stony'. It appears frequently in extended ***-iko-*** as a suffix indicating appurtenance, as Gk. *hipp-ikós* 'having to do with horses', Lat. *bell-icus* 'pertaining to war'.

NOTE. Related is ***-isko-***, found in Gmc. and Bal.-Sla. to indicate affiliation or place of origin. The suffix ***-ko-*** was apparently also used as hypocoristic or diminutive, *cf.* Ved. *putra-ká-*, 'little son (*putrá-*)', *avi-kā́-* 'ewe-lamb' (*avi-* 'sheep'); *cf.* Slavic **-ĭko-* in O.C.S. *ovĭ-ca* 'sheep', *otĭ-cĭ* (Russ. *otec*) 'father', etc. (Meillet 1961, Fortson 2004), or Lat. forms in ***-ko-*** for diminutives, as *-cus* or *-culus* (combined with ***-lo-***, see below), as well as Hittite, after Shields (*Hittite* neka- *and the origin of the Indo-European diminutive suffix* *-ko-, 1998). The older function was possibly simply adjectival. Miller (*Latin suffixal derivatives in English and their Indo-European ancestry*, 2006).

The suffix ***-ro-*** was added to the zero-grade of an adjectival root to form that root's free-standing adjectival form, and was usually accented; as, **rudhrós**, red.

The suffix ***-tó-*** forms passive verbal adjectives (*v.i.* §7.7), and also possessive adjectives, as Lat. *barbā-tus* 'bearded', Eng. *beard-ed*, O.C.S. *bogatŭ* 'wealthy'.

Stems in ***-nt-*** form adjectives (viz. in ***-ment-/-went-***), but are mostly found within the verbal system as present participles.

Words in ***-ter-*** are nouns, and adjectives are derived usually in ***-trjo-*** and others.

Nouns in ***-ti*** make adjectives in ***-tjo-***, or ***-tiko-***, usually with an ethnic meaning.

IE ***-lo-*** formations are found in a variety of adjectival functions, including ancient hypocoristics (shorter forms of a word or given name), as well as (later) diminutives.

NOTE. *Cf.* Lat. *porculus* 'small pig', MHG *verhel* (Germ. *Ferkel*), Lith. paršẽlis 'piglet', sūnẽlis 'little son', etc. or Goth. *Wulfila*, O.H.G. *Wolfilo* lit. 'little wolf' (according to Senn, Krahe and Meid, Risch, etc.), while O.Ir. *Túathal* (personal name; *cf. túath* 'tribe, people'), cited by Jurafsky (1996) is possibly not a diminutive, Miller (2006).

The accent is sometimes used to distinguish thematic nouns from adjectives.

NOTE. There are sometimes secondary processes that displace the accent from an adjective to create a noun; *cf.* Gk. *leukós* 'white', *léukos* 'white spot'.

5.3.3. Common adjectival suffixes from prepositions and examples include:

- In -**tero**: **próteros**, **énteros**, **éksteros**, **níteros**, etc.
- In -**no**: **úpernos**, Lat. *supernus*, **éksternos**, Lat. *externus*.
- In -**jo**: **enjos**, *cf.* O.Ir. *inne 'interior zone'*, O.Ind. *ni-já-*, Goth. *inna*; **autjos**, **ántitjos**, **preitjos**, *cf.* Ltv. *prìe(k)ša*, O.Ind. *ní-tya-*, Lit. *įščios*, Ltv. *įščios* 'intestine'.
- In -**qo**: **wiqos**, *diverse* (*cf.* O.Ind. *viśva-*, *'all'*), **niqos**, *inferior* (*cf.* Gmc. **nihuuela*), **proqos** *near/far* (*cf.* Lat. *procul/prope/proximus*), **seqos**, *isolated* (*cf.* Lat. *secus*, *sequius*, Corn *heb*, Bret. *hep*, O.Ir. *sech*; but Lat. *antīqus* <**anti-$h_3$qo-*).
- In -**qo**: **áporos**, *cf.* O.Ind. *apara-*.
- In -**mo**: **epiromo**- (*cf.* O.Ir. *iarum*, Alb. *i èpërm*), Lat. *immus*, *summus*.

5.4. COMPARISON OF ADJECTIVES

5.4.1. In Proto-Indo-European, as in English, there are three degrees of comparison: the positive, the comparative and the superlative.

5.4.2. The adjective in its natural or 'positive' state may be made comparative and superlative by the addition of suffixes.

5.4.3. The comparative, a difference of grade between two compared values, is generally formed by adding the primary comparative suffix ***-jos-*** to the root in e-grade (if there was one), regardless of the grade or stem of the generic adj. Thus from **swād-ús**, comp. **swād-jōs**, *sweeter*, rather than ˣ***swādu-jōs***, or from **dḷnghos**, comp. **dlegh-jōs**, *longer*, rather than ˣ***dḷngh-jōs***; also, from **kartús**, **kret-jōs**, *harder*, but from **mag-nos** (no-stem) **mag-jōs**, *bigger* (Lat. *maiior*), from **sen-os**, **sen-jōs**, *older* (*cf.* Skt. *san-yas*, Lat. *senior*), etc.

NOTE. "Older (probably PIE) was *-is*, which is preserved in adverbs: Lat. ntr. *maius* 'greater' < **-ios*, adv. *magis*; Goth. *min* 'less' < **minn-is*, *mais* 'more' > **meh₂-is* (*cf.* E. *more*)." According to Sihler (1995), "[t]he suffix *-yos- added to a root X originally meant 'X to a pronounced degree; very X'. This is essentially the force of the affix in InIr. Pragmatically, of course, a statement like *fruit is sweet, but honey is very sweet* is equivalent to *fruit is sweet, but honey is sweeter*, and that is the basis for the evolution of the paradigmatic comparative (...)." This origin is probably behind its use as augmentative and pejorative in some languages.

Also, the intensive/comparative was added directly to the root (in full grade) rather than to the stem of the adjective, in accordance with the "view that the original meaning of the suffix was different from our notion of a paradigmatic comparative, which would be a derivative of the generic itself (as is clearly the case in NE *damnedest* and L *difficilior*). Thus Vedic *átavyas-*, a form with both the intensive suffix and the privative prefix, means 'not very strong' (from *tavyás-* 'very strong') rather than 'very unstrong; very weak'. That is, it is a privative based on an intensive, not the other way around like the NE comparative *untidier*." *Cf.* O.Ir. *sír*, cp. *sía<*sējós*, *'longus, longior'*; *lán* (*plēnus cf. lín 'numerus'*), cp. *lia<*plējós* (Lat *ploios*, Gk. *pléos*); *cf.* Lat. *ploirume*, zero-grade Lat. *maios*, O.Ir. *mía*. So, for **júwen-** we find Umb. cp. *jovie<*jowjē-s*, O.Ir. *óac 'iuuenis'*, *óa 'iunior'*; *óam 'iuuenissimus'*, O.Ind. *yúva(n)- (yū́naḥ)*, cp. *yávīyas-*, sup. *yáviṣta-ḥ*.

The form ***-jos-*** varies allophonically with ***-ijos-***, *cf.* **new-jōs**, **new-ijōs**, *newer*. According to Meier-Brügger, "[*-ijos] replaces [*-jos] in nominative singular masculine and feminine forms with the structure KV̄.K- and KVR.K-; whereas, according to rules of phonetics, *-jos- is expected in forms with three or more syllables."

The inflection of the comparative is that of the hysterodynamic inflection for s-stems: singular nom. masc./fem. ***-jōs***, acc. masc./fem. ***-josm̥***, nom.-acc. neu. ***-jos***, gen. ***-jesos***, dat. ***-jesei***, loc. ***-jesi***; plural masc./fem. ***-joses***, acc. masc./fem. ***-josn̥s***, nom.-acc. neut. ***-jōs***, gen. ***-jesom***, dat. ***-jesbhos***, etc.

NOTE. This declension comes from an older ablauting **-´jōs*, acc. m.f. **-jés-m*, gen. **-is-ós*, dat. **-is-éi*, loc. *-jes-i, dat. pl. -is-bh´-*, etc. Sihler (1995). Beekes (1995):

The suffix ***-(t)er-o-*** is the basis for the secondary comparative forms; as, from **upo**, *up, upon,* **úperos** (*cf.* O.Ind. *úpar-a-*) *beneath, nearer*.

NOTE. The suffix ***-(t)ero-*** is the **-o-** adjective form of adverbs ending in ***-(t)r̥*** and ***-(t)er***; as, **sup**, under, **sup-er-**, *over*, and **sup-er-o-**, *found above*; **pro**, *at the front*, forward, and **pró-ter-o-**, *toward the front, earlier*. Adverbs and adjectives that were derived from them were capable of marking relative contrast, e.g. in the case of opposites or selection from a pair; *cf.* from **sem-**, *one*, **sm̥-ter-o**, *the other of two in a unity*. The original use of this suffix was then probably to convey the idea of binary contrast to something else, rather than intensive; as, **qóteros**, *which (of two)?*, **enteros**, *the other* (also *second, v.i.* §5.5.2) in contrast to **aljos**, *(an)other*. Sihler (1995), Meier-Brügger (2003).

5.4.4. The superlative marks the highest grade among two compared values. The same suffix (with the ablaut ***-is-***) is the base for a common suffix ***-is-tos*** (<*-*ist(h$_2$)o-*, *cf.* Skt. *-iṣṭha-*, Gk. *-istos*, Goth. *-ista*), and ***-t-m̥os*** (*cf.* Skt. *-tamas*, Gk. *-tato-*, *-tamo-*), and (possibly a combination of ***-is-tos*** and ***-t-m̥os***) ***-is-m̥os*** (Ita.-Cel. **-isamo-*); as, **sénistos**, *oldest*, **mágistos**, *biggest* (Gk. *megistos*, Lat. *maximus<*magisamos*), **néwistos**, *newest*, etc.; probably common to certain numeral suffixes.

NOTE. As stated by Sihler (1995), "a complex of two separate elements *-m̥- and *-mo- is indefensible morphologically. An original PIH *-(t)mHo- solves the phonological problem, but there is no reason otherwise to suppose the presence of a laryngeal". This form in *-m̥mo- is also preferred by Fortson (2004) among others, while a laryngeal is preferred e.g. in Meier-Brügger (2003). Again, the auxiliary vowel in a sequence *T-RE is the most logical assumption (Adrados–Bernabé–Mendoza 1995-1998), hence LIE *-mo/- °mo-.

Superlative of the secondary comparative is made in **-m̥o-**; *as,* **úper-m̥o-**, **sup-m̥os** (Lat. *summus*), from **n̥dherós**, *underly*, **ńdh-m̥os** (Lat. *infimus,* Skt. *ádhamas*), from **entós**, *inside*, **ént-m̥os**, (Lat. *intimus*), *innermost.*

NOTE. While adjectival suffixes ***-jos-***, ***-istos***, are added to the root (in e-grade) without extensions, ***-teros*** and ***-m̥os*** are added with the extensions.

Suffixes ***-jo-***, ***-tero-***, and ***-is-to-***, had probably an original nominal meaning.

NOTE. Thus, the elongations in ***-jos-*** had a meaning; as in Latin, where *iuniores* (<*jun-jos-es) and *seniores* (<*sen-jos-es) were used for groups of age; or those in ***-teros***, as **mātérterā* 'aunt on the mother's side', **ekwā́teros* lit. 'the horsy one' (in contrast to 'ass'), 'mule', Sihler (1995). Forms like **jun-jos-es* were not common in PIE, although indeed attested in different dialects.

5.5. NUMERALS

5.5.1. CLASSIFICATION OF NUMERALS

Indo-European numerals may be classified as follows:

I. Numeral adjectives:

1. Cardinal numbers, answering the question *how many?* as, **oinos**, *one*; **dwōu**, *two.*

2. Ordinal numbers, adjectives derived (in most cases) from the cardinals, and answering the question *which in order?* as, **prāmos,** *first*; **ónteros**, *second.*

3. Distributive numerals, answering the question *how many at a time?* as, **semli**, *one at a time*; **dwisni**, *two by two.*

II. Numeral adverbs, answering the question *how often?* as, **dwis**, *twice*, **tris**, *thrice.*

5.5.2. CARDINALS AND ORDINALS

1. These two series are as follows, from one to ten:

	Cardinal	*Eng.*	*Ordinal*	*Eng.*
1.	**oinos, oinā, oinom**	*one*	**prāmos**	*first*
2.	**dwōu, dwāi, dwoi**	*two*	**ónteros**	*second*
3.	**trejes, trja/trī, trísores**	*three*	**tritjos**	*third*
4.	**qétwores**	*four*	**qetwr̥tos**	*fourth*
5.	**penqe**	*five*	**penqtos**	*fifth*
6.	**s(w)eks**	*six*	**s(w)ekstos**	*sixth*
7.	**septḿ**	*seven*	**séptm̥os**	*sevent*
8.	**oktṓu**	*eight*	**óktŏ̄wos**	*eighth*
9.	**newn̥**	*nine*	**neunos**	*ninth*
1	**dekm̥**	*ten*	**dékm̥tos**	*tenth*

NOTE. From root ***oi***-, PII *ai-kas* (<**oi-k-os*), CA *ei-kos*, PGk *oi-wos*. For **prāwos** (<**prəHwos*<**pr̥*h_2*-wo-*), *first*, *cf.* O.Ind. *pūrva-*, O.C.S. *prŭvŭ*. For **prāmos**, (<**prəHmos*<**pr̥*h_2*-mo-*), *cf.* Gk. Dor. *pratos* (<**prā-wo-to*<**prā-mo-*), Lith. *pìrmas*, O.Eng. *forma*, or Goth. *fruma* (maybe also in Lat. *prandēre* < **prāmdo-dejom* 'first eating'); Lat. *prīmus* (<**prī-isamos*<**prei-isamos*, Pael. *prismu*). All forms are probably related through the same root as in particle **prŏ̄**, *forth*, thus originally meaning 'foremost' or similar. For. fem. **trja/trī**<**triH*, *three*, *cf.* Skt. *trī*, Gk. *tría*, Lat. *tria*, *U. triia*, *Goth. þrija*, O.Ir. *tre*, but. It seems that **weks**, *six*, could have been the 'original' PIH form, to which an ***s***- from **septḿ** was added; it would have lost the -***w***- later (Sihler 1995).

The ordinals were formed by means of the thematic suffix -o-, which caused the syllable before the ending to have zero-grade. The newer suffix -to- was the most productive in Late Indo-European.

NOTE. For internal reconstruction in PIH, Late Indo-European and early dialects, see Szemerényi (1970). For eighth, Beekes (1995) reconstructs an original short vowel *h_3*kt(e)*h_3*wó-* *cf.* gr. *ogdo(w)os*, but *cf.* for lengthened grade Lat. *octāuus* <**oktōwos* <**e*h_3*-w-*. An original ****dekm̥t-ó***- is reconstructed, later metanalysed into the attested **dékm̥-to**- (Sihler 1995). The same could be said of most ordinals, apparently from earlier zero-grade forms and accent on the ending, Sihler (1995) and Beekes (1995), but recognised as having been replaced already in parent language; as, ***tr̥jó-* → **trijó-* 'third'.

2. The forms from eleven to nineteen were usually formed by placing the number and then **dekm̥**, *ten*. Hence Late Indo-European used the following system:

	Cardinal	*Ordinal*
11.	**sémdekm̥ / oinos dekm̥**	**sémdekm̥tos / prāmos dékm̥tos**
12.	**dwōu dekm̥**	**éteros dékm̥tos**
13.	**trejes dekm̥**	**tritjos dékm̥tos**
14.	**qétwores dekm̥**	**qetwr̥tos dékm̥tos**
15.	**penqe dekm̥**	**penqtos dékm̥tos**
16.	**s(w)eks dekm̥**	**s(w)ekstos dékm̥tos**
17.	**septḿ̥ dekm̥**	**séptmos dékm̥tos**
18.	**oktṓ dekm̥**	**óktō̆wos dékm̥tos**
19.	**newn̥ dekm̥**	**newnos dékm̥tos**

NOTE. Eleven and twelve were already fossilised collocations in O.Lat. *undecim* (<**oinodecem*), O.Ind. *áikadaśa*, probably from ***oinom dekm̥t*** (Sihler 1995). For a frozen *thirteen*, *cf.* Skt. *trayodaśa*, Lat. *trēdecim* (<**trēsdecem*).

Also Gmc. and BSl. apparently from **óinoliqa* 'one left', **dwṓliqa* 'two left', with ordinals **óinoliqtos*, **dwṓliqtos*, although the exact reconstruction of these forms is problematic (Beekes 1995).

3. The tens are normally formed with the units and suffix ***-dkm̥ta*** *"group of ten"*.

	Cardinal	*Ordinal*
20.	**(d)widkm̥tī**	**(d)wídkm̥tm̥os**
30.	**trídkm̥ta**	**trídkm̥tm̥os**
40.	**qetwŕ̥dkm̥ta**	**qetwŕ̥dkm̥tm̥os**
50.	**penqédkm̥ta**	**penqédkm̥tm̥os**
60.	**s(w)éksdkm̥ta**	**s(w)éksdkm̥tm̥os**
70.	**septḿ̥dkm̥ta**	**septḿ̥dkm̥tm̥os**
80.	**oktṓdkm̥ta**	**oktṓdkm̥tm̥os**
90.	**néwn̥dkm̥ta**	**néwn̥dkm̥tm̥os**
100.	**(d)km̥tóm**	**dkm̥témtm̥os**

NOTE. These forms are traditionally reconstructed for LIE with lengthened preceding vowel or resonant (as a conventional writing of LIE uncertain output for *RH), based on comparative evidence alone (e.g. Sihler 1995, Adrados–Bernabé–Mendoza 1995-1998), but internal reconstruction might explain the development of all attested forms more elegantly following the Leiden school (Kortlandt, Beekes, De Vaan, etc.), with the hypothesis that the glottal stop of the *d* in **dkm̥tóm** with the preceding vocalic resonant caused the development toward outputs similar to those of *RH; i.e. -**R?kṃta** <**-HkṃtəH* < **-h$_1$kṃth$_2$* <**-dkṃt-(h$_2$?)*. Hence our selection of writing an etymological ***d***- to represent the old glottal stop, that had the common effect in the attested dialects of lengthening the preceding vowel (or vocalic resonant). The ending -**ă̄**, comes from neuter ending **-(e)h$_2$*, which by convention we write -**a**. See e.g. at <http://eprints.ucm.es/tesis/19911996/H/3/AH3005401.pdf> Lujan's tesis on numerals, with a full review of the available reconstructions (Lillo, Szemerényi, Mallory), Fortson (2004), or Kortlandt's original article from 1983, available at <https://openaccess.leidenuniv.nl/bitstream/1887/1877/1/344_043.pdf>.

4. The hundreds are made as compounds of two numerals, like the tens:

	Cardinal	*Ordinal*
200.	**dwikṃtos**	**dwikṃtémtṃos**
300.	**trikṃtos**	**trikṃtémtṃos**
400.	**qatwṛkṃtos**	**qatwṛkṃtémtṃos**
500.	**penqekṃtos**	**penqekṃtémtṃos**
600.	**sekskṃtos**	**sekskṃtémtṃos**
700.	**septṃkṃtos**	**septṃkṃtémtṃos**
800.	**oktōkṃtos**	**oktōkṃtémtṃos**
900.	**newṇkṃtos**	**newṇkṃtémtṃos**
1000.	**sṃgheslom**	**sṃgheslotṃos**

NOTE. For n. (**sṃ**)**gheslom**, *thousand*, *cf.* Skt. *n. sa-hásra-m*, Av. *ha-zaŋra*, from PII ***sa-ĝhasla-m***; from i-stem adjective **gheslijos**, -**ā**, -**om**, '*having a thousand, thousand-fold*', *cf.* Skt. *sahasríya-*, Gk. *khīl(l)ioi*< PGk ***khesl-ij-o-*** (Sihler 1995), Lat. *n. mīlle*, (*n. pl*) *mīlia*, possibly from an original fem. abstract **sṃ-ih$_2$ ghesl-i*, or **sm-ih$_2$ ghsl-ih$_2$*; for fem. **sm-ih$_2$*, *cf.* Gk. *mía*. Both Lat. **mīl(l)i* and *mīlia* "might be postulated as free forms within the same synchronic structure" J. Gvozdanović (1992) against a starting point **-ijă̄* (E. Hamp, 1968). For the ordinal, *cf.* Skt. *sahasra-tama*.

A difficult to reconstruct **tū́sṇtī<*tū́s-kṃt-ij-os*? 'fat hundred'?, is found (Mallory–Adams 2007) in Northern IE; *cf.* Gmc. *þūsund-i*, pl. *þūsundjōs*, Toch. *tumame*, Bal. *tūksunt-i*, O.Prus. *tūsimtons*, Sla. **tīsǫt-j-ā*.

5. The other numerals are made similar to the tens, with the units in first place; as, **oinā widkṃtī**, f. *twenty-one*; m. **qétwores tridkṃta**, *thirty-four*.

NOTE. For the simple type **oinos widkṃtī**, *cf.* Skt. *éka-viṅśati* (in compounds where the unit could be inflected); with copulatives, *cf.* Lat. *unus et uiginti*, Bret. *unan-warn-ugent*, Ger. *einundzwanzig*, Du. *eenentwintig*, Fris. *ienentweintich*, Da. *enogtyve*, etc.

The normal order of composite numerals is units+tens, and there was a natural tendency to follow a 'units+tens+hundreds+...', *cf.* Skt. *ekādaśaṃ sahasram*, lit.

'one ten thousand', *one thousand and eleven.* So e.g. **penqe dekm̥ km̥tóm**, *one hundred and fifteen,* **oinom qatwŕdkm̥ta septm̥km̥tos**, *seven hundred and forty-one.*

All numbers signal the ordinal; as, **prāmos widkm̥tm̥os**, (masc). *twenty-first,* **tritjā trídkm̥tm̥ā trikm̥témtm̥ā**, (fem.) *three hundred thirty-third.*

6. Numerals were often inserted as prefixes of possessive compound forms, of the type **qatwr̥-pods,** *four-footed, quadruped.* As first members, numbers 1-4 had a special zero-grade form: **sm̥-**, *one-;* **dwi-**, *two-,* **tri-**, *three-, and* **q(a)tur-** [**q(a)twr̥-** before consonant], *four-.*

NOTE. The 'original' zero-grade **qtwr̥-**, **qtur-**, appears usually with an inserted *schwa secundum*, generally LIE [a], i.e. **qatwr̥-**, **qatur-**; also, PGk ***qetwr̥-***, ***qetur-***. See §2.6.6.

5.5.3. DECLENSION OF CARDINALS AND ORDINALS

Of the cardinals **oinos**, **dwōu**, **trejes** (and dialectally **qétwores**), are declinable.

a. The declension of **oinos, -ā, -om** has often the meaning of *certain, a, single, alone*; as, **oinos dinos**, *a certain day.* Also, as a simple numeral, it agrees with a plural noun of singular meaning. The plural occurs also in phrases like **oinōs álterōsqe**, *one party and the other one* (*the ones and the others*).

The root **sem-**, in **semos**, *one*, refers the unity as a whole, found in adj. **somós**, *equal.*

NOTE. Gk., Arm., Toch., show an old declension, found in frozen compounds in Late Indo-European: masc. nom. **sems*, acc. **sēm* (<***sem-m*) neu. nom.-acc. **sem* (gen.-abl. **smós*, dat. **smei*, loc. **sem(i)*, ins. **smē*), and fem. **smja/ī* (acc. **smja/īm*, gen.-abl. **smjās*, dat. **smjāi*, loc. **smjā(i)*, ins. **smjā*). Beekes (1995), Ringe (2005).

c. The inflection of **dwōu**, *two*, is irregular, connected to issues concerning the dual:

	masc.	*fem.*	*neu.*
N.-V.-A.	**dwōu**	**dwāi**	**dwoi**
GEN.	**dwous**		
DAT.-ABL.	**dwobhós/dwomós**		
LOC.	**dwou**		
INS.	**dwobhís/dwomís**		

NOTE. Apparently an older *n./f.* **dwoi** was separated into a newer Late Indo-European *f.* **dwāi**. Also, IE **ambhōu**, *both*, from **ambhí**, is inflected like **dwōu**; for adjective **ambhojos**, *cf.* Skt. *ubháya-*, O.C.S. *oboji*, Lith. *abejì* (Beekes 1995).

c. The inflection of **trejes**, *three*, is mostly a regular i-stem one:

	masc.	*fem.*	*neu.*
NOM.-VOC.	**trejes**	**trja/trī**	**trísores**
ACC.	**trins**	**trjans/trīns**	**trísores**
GEN.	**trijō̆m**		
DAT.-ABL.	**tribhós/trimós**		
LOC.	**trisú**		
INS.	**tribhís/trimís**		

NOTE. Ringe (2006) reconstructs the fem. **trís(o)res** as ***tisres***, as does Luján, and its declension is thus separated into **tisrn̥s*, **tisróHom*, **tisr̥mós*, **tisr̥sú*, **tisr̥bhí*.

The inflection attested of **qétwores** or **qetwores** seems to have followed an old accent-ablaut paradigm acc. **qet-wór-ns**, gen. **qet-ur-ō̆m**, loc. **qet-wr̥-sú**, etc..

NOTE. A feminine form **qétes(o)res** (see Ringe 2006, Luján; but **kʷetu-sre-* for Beekes 1995) is found in Celtic and Indo-Iranian, deemed therefore usually an old PIE formation (although in decline, given that most old IE languages had already lost it), or an innovation based on **trís(o)res**. It might have been declined as acc. **qét-esr-ns**, gen. **qet-esr-ō̆m**, loc. **qet-esr-sú**, etc. (Ringe 2006). Tocharian, Italic, and Gothic show no gender distinction; all such finds indicate either an old common LIE trend of disuse of inflection for this number, or dialectal innovations. A neuter **qetwṓr** <**kʷetworH* is found in Greek and Balto-Slavic. It was declined as acc. ***qét-wṓr***, gen. ***qet-ur-ō̆m***, loc. ***qet-wr-sú***, etc. Sihler (1995), Adrados–Bernabé–Mendoza (1995-1998).

d. The ordinals are adjectives of the **o** and **ā** declensions, and are regularly declined.

6.3.2. Cardinals and ordinals have the following uses:

a. Only compound numbers have no gender or flexion; as, **penqédkm̥ta kmtóm** m., f., n. *hundred and fifty*; numbers including one, two, or three have gender and flexion; as, **oinā séksdkm̥ta**, (*fem.*) *sixty-one*, **dwāi widkm̥tī**, (*fem.*) *twenty-one*, **trísores qetwŕ̥dkm̥ta**, (*neu.*) *forty-three*, **oinom widkm̥tī putla**, (*masc. acc.) 21 children*.

b. The highest denomination generally stands last, the next before it, etc., and the unit is first; as, **qétwores séksdkm̥ta septm̥km̥tom sm̥gheslom**, *1764*.

c. LIE had no special words for *million*, *billion*, *trillion*, etc. They were expressed by multiplication. From common loan *million*, from Lat. *mille* 'one thousand', we could reconstruct **sm̥ghéslijōn**, *million*, **dwighéslijōn**, *billion*, **trighéslijōn**, *trillion*, etc.

d. A common expression in PIE is the adverbial use of the accusative singular neuter of the ordinal; as, **prāmom**, *firstly*; **ónterom**, *secondly*, etc.

e. Fractions are expressed, as in English, by cardinals in the numerator and ordinals in the denominator. The neuter is generally used for substantivised ordinals, or the feminine with noun 'part'; as, *n.* **dwōi septm̥a** (or *f.* ***dwāi septm̥āi pr̥tes***) *two-sevenths*; *n.* **trísores óktōwa**, *three-eighths*.

When the numerator is one, it is usually omitted: **tritjom**, *one-third*; **qétwr̥tom**, *one-fourth*, and so on.

NOTE. Indo-Iranian exhibits an old trend to omit the parts in which it is divided, if only one is left; as, ***dwāi pr̥tes***, *two-thirds* ("*two parts*"), ***trja pr̥tes***, *three-fourths*, etc.

The compositional **sēmi-**, *half-*, is combined with ordinals to express cardinals plus *half*; as, **sēmi-tritjos**, *two and a half*, lit. '*having a half of the third (item)*'.

NOTE. For IE 'half', *cf.* Lat. adj. ***dwismedhjos***, noun ***dwismedhjom***, 'divided medially'; however, proper forms meaning 'divided in two' are reconstructed from multiplicatives, *v.i.*

f. In approximatives, the old disjunctive use of numerals was made by collocations of adjacent cardinals in ascending order, e.g. **penqe seks septḿ**, *five, six*, or *seven*. A common IE **penqe septḿ** (for **penqe septm̥we**), *five or seven*, is also possible.

g. Time periods are made with compounds:

For years, as **dwiatnjom**, *a period of two years*, **triatnjom**, **qaturatnjom**, **sm̥gheslijatnjom**, *millenium*, etc.

For days, as **dwidjówijom**, *a period of two days*, **tridjówijom**, **qatwr̥djówijom**.

For months, as **dwimēnstris**, *a period of two months*, *bimester*, **trimēnstris**, *trimester*, **qatwr̥mēnstris**, **seksmēnstris**, *semester*, etc.

NOTE. For month names, a compound with ***mēns-ri-*** is followed; as, **septm̥mēnsris**, *september*, **oktōmēnsris**, *october*, etc.

5.5.4. DISTRIBUTIVES

1. Distributive numerals are number words which express group membership. They are used mainly in the sense of *so many apiece* or *on each side*, and also in multiplications. They answer to the question *how many of each? how many at a time?*

2. The oldest formations are collocations of geminated cardinals, with both members inflected; as, **semos semos**, **oinos oinos**, *each one*, **penqe penqe**, *each five*, etc.

NOTE. For this kind of distributives, *cf.* Gk. *tri tri*, O.Ind., *éka- eka-*, Zor. Pahl. *ēk ēk*, Pers. *das das*, Parth. Sogd. *'yw 'yw*, Arm. *tasn tasn*, Toch. A *sam sam*, B *ṣeme ṣeme, okt okt, ñu ñu*; also in Hittite iterated groups, in place of distributives, *1-aš 1-aš, 1-an 1-an*.

This is also found in nouns, *cf.* Lat. *alteros alterom* 'each other', O.Ind. *díve díve*, 'each day'; Myc. *we-te we-te* 'each year'; etc.

3. Some PIE distributives were formed with adj. suffix ***-(s)no-***, and abstract/collective suffix **-ī**; as, **dwīsnī**, *two at a time, two each*, **trisnī**, **qátrusnī**.

NOTE. For this formation e.g. **dwīsnī**, *cf.* Lat. *bīnī*, Gmc. **twiznaz* (<**dwisnōs*, *cf.* O.N. *tvenner*, O.H.G. *zwirnēn*, O.Eng. *twīn*, Du. *twijn*), Russ. *dvójni*, Lith. *dvynù*, Arm. *krkin*, Lyc. *kbisñni*. Also, it is believed that ***oi-no-*** was originally the first member of that series (remember dialectal PGk ***oi-wos***, PII ***oi-kos***), meaning 'singleness, unity', before replacing ***sem-***. Distributives for higher numerals were later expressed in IE languages using a word that meant 'each', as, Eng. *each*, Fr. *chaque*, Alb. *kaa*, Bret. *cach*, etc.

4. Distributives can be used to express percentage; as, for 'twenty percent', **dekm̥ dekm̥ dwōu**, *two for each ten*, **km̥tóm km̥tóm widkm̥tī**, *twenty for each hundred*.

5.5.5. NUMERAL ADVERBS

1. The so-called numeral adverbs are a distinctive class of adverbs which specifically answer the question **qoti**, *how many times? how often?*

2. The most common ones are formed with zero-grade and a lengthening in **-s**; as, **semli**, *once*, **dwis**, *twice*, **tris**, *thrice*, and **qatrus** (<**kʷətwr̥-s*), *four times*.

NOTE. For NWIE **semli**, *cf.* O.Lat. *semol*, Umb. *sumel*, Goth. *simble*, O.H.G. *simlē*, O.Ir. *amal*; for the expected **sm̥ni-*, maybe Hitt. *šani*. PII ***sm̥-qŕ̥t***, from **-qr̥t**, *v.i.*; PGk ***sm̥-pn̥qus***, *alone*, *cf.* Gk. *hapaks*, Hitt. *pa-an-ku-uš*, L. *cūnctus*. For the rest, e.g. **tris**, *cf.* Lat. *ter*, Myc. *ti-ri-se-roe* (<*Tris-(h)ḗrōhei*), Gk. *tris*, O.Ind. *triḥ*, Goth. *driror*, O.Ir. *thrí*, Luv. *tarisu*, Lyc. *trisu*. Higher numbers are found in Lat. and maybe behind Hitt. *3-iš*, 10-*iš*, 20-*iš*, 30-*iš*, etc. See Sihler (1995).

3. Some old compounds are also found in ***-ki***.

NOTE. A certain reconstruction is difficult, though; *cf.* Hitt. *-an-ki*, Gmc. *zwis-ki*, Gk. *-ki*, Indian **-ki* (*cf.* Sogd. *-ky*, Yaghnobi *īki īki* 'one by one, one each', Chorasmian -*c*); maybe also in Arm. *erkics*. Variant Gk. *-kis*, Hitt. *-kis* are probably due to assimilation to the type

dwis, *twice, twofold*. For higher numbers, probably an innovation, *cf.* Greek numeral adverbs in *-a-kis*, and Hittite in *-an-ki*, maybe from a common PIE **-n̥ki*.

4. A system of simple collocations is used, placing the cardinal number before a noun meaning 'time'; as, **penqe qŕtewes**, *five times*, **oktṓ qŕtewes**, *eight times*, and so on.

NOTE. For *m.* **qṛtus**, *time*, *cf.* O.Ind. *-kṛtwaḥ* (<**k^{w}ŕt-wn̥t-m̥*, see Hollifield 1984), Bal. **kar̃t-a-*, Sla. **kortŭ*, O.Ir. *cruth*, O.Welsh *pryd*. For (rare) compounds, viz. ***sṃ-qṛt***, *once*, *cf.* O.Ind. *sa-kṛt*, Av. *ha-kərət*; *cf.* also Umb. *trioper* 'three times', Osc. *petiropert* 'four times'.

5.5.6. MULTIPLICATIVES

1. Multiplicatives like *single, double, triple*, etc. which answer the question *how many fold?*, had a variety of compounds for the first numerals.

2. The oldest PIE multiplicatives found were collectives, made in ***-jo-***, ***-t-*** and ***-k-***; as, **óinokos**, *single, sole, unique*, **dwojós**, *two-fold, group of two, duad*, **trejós**, *three-fold, triad*, **qetwerós**, *four-fold, group of four*, **penqstís**, *group of five*, **dekḿts**, *group of ten, decade.*

NOTE. For North-West common **óinokos**, *cf.* Gmc. **ainagas* (*cf.* Goth *ainahs*, O.N. *einga*, O.Eng. *anga*, O.Sax. *enag*, O.H.G. *einac*), O.C.S. *inokŭ*, Lat. *unicus* (<**oine-kos? or *oino-ikos?*); suffix ***-ko-*** is also found in O.Ind. *-śáḥ*, Gk. *-kás*, Hitt. *-kaš*. For PIE **dwojós**, **trejós**, *cf.* Ved. *tvayá-*, *trayá*, Myc. *duwojo-/dwojo-*, Gk. *doiós*, O.H.G. *zwī*, g. *zwīes*, Lith. *dvejì*, *trejì*, O.C.S. *dĭvojĭ*, *trojĭ*, O.Ir. *trēode*. For **qetwerós**, *cf.* Skt. *catvarám*, O.C.S. *četvori*, Lith. *ketverì*, Lat. *quaternī*. Apart from **-jo-**, common PIE collectives are found in ***-t-***, usually ***-ti-***, as **penq-s-tis**, *group of five, fist*, *cf.* O.Ind. *paṇktí-*, Av. *sastí-*, *xsvasti-*, O.C.S. *pęstĭ*, *-tĭ*, Lith. *-t-*, *-ti-*, Gmc. *funxstiz* (*cf.* Goth. *fūst*), O.Ir. *bissi*, O.Welsh *bys*, but also **-ts**, as, **dekḿ-ts**, Gk. δεκάς (*dekás*), Lat. **dekents>*dekients*, spreading **j-n̥ts* as new formant, into Gk. πεντάς (*pentás*), then τριάς (*triás*), etc. Lat. **quinquens>quinquiens*, then *triēns*, etc; *cf.* e.g. neuter plurals **widkṃtī** (interpreted as dual), lit. *'a group of two decades, double decads'*, *twenty*, **tridkṃta**, '*triple decads*', *thirty*, and so on.

4. Proportional or relative numerals express how many times more (or less) one thing is than another; they are made as follows:

a. in ***-plós***, as **sṃplós**, *simple*, **dwiplós**, *two-fold, double, twice as much, twice as large*, **triplós**, *three-fold, triple.*

NOTE. For ***dwi-plos***, *cf.* Lat. *duplus*, Hom. Gk. f. acc. *diplḗn* (<*dwi-plā́-m*) Umbr. *dupla*, Goth. *twei-fls*, O.H.G. *zvī-fal*, "*doubt*", O.Ir. *dīabul*, maybe Av. *bi-fra-* '*comparison*', Lyc. B *dwiplẽ*. ***sṃ-plos*** is found in Gk. ἁ-πλός (*ha-plós*), Lat. *simplus*, ***tri-plos*** is found in Gk. τριπλοῦς (*triplous*), Lat. *triplus*, Umb. *tripler*. For -**plos** (*cf.* Arm. *-hal*), a connection with PIE **pel-**, *fold*, is usually assumed.

b. in ***-pḷks***, as, **dwipḷks**, '*with two folds*', *duplex*, **tripḷks**, '*with three folds*'.

NOTE. For **pḷk-**, also reconstructed as from root **pel-**, *cf.* Lat. *-plicare*, Gk. *plekō* <**pl-ek*, 'to fold'. For **dwipḷks**, *cf.* Lat. *duplex*, Gk. δίπλαξ (*díplaks*), Umbr. *tuplak*.

c. with verbal adjective ***-pḷtós***, *folded*, is used to denote something divided in *n* parts; as, **dwipḷtós**, *an object folded in two*.

NOTE. *Cf.* Gk. *-plasio-*<**-platio-*<**pḷt-jo-s*, a derivative that could express 'belonging to the class of objects folded in two' (Gvozdanović, 1992); maybe also here i-stem O.Ir. *trilis*<**tripḷtis*? For **dwipḷtós**, *cf.* Gk. διπλάσιος (*diplásios*), Ger. *zwifalt*. A similar form is in Gmc. **poltos* 'fold'.

d. with suffix ***-dhā***, as **dwidhā**, *two-fold, divided in two parts*.

NOTE. *cf.* Skt. *duví-dha*, *dve-dha*, Gk. διχθά <*δι-θα (*di-thá*) and maybe also (with the meaning 'half') O.N. *twēdi*, O.Eng. *twǣde*, O.H.G. *zwitaran*, O.Ir. *dēde*, Hitt. *dak-ša-an*.

6. PRONOUNS

6.1. ABOUT THE PRONOUNS

6.1.1. Pronouns are used as nouns or as adjectives. They are divided into the following seven classes:

1. Personal pronouns: as, **egṓ**, *I*.

2. Reflexive pronouns: as, **se**, *himself*.

3. Possessive pronouns: as, **n̥serós**, *our*.

4. Demonstrative pronouns: as, **so**, *this, that*.

5. Relative pronouns: as, **jos**, *who*.

6. Interrogative pronouns: as, **qis?** *who*?

7. Indefinite pronouns: as, **qis**, *anyone*.

6.1.2. Like adjectives, pronouns are declined for case and number and – except for the personal and reflexive pronouns – for gender. Pronouns have a special declension, differing from the nominal declension in several respects.

6.2. PERSONAL PRONOUNS

6.2.1. The personal pronouns of the first person are **egṓ**, *I*, **wejes**, *we*; of the second person, **tū**, *thou*, **juwes**, *you*. The personal pronouns of the third person - *he, she, it, they* - are wanting in Indo-European, an anaphoric (or even a demonstrative) being used instead.

NOTE. Late Indo-European had no personal pronouns for the third person, like most of the early dialects attested. For that purpose, a demonstrative was used instead; as, from ***ki***, ***id***, *cf.* Anatolian *ki*, Gmc. *khi-*, Lat. *cis-*, *id*, Gk. *ekeinos*, Lith. *sis*, O.C.S. *si*, etc.

6.2.2. Since every finite verb form automatically indicates the 'person' of the verb, the nominal pronoun forms are already adequately marked. Therefore, pronouns are not generally used in verbal sentences; they might be used to mark insistence, though: **esmi**, *I am*; **egṓ esmi**, *me, I am*.

In comparison with the orthotonic forms, often strengthened by particles, the special enclitic forms feature the minimal word stem and may be used in multiple cases.

NOTE. Tonic forms are fully stressed (emphatic or contrastive), while enclitic are unstressed clitic object pronouns; these are clearly attested in Anatolian, Indo-Iranian,

Greek, Balto-Slavic and Tocharian. They are mostly reduced versions of the full forms, and it is a common resource write them added to the preceding verb, *cf.* Hitt. *-mu*, O.Lith. *-m(i)*.

6.2.3. The personal (non-reflexive) pronouns are declined as follows:

First Person

	Singular **eg-, me-**		*Plural* **we-, no-**	
	Orthotonic	*Enclitic*	Orthotonic	*Encliti*
NOM.	**eg(h)óm, egṓ**, *I*		**wejes, n̥smés**, *we*	
ACC.	**mewóm**, *me*	***me***	**n̥smé, nōns**, *us*	***nos***
GEN.	**mene**, *of me*	***mo***	**n̥seróm**, *of us*	***nos***
DAT.	**meghei**,	***moi***	**n̥sméi, nosbhos**	***nos***
LOC.	**mei**		**n̥smí, nosi**	
INS.	**mojo**		**nosbhis**	
ABL.	**med**		**n̥sméd**	

Second Person

	Singular **tu-, te-**		*Plural* **ju-, we-**	
	Orthotonic	*Enclitic*	Orthotonic	*Encliti*
NOM.	**tū, tu**, *thou*		**juwes, jusmés**, *you*	
ACC.	**tewóm**, *thee*	***t(w)e***	**jusmé, wōns**, *you*	***wos***
GEN.	**tewe**; *of thee*	***t(w)o***	**wesróm**, *of you*	***wos***
DAT.	**tebhei, tebhjo**	***t(w)oi***	**jusméi, wosbhos**	***wos***
LOC.	**t(w)ei**		**jusmí, wosi**	
INS.	**t(w)ojo**		**wosbhis**	
ABL.	**t(w)ed**		**jusméd**	

NOTE. A comprehensive comparison of the reconstructed forms is at the end of this book:

1) For 1st P. Nom. **eghóm** (<*egh$_2$-óm*), emphatic from **egṓ** (<*eg-óh$_2$*), *cf.* O.Ind. *ahám*, Av. *azəm*, Hom.Gk. *εγων*, Ven. *ehom*.

2) Enclitics **moi**, **mei**, and **t(w)oi**, **t(w)ei**, are found in genitive, dative and locative, but they are deliberately specialised in this table.

3) 1st sg. dative is often found reconstructed as ***mebhi/mebhei***, following the 2nd pl. **tebhei/tebhi**.

4) ***-es*** endings in nom. pl., **n̥smés**, **(j)usmés** (<*juswés*?) attested in Att.-Ion. Greek and Gothic.

5) An older **ju(s)wes** is probably behind the generally reconstructed nominative *jūHs?* based on Balto-Slavic (and Germanic) forms, which would therefore be a contraction of the original form (*cf.* Skt. *yū-yám*, Gk. *u-meis*, Lat. *uōs*, Cel. *s-wīs*, Goth. *iz-wis<*uz-wes?*)

6) Zero-grade forms in ***jus***- are also found as ***us***- (from ***wes***-? *cf.* Goth. *izwis*<**uswes?*).

7) Possibly accusatives **jusmé**<**jusmēn*<***jusmens*, and **n̥smé**<**n̥smēn*<***n̥smens*.

8) Probably acc. pl. ***nos-m-s*→**nōns** and ***wos-m-s*→**wōns**.

8) Gen. **nŏsom**, **wŏsom**, is also attested.

9) Osc.-Umb., O.Ind. variant (orthotonic) series of Acc. Sg. in -***m***, as ***mēm***(***e***), ***twēm***, ***tewem***, ***usóm***, ***s(w)ēm***.

10) Dual forms (in *-h_1) are for the 1st nom. **wē**, acc. tonic **n̥wé**, enclitic **nō**; for the 2nd **jū**, acc. tonic **ūwé**, enclitic **wō**.

For the personal pronouns of the third person singular and plural, the anaphoric **i**- is used. See §6.5 and §6.6 for more details on its use and inflection.

6.3. REFLEXIVE PRONOUNS

6.3.1. Reflexive pronouns are used in the accusative and the oblique cases to refer to the subject of the sentence or clause in which they stand, meaning '(one)self'.

They do not have a nominative case, do not distinguish number, and can be used with any of the three persons.

se, *-self*

ACC.	**se**, *myself, yourself, him-/her-/itself, ourselves, yourselves, themselves.*
GEN.	**sewe**, ***soi***, *of myself, yourself, him-/her-/itself, ourselves, themselves.*
ABL.	**swed**, *by/from/*etc. *myself, yourself, him-/her-/itself, ourselves, themselves.*
DAT.	**sebhei**, ***soi***, *to myself, yourself, him-/her-/itself, ourselves, themselves..*
L.-I.	**sei**, *in/with myself, yourself, him-/her-/itself, ourselves, themselves..*

NOTE. Particular IE languages show an old **swoi** and **swe**, *cf.* Gk. Lesb. ϝε. According to J.T. Katz precisely this **swe** is regarded as ancient and **se** as secondary. In contrast, G.E. Dunkel connects **se/soi**, which he considers more ancient, with the demonstrative pronoun **so**.

6.3.2. The reciprocals *one another*, *each other*, were expressed like the distributives (*v.s.* §5.5.4), with the first member in the nominative, and the second in the accusative (or other oblique case); as, **aljos aljom**, **onjos onjom**, etc.; as,

NOTE. *Cf.* Hitt. *1-aš 1-an ku-w-aš-ki-it* 'one killed the other continuously', O.Ind. *anyonya-*<**anyás anyám*, Av. *aniiō.aniia-*, Chor. *nywny*, Gk. *allālo-*<**alos allon*, **alloi allous* 'one another', Lat. *aliī aliōs*, *alterius alterum*; for ***oinos álterom***, *cf.* Latin *unus alterum*, Eng. *one another*, Ger. *einander*, etc. Reciprocity is one of the principal meanings of middle voice forms, *v.i.* §7.1.2.

6.4. POSSESSIVE PRONOUNS

6.4.1. From the bases of the personal pronouns, the oldest possessive pronouns were **mos**, *mine*, **n̥smós**, *ours*, **twos**, *thine*, **usmós**, *yours*, **swos**, *own*.

NOTE. So e.g. in Gk. *emós* (<**$h_1$mós*), *ammos*, *sós*, *ummos*, *hos*, Av. *ma-*, *θwa-*, O.Ind. *twa-*. Variants exist in ***tewós*** (as Gk. teϝós, Lat. *tuus*), ***sewós*** (as Gk. heϝós, Lat. *suus*), explained as neologisms, but "which may well be as early as Late PIE" (Sihler 1995).

6.4.2. The common Late Indo-European possessives were formed from the same bases with suffixes ***-(i)jo-*** in the singular, ***-(t)ero-*** in the plural; as, **méwijos**, **menjos**, *my*, **n̥serós**, *our*, **téwijos**, *thy*, **userós**, *your*, **séwijos**.

NOTE. For such common PIE forms, similar to the genitives of the personal pronouns (*v.s.* §6.2), *cf.* Gk. *ēméteros* (<*n̥smé-tero-*), *uméteros* (<*usmé-tero-*), O.Lat. *noster* (<*nos-tero-*) *uoster* (<*wos-tero-*), Goth. *unsara-*, (<*n̥s-ero-*), *izwara-* (<*wesw-ero-?*), etc. all used as possessive pronouns; for the singular, *cf.* Lat. *meus*, O.C.S. *mojĭ*, Goth *meina-*, etc. O.Ind. *madīya-*, *twadīya*, etc. were formed from the ablatives *mad*, *twad*, etc., while possessives *mamaka-*, *asmāka-*, *jusmāka-*, were made from the genitives. See Szemerényi (1970), Adrados–Bernabé–Mendoza (1995-1998), Meier-Brügger (2003).

6.4.3. Possessives are declined like adjectives of the first type, in ***-os***, ***-ā***, ***-om***.

NOTE. PIE **swos**, **séwijos**, are only used as reflexives, referring generally to the subject of the sentence. For a possessive of the third person not referring to the subject, the genitive of the anaphoric must be used. Thus, **paterm̥ séwijom chenti**, *(s)he/it kills his [own] father*; but **paterm̥ esjo chenti**, *(s)he/it kills his [somebody* (m.) *else's] father*. See below §10.1.2 for more on its use.

6.5. ANAPHORIC PRONOUNS

6.5.1. Anaphora is an instance of an expression referring to another, the weak part of the deixis. In general, an anaphoric is represented by a pro-form or some kind of deictic. They usually don't have adjectival use, and are only used as mere abbreviating substitutes of the noun.

NOTE. Old anaphorics were usually substituted in modern IE languages by demonstratives.

They are usually integrated into the pronoun system with gender; only occasionally some of these anaphorics have been integrated into the personal pronouns system in Indo-European languages.

6.5.2. Indo-European has a general anaphoric pronoun, **is**, **ja/ī id**, an old demonstrative pronoun with basis on PIE root **i-** with ablaut **ei-**.

NOTE. PIE root **i-** is also the base for common relative **jo-**. Demonstrative **is**, **ja/ī**, **id**, with anaphoric value, "he/she/it", in Italic (e.g. Lat. *is*, *ea*, *id*), Germanic (e.g. O.H.G. *ir*, *er/iz, ez*), Baltic (e.g. Lith. *jìs/jì*), Greek (e.g. Cypriot *ín*), Indo-Iranian (e.g. Skt. *ay-ám, iy-ám, i-d-ám*).

6.5.3. The other demonstrative pronoun, **so, sā, tod**, functions as anaphoric too, but tends to appear leading the sentence, being its origin probably the relative. They are also used for the second term in comparisons.

NOTE. Demonstrative **so, sā, tod** is also widely attested in Celtic (e.g. O.Ir. *-so/-d*), Italic (e.g. Lat. *is-te, is-ta, is-tud*), Germanic (e.g. Goth. *sa, sō, þata*, O.Eng. *sē, sēo, þæt*, O.H.G. *der, die, daz*), Baltic (e.g. Lith. *tàs, tà*), Slavic (e.g. O.C.S. *tŭ, ta, to*), Alb. *ai, ajo*, Gk. *ho, hē, tó*, Indo-Iranian (e.g. Skt. *sá*, sā́, *tát*), Toch B *se, sā, te*, Arm. *ay-d*, Hitt. *ta*. Modern IE languages have sometimes mixed both forms to create a single system, while others maintain the old differentiation.

6.6. DEMONSTRATIVE PRONOUNS

6.6.1. The function of demonstrative pronouns, *deixis*, includes an indication of position in relation to the person speaking. It is possible to express a maximum of four (generally three) different degrees of distance; as, *I-deixis* (here, near the speaker), *thou-deixis* (there, near the person addressed), *that-deixis* (there, without a particular spatial reference), *yonder-deixis* (yonder, over there).

6.6.2. The demonstrative pronouns **so**, *this, that*, and **is**, *this one, that one*, *"the (just named)"*, are used to point out or designate a person or thing for special attention, either with nouns, as adjectives, or alone, as pronouns, and are declined as follows:

so, sā, tod, *this, that*

	Singular			*Plural*		
	masc.	*neu.*	*fem.*	*masc.*	*neu.*	*fem.*
NOM	**so(s)**	**tod**	**sā**	**toi**	**tā**	**tāi**
ACC.	**tom**		**tām**	**tons**		**tāns**
GEN.	**tosjo**		**tosjās**	**toisom**		**tāsom**
ABL.	**tosmōd**		**tosjās**	**toibhos/toimos**		**tābhos/tāmos**
DAT.	**tosmōi**		**tosjāi**	**toibhos/toimos**		**tābhos/tāmos**
LOC.	**tosmi**		**tosjāi**	**toisu**		**tāsu**
INS.	**toi**		**tosjā**	**tōis**		**tābhis/tāmis**

NOTE. Variants are observed in the attested dialects: 1) Nom. **so** (before all consonants) is also found as **sos** in Old Indian, Greek and Gothic (in all other circumstances), and as **se** in Latin (*cf.* Lat. *ipse*). 2) Nom. **sā** is found as **sja/sī** in Germanic and Celtic. 3) Nom. Pl.

tāi is general, while **sāi** is restricted to some dialects, as Attic-Ionic Greek, possibly from original fem. **tā* and masc. **to* (Meier-Brügger 2003). However, linguists like Beekes (1995) or Adrados–Bernabé–Mendoza (1995-1998) reconstruct the nominative form in ***s***- as the original Proto-Indo-European form. 4) Forms in **tes**- for the feminine singular forms are supported by findings in Germanic, mainly (Beekes 1995). 5) The instrumental singular forms are difficult to reconstruct with the available data, but the dative is also often reconstructed as **tosmei**, along with **tosmōi**.

is, ja, id, *this one, that one*

	Singular			*Plural*		
	masc.	*neu.*	*fem.*	*masc.*	*neu.*	*fem.*
NOM	**is**	**id**	**ja/ī**	**ejes**	**ī/ja**	**jās**
ACC.	**im**		**jam/īm**	**ins**		**jāns**
GEN.	**esjo**		**esjās**	**eisom**		
ABL.	**esmōd**		**esjās**	**eibhos/eimos**		
DAT.	**esmōi**		**esjāi**	**eibhos/eimos**		
LOC.	**esmi**		**esjāi**	**eisu**		
INS.	**ei**		**esjā**	**eibhis/eimis**		

NOTE. Some emphatic forms exist; as, ***ejóm*** for **is**, ***idóm*** for **id**; ***ijóm*** for **ja**.

6.6.2. Distance degrees in demonstratives might be classified as follows: **kos**, **kā**, **kod** (also **ghei-ke**, **ghāi-ke**, **ghod-ke**), *I-deixis*, '*this here*', **oisos**, **oisā**, **oisom**, *thou-deixis*, '*this there*', general **so**, **tod**, **sā**, *that-deixis*; **elne**, **elnā**, **elnod**, *yonder-deixis*.

NOTE. While there is no definite or indefinite article in PIE, and nouns might be translated as indefinite or definite depending on the context – as in Sanskrit or Latin –, when the difference is crucial demonstratives are used. See §10.4.3.

6.6.3. Deictic particles which appear frequently with demonstrative pronouns include -***ke***/-***ko***-, *here*; -***ne***-/-***no***-, *there*; -***wo***-, *away*, *again*.

NOTE. For PIE ***i***-, ***se***-, *he*, *cf.* Lat. *is*, O.Ind. *saḥ*, *esaḥ*, Hitt. *apā*, Goth. *is*, O.Ir. *(h)í*.

For -***ke***/-***ko***-, in (**e**)**ke**, **ghei**-(**ke**), *this* (*here*), *cf.* Hitt. *kās*, *eda* (def.), Lat. *hic* (<**ghe-i-ke*), Goth. *hi-*, *sa(h)*, O.Ir. *sin*, O.C.S. *sĭ*, *si*, *se*, Lith. šìs, *ši*.

For **ke-enos**, *cf.* Gk. *keĩnos* (<**ke-enos*), O.N. *hánn*, *hann*, 'he'; for ***au***-, *away*, *again*, *cf.* Gk. *houtos*, O.Ind. *a-sau*, *u-*, Av. *ava-*, OCS. *ovĭ...ovĭ*.

For ***se***-, ***te***-, in **oi-se**, **is-te**, **ene**, *this* (*there*), *cf.* Lat. *iste*, Gk. *οιος* (<**oihos*), O.Ind. *enam* (clit.).

For **en-**, *cf.* O.C.S. *onĭ*, Lith. *anàs* 'that'.

For **-ne**, **-no-**, *that*, *cf.* Lat. *ille* (<**el-ne*), *ollus* (<**ol-nos*), Gk. *keĩnos* (<**ke-enos*), Goth. *jains*.

Common derivatives **kei**, *here* (loc. from **ke**), **num-ke**, *now* (from **nū**, *now*), or **i-dhei**, *there*, **tom-ke**, *then* (from **tom**, *then*).

Latin *(c)ibī, (c)ubī* are frequently found reconstructed as PIE **ibhi*, **qobhi* (*cf.* Hitt. *kuwaapi(t)*, see Kloekhorst 2007), but it is not difficult to find a common origin in PIE ***i-dhei***, ***qo-dhei*** for similar forms attested in different IE dialects; *cf.* Lat. *ubī*, Osc. *puf*, O.Ind. *kuha*, O.Sla. *kude*, etc.

6.7. INTERROGATIVE AND INDEFINITE PRONOUNS

6.7.1. INTRODUCTION

1. There are two forms of the interrogative-indefinite pronoun in Proto-Indo-European, and each one corresponded to a different class: **qi-** (with ablaut **qei-**) to the substantive, and **qo-** to the adjective pronouns.

SUBSTANTIVE	*ADJECTIVE*
qis bhéreti? *who carries?*	**qos wīrós bhéreti?** *what man carries?*
qid widḗjesi? *what do you see?*	**qom autom widḗjesi?** *which car do you*

NOTE. In the origin, **qi-/qo-** was possibly a noun which meant 'the unknown', and its interrogative/indefinite sense depended on the individual sentences. Later both became pronouns with gender, thus functioning as (orthotonic) interrogatives or (enclitic) indefinites (Szemerényi, 1970). The form **qi-** is probably the original independent form (compare the degree of specialisation of **qo-**, further extended in IE dialects), for which **qo-** could have been originally the o-grade form (Beekes 1995, Adrados–Bernabé–Mendoza 1995-1998).

The substantive interrogative pronoun in PIE was **qi-**, whereas **qo-** was used to fill adjectival functions (Meier-Brügger 2003, Sihler 1995). Some IE dialects have chosen the o-stem only, as Germanic, while some others have mixed them together in a single paradigm, as Indo-Iranian, Balto-Slavic or Italic. *Cf.* Sktr. *kaḥ*, Av. *ko*, Gk. *tis*, Lat. *qui*, *quae*, *quod*; *quis*, *quid*, Osc. *pisi*, Umb. *púí*, *svepis*, O.Pers. *čiy*, Pers. *ki*, Phryg. *kos*, Toch. *kus/kŭse*, Arm. *ov*, *inč'*, Gmc. **khʷo-* (*cf.* Goth. *hwas*, O.N. *hverr*, O.S. *hwe*, O.E. *hwā*, Dan. *hvo*, O.Fris. *hwa*, O.H.G. *hwër*), Lith. *kas*, Ltv. *kas*, O.C.S. *kuto*, Rus. *kto*, Pol. *kto*, O.Ir. *ce*, *cid*, Welsh *pwy*, Alb. *kush*, Kam. *kâča*; in Anatolian, compare Hitt. *kuiš*, Luw. kui-, Lyd. *qi-*, Lyc. *tike*, and Carian *kuo*.

2. The substantive interrogative pronoun **qis?** *who?* **qid?** *what*?, declined like **i-**:

	Singular			*Plural*		
	m.	*f.*	*n.*	*m.*	*f.*	*n.*
NOM.	**qis**		**qid**	**qejes**		**qī/qja**
ACC.	**qim**			**qins**		
GEN.	**qesjo**			**qeisom**		
ABL.	**qesmōd**			**qeibhos/qeimos**		
DAT.	**qesmei**			**qeibhos/qeimos**		
LOC.	**qesmi**			**qeisu**		
INS.	**qī**			**qeibhis/qeimis**		

NOTE. PIE **-qe**, *and*, is probably derived from the same root, and was originally a modal adverb meaning 'as, like'; e.g. **patḗr mātērqe**, *father like mother* (Szemerényi 1970). Similarly, **jo-** is probably behind Hitt. *-ya*.

3. The adjective interrogative pronoun, **qos? qā?** *who (of them)?,* **qod?** *what kind of? what one?*, is declined throughout like the relative:

	Singular			*Plural*		
	m.	*f.*	*n.*	*m.*	*f.*	*n.*
NOM.	**qos**	**qā(i)**	**qod**	**qoi**	**qās**	**qā**
ACC.	**qom**	**qām**		**qons**	**qāns**	
GEN.	**qosjo**			**qoisom**		
ABL.	**qosmōd**			**qoibhos/qoimos**		
DAT.	**qosmōi**			**qoibhos/qoimos**		
LOC.	**qosmi**			**qoisu**		
INS.	**qoi**			**qoibhis/qoimis**		

NOTE. Italic had a dat.-abl. *k^wois < **k^wōis** (de Vaan, p. 508). Apart from the instrumental in -ei, parallel to instrumental *k^wiH_1 , an instrumental in -iH_1 is proposed (de Vaan, página 522).

4. The indefinite pronouns **qi-/qo-**, *any one, any*, are declined like the corresponding interrogatives.

SUBSTANTIVE	**qis**, *anyone*; **qid**, *anything*
ADJECTIVE	**qos**, **qā**, **qod**, *any*

5. PIE had other interrogative or relative particle, ***me-/mo-***.

NOTE. It survived in Celtic (e.g. Bret *ma, may* 'that'), Anatolian (Hit. *masi* 'how much'), and Tocharian (Toch. A *mänt* 'how'). For more on this question, see the article <http://www.indogermanistik.uni-muenchen.de/downloads/publikationen/publ_hackstein/discoursesyntax.pdf>.

6.7.2. COMPOUNDS

1. The pronouns **qi-** and **qo-** appear in different combinations:

a. The forms can be repeated, as in substantive **qisqis**, *anyone*, **qidqid**, *anything*, or adjective **qāqos**, **qāqā**, **qāqod**, *whoever*.

NOTE. For this use, similar to the distributive ones, e.g. **qāqos**, *whoever*, *cf.* Gaul. *papon*, O.Ir. *cāch*, O.C.S. *kakŭ*, Lith. *kók(i)s*, and also Gk. *εκατερος, εκαστος*, O.Ind. *pratieka*, Hitt. *kuissa*, Goth. *ainhvaþaruh*; for **qisqis**, *anyone*, *cf.* Gk. *τις, οστις*, O.Ind. *kim kid, kacit, kaścana, kopi*, Hitt. *kuis kuis, kuis-as kuis*, Lat. *quisquis, quīlĭbĕt, quīvis*, Goth. *hvazuh, hvarjizuh*, Arm. *in-č*.

Other common PIE forms include **solwos**, *all*, *cf.* Gk. *ολοι*, O.Ind. *visva, sarva*, Hitt. *hūmant-*, O.Ir. *u(i)le*; **enis**, *certain*, *cf.* Gk. ἔνιοι, O.Ind. *ekaścana* Lat. *quīdam*; **álteros**, **ónteros**, *the other*, from **aljos**, **onjos**, *some other*, etc.

b. In some forms the copulative conjunction **-qe** is added to form new pronouns, usually *universals*; as, **qiskomqe**, **qisimmoqe**, *whoever*. Indefinites **itaqe**, *and also*, **toqe**, *also*, **joqe**, *and*.

NOTE. *Cf.* Gk. *τις αν, τις εαν*, O.Ind. *yaḥ kaś cit, yo yaḥ, yadanga*, Hitt. *kuis imma, kuis imma kuis, kuis-as imma (kuis)*, Lat. *quiscumque*, Goth. *sahvazuh saei*, Ger. *wer auch immer*, O.Ir. *cibé duine*, Russ. *кто бы ни*;

c. Some forms are made with prefixes, like (substantive) **edqis**, *some(one) among many*, **edqid**, *something*, (adjective) **edqos**, **edqā**, **edqod**, *whether, some*. Other forms with suffixes; as, **qéjespejoi**, *some*.

NOTE. For (**ed**)**qis**, *cf.* Gk. *τις*, O.Ind. *anyatama*, Hitt. *kuis ki*, Lat. *ecquis, quis, aliquis*, Goth. *hvashun*, Russ. *edvá*, O.Ir. *nech, duine*. For **qéjespejoi** *cf.* Gk. *οιτινες*, O.Ind. *katipaya*, Hitt. *kuis ki*, Russ. *несколько*.

d. The negatives are usually composed with negation particles, usually **ne**; as, **neqis**, *nobody*, **neqid**, *nothing*, **neqom**, *never*; but **neqos**, *someone*.

NOTE. For **neqis**, *nobody, no one*, *cf.* Gk. *ουδεις*, O.Ind. *na kaḥ*, Hitt. *UL kuiski*, Goth. (*ni*) *hvashun*, Gaul. *nepon*, O.Ir. *ní aon duine*, Lat. *nec quisquam*, Russ. *никто*.

e. It is also found as in compound with relative **jo-**; as, **jos qis**, *anyone*, **jod qid**, *anything*, *cf.* Gk. *hóstis hótti*, Skt. *yás cit, yác cit*.

f. With identity or oppositive forms; as, **qidpe**, *indeed*, **aljodhei**, *elsewhere*.

2. There are compounds with numerals; as, **ghei-sem**, *exactly so, in this one way*.

NOTE. *Cf.* Hitt. *ki-ššan* 'thus, in the following way', from ***ghei-sem***, *'in this one way, exactly so'*, also found in *eni-ššan* 'thus, in the manner mentioned', *apeni-ššan* 'thus, in that way', etc. For **ne-oinom**, *'no one', none, not any*, *cf.* Eng. *none*, Ger. *nein*, maybe Lat. *nōn*. Also, Latin *nūllus* (<***ne-oinolos***, *'not any'*), *none, null*.

3. Reflexives are found in **jota sei**, *alike, nearly*, **sweike**, *thus*, **swāi**, *so*, etc.

6.7.3. CORRELATIVES

1. Many pronouns, pronominal adjectives and adverbs have corresponding demonstrative, relative, and interrogative-indefinite forms in Indo-European. Such parallel forms are called correlatives, and some common forms are the following:

Demonstrative	*Relative in* **jo-**	*Interrogative*
so, sā, tod *this, that*	**jos, jā, jod** *who, which*	**qis? qid?, qos? qā? qod?** *who?, what? which?*
ita *so*	**jota** *so*	**qota?** *how?*
tālis *so constituted*	***jālis*** *as*	**qālis?** *of what sort?*
tām *that way*	***jām*** *which way*	**qām?** *how, in what way?*
tom, todā́ *then*	**jom** *when*	**qom? qodā́?** *when?*
idhei, tor *here, there*	**jodhei** *where*	**qor? qodhei?** *where?*
tŏ̄i *thither*	***jŏ̄i*** *whither*	**qŏ̄i? qote?** *whither?*
totrōd *from there*	**jomde** *wherefrom*	**qomde? qotrōd?** *from which?*

totjos *so many*	**jotjos** *as many*	**qotjos?** *how many?*
toti *so often*	**joti** *as often*	**qoti?** *how often?*
tā́wn̥ts *so much/large*	**jā́wn̥ts** *as much/large*	**qā́wn̥ts?** *how much/large?*
to(s)jo *of whom/which*	**josjo** *whose*	**qosjo?** *pertaining to*
íteros *(an)other*	**jóteros** *which (of two)*	**qóteros?** *which (of two)?*
tori *therefore*	**jori** *wherefore*	**qori?** *why?*

NOTE. Relative forms in italics are inferred following the general paradigm, because its reconstruction is missing with the available comparative data. The rest of them are reconstructed in Mallory–Adams (2007), Szemerényi (1996), Sihler (1995), among others. For pronoun **jāwod-**, *so long as, so far, cf.* O.Ind *jāvat,* gr. ἕως < **jānts* < ***jāwods***?, although both forms could be from **jāwnts**. A pronoun **tāwod**-<**teh₂wod-* 'so many, so long' is found in Gk. *téōs,* 'so long, meanwhile', Indo-Iranian (e.g. Skt. *e-tā́vat* 'so much, so many; so great, so far'), and Tocharian (e.g. Toch B *tot* 'so much, so many; so great; so far'); see below Conjunctions, § 8.5. For support of the **jāwnt-** form, *cf.* ***tawn̥t-*** in Lat. *lātrīna* <**lawatrīna*); however, Lat. *tantum* is reconstructed as **teH₂n̥t-*→***tānt-*** (Hackstein, de Vaan).

6.8. RELATIVE PRONOUNS

6.8.1. There are two general pronominal stems used as relative pronouns, one related to the anaphorics (**jo-**), and one to the interrogative-indefinites (**qi-**/**qo-**).

NOTE. The interrogative pronoun is also used as indefinite in all IE languages. In some it is used additionally as relative, without differentiation in Anatolian, with it in Italic (e.g. Lat. *quo-* opposed to *quis*), Tocharian, later Celtic, Germanic and Baltic; the other group, comprising Aryan, Greek, Phrygian and Slavic kept using the PIE relative pronoun **jo-** (<**Hjo-*), from the anaphoric root **i-**; *cf.* Gk. *hós, hē, ho,* Skt. *yás, yā, yad,* Av. *ya-*, Phryg. *ios,* Sla. *i-že,* Cel. *io,* Goth *ja-bai,* maybe Hitt. *ya,* Toch. A *yo.* Despite Szemerényi (1970), who considers it mainly a S.LIE innovation, only Proto-Italic shows no traces of the common PIE relative, and because of that it is generally considered lost in that branch, not an innovation of the others.

6.8.2. PIE forms in **jo-** introduced appositive-explicative relative clauses, while those in **qi-**/**qo-** introduced attributive-restrictive clauses. For more information, see below §10.5.3.

6.8.3. IE relative pronoun **jos, jā, jod**, the o-stem derivative from **i-**, is inflected like **so, sā, tod**.

6.9. OTHER PRONOUNS

6.9.1. Identity pronouns are those generally called intensifiers or emphatic pronouns, expressions like Eng. '*x-self* (*himself, herself, myself, oneself*, etc.), Ger. *selbst, selber*, Lat. *ipse*, Ita. *stesso* or Russ. *sam*.

Proto-Indo-European formations that function as identity pronouns stem from a common **epe**, *self*; as, **se epse**, **s(w)el (e)pe**, *-self*.

NOTE. *cf.* Hitt. *apāsila*, O.Lat. *sapsa, sumpse, ipse*, Goth. *silba*, O.Ir. *fessin, fadessin* (>*féin*), Russ. *сам*.

6.9.2. Oppositive pronouns are usually derived from suffix ***-tero-***; as, **qóteros?** *which of two?* **íteros**, *another*, **álteros**, *the other one*, **próteros**, *first (of two)*.

NOTE. For **qóteros**, *cf.* Lat *uter*, O.Eng. *hwæðer* (Eng. *whether*), Lith *kataràs*, OCS *koteryjĭ*, Gk. *póteros*, Skt. *katará-*; from this word is Latin *neuter*<**neqóteros**, '*neither one nor the other*'. For **sn̥terí**, *missing*, *cf.* Gmc. **sun-dr-* (e.g. Ger. *sonder*), Gk ατερ (*ater*), O.Ind. *sanutar*; from **sni**, *apart*, *cf.* Lat. *sine* 'without', Goth. *sundrō*, O.Sla. *svene*, O.Ir. *sain* 'different'.

6.9.3. Adjectival pronouns include identity as well as oppositive pronouns; as, **somós**, *the same*, or **aljos, onjos**, *the other*.

NOTE. Such nominal forms, properly categorised as vaguely belonging to the field of pronuns, receive pronominal inflection. For adj. **somós**, *equal, same, cf.* Gmc. **samaz*, Gk. ὁμός, ὁμοῦ, ὁμαλός, Skt. *samaḥ*, Av. *hama*, O.C.S. *самъ*, O.Ir. *som*. The best attested pronominal adjective is **aljos, aljā, aljom**, *other* (*cf.* Gk. *állos*, Lat. *alius*, Goth. *aljis*, O.Ir. *ail*, Toch. B *alyek*).

7. VERBS

7.1. INTRODUCTION

7.1.1. VOICE, MOOD, TENSE, PERSON, NUMBER

1. The inflection of the verb is called its conjugation.

2. Through its conjugation the verb expresses voice, mood, tense, person and number.

3. The voices are two: active and middle (or more exactly *middle-passive*).

4. The moods were up to five:

a. The indicative, for plain statement of objective fact.

b. The imperative, for commands.

c. The optative, for intentions or hopes for action.

d. The subjunctive, for potentiality, possibility.

NOTE. An old injunctive is also reconstructed to account for S.LIE forms; *v.i.* §7.4.2.

5. The general tenses are three, *viz.*:

a. The present.

b. The past.

c. The future.

NOTE. The so-called *future stem* is generally believed to have been an innovation in post-LIE, not spreading to some dialects before the general split of the proto-languages; however, the distinction between a present and a future tense is common to all IE languages.

6. The aspects were up to three:

a. For continued, not completed action, the present.

b. For the state derived from the action, the perfect (or more exactly *stative*).

c. For completed action, the aorist.

7. There are three verbal tense-stems we will deal with in this grammar:

I. The present stem, which gives the present with primary endings and the imperfect with secondary endings.

II. The aorist stem with secondary endings, giving the aorist (always past), usually in zero grade, with dialectal augment.

III. The perfect stem, giving the perfect, only later specialised in present and past.

NOTE. From this reconstructed original PIE verbal system, a future stem was created from some present stem formations. The aorist merged with the imperfect stem in Northwestern dialects, and further with the perfect stem in Germanic, Italic, Celtic and Tocharian. The aorist, meaning the completed action, is then reconstructed as a third PIE aspect, following mainly the findings of Old Indian, Greek, and also – mixed with the imperfect and perfect stems – Latin.

8. The persons are three: first, second, and third.

9. The numbers in the Indo-European verb are two: singular and plural, and it is the only common class with the noun. It is marked very differently, though.

NOTE. The reconstructed dual in the verbal system seems to have been a late development, systematised only after the LIE split in some dialects, and disappeared in others, see §3.5.

7.1.2. VOICE

1. In grammar, voice is the relationship between the action or state expressed by a verb and its arguments.

2. When the subject is the agent or actor of the verb, the verb is said to be in the active. When the subject is in some way affected by the verbal action, it is said to be in the middle-passive.

NOTE. For Clackson (2007): "The middle is the voice used to denote that the subject is in some way affected by the verbal action. Thus, for transitive verbs the active typically represents the subject as the actor, and the middle represents the subject as the undergoer. For intransitive verbs the middle is preferred when there is some notion of control over the verbal action (hence the middle inflection of 'think' and 'speak'), but if the verb denotes an event or action where the participant cannot have control, the active is used (thus 'be', 'vomit' and 'wait')."

2. The active and middle-passive voices in Indo-European generally correspond to the active and passive in English. The middle had these uses in LIE (Clackson 2007):

a. Personal involvement, or sense of benefaction for the subject; as, Skt. *yájati* (active) '(s)he performs a sacrifice' (said from the priest), and *yájate* '(s)he performs a sacrifice' (said of person for whose benefit the sacrifice is made).

b. Reflexivity, generally referring to an action whose object is the subject, or an action in which the subject has an interest or a special participation; as, Greek

lówō (active), *I wash*, **lówomar** (middle), *I wash myself*, or **wéstijetor**, *(s)he dresses (him/herself), (s)he gets dressed.*

c. Reciprocity; as, Hitt. *appanzi* (active) 'they take', Hittite *SU-za appantat* (lit. hand take-*middle*) 'they took each other by the hand'.

b. Passivity, usually meaning that an action is done. This is the default meaning in Italo-Celtic and Germanic, also found in the Greek and Anatolian middle; as, **stoighōs péwontor**, *streets are (being) cleaned.*

NOTE. According to Fortson (2004): "The middle could also express the passive voice, which indicates that the subject is acted upon by someone else: 'is being fought', 'was washed'. A tradition of scholarship rejects positing a passive voice for PIE because there was no separate set of passive endings. But all the daughter languages that have a separate passive conjugation have developed it in whole or in part from the PIE middle endings, and it seems best to regard the middle as having been, in fact, a mediopassive or middle-passive – capable of expressing either voice depending on the context."

3. Apart from this middle-passive voice system, the relic of an old impersonal -**(ĕ̄)r** desinence is reconstructed for LIE times.

NOTE. This desinence begins in the third person (singular or plural), according to Jasanoff (*"The* r-*endings of the Indo-European middle", Sprache 23*, 1977) and Szeméreny (1985), and probably not as middle mark, as proposed by Kuryłovicz (*Indogermanische Grammatik II Akzent-Ablaut*, 1968) and Bader (*"Relations de structure entre les desinences d'infectum et de perfectum en latin", Word 24*, 1968); it is indeed probably at the origin of middle-passive primary endings in -**r**, though, but was apparently used as impersonal mark within the active voice. It is the oldest reconstructed meaning of the -**r** ending, and it is only found originally in the 3rd sg. and 3rd pl. (probably originally without lengthening or distinction of singular vs. plural). The ending is reconstructed as *-(ĕ̄)r. It is found in Italo-Celtic, Germanic (*cf.* O.H.G. *skritun*), Tocharian, Old Indian, and possibly in Armenian. Adrados–Bernabé–Mendoza (1995-1998).

It marked impersonality, as in Celtic impersonal verbal forms; it is similar to Eng. 'there' in 'there are three books', and equivalent to Ger. '*es wird*' in '*es wird geschlafen*', or Spa. '*se*' in '*aquí se duerme*'. It was attached directly to the present, aorist or perfect stem. So e.g. ***kei sweper***, *one sleeps here*, '*it is slept here*', ***edjēu wr̥gjer***, *today one works*, '*it is worked today*'.

4. Some verbs are only active; as, **esmi**, *be*, **edmi**, *eat*, or **dōmi**, *give*.

5. Many verbs are middle-passive in form, but active or reflexive in meaning. These are called deponents in Latin; as, **gnāskōr**, *be born*, **keimōr**, *lie, lay*; **séqomar**, *follow*, etc.

7.1.3. MOODS

1. The mood in which a verb appears expresses the speaker's attitude or stance taken towards the action – whether (s)he is asserting that it is factual, or indicating a wish that it were or were not true, or reporting the action second-hand, or indicating a contrafactual condition (Fortson 2004).

NOTE. While the oldest PIE had possibly only indicative and imperative, a subjunctive and an optative were common in Late Indo-European, both used in the present, perfect and aorist. Not all dialects, however, developed those new formations further into a full system.

2. The indicative mood is used for most direct assertions and interrogations, with the action described as fact.

3. The imperative is used for exhortation, entreaty, or command.

3. The subjunctive mood is used for actions described as completely theoretical, generally with a future meaning, frequently translated by means of the auxiliaries *may*, *might*, *would*, *should*.

c. The optative is used to express wishes, hopes, and various other non-factual modalities.

7.1.4. ASPECT

1. Aspect is a grammatical category that refers to the type of action indicated by a verb. Actions can be done once or repeatedly, to completion or not, or be ongoing with neither a true beginning nor end.

2. According to the generally accepted view, the imperfect and aorist were distinct aspectually, the imperfect expressing incomplete or ongoing action in past time (imperfective aspect), the aorist indicating completed or punctual (one-time) action in past time (perfective aspect).

3. The perfect or *stative* referred to a current state derived from the action (resultative aspect), without a temporal reference.

NOTE. A number of archaic examples of the perfect, especially in Indo-Iranian and Greek, refer to states in present time; so e.g. Lat. *meminit* 'remembers', Gk. *mémone*, Goth. *man* 'is mindful of', 'thinks'. Furthermore, the singular perfect endings are sued to inflect a class of presents in Anatolian, the so-called ḫi-conjugation. These facts together have led researchers to believe that the PIE perfect was a stative. In the dialects attested, however, except for relic forms like these, perfect forms express past tense; to explain this development, it is usually said that the PIE stative perfect had (or optionally had) resultative overtones ('is in a state resulting from having done X', therefore 'has done X'). Fortson (2004).

The Late Indo-European aspectual system might be so depicted, using a amore exact vs. the traditional notation:

Process	Aspect	Aspect (traditional)	Tense	Tense (traditional)
Stative	Stative	Perfect system	(unmarked)	Perfect tense
Eventive	Perfective	Aorist system	(unmarked)	Aorist tense
	Imperfective	Present system	Present	Present tense
			Past	Imperfect tense

The terminology around the stative, perfective and imperfective aspects can be confusing. The use of these terms in this table is based on the reconstructed meanings of the corresponding forms in PIE and the terms used broadly in linguistics to refer to aspects with these meanings. In traditional PIE terminology, the forms described in the above table as *stative*, *perfective* and *imperfective* are known as the perfect, aorist and present systems. The present/imperfective system in turn can be conjugated in two tenses, described here as present and past but traditionally known as present and imperfect. The traditional terms are based on the names of the corresponding forms in Ancient Greek (also applied to Sanskrit), and are commonly encountered. The existence of the terms 'perfect' and 'perfective', with quite different semantics, is especially problematic, and is a perennial source of confusion in linguistics as a whole.

7.1.5. TENSES OF THE FINITE VERB

The tenses of the indicative have, in general, the same meaning as the corresponding tenses in English:

a. Of continued action

I. Present: **deikō**, *I show, I am showing, I do show*

II. Imperfect: **deikom**, *I was showing, I used to show*

b. Of completed action or the state derived from the action

V. Aorist: **dikóm**, *I showed, I had shown, I have shown*

c. Of state derived from the action

IV. Perfect: **doika**, *I am in a state derived from having shown.*

7.2. FORMS OF THE VERB

7.2.1. THE VERBAL STEMS

1. The actual forms of the tenses and moods were made from tense-stems, of which there were up to four for each verb, called (1) the present, (2) the aorist, (3) the perfect; and also (4) future stems in post-LIE times.

NOTE. There are some characteristic forms of each stem, like the suffix -***n***- or -***sko***, which give mostly present stems. Generally, though, forms give different stems only when opposed to others.

2. The different stems are used in the verbal conjugation as follows:

STEMS	WHERE USED
Present	Present and Imperfect (active and middle-passive)
Aorist	Aorist (active and middle-passive)
Perfect	Perfect
Future	*Future*

3. There are some monothematic verbs, as **esmi**, *be*, or **edmi**, *eat* – apparently remains of the oldest PIE. And there are also some traces of recent or even nonexistent mood oppositions. To obtain this opposition there are not only reduplications, lengthenings and alternations, but also ablaut and accent shifts.

NOTE. Not every verb could form all three tense-stems. Quite a few did not form perfects, for example, and derived verbs only had present stems in PIE. IEDs did usually however innovate additional tense-stems for these verbs.

4. Most Late Indo-European verbs are built with a series of derivational suffixes that alter the root meaning, creating denominatives and deverbatives. The first are derived from nouns and adjectives; as, **torsējō**, *dry, "make dry"*, from **ters**-, *dry*, or **newājō**, *make new*, from **new**-, *new*. The last are derived from verbs, as **widējō**, *see*, from **weid**-, *see, know*.

NOTE. It is not clear whether these deverbatives – causatives, desideratives, intensives, iteratives, etc. – are actually derivatives of older PIE roots, or are frozen remains, formed by compounds of older PIE independent verbs added to other verbs, the ones regarded as basic.

5. Reduplication is another common resource; it consists of the repetition of the root, either complete or abbreviated; as, **sisdō**, *sit down, settle down*, from **sed**-, *sit*, **gígnōskō**, *know*, from **gnō**-, **mímnāskō**, *remember*, from **men**-, *think*, etc.

6. Thematic **e/o** has no meaning in itself, but it helps to build different stems opposed to athematics. Thus, It can be used to oppose a) indicative athematic to subjunctive thematic, b) present thematic to imperfect athematic, c) active to middle voice, etc. Sometimes accent shift helps to create a distinctive meaning, too.

7. Stems are inflected, as in the declension of nouns, with the help of vowel grade and endings or *desinences*.

7.2.2. VERB-ENDINGS

1. Every form of the finite verb is made up of two parts:

I. The stem. This is the root or an extension, modification or development of it.

II. The ending or *desinence*, consisting of:

a. The signs of mood and tense.

b. The personal ending.

So e.g. the root **deik-**, *show*, lengthened as thematic present verb-stem ***deik-e/o-***, *to show*, and by the addition of the personal primary ending ***-ti***, becomes the meaningful **déik-e-ti**, *he shows*.

2. Verbal endings can thus define the verb stem, tense and mood. Fortson (2004):

DESINENCES	WHERE USED
Primary active	present indicative active, active subjunctives
Secondary active	imperfect and aorist indicative active, active optatives
Primary middle-passive	present indicative middle, middle subjunctives
Secondary middle-passive	imperfect and aorist indicative middle, middle optatives
Perfect	perfect

3. The primary series indicates present and future; sg. ***-mi, -si, -ti***, and 3rd pl. ***-nti*** are the most easily reconstructed LIE formations. The secondary endings indicate past; sg. ***-m, -s, -t*** and 3rd pl. ***-nt***. The subjunctive is marked with primary desinences, while the optative is usually marked with secondary endings. The imperative has Ø or special endings.

The secondary endings are actually a negative term opposed to the primary ones. They may be opposed to the present indicative, they may indicate indifference to tense, and they might also be used in the present.

They can also mark the person; those above mark the first, second and third person singular and third plural.

Also, with thematic vowels, they mark the voice: ***-ti*** active primary | ***-t*** active secondary; ***-tor/-toi*** middle primary | ***-to*** middle secondary.

4. The augment appears in Ind.-Ira., Gk., and Arm., to mark the past tense (i.e., the aorist and the imperfect). It was placed before the stem, and consisted

generally of a stressed ***é***-, which is a dialectal Graeco-Aryan feature not found in N.LIE.

ACTIVE ENDINGS

1. The characteristic active primary endings are singular ***-mi***, ***-si***, ***-ti***, 3rd plural ***-nti***, while the secondary don't have the final ***-i***, i.e. sg. ***-m***, ***-s***, ***-t***, 3rd pl. ***-nt***.

NOTE. The secondary endings are believed to be older, being originally the only verbal endings available. With the addition of a deictic ***-i***, termed the *'hic et nunc'* particle (Latin for 'here and now'), the older endings became secondary, and the newer formations became the primary endings. It may have been the same as the ***-i*** found in pronominal and adverbial forms. Adrados–Bernabé–Mendoza (1995-1998), Fortson (2004). Compare a similar evolution in Romance languages from Lat. *habere*, giving common Fr. *il y a* 'there (it) is', or Cat. *i ha* 'there is', while the Spanish language has lost the relationship with such older Lat. *I* 'there', viz. Spa. *hay* 'there is' (from O.Spa. *ha+i*), already integrated within the regular verbal conjugation of the verb *haber*.

2. These desinences are used for all verbs, whether athematic or thematic; as, **esti**, *he is*, or **déiketi**, *he shows*. However, in the 1st sg., thematics end in ***-ō***; as, **deikō**.

NOTE. These endings in ***-ō*** are probably remains of an older situation, in which no ending was necessary to mark the 1st sg. (that of the speaker), and therefore, even though a desinence ***-m*** became general with time, the older formations prevailed, along with a newer thematic ***-o-mi***.

3. The thematic and athematic endings of the active voice are reconstructed as follows:

		Athematic		*Thematic*	
		Primary	Secondary	Primary	Secondary
Sg.	1.	***-mi***	***-m***	***-ō***	***-om***
	2.	***-si***	***-s***	***-esi***	***-es***
	3.	***-ti***	***-t***	***-eti***	***-et***
Pl.	1.	***-mes***	***-me***	***-omos***	***-omo***
	2.	***-te***	***-te***	***-ete***	***-ete***
	3.	***-n̥ti***	***-n̥t***	***-onti***	***-ont***

NOTE. About the reconstruction of PIE active endings:

1) 1st p. pl. thematic endings ***-o-mo***, ***-o-mos***, are found in Italic (Lat. *-mus*), Celtic (O.Ir. **-mo* or **-mos*), Balto-Slavic (*cf.* Pruss. *-mai*, O.C.S. *-mŭ<*-mo*, **-mos* or **-mom*), and from ***-mo-*** or ***-me-***, in Germanic (*cf.* Goth. *-m*) and Indo-Iranian (*cf.* O.Ind. *-ma*). Primary Thematic ending ***-o-mo-*** does not have a clear 'original' PIE ending, but an ***-s*** the most

logical choice, given the contrast between primary endings ***-mes***/***-me***. So in Ringe (2006). Beekes (1995) tentatively reconstructs ***-o-mom-***.

2) 2nd P. Pl. ending athematic ***-the*** (<*-*tHé*) is only found differentiated in PII, while in the other dialects it would have evolved as a common ***-te***.

3) Athematic desinences in *-*enti*, as found in Mycenaean and usually reconstructed as proper PIE endings, weren't probably common PIE desinences. Compare Att. Gk. *-aasi* (<-*ansi*<-*anti*), or O.Ind. *-ati*, both remade from an original zero-grade PIE *-*n̥ti*. In fact, Mycenaean shows some clearly remade examples, as Myc. *e-e-esi*<**esenti* (*cf.* Ion. εων), or *ki-ti-je-si* (<*ktíensi*).

MIDDLE-PASSIVE AND PERFECT ENDINGS

1. The middle-passive endings are generally those of the active voice with a characteristic middle voice ***-o***, in which the primary endings have an additional ***-i*** or ***-r***, depending on the dialects.

NOTE. In the moods, the endings attested are the same. Only dialectally were some new endings developed to differentiate the subjunctive.

2. There were apparently two possible set of endings already in Late Indo-European: either because the original primary ***-r*** endings were replaced by the endings in ***-i***, or because both came to be used with the same meaning by different dialects at the same time, with an expansion of that use through neighbouring contact zones. Syncretic trends led in any case to dialectal specialisation of both marks into the known (middle, middle-passive or passive) systems attested.

NOTE. Italic, Celtic, Tocharian, and Phrygian had mediopassive primary endings in ***-r*** (*cf.* Lat. *-tur*, O.Ir. *-tha(i)r*, Toch. *-tär*, Phryg. *-tor*), whilst others show ***-i*** (*cf.* Skt., Av. *-te*, Gk., Toch. *-tai*, Goth. *-da*); both forms coexisted in Anatolian (with *-r* as primary ending, combined with *-i cf.* Hitt. *-ta-r-i*, *nta-r-i*), in Tocharian (with *-r* as primary ending, *-i* as secondary), Indo-Iranian (with *-r-* passive forms), and afield *cf.* also Germanic (with remains of forms in *-r* with impersonal value, *cf.* O.H.G. *skritun*).

From these finds it is thought that ***-r*** was the old 'original' primary middle marker (possibly taken from the impersonal mark, *v.s.* §7.1.2), corresponding to the ***-i*** of the active. Both mediopassive endings (***-r*** and ***-i***) coexisted already in the earliest reconstructible PIE, and ***-i*** probably began to replace the old impersonal ***-r*** as the general middle marker already by Late Indo-European, as the Anatolian endings ***-r-*** and Sanskrit remains of middle forms in ***-ro-*** show. In the northern dialects ***-r*** became later specialised for the passive constructions or disappeared. It is therefore reasonable to think that while the general trend in N.LIE was to keep (or generalise) the middle-passive with primary endings in ***-r***, in S.LIE the middle-passive in **-i** gradually replaced the older endings. Endings in ***-r*** generalised in Phrygian and impersonal ***-r*** in Armenian (both S.LIE dialects), and endings in ***-i*** generalised in Germanic (a N.LIE dialect), which also shows traces of an old **-r**, further complicate the situation, showing that specialisation trends – at least in a post-IED period – were not uniform.

Fortson (2004): "This *-*r* is now generally thought to have been the primary middle marker, corresponding to the *-*i* of the active. Middles in Anatolian, Italic, Celtic, Tocharian, and Phrygian preserve this -*r*, but it has been replaced by the -*i* of the active in Indo-Iranian, Greek, Germanic, and Albanian".

Clackson (2007): "The morph *-*r* appears therefore to have acted as the analogue to *-*i* in the active endings and originally marks the 'here and now' of middles. This explanation, proposed by Cowgill (1968:25-7), also accounts for the absence of *-*r* in Greek and Vedic middle endings: at one stage these languages must have replaced the primary marker *-*r* with *-*i* on the analogy of the active endings."

Ringe (2006) also considers the *hic-et-nunc* particle of the mediopassive to have been *-*r* rather than *-*i*, having been replaced by the spread of active *-*i*.

Beekes (1995) considers the addition of *-*r* or *-*i* to the 'original' (secondary) endings to be a late development from a PIH point of view: "From this it follows that the -*r* was not characteristic of the primary endings. But neither was the -*i* of Sanskrit and Greek the marker of the primary ending in PIE, because the languages which generalized the -*r* show no trace of the -*i*. That on the other hand especially the marker of the primary endings of the active (the -*i*) in some languages was also used for the middle, is understandable. The conclusion is that there was no opposition between primary and secondary (...) we shall see that the perfect endings can be considered as secondary endings of the middle (...)".

Adrados–Bernabé–Mendoza (1995-1998) also deem both marks *-*r* and *-i to have coexisted parallel to each other as systems to mark the primary endings, as a late development.

3. The thematic and athematic endings of the middle-passive, reconstructed from a Northern Late Indo-European point of view, are as follows:

MIDDLE-PASSIVE AND PERFECT ENDINGS

	ATHEMATIC		*THEMATIC*		*STATIVE*
	Primary	*Secondary*	*Primary*	*Secondary*	
Sg.	***-mar***	***-ma***	***-ōr***	***-a***	***-a***
	-sor	***-so***	***-esor***	***-eso***	***-tha***
	-tor	***-to***	***-etor***	***-eto***	***-e***
Pl.	***-mesdha***	***-medha***	***-omesdha***	***-omedha***	***-mé***
	-(s)dhwe	***-dhwe***	***-e(s)dhwe***	***-odhwe***	***-té***
	-n̥tor	***-n̥to***	***-ontor***	***-onto***	***-(ḗ)r***

NOTE. 1) The Southern Late Indo-European middle primary endings in ***-i*** are easily reconstructed for the singular, ***-ai***, ***-soi***, ***-toi***, and the 3rd plural ***-ntoi***, even though Toch. B

(secondary endings) *-tai*, *-te*, *-nte* still suggest to some (Neu 1968) that the original PIE were *-sai, *-tai, *-ntai, instead of the general opinion. Dialectal Greek forms in the singular point to an alternative 1st sg. ***-oi***. A full discussion of the reconstruction is found e.g. in Villanueva Svensson's <http://eprints.ucm.es/tesis/fll/ucm-t26697.pdf>.

Villanueva Svensson (2003), Malzahn (2010) reconstruct the 1st p. sg. in *-H_2e-r / *-H_2e-i but also allowing for a form without *-e-. That would explain Latin thematic ending *-ōr* <*-o-a-r <*-o-h_2e-r /*-o-h_2-r, hence MIE ***-ōr*** for thematics, ***-ar*** for athematics.

2) The forms of the 1st and 2nd person plural were apparently the same in both systems. Greek, Indo-Iranian, and Anatolian dialects show middle-passive 2nd plural forms in ***-medha*** (<*-med^h-h_2, O.Ind. *-mahe*, Gk. *-metha*, Toch. *-ämtä-*), ***-mesdha*** (<*-mesd^h-h_2, *cf.* Gk. *-mestha*, Hitt. *-wašta-*), Toch. *-cär* (*cf.* Toch. *-t*<***-dhwe***), O.Ind. *mahi*>*-megha, and ***-men***, *cf.* Gk. *-men*, Hitt. *-wen-i*. Among others, Malzahn (2010) reconstructs a system that includes forms ***-mesdha/-mosdha***, ***-dhwer/-dhwor*** (and ***-dhwei/-dhwoi***); for Noyer in his useful article on PIE verbs (with conjugated examples), <http://www.ling.upenn.edu/~rnoyer/courses/51/PIEVerbs.pdf>, the variants include secondary ***-medha***, primary ***-mosdha***, and ***-dhwe***, without ***-i/-r*** ending.

1st pl. *-mo(s)r, Lat. *-mur*, and 2nd P. Pl. Osc. *-ter*, Hitt. *-ttumari*,. In Ita.-Cel. a form *-ntro has been related to the perfect, hence related to the 'original' paradigm with an 3rd p. pl. secondary ***-ro***, primary ***-ro-r***?; a 3rd p.sg. **-o**, ***-or*** is also reconstructible.

4) The forms in **-r** are reconstructed according to Kortlandt (1979), Sihler (1995), Beekes (1995), Villanueva Svensson (2003), Fortson (2004), and Clackson (2007); all of them make a similar account of the 'older' paradigm, which includes the forms 3rd sg. prim. **-or**, sec. **-o**, 3rd pl. prim. **-ro**, sec. **-ront**, attested in scattered remains in Hittite, Sanskrit, Tocharian, Sabellian, and Old Irish, what suggest that they were the 'original' ones, being replaced by the common endings. The old middle-passive ending system was then apparently sg. ***-a-***, ***-tha-***, ***-o-/-to-***, pl. ***-ro-/-nto-***, to which primary endings were attached in *-i*, *-so-i, *-to-i , *-nto-i, or in *-r*, *-ar, *-tar, *-or, pl. *-ro-r?/*-ntor, from older *-h_2-, *-th_2-, *-o, pl. *-r.

Kortland's article distinguishes between middle transitive and intransitive, in <https://openaccess.leidenuniv.nl/bitstream/handle/1887/1867/344_033.pdf?sequence=1>, an idea that has not had much echo. Also, it is unclear in the article the distinction between thematic and athematic desinences.

These endings share similarities with the perfect ones, *cf.* *-h_2e, *-th_2e-, *-e, pl. *-mé-, *-é, *-ḗr. About the different writing of *-th_2e-, as ***-tha*** or ***-ta***, it is not only restricted to Proto-Indo-Iranian; *cf.* perf. Gk. *oĩstha*.

This similarity of perfect and 'original' middle endings is explained differently according to the available theories on the prehistory of PIE verb (through internal reconstruction), apparently involving complicated syncretic and innovative trends regarding the voices, tenses and aspects. However, what seems clear from the later developments attested in the older IE languages, is that the synchronic picture of the Late Indo-European middle and perfect verbal ending system had to be near to the one depicted above.

DUAL ENDINGS

A complete reconstruction of the dual endings is not possible, because there is too little and contradictory data, probably because of the late development of the verbal dual (see above §3.5 for more on the nominal dual).

Only the active paradigm shows common endings:

		Primary	*Secondary*
Du.	1.	***-wes***	***-we***
	2.	***-t(h)os***	***-tom***
	3.	***-tes***	***-tām***

NOTE. Dual endings are found in Ind.-Ira., Gk., BSl. and Gmc., but apart from a common 3rd prim. ***-tom*** / sec. ***-tām*** in O.Ind. and Gk., there is only a general (usually incomplete) paradigm 1st ***w-***, 2nd & 3rd ***t-***, with different lengthenings in **-e/-o*, **-es/-os*, **-ā*. This table has ben taken from Beekes (1995). Fortson (2004) reconstructs an uncertain ***-to-*** for 2nd and 3rd. Only Beekes tentatively reconstructs uncertain middle endings for the parent language.

7.2.3. THE THEMATIC VOWEL

1. Stem vowels are – as in nouns – the vowel endings of the stem, especially when they are derivatives. They may be **i**, **u**, **ā**, **ē** (and also **ō** in roots). But the most extended stem vowel is **e/o** (also lengthened **ē/ō**), called thematic vowel (see above §2.6) which existed in PIH before the split of the Anatolian dialects, and which had overshadowed the (older) athematic stems already by Late Indo-European. The *thematisation* of stems, so to speak, relegated the athematic forms especially to the aorist and to the perfect; many old athematics, even those in ***-ā-*** and ***-ē-***, are usually found extended with thematic endings ***-je/o-***.

NOTE. The old thematics were usually remade, but there are some which resisted this trend; as **edmi**, *I eat*, **dōti**, *he gives*, or **idhi!** *go!*

The stem vowel has sometimes a meaning, as with ***-ē-*** and ***-ā-***, which can indicate state. There are also some old specialisations of meanings, based on oppositions:

a. Thematic vs. athematic:

- Athematic indicative vs. thematic subjunctive. The contrary is rare.

- Thematic present vs. athematic aorist, and *vice versa*.

- It may also be found in the middle-active voice opposition.

b. Thematic stem with variants:

- The first person, thematic in lengthened **-ō**.
- Thematic **o** in 1st sg. & pl. and 3rd pl.; **e** in 2nd and 3rd sg. and 2nd pl. There are also archaic 3rd pl. in **e**, as **senti**, *they are*.

c. Opposition of thematic stems. This is obtained with different vowel grades of the root and by the accent position.

2. In the so-called *semithematic* inflection, ahematic forms alternate with thematic ones.

NOTE. The semithematic inflection is for some an innovation of LIE, which didn't reach some of the dialects, while for other scholars it represents a situation in which the opposition thematic-athematic and the accent shifts of an older PIE system had been forgotten, leaving only some mixed remains within an already generalised LIE regular thematic verbal system.

7.3. THE CONJUGATIONS

7.3.1. Conjugation is the traditional name of a group of verbs that share a similar conjugation pattern in a particular language, a verb class. Late Indo-European shows regular conjugations, and all verbs may be conjugated in any person, number, tense, mood and voice by knowing which conjugation it belongs to.

NOTE. According to Clackson (2007): "In order to explain the number of different stem formations with the same function, Meillet supposed that in the parent language not just one present stem was opposed to one aorist stem, but rather it was possible to form several present and aorist stems from the same root. These stems were held to show different 'nuances' of aspectual meaning (or, to use the German term, *Aktionsart*), such as punctual, repeated or incipient action. Each root could show a wide variety of different formations, none of which presupposed the other. (...)

However, better knowledge of the earliest attested IE languages has led to a revision of this view, and researchers have increasingly become aware that if two stems can be reconstructed for PIE, one may represent an archaism and the other an innovatory replacement. Thus athematic verbs are in general a relic class, replaced over the history of individual languages by thematic formations. Motivation for the replacement of athematic verbs is not difficult to find: the juxtaposition of root-final consonants and the athematic endings (mostly consonant-initial) led to clusters which were often simplified or otherwise altered, so that the boundary between root and desinence, or suffix and desinence, became opaque to speakers. In some languages, paradigms still survive which exemplify the extent to which regular phonological developments can conceal the form of the root and the suffix. (...)"

7.3.2. A reference classification of PIE verbs into conjugations is the *Lexikon der indogermanischen Verben* (2001), supervised by H. Rix. It offers a conservative approach, not including much information on the Hittite verb (and thus Anatolian), being thus very interesting as a real approach to a living Late Indo-European verb.

NOTE. Nevertheless, it features a PIH phonetic reconstruction, and looks for the 'original' pre-LIE lexicon, what makes the work fit somewhere between the conventional PIH reconstruction and the modern PIH/LIE distinction, being thus somehow inconsistent, and at best showing a picture of a *pre-LIE* verbal system. It is therefore complex for a simple grammar, and indeed not directly applicable to an IED scheme, in which some athematic paradigms had been lost (or frozen into scarce, hence irregular examples), while newer verbs (and remade ones) further split within the most productive classes. Nevertheless, it is no doubt the most comprehensive work to date on the Proto-Indo-European verb.

7.3.3. The most important LIV verbal classes is as follows (Meier-Brügger 2003):

LIV	STEM CLASS	Examples
1a	Present, athematic, amphidinamic root	*g^{wh}en-ti/*g^{wh}n-énti
1b	Present, athematic, acrodynamic root	*stēu-ti/*stéw-n̥ti
1g	Present, athematic, with -e- reduplication	*d^{h}é-d^{h}oh$_{1}$-ti/*d^{h}é-d^{h}h$_{1}$-n̥ti
1h	Present, athematic, with -i- reduplication	*sti-stéh$_{2}$-ti/*sti-sth$_{2}$-énti
1i	Present, thematic, with -i- reduplication	*gi-gn̥h$_{1}$-é-ti
1k	Present, athematic, with nasal Infix	*li-né-k^{w}-ti/li-n-k^{w}-énti
1n	Present, thematic suffix -e-, e grade root	*b^{h}ér-e- ti
1o	Present, thematic suffix -é-, zero grade root	*g^{h}r̥h$_{3}$-é- ti
1p	Present, thematic suffix -ské-, zero grade root	*g^{w}m̥-ské- ti
1q	Present, thematic suffix -jé-, zero grade root	*gn̥h$_{1}$-jé-toi
2a	Aorist, athematic, root	*g^{w}em-t
2b	Aorist, athematic, suffix -s-	*prek-s-n̥t
2c	Aorist, thematic, reduplicated	*we-uk^{w}-e-t
3a	Perfect, reduplicated	*g^{w}e-g^{w}om-/g^{w}e-g^{w}m-

7.3.4. We have divided the Late Indo-European verbs in two main conjugation groups: athematic and thematic. The latter were the most productive and abundant ones in IEDs, and often replaced the older athematics by means of derivation.

Athematic and thematic groups are, in turn, subdivided into four and eight subgroups respectively.

A. THE THEMATIC CONJUGATION

The thematic conjugation group is formed by the following 8 subgroups:

I. Root verbs with root vowel **e** in the present and **o** in the perfect:

a. Triliteral: **deikō**, **dikóm**, **doika**, **deiksō**, *show*, etc.

b. Concave: **teqō**, **teqóm**, **toqa/tōqa**, **teqsō**, *escape*, **séqomai**, *follow*, etc.

NOTE. For IE **teqō**, *cf.* O.Ir. *téchid/táich* (<**e/ō**).

II. Concave root verbs with non-regular perfect vocalism. Different variants include:

a. **labhō**, **lābha**, *take*; **lawō**, **lāwa**, *enjoy*, **slabai**, **slāboma**, *fall* (Middle Voice); **aisdai**, *praise*.

NOTE. Compare Gk. *αιδομαι*, O.ind. *ile*, Gmc. part. *idja-*.

b. **kano**, **kékana/kékāna**, *sing*.

c. **legō**, **lēga**, *join, read, decide*.

d. **lowō**, **lōwa**, *wash*.

e. **rādō**, **rāda**, *shuffle, scrape, scratch*.

f. **rēpō**, **rēpa**, *grab, rip out*.

g. **rōdō**, **rōda**, *gnaw*.

III. *Verba vocalia*, i.e., thematic **-ā́-je/o-**, **-ē̆-je/o-**, **-í-je/o-**, **-ú-je/o-**:

a. **amājō**, *love*.

e. **lubhējō**, *love, desire*.

i. **sāgijō**, *look for, search*.

u. **argujō** *reason, argue* (*cf.* Lat. *arguō*, Hitt. *arkuwwai*).

o. Causative-iteratives in **-*ejo*-**: **bhoudhejō**, *wake somebody up*.

NOTE. Jassanoff in <http://www.people.fas.harvard.edu/~jasanoff/pdf/Stative%20*-e-%20revisited.pdf> discards the PIE nature of Gk. aorists in **ē**.

IV. Verbs in **-*je/o*-**:

a. Triliteral: **kupjō**, **kupóm**, **koupa**, **keupsō**, *demand, desire, tremble*.

b. Concave: **jakjō**, **jēka**, *throw*.

c. *Lamed-he*: **parjō**, **pepōra/péprōka**, *produce*.

d. Reduplicated Intensives: **kárkarjō**, *proclaim*, *announce* (*cf.* Gk. καρκαίρω, but Skt. *carkarti*).

V. Intensives-inchoatives in ***-ske/o-***:

a. Of mobile suffix: **swēdhskō**, **swēdhjóm**, **swēdhwa**, **swēdhsō**, *get used to.*

b. Of permanent suffix: **pr̥skṓ**, *inquire.*

VI. With nasal infix or suffix:

a. Perfect with **o** vocalism: **jungō, jugóm, jouga, jeugsō,** *join.*

b. Reduplicated perfect: **tundō**, **tétouda/tútouda**, *strike.*

c. Convex: **bhrangō**, **bhrēga**, *break.*

d. Nasal infix and perfect with **o** root: **gusnō**, **gousa** (*cf.* Lat. *dēgūnō*, *dēgustus*)

e. Nasal infix and reduplicated perfect: *cf.* Lat. *tollō*, *sustulii* (***supsi+tét-***), *lift.*

VII. With reduplicated present:

a. **sisō**, **sēwa**, *sow.*

b. **gignō**, **gegona**, **gégnāka**, *produce.*

VIII. Other thematics:

- **pl̥dō**, **pépola**.
- **widējō**, **woida**, *see.*
- etc.

B. THE ATHEMATIC CONJUGATION

Verbs of the second or athematic conjugation group may be subdivided into:

I. Monosyllabic:

a. In consonant: **esmi**, *be*, **edmi**, *eat*, **ēsmai**, *find oneself, be.*

b. In **ā** (<*-h_2): **snāmi**, *swim*, **bhāmai**, *speak.*

c. In **ē** (<*-h_1): **bhlēmi**, *cry*, **(s)rēmai**, *calculate.*

d. With nasal infix: **leiq-** (***lineqti/linqn̥ti***), *leave*, **kleu-** (***kl̥neuti/kl̥nunti***), *hear*, **peu-** (***punāti/punānti***), *purify*, etc.

NOTE. These verbal types appear mostly in Indo-Iranian and Hittite examples, and could therefore be more properly included in the suffixed (BIVc) type below.

e. Others: **eimi**, *go*, etc.

II. Reduplicated:

a. **(sí)stāmi**, *stand.*

b. **(dhé)dhēmi**, *set, place, do.*

c. **(jí)jēmi**, *throw, expel.*

d. **(dí)dōmi**, *give.*

e. **(bhí)bheimi**, *fear.*

f. **kī́keumi/kuwóm/kékuwa**, *strengthen.*

III. Bisyllabic:

a. **wémāmi**, *vomit.*

NOTE. These verbal types appear mostly in Indo-Iranian and Hittite examples, and could therefore be more properly included in the suffixed (BIVc) type below.

b. **bhleumi**, *weaken*, (*cf.* Goth. *bliggwan*, "*whip*").

NOTE. This verb might possibly be more correctly classified as **bhleujō**, within the *verba vocalia*, type AIIIu in ***-u-jo-*** of the thematic group.

IV. Suffixed:

a. In **-nā-** (<**-neh₂*): **pr̥nāmi**, *grant, sell* (*cf.* Gk. περνημι, O.Ir. *ren(a)id,* etc.), **qrī́nāmi**, *buy* (*cf.* O.Ind. *krīnāti,* O.Ind. *cren(a)im,* gr. πρίαμαι, etc).

b. In **-nu-**: **r̥neumi**, *rise (up).*

c. With nasal infix: **lineqmi** (***linqō***), **bhenegmi** (***bhegō***), **amneghti** (***amghō***)

NOTE. For these verbs Old Indian shows zero grade root vowel and alternating suffixes.

7.4. THE FOUR STEMS

7.4.1. TENSE-STEMS AND VERB DERIVATION

1. In the earliest reconstructible PIE, secondary verbs existed probably only in the present-tense system, and had no perfect or aorist forms – although presumably they could be conjugated in the imperfect, since it forms part of the imperfective/present system.

NOTE. Even some of the primary verbs were missing perfect and aorist forms, or had forms with unpredictable meanings, and many primary verbs had multiple ways of forming some or all of their aspects. Furthermore, evidence from Old Indian indicates that some secondary verbs in PIE were not conjugated in the subjunctive or optative moods.

Collectively, all of this indicates that in PIH, especially early on, all of the aspects and moods were probably part of the derivational rather than inflectional system. That is, the various tenses, aspects and moods were originally independent lexical formations. Furthermore, a basic constraint in the verbal system might have prevented applying a derived form to an already-derived form (Rix 1986).

That old dynamic situation reconstructed for the PIH conjugation is similar to the system found in Late Indo-European, where old desiderative present stems are generalised as new future stems in a post-LIE period, without the possibility of conjugating it in the subjunctive or optative moods, or even create participles (see below §7.4.2).

2. With verb creation we refer to the way verbs are created from nouns and other verbs by adding suffixes and through reduplication of stems.

3. There are generally two kinds of suffixes: root and derivative; they are so classified because they are primarily added to the roots or to derivatives of them. Most of the PIE suffixes (like ***-u-***, ***-i-***, ***-n-***, ***-s-***, etc.) are root suffixes. The most common derivational suffixes are studied in the following sections.

4. Reduplication is a common resource of many modern languages. It generally serves to indicate intensity or repetition in nouns, and in the Proto-Indo-European verb it helped create present stems (especially intensives), and more frequently it marked the different stems, whether present, aorist or perfect.

5. Examples of the stems found for PIE verbal root **leiq-**, *leave*, include:

- Present stem nasal **li-n-qe/o-** (*cf.* Gk. *limpánō*, Lat. *linquō*, *-ere*, O.Ir. -*léici*), and also PII athem. **li-n-eq-e/o-** (*cf.* Ved. *riṇákti*, Av. *irinaxti*)
- Aorist stem **liq-é/ó-** (*cf.* Ved. *rikthās*, Gk. *élipon*, Lat. *līquī*)
- Perfect stem **(lé-)loiq-** (*cf.* Ved. *rireca*, Gk. *léloipen*, Goth. *laihv*, O.Pruss. *po-lāikt*, O.Lith. *liekti*)
- Desiderative/Future stem **leiq/liq-se/o-** (*cf.* Gk. *leípsō*).
- Causative-Iterative derivative present stem **loiq-éje-** (*cf.* Ved. *recayati*, Lith. *laicaũ*, *laikýti*)

ACCENT-ABLAUT IN INFLECTION

Thematic stems, including subjunctives, had fixed accent on the stem.

In athematic stems, the accent usually alternated in PIE, falling on the endings in the middle-passive and the nonsingular active, but on the preceding syllable in the singular active.

However, s-aorists seem to have had fixed accent on the root, and it appears that there were a few root presents that exhibited a similar pattern; and reduplicated presents (but not perfects) seem to have had a fixed accent on the reduplicating syllable (Ringe 2006).

NOTE. No matter what the accentual pattern was, there was normally a difference in ablaut between the singular active and all other forms of athematic stems. The commoner attested patterns are exemplified in the paradigms shown in §§7.8.1, 7.8.2.

Obviously, the inflection of thematic stems was simpler and easier to learn. In the development of Northwestern dialects, nearly all presents would become thematic.

7.4.2. THE PRESENT STEM

PRESENT ROOT STEM

A pure root stem, with or without thematic vowel, can be used as a present, opposed to the aorist and perfect. Present verbal roots may be athematic and thematic. The athematics were, in Late Indo-European, only the remains of an older system.

CLASS BIa – Monosyllabic Athematic

[LIV types 1a & 1c, Old Indian 2nd class] Monosyllabic athematic root presents ending in consonant or resonant; their inflection is usually made:

- in the active voice sg., root vowel ***e*** and root accent.
- in the active voice pl. and middle voice, root vowel ∅ and accent on the ending.

The most common example is **es-mi**, *to be*, which has a singular in ***es***- and plural in ***s***-. There are also other monosyllabic verbs, as **chen-mi**, *to strike*, **ed-mi**, *to eat*, **wek-mi**, *to will*, etc.

NOTE. There was a general tendency within Late Indo-European to use thematic verbs instead of the old athematic ones. "The athematic verbs have been largely replaced by those of the thematic type" Beekes (1995).

BIe.- Other monosyllabic athematic root stems, as **ei-mi**, *go*; these follow the same declension.

		ed-, *eat*	**chen-**, *kill*	**ei-**, *go*	**es-**, *be*
Sg.	1.	**edmi**	**chenmi**	**eimi**	**esmi**
	2.	**edsi**	**chensi**	**eisi**	**esi**[ii]
	3.	**esti**[i]	**chenti**	**eiti**	**esti**
Pl.	1.	**dmes**	**chn̥més**	**imés**	**smes**
	2.	**dte**	**chn̥té**	**ité**	**ste**
	3.	**denti**	**chn̥enti**	**jenti**	**senti**

[i] post-LIE **ésti**(<**etsti?*)<**édti*. [ii] please note PIE ***es***- + -***si*** = **esi**.

NOTE. In an old inflection like that of the verbal root **es**, i.e. sg. **esmi**, pl. **smés**, sometimes a semithematic alternative is found. Compare the paradigm of the verb *be* in Latin, where zero-grade and o vowel forms are found: ***s-omi*** (*cf.* Lat. *sum*), not **es-mi**; ***s-omos*** (*cf.* Lat. *sumus*), not **s-me**; and ***s-onti*** (*cf.* Lat. *sunt*), not **s-enti**. Such inflection, not limited to Latin, has had little success in the Indo-European verbal system, at least in the older IE languages attested. There are, however, many examples of semithematic inflection in non-root verbs, what could mean that an independent semithematic inflection existed in PIE, or, more likely, that old athematic forms were remade and mixed with the newer thematic inflection (Adrados–Bernabé–Mendoza 1995-1998).

The middle voice forms that correspond in terms of formation are treated separately as zero grade root statives in LIV (type 1c); only two cases are certain.

CLASS BIII – Disyllabic Athematic

Disyllabic athematic root stems that make the present in full/Ø root vowel; as, **wémāmi**, *vomit*, **bhleumi**, *weaken*.

The alternative Ø/full root vowel is generally reserved for the aorist.

CLASSES BIb & BIc – Narten Present

[LIV type 1b, *Narten present*] Root athematic stems with alternating long/full root vowel and fixed root accent, acrodynamic; as, **stēu-ti**, 3rd pl. **stéw-n̥ti**. They are conjugated frequently in the middle voice.

NOTE. The so-called Narten verbs (**Hreg-*, **Hed-*, **genH-*, **tek-*, **sed-*, etc) have been the object of some controversy. Schindler presented in 1993 a document with stems that presented lengthened grade where a grade guṇa was expected, and e-grade where we would expect zero grade. There are two schools of thought that partially dismantle the arguments exposed by Schindler: Kortland proposes an alternative reconstruction to Narten for certain verbs of Old Indian, in his article 'Accent and ablaut in the Vedic verb', <www.kortlandt.nl/publications/art188e.pdf>. Also, de Vaan considers that "the Avestan pillar under the theory of 'Narten' roots has collapsed", in his article found at <http://leidenuniv.academia.edu/MichieldeVaan/Papers/791187/Narten_roots_from_the_Avestan_point_of_view>, Narten roots from the Avestan Point of View (2004), something that Ryan Paul Sandell supports in his thesis (2009). However, Nikolaev considers that de Van hasn't take into account secondary Narten phenomena, and especially the zero grade of the suffixed stem, or with endings of the Narten forms (*cf.* Toch. A *samantar*).

CLASS AI – bhárati/tudáti

[LIV types 1n & 1o – Old Indian 6th Class] Thematic root stems with e grade and thematic suffix **-*e*/*o*-** before the endings. A common example is **bhér-e-ti**, 'bears'. Thematic inflection shows two general old paradigms:

a. Root vowel **e** and root accent, as **déiketi**, *(s)he/it shows.*

b. Root vowel ∅ and accent on the theme vowel.

NOTE. The b-types are called *tudáti*-presents from a representative example in Ved. *tudáti* 'beats' < **(s)tud-é-ti*, a verb that forms a common LIE nasal infix present **(s)tu-né-d-**. There seems to be no certain present reconstructible for common PIE, according to Beekes (1995). The '*tezzi* principle' (Malzahn 2010) supports that a new present stem is created based on a past one, the aorist; thus Hitt. *tēzzi* 'says' <**d^heh_1-ti* < aor.**d^heh_1-t* (*cf.* Lyc. *tadi* 'put' (Jasanoff 2003).

The a-type appears usually in the present, and the b-type in the aorist – pres. **déiko** vs. aor. **dikóm** –, although apparently both could appear in both stems in PIE. In fact, when both appear in the present stem, the a-type is usually a durative – meaning an action not finished –, while b-type verbs are terminatives or punctuals – meaning the conclusion of the action. This semantic value is not general, though, often found only in Graeco-Aryan dialects. The a-type present stems correspond to LIV type 1n, while the b-type present stems correspond to LIV type 1o.

NOTE. The newer inflection is, thus (in a singular/plural scheme), that of full/full vocalism for present, ∅/∅ for aorist. The athematic root inflection in full/∅ appears to be older than the thematic one. The thematic inflection therefore probably overshadowed the athematic one by Late Indo-European, and there are lots of examples of coexisting formations, some of the newer being opposed to the older in meaning.

PRESENT REDUPLICATED STEM

Depending on its formation, present stems may show either *full* reduplication, sometimes maintained throughout the conjugation, or *simple* reduplication, which normally consists of the initial consonant of the root followed by **-i-**.

Depending on its meaning, reduplication may have a general value (of iteration or intensity), or simply opposed values in individual pairs of *basic verb vs. deverbative*, helping to distinguish the verb in its different forms.

Simple reduplication is made:

- With *consonant* + ***i***,

  - in athematic verbs; as, **bhi-bher-**, *carry* (from **bher-**),

  - in thematic verbs; as, **gi-gnō-sko-**, *know* (from **gnō-**), etc. **si-sdo-**, *sit down,* (from zero-grade of **sed-**, *sit*),

  - Some intensives have half full, half simple reduplication, as in **dei-dik-**, *show* (from **deik-**).

- There are other forms with ***-w, -u***, as in **leu-luk-**, *shine* (from **leuk-**, *light*).

- There are also some perfect stems with ***i***.

- With *consonant* + ***e/ē***, as **dhe-dhē-**, **de-dō-**, etc.

Simple reduplication in ***e*** appears mainly in the perfect, while ***i*** is characteristic of present stems. Reduplication in ***e*** is also often found in intensives in S.LIE.

CLASS BII – Athematic in -i-/-e-

[LIV types 1g & 1h] Athematic present with ***-i-*** or ***-e-*** reduplication. Roots with long vowel (as **dhē-**, **stā-** or **dō-**) are rare in present stems, usually reserved for the aorist. The reconstructed PIH paradigm of **stā-** is given here for comparison.

		dhē-, *do*	**dō-**, *give*	**stā-**, *stand*	**steh$_2$-, stand*
Sg.	1.	**dhédhēmi**	**(dí)dōmi**	**(sí)stāmi**	**(sí)steh$_2$mi*
	2.	**dhédhēsi**	**(dí)dōsi**	**(sí)stāsi**	**(sí)steh$_2$si*
	3.	**dhédhēti**	**(dí)dōti**	**(sí)stāti**	**(sí)steh$_2$ti*
Pl.	1.	**dhedhamés**	**(di)damés**	**(si)stamés**	**(si)sth$_2$més*
	2.	**dhedhaté**	**(di)daté**	**(si)staté**	**(si)steh$_2$té*
	3.	**dhedhanti**	**(di)danti**	**(si)stanti**	**(si)sth$_2$ṇti*

NOTE. 1) Reduplication didn't affect the different root vowel grades in inflection, and general accent rules were followed; as, **bíbherti-bibhṛmés**, **sístāmi-sistamés**, etc.

2) Most athematic verbs are usually reconstructed with an accent-ablaut paradigm (as in Sanskrit, or the assumed older situation in PIE), but another simple columnar accent could have been possible, as in Greek, probably from a LIE trend to simplify the system, similarly to the simplified nominal accent-ablaut paradigm; it could read post-LIE **dhédhames**, **dhédhate**, **dhédhanti**, or **dídames/dames**, **sístames/stames**, etc.

3) Formal reduplication was optional in Late Indo-European, its generalisation being a Graeco-Aryan feature; as, **dédōmi/dídōmi** vs. **dōmi**, **gígnōskō** vs. **gnōskō**, etc.

4) Reduplication reconstructed in **-e-** (*cf.* for **dhe-dhē-** Skt. *dádhāti*, O.Lith. *desti*, O.C.S. *deždǫ*, Lat. *re-ddo*?; for **dé-dō-**, Skt. *dádati*) is also found in ***-i-*** (*cf.* for **dhí-dhē-**, Gk. *títhēmi*; for **dí-dō-** Gk. *dídōmi*, Celtib. *didonti*). The LIV classifies Greek forms in ***-i-*** as from an original PIE ***-e-*** assimilated to the ***-i-*** class, but there is no certainty in that assumption for all cases, given that reduplication appears not to have been obligatory in PIE. A general reduplication in ***-e-*** for **dhē-** seems to be well established for most languages, though. As Fortson (2004) states: in many examples of the type from the daughter languages, the reduplicating syllable has ***-i-*** rather than ***-e-***, as in Vedic Skt. *jí-gā-ti* 'he goes' and Gk. *dí-dō-mi* 'I give'. This pattern probably spread from thematic reduplicated presents like Gk. *gígnomai* 'I become'. Or, after Beekes (1995): "It is unclear

when e and when I were used. Skt *dádāmi*, Gr. *dídōmi* 'to give' perhaps suggest that both forms appeared in the same paradigm."

CLASS AVII – Thematic in -i-

[LIV type 1i] Thematic present with **-i-** reduplication is clearly a secondary development from the LIV type 1h. Common examples are **gi-gnō**, *beget*, **pi-bō**, *drink*.

CLASS BIVd – Intensives

[LIV type 6a] Stem formations of the action type 'intensive', meaning "repeated bringing about of a state of affairs", have an (almost) complete reduplication of the root (only an occlusive at the end of the root was not repeated); as, **wer-w(e)rt-**, *to turn*, **dei-dik-(sk)-**, *to indicate*, **qér-qr-**, *to do again and again*, from **qer-**, *cut (off), carve*.

Full reduplication, normally found in the present stem, repeats the root or at least the group *consonant/resonant+vowel+consonant/resonant*. **gal-gal-**, *talk*, **bher-bher-**, *endure*, **dr̥-dr-**, **mr̥-mr-**, *whisper*, *murmur*, etc.

Full reduplication is also that which repeats a root with *vowel+consonant/resonant*; as, **ul-ul-**, *howl* (*cf.* Lat. *ululāre*).

NOTE. Examples include Greek πορφυρω, παμπαινω, γαργαιρω, μορμορω, μερμηριζω, καγχαλαω, μαρμαιρω, δενδιλλω, λαλεω, and, in other IE dialects, Slavic *glagoljo*, Latin ('broken' reduplication with different variants) *bombico, bombio, cachinno, cacillo, cracerro, crocito, cucullio, cucurrio, curculio, didintrio, lallo, imbubino, murmillo, palpor, pipito, plipio, pipio, tetrinnio, tetrissito, tintinnio, titio, titubo*, etc.

PRESENT CONSONANT STEM

IN -s-

A present-tense thematic suffix *-(e)s-* is found, for example in **kleu-sō**, *obey, be obedient*, **g-esō**, *carry* (**h₂g-es-*, from **h₂eg-* → **agō**), **aug-sō**, *grow* (*cf.* Gk. *aéksō*, Lat. *augeō*).

Thematic **-s-** also makes desideratives which are the basis of post-LIE futures, *v.i.*

Extended **-s-** stems, as **-sk-** and **-st-**, are almost all thematic.

NOTE. Thematic suffix ***-ste/o-*** has usually an expressive meaning, meaning *sounds* most of the times; as, ***bhr̥stō***, *burst, break* (from **bhresjō**, *shatter*).

CLASS AV – In -ske/o-

[LIV type 1p].- Thematic suffix ***-ske/o-*** is added to roots in the zero-grade, especially to monosyllabics and disyllabics, and make iterative (or inchoatives); as, **pr̥k-skṓ** (from **prek-**), *ask, ask repeatedly*, **cm̥-skṓ**, *walk about* (*cf.* **cemjō**, *come*), **gnō-skō** (from **gnō-**), *know*.

It can also be added to reduplicated stems, as **dí-dk-skō** (from **dek-**), **gí-gnō-skō**, and to lengthened roots, especially in **ī, u, ē, ā**, as **krē-skō** (from **ker-**).

NOTE. Several verbs reconstructed for PIE with this ending refer to asking or wishing. Sometimes these deverbatives show limited general patterns, creating especially iteratives (with repeated, habitual or background action, i.e. durative sens, *cf.* Hitt. *walḫ-iški-zzi* 'beats repeatedly, beats several objects', Gk. *pheúgeskon* 'they would habitually flee'), but also inchoatives (indicating beginning or inception of an action or state, *cf.* Lat. *rubē-sc-ere* 'to grow red'), causatives, and even determinatives or terminatives. Apparently, the same -***ske/o***- can also produce denominal duratives like **medhuskō**, get *drunk* (from **medhu**, *mead, intoxicating drink*) or **wodskō**, *wash* (from **wod-**, *water*). (Piotr Gąsiorowski, n.d.)

This lengthening in -***sk***- seems to have been part of present-only stems in LIE; *cf.* Lat. *flōrescō/flōruī*, Gk. *κικλησκω/κεκληκα*, and so on. Cases like LIE verb **pr̥kskṓ**, *ask, demand* (*cf.* O.H.G. *forscōn*, Ger. *forschen*, Lat. *poscō>por(c)scō*, O.Ind. *pr̥cch*, Arm. *harc'anem*, O.Ir. *arcu*), which appear in zero grade throughout the whole conjugation in different IE dialects, are apparently exceptions of the PIH verbal system; supporting a common formation of zero grade root iterative presents, compare also the form **(e)ské/ó-** (<*h₁skó*), the verb **es-** with 'existential' sense, as O.Lat. *escit*, "*is*", Gk. *ẽske*, "*was*", Hom. Gk. *éske*, Pal. *iška*, etc.

Supporting the theory that -***sk*** has a newer development than other lengthenings is e.g. the Hittite formation *duskiski(ta)* (*cf.* O.Ind. *túsyate*, *'satisfaciō'*, O.Ir. *inna tuai 'silentia'*), which indicates that in Anatolian (hence possibly in Indo-Hittite as well) such an ending – unlike the other endings shown - was still actively in formation.

CLASSES BIVb & AVI – Nasal Presents

[LIV type 1k – Old Indian class 7] Stems in -***n***- are said to have a *nasal suffix* or a *nasal infix* – a morpheme placed inside another morpheme. They may be athematic or thematic, and the most common forms are -***n***, and extended -***neu***-/-***nu***-, -***nā***-.

The so-called *nasal presents* are thematic and thematics with nasal infix **-n-**, typically active transitives. The distribution of the ablaut grades was the same as in root presents: full grade in the singular active, zero-grade elsewhere.

The infix was inserted into the zero-grade of the root, between its last two sounds (generally a resonant or high vowel followed by a consonant), i.e. in CeRC- roots, the produced the characteristic alternation CR-né-C-/CR-n-C-; as, from **jug-**, 3rd sg. nasal present 3rd sg. **ju-né-g-ti**, *he yokes*, 3rd pl. **ju-n-g-énti**; **ku-n-és-mi**, *kiss*.

Other examples include **li-ne-q-mi**, becoming thematic **li-n-q-ō**, *leave*; other thematics include **pu-n-g-ō**, *prik*, **bhu-n-dh-ō**, *be aware*. Other stems with nasal infix became *verba vocalia*; as, **dhre-n-g-ājō**, *hold*; **pla-n-t-ājō**, *plant*.

CLASSES BIVc & AVI – In -neu-

[LIV type 1l – Old Indian classes 5, 8] Athematic nasal infix present **-néu-/-nu-** usually enforcing the weak vocalism of the root, as in **str̥-neu-mi**, becoming thematic **ster-n(u)-ō**, *spread*, **r̥-neu-mi**, *set into motion*, etc.

NOTE. Derivative **kl̥neumi** is difficult to reconstruct with certainty; often interpreted as with infix **-n-**, i.e. ***kl̥-n-eu-***, it has been proposed that it is a zero-grade suffixed ***klu-neu-***, *cf.* Buddh. Skt. *śrun*; Av. *surunaoiti*; Shughni *çin*; O.Ir. *cluinethar*; Toch. A and B *käln*. Skt. *śr̥no-/śr̥nu-* < **kluneu-/klunu-* would show a loss of *u* analogous to the loss of *i* in *tr̥tī́ya-* '*third*' < IE ***tritijo-***.

It produced (often transitive and vaguely causative) athematic verbs that refer to the beginning or termination of an action (the so-called inchoatives), or suggest that something is done once (rather than repeated) (Piotr Gąsiorowski, n.d.).

A rarer variant of this pattern involves ***-nu-***, ***-ne/o-***, formations with stress alternating between the full-vowel root and the inflection.

NOTE. Other forms (possibly derived from inflected ***-neu-*** and ***-nei-***) include ***-nwe/o-***, ***-nje/o-***. These formations seem to be very recent in Late Indo-European. In Greek it is frequent the nasal suffix **-an-**. Others as ***-nwe/o-***, ***-nje/o-***, appear often, too; as Gk. *phthínuo*, Goth. *winnan* (from **wenwan*); Gk. *iaíno*, *phaínomai* (from **bhā-**) and O.Ind. verbs in *-nyati*.

CLASS BIVa – In -nā-

[LIV type 1m – Old Indian class 9] Athematic nasal infix **-nā-**; as, **pr̥-nā-mi**, *grant, sell*, **qrī́-nā-mi**, *buy*, **dm̥-nā-mi**, *to subdue*, etc.

IN OCCLUSIVE

Indo-European roots could be lengthened with an occlusive to give a verb stem, either general or present-only. Such stems are usually made adding a dental ***-t-***, ***-d-***, ***-dh-*** (as **plek-tō**, *plait*, from **plek-**, *weave*) or a guttural ***-k-***, ***-g-***, ***-gh-*** (as **dha-k-jō**, *do*), but only rarely with labials or labiovelars. They are all thematic, and the lengthenings are added to the root.

PRESENT VOWEL STEM

CLASS AIV – Primary je/o-Presents

[LIV types 1q & 1r – Old Indian 4th class] Some roots and derivatives (deverbatives or denominatives) form the thematic verb stems with ***-je/o-***, usually added to stems ending in consonant. These are called primary **je/o**-presents (not to be confused with "primary" in the meaning "non-past" of verbal endings).

NOTE. According to the LIV, it forms thematic durative verbs, conveying "a subject's state of being without stressing the entry of the subject into the state of being"; as **kapjō**, *take, seize*, **mr̥sjō**, *not heed, ignore* (from **mors-**, *forget*), **oqjō**, *eye* (from noun **oqos**, *eye*, *cf.* **oqō**, *see*).

In these cases, the root grade is usually Ø; as, **mn-jṓ**, from **men-**, *think*, **bhudh-jō**, *wake up*, from **bheudh-**; but the full grade is also possible, as in **spek-jō**, *look*, **lā-jō**, from **lā-**, *bark*.

NOTE. Fortson (2004): "The type with zero-grade of the root and accented suffix, characteristically used with intransitives, may have been restricted to middle inflection originally, which would explain why in some branches (Indo-Iranian, Armenian) it came to be used to form the passive."

These verbs may be deverbatives – normally iteratives or causatives – or denominatives. With an iterative-causative action type [LIV type 4b], *cf.* **swopjō**, *lull to sleep*, from **swep-**, *sleep*.

They served especially to form verbs from nouns and adjectives, as, from **nōmn̥**, *name*, **nōmnjō**, *name* (*cf.* Gk. *onomainō*, Got. *namnjan*), from **melit**, *honey*, **ml̥itjō**, *take honey from the honeycomb* (as Gk. *blíttō*), etc.

NOTE. Equivalent stems in thematic ***-u-e/o-*** are rarely found in the present, but are often found in the past and perfect stems. Stems in ***-u-*** show then an opposed behaviour to those in ***-i-***, which are usually found in present stems, and rarely in past or perfect stems. In present stems, ***-u-*** is found in roots or as a suffix, whether thematic or athematic, giving a stem that may normally appear as the general stem of the verb. It is therefore generally either part of the root or a stable lengthening of it (*cf.* **gheu-/ghō-**, **pleu-/plō-**, etc.).

CLASS AIII – Verba Vocalia

[LIV types 1q & 1r – Old Indian 4th class] The preceding vowel may be an ***-ā-***, ***-ē-***, ***-i-*** or ***-u-***, sometimes as part of the root or derivative, sometimes as part of the suffix. Possible suffixes in ***-je/o-*** are therefore also the so-called *verba vocalia*, ***-ā́je/o-***,***-ḗje/o-***, ***-íje/o-***, and ***-úje/o-***.

Class AIIIa – Factitives

[LIV type 7] Roots or stems in ***-ā-*** (<*$*$-eh$_2$-/*$*$-h$_2$-*), added to the weak form of a root to produce athematic or thematic stems mixed with ***-i-***, generally indicating "the entry of the subject into a new state of being"; as, **am-ā-jō**, *love*, **sēd-ā-jō**, *settle* (*cf.* **sed-ejō**).

NOTE. Athematic presents in **-ā-** are classified in LIV as "fientive stems", like **mnā-**, *become furious*, from **men-**, *hold a thought.*

Some find apparently irregular formations as Lat. *amō*, "*I love*", from an older ***amā́-je/o-***, mixed with ***-i-***; however, they are sometimes reconstructed as from **amā-*, i.e. in **-ā** without ending (*cf.* Lat. *amas, amat,...*), as in Adrados–Bernabé–Mendoza (1995-1998); against it, compare common IE formations as Umb. *suboca* 'invoke', Russ. *délaiu*, and so on.

Added to thematic adjectival stems it was used to form *factitives*, verbs meaning 'to make something have the quality of the adjective', especially when opposed to statives in **-ē-** (*cf.* Hitt. *maršaḫ-marše-*, Lat. *clarāre-clarēre, albāre-albēre, nigrāre-nigrēre, liquāre-liquēre*); as, from **new-o-**, *new*, **new-ā-jō**, *make new*,

They may also form statives or duratives. But there are also many deverbatives in **-ā-** without a special value opposed to the basic verb.

NOTE. Stems in **-ā-** help create (usually athematic) subjunctives and aorists. **-ā-** is less commonly used than **-ē-** to make iterative and stative deverbatives and denominatives.

Class AIIIe – Statives

[LIV type 8] Thematic stems in ***-ē-***, mixed with ***-i-***. Sometimes the ***-ē-*** is part of the root, sometimes it is a suffix added or substituting the ***-e-*** of the stem.

NOTE. These stem formations are defined in LIV as of the "essive" action type, conveying "a subject's state of being...without stressing the entry of the subject into the state of being" (see above Class AIV). Its stem ending is reconstructed as **-h$_1$jé-*, as a derivative of **-jé-*, upon the *fientives* with **-eh$_1$-/-h$_1$-*.

They may form verbs of state (or *statives*) if added to and adjectival root thematic in **e/o**, meaning 'have the quality of the adjective', as **rudhējō**, *be red*, **albhējō**, *be white*, with a stative value, **lubhējō**, *be dear, be pleasing*, **senējō**, *be old*, etc.

It is also found in combination with ***-s-*** in ***-ē-s-***, ***-ē-ske/o-***, yielding intransitive verbs denoting change of state ('become *X*'); as, **rudhēskō**, *turn red*, **senēskō**, *get old* (Piotr Gąsiorowski n.d.).

CLASS AIIIo – Causative-Iteratives

[LIV type 4a] The co-called *causative-iterative* stems show root in o-grade and accented thematic suffix in ***-éjo-***, conveying the meaning "a cause of bringing about a state of affairs, or the repeated bringing about of a state of affairs"; as, from **sed-**, *sit*, **sodejō**, *cause to sit*, from **men-**, *think*, **monejō**, *remind, advise*; **wortejō**, *cause to turn*, from **wert-**, turn, from **wes-**, *dress*, **wosejō**, *clothe, put on clothes*, (*cf.* Hitt. *waššizzi*, Skt. *vāsáiati*, Ger. *wazjan*, Alb. *vesh*), **sedejō**, *be sitting* (*cf.* **sed-**, *sit*), **bhoudhejō**, *wake somebody up* (*cf.* **bheudhō**, *awake*), **ṛghejō**, *incite* (*cf.* **ṛgujō**, *reason, discuss*), etc. And it is also used to form denominatives, as **wosnejō**, *buy, sell*, from **wesnom**, *sale*.

It formed non-causatives, too; as, from **leuk-**, *light*, **loukéjō**, *shine* (*cf.* Hitt. *lukiizzi*, Skt. *rocáyati*, Av. *raočayeiti*, O.Lat. *lūmina lūcent*).

NOTE. It is sometimes difficult to know if the original form was ***-éje/o-*** or ***-ḗje/o-***, because the former is apparently attested only in Anatolian, Indo-Iranian, Greek and Armenian (*cf.* Arm. Gen. *siroy*, "*love*", *sirem*, "*I love*"<****keire-jé-***); Greek loses the ***-j-*** and follows (as Latin) the rule '*uocālis ante uocālem corripitur*', what helps metrics. However, Greek had probably a present with long **ē** (as in non-liquid future and perfect). Mycenaean doesn't help clarify uncertain reconstructions; moreover, it is often accepted that some forms in O.Ind. *-ayati* are isolated. See Appendix II – *Guide to the Reader* for dubious reconstructions.

DESIDERATIVES AND THE FUTURE STEM

[LIV type 5] Following the LIV, the desiderative action type conveys "the subject's desire or intent to bring about a state of affairs". These stems are built with a thematic **-s-** ending. *cf.* **wéid-se/o-**, '*want to see, go to see*', hence '*visit*', as Lat. *vīsere*, Goth. *gaweisōn*, O.S. O.H.G. *wīsōn*, a deverbative from root **weid-**, from which the general present stem is **wid-ḗje/o-**, *see*.

NOTE. Aorist stems in ***-s-*** are usually athematic. Sometimes the ***-s-*** marked the subjunctive. Because of its common use in verbal inflection, deverbatives with a lengthening in ***-s-*** aren't generally opposed in meaning to their basic stems, and there was no general common meaning reserved for the extended stem in ***-s-***. Compare Lat. *pressī* <* *pres-sai* vs. Lat. *premō*; Lat. *tremō* vs. a Gk. τρεω<**tre-sō*, O.Ind. *trásate* 'he is frightened'.

Some of their descendants function as futures, hence the assumption that future formations in IEDs come from LIE desideratives/causatives. Present stems, usually formed with extensions in **-s-** (and its variants), became with time a regular part of the verbal conjugation in some dialects, whilst disappearing in others.

NOTE. It is assumed then that PIE did not have a future stem. That might seem strange, but it is possible to express future tense without having a special formation ('I do it tomorrow'). Gothic, for example, is an IE language that didn't have an especial future formation. Nevertheless, the development of the earliest languages attested show that within the post-LIE times a future stem must have been developed.

[LIV type 5a] Desiderative/causative stems were usually made in IEDs with root vowel ***e***, i.e. in full-grade, with a suffix ***-s-***<**-(H)s-*:

1. Thematic ***-s(j)e/o-***; as, **do-sjé-ti**, 'he intends/wants to give', later 'will give' or 'about to give' (*cf.* Skt. *dā-ṣyắ-mi*, Lith. *dúosiant-*).

NOTE. A common origin of the future in ***-s-*** is found in Sanskrit, Balto-Slavic, Italic (Sabellian), and in Celtic futures in ***-sje/o-*** (*cf.* O.Russ. *byšęštĭ*<**bʰuH-sjont-* 'about to be', Gaul. *pissíiumi* 'I will see'), and Doric Greek in ***-sēje/o-***, ***-sje/o-***. *Cf.* also Hom. Gk. *kaléō* <**kal-e-sō* 'I will call', Classical Greek and Archaic Latin in ***-se/o-*** (*cf.* O.Lat. *faxō*<**dhak-sō* 'I will make', O.Lat. *peccas-sō*, from *peccāre*, etc. and Gk. *dḗk-s-o-mai* 'I will bite' to active present *dáknō* 'I bite'). *Cf.* from **derk-**, *see*, Skt. *drakṣyáti* 'he shall see', and Gk. *dérksomai* 'I shall see'. Some more dialectal extensions are found appearing before the ***-s-*** endings; as, ***-i-s-*** in Indo-Iranian and Latin, ***-e-s-*** in Greek and Osco-Umbrian.

For the future stem coming from sigmatic aorist stem, Adrados–Bernabé–Mendoza (1995-1998): "Homeric Greek aorists *dúseto*, *bḗseto*, are exactly parallels to future *dúsomai*, *bḗsomai*, remains of the same sigmatic thematic stem, and not remade forms as Leumann (1952-53) and Prince (1970) proposed."

2. An athematic future in **-s-** is found in Italic (*cf.* Umbr. *fu-s-t* 'he will be') and Baltic (Lith. *bùs* 'he will be').

3. [LIV type 5b] A reduplicated desiderative with i-reduplication and a suffix *-(*h_1*)*se-*, found in Indo-Iranian and Celtic; as, **wi-wn̥-sō**, *overpower, win*, from **wen-**, *overpower, win*; from **chen-**, *slay*, **chi-chnā-se-ti**<**gʷi-gʷn̥-$h_1$se*, *wants to slay, will slay* (*cf.* Ved. Skt. *jíghāṃsati* 'wants to slay', O.Ir. fut. (-)*géna* < Cel. **gʷi-gʷnā-se-ti* 'will slay'); **di-dr̥k-sō**, *want to see.*

It seems that future stems originated already within a disintegrating post-LIE community, which tended to integrate the known **-s-** desiderative present stem formation paradigm into the conjugation system, so that it became possible to create systematic futures of all verbs.

IMPERFECT AND INJUNCTIVE

The present stem was used to form the present tense and the imperfect, which – as already said – is usually thought to have signified durative or repeated action in the past time (*was going, used to go*). Formally it was usually identical to the present stem, except that secondary endings were used instead of primary. 1st sg. -***m*** is the same in both thematic and athematic imperfects.

NOTE. Fortson (2004) continues: "The original type is best preserved in Anatolian, Indo-Iranian, and Greek: for example, Hitt. (preterite) *daškinun* 'I (repeatedly) took', Vedic Skt. *ábharam* 'I was carrying', Av. *barəmz* 'I was carrymg', and Gk. *épheron* 'I was carrying' (...) Outside of these branches, the IE imperfect has either been completely lost, or merged with the aorist. In those branches where the imperfect was lost, a new imperfect conjugation was often innovated (as in Italic and Slavic), sometimes of obscure origin (as in Celtic)."

Indo-Iranian, Greek, Armenian and Phrygian attest a prefix called the augment that was added to past-tense forms. It is reconstructible as **e-**; as, imperfect **é-bher-e-t** 'he *was carrying*' (*cf.* Ved. Skt. *ábharat*, Gk. *éphere*, Arm *eber*), or aorist **e-dhē-** 'placed' (*cf.* Phrygian *edaes* 'he placed').

NOTE. The great success of that particular augment (similar to other additions, like Lat. *per-* or Gmc. *ga-*) happened apparently later in those proto-languages. Vedic Sanskrit clearly shows that augment was not obligatory, and for Proto-Greek, *cf.* Mycenaean *do-ke/a-pe-do-ke*, Myc. *qi-ri-ja-to*, Hom. Gk. πριατο, etc. It is often shown in most PIE grammars because (Brugmannian) tradition in IE studies has made augment seem obligatory for PIE.

According to Meier-Brügger (2003): "The PIE augment *(h_1)é* was quite probably an adverb with the meaning 'at that time' and could be employed facultatively where indicative forms of present and aorist stems were combined with secondary endings to produce a clear past tense (...) The establishment of the augment as a norm in the indicative aorist, indicative imperfect, and indicative pluperfect took place in a post-Proto-Indo-European phase. Other IE languages such as Latin or Germanic developed their own suffixal means of indicating past tense forms."

The augment is in fact related to the so-called 'injunctive mood', defined as augmentless past-tense forms that appear in Indo-Iranian and Ancient Greek, of obscure function, much discussed by scholars. "Their precise function or functions are still not fully clear. In Homer, injunctives are interchangeable with past tenses but sometimes have gnomic force (that is, are used to express general truths). In Indo-Iranian, injunctives can indicate intent, futurity, and some quasi-modal meanings, and were also used in commands, especially prohibitions" (Fortson 2004).

7.4.3. THE AORIST STEM

AORIST ROOT STEM

[LIV type 2a] Monosyllabic athematic root aorists are formed by adding the secondary endings directly to the full grade of the root in the active singular, and to the zero-grade of the root elsewhere. They are usually opposed to presents:

- In **-neu-**; as, pres. **kl̥neumi**, aor. 3rd p. sg. **kleum**, 3rd p. pl. **klwent**, *hear*, or pres. **qr̥neumi** vs. aor. **qerm**, *make, do*, etc.
- Reduplicated; as, pres. **sí-stā-mi**, *I stand*, aor. 1st sg. **stā-m**, *I stood*, 3rd pl. **sta-nt**, *they stood*; pres. **dhé-dhē-mi**, *I do, I put*, aor. **dhē-m**, *I did*, pres. **pí(m)-plē-mi**, *I fill*, aor. **plē-m**, *I filled*.
- In ***-ske/o-***, ***-je/o-***; as, pres. **cm̥skṓ**, *I walk about/come*, aor. 3rd sg. **cḗm-t**, *he walked about*, 3rd pl. **c(e)m-ént**, *they walked about*.

NOTE. We may divide in two schools the positions regarding the Latin preterite with internal long vowel, of the type *uēnī, lēgī*; either originally from IE aorists or from perfects. The Meiser school considers it evolved from the perfect stem (e.g. González Fernández, *El perfecto radical latino*, 1981). It would then be derived from the 'perfect of state', i.e. *uēn-* <**gʷēm*, prevailing over the less defined aorist stem **uen(e)-*. The other school is represented by Kortlandt, supporting that *uēnī* continues an original aorist stem with a long vowel. Nikolaev mentions Meiser's position, without discussing it, in his article <http://scholar.harvard.edu/nikolaev/files/nikolaev_tocharian_a_samantar.pdf>. An alternative to aorist **cēmt** vs. **cemt** would be to use as aorist for this verb the same as for **cemjō**, **ludhóm** (<**h₁ludh-*).

- Thematic presents; as, pres. **ghewō**, *I pour*, aor. **gheum**, *I poured*.

Thematic aorist root stems are usually made in Ø/Ø root vowel grade, secondary endings, and sometimes reduplication; as, pres. **deik-ō**, aor. **dik-óm**, pres. **linq-ō**, *I leave*, aor. **liq-óm**, *I left*, pres. **wid-ḗjō**, aor. **wid-óm**; *cf.* also from **leudh-** *go/come*, **ludhóm**, *I went, I came*, most commonly used as aorist of **cemjō** (<**cm̥jō**), *I come*.

NOTE. As already seen, these stems could form aorists and presents: The ***liqé/ó-*** form (i.e. zero grade and accent on thematic vowel) is usually reserved for the aorist stem, while the ***leiqe/o-*** form (i.e. full grade) is rarely found in the aorist – but, when it is found, the present has to bc differentiated from it. This is made (1) with vowel opposition, i.e., full grade, o-grade or zero grade, (2) thematic vowel, or (3) with secondary phonetic differentiations (as accent shift).

AORIST REDUPLICATED STEM

[LIV type 2c] Aorist reduplicated stems are usually thematic, with a general vowel ***e*** (opposed to the ***i*** of the present), zero-grade root vowel (general in aorists); as, **chenmi/che-chn̥-om**, *murder, kill*; **weqmi/we-uq-om**, *say, speak*;

NOTE. Fortson (2004): "(...) reduplicated aorists typically have causative meaning, such as Ved. Skt. *á-pī-par-as* 'you made cross over', Gk. *dé-da-e* 'he taught' (<'caused to know'), and Toch. A *śa-śärs* 'he made known'." *Cf.* also Lat. *momordit, totondit, spopondit*, etc., or O.Ind. *atītaram, ajījanam*, etc.

In roots which begin with vowel, reduplication is of the type *vowel+consonant*.

Some roots which begin with vowel form also reduplicated aorists; as **ag-ag-om** (as Gk. ηγαγον, where η<ā<*é+a – Wackernagel, hence **é-agagom*).

AORIST CONSONANT STEM

[LIV type 2b] The most common consonant stem is the sigmatic aorist, formed with the suffix -***s***-, generally athematic.

The -***s***- is added usually to the root, whether monosyllabic or disyllabic, in consonant or vowel, opposed to the present. Such root aorists usually show lengthened e-grade in the active voice, and zero grade in the rest; as, pres. **pí(m)plēmi**, *I fill*, aor. **plēsm**, *I filled*, 3rd pl. **plesn̥t**, *they filled*; **qērsm̥**, *I made*, 3rd pl. **qr̥sn̥t**, *they made*, from **qer**-, *make*; **dēik-s-m**, *I indicated,* **wēgh-s-m**, *I carried, I conveyed*, etc.

NOTE. Lengthened vocalism in sigmatic aorists was probably an innovation in Late Indo-European. For lengthened grade, *cf.* maybe Latin forms like *dīxī* (<**dēik-s-*), *uēxī* from *uehō* (*cf.* O.Ind. *ávāk-ṣam* from *váhāmi* 'drive'), *rēxī* from *regō*, etc., or Toch. B *preksa*, A *prakäs* (<**prēk-s-ā*), according to Lindeman (1968). Without lengthening (i.e. full grade) they are found in Greek and in the s-aorist middle in Indo-Iranian, *cf.* Gk. *élekse*<**é-leg-s-* 'he said'. For Beekes (1995), the lengthened grade "perhaps it has disappeared through regular sound developments (**dēik-* → *deik-*, Osthoff's Law)."

It could also be added to a vowel **ā**, **ē**, **ō**, with the same stem as the present, or to the noun from which the verb is derived; as, pres. **alkējō**, aor. **alkēsom**, *grow*.

The general system of thematic present vs. sigmatic aorist stems may be so depicted: **-ēje/o-** vs. **-ēs-**; **-āje/o-** vs. **-ās-**; **-je/o-** vs. **-is-**; **-je/o-** vs. **-ās-**; **-je/o-** vs. **ēs-**; and **-e/o-** vs. **-ās-**.

Monosyllabic or disyllabic sigmatic aorist root stems in **i**, **u**, **ā**, **ē**, **ō**, have a fixed vowel grade; as, aor. **pewism**, **pewisn̥t**, *purify*.

NOTE. Aorist stem formation in -***i***-, -***ē***-, -***ā***- is still less common. Other common formations in -***s***- include the following: In -***is***- (Latin and Indo-Aryan), -***es***- (Greek), as *genis-* from **gen**-, *beget*, *wersis-* from **wers**-, *rain*; also, *cf.* Lat. *amauis* (*amāuistī*, and *amāuerām*<*-*wisām*), etc. In -***sā***-, attested in Latin, Tocharian and Armenian. Also attested are aorists in -***sē***-, thematic -***sje/o***-, etc.

Stems in ***-t-*** function usually as aorists, opposed to present stems, especially in Italic, Celtic and Germanic.

NOTE. While the use of ***-t*** for persons in the verbal conjugation is certainly old, the use of an extension in ***-t-*** to form verbal stems seems to be more recent, and mainly a North-West IE development.

Stems in ***-k-*** are rare, but there are examples of them in all forms of the verb, including aorists.

AORIST VOWEL STEM

Aorists in ***ā***, ***ē***, are very common, either as root stems with athematic inflection, or mixed with other endings, e.g. ***-u-***.

NOTE. As already said, stems extended in ***-u-*** are rarely found in present stems, but are frequent in past stems; the opposite is true for ***-i-***.

When opposed to a present, stems extended in ***-ā***, ***-ē***, are often aorists. Possible oppositions present stem vowel vs. aorist stem vowel include:

- Present thematic in ***-i-*** vs. aorist athematic in ***-ē***, ***-ā***; as, **mn̥jō** vs. **mn̥ḗm**, *consider*, **alkējō** vs. **alkā́m**, *protect*.
- Present thematic in **e/o** vs. aorist athematic in ***-ē***, ***-ā***; as, **legō-legēm**, *collect*.

NOTE. The preterite in *-ā*, common to Tocharian, Italic, and Baltic, has been discussed by Jasanoff, Nikolaev, Fellner, or Malzahn among others, in already mentioned works, although the information that we have on this question remains limited.

The use of stems in ***-u-*** is usually related to the past, and sometimes to the perfect. Such endings may appear as ***-we/o-***, often ***-āwe/o-***, ***-ēwe/o-***; as, **plēu-**, from **plē-**, **sēu-**, from **sē-**, **gnōu-**, from **gnō-**.

Endings ***-i-/-ī-*** are scarcely used for aorists, but they appear in some stems used both for present and aorist stems; as, **awisdhijō** vs. **awisdhijóm**, *hear*, Lat. *audĭo, audĭui.*

7.4.4. THE PERFECT STEM

[LIV type 3a] The perfect stem has **ŏ̄** or lengthened root vowel and special perfect endings, sg. ***-a***, ***-tha***, ***-e***, pl. ***-mé, -té, -(ḗ)r***, which are only used in the perfect indicative.

In Gk. and Ind.-Ira., the stem was often reduplicated, generally with vowel ***e***; in Latin and Germanic, reduplication is often absent.

NOTE. Historically the perfect was possibly a different stative verb, a deverbative from the root with certain formation rules, which eventually entered the verbal conjugation, meaning the state derived from the action of the present stem. PIE perfect did not have a tense or voice value.

Root vowel is usually **ō̆/∅**, i.e. o-grade in the singular and zero-grade in the plural; for a contrast pres. 1st sg./ perf. 1st sg. / perf. 3rd pl., *cf.* **gígnō / gé-gon-a / ge-gn̥-mé**, *know*; **bhindh-ō / bhondh-a / bhn̥dh-mé**, *bind*; **bheudhō / bhoudh-a / bhudh-mé**, *wake up*.

NOTE. 1) for different formations, *cf.* **kan-ō / (ké)kan-a / kn̥-mé**, *sing*, *cf.* O.Ir. *cechan, cechan, cechuin (and cechain), cechnammar, cechn(u)id, cechnatar.*; **d-ō-mi / de-d-ai**, *give*, *cf.* O.Ind. *dadé*, Lat. *dedī*. 2) For examples of root vowel **ā**, *cf.* Lat. *scābī*, or Gk. *τεθηλα*, and for examples with root vowel **a**, *cf.* Umb. *procanurent* (with ablaut in Lat. *procinuerint*) – this example has lost reduplication as Italic dialects usually do after a preposed preposition (*cf.* Lat. *compulī, detinuī*), although this may not be the case (*cf.* Lat. *concinuī*).

2) There are also perfects with lengthened root vowel; as, from Latin **sedē-jō**, perf. **sēd-a**, sit; **ed-ō**, perf. **ēd-a**, *eat*; **cem-jō**, perf. **cēm-a**, *come*; **ag-ō**, perf. **āg-a**, *act*; from Germanic, **sleb-ō**, perf. **séslēb-a**, *sleep*; etc.

Reduplication is made in ***e***, and sometimes in ***i*** or ***u***.

NOTE. Apparently, in Indo-Iranian and Greek dialects reduplication was obligatory, whereas in North-West Indo-European it wasn't. For an older nonobligatory reduplication, there is common PIE perfect **woistha** (<**woid-th*$_2$*e*), *know*, from **weid-**, *see* (hence the stative meaning '*state derived from having seen*'?), *cf.* O.Ind. *véttha*, Gk. *(w)oīstha*, Goth. *waist*. *Cf.* also afield Gk. εγνωκα, Lat. *sēuī* (which seems old, even with Goth. *saiso*), Lat. *sedī*, from *sedeō* and *sīdo*, which do not let us reconstruct whether the original form is ***sesdāi*** or ***sēdāi***.

There could have been a hesitant pluperfect formation in PIE, which would have been easily constructed by adding secondary athematic endings to the perfect stem.

NOTE 1. The secondary endings marked a past tense, the old perfect became then a present. It is found reconstructed for PIE e.g. in Adrados–Bernabé–Mendoza (1995-1998), and J.T. Katz in <http://www.princeton.edu/~pswpc/pdfs/katz/070702.pdf>. In <https://openaccess.leidenuniv.nl/bitstream/handle/1887/1919/344_092.pdf?sequence=1 >, Kortlandt, however, about the pluperfect in Proto-Germanic, deems the pluperfect a post-PIE formation.

NOTE 2. The perfect middle seems to have been an early dialectal formation, too. It was made by opposing a new perfect formation to the old one, so that the old became only active and the newer middle. Such formations were generalized in the southern dialects, but didn't succeed in the northern ones. The new perfect middle stem was generally obtained with the perfect stem in zero-grade and middle endings.

NOTE 3. A special past is found in IE dialects of Europe (i.e., the North-West IE and Greek), the compound past, sometimes called *future past*, which is formed by two elements: a verbal stem followed by a vowel (***-ā***, ***-ē***, ***-ī***, ***-ō***), and an auxiliary verb, with the meanings *be* (***es-***), *become* (***bheu-***), *do* (***dhē-***), or *give* (***dō-***). Although each language shows different formations, they all share a common pattern, and therefore probably had a common origin traceable to post-LIE, unstable at first and later systematized in the early proto-languages. The first element of the compound is derived from a root or a stem with vowel ending, either the present or the aorist stem - generally with lengthened grade. They are past formations similar to the others (imperfects and aorists), but instead of receiving secondary endings, they receive a secondary stem (like the perfect). The second element is an auxiliary verb; as, ***dhē-*** in Greek and Germanic, ***bheu-*** in Latin and Celtic, and ***dō-*** in Balto-Slavic. Their specific Past meaning vary according to the needs of the individual dialects (Adrados–Bernabé–Mendoza 1995-1998).

7.5. MOOD STEMS

7.5.1. INDICATIVE

The indicative expresses the real action, and it is the default mood; the other ones were specialised in opposition to it. It appears in the three verbal stems. The following table depicts the minimal verbal stem system attested for IEDs, according to finds from Vedic Sanskrit and Ancient Greek (Clackson 2007):

	Present	Aorist	Perfect	*Future?* [ii]
Indicative	past & non-past active & middle	past active & middle	[no voice/tense opposition]	*non-past* *active & middle*
Subjunctive	active & middle	active & middle	[no voice opp.][i]	-
Optative	active & middle	active & middle	[no voice opp.][i]	-
Imperative	active & middle	active & middle	-	-
Infinitive	active & middle?	active & middle?	-	-
Participle	active & middle	active & middle	[no voice opp.]	-

[i] The moods in the perfect were probably developed late in the history of the proto-language (see §7.4.1). Adrados–Bernabé–Mendoza (1995-1998), Fritz (Meier-Brügger, 2003), Fortson (2004), Clackson (2007), among others attribute their development to a late innovation, probably a Graeco-Aryan one. For a reconstruction of a PIE moods in the perfect, see Beekes (1995), Ringe (2006). Given that Northwestern dialects tended to merge later perfect, aorist and imperfect into a common *preterite*, it is probably safe to assume that in any case mood distinctions for the perfect were not much used in NWIE.

[ii] With the *future* we refer to the post-LIE stem incorporated into the conjugation of a certain verb. Those desideratives with present stems in thematic ***-s-*** reconstructed for LIE

(of which the LIV cites more than 100 examples, with almost 40 of them certain) could have in turn their own present, aorist, perfect, and even future stems.

The general mood system might be so depicted:

	Indicative	Imperative	Optative	Subjunctive
Function	action described as fact	commands	wishes, hopes	action described as completely theoretical
Charact.	default mood	not conjugated in the first person special personal endings	ablauting athematic **-ī/*jē*-**, thematic ***-oi-*** affixed to stem secondary endings	thematic **-e/o-** suffix affixed to stem primary endings

7.5.2. IMPERATIVE

The imperative, used to express direct commands, had probably in PIH the same basic stem of the indicative, and was used without ending, in a simple expressive-impressive function, of exclamation or order. Imperatives are the equivalent in verbal inflection to the vocative in nominal declension.

NOTE. In Late Indo-European a new system was derived from this older scheme, a more complex imperative system, featuring person, tense and even voice.

The general athematic 2nd sg. imperative ending was -Ø; as in **ei!** *go!* from **eimi**; or **es!** *be!* from **esmi**. An ending ***-dhí*** seems to have been common in LIE too; as, **i-dhí**! *go!*, **s-dhí**! *be!*

The thematic 2nd singular imperative was the bare thematic stem; **bhere!** *carry!*, **age!** *do! act!* The 2nd pl. ends in ***-te***, as **bhérete!** *carry!*, **agete!** *do! act!*

The thematic and athematic 3rd sg. and 3rd pl. have a special ending ***-tōd***.

NOTE. Endings in *-*u*, i.e. 3rd sg. *-*tu*, 3rd pl. *-ntu, are also reconstructed (see Beekes 1995) from forms like Hitt. *paiddu* 'let him go', or Skt. *é-tu*, 'go'; the inclusion of that ending within the verbal system is, however, difficult. A common IE ending ***-tōd*** (*cf.* Skt. -*tā̆t*, Gk. -*tō*, O.Lat. -*tōd*, Celtib. -*tuz*, Goth. -*dau*), on the other hand, may obviously be explained as the introduction into the verbal conjugation of a secondary ablative form of the neuter pronoun **tod**, *this*, a logical addition to an imperative formation, with the sense of '*here*', hence '*now*', just as the addition of **-i**, '*here and now*' to oppose new endings to the older desinences (Adrados–Bernabé–Mendoza 1995-1998, Fortson 2004). This formation was further specialised in some dialects as future imperatives.

In root athematic verbs, plural forms show Ø vowel and accent on the ending; as, **s-entōd**! *be they!*

For Late Indo-European, only the person distinctions of the active voice are reconstructed with certainty. Common middle forms include the bare stems plus middle desinences; as, 2nd sg. ***-s(w)e/o*** (*cf.* Skt. *-sva*, Gk. *lúou<*lúe-so*, Lat. *sequere<*seque-se*, Ira. **-swe/o*), 2nd pl. ***-dhwe***, *cf.* Gk. *lúes-the*, O.Ind. *bháva-dhvam*. Beekes (1995), Sihler (1995).

		Athem.	*Them.*	*Middle*
Sg.	2.	-Ø, (***-dhí***)	***-e***	***-so***
	3.	***-tōd***	***-etōd***	***(-to)***
Pl.	2.	***-te***	***-ete***	***-dhwe***
	3.	***-ṇtōd***	***-ontōd***	***(-nto)***

NOTE. Forms for the 3rd person are uncertain, although a common sg. ***-tōd*** (from the active voice) is reconstructed; *cf.* Skt. *-tāt*, Gk. *-sthō* (*sth-* from plural and *-ō* from *tōd*), Lat. *-tōd*. Middle secondary endings 3rd sg. ***-to***, 3rd pl. ***-nto***, are tentatively reconstructed by Beekes (1995) as imperative marks with basis on the Sanskrit (*-tām*, *-ntām*) and Hittite (*-taru*, *-antaru*) endings.

7.5.3. SUBJUNCTIVE

1. The subjunctive is normally formed by the addition of the thematic vowel to the verb stem (be it athematic or already thematic), followed apparently by primary endings (although in Indo-Iranian both primary and secondary endings were used).

The subjunctives made from thematic verbs end therefore usually in so-called 'doubled' thematic vowels, i.e. ***-ē***, ***-ō***, and ***-ā***, always opposed to the indicative. These are sometimes called *athematic* subjunctives.

NOTE. The reader should take on account that the classification of forms in ***-ā***, ***-ē***, ***-ō***, as "athematic" is purely conventional; so, for example, Dahl considers them as two thematic stem allomorphs, terming them long-vowel-subjunctive [=athematic] against short-vowel-subjunctive [=thematic]. See <http://folk.uio.no/eysteind/PaperICHL.pdf>.

2. The subjunctive always has full grade in the root, and is usually made following these rules:

a. Indicative athematic vs. subjunctive thematic; as, ind. **esmi**, *I am*, **senti**, *they are*, subj. **esō**, *(if) I be*.

b. Indicative thematic vs. subjunctive with lengthened thematic vowel; as, ind. **bhéresi**, *you carry*, Sub. **bhérēsi**, *you may carry*, *(if) you carried*.

NOTE. Following Meier-Brügger, "[t]he subjunctive suffix is PIE *-e-, In the case of athematic verbal stems, the rule is [where K=Consonant] -K+Ø- (indicative stem), -K+e-

(subjunctive stem); correspondingly, that of thematic verbs is -e+∅ - (indicative stem), -e+e- (subjunctive stem)."

3. Subjunctives could also be formed in the same way from root and s-aorists, where likewise the full grade of the aorist stem was used (Fortson 2004).

NOTE. As indicated by first-person subjunctives like Ved. *kr̥ṇavā* 'I will do', Old Avestan *yaojā* 'I will yoke', Gk. *phérō* 'let me carry', and Lat. *erō* 'I will be', the 1st singular ended in -***ō*** rather than -***mi*** (Fortson 2004).

7.5.4. OPTATIVE

The optative mood is a volitive mood that signals wishing or hoping, as in English *I wish I might, I hope it may, I wish you could*, etc. It is made with the following suffix, and secondary endings.

1) In the athematic flexion, a general alternating suffix **-jē-**/**-ī-** with full-grade in the singular and 3rd pl. and zero-grade elsewhere; as, **s-jḗ-m**, *may I be*, **s-ī-mé**, *may we be*, **es-ī-nt**, *may they be*.

NOTE. "The stress was on the ending in the 1st and 2nd pl. forms of the mobile paradigms, and evidently also in the sg. forms of the middle voice, but not in the 3rd pl. forms, where a number of indications point to original root stress", as Lat. *velint,* Goth. *wileina,* and O.C.S. *velętъ*. But, Vedic *-ur* appears "in all those athematic forms where the stress is either on the root or on a preceding syllable". For more on this question, see <https://openaccess.leidenuniv.nl/handle/1887/2878>, Kortlandt (1992).

2) When the stress is fixed, it is ***-oi-*** in the thematic flexion, and **-ī-** in the athematic (e.g. Narten presents); as, **bher-oi-t**, *may he carry*.

NOTE. This is probably the thematic -***o***- plus the zero-grade Optative suffix -***i***- (<*i-h_1-), i.e. originally *-o-ih_1-, or maybe *-o-jh_1-, see Hoffmann (1976). Optative endings might yield a reconstruction of vocalic resonants in PII, PGk from ***-o-jm̥***, ***-o-jn̥t***.

3) In the 1st person middle the *thematic* ending is found (*cf.* Skt. *bruv-īyá*); as, **s-īj-á**, **bhér-oj-a**.

Athematic stems have usually root vowel in zero-grade, while thematic stems show no ablaut.

NOTE. For athematic optatives form the present with zero-grade; *cf.* Lat. *siēm*, *duim*, Gk. *ισταιην*, *διδοιην*, *τιθειην*, O.Ind. *syaam* (*asmi*), *dvisyām* (*dvesmi*), *iyām* (*emi*), *juhuyām* (juhkomi), *sunuykām* (*sunomi*), *rundhyām* (*runadhmi*), *kuryām* (*karomi*), *krīnīyām* (*krīnāmi*), etc. Exceptions are Lat. *uelim* (not *uulim*), Goth. (concave) *wiljau*, *wileis*, etc.

Sigmatic aorists seem to have formed originally their optative directly with the verbal stem.

NOTE. It is not clear whether the oldest PIE allowed the sigmatic aorist to form the optative, as did Old Greek. Kortlandt clearly supports this possibility in

<https://openaccess.leidenuniv.nl/bitstream/handle/1887/2878/344_066.pdf?sequence=1>, regarding the Eolic optative, whilst Jasanoff, in a parallel article at <http://www.people.fas.harvard.edu/~jasanoff/pdf/Ablaut%20of%20the%20root%20aorist%20optative.pdf> considers that "we may take it as given that there was no aorist optative in s-ih_1 in late PIE. The s-aorist based its synchronic optative directly on the verbal root." Both authors also differ in the reconstruction of the optative of ***wel-***, *wish*. More recently, Jasanoff has published another article on the optative, that can be find at <http://www.people.fas.harvard.edu/~jasanoff/pdf/Notes%20on%20internal%20history%20of%20PIE%20optative.pdf>, and where he continues his reconstruction.

7.7. NOUN AND ADJECTIVE FORMS

7.7.1. INFINITIVES

1. The infinitives are indeclinable nouns with non-personal verbal functions, which can be as many as inflection, voice, aspect and even time.

2. The oldest infinitives are the verbal nouns, casual forms inflected as nouns, sometimes included in the verbal inflection. A verbal noun is a declinable substantive, derived from the root of a verb.

NOTE. Infinitives are, thus, old nouns reinterpreted as forming part of the verbal conjugation, probably within the Late Indo-European period. As Meier-Brügger (2003) notes, "The development of means of differentiation of voice, aspect, and tempus in the infinitive formations is post-Proto-Indo-European."

The difference in syntax is important: the verbal noun is constructed as a substantive, thus e.g. with the object in the genitive; as, **wīrosjo chentis**, *the murder of a man*. Such a formation is opposed to an infinitive with an accusative; as, **wīróm chentum**, *to murder a man*.

3. Verbal nouns were, thus, the normal way to express the idea of a modern infinitive in PIE. They were formed with the verbal stem and usually a nominal suffixes ***-ti-***, ***-tu-***; as, **statis** (<**sth$_2$-ti-*), *standing, placing*, from **stā-** (<**steh$_2$-*) *stand*; **cem-tus**, *coming*, from **cem-**, *come*.

NOTE. *Cf.* Skt *sthíti-* 'stay, sojourn', Grk *stásis* 'place, setting, erection [of a statue]', Lat *statim* 'firmly, steadfastly', Eng. *stead*. Mallory–Adams (2007). Some IE dialects chose later between limited noun-cases of those verbal nouns for the infinitive formation, generally Acc., Loc., Abl.; compare Lat. **-os* (sibilant neuter), Gmc. **-on-om* (thematic neuter), etc.

4. In Late Indo-European, a common infinitive suffix ***-tu-*** (and more limited ***-ti-***) seems to have been usually added to the accented strong verbal root, conveying the

same meaning as the English infinitive; as, **stătum**, *to stay*, opposed to the weak, unaccented form in participle **statós**, *placed.*

NOTE. For generalised IE infinitive formation in ***-tu*** [generally ***-tu-m***, i.e. the accusative of the abstract noun suffix ***-tu-***, often called *supine* (solely used with verbs of motion to indicate purpose)], *cf.* Skt. *-tus, -tum* (acc.), Gk. *-tós*, Av. *-tos* (gen.), *-tave, -tavai* (dat.), *-tum*, Lat. (active & passive supine) *-tum* (acc.) *-tū* (dat.-loc.) *-tui* (dat.), Prus. *-twei* (dat.) *-tun, -ton* (acc.), O.Sla. *-tŭ* (supine), Lith. *-tų*, etc.; for ***-ti-***, *cf.* Ved. *-taye* (dat), BSl., Cel. *-ti* (loc.), Lith. *-tie* (dat.), etc.; also, in ***-m-en-***, *cf.* Skt. *-mane*, O.Gk. *-men(ai)*, etc. On the infinitive, it is interesting to read Keynada's thesis Infinitives in the Rigveda (2003). The thesis is readily available on the web (at least in 2012), but you can always ask for a copy at his website <http://www.keydana.de/>.

Also, a common ending ***-dhjāi*** added to the verbal stem formed common middle infinitives.

NOTE. The reconstructed ***-dhjāi*** (Haudry), is the basic form behind Ved. *-dhyai*, Gk. Middle *-σθαι*, Umb. *-fi*, Toch. *-tsi*, as well as Latin gerunds and the Germanic **-dhjōi* (Rix 1979), all related to an original middle infinitive (Beekes 1995, Sihler 1995), although appearing in both active and passive formations (Fortson 2004). Other forms include ***-u-***, ***-er/n-***, -(***e***)***s-***, extended ***-s-***, ***-u-***, ***-m-***, also Gmc. ***-no-*** (as Goth. *ita-n<*edo-no-*), Arm. ***-lo-***, etc.

7.7.2. PARTICIPLES

1. The participles are adjectives which have been assimilated to the verbal system, expressing tense and voice; like other adjectives, they have nominal inflection.

NOTE. The reconstructed Proto-Indo-European shows an intense reliance on participles, and thus a certain number of participles played a very important role in the early language.

2. Those in **-nt-**, fem. **-nt-ja/ī**, are the older ones, and form participles of active voice to present or aorist stems.

NOTE. In Anatolian, this participle is semantically equivalent to verbal adjectives in ***-tó-***.

In athematics it seems that an ablauting suffix **-e/ont** with full and zero grade coexisted in the declension of present participles; *cf.* **s-ent-**(also **s-ont-**)/**s-n̥t-**, *who exist, being*, **weq-ont-/uq-n̥t-**, *who speaks, speaking*, **dhe-dhē-nt-/dhe-dha-nt-**, *placing*, **jung-ent-/jung-n̥t-**, *joining*, **d-ent-**, *eating* (from which **dentis**, *tooth*), **j-ent-**, *going*, **chn-ent-**, *killing*, **ag-ent-**, *driving, guiding*, etc.

NOTE. For ***s-n̥t-*** instead of **sent-**, *cf.* ***ap-sn̥t-*** (for ***apo-we-s-ent-is***) in Lat. *(ab)sent-*, Myc. pl. *(a-p)e-a-sa*, i.e. *ap-ehassai* (with *-assa-<*-n̥t-ih₂-*). A. Morpurgo Davies (1978, reviewed in Meier-Brügger 2003) considered that "[a]s far as we know, there is no reason to attribute **h₁s-ent-* to Proto-Greek."

In thematics, a form ***-o-nt-*** (i.e. ***-nt*** added to the thematic vowel) is generalised as, **bher-ont-**, *who carries, carrying*.

NOTE. The suffix ***-o-nt-*** shows no generalised ablaut full-grade/zero-grade paradigm in IEDs. It is safe to assume no accent-ablaut change for North-West IE, and probably also for LIE, as "[i]t remains to be seen whether the thematic forms were originally declined as **-ont-/*-nt-* (as in Vedic), and were only secondarily reinterpreted as **-o-nt-*", as some have posited; Meier-Brügger, 2003 (reviewing Rix 1976, Szemerényi 1990).

Also, some questions about the participles are not easily reconciled: in Latin, they are formed with **e** ending for stems in **-i-**; in Greek, they are formed in **o** and are consonantal stems. Greek, on the other hand, still shows remains of the thematic vowel in participles of *verba vocalia* ***-ājont-***, ***-ējont-***, etc. Latin doesn't.

Aorist active participles were formed similarly to present participles, as the root aorist participle **stā-nt-**, *having stood* (*cf.* Ved. *sthānt-*, Gk. *stant-*), s-aorist **dhech-s-ṇt-** ['d^{h}ek-sn̥t], *having burnt*, **dēik-s-ṇt-**, *having indicated*,

3. The perfect active participle has an ablauting suffix ***-wos-/-us-***, fem. ***-us-ja/ī***; as, **weid-wós-**, **wid-us-ja**, *knowing*, '*who is in a state of having seen*', from **weid-**, *see*; **bher-wós-**, '*who is in a state of having carried*'. Common is the reduplicated Perfect stem; as, **qe-qṛ-wós-**, *making*, from **qer-**.

For the declension of these participles in ***-nt-*** and ***-wos-***, see above §5.2.

4. The middle participles have a common suffix ***-mṇo-*** for athematic, ***-o-mṇo*** in thematics; as, **bhéro-mṇos**, *carrying (oneself, for oneself)*, **álo-mṇos**, *who feeds himself, nurtured*, from **alō**, *raise, feed* (*cf.* Lat. *alumnus*), **dhē-mṇā**, *the one who gives suck*, from **dhē-i-**, *suck* (milk), *suckle* (as Av. *daēnu-*, Lat. *femina*, '*woman*').

NOTE. On the *-mXno- question, where X is a vowel or laryngeal or even laryngeal+vowel, while Melchert (1983) or Szemerényi (1990) support an original **-mn-o-**, a competing hypothesis is Fritz's one with an original **-m$h_1$eno-*, into variants **-m$h_1$no-* and then *-mno-*, in which "the laryngeal disappears when the suffix is added to a root or stem with a non-syllabic final position preceding the full vowel e. The non-laryngeal full grade form **-meno-* would then have the newly constructed zero grade form **-mno-*" (Meier-Brügger 2003). The differentiation of the perfect **-mh_1n-ó-* vs. the present **´-o-m$h_1$no-* in the various IE languages may be traced back to the athematic/thematic dichotomy (Rix 1976). For an explanation on the auxiliary vowel in Adrados–Bernabé–Mendoza (1995-1998), see §2.3.

5. In addition to participles, PIE had verbal adjectives in ***-tó-*** and ***-nó-***, added usually to the zero-grade of a verbal stem that indicated completed action, and were semantically like past participles in English. If the verb they were formed

from was transitive (like *eat*), the verbal adjective was passive and past in tense (*eaten*), but if the verb was intransitive (like *go*), the verbal adjective was simply past in tense (*gone*) Fortson (2004). Examples include **chn̥-tós**, *slain*, from transitive **chenmi**, *murder*, *cf.* Skt. *hatá-*, Gk. *-phatós*, **sjū-tós**, *sewn*, from **sisō**, **tn̥-tós**, *stretched*, **klŭ̄tós**, *heard*; **cm̥-tós**, *(having) come*, from intransitive **cemjō**, *come*.

a. General ***-tó-***, added usually to zero-grade roots; as, **altós**, *grown*, **dhatós**, *placed*, **kaptós**, *taken*, **liqtós**, *left*, etc. Exceptions include e.g. **gnōtós**, *having been understood*.

b. Old (not generalised) ***-nó-*** and its variants; as, **plēnós**, '*(having been) filled up*', *full*, **bhidhnós**, *'having been split'*, *parted*, *bitten*; **wr̥gnós**, *worked*.

NOTE. For **plēnós**, from **pel-**, *fill*, an adjective which was not part of the verbal paradigm, *cf.* Skt. *pūrṇá-*, Lat. *plēnus* (vs. past participle *–plētus* 'filled'), Goth. *fulls* (double *-ll-* < **-ln-*), O.Ir. *lán*, Lith. *pìlnas*. Also, the common PIE verb is found from this root, **plḗnāmi**, *fill*, *cf.* O.Ind. *pr̥ṇā́ti* Goth. *fullnan*, Ger. *füllen*, O.Ir. *lín(a)im*, Arm. *lnum*, and root Gk. *píplēmi*.

Verbal adjectives in ***-mó-***, ***-ló-***, functioned as past participles in individual languages; as, present passive participle in Balto-Slavic *-mo-*, *cf.* O.C.S. *něsomŭ*, Lith. *nēšamas* 'being carried', perhaps Anatolian, *cf.* Luv. *kīšammi-* 'combed'. For its old use, *cf.* ***prāmós***, *foremost*, *first*, from **per-**, *v.s.* §5.5.2; however, Latin *prīmus* is usually reconstructed as from ***prei-isamós*** (*cf.* Paelignian *prísmū*), but possibly superlative ***pr̥w-isamós***, from the same root as common PIE **prāmos**, **prāwos**, *first*, is the solution (see Szemerényi 1970, Adrados–Bernabé–Mendoza 1995-1998).

7.7.3. GERUNDIVES AND ABSOLUTIVES

1. Verbal adjectives are not assimilated to the verbal system of tense and voice. Those which indicate need or possibility are called gerundives.

NOTE. Verbal adjectives and adjectives (as verbal nouns and nouns) cannot be easily differentiated.

2. Whereas the same participle suffixes are found, i.e. ***-tó-***, ***-nó-***, ***-mó-***, there are two forms especially identified with gerundives in IEDs:

a. ***-ló-*** and ***-li-*** are found in Latin, Balto-Slavic, Tocharian and Armenian; as, **n̥bherelós**, *unbearable*, **ágilis**, *agile*, etc.

NOTE. For suffix ***-lo-*** as a participle suffix, *cf.* Russ. *videlŭ*, Lat. *credulus*, *bibulus*, *tremulus*, etc.

b. ***-jó-*** (a common lengthening to differentiate adjectives) is sometimes a gerundive of obligation, as well as forms in ***-tu-***, ***-ti-***, ***-ndho-***, etc.; as, **dhr̥sjós**, *that has to be dared*; **gnōtinós**, *that has to be known*; **gnā́skendhos**, *that has to be born*, **awisdhíjendhos**, *that has to be heard*; and so on.

NOTE. Some forms in ***-ndhos*** seem to retain a so-called *fossil proto-gerundive* (Meiser 1998), from an archaic ending **-dnós*, whose meaning lack the passive obligation common to the gerundive; so e.g. **mlāje-dnós*>O. Lat. **blandos*, **rotodnós* (Lat. *rotundus*), *round*, or **seqodnós* (Lat. *secundus*). Outside Latin it is possibly found e.g. in Gk. *tēkedṓ* 'consumption' or **phagedṓn* (*cf.* Gk. *phagédaina* 'gangrene'); see Blanc (2004) in <http://www.cairn.info/publications-de-Blanc-Alain--7916.htm>.

Jasanoff dismisses this so-called *lex unda*, proposing an 'original' ***-tino-***, in his article <http://www.people.fas.harvard.edu/~jasanoff/pdf/Latin%20gerundive%20(preprint).pdf >. We would have then a group of passive participles-gerundives, which indicate possibility/obligation, built by agglutination of two suffixes; as, ***-ti-no-***, ***-i-jo-*** (*cf.* O.Ind. *ramanīya*, *miśranīya*), ***-tew-(ij)o-***, ***-ti-mo-*** (*cf.* Gk. *aidesimos*), O.C.S. *pečalьnъ* 'deplorable' (*cf.* O.Ir. *fedelm*), Lat. *amābilis*, etc. Jasanoff also presents abstracts in *-**(n)ti**-*, which are behind the Latin gerund.

c. A future (or obligation) passive gerundive ending, ***-téw(ij)os***, existed in Late Indo-European; as, **legtéw(ij)os**, *which has to be said, read or gathered*. Because of its passive use, it may be used only with transitive verbs.

NOTE. For the absolutive use of ***-téw(ij)os***, *cf.* Gk. *-τεος*, O.Ind. *-tavya*, O.Ir. *-the*, etc., probably all from verbal adjectives in ***-tu-***, full grade ***-tew-***, usually lengthened with common gerundive ending ***-ij-***.

d. ***-mn̥***, with a general meaning of 'able'; as, **mnāmn̥**, *mindful*.

NOTE. For the 'internal derivation' (after the German and Austrian schools) of this PIE suffix ***-mn̥***→**-mon*, *cf.* Gk. *mnēma* < **mń-mn̥** 'reminder', Gk. *mnḗmon* < **mnāmn̥** 'who remembers'; compare also Skt. *bráhman* 'prayer', Skt. *brahmán* 'brahman', etc.

3. The adverbial, not inflected verbal adjectives are called absolutives or gerunds. They were usually derived from older gerundives.

NOTE. PIE speakers had to use verbal periphrases or other resources to express the idea of a modern gerund, as there were no common reconstructible PIE gerunds. Just like verbal nouns were the usual basis to express the idea of infinitives, verbal adjectives (and especially gerundives) were a common PIE starting point to create gerunds.

7.8. CONJUGATED EXAMPLES

7.8.1. THEMATIC VERBS

I. PRESENT STEM

ACTIVE

loutum, *to wash* (present stem ***low-o-***)

		Indicative	*Subjunctive*	*Optative*	*Imperative*	IMPERFECT
Sg.		**lowō**	**lowō**	**lowoim**	-	**lowom**
		lówesi	**lówēsi**	**lowois**	**lowe**	**lowes**
		lóweti	**lówēti**	**lowoit**	**lówetōd**	**lowet**
Pl.		**lówomos**	**lówōmos**	**lówoime**	-	**lówomo**
		lówete	**lówēte**	**lówoite**	**lówete**	**lówete**
		lówonti	**lówōnti**	**lowoint**	**lówontōd**	**lowont**

deiktum, *to show* (present stem ***deik-o-***)

	Indicative	*Subjunctive*	*Optative*	*Imperative*	IMPERFECT
Sg.	**deikō**	**deikō**	**deikoim**	-	**deikom**
	déikesi	**déikēsi**	**deikois**	**deike**	**deikes**
	déiketi	**déikēti**	**deikoit**	**déiketōd**	**deiket**
Pl.	**déikomos**	**déikōmos**	**déikoime**	-	**déikome**
	déikete	**déikēte**	**déikoite**	**déikete**	**deikete**
	déikonti	**déikōnti**	**deikoint**	**déikontōd**	**déikont**

weistum (<***weid-tum***), *to see* (present stem ***wid-ḗjo-***)

	Indicative	*Subjunctive*	*Optative*	*Imperative*	IMPERFECT
Sg.	**widējō**	**widējō**	**widējoim**	-	**widējom**
	widḗjesi	**widḗjēsi**	**widējois**	**widēje**	**widējes**
	widḗjeti	**widḗjēti**	**widējoit**	**widḗjetōd**	**widējet**
Pl.	**widḗjomos**	**widḗjōmos**	**widḗjoime**	-	**widḗjomo**
	widḗjete	**widḗjēte**	**widḗjoite**	**widḗjete**	**widḗjete**
	widḗjonti	**widḗjōnti**	**widējoint**	**widḗjontōd**	**widḗjont**

MIDDLE-PASSIVE

loutum, *to wash* (present stem ***low-o-***)

	Indicative	*Subjunctive*	*Optative*	IMPERFECT
Sg.	**lowōr**	**lówōmar**	**lówoima**	**lowa**
	lówesor	**lówēsor**	**lówoiso**	**lóweso**
	lówetor	**lówētor**	**lówoito**	**lóweto**
Pl.	**lówomesdha**	**lówōmesdha**	**lówoimedha**	**lówomedha**
	lówedhwe	**lówēdhwe**	**lówoidhwe**	**lówedhwe**
	lówontor	**lówōntor**	**lówointo**	**lówonto**

deiktum, *to show* (present stem ***deik-o-***)

	Indicative	*Subjunctive*	*Optative*	IMPERFECT
Sg.	**deikōr**	**déikōmar**	**déikoima**	**deika**
	déikesor	**déikēsor**	**déikoiso**	**déikeso**
	déiketor	**déikētor**	**déikoito**	**déiketo**
Pl.	**déikomesdha**	**déikōmesdha**	**déikoimedha**	**déikomedha**
	déikedhwe	**déikēdhwe**	**déikoidhwe**	**déikedhwe**
	déikontor	**déikōntor**	**déikointo**	**déikonto**

weistum, *to see* (present stem ***wid-ḗjo-***)

	Indicative	*Subjunctive*	*Optative*	IMPERFECT
Sg.	**widējōr**	**widḗjōmar**	**widḗjoima**	**widēja**
	widḗjesor	**widḗjēsor**	**widḗjoiso**	**widḗjeso**
	widḗjetor	**widḗjētor**	**widḗjoito**	**widḗjeto**
Pl.	**widḗjomesdha**	**widḗjōmesdha**	**widḗjoimedha**	**widḗjomedha**
	widḗjedhwe	**widḗjēdhwe**	**widḗjoidhwe**	**widḗjedhwe**
	widḗjontor	**widḗjōntor**	**widḗjointo**	**widḗjonto**

II. AORIST STEM

ACTIVE

loutum, *to wash* (aorist stem sigmatic ***lou-s-***)

	Indicative	*Subjunctive*	*Optative*
Sg.	**lousm̥**	**lousō**	**lousīm**
	lous	**lousesi**	**lousīs**
	loust	**louseti**	**lousīt**
Pl.	**lousme**	**lóusomos**	**lóusīme**
	louste	**lóusete**	**lóusīte**
	lousn̥t	**lousonti**	**lousīnt**

deiktum, *to show* (aorist stem ***dik-ó-***, zero-grade)

	Indicative	*Subjunctive*	*Optative*
Sg.	**dikóm**	**dikṓ**	**dikóim**
	dikés	**dikḗsi**	**dikóis**
	dikét	**dikḗti**	**dikóit**
Pl.	**dikome**	**dikōmos**	**dikoime**
	dikete	**dikēte**	**dikoite**
	dikónt	**dikṓnti**	**dikóint**

NOTE. For original **dikóm**, *cf. diśáti*, Gk. *ἄδικος*, etc.

weistum, *to see* (aorist stem ***wid-ó-***, zero-grade)

	Indicative	*Subjunctive*	*Optative*
Sg.	**widóm**	**widṓ**	**widóim**
	widés	**widḗsi**	**widóis**
	widét	**widḗti**	**widóit**
Pl.	**widome**	**widōmos**	**widoime**
	widete	**widēte**	**widoite**
	widónt	**widṓnti**	**widóint**

NOTE. For PIE accent on the optative suffix, following the accent on the thematic vowel of certain Aorist formations, *cf.* O.Ind. them. aor. opt. sg. *vidé-s* (<****widói-s***).

MIDDLE-PASSIVE

loutum, *to wash* (aorist stem ***lou-s-***, sigmatic)

		Indicative	Subjunctive	Optative
Sg.		**lousma**	**lousōr**	**lóusīma**
		louso	**lóusesor**	**lóusīso**
		lousto	**lóusetor**	**lóusīto**
Pl.		**lóusmedha**	**lóusomesdhā**	**lóusīmedha**
		lousdhwe	**lóusedhwe**	**lóusīdhwe**
		lousn̥to	**lóusontor**	**lóusīnto**

deiktum, *to show* (aorist stem ***dik-ó-***, zero-grade)

		Indicative	Subjunctive	Optative
Sg.		**diká**	**dikṓr**	**dikoima**
		dikeso	**dikēsor**	**dikóiso**
		diketo	**dikētor**	**dikoito**
Pl.		**dikómedha**	**dikṓmesdhā**	**dikóimedha**
		dikedhwe	**dikēdhwe**	**dikoidhwe**
		dikonto	**dikōntor**	**dikointo**

weistum, *to see* (aorist stem ***wid-ó-***, zero-grade)

		Indicative	Subjunctive	Optative
Sg.		**widá**	**widṓr**	**widoima**
		wideso	**widḗsor**	**widoiso**
		wideto	**widētor**	**widoito**
Pl.		**widómedha**	**widṓmesdhā**	**widóimedha**
		widedhwe	**widēdhwe**	**widoidhwe**
		widonto	**widōntor**	**widointo**

III. PERFECT STEM

loutum, *to wash* (perfect stem ***lōu-*/*lou-***)

	Indicative	*Subjunctive*	*Optative*
Sg.	**lōwa**	**lōwō**	**loujḗm**
	lōutha	**lōwēsi**	**loujḗs**
	lōwe	**lōwēti**	**loujḗt**
Pl.	**loumé**	**lṓwōmos**	**lowīmé**
	louté	**lṓwēte**	**lowīté**
	lowḗr	**lōwōnti**	**lowī́nt**

deiktum, *to show* (perfect stem ***doik-*/*dik-)***

	Indicative	*Subjunctive*	*Optative*
Sg.	**doika**	**doikō**	**dikjḗm**
	doiktha	**doikesi**	**dikjḗs**
	doike	**doiketi**	**dikjḗt**
Pl.	**dikmé**	**dóikomos**	**dikīmé**
	dikté	**dóikete**	**dikīté**
	dikḗr	**doikonti**	**dikī́nt**

weistum, *to see* (perfect stem ***woid-*/*wid-***, *know*)

	Indicative	*Subjunctive*	*Optative*
Sg.	**woida**	**woidō**	**widjḗm**
	woistha[i]	**woidesi**	**widjḗs**
	woide	**woideti**	**widjḗt**
Pl.	**widmé**	**wóidomos**	**widīme**
	wisté[ii]	**wóidete**	**widīte**
	widḗr	**woidonti**	**widī́nt**

[i] From ***woid-tha***. [ii] From ***wid-té***.

7.8.2. ATHEMATIC INFLECTION

I. PRESENT STEM

ACTIVE

estum, *to be* (present stem ***es-/s-***)

	Indicative	*Subjunctive*	*Optative*	*Imperative*	IMPERFECT
Sg.	**esmi**	**esō**	**sjēm**	-	**esm̥**
	esi	**ésesi**	**sjēs**	**es/sdhí**	**es**
	esti	**éseti**	**sjēt**	**estōd**	**est**
Pl.	**smes**	**ésomes**	**sīme**	-	**sme**
	ste	**ésete**	**sīte**	**(e)ste**	**ste**
	senti	**esonti**	**sīnt**	**sentōd**	**sent**

NOTE. Proto-Indo-European verb **es-**, *be*, *exist*, originally built only a durative aspect of present, and was therefore supported in some dialects (as Gmc., Sla., Lat.) by the root **bheu-**, *be*, *exist*, which helped to build some future and past formations.

kleutum, *to hear* (present stem ***kl̥neu-/kl̥nu-***, with nasal infix)

	Indicative	*Subjunctive*	*Optative*	*Imperative*	IMPERF.
Sg.	**kl̥neumi**	**kl̥newō**	**kl̥nujḗm**	-	**kl̥newm̥**
	kl̥neusi	**kl̥néwesi**	**kl̥nujḗs**	**kl̥néu/kl̥nudhí**	**kl̥néus**
	kl̥neuti	**kl̥néweti**	**kl̥nujḗt**	**kl̥neutōd**	**kl̥néut**
Pl.	**kl̥numés**	**kl̥néwomos**	**kl̥nwīmé**	-	**kl̥numé**
	kl̥nuté	**kl̥néwete**	**kl̥nwīté**	**kl̥nuté**	**kl̥nuté**
	kl̥nunti	**kl̥néwonti**	**kl̥newīnt**	**kl̥nwentōd**	**kl̥núnt**

NOTE. Indicative forms could have possibly been read with a columnar accent in a post-Late Indo-European period, i.e. **kl̥numes**, **kl̥nute**, opt. **kl̥nwīme**, **kl̥nwīte**, imp. **kl̥nudhi**, as in Greek.

The 3rd pl. optative had full-grade root vowel, see Kortlandt (1992), Beekes (1995).

stātum, *to stand* (present stem ***(si)stā-/(si)sta-***, reduplicated)

	Indicative	Subjunctive	Optative	Imperative	IMPERFECT
Sg	**(sí)stāmi**	**stájō**	**(si)stajḗm**	-	**(si)stām**
	(sí)stāsi	**stájesi**	**(si)stajḗs**	**stā/stadhí**	**(si)stās**
	(sí)stāti	**stájeti**	**(si)stajḗt**	**stātōd**	**(si)stāt**
Pl.	**(si)stamés**	**stájomos**	**(si)staīmé**	-	**(si)stamé**
	(si)staté	**stájete**	**(si)staīté**	**staté**	**(si)staté**
	(si)stanti	**stájonti**	**(si)staī́nt**	**stanti**	**(si)stant**

NOTE. Indicative forms were possibly read in post-LIE period with columnar accent, as **sístames**, **sístate**, etc. or **stames**, **state**, etc.

The optative formations show zero-grade stem **sta-**, and the accent is written to distinguish -**a**-**ī**- from a diphthong -**aī**-.

For **sta-jo-** as a thematic subjunctive (*cf.* O. Gk. subj. 1st pl. στείομεν (< PGk *stejo-* < LIE **stəjo-* > NWIE ***stajo-***), from Gk. ἵστημι; also, θείομεν (<PGk *dhejo-* < LIE **dhəjo-* > NWIE ***dhajo-***) from τίθημι, IE **dhē**-; δείομεν (<PGk *dejo-* < LIE **dəjo-* > NWIE ***dajo-***) from Gk. δίδωμι, IE **dō**; and so on.

MIDDLE-PASSIVE

kleutum, *to hear* (present stem ***kl̥neu-/kl̥nu-***, with nasal infix)

	Indicative	Subjunctive	Optative	IMPERFECT
Sg.	**kl̥numár**	**kl̥néwomar**	**kl̥nwīmá**	**kl̥numá**
	kl̥nusór	**kl̥néwesor**	**kl̥nwīsó**	**kl̥nusó**
	kl̥nutór	**kl̥néwetor**	**kl̥nwītó**	**kl̥nutó**
Pl.	**kl̥numesdha**	**kl̥néwomesdha**	**kl̥nwīmedha**	**kl̥numédha**
	kl̥nudhwé	**kl̥néwedhwe**	**kl̥nwīdhwé**	**kl̥nudhwé**
	kl̥nuntór	**kl̥néwontor**	**kl̥nwīntó**	**kl̥nuntó**

NOTE. In a post-LIE period a common columnar accent would have been also possible; viz. **kl̥numar**, **kl̥nusor**, etc.

stātum, *to stand* (present stem ***(si)stā-/(si)sta-***, reduplicated)

	Indicative	*Subjunctive*	*Optative*	*IMPERFECT*
Sg.	**(si)stamár**	**stajōr**	**(si)staīmá**	**(si)stama**
	(si)stasór	**stájesor**	**(si)staīsó**	**(si)staso**
	(si)statór	**stájetor**	**(si)staītó**	**(si)stato**
Pl.	**(si)stamesdha**	**stájomesdha**	**(si)staīmedha**	**(si)stámedha**
	(si)stadhwé	**stájedhwe**	**(si)staīdhwé**	**(si)stadhwe**
	(si)stantor	**stájontor**	**(si)staīntó**	**(si)stanto**

II. AORIST STEM

ACTIVE

kleutum, *to hear* (aorist ***klew-/klu-***)

	Indicative	*Subjunctive*	*Optative*
Sg.	**klewom**	**klewō**	**klujḗm**
	klewes	**kléwēsi**	**klujḗs**
	klewet	**kléwēti**	**klujḗt**
Pl.	**klwome**	**kléwōmos**	**klwīmé**
	klwete	**kléwēte**	**klwīté**
	klwont	**kléwōnti**	**klwīnt**

NOTE. For aorist **klew-/klu-** *cf.* Gk. ἔ-κλυον, O.Ind. *áśrot.*

stātum, *to stand* (aorist stem ***stā-***)

	Indicative	*Subjunctive*	*Optative*
Sg.	**stām**	**stajō**	**stajḗm**
	stās	**stájesi**	**stajḗs**
	stāt	**stájeti**	**stajḗt**
Pl.	**stamé**	**stájomos**	**staīmé**
	staté	**stájete**	**staīté**
	stănt	**stajonti**	**staīnt**

MIDDLE-PASSIVE

kleutum, *to hear* (aorist stem ***kluw-***)

	Indicative	Subjunctive	Optative
Sg.	**klwá**	**kléwōr**	**klwīmá**
	klwesó	**kléwēsor**	**klwīsó**
	klwetó	**kléwētor**	**klwītó**
Pl.	**klwomesdha**	**kléwōmesdha**	**klwīmedha**
	klwedhwé	**kléwēdhwe**	**klwīdhwé**
	klwontó	**kléwōntor**	**klwīntó**

stātum, *to stand* (aorist stem ***stā-***)

	Indicative	Subjunctive	Optative
Sg.	**stāmá**	**stajōr**	**staīmá**
	stāsó	**stájesor**	**staīsó**
	stātó	**stájetor**	**staītó**
Pl.	**stamedha**	**stájomesdha**	**staīmedha**
	stadhwé	**stájedhwe**	**staīdhwé**
	stantó	**stájontor**	**staīntó**

III. PERFECT STEM

kleutum, *to hear* (perfect stem ***ké-klou-/ké-klu-,*** reduplicated)

	Indicative	Subjunctive	Optative
Sg.	**kéklowa**	**kéklowō**	**keklujḗm**
	kékloutha	**kéklowesi**	**keklujḗs**
	kéklowe	**kékloweti**	**keklujḗt**
Pl.	**keklumé**	**kéklowomos**	**keklwīmé**
	kekluté	**kéklowete**	**keklwīté**
	keklwḗr	**kéklowonti**	**keklwī́nt**

stātum, *to stand* (perfect stem ***se-stā-/se-sta-***, reduplicated)

	Indicative	*Subjunctive*	*Optative*
Sg.	**sestā**	**séstājō**	**sestajḗm**
	séstātha	**séstājesi**	**sestajḗs**
	sestā	**séstājeti**	**sestajḗt**
Pl.	**sestamé**	**séstājomos**	**sestaīmé**
	sestaté	**séstājete**	**sestaīté**
	sestā́r	**séstājonti**	**sestaī́nt**

NOTE. For reduplicated ***s(t)e-sta-*** (with different accent paradigms, often reconstructed with stress on the root), *cf.* O.Ind. perf. *tastháu*, Av. *-šastarə*, Gk. *héstamen*, O.Ir. *-sestar*.

7.8.3. COMMON PIE STEMS

I. THEMATIC VERBS

1. Root:

- Present **lowō**, *I wash*, aorist **lousm̥**, perfect **lélowa**.
- Present **serpō**, *I crawl*, aorist **sr̥póm**.
- Present **bherō**, *I carry*, aorist **bhērm**, perfect **bhébhora**.
- Present **bheugō**, *I flee*, aorist **bhugóm**.
- Present **bheidhō**, *I believe, persuade, trust*, aorist **bhidhom**.
- Present **weqō**, *I speak*, aorist (them. redupl.) **weuqom**.
- Present **tremō**, *I tremble*, aorist **tr̥mom**.

NOTE. A particular sub-class of thematic presents without suffix is of the type Skt. *tudáti*, which have present stems with zero-grade root-vowel, as **glubhō/gleubhō**, *skin*.

2. Reduplicated:

There are many reduplicated thematic stems, analogous to the athematic ones:

- Present **gignō**, *I beget*, (from **gen-**), aorist **gnom/genóm**, perfect **gégona**, p.part. **gnātós**.

NOTE. For **gnātós**, *cf.* O.Ind. *jātás*, Av. *zāta-*; Lat. *nātus*, Pael. *cnatois*, Gaul. f. *gnātha* "*daughter*"; O.N. *kundr* "*son*", also in compound, *cf.* Goth. *-kunds*, " *be a descendant of* ", O.E. *-kund*, O.N. *-kunnr*.

- Present **pibō**, *I drink* (<reduplicated ***pí-pō***, from **pōi-**).
- Present **mimnō**, *I remember*, (from **men-**).

3. In ***-je/o-***, some of them are causatives:

- Present **spekjō**, *I watch*, aorist **speksm̥**, p.part. **spektós**.

- Present **tenjō**, *I stretch*, aorist **tnom/tenóm**, perfect **tétona**, p.part. **tn̥tós**.

4. *Verba vocalia*:

- Present **widējō**, *I see, I know*, aorist **widóm**, perfect **woida** p.part. **wistós** (<***wid-tós***).
- Present **monejō**, *I make think, warn*, as Lat. *moneo*, from **men-**, *think*.
- Present **tromejō**, *I make tremble*, from **trem-**, *tremble*.

5. In -***ske/o***-:

- Present **pr̥skṓ**, *I ask, demand, inquire* (*cf.* Lat. *posco*, Ger. *forschen*) from **prek-**, *ask*.
- Present **gnāskōr**, *I am born* (*cf.* Lat. *gnascor*), p.part. **gnātós**, from zero-grade of **gnō-**, *beget*.
- Present **(gí)gnoskō**, *I begin to know, I learn*, from **gnō-**, *know*.

6. With nasal infix:

- Present **jungō**, *join* (from **jeug-**), aorist **jeugom**; p.part. **jugtós**.

NOTE. Compare O.H.G. *(untar-)jauhta* (as Lat. *sub-jugaui*), Lat. *jungō, -ere, -nxi, -nctus*, Gk. ζεύγνῡμι, ζεῦξαι ζυγηναι; O.Ind. *yunákti* (3. Pl. *yuñjánti* = Lat. *jungunt*), *yuñjati*, full-grade *yōjayati* (<***jeugējeti***); Av. *yaoj-, yuj-*; Lit. *jùngiu, jùngti*, etc. For past participles (with and without present infix -***n***-), compare O.E. *geoht, iukt*, Lat. *junctus*, Gk. δεπθηόο, O.Ind. *yuktá-*, Av. *yuxta-*, Lit. *jùngtas*, etc.

II. ATHEMATIC VERBS

1. Root: They are the most archaic PIE verbs, and their present conjugation is of the old type singular root vowel in full-grade, plural root vowel in zero-grade.

- Present **esmi**, *I am*.
- Present **eimi**, *I go*.
- Present **bhāmi**, *I speak*.

NOTE. The verb *talk* is sometimes reconstructed as PIE **āmi, I talk, and* imperfect **ām, I talked/have talked*; for evidence of an original ***ag(h)-jō***, compare Lat. *aiō*, Gk. *ηv*, Umb. *aiu*, Arm. *asem*. Thus, this paradigm would rather be thematic, i.e. present **ag(h)jō**, *I talk*, vs. imperfect **ag(h)jóm**, *I talked/have talked*.

- Present **edmi**, *I eat*.

NOTE. Note that its early present participle ***dent-***, "*eating*", was frozen as substantive **dentis**, meaning "*tooth*".

- Present **welmi**, *I want*.

2. Reduplicated:

- Present **(sí)stāmi** (from **stā-**, *stand*), aorist **stām**, p.part. **statós**.
- Present **déidikmi** (from **deik-**, *show*), aorist **dēiksm̥**, perfect **dédoika**, p.part. **diktós**.
- Present **dhédhēmi** (from **dhē-**, *do*, *make*), aorist **dhēm**, p.part. **dhatós**.
- Present **dídōmi** (from **dō-**, *give*), aorist **dōm**, p.part. **datós**.
- Present **jíjēmi**, *expel*, aorist **jem**.

NOTE. For evidence on an original PIE **jíjēmi**, and not ˣ***jíjāmi*** as it is sometimes reconstructed, *cf.* Lat. pret. *iēcī*, a form due to its two consecutive laryngeals, while Lat. *iaciō* is a present remade (J. González Fernández, 1981).

3. With nasal infix:
   - **kl̥néumi**, *hear* (from **kleu-**), aorist **klewom**, perfect **kéklowa**, p.part. **klŭ̄tós**, *heard*, also '*famous*'.
   - **punémi**, rot (from **pew**), aorist **pēwsm̥**.

7.9. VERBAL COMPOSITION

Verbs were often combined with adverbs to modify their meaning. Such adverbs were called preverbs and in the first instance remained separate words. Over time they tended to join with verbs as prefixes.

NOTE. For more on preverbs, see below §10.6.1.

Occasionally, verbs were compounded with a non-adverbial element, such as a noun. The most familiar example of this is **kréd-dhē-mi**, *believe, trust*, literally '*place one's heart in*', *cf.* Vedic Skt. *śrád dadhāti*, Lat. *crēdō*, and O.Ir. *cretim* (Fortson 2004).

7.10. THE VERBAL ACCENT

The finite verb of a LIE main clause was normally placed following the subject and the object, at the end of the sentence, where the sentence accent usually decreases. However, when the verb was stressed at the beginning of the sentence, or in a subordinate clause, it carried its normal accent.

NOTE. Fortson (2004): "In Vedic Sanskrit, main-clause finite verbs that do not stand at the beginning of their clause are written in the manuscripts without accent marks. In Greek, the rules for accenting verbs are different from those for nouns, and resemble the accentuation of strings of clitics; this suggests an affinity between the prosody of verbs and the prosody of chains of weakly stressed or unstressed particles. In Germanic heroic poetry, fully stressed words alliterate with one another, but certain verbs, together with unstressed pronouns and particles, do not participate in alliteration; this suggests weaker prosodic status for those verbs. In certain Germanic languages, such as modem German, verbs are required to be the second syntactic unit in main clauses, which is the same position taken by many unstressed sentence particles elsewhere in Indo-European (Wackernagel's Law)".

Meier-Brügger (2003) also states that "[r]esearchers agree that Vedic generally reflects the fundamental characteristics of Proto-Indo-European, and thus, that the finite verb in a main clause was unstressed (...) It remains disputed whether the second position of the finite verb, common to modern Germanic languages such as German, originated from the inherited phenomenon of enclitics, or whether it appeared secondarily". On that, Wackernagel (1892) "the German rule of word order was already valid in the mother language".

Finite verbs were therefore prosodically deficient in PIE, they could behave as clitics, i.e. they had no stress and formed an accentual unit with a neighbouring stressed word. However, they were fully stressed when moved to the front of a clause for emphasis or contrast, or when occurring in subordinate clauses. See below §10 *Syntax*.

8. PARTICLES

8.1. PARTICLES

8.1.1. Adverbs, prepositions, conjunctions and interjections are called particles. They cannot always be distinctly classified, for many adverbs are used also as prepositions and many as conjunctions.

8.1.2. Strictly speaking, particles are usually defined as autonomous elements, usually clitics, which make modifications in the verb or sentence, but which don't have a precise meaning, and which are neither adverbs nor preverbs nor conjunctions.

8.1.3. Indo-European has some particles (in the strictest sense) which mark certain syntax categories, classified as follows.

8.1.4. Emphatics or generalisers may affect the whole sentence or a single word, usually a pronoun, but also a noun or verb.

i. The particles ***-ge/-gi***, ***-ghe/-ghi***, usually strengthen the negation, and emphasise different pronouns; as, **egṓge**, *'I (for one), as for myself, I...'*, **neghí**, *certainly not.*

NOTE. The origin of these particles is possibly to be found in the same root as PIE **-qe**, acquiring its coordinate value from an older use as word-connector, from which this intensive/emphatic use was derived. Compare O.Ind. *gha, ha, hí*, Av. *zi*, Gk. *ge, -gí, -χí*, Lith. *gu, gi*, O.Sla. *-go, že, ži*, Also, compare, e.g. for intensive negative **neghi**, O.Ind. *nahí*, O.E. *nek*, Balt. *negi*. If compared with Gk. *-thé*, O.Ind. *gha, ha*, O.Sla. *-že, -go*, and related to **-qe**, a common PIH particle ***g***^{w}***he/o*** might tentatively be reconstructed.

ii. **e** comes probably from the pronoun **i-**, *v.s.* §6.5, §6.6. It appears e.g. in **e-djēu**, *today*, **e-so**, *this*, etc.

iii. **i**, e.g. in **num-í**, *now*.

iv. **ke**, *here, this*, *cf.* Lith. *šè'*, Lat. *-c(e)*, O.Lat. *hocce <*hod-ce.*

v. **u**, *cf.* Skt. *u*, Gk. *hoũtos*, Goth. *u*.

vi. **tar**, *cf.* Luv. *-tar*, Hom. Gk. *tar*. It appears to have been especially used with interrogatives, **qis tar?**, *who (indeed)? cf.* Luv. *kuiš-tar* = Hom. Gk. *tís tar*.

NOTE. Although the article of Katz is brilliant, it is not clear whether Gk. *tar* might also be reconstructed as **k*^{w}*e+ar*, as well as Gk. *aute* as **Hu+k*^{w}*e* <http://www.jstor.org/pss/4427613>.

vii. **kem**, a modal particle; *cf.* Hitt. *-kan*, Gk. *ke(n)*, Ved. *kám*.

8.1.5. Verb modifiers:

a. The old ***-ti*** had a middle value, i.e. reflexive.

NOTE. This is a very old value, attested in Anatolian, *cf.* Hitt. *za*, Pal. *-ti*, Luw. *-ti*, Lyd. *-(i)t*, Lyc. *-t/di*.

b. The modal **-man**, associated with the indicative, expresses potentiality (when used in present) and irreality (in the past).

NOTE. It is probably the same as the conjunction **man**, *if*, and closely related to **-ma**, *but*.

c. The negative particle **mē**, **nē**, associated with the indicative or forms indifferent to the moods.

NOTE. Sometimes, the intermediate syllable in Lat. *dōnique* (*dōnicum*) has been reconstructed as **-nē/ne-* (see for example Fortson's article on Latin and Sabellic at <http://muse.jhu.edu/journals/american_journal_of_philology/v131/131.1.fortson.pdf> p. 23) and **-na-*.

8.1.6. Sentence categorisers indicate the class of sentence, whether negative or interrogative.

i. Absolute interrogatives were introduced by special particles, generally **an**.

NOTE. The origin could be the "non-declarative sense" of the sentence. It has been proposed a common origin with the negative particle **ne/n̥**.

ii. Negation has usually two particles, etymologically related:

- Simple negation is made by the particle **ne**, and lengthened with ***-i***, ***-n***, ***-d***, etc.; as, emphatic **nei**, *not at all*. From the same root is the privative prefix **n̥-**, *un-* (*cf.* Hitt. *am-*, Skt. and Gk. *a(n)-*, Lat. *in-*, Eng. *un-* etc.).
- Mood negation or prohibitive (used with verb forms in negative commands) is the particle **mē**, general west IE **nē**.

NOTE. For PIE **mē**, compare Gk. μή, O.Ind.,Av.,O.Pers. *mā*, Toch. *mar/mā*, Arm. *mi*, Alb. *mos*. In some PIE dialects (as generally in west IE), **nē** (from **ne**) fully replaced the function of **mē**, *cf.* Goth. *ne*, Lat. *nē*, Ira. *ni*. It is not clear whether Hitt. *lē* is ultimately derived from **mē** or **nē**. For ***ne oinom***, *not ever*, *not at all*, *cf.* Lat. *nōn*, Eng. *none*, Gk. *ou* from **ne* h_2*oiu*.

8.1.7. Sentence connectives introduce independent sentences or connect different sentences, or even mark the principal sentence among subordinates.

so and **to**, which are in the origin of the anaphoric pronoun.

nu, *now*, which has an adverbial, temporal-consecutive meaning; *cf.* Skt. *nú*, O.C.S. *nyne*, Lith. *nù*, Hitt. *nu*, Gk. *nu*, Lat. *nunc*, O.Ir. *nu*, Goth. *nu*.

de; postpositive, *cf.* Gk. *dé*.

ar, *and, thus, therefore*, an introductory or connective particle, which is possibly the origin of some coordinate conjunctions; *cf.* Lith. *ir* '*and, also*', Gk. ra, ar, ára '*thus, as known*'. Also reconstructed as **-r̥**.

ne, *thus*, *cf.* Lat. *ne*, Gk. *ne*, Skt. *ná*, Lith. *nei*.

-pe, *cf.* Lith. *kaĩ-p* 'how', Lat. *quip-pe* 'because'.

sma, *truly*, *cf.* Skt. *smá*, Gk. *mēn*.

swod, *as, like*, *cf.* Av. *hvat*, Goth. *swa*.

tu, *cf.* Skt. *tú*, O.C.S. *thu-s*, Goth. *dau(h)*, Ger. *doch*.

8.2. ADVERBS

8.2.1. There is a class of invariable words, able to modify nouns and verbs, adding a specific meaning, whether semantic or deictic. They can be independent words (adverbs), prefixes of verbal stems (preverbs) – originally independent but usually merged with them – and also a nexus between a noun and a verb (appositions), expressing a non-grammatical relationship, normally put behind, but sometimes coming before the word.

NOTE. In PIE the three categories are only different uses of the same word class; they were eventually classified and assigned to only one function and meaning in the different languages attested. In fact, adverbs are often clearly distinguished from the other two categories in the history of Indo-European languages, so that they change due to innovation, while preverbs and appositions remain the same and normally freeze in their oldest attested positions.

8.2.2. Adverbs come usually from old particles which have obtained a specific deictic meaning. Traditionally, adverbs are deemed to be the result of oblique cases of old nouns or verbal roots which have frozen in IE dialects, thus loosing inflection.

8.3. DERIVATION OF ADVERBS

8.3.1. Adverbs were regularly formed in PIE from nouns, pronouns and adjectives.

8.3.2. From pronouns we find adverbs made as follows:

i. With a nasal lengthening; as, **tām**, *at that point*, **jāmi**, *already*, **teni**, *until*, **kina**, *from this side*, **dom**, *still*, **num-**, *now*, **nom**, *so*.

NOTE. Those in ***-ām*** are interpreted as being originally acc. sg. fem. of independent forms.

ii. An ***-s*** lengthening, added to the adverb and not to the basic form, giving sometimes alternating adverbs; as, **ap/aps**, **ek/eks**, **ambhí/ambhís**, etc.

iii. An ***-r*** lengthening; as, **tor**, **kir**, etc. which is added also to other derived adverbs. It is less usual than the other two.

NOTE. Compare for such lengthenings Goth. *hwar*, *her*, (O.E. *where*, *hier*), Lat. *cur*, O.Ind. *kár-hi*, *tár-hi*, Lith. *kur*, Hitt. *kuwari*. Also, IE ***qor-i***, ***tor-i***, ***kir-i***, etc. may show a final circumstantial ***-i***, probably the same which appears in the oblique cases and in the primary verbal endings, and which originally meant 'here and now'.

8.3.3. Some older adverbs, derived as the above, were in turn specialised as suffixes for adverb derivation, helping to create compound adverbs from two pronoun stems:

a. From **dē**, *from upwards*; as, **imde**, *from there*; or nasal ***-dem***.

b. Possibly from root **dhē-**, *put, place*, there are two particles which give suffixes with local meaning 'here', from stems of pronouns, nouns, adverbs and prepositions, **-d(h)em**, and **-dhei/-dhi**; as **idhei**, *there*, **n̥dhi**, *in excess*.

NOTE. For **-dem**, *cf.* Lat. *idem*, *quidam*, O.Ind. *idān-im*; for **-dhem**, **-dhi**, Gk. *-then*, *-tha*, *-thi*. For the origin of these adverbs in ***-bhi***, and for adverbs in ***-is*** (Gk. *mogis*, etc.), see <http://www.people.fas.harvard.edu/~jasanoff/pdf/Following%20the%20trail.pdf> from Jasanoff.

c. Some adverbial suffixes with mood sense – some with temporal sense, derived from the older modal; as, **ita**, *so*, **uta**, *rather*, **anta**, *towards*, etc.; and **itim**, *item*, **autim**, *otherwise*, **uti**, *out*, etc.

NOTE. Compare from PIE ***-ta*** (<*$-th_2$), Lat. *iti-dem, ut(i), ita*, Gk. *protí, au-ti*, O.Ind. *iti, práti*; from ***-t(i)m***, Lat. *i-tem*, Gk. *ei-ta, epei-ta*, O.Ind. *u-tá*.

d. In **-d**: *cf.* Lat. *probē*, Osc. *prufēd*; O.Ind. *pascāt, adharāt, purastāt.*

e. In **-nim**: *cf.* Osc. *enim* 'and', O.Ind. *tūsnim* 'silently', maybe also *idānim* is **idā-nim*, not **idān-im*.

f. In **-tos**: *cf.* Lat. *funditus, diuinitus, publicitus, penitus*; O.Ind. *vistarataḥ* 'in detail', samkṣepataḥ, *prasangataḥ* 'occasionally', *nāmattaḥ* 'namely', *vastutaḥ* 'actually', *mata* 'by/for me'.

g. In **-ks**: *cf.* Lat. *uix*, Gk. περιξ, O.Ind. *samyak* 'well', *prthak* 'separately', Hitt. *hudak* 'directly'.

8.3.4. From nouns and adjectives (usually neuter accusatives), frozen as adverbs already in Late Indo-European. The older endings to form adverbs are the same as those above, i.e. generally ***-i***, ***-u*** and ***-(i)m***.

Common cases of substantives and adjectives include the following, from which mainly the accusative and locative were productively used (Beekes 1995):

The nominative might be behind **edjēu**, *today* (*cf.* Lat. *hodiē*, O.Ir. *indiu*, Welsh *heddyw*, Skt. *adyā́*).

The accusative singular is found very often in adverbs:

- Of content: One of the most extended adverbs was neuter nominative-accusative singular of the adjective for 'great', used to mean 'greatly', **mega** (*cf.* Hitt. *mēk*, Ved. *máhi*, Gk. *méga*, O.N. *mjǫk*); also, we could infer **plēim**, *much*, from **plēis**, *more* (*cf.* Gk. *polú*, O.C.S. *mŭnogo*, Lat. *multum*, Goth. *filu*).
- Of space or time: **prāmom**, *firstly*; **éterom**, *secondly*, already seen.
- Of direction: *cf.* Lat. *domum*<**domom**, *'housewards'*, Skt. *dūrám* < **dūróm**, *'in (toward) the distance'*.
- From an apposition: **partim**, partly.

The genitive is seen in words which indicate place and time; as, **noqtjos**, *at night* (*cf.* Gk. *nuktós*, Goth. *nahts*).

The ablative indicates the origin of something; as, Skt. *dūrā́t* < **dūród**, *'from far away'*.

The locative is often found; as, **péruti**, *in the previous year* (*cf.* Skt. *párut*, Gk. *peruse*, Ir. *uraid*, M.H.G. *vert*), **témesi**, *in the dark* (*cf.* Skt. *támas*, Lat. *temere*, 'blindly'), **domoi**, *at home* (*cf.* Gk. *oíkoi*, Lat. *domi*), **dhghjesi**, *yesterday* (*cf.* Skt. *hyás*, Alb. *dje*, Gk. *khthés*, Lat. *herī*, O.Ir. *in-dé*, Goth. *gistra-*), etc.

The instrumental is found in **diwḗ**, *during the day*, **noqtī**, *during the night* (*cf.* Skt. *dívā*, O.C.S. *noštjo i dĭnĭjo*).

NOTE. Jasanoff (2003) also considers to have found the remains of an allative (Lat. *quō* <**$k^w oH_2$*(e) *'whither'*).

8.4. PREPOSITIONS

8.4.1. Prepositions were not originally distinguished from adverbs in form or meaning, but have become specialised in use. Originally postpositions, most eventually became prepositions, being its original placement attested in Anatolian, Indo-Iranian, Sabellic, and sometimes in Latin and Greek.

NOTE. They developed comparatively late in the history of language. In the early stages of the Proto-Indo-European language the cases alone were probably sufficient to indicate the sense, but, as the force of the case-endings weakened, adverbs were used for greater precision. These adverbs, from their common association with particular cases, became prepositions; but many retained also their independent function as adverbs.

8.4.2. Prepositions are regularly used either with the accusative or with the oblique cases.

8.4.3. Some examples of common PIE adverbs/prepositions are:

ad, *to, by, near*; *cf.* Lat. *ad*, Goth. *at*.

ambhí, *on both sides, around*; *cf.* O.Ind. *abhí*, Gk. *amphi, amphis*, Lat. *am, amb-*, Gaul. *ambi*, O.Ir. *imb-*, O.H.G. *umbi* (as Eng. *by*, Ger. *bei*).

ana, *to*; *on, over, above*. *Cf.* O.Ind. *ána*, Gk. *ánō, aná*, Goth. *ana*, O.C.S. *na*.

antí, *opposite, in front*. *Cf.* O.Ind. *ánti, átha*, Gk. *antí*, Lat. *ante*, Goth. *and*, Lith. *añt*; Hitt. *ḫanti*.

apo, **po**, *from*; *out*. *Cf.* O.Ind. *ápa*, Gk. *apo, aps, apothen*, Lat. *ab, abs*, po- Goth. *af*, Slav. po-.

apóteri, *behind*.

au-/we-, *out, far*. *Cf.* O.Ind. *áva, vi-*,Lat. *au-, uē-*, Gk. *au, authi, autár*, O.Ir. *ó, ua*, Toc. *-/ot-*, O.C.S. *u*.

dē/dō, *from, to*. *Cf.* Skt. *-dā́*, Lat. *dē*, O.Ir. *dí*, O.C.S. *-da*. Also behind O.H.G. *zādal*.

deks(í), *at the right side*. *Cf.* Skt. *dákṣiṇa-*, Lith. *dēšinas*, Gk. *deksiós, deksíteros*.

ek(sí) (<*h_1eg^h-s-), *out*. *Cf.* Gk. *ek(s)*, Lat. *ex*, Gaul *ex-*, O.Ir. *ess-*.

ektós, *except*.

en(i)/n̥, *in*. *Cf.* O.Ind. *ni, nis*, Gk. *en, ení*, Lat. *in*, Goth. *in*, Lith. *in*, O.C.S. *on, vŭ*.

enter, *between, within, inside*; *cf.* Skt. *antár*, Lat. *inter*, O.Ir. *eter*, O.H.G. *untar*, Alb. *ndër*.

entós, *even, also*.

epi, **opi**, **pi**, *on, upon, by, at, towards here, around, circa*. *Cf.* Gk. *epi, opi, pi*, O.Ind. *ápi*, Av. *áipi*, Lat. *ob, op-, -pe*, Osc. *úp-*, Gmc. *ap-, ep-*, Arm. *ev*, Lith. *ap-*, O.Ir. *iar, ía-, ei-*, Alb. *épërë*, etc.

eti, *even, also*; over. *Cf.* O.Ind. *áti, átaḥ, at*, Gk. *eti*, Lat. *et*, Goth. *iþ*, O.C.S. *otŭ*.

kn̥ta, *by, along, down*. *Cf.* Hitt. *katta*, Gk. *káta*, O.Ir. *cét*, O.W. *cant*. Perhaps from **kom**.

ko(m), *together, with; near*. *Cf.* Lat. *cum*, Ir. *co*, Goth. *ga-*.

meta, *between, with*. *Cf.* Gk. *méta*, Goth. *miþ*, Ger. *mit*.

n̥dhos, n̥dher(í), *down, under*. *Cf.* Av. *aϑairi*, O.Ind. *ádhaḥ, ádhara-*, Lat. *infra, inferus*, Goht. *undar*, Gmc. *under-*.

n̥dhi, *more, over*. *Cf.* O.Ind. *ádhi*, Gk. *éntha*.

ni, *downward, down, under*. *Cf.* Skt. *ní*, O.C.S. *ni-zŭ*, , and also in the word for 'nest', **ni-sd-o-** (from **sed-**, *sit*).

níteros, *down, below, inferior*. *Cf.* Skt. *nitáram*, O.H.G. *nidar*, Eng. *nether*, etc.

obhi, **bhi**, *in the middle; around, from, to*, etc. *Cf.* Lat. *ob* 'towards, to', O.Ind. *abhi*, Av. *aiwi*, Goth. *bi*.

ólteri, *beyond*.

per(i), *over, around, through*. *Cf.* O.Ind. *pári*, Gk. *péri*, Lat. *per*, O.Pruss. *per*, Alb. *për*.

perti, *through, otherwise*.

pos/posti/pósteri, *behind*.

poti, *toward*, *cf.* Av. *paiti*, Gk. *póti*.

pósteri, *afterwards*.

postrōd, *backwards*.

pra, *next to*.

prāi, *at the front, in front, ahead*. *Cf.* O.C.S. *prědŭ*, Lat. *prae*.

prā́iteri, *along(side)*.

pro, *in front, opposite; before; forwards, ahead*. *Cf.* O.Ind. *prá*, Gk. *pró*, Lat. *prōd-*, O.Ir. *ro-*, Goth. *fra* (Eng. *from*), O.Pruss. *pra, pro*, Lith. *pra*.

próteri, *in front of*.

pros, *before, ahead*. *Cf.* Skt. *purás*, Gk. *páros*. Maybe here Goth. *faúra* (Eng. *for*).

proti, *(over) against*. *Cf.* Skt. *práti*, O.C.S. *protivŭ*, Gk. *próti, pros*.

rōdhí, *because (of)*.

sn̥i, sn̥eu, *without*. *Cf.* Skt. *sanu-tár*, Toch. *sne/snai*, Gk. *áneu*, Lat. *sine*, O.Ir. *sain*.

NOTE. The preposition for 'separately, without' is found reconstructed as locative **sn̥ah*$_2$*i* (Klingechmitt), dative **sn̥h*$_2$*-éi*, locative of a collective **sn̥h*$_2$*-éh*$_2$*-i* (Hackstein), and directive snai (Peters).

sn̥ter(i), *separately*, *Cf.* Gk. *áter*, M.H.G. *sunder*.

som, *together*. *Cf.* Skt. *sám*, O.C.S. *sŭ*, Lith. *sam-*.

trās, **trāntis**, *through*. *Cf.* Skt. *tirás*, O.Ir. *tar*, Lat. *trans*, O.Ir. *tre*. From the same root Goth. *þairh*.

ud(sí), *on high*. *Cf.* Skt. *úd*, O.C.S. *vy-*, Goth. *ūt* (Ger. *aus*).

upér(i), *on, over, above*. *Cf.* O.Ind. *upári*, Gk. *hupér*, Lat. *s-uper*. O.Ir. *for*, Goth. *ufar*, Arm. *(i) ver*.

upo, *under, down, below*. O.Ind. *úpa*, Gk. *hupó*, Lat. *s-ub*, O.Ir. *fo*, Goth. *uf*.

wī, *separately*.

NOTE. Further information e.g. in <http://eprints.ucm.es/tesis/fll/ucm-t26697.pdf>.

8.5. CONJUNCTIONS

8.5.1. Conjunctions, like prepositions, are closely related to adverbs, and are either petrified cases of nouns, pronouns and adjectives, or obscured phrases: as, **jod**, an old accusative. Most conjunctions are connected with pronominal adverbs, which cannot always be referred to their original case-forms.

8.5.2. Conjunctions connect words, phrases or sentences. They are divided in two main classes, coordinate and subordinate.

8.5.3. Coordinates are the oldest ones, which connect coordinated or similar constructions. Most of them were usually put behind and were normally used as independent words. They are:

i. Copulative or disjunctive, implying a connection or separation of thought as well as of words; as, **-qe**, *and*, **-wē**, *or*, **toqe**, *also*, **joqe**, **atqe**, *and*, **itaqe**, *and also*, **neqe**, *nor*, **enim**, *and*.

NOTE 1. Postpositive particles were placed directly after the word (or first word of the phrase or clause) that was being conjoined or disjoined; **-qe**, it can be put once or twice; *cf.* Lat. *arma uirumque canō*, 'Arms and the man I sing', Lat. *senātus populusque* 'the senate and the people', Skt. *devā́ś ca ásurās ca*, 'Gods and Asuras', Gk. *patḗr andrõn te theõn te* 'father of men and gods'. The same can be said of **-we**, *cf.* Skt. *náktaṃ vā dívā vā*, 'during the night or during the day'.

NOTE 2. For PIE **neqe**, compare Lat. *ne-que*, Gk. οὔ-τε, Arm. *o-c*, O.Ir. *nó, nú*, Welsh *ne-u*, O.Bret. *no-u*, Alb. *a-s*, Lyc. *ne-u*, Luw. *na-pa-wa*, and for PIE **mēqe**, in Greek and Indo-

Iranian, but also in Toch. *ma-k* and Alb. *mo-s*. The parallel **newe** is found in Anatolian, Indo-Iranian, Italic and Celtic dialects.

ii. Adversative, implying a connection of words, but a contrast in thought: as, **ma**, *but*, **auti**, *or*, **autim**, **perti**, *otherwise*, **ati**, *but*, **ōd**, *and*, *but*, **ektós**, *excepted*.

NOTE. Adversative conjunctions of certain antiquity are **at(i)** (*cf.* Goth. *adh-*, Lat. *at*, Gk. *atár*), **(s)ma/(s)me** (*cf.* Hitt.,Pal. *ma*, Lyd. *-m*, Lyc. *me*, Gk. *má*, *mé*, Messap. *min*), **auti** (*cf.* Lat. *autem*, *aut*, Gk. *aute*, *authis*, *autis*, *autár*), **ōd**, *and*, *but* (*cf.* O.Ind. *ād*, Av. *(ā)at*, Lith. *o*, Sla. *a*), etc. In general, the oldest IE languages attested use the same copulative postpositive conjunctions as adversatives, their semantic value ascertained by the context.

iii. Causal, introducing a cause or reason: as, **nam**, *for*.

iv. Illative, denoting an inference: as, **tori**, *therefore*, **ar**, *thus*, *therefore*, **ita**, **swāi**, *so*, **ṇdha**, *then*, **s(w)eike**, *thus*.

8.5.4. Subordinates connect a subordinate or independent clause with that on which it depends. They were introduced in PIE generally with relative clauses. The (rare) conjunctions that could have subordinate value included:

a. **jō/jōd**, *how, as*; **jod/qod**, *that*; **jāwod**, *so long as*; all have a general subordinate value, usually relative, final or conditional.

NOTE. For common derivatives of PIE **jo**, related to the relative pronoun, compare for **jod**, **qod**, *that*, Skt. *yád*, Gk. *hó*, *hóti*, Lith. *kàd*, Lat. *quod*, Goth. *þat-ei*; for **jō**, **jōd**, *how*, as, Skt. *yā́d*, Av. *yā*, Gk. *hō(s)*, Myc. *jodososi* /*jō-dōsonsi*/ 'as they shall give'; for **jāwod** *cf.* Skt. *yavā́t*, Gk. *hēos*>*héōs*; for **-jo** (probably replaced by **-qe**) Hitt. *-a*/*-ya*, Toch. *-*/*yo*.

b. Conditional, denoting a condition or hypothesis; as, **mān**, *if*, **ei**, *in that case*, **nemān**, *unless*, **sēd**, **sni**, *apart*.

NOTE. For **ei**, possibly related to **i-**, hence to **jo**, *cf.* Goth. *-ei*, Gk. *eí*, O.C.S. *i*, Lat. *s-ī*.

c. Comparative, implying comparison as well as condition; as, **mān**, *as if*.

d. Concessive, denoting a concession or admission; as, **eti**, *even*, **an**, *perhaps*, **au**, *howbeit, although*, **perom**, *besides*.

NOTE. For **eti**, *even*, *and*, *cf.* Lat. *et*, Gk. *eti*, maybe nasalised ***ṇti*** in Germanic *und-*, as Goth., Eng. *and*.

e. Temporal: as, **antí**, **prāi**, *before*, **pos(ti)**, *after*.

g. Final, expressing purpose; as, **uta**, *in order that*, **ne**, *that not*.

h. Causal, expressing cause; as, **jodqid**, *because*.

8.6. INTERJECTIONS

Interjections are natural exclamations of pain, surprise, horror and so forth, and they are onomatopoeic in nature.

These are the most common IE interjections, not taking into account pure examples of onomatopoeia, like *boom!* and the like (from Beekes 1995, Mallory–Adams 2007):

ā (surprise, pain); *cf.* Skt. *ā*, Lith. *(a)à*, Gk. *ã*, Lat *ā*, *ah*, Goth. *o*.

ai (surprise, pity); *cf.* Skt. *e*, *ai*, Av. *āi*, Lith. *aĩ*, *ai*, Gk. *aí*, *aiaĩ*, Lat. *ai*.

bhā, *truly*; *cf.* Av. *bā(t)*, Lith. *bà*, Gk. *phḗ*. *Cf.* also **bhod**, Hitt. *pat* (Kloekhorst 2008), Pol. *bo*.

bheu, **bhū** (pain); *cf.* Gk. *pheu*, *phū*, Lat. *fū*, *fi*.

ē (exclamation, vocative-particle); *cf.* Skt. *ā́*, Lith. *é*, Gk. *ẽ*, Lat. *eh* (*ē-castor* 'by Castor'); perhaps O.H.G. *nein-ā* 'oh no';

ō (exclamation, vocative-particle); *cf.* Gk., Lat. *ō*, O.Ir. *á*,*a*, Lith., Goth. *o*, Eng. *oh*.

eheu (complaint); *cf.* Skt. *aho*, Lat. *eheu*.

ha (surprise); *cf.* Skt. *ha*, Gk. *hā*, Lat. *hā*, M.H.G. *ha*.

ha ha (laughter); *cf.* Skt. *ha ha*, Russ. *xa xa*, Gk. *hà há*, Lat. *hahae*, N.H.G. *ha ha*. Compare **khákhatnos**, *laugh*, and the verb Skt. *kákhati*, C.S. *xoxotati*, Arm *xaxank* 'laughter', Gk. *kakházō*, Lat. *cachinnō*, O.H.G. *kachazzen*, suggesting that one may have laughed ***kha kha!*** earlier in PIE (Beekes 1995).

wai! *woe, alas!* (grief); *cf.* Latv. *wai*, Arm. *vay*, Lat. *vae*, O.Ir. *fáe*, W. *gwae*, Goth. *wai*, Eng. *woe*. Lat. *vae victis* 'woe to the vanquished'.

PART III

SYNTAX

Like Pāṇini, we haven't made – and probably couldn't make – any conventional selection of the *proper* IE syntax, since "[t]o do so explicitly and incontrovertibly would be difficult in any language, given several ways of expressing the same idea and various other ways of expressing closely similar ideas" (Coulson 2003). We have nevertheless collected some studies on the common PIE syntax, with examples attested in the older dialects, so that the natural means of expression of Proto-Indo-Europeans – their *principles* and *parameters* (Chomsky-Lasnik 1993) – are properly exposed, for the learner to adopt the correct setting.

The most comprehensive summary available on PIE morphosyntax was written by Matthias Fritz in Indo-European Linguistics (Michael Meier-Brügger, 2003), pp. 238-276.

The most comprehensive, widely referenced work on sentence syntax is still Winfred Philipp Lehmann's Proto-Indo-European Syntax (1974). It has been made available online for free at the University of Texas at Austin – Linguistics Research Center <http://www.utexas.edu/cola/centers/lrc/books/pies00.html>.

Excellent recent works on syntax include Benjamin W. Fortson IV Indo-European Language and Culture (2004), pp. 137-153, and James Clackson's Indo-European linguistics (2007), pp. 157-186.

Their texts have been adapted to this grammar, omitting specialised comments, references to academic articles, or the source of examples in the different old IE languages, so that any reader interested in further information on IE syntax should read the original works.

Collection of texts arranged and adapted by Carlos Quiles

9. MORPHOSYNTAX

9.1. VERBAL MORPHOSYNTAX

In addition to its lexical meaning, the finite verb consists of grammatical categories, which are in turn composed of the following five dimensions: person, number, mode, tense-aspect, and diathesis.

There are three categories of number (singular, dual and plural), four modes (indicative, imperative, subjunctive, optative), three tense-aspects (present, aorist, perfect), and three voices (active, middle, passive).

9.1.1. PERSON

1. There are three dimensions in person, classified according to classical grammarians: In the singular, the first person indicates the speaker; the second, the person to whom he speaks; and the third, that about which one speaks.

The first person refers to an object thought of as animated, whether a human being or not. The second person refers to the being or object thought of as listening. The third person may indicate living beings or objects.

The 1st plural may indicate that there is more than one speaker, and the 2nd plural that there are more than one listener, but they could refer to the speaker or listener as groups (M. Fritz 2003).

NOTE. "The distinction between the inclusive first person plural ('we', i.e. including the speaker, his group, and the listener) and exclusive first person plural ('we', i.e. the speaker and his group, without the inclusion of the listener) cannot be reconstructed as Proto-Indo-European. That which is true of the plural, also applies to the dual" (M. Fritz 2003)

9.1.2. TENSE-ASPECT AND MOOD

TENSE-ASPECT

The Proto-Indo-European tense-aspect system shows three common formations: perfect or *stative* stem (expressing a state of being), present or *imperfective* stem (depicting ongoing, habitual or repeated action), and aorist or *perfective* stem (depicting a completed action or actions viewed as an entire process). In the indicative mood the present or imperfect stem was conjugated in two tenses: present and past.

NOTE. In the post-Proto-Indo-European period, there were, aside from the languages that continued the use of the subjunctive, various other means of expressing future actions, including a new future stem formation, *v.s.* §7.4.2. Periphrastic future was express by means of an auxiliary verb, usually meaning "become" in North-West IE, while Hittite had "come" o "go" (*cf.* Hitt. *uwami/paimi*) + present. Vedic had also a form in *-tar-* (*nomen agentis*) + copula.

Examples (Fritz 2003):

a) Present: Lat. *aperiuntur aedes* 'the house is opened'; Gk. *nóston dízdnai meliēdéa* 'You seek honey-sweet homecoming', Ved. *dákṣiṇā́śvam dákṣiṇā gā́ṃ dadāti* 'the Dakṣiṇā gives a steed, the Dakṣiṇā gives a cow'.

b) Imperfect: Lat. *nam ego ibam ad te* 'for I came to you'; Gk. *mála gàr kraterō̃s emákhonto* 'for they fought very hard'.

c) Aorist: Gk. *tón rh' ébale prō̃tos* 'It was him that he hit first'; Ved. *rayíṃ ca putrā́m̐ś cādād* 'He gave riches and sons'.

d) Perfect: Lat. *servos es, liber fuisti* 'A slave you are; free you have been'; Gk. *kakà dè khroḯ eímata eĩmai* 'I clothe bad garment on my skin'; Ved. *apó rireca* 'he released the water'.

INDICATIVE

The indicative is used for statements to which the speaker lends validity: By using the indicative, the speaker gives his statement the character of a true statement. Whether or not the contents of the statements in fact correspond to reality, is of course uncertain (M. Fritz 2003).

Examples – Gk. *epí khthonì baínei* '(s)he runs on the earth'; Ved. *candrámā apsvàntár ā́ suparṇó dhāvate diví* 'the beautifully winged moon runs in the waters across the sky'.

IMPERATIVE

According to M. Fritz (2003), the imperative holds a special place in the verbal paradigm, "similar to that in the nominal paradigm occupied by the vocative, which is equally directed to a listener, and with which the imperative shares the formal characteristic of having a singular form which is composed of the stem without an ending, with no sign of its connection to the sentence."

Examples – Lat. *habe bonum animum* 'have good courage'; Gk. *áll' áge mímnete pántes* 'come now, stay'; Ved. *tā́m̐ indra sáhase piba* 'Drink this, oh Indra, for strength'.

SUBJUNCTIVE AND OPTATIVE

"According to Delbrück's investigations of fundamental notions (*Ai. Syntax* 1888), the subjunctive mood expresses a will, while the optative mood expresses a wish. It is important to note that the will or the wish (as the case may be) that is meant is that of the speaker, and not that of the subject, or, more precisely stated, that of the actor that is designated by the nominative form. The wish of the subject was originally expressed through its own derivational verbal form, namely, the desiderative" (M. Fritz 2003).

1. The subjunctive, which originally indicates the future, has three main functions (Mendoza 1998):

- In its *voluntative* function, it indicates the will of the speaker; as, Gk. *mḗpō ekeîse íōmen* lit. 'not-yet there-to we-should-go'; Ved. *sá devā́n éhá vaksati* lit. '(that) he the-gods here should-bring'.
- In its *deliberative* function, it indicates the deliberation of the speaker; as, Gk. *pêi gàr... íō* lit. 'where-to, then...I-shall-go?'; Ved. *kathā́ mahé rudríyāya bravāma* lit. 'how from-the-great-court of-Rudra we-shall-talk?
- In its *prospective* function, it serves to express things that happen in the future; as, Gk. *ei de' ke mè dṓōsin, egṑ dé ken autos hélōmai* 'if Ptc. Ptc. they-give not (to me), I Ptc. Ptc. myself will-take (it)' .

According to M. Fritz (2003), "the subjunctive is used to express his will when he considers that it is within his power to bring about the verbal action. A declaration of will in a strict sense is only possible when the speaker has direct influence on events, such that that which is desired may also be executed. This means that a true expression of will may only be in the first person singular, while all other cases are equally requests. If the first person subjunctive is taken as a request made of oneself, a connection to the second and third person subjunctive is possible in which the speaker has no direct influence on the realization of the verbal action, so that the statement may only be understood as a request. A further connection may be made with the 1st person plural, in which the speaker communicates his own will, and at the same time directs a request to others."

Examples (Fritz 2003):

a) 1 sg.: Lat. *quod perdundumst properem perdere* 'what may be lost, I will/want to hurry up and lose'; Gk. *áll' áge oí kaì egṑ dō̃ kseínion* 'thus I will/want to give a gift of welcome also to him'; Ved. *purāṇā́ vāṃ vīryà prá bravā jáne*, 'your earlier heroic deeds I will/want to announce to all people'; Ved. *prá nú vocā sutéṣu vām* 'On the occasion of the pressing, I thus will/want to announce the heroic deeds of both of you'.

b) 1 pl.: Gk. *nũn dè mnēsṓmetha dórpou* 'now we will/want to think about the meal'; Ved. *svastáye vāyúm úpa bravāmahai* 'We will/want to call to Vaayu for the sake of welfare'.

c) 2nd person: Lat. *taceas* 'you should remain silent'; Ved. *abhī́ ṣú naḥ sákhīnām avitā́ jaritr̥̄ṇā́m satám bhavāsi ūtíbhiḥ* 'you, oh helper of the singer's friends, will/should protect us well with a hundred helps'.

d) 3rd person: Lat. *sed uti adserventur magna diligentia* 'but they should be guarded with great care'; Gk. *oú gár tís me bíēi ge hekồn aékonta díētai* 'For none will/should force me to leave against my own will'; Gk. *kaí poté tis eípēisi kaì ópsigónōn anthrṓpōn* 'and one day, even one of the descendants will say'; Ved. *sá sunvaté ca stuvaté ca rāsate* 'who will/should give both to him who presses, and to him who prizes'; Ved. *sá no víśvāni hávanāni joṣad* 'That man will/should be friendly and take receipt of all our sacrifices'.

2. The optative, which originally indicates possibility, has three functions (Mendoza 1998):

- A desiderative function, expressing the wish of the speaker; as Gk. *eíth hōs hēbṓoimi* lit. 'I-wish that I-would-be-young'; Ved. *ahám prathamáḥ pibeyam* lit. 'I the-first want-to-drink'.
- An exhortative function; as, Gk. *kẽrúks tís hoi hépoito* lit. '(that) herald one him accompanies'.
- A potential function expressing possibility or potentiality; as, Gk. *nûn gár ken héloi pólin* lit. 'now really ptc can-take the-city'.

According to M. Fritz (2003), "when the optative is used to express a wish, the speaker indicates that he is not directly able to bring about the verbal action. The optative proves to be more uniform that the subjunctive, given that in its cupitive function, the optative, independently of the category of person, always indicates a simple wish of the speaker, regardless of his influence on the realization of the verbal action."

Examples of the potential function: – Lat. *nec me miserior femina est neque ulla videatur magis* 'a more miserable woman than myself does not exist, and will most probably never be seen'; Lat. *roget quis* 'one might ask'; Gk. *oú tis keínon anḕr alalḗmenos elthṑn' allḗllōn peíseie gunaĩká te kaì phílon huión* 'a man, who comes travelling with news of that, could not convince his son and the woman';

Ved. *víśvo devásya netúr márto vurīta sakhyám* 'each mortal will likely desire the friendship of the leading god'.

Examples of the desiderative function:

a) 1st person: Gk. *nũn dè kléos esthlón apoímēn* 'and now I would like to wrest noble fame'; Ved. *víśvābhir gīrbhír abhí pūrtím aśyām* 'by all songs, I would like to obtain fulfillment'; Ved. *syā́méd índrasya sármani* 'we would like to be under Indra's protection'.

b) 3rd person: Lat. *ut illum di deaeque senium perdant* 'that elder is the one that the gods and the goddesses would like to ruin'; Gk. *humĩn mèn theoì doĩen* 'to you indeed, the gods like to give'; Gk. *all'autou gaĩa mélaina' pãsi khánoi* 'the black earth should open to all precisely here'; Ved. *devám̥ vo devayajyáyāgnim īḷīta mártyaḥ* 'the mortal should praise your god Agni through worship'.

In terms of content, the similarity between the prospective function of the subjunctive and the potential function of the optative is evident in the comparison of Gk. *kaí poté tis eípēisin* 'one day, someone will say' and Gk. *kaí poté tis eípoi* 'one day, someone will in all likelihood say'.

9.1.3. VOICE

1. Active and middle voices are distinguished formally by their endings, see above.

NOTE. According to Fortson (2004), "in traditional grammatical usage, active means that the subject is doing the action rather than being acted upon, while middle means the subject is either acting upon itself or is in some other way "internal" to the action. This rough guideline works reasonably well for verbs that could inflect in either voice (...) But in many other cases, the distinction between active and middle inflection was purely a formal one: there were some verbs that inflected only in the active and others only in the middle, without clear difference in meaning. Verbs having only middle inflection are often called middle verbs. (Students familiar with Latin can think of these as equivalent to the Latin deponent verbs – active in meaning but having only passive endings, which come historically from the PIE middle.)."

For Clackson (2007): "Combining the functions of the middle in opposition to the active and the semantics of the lexical stems which are associated with the middle, we can say something of the prototypical use of the middle, which appears to be dependent on how speakers view the semantic role of the subject. The middle is the voice used to denote that the subject is in some way affected by the verbal action. Thus, for transitive verbs the active typically represents the subject as the actor, and the middle represents the subject as the undergoer. For intransitive verbs the middle is preferred when there is some notion of control over the verbal action (hence the middle inflection of 'think' and 'speak'), but if the verb denotes an event or action where the participant cannot have control, the active is used (thus 'be', 'vomit' and 'wait')."

3. The function of the category 'passive', which appears in many IE languages, but did not exist as a grammatical category in Proto-Indo-European, was performed by the middle voice (Fritz 2003, Fortson 2004, Clackson 2007). The various IE languages that feature a passive voice each formed it independently from each other (Fritz 2003).

9.2. NOMINAL MORPHOSYNTAX

9.2.1. NOMINATIVE

According to M. Fritz (2003), the nominative "indicates the theme of the sentence which, in a non-marked sentence, is placed in sentence-initial position. Other sentence elements are also thematized in taking the sentence-initial position, which, in the non-marked sentence, is reserved for the subject."

"The Proto-Indo-European nominative does not indicate the subject of an action in the logical sense, but rather in the sense that appears to the observer to be bearer and middle-point of the action that is expressed by the verb" (Delbrück 1879).

The concept of the subject is itself difficult to grasp; for H.-J. Sasse it is "a syntactical relation with semantic and pragmatic functions... [the] sentence element that is indicated as the subject has a doubled function as it is both pragmatic (as an indicator of the topic of the sentence) and semantic (as an identifier of the agent). This double-function finds expressing in its syntactical characteristics (Sasse, 1982).

9.2.2. VOCATIVE

According to M. Fritz (2003), the vocative is the nominal form that is used for addressing a listener. There is only a distinct vocative in the singular, and even then, not all nominal paradigms feature a separate vocative form. Where there is no separate vocative, its function is taken by the nominative. The same occurs when two actions of addressing are linked: While the first is in the vocative, the second is in the nominative. – Examples: Gk. *Zdeũ páter...Ēéliós th'* 'Oh father Zeus (voc.) ... and Helios (nomin.)'; Ved. *ágna índraś ca* 'Oh Agni (voc.) and Indra (nomin.)'.

NOTE. On the *vā́yav índraś ca* construction, Fortson (2004): "It was apparently a rule of PIE grammar that when two vocatives were conjoined, the one preceding the conjunction was put in the nominative rather than the vocative case. Almost all the examples of this come from Vedic, as in the phrase *vā́yav índraś ca* "o Indra and Vayu" after which the construction is named. In this example, the god Vayu's name is in the vocative but Indra's is in the nominative, as it precedes the conjunction *ca* 'and'. The sole example outside Indo-Iranian is from an archaic passage in the Iliad" already seen, *Zdeũ páter...Ēéliós th'*.

i. The vocative element in the sentence receives no accent. – Example: Ved. *asmé ū ṣú vr̥ṣaṇā mādayethām* 'Enjoy yourselves nicely, you two heroes, in our company'.

ii. In Old Indian, when the vocative forms a sentence of its own, and is thus in sentence-initial position, it receives stress, regardless of its normal nominal accent, on its first syllable, i.e. on the first syllable of the sentence. In this case, sentence stress is meant and not word stress. – Example: Ved. *dévā jī́vata* 'Gods! Live!'

9.2.3. ACCUSATIVE

According to M. Fritz (2003), the accusative has the following functions:

a) Accusative of direction: it expresses that the verbal action bears an orientation in terms of space; as, Gk. *érkhesthon klisíēn* 'go both of you to your tent'; Gk. *hósoi keklḗato boulḗn* 'who where summoned for consultation'; Ved. *yadā́ múkhaṃ gachaty áthodáraṃ gachati* 'if it goes to the mouth, then it goes to the stomach'.

b) Accusative of extent: is further used to express spatial or chronological expanse; as, Lat. *noctem in stramentis pernoctare* 'to pass one night in the straw'; Gk. *douròs erō̃ēn* 'at a spear throw's distance'; Gk. *kheĩma* 'in the winter'; Ved. *saptádaśa pravyādhā́n ājíṃ dhāvanti* 'they run a race for a distance of seventeen times the range of one shot'; Ved. *só asvatthé saṃvatsarám atiṣṭhat* 'he remained in the Asvattha (tree) for one year'.

c) Accusative of relation: it expresses the relation of the verbal action to a referent in a non-spatial sense; as, Lat. *indutum...pallam* 'clothed in a dress'; Gk. *melaíneto dè khróa kalón* 'and she was reddened on her beautiful skin'; Ved. *nàinaṃ kr̥tākr̥té tapataḥ* 'neither things done, nor things undone hurt this one'.

d) Object accusative: it indicates the direct object in the case of transitive verbs; as, Ved. *jíghran vái tád ghrātávyaṃ ná jighrati* 'truly smelling, he smells not what is to be smelled'.

e) Accusative of content: used when the contents of a verb are additionally expressed through a noun which appears in the accusative; as, Lat. *quod bonis bene fit beneficium* 'which charitable act is well direct to the good'; Gk. *álloi d' ámph' állēisi mákhēn emákhonto néessin* 'here and there they fought the fight for the ships'; Ved. *yád yā́maṃ yā́nti vāyúbhiḥ* 'when they go the way with the winds'.

9.2.4. INSTRUMENTAL

According to M. Fritz (2003), the instrumental case indicates that which accompanies the verbal activity. This meaning forms the basis from which other meanings have developed:

a) Instrumental of accompaniment: in the case of a person, it indicates that the person executes, or helps to execute the action; as, Lat. *postquam utrimque exitum est maxuma copia* 'after they marched up in great numbers on both sides'; Gk. *enthád' hikáneis nēí te kaì hetároisi* 'you arrive here with the ship and the companions'; Ved. *devó devébhir ā́ gamat* 'the god should come here with the gods'; Ved. *víśvair ū́mebhir ā́ gahi* 'come here with all helpers'; Ved. *divá stave duhitā́ gótamebhiḥ* 'the daughter of the heavens is prized by the Gotamas'.

b) Instrumental of means: in the case of inanimate objects, the instrumental indicates the means by which the verbal action is executed; as, Lat. *neque etiam queo / pedibus mea sponte ambulare* 'and I cannot even walk around independently on my own feet'; Lat. *vehimur navi* 'we sail with the ship'; Gk. *kephalē̃i kataneúsō* 'I will nod with my head'; Gk. *péteto pnoiē̃is anémoio* 'he flew with a breath of the wind'; Ved. *śatáṃ cákṣāṇo akṣábhiḥ* 'the god that sees with a hundred eyes'; Ved. *nāvéva yā́ntam* 'as to those who go with the ship'.

c) Instrumental of route: Lat. *nemo ire quemquam publica prohibet via* 'no one hinders another from walking on a public street'; Lat. *terra marique* 'on earth and sea'; Ved. *antárikṣeṇa pátatām* 'which fly in the air'; Ved. *éhá yātam pathíbhir devayā́naiḥ* 'comes this way on divine paths'; Ved. *mitrásya yāyām pathā́* 'I would walk on Mitra's path'.

d) Instrumental of constitution: Lat. *amphoram defracto collo* 'an amphora with a broken neck'; Myc. *ti-ri-po e-me po-de* i.e. *tripos hemē podē* 'a tripod with one leg'; Ved. *dyā́m iva stŕ̥bhiḥ* 'like the heavens with the stars'.

e) Instrumental of accompanying circumstances: in the indication of temporal circumstances, the instrumental bears a resemblance to the temporal locative; as,

Gk. *tetiēóti thumō̃i* 'with a worried temperament'; Gk. *phthóngōi eperkhómenai* 'coming forward with noise'; Ved. *út sū́ryo jyótiṣā devá éti* 'up comes the divine sun with light'; Ved. *índram ā́ viśa bṛhatā́ rávena* 'go to Indra with great noise'.

f) Instrumental of reason: Lat. *nam mihi horror membra misero percipit dictis tuis* 'for fright seizes from poor me my limbs because of your words'; Gk. *gēthosúnēi* 'out of joy'; Skt. *sá bhīṣā́ ní lilye* 'he hid himself out of fear'.

g) Instrumental of comparison: Lat. *qui omens homines supero antideo cruciabilitatibus animi* 'I, who supersede all men, surpass in tortures of the heart'; Gk. *eurúteros d' ṓmoisin* 'wider, however, than the shoulders'.

9.2.5. DATIVE

According to M. Fritz (2003), the dative had the following uses:

a) Relational dative: when used to indicate people, the dative indicates an actor or actors who receive (action; [indirect] object dative) or possess (state; possessive dative); as, Lat. *nullan tibi lingua est?* 'have you no tongue?'; Lat. *tibi me exorno ut placeam* 'I adorn myself for you, in order to please'; Lat. *quoniam vox mihi prope hic sonat?* 'what voice thus sounds for me so near?'; Lat. *nunc tibi amplectimur genua* 'now we shall seize your knees'; Lat. *mihi quidem atque oculis meis* 'indeed for me and my eyes'; Gk. *hoí d' ḗnteon allḗloisin* 'and they met one another'; Gk. *tõide d' egṑn autòs thōrḗksomai* 'and for this one I will arm myself'; Gk. *autoùs dè helṓria teũkhe kúnessin* 'and he gave them to the dogs as prey'; Gk. *mēdé moi hoútōs' thũne* 'do not rage so to me'; Gk. *toĩsi dè thumòn enì stḗthessin órine* 'and he stirred the soul in their chests'; Gk. *daímosin eĩnai alitrós* 'to be a sinner to the gods'; Ved. *dádhāti rátnaṃ vidhaté...mártyāya* 'he distributed wealth to the devoted mortal'; Ved. *devā́n devayaté yaja* 'sacrifice to the gods for the worshipper of gods'; Ved. *átithis cā́rur āyáve* 'a dear guest for the son of Āyu'.

b) *Dativus finalis*: when applied to abstract nouns, the dative indicates that the noun is the goal of an action; as, Lat. *ut quaestui habeant male loqui melioribus* 'that they have it as a gain, that they speak badly of their betters'; Lat. *khármēi prokaléssato* 'he called out to battle'; Lat. *ūrdhvás tiṣṭhā na ūtáye* 'be there upright to support us'.

9.2.6. ABLATIVE

According to M. Fritz (2003), the ablative expresses the place of origin of the verbal action. Accordingly, the ablative is principally featured when a *locatum* moves, or is moved, away from a *relatum*. Its functions include:

a) Ablative of place of origin: refers to a spatial idea, relating to separation, which is accompanied by a movement away; as, Lat. *primus cubitu surgat* 'he gets up out of bed first'; Lat. *cunctos exturba aedibus* 'drive all from the house'; Gk. *neỗn mèn ekhṓrēsan* 'they retreated from the ships'; Gk. *ouk án dḕ tónd' ándra mákhēs erúsaio* 'could you not push this man from the fight?'; Ved. *īyúr gā́vo ná yávasād ágopāḥ* 'they went like cows from the field without a herdsman'; Ved. *tvám̩ dásyūm̐r ókasa agna ājaḥ* 'you, oh Agni, drive the Dasyus from their homeland'.

b) *Ablativus originis*: it is used to indicate the object in relation to which a compared object differs; as, Lat. *quo de genere natust* 'from which family he originates'; Ved. *śukrā́ kr̥ṣṇā́d ajaniṣṭa* 'the shining one was born from the darkness'; Ved. *ásataḥ sád ajāyata* 'from the non-being came the being forth'.

c) *Ablativus separativus*: Gk. *oút' oũn esthḗtos deuḗseai* 'and you will not lack in clothing'; Gk. *mēdé m' éruke mákhēs* 'do not hold me back from battle'.

d) *Ablativus comparationis*: Lat. *levior pluma est gratia* 'thanks is lighter than a feather'; Gk. *eĩo khérēa mákhēi* 'worse than he in battle'; Gk. *polú glukíōn mélitos* 'much sweeter than honey'; Ved. *svādóḥ svā́dīyo* 'sweeter than sweets'; Ved. *sáhasaś cid sáhīyān* 'stronger even than the strong'.

9.2.7. GENITIVE

According to M. Fritz (2003), the genitive had the following functions:

a) Partitive: in its partitive root meaning the genitive expresses that a part is meant of the noun in the genitive case; as, Lat. *modius...salis* 'a scoop of salt'; Gk. *lōtoĩo phagṓn* 'eating of lotus'; Gk. *ēoũs* 'in the morning'.

b) *Genitivus qualitatis*: Lat. *lauri folia* 'leaves of the laurel'; Gk. *kṓpē d' eléphantos epẽen* 'a handle of ivory was on it'.

c) *Genitivus possessivus*: Lat. *patris amicus* 'the father's friend'; Gk. *Diós Ártemis* 'Artemis (daughter) of Zeus'; Gk. *patrós d'eím' ágathoĩo* 'and I am (the son) of a noble father'.

d) *Genitivus relationis*: it is used in comparisons to indicate that with which something is compared; as, Lat. *monstri ... simile* 'similar to a miracle'; Gk. *ḗ trípodos peridṓmethon ēè lébētos* 'both of us are betting a tripod and a basin'; Gk. *ḗpsato goúnōn* 'she touched the knee'.

The genitive may often replace other cases without expressing their meaning; it lends an additional partitive meaning to the meaning that the expected case would have brought

9.2.8. LOCATIVE

According to M. Fritz (2003) , the locative had these uses:

a) Locative of place: the local meaning of the locative is not limited to a certain part of the object, but rather may just as well pertain to its interior, exterior, or environment; Lat. *homo idem duobus locis ut simul sit* 'that the same man should be in two places at the same time'; Gk. *aithéri naíōn* 'living in the heavens'; Gk. *ésti dé tis nē̃sos méssēi alí* 'there is an island in the middle of the sea'; Gk. *óreos koruphē̃i* 'on the peak of the mountain'; Gk. *eũt' óreos koruphē̃isi Nótos katékheuen omíkhlēn* 'as when Notos (=the south wind) pours fog down from the mountain top'; Ved. *mádhye ... samudré* 'in the middle of the sea'; Ved. *ā́ yó víśvāni vā́ryā vásūni hástayor dadhé* (lit. who all desirable-ACC. goods-ACC. hand-LOC-DU put-PERF-3-sg-med.) 'who holds all treasures that one could desire to have in his own hands'; Ved. *áhann áhim párvate śiśriyāṇám* 'he smote the dragon that had occupied the mountain'; Ved. *párvatasya pr̥ṣṭhé* 'on the back of the mountain'; Ved. *sárasvatyām revád agne didīhi* 'shine beautifully on the Sarasvati (river) oh Agni'; Ved. *tásmin ní jahi vájram* 'Strike him with the cudgel!'.

b) *Locativus temporalis*: when the noun indicates, e.g. a unit of time, the use of the locative only reveals the original spatial metaphor that underlies the concept of a temporal relation; as, Lat. *tempore uno* 'at one time'; Gk. *ṓrē* 'in the spring'; Gk. *ḗmati tō̃i* 'on this day'; Ved. *yáṃ devā́sas trír áhann āyájante* 'whom the gods summon three times a day'.

c) *Locativus conditionis*: the spatial idea may be carried over to the most various circumstances; as, Ved. *vidáthe santu devā́ḥ* 'the gods should be present at the sacrifice'; Ved. *víśve devā haviṣi mādayadhvam* 'all of you gods amuse yourselves at the pouring of libations'.

9.2.9. CASE FORMS: ADVERBIAL ELEMENTS

Nonmandatory case forms are found in great variety, as may be determined from the studies of substantival inflections and their uses. Five groups of adverbial elements are identified: (1) circumstance, purpose, or result; (2) time; (3) place; (4) manner; (5) means (Lehmann 1974).

CIRCUMSTANCE, PURPOSE OR RESULT

Additional case forms may be used to indicate the purpose, result, or circumstance of an action. So e.g. the instrumental in Skt. *mr̥ḷáyā naḥ suastí* 'Be gracious to us for our well-being' (Lehmann 1974).

The dative was commonly used in this sense, as in the infinitival form Skt. *prá ṇa ā́yur jīváse soma tārīḥ* 'Extend our years, soma, for our living [so that we may live long]; Hitt. *nu-kan ^{m}Nana-Luin kuin DUMU.LUGAL ANA ^{m}Nuwanza haluki para nehhun* 'and the prince NanaLUiš whom I sent to Nuwanza to convey the message' where Hittite dative noun *haluki* 'message' (Raman 1973).

When an animate noun is involved, this use of the dative has been labelled the indirect object; as, Skt. *riṇákti kr̥ṣṇī́ raruṣā́ya pánthām* (lit. he-yields black to-ruddy path) 'Black night gives up the path to the red sun'.

NOTE. As these examples may indicate, the dative, like the other cases, must be interpreted with reference to the lexical properties of the verbal element.

TIME

A further adverbial segment in sentences indicates the time of occurrence. The cases in question are various, as in Skt. *dívā náktaṃ śárum asmád yuyotam* 'By day and during the night protect us from the arrow'. The nominal form *dívā* 'by day', which with change of accent is no longer an instrumental but an adverbial form outside the paradigm, and the accusative *náktaṃ* 'during the night' differ in meaning. The instrumental, like the locative, refers to a point in time, though the "*point*" may be extended; the accusative, to an extent of time. Differing cases accordingly provide different meanings for nouns marked for the lexical category *time* (Lehmann 1974).

PLACE

According to Fritz (2003), "The Proto-Indo-European cases with local meaning are the locative, accusative, and the ablative. These cases designate a general spatial relationship between two objects, which include places (which are concrete objects) and actions (in which concrete persons or objects participate). The locative simply organizes spatially. With the accusative and the ablative, the concept of direction comes into play, with each indicating an opposing direction:

The accusative indicates that the verbal action is oriented toward the object referent; the ablative indicates that the verbal action is oriented away from the object referent. These local dimensions then serve – in a process of transfer that is itself the result of cognitive reflection – equally to describe temporal relations and other circumstances."

A. The accusative indicates the goal of an action, as in Lat. *Rōmam īre* 'go to Rome', Hitt. *tuš alkištan tarnahhe* 'and those (birds) I release to the branch' (Otten and Souček 1969).

B. The instrumental indicates the place "over which an action extends" (Macdonell 1916): *sárasvatyā yānti* 'they go along the Sarasvatī'.

C. The ablative indicates the starting point of the action: *sá ráthāt papāta* 'he fell from his chariot'; and the following example from Hittite (Otten and Souček 1969): *iššaz (š)mit lālan AN.BARaš [d]āi* 'He takes the iron tongue out of their mouths'.

D. The locative indicates a point in space, e.g., Skt. *diví* 'in heaven' or the locative *kardi* 'in heart', in the following Hittite example (Otten and Souček): *kardi-šmi-i̯a-at-kán dahhun* 'And I took away that [illness which was] in your heart'.

Nouns with lexical features for place and for time may be used in the same sentence, as in Skt. *ástam úpa náktam eti* 'He goes during the night to the house'. Although both nouns are in the accusative, the differing lexical features lead to different interpretations of the case. In this way, inflectional markers combine with lexical features to yield a wide variety of adverbial elements.

MANNER

Among the adverbial elements which are most diverse in surface forms are those referring to manner. Various cases are used, as follows (Lehmann 1974).

A. The accusative is especially frequent with adjectives, such as Skt. *kṣiprám* 'quickly', *bahú* 'greatly', *nyák* 'downward'.

B. The instrumental is also used, in the plural, as in Skt. *máhobhiḥ* 'mightily', as well as in the singular, *sáhasā* 'suddenly'.

Similar to the expression of manner is the instrumental used to express the sense of accompaniment: Skt. *devó devébhir ā́gamat* 'May the god come [in such a way that he is] accompanied by the other gods'.

C. The ablative is also used to express manner in connection with a restricted number of verbs such as those expressing 'fear': *réjante víśvā kṛtrímāṇi bhīṣā́* 'All creatures tremble fearfully'.

MEANS

Adverbial expressions of means are expressed especially by the instrumental; as, Skt. *áhan vṛtrám ... índro vájreṇa* 'Indra killed ... Vṛtra with his bolt'. The noun involved frequently refers to an instrument; *cf.* Hitt. *kalulupuš šmuš gapinit hulaliemi* (lit. fingers their with-thread I-wind) 'I wind the thread around their fingers'.

Animate nouns may also be so used. When they are, they indicate the agent: *agnínā turvā́ṣaṃ yáduṃ parāváta ugrā́ devaṃ havāmahe* 'Through Agni we call from far Turvasa, Yadu, and Ugradeva'. This use led to the use of the instrumental as the agent in passive constructions (Lehmann 1974).

10. SENTENCE SYNTAX

10.1. THE SENTENCE

A sentence is a form of words which contains a statement, a question, an exclamation, or a command.

The fundamental order of sentences in PIE appears to be OV. Support for this assumption is evident in the oldest texts of the materials attested earliest in the IE dialects. Examples of this include the following, from Fortson (2004): Hitt. *nu=za* *ᴹᵁˢ̌illuyankaš ᴰIM-an tarahta* 'And the serpent overcame the Stormgod'; Ved. *maruto ha enam na ajahuḫ* 'Indeed the Maruts did not abandon him'; Lat. *Eumolpus tanquam litterārum stūdiōsus utīque ātrāmentum habet* 'Eumolpus, so interested in learning, surely has (some) ink'; Runic *ek hlewagastiz holtijaz horna tawido* 'I, Hlewagastiz of Holt, made (this) horn'; Toch. A. *kāsu ñom-klyu tsraṣiśśi śäk kälymentwaṃ sätkatar* 'Good fame of the strong spreads out in ten directions'.

NOTE. Lehmann (1974): "The fundamental order of sentences in these early dialects cannot be determined solely by frequency of sentence patterns. For, like other linguistic constructions, sentence patterns manifest marked as well as unmarked order. Marked order is expected in literary materials. The documents surviving from the earliest dialects are virtually all in verse or in literary forms of prose. Accordingly many of the individual sentences do not have the unmarked order, with verb final. For this reason conclusions about the characteristic word order of PIE and the early dialects will be based in part on those syntactic patterns that are rarely modified for literary and rhetorical effect: comparative constructions, the presence of postpositions and prepositions, and the absence of prefixes (...)."

Lehmann is criticised by Friedrich (1975) who, like Watkins (1976) and Miller (1975), support a VO prehistoric situation, probably SVO (like those found in 'central' IE areas), with non-consistent dialectal SOV findings. In any case (viz. Lehmann and Miller), an older PIH OV (VSO for Miller), as attested in Hittite, would have been substituted by a newer VO (SOV for Miller, later SVO through a process of verb transposition) – thus, all Indo-European dialects attested have evolved (therefore probably from a common post-Proto-Indo-European trend) into a modern VO.

Fortson (2004): "Part of the problem with it is arriving at a clear definition of a verb-final language. In the strict sense, a verb-final language is one where the verb always comes at the end of each clause unless other factors intervene. The only well-known older PIE language that meets this criterion is Hittite. No matter what the genre, no matter how stylistically marked the text, the verb in Hittite is always clause-final, with one exception – when it is fronted to the beginning of the clause for emphasis or contrast (...). None of the other old IE languages behaves so rigidly (...); there is essentially no position in the clause (on the surface at least) where the verb cannot appear.

It is usually stated that in these languages, the pragmatically neutral order is SOV. This may, in fact, be true, at least of some of them (such as Latin); but with so many word-order permutations possible (and frequent), clearly they cannot be called "verb-final" in the same way as Hittite. There are any number of reasons, according to current theory, why a verb may or may not appear as the last word in its clause."

Clackson (2007): "The investigation of PIE word order in terms of rigid SVO and SOV patterns was rightly criticised as a 'pseudo-problem' by Watkins in a much-cited article of 1976. It would be wrong, however, to think that because word order cannot be expressed in terms of strict SOV or SVO patterns it is somehow unimportant, or that it was free. If PIE were a 'non-configurational' language, with completely freeword order, we would still have to explain why the unmarked place of the verb is sentence-final in Hittite, Sanskrit and Latin, and why word comparisons which reflect original juxtapositions of noun and dependent genitive agree in showing the order genitive – head noun (...) Agreements such as these could lead to the conclusion that the unmarked order was SOV for the PIE sentence, and head-final for the PIE noun phrase. But variation from these patterns is widely attested, particularly in poetic or highly stylised texts, which make up a large part of our corpus of many early IE languages."

10.1.1. KINDS OF SENTENCES

1. PIE sentences were either nominal, i.e. formed by nouns, or verbal, if they included a verb.

2. Sentences are formed by a subject and a predicate. The subject of a sentence is the *person or thing spoken of.* The predicate is *that which is said* of the subject.

a. The subject is usually a noun or pronoun, or some word or group of words used as a noun. However, because the personal endings of verbs encode the subject in them, it is not grammatically necessary to use an overt personal pronominal subject in addition. When subject pronouns occur, it is usually said that its use is emphatic (Fortson 2004); as, Lat. *sīcutī <u>ego</u> accēpī* '*as <u>I</u> understand it*' (Sallus, Bellum Catilinae 6.1), where 'I' serves to contrast his own understanding with the opinion of others.

However, in nominal sentences, an overt pronominal subject is generally required for clarity; as, O.Pers. <u>*adam*</u> *navama*, '<u>I</u> (am) the ninth'.

The syntax of possessive **swos**, *own*, is treated by Fortson (2004): "Reflexive adjectives (and pronouns) refer back to the grammatical subject of a sentence. But the possessive "swo-" had broader usage, to judge by the daughter languages: it could refer back not to the grammatical subject, but to newly introduced discourse material or to an older topic that is returned to. As an example of the former, consider Ved. *tráya índrasya sómaḥ sutā́sah santu devásya své kṣáye sutapā́vnaḥ* 'Let the three somas be pressed for the god Indra in the soma drinker's own house' (translation following Brent Vine; *soma* was an intoxicating sacred drink). Here the grammatical subject is *tráya. .. sómaḥ* 'the three somas' and the possessive *své* refers to the soma-drinker, who is newly introduced. Similar behavior can be found in other older IE languages."

b. The predicate of a sentence may be a verb (as *the dog runs),* or it may consist of some form of **esmi**, *be*, and a noun or adjective which *describes* or *defines* the subject (as *It is good).* Such a noun or adjective is called a predicate noun or adjective.

3. In Proto-Indo-European, simple sentences may be composed of only one word, a noun or a verb; as, 'God!' or '(it) rains'.

NOTE 1. Nominal sentences of this type are usually interjections and vocatives. Verbal sentences of this type include imperatives (at least of 2nd sg.) and impersonal verbs, which had never a subject in the oldest dialects attested; as, for Eng. *(it) rains*, *cf.* Goth. *rigneiþ*, Lat. *pluit*, Gk. ὕει, Skt. *várṣati.* It is believed that when IE dialects became SVO in structure, so that a subject was required, the third singular anaphoric pronoun, corresponding to *it*, German *es*, French *il*, etc., was introduced as subject in such sentences. Such pronouns were introduced because SVO languages must have subjects in sentences, as do intransitive verbs in any OV language. Such verbs could be supplemented by substantives in various cases, among them the accusative. These constructions are especially prominent for verbs referring to the emotions; as, Skt. *kitavā́ṃ tatāpa* (lit. with-regard-to-the-gambler there-is-pain) 'it pains the gambler', Lat. *miseret, pudet, taedet* 'It makes one pitiful, ashamed, bored'. Compare also Cicero's Lat. *eōrum nōs miseret* (lit. 'of-them us it-makes pitiful/there-is-pity') 'we feel pity for them' or O.H.G. *thes gánges thih nirthrúzzi* (lit. 'of-the way you may-there-not-be-weariness') 'Do not let yourself be wearied of the way'. In PIE sentences various case forms could be used with verbs. The simplest sentences may consist of verbs accompanied by nouns in seven of the eight cases; only the vocative is not so used. The nouns fill the role of objects or, possibly better stated, of complements (Lehmann 1974).

NOTE 2. Besides the simple sentence which consists only of a verb, a simple sentence in the early dialects and in PIE could consist of a verb accompanied by a noun or pronoun as complement. A subject however wasn't mandatory. Nor were other constructions which may seem to be natural, such as indirect objects with verbs like 'give'. The root **dō-* or in its earlier form **deH-* had in its simplest sense the meaning 'present' and was often unaccompanied by any nominal expression (Lehmann 1974).

10.1.2. NOMINAL SENTENCE

1. Nominal sentences, in which a substantive is equated with another substantive, an adjective, or a particle, make up one of the simplest type of sentence in PIE.

Such a type of sentence is found in almost every IE dialect; *cf.* (Lehmann 1974) Hitt. *attaš aššuš* 'the father (is) good', Skt. *tvám váruṇa*, 'you (are) Varuna', O.Pers. *adam Dārayavauš* 'I (am) Darius', Gk. *emoì d' ákhos* 'and to me (there is) pain', Lat. *omnia praeclara rara 'all the best things (are) rare'*. Apart from a noun or adjective, the predicate could be an adverb; as, Hitt. *ᵐŠippa-LÚ-iš=wa=kan ŪL anda* 'Sippazitis (is) not in (it)'; Gk. *metà dè glaukõpis Athénē* 'and Athena of glaucous eyes (was) with (them)'.

In all dialects, however, such sentences were restricted in its use to a especially formal use or, on the contrary, they are found more often than originally in PIE. Thus, in Latin and Germanic dialects they are found in proverbs and sayings, as in Old Irish; in Greek it is also found in epic and poetry. In Balto-Slavic dialects the pure nominal sentence has become the usual type of nominal sentence, even when the predicate is an adverb or an adverbial case. However, such a use, which is more extended in modern dialects (like Russian) than in the older ones (as Old Slavic), is considered the result of Finno-Ugrian influence. (Lehmann 1974).

2. An action, state, or event could be syntactically backgrounded using a construction called an absolute. Typically the absolute consisted of a noun modified by a participle – semantically equivalent to a subject plus verb – in an oblique case (Fortson 2004).

Thus Latin has ablative absolutes (*hīs rēbus gestīs* lit. 'these things having been done', i.e. 'after these things were done' or 'because these things were done'), Greek has genitive absolutes (Homeric *aékontos emeĩo* 'with me being unwilling', *pàr émoige kaì hálloi hoi ké mé timḗsousi*, 'near me (there are) others who [particle] will praise me'), Vedic Sanskrit has locative absolutes (*ucchántyām uśási* 'with dawn shining forth', or *havyaír agnír mánuṣa īrayádhyai*, 'Agni must be prayed with the sacrifices of men',), and Gothic and Old Church Slavonic have dative absolutes (Goth. *imma rodjandin* and O.C.S. *jemu glagoljǫščemu* 'with him speaking, while he is/was speaking').

NOTE. PIE surely had such constructions too, although which case or cases were used is debated.

3. In addition to such expansions by means of additional nouns in nonrequired cases, sentences could be expanded by means of particles.

NOTE. For Lehmann (1974), three subsets of particles came to be particularly important. One of these is the set of preverbs, such as **ā**. Another is the set of sentence connectives, such as **nu**. The third is the set of qualifier expressions, e.g., PIE **nē/mē** *'(must) not'*. An additional subset, conjunctions introducing clauses, will be discussed below in the section on compound clauses. Preverbs are distinctively characterised by being closely associated with verbs and modifying their meaning. In their normal position they stand directly before verbs (Watkins 1964).

Generally, thus, concordance governed both members of the pure nominal sentence. Unlike the personal verb and its complements (governed by inflection), the nominal sentence showed a strong reliance on concordance between subject and predicate as a definitory feature: both needed the same case, and tended to have the same number and gender (Lehmann 1974).

THE COPULATIVE VERB

Nominal sentences are not always simple clauses without copula; examples are found with an explicit copula with stylistic and semantic change (Ramat 1993): Hitt. LÚ.ULÙ.LU=*k*u GUD=*ku* UDU=*ku* *ēšzi* 'whether he is man or ox or sheep'.

The copulative verb **esmi** is only necessary when introducing late categories in the verbal morphology, like time and mood. Therefore, when the mood is the indicative, and the time is neuter (proverbs without timing, or present with semantic neuter) there is no need to use **esmi**.

NOTE. The basic form of nominal sentences has been a matter of dispute. Some Indo-Europeanists propose that the absence of a verb in nominal sentences is a result of ellipsis and assume an underlying verb **esmi** (Benveniste 1950). They support this assumption by pointing to the requirement of such a verb if the nominal sentence is in the past tense; *cf.* Hitt. *ABU.I̯A genzuu̯alaš ešta* 'My father was merciful'. On the contrary, Meillet (1906-1908), followed by Lehmann (1974) and Mendoza (1998), consider that nominal sentences did not require a verb but that a verb might be included for emphasis. This conclusion may be supported by noting that the qualifiers which were found in PIE could be used in nominal sentences without a verb. As an example we may cite a Hittite sentence which is negative and imperative, *1-aš 1-edani menahhanda lē idāluš* 'One should not be evil toward another one'. Yet, if a passage was to be explicit, a form of **esmi** could be used, as in Skt. *nákir indra tvád úttaro ná jyā́yāṅ asti* "No one is higher than you, Indra, nor greater'.

Fritz (in Meier-Brügger 2003): "Nominal phrases are not simply verbal phrases without a finite verb (with what is called ellipsis of the copula), but rather constitute an independent type of clause. Thus, the predicate noun in nominal phrases is always stressed, unlike the verbal predicate in verbal phrases. In fact the term 'elipsis' is not exact, since the copula is not essential. Contrarily, the use of the copula should rather be seen as an adaptation to the common pattern of verbal phrases, which always feature a finite verb form. This use of the copula is in fact a sort of explicative signification, in which the content of the copula is expressed through the connection of the various sentence elements and is given particular emphasis alone through an independent linguistic symbol of comparable meaning."

On the original meaning of **esmi**, since Brugmann (1925) it is reconstructed as '*exist*' hence its use as a copulative verb through constructions in which the predicate express the existence of the subject, as in Hom. Gk. *eím' Odusseús Laertiádēs, hós...* 'I am Odisseus, son of Laertes, the one who...' (Mendoza 1998).

10.1.3. VERBAL SENTENCE

The simplest structure of the common Indo-European sentence consists of a verb, i.e. the carrying out of an action. In it, none of the verbal actors (subject and object) must be expressed – the subject is usually not obligatory, and the object appears only when it is linked to the lexical nature of the verb.

NOTE. The oldest morphological categories, even time, were expressed in PIE through lexical means, and remains are found of such a system; *cf.* Hitt. *-za* (reflexive), modal particles in Gk. and O.Ind., modal negation in some IE dialects, or the simple change in intonation, which made interrogative or imperative a declarative sentence – in fact, the imperative lacks a mark of its own.

The relationship between the subject and the object is expressed through the case.

There is no clear morphological distinction between transitive and intransitive verbs in Proto-Indo-European.

NOTE. Some Indo-European dialects have specialised certain verbal suffixes as transitives (causatives) or intransitives, as Gk. *-en*, Gmc. *-io*, Lat. *-a*, etc., while in some others a preverb combined with a verbal root makes the basic verb transitive or intransitive.

When subjects are explicitly expressed, the nominative is the case employed.

NOTE. Expression of the subject is the most prominent extension of simple sentences to include more than one substantival expression. Apart from such explicit mention of the subject, predicates may consist of verbs accompanied by two or more nouns, in cases which supplement the meanings of the verbs (see below). Such constructions must be distinguished from the inclusion of additional nouns whose case forms indicate adverbial use.

PREDICATES WITH TWO OR MORE SUBSTANTIVES

Few verbs are mandatorily accompanied by two nouns (Lehmann 1974):

1. The use of the dative in addition to the accusative. This is made almost obligatory with verb **dō-**, give; as in Skt. *tā́bhiām enaṃ pári dehi* (lit. those-two-DAT. him-ACC. over you-give), 'Give him over to those two'; Gk. *dō̂ra phérein tō̂i patrí* 'give presents to the father' (Mendoza 1998).

2. The instrumental and ablative, as Skt. *áhan vṛtrám ... índro vájreṇa* 'Indra killed ... Vrtra with his bolt'; Skt. *tvám̩ dásyūm̐r ókaso agna ājaḥ* 'You drove the enemies from the house, O Agni'.

NOTE. While the addition to these sentences which is indicated by the nouns in the instrumental and the ablative is essential for the meaning of the lines in their context, it does not need to be included in the sentence for syntactic reasons.

3. The causative accompanied by two accusatives, as Skt. *devā́m̐ uśataḥ pāyayā havíḥ* (lit. gods desiring you-cause-to-drink libation) 'Make the desiring gods drink the libation'.

In such sentences the agent-accusative represents the object of the causative element: as Arthur A. Macdonell indicated (1916), in a corresponding simple sentence this noun would have been given in the nominative, as Skt. *devā́ havíḥ pibanti* 'The gods drink the libation'.

Accordingly a simple verb in PIE was at the most accompanied by one substantive, unless the additional substantive was complementary or adverbial.

10.2. SENTENCE MODIFIERS

10.2.1. INTONATION PATTERNS

1. According to Fritz (in Meier-Brügger 2003), with regard to sentence accent, one may note that the word that begins the sentence is stressed. Sentence-initial position implies the function of establishing the topic: In nominative language, the subject in sentence-initial position is considered the normal, unmarked type. In interrogative sentences, the nominal element, about which the question is asked, establishes the theme. It is thus the interrogative pronoun that begins the sentence

NOTE. An enclitic is added as a second word in the sentence; a further enclitic is added as a third word. This is known as the (Delbrück-)Wackernagel Law, see §10.6.4.

2. The sentence was characterised in PIE by patterns of order and by selection (Lehmann 1974):

A. Selection classes were determined in part by inflection, in part by lexical categories, most of which were covert.

NOTE. Some lexical categories were characterised at least in part by formal features, such as abstract nouns marked by ***-ti-***, nouns in the religious sphere marked by ***-u-*** and collectives marked by **-h*.

B. In addition to characterisation by means of order and categories of selection, the sentence was also delimited by intonation based on variations in pitch.

2. To the extent that the pitch phonemes of PIE have been determined, a high pitch may be posited, which could stand on one syllable per word, and a low pitch, which was not so restricted.

Words were characterised on one syllable by a high pitch accent, unless they were enclitic, that is, unmarked for accent.

3. Accented words could lose their high pitch accent if they were placed at specific positions in sentences:

A. Vocatives lost their accent if they were medial in a sentence or clause; and finite verbs lost their accent unless they stood initially in an independent clause or in any position in a dependent clause in Vedic. These same rules may be assumed for PIE. On the basis of the two characteristic patterns of loss of accent for verbs, characteristic patterns of intonation may also be posited for the IE sentence.

B. Judging on the basis of loss of high pitch accent of verbs in them, independent clauses were characterised by final dropping in pitch. For in unmarked order the verb stands finally in the clause; as, *purodhā́m evá <u>gacchati</u>* (lit. priesthood verily he-attains) '<u>He attains</u> the priesthood'.

C. In marked order on the other hand it stands initially. H. S. Ananthanarayana investigated the accent patterns in accented Vedic texts, particularly in the Taittirīya Brāhmaṇa, and concluded on the basis of the interpretation of sentences with similar lexical material that sentences with initial verb are marked.

Thus, in contrast with the previous example, the following indicates "emphasis" of the verb (Ananthanarayana 1970): *<u>gácchati</u> pratiṣṭhā́m* '<u>He attains</u> stability' Since *gacchati* in the other example has no high pitch accent, and since other such sentences have a similar distribution of accents, it may be concluded that sentences with normal, unmarked meaning have a final lowered pitch accent. This might be indicated with #.

Clauses, however, which are marked either to convey emphasis or to indicate subordination, do not undergo such lowering. They may be distinguished with final || (Ananthanarayana 1970): *yát stríyam <u>upeyā́t</u>* || *nírvīryas <u>syā́t</u>* # (lit. if woman he-may-approach impotent he-may-become) 'If he were to approach a woman, he might become impotent'.

The intonation pattern indicated by # apparently conveyed the notion of a simple, nonemphatic utterance, whether a statement, question, or command: *kásmai nú satrám āsmahe* # (lit. why indeed sacrifice we-perform) 'Why should we perform sacrifice?'

The intonation pattern indicated by || apparently conveyed the notion of an emotional or emphatic utterance or one requiring supplementation, as by another clause. These conclusions are supported by the patterns found in Germanic alliterative verse. For, as is well known, verbs were frequently placed by poets in the fourth, nonalliterating, metrically prominent position in the line: *þeodcyninga þrym gefrūnon* (lit. of-people's-kings glory we-heard-of) 'We heard of the glory of the kings of the people'.

This placing of verbs, retained by metrical convention in Germanic verse, presumably maintains evidence for the IE intonation pattern. For, by contrast, verbs could alliterate when they stood initially in clauses or in subordinate clauses; *egsode eorlas, syððan ǣrest wearð* (lit. he-terrified men since first he-was) 'He terrified men from the time he first was [found]'; *þenden wordum wēold wine Scyldinga* (lit. as-long-as with-words he-ruled the-friend of-the-Scyldings) 'As long as the friend of the Scyldings ruled with his words.'

The patterns of alliteration in the oldest Germanic verse accordingly support the conclusions that have been derived from Vedic accentuation regarding the intonation of the Indo-European sentence, as do patterns in other dialects.

D. Among such patterns is the preference for enclitics in second position in the sentence (Wackernagel 1892). Words found in this position are particles, pronouns, and verbs, which have no accent in Vedic texts. This observation of Wackernagel supports the conclusion that the intonation of the sentence was characterised by initial high pitch, with the voice trailing off at the end. For the enclitic elements were not placed initially, but rather they occupied positions in which unaccented portions of words were expected, as in Skt. *prāvepā́ mā bṛható mādayanti*, 'The dangling ones of the lofty tree gladden me'. The pronoun *mā* 'me', like other such enclitics, makes up a phrase with the initial word; in this way it is comparable to unaccented syllables of individual words, as in Skt. *pravātejā́ íriṇe várvṛtānāḥ* (lit. in-windy-place on-dice-board rolling) '[born] in a windy place, rolling on the dice-board'.

10.2.2. SENTENCE DELIMITING PARTICLES

1. The particles concerned are PIE **nu**, **so**, **to**, all of them introductory particles.

Their homonymity with the adverb **nu**, **nun** and the anaphoric pronoun was one of the reasons earlier Indo-Europeanists failed to recognise them and their function. Yet Delbrück had already noted the clause-introducing function of Skt. *sa* (1888), as in Skt. *tásya tā́ni śīrṣā́ṇi prá cicheda.* (lit. his the heads off he-struck) *sá yát somapā́nam ā́sa tátaḥ kapíñjalaḥ sám abhavat* (lit. Ptc. what soma-drinking it-was from-that hazel-hen [grouse] together it-became] 'He struck off his heads. From the one that drank soma, the hazel-hen was created'. Delbrück identified *sa* in this and other sentences as a particle and not a pronoun, for it did not agree in gender with a noun in the sentence. But it remained for Hittite to clarify the situation.

In Hittite texts the introductory use of the particles is unmistakable (J.Friedrich 1960); *ta* and *šu* occur primarily in the early texts, *nu* in the later, as illustrated in the following Old Hittite example (Otten and Souček 1969): *šer-a-ššan GAD-an pešiemi šu- uš LÚ-aš natta aušzi* (over-and-Ptc. cloth I-throw Ptc.- them man not sees) 'I throw a cloth over it and no one will see them' (Lehmann 1974).

2. Besides such an introductory function (here as often elsewhere translated 'and'), these particles were used as first element in a chain of enclitics, as in *n-at-ši* 'and it to-him', *nu-mu-za-kan* 'and to-me self within' and so on.

In Homeric Greek such strings of particles follow different orders, but reflect the IE construction, as in: *oudé nu soí per entrépetai phílon êtor, Olúmpie* (lit. not-indeed and to-you but it-turns 'dear' heart Olympian) 'But your heart doesn't notice, Zeus'. As the translation of *per* here indicates, some particles were used to indicate the relationships between clauses marking the simple sentence (Lehmann 1974).

3. Many simple sentences in PIE would then be similar to those in Hittite and Vedic Sanskrit. Among the simplest is Skt. *tám índro didveṣa* 'Indra hated him'. Presumably *tam* is a conflated form of the particle *ta* and the enclitic accusative singular pronoun; the combination is attested in Hittite as *ta-an* (J. Friedrich 1960). Similar examples from the other early dialects could be cited, such as the Italic inscription of Praeneste, or the Germanic Gallehus inscription: *Ek HlewagastiR HoltijaR horna tawido*, 'I, Hlewagastir of Holt, made the horn'. In these late texts, the subject was mandatory, and accordingly two nominal forms

had come to be standard for the sentence. If however the subject is not taken into consideration, many sentences contained only one nominal element with verbs, in the early dialects as well as in PIE (Lehmann 1974).

10.3. VERBAL MODIFIERS

10.3.1. DECLARATIVE SENTENCES

1. The injunctive has long been identified as a form unmarked for mood and marked only for stem and person. It may thus be compared with the simplest form of OV languages.

By contrast the present indicative indicates "mood". We associate this additional feature with the suffix ***-i***, and assume for it declarative meaning.

2. As Lehmann (1974) says, "Yet it is also clear that, by the time of Vedic Sanskrit and, we assume, Late PIE, the injunctive no longer contrasted directly with the present indicative. We must therefore conclude that the declarative qualifier was expressed by other means in the sentence. We assume that the means of expression was an intonation pattern. For, in normal unmarked simple sentences, finite unaccented verbs stood finally in their clause, as did the predicative elements of nominal sentences; Delbrück's repeatedly used example may be cited once again to illustrate the typical pattern: *víśaḥ kṣatríyāya balíṃ haranti* 'The villagers pay tribute to the prince'. Since the verb *haranti* was unaccented, i.e., had no high pitch, we may posit for the normal sentence an intonation pattern in which the final elements in the sentence were accompanied by low pitch."

Lehmann (1974) supports this assumption by noting that a distinctive suprasegmental was used in Vedic to distinguish a contrasting feature, *interrogation* or *request* (Wackernagel 1896). This marker, called *pluti* by native grammarians, consisted of extra length, as in *ágnā3i* 'O fire' (3 indicates extra length). But a more direct contrast with the intonation of simple sentences may be exemplified by the accentuation of subordinate clauses. These have accented verbs, as in the following line from the Rigveda: *antáś ca prắgā áditir bhavāsi* 'If you have entered inside, you will be Aditi'. As the pitch accent on *ágā* indicates, verbs in subordinate clauses maintained high pitch, in contrast with verbs of independent clauses like *bhavāsi*. We may conclude that this high pitch was an element in an intonation pattern which indicated incompleteness, somewhat like the pattern of contemporary English.

3. Evidence from other dialects supports the conclusion that, in late PIE, declarative sentences were indicated by means of an intonation pattern with a drop in accentuation at the end of the clause.

NOTE. In Germanic verse, verbs of unmarked declarative sentences tend to occupy unaccented positions in the line, notably the final position (Lehmann 1956). Although the surface expression of accentuation patterns in Germanic is stress, rather than the pitch of Vedic and PIE, the coincidence of accentuation pattern supports our conclusions concerning PIE intonation.

10.3.2. INTERROGATIVE SENTENCES

1. The interrogation was apparently also indicated by means of intonation, for some questions in our early texts have no surface segmental indication distinguishing them from statements, for example, Plautus *Aulularia* 213, *aetatem meam scis*, 'Do you know my age?'.

NOTE. Only the context indicates to us that this utterance was a question; we may assume that the spoken form included means of expressing interrogation, and in view of expressions in the later dialects we can only conclude that these means were an intonation pattern.

2. Questions are generally classified in two groups:

- Those framed to obtain confirmation, yes/no questions (*Bestätigungsfragen*). This feature accompanies statements in which a speaker sets out to elicit information from the hearer.
- Those framed to obtain clarification *(Verdeutlichungsfragen).*

3. Yes/no questions (*Bestätigungsfragen*) were made (Clackson 2007):

a) By an intonation pattern alone, as noted above. That is the reconstruction favoured by most of those who have addressed the issue (Delbrück 1893-1900, Meier-Brügger 2003), because of the finds in Hittite and Vedic Sanskrit. It might therefore be considered one of the oldest means to express interrogation of any type, including yes/no questions. This is most probably the older situation in PIE.

b) Disjunctive questions can be formed by juxtaposition of a verb with a negated verb, as in the following example of Vedic Sanskrit prose text (3 indicates extra length): *chinátti sā́ ná chinattī3* [cuts she not cuts *pluti*] 'Does she divide or not?'..

NOTE. For Clackson (2007): "These different reconstructed hypotheses are not mutually exclusive: it is possible that different types of 'yes-no' question formation existed alongside each other in PIE. Indeed, systems of marking through intonation exist alongside other systems in many languages of the world. In French, for example, there are three different ways of forming 'yes-no' questions: *Il vient?, Est-ce qu'il vient?* and *Vient-il?* all mean 'Is he coming?'."

c) By an interrogative affix or particle. Such means of expression for interrogation are found in most IE languages, apparently from a late development, since the particles used are different. Two of them have been reconstructed for PIE, though:

i. The particle ***nu***, found in Greek and Vedic Sanskrit as interrogative particle, is also extremely widely used in non-interrogative sentences in Hittite, as well as in Sanskrit and Greek. It was probably then mainly a S.LIE resource.

ii. Lehmann (1974), following Delbrück (1893-1900) and Eichner (1971) argues that Lat. *-ne*, was the original interrogative particle, since its post-placement accorded with the typology of OV languages, in which interrogative particles are placed sentence finally. According to Minton Warren, it "occurs about 1100 times in Plautus and over 40 times in Terence" (1881). Besides expressions like Lat. *egone* 'Me?', sentences like the following occur (Plautus *Asinaria* 884): *Aúdin quid ait? Artemona*: *Aúdio*. 'Did you hear what he is saying? Artemona: yes'.

Other evidence for a postponed particle for expressing interrogation is found in Avestan, in which *-na* is suffixed to some interrogatives, as in Av. *kas-nā* 'who (then)?'; and in Germanic, where *na* is found finally in some questions in Old High German. Old Church Slavic is more consistent in the use of such a particle than are these dialects, as in *chošteši li* 'Do you wish to?' This particle is also used in contemporary Russian.

The particle used to express interrogation in Latin, Avestan, and Germanic is homophonous with the particle for expressing negation, PIE **ne**.

NOTE. It is not unlikely that LIE **an** of questions is behind same ***ne/n̥*** particle used for the negative. As the interrogative particle, however, it has been lost in most dialects. After Lehmann (1974), its loss is one of the indications that late PIE was not a consistent OV language. After Mendoza, the fact that such interrogatives of a yes/no-answer are introduced by different particles in the oldest attested dialects means that no single particle was generalised by Late Indo-European; *cf.* Goth. *niu*, Lat. *-ne, nonne, num*, Gk. ἦ, νὐ , Skt. *nu*, Sla. *li*. However, the common findings of Hittite, Indo-Iranian, Germanic and Latin are similar, if not the same.

4. The partial interrogative sentences are those which expect an aclaratory answer (*Verdeutlichungsfragen*), equivalent to English 'What...?', 'Where...?', 'Who...?', and so on. They are introduced in PIE by pronominal or adverbial forms

derived from interrogative **qi-/qo-**, always placed initially but for marked sentences, where a change in position is admitted to emphasise it.

NOTE. In some languages, interrogatives may be strengthened by the addition of posposed particles with interrogative sense, as in Av. *kaš-na* (<*k^{w}*os-ne*). Such forms introduce indirect interrogatives when they ask about a part of the sentence. Indirect interrogatives in the form of total interrogatives (i.e., not of yes/no-answer) are introduced by particles derived from direct interrogative particles (when there are) or by conditional conjunctions; as Hitt. *man*.

5. According to Clackson (2007), question words are typically fronted and followed by enclitics, as Vedic *kás* ***te*** *mātáraṃ vidhávām acakrat* (lit. who you-gen mother-acc widow-acc he-made) 'Who made **your** mother a widow?'; Vedic *kásya bráhmāni jujusur yúvānaḥ* lit. 'of whom the formulas like the-young-men?';

Where an element precedes the question word, it makes sense to interpret this as a left-detached element, and it appears that in Vedic Sanskrit, as in Hittite, left-detachment does not count in the calculation of second position; as Vedic *índraḥ kím* ***asya*** *sakhyé cakāra* (lit. Indra-nom what-acc he-gen friendship-loc he-did), 'As for Indra, what did **he** do in his friendship?'; Vedic *brahmā kó* ***vaḥ*** *saparyati* 'priest which **you** honors?' See §10.6.3 for more on emphasis.

10.3.3. NEGATIVE SENTENCES

1. Indications of negation, by which the speaker negates the verbal means of expression, commonly occupy third position in the hierarchy of sentence elements.

2. We can only posit the particles **ne** and **mē/nē**, neither of which is normally postposed after verbs.

NOTE. For prohibitive particle **mē**, compare Gk. mḗ, O.Ind.,Av.,O.Pers. *mā*, Toch. *mar/mā*, Arm. *mi*, Alb. *mos*. In other IE dialects it appears as **nē**, *cf.* Goth. *ne*, Lat. *nē* (also as modal negation), O.Ir. *ni*. It is not clear whether Hitt. *lē* is ultimately derived from **mē** or **nē**, although Clackson (2007) reconstructs a common Anatolian *nē, due to Luv. *ni(s)*, Lyc. *ni*. Although **mē** is sometimes reconstructed as the 'original' PIE particle, the Anatolian finds don't let us decide which form is older. Apparently, S.LIE and Tocharian had **mē**, while Anatolian and North-West IE seem to have used **nē**.

PIE **ne** is found as Goth.,O.H.G. *ni*, Lat. *nĕ-* (e.g. in *nequis*) O.Ind. *ná*, O.Sla. *ne*, etc. Sometimes it is found in lengthened or strengthened forms as Hitt. *natta*, Lat. *non*, Skt. *ned*, etc. A common PIE lengthened form is **nei**, which appears in Lat. *ni*, Lith. *neî*, Sla. *ni*, etc.

3. The negative element **ne** was not used in compounding in PIE (Brugmann 1904); the privative prefix **n̥**-, *un*-, had this function.

Comparative evidence suggests, following Fortson (2004), that certain classes of words were preferentially negated not with the adverb but with the privative prefix; among these words were participles and verbal adjectives. Greek and Latin, for example, ordinarily use their negative adverbs when negating participles, but some fixed archaic constructions point to an earlier time when the privative prefix was used instead, as Homeric Gk. *a-ékontos emeĩo* 'with me being unwilling, against my will', Lat. *mē īn-sciente* 'with me not knowing', *in-uītus* 'unwilling' (later replaced by *nōn uolēns* 'not willing'), *im-prūdēns* 'not knowing beforehand' (later *nōn prouidēns*). Compare also Av. *an-usaṇt-* 'not wanting', Goth. *un-agands* 'not fearing'.

4. In the oldest languages, negation seems to have been preverbal; Vedic *nákis*, Gk. *oú tis, mḗ tis*, Lat. *nēmo*, OHG *nioman* 'no one', and so on. If the negation has scope over a single word or constituent, it usually directly precedes that constituent. Sentential negation typically directly precedes the verb, as in English. But it could also be moved toward the front of the sentence for emphasis. (Fortson 2004).

NOTE. Moreover, there is evidence for proposing that other particles were placed postverbally in PIE (Delbrück 1897). Delbrück has classified these in a special group, which he labels *particles*. They have been maintained postpositively primarily in frozen expressions: *ē* in Gk. *egṓnē, ge* in *égōge* 'I' (Schwyzer 1939). But they are also frequent in Vedic and early Greek; Delbrück (1897) discusses at length the use of Skt. *gha*, Gk. *ge*, and Skt. *sma*, Gk. *mén*, after pronouns, nouns, particles, and verbs, *cf.* Lat. *nōlo* < *ne volo*, Goth. *nist*< *ni ist*, and also, negative forms of the indefinite pronoun as O.Ind. *mā́-kis, ná-kis*, Lat. *ne-quis*, etc. which may indicate an old initial absolute position, which could be also supported by the development of correlative forms like Lat. *neque*, etc., which combine negation and coordination. Lehmann, on the contrary, believes in an older postposed order, characteristic of OV languages, because of the usually attributed value of emphasis to the initial position of negation, postverbal negation examples (even absolute final position in Hittite and Greek), the old existence of the form ***nei***, as well as innovative forms like Lat. *ne-quis* or Gk. *oú-tis* (Lehmann 1974).

It is therefore safe to assume that in post-LIE times negation was usually preverbal, as in modern Romance languages (*cf.* Fr. *n'est*, Spa. *no es*, etc.), but it could be placed word-initially in emphatic contexts, and it is also found postponed in some archaic lexical or syntactic remains of the older IE languages, as it is found in modern Germanic languages (*cf.* Eng. *is not*, Ger. *ist nicht*, etc.).

5. Prohibitive sentences have a different negative particle, **mē/nē**. The older IE languages seem to have used the unmarked indicative (the so-called 'injunctive') for prohibitions, as some relic forms in Vedic might show. In Tocharian and Hittite, the tense-marked indicative was used. However, the tendency to replace the indicative with the imperative in prohibitions is seen in Greek and Latin, where the imperative became the marker of all commands, being **mē/nē** the modal negative.

For example, following Clackson (2007), while the 'original' situation would have been **cemt**, *he came* (aorist), **ne cemt**, *he did not come* (aorist), **cemje**, *come*, ***mē/nē cemjes***, *stop coming*, this was reinterpreted and the imperative was used instead (hence a negative particle added to the positive utterance), i.e. **mē/nē cemje**, *stop coming*.

NOTE. Clackson (2007) continues: "Note also that several languages have opted to use modal forms (subjunctive and optative) in prohibitions. The most likely explanation for this is that speakers have extended the secondary functions of these modal forms, which include marking requests, wishes and other directive expressions, to embrace negative commands as well."

According to Clackson (2007), some older IE languages show a difference between *inhibitives*, commands to stop doing something that the hearer is engaged in, and *preventatives*, commands or warnings not to do something in the future; that differentiation is found in Indo-Iranian, Tocharian, and apparently in Celtic too. Although the constructions differ, the Indo-Iranian differentiation could have been the original one: the present stem forms inhibitives, while the aorist stem forms preventatives.

10.4. NOMINAL MODIFIERS

10.4.1. ADJECTIVE AND GENITIVE CONSTRUCTIONS

1. Proto-Indo-European attributive adjectives were normally preposed.

Delbrück (1900) summarises the findings for Vedic, Greek, Latin, Lithuanian, and Germanic, giving examples like the following from Vedic: *śvetā́ḥ párvatāḥ* 'white mountains'. Lehmann (1974) adds an example of Hitt. *šuppi watar* 'pure water'.

In marked constructions adjectives might be postposed, as in Ved. *áśvaḥ śvetáḥ* 'a white horse, a gray'.

2. The position of the attributive genitive is the same as that of the attributive adjective. A striking example is given from the Old English legal language (Delbrück 1900): *ōðres mannes hūses dura* 'the door of the house of the other man'.

3. Like the adjective construction, the attributive-genitive construction may have the modifier postposed for marked effect, as is *sómasya* in Skt. *kíṃ nas tátaḥ syād íti? prathamabhakṣsá evá sómasyarā́ jña íti* (lit. what us then it-might-be Ptc. first-enjoyment Ptc. of-soma) 'What might then happen for us? The first enjoyment of [Prince] Soma'. (Delbrück 1878)

NOTE 1. The relatively frequent marked use of the genitive may be the cause for the apparently free position of the genitive in Greek and Latin. The ambivalent order may also have resulted from the change of these languages toward a VO order. But, as Delbrück indicates, the preposed order is well attested in the majority of dialects. This order is also characteristic of Hittite (J. Friedrich 1960).

NOTE 2. In accordance with Lehmann's (1974) views on syntactic structure, the attributive genitive, like the attributive adjective, must be derived from an embedded sentence. The sentence would have a noun phrase equivalent with that in the matrix sentence and would be a predicate nominal sentence. Such independent sentences are attested in the older dialects. Delbrück gives a number of examples, among them: Skt. *aṣṭaú ha vaí putrā́ ádites* (eight Ptc. Ptc. sons of-Aditi) 'Aditi had eight sons'; Skt. *áhar devā́nām ā́sīt* (lit. day of-gods it-was) 'Day belonged to the gods'. These sentences accordingly illustrate that the genitive was used in predicate nominative sentences to convey what Calvert Watkins has labelled its primary syntactic function: the sense "of belonging". When such a sentence was embedded in another with an equivalent NP, the NP was deleted, and the typical genitive construction resulted. Hittite also uses ***s*** as a genitive as well as a nominative marker. For "genitives" like *haššannaššaš* '(one) of his race' can be further inflected, as in the accusative *haššannaš-šan '(to one) of his race'* (J. Friedrich).

4. Fortson (2004): Common to all the older languages was the ability of nouns and their modifiers to be separated by intervening elements, yielding what are called discontinuous or distracted noun phrases (a construction called *hyperbaton* in Greek and Latin grammar): Cuneiform Luv. *alati awienta Wilušati* 'they came from steep Wjlusa' (KBo 4.11:46), Gk. *ándra moi énnepe Moũsa polútropon* 'tell me, Muse, of the resourceful man' *(Odyssey* 1.1), Lat. *magnā cum laude* 'with great praise', Old Irish *Marta for slúaig saithiu* 'on the swarm of the host of March' *(Felire Oengusso,* March 31). Distraction of other types of phrases was common as well. The technical details of distraction are not well understood; in some cases, it is the result of part of a phrase being moved to a position of emphasis or contrast.

10.4.2. COMPOUNDS

1. *Nominal compositum* or nominal composition is the process of putting two or more words together to form another word. The new word, called a compound word, is either a noun or an adjective, and it does not necessarily have the same meaning as its parts.

2. According to their meaning, compounds can be broadly classified in two types (Fortson 2004):

a. Endocentric (or determinative), as *blackbird*, '(a type of) black bird', when the compound is essentially the sum of its parts, and its referent (a type of bird) is one of the compound members itself (usually the second one, as here). Examples include Skt. *Siṃha-puras* 'Lion City' (Singapore), Ger. *Blut-wurst* 'blood sausage'.

b. Exocentric or possessive compounds (usually called *bahuvrihis*, see below), illustrated by Eng. *redthroat*, is more than the sum of its parts and refers to something outside itself: the referent is not a type of throat, but a type of bird possessing a red throat. Examples include O.Ir. *Fer-gus* 'hero-strength = having a hero's strength', Gk. *Aristó-dēmos* 'best people = having the best people'.

It is frequently said that bahuvrihis typically have o-grade of the ablauting syllable of the second compound member. Such is indeed the case in such forms as Gk. *eu-pátōr* (<**su-patōr**) 'having a good father', and Umbrian *du-purs-* (<**dwi-pods**) 'having two feet'. These o-grades are likely to be survivals of old ablauting inflection rather than engendered directly by the process of compounding.

3. In the derivation of compounds special compounding rules apply.

The verbal compounds in a language observe the basic order patterns, For PIE we would expect an older OV order in compounds, as e.g. Skt. *agnídh-* 'priest' < *agni 'fire'* + *idh 'kindle.'*

NOTE. A direct relationship between compounds and basic syntactic patterns is found only when the compounds are primary and productive. After a specific type of compound becomes established in a language, further compounds may be constructed on the basis of analogy, for example Gk. *híppagros 'wild horse'*, in contrast with the standard productive Greek compounds in which the adjectival element precedes the modified, as in *agriókhoiros* 'wild swine' (Risch 1944-1949). Here we will consider the primary and productive kinds of compounds in PIE.

4. Two large classes and other minor types are found:

A. The synthetics (noun+noun), which make up the majority of the PIE compounds:

a. Pure synthetics, i.e. noun+noun.

NOTE. While both members of the compound can be changed without a change in meaning, some rules govern these compounds (Mendoza 1998);

- *phonetic*: there is a preference for a succession of high vowels – low vowels, and for labial or labialised sounds in the second term (Wackernagel 1928).
- *prosodic*: the law of growing members, i.e. the tendency to place the shorter member before the longer one; that rule is followed in *dvāndvā* (copulative compounds of two names in the dual number, *cf.* Skt. *Mitrā-Váruṇā*, 'Mitra and Varuna', *Dyā́vā-pṛ̥thivī* 'sky and earth'), but also concerning paratactic members, *cf.* Gk. *álloi mèn rha theoí te kaì anéres híppokorustaí* (Behagel 1923).
- *semantic*: since Krause (1922) it is believed that the most important, near and logical notions are put in first place; i.e. compounds are subject to the principles of 'importance' and 'sequence' (Bednarczuck 1980).

b. Sinthetics in which the first element is adverbial, i.e. adverb+noun.

B. The bahuvrihis.

c. Adjective + nouns, apparently not so productive in PIE as in its dialects.

d. A small number of additive compounds.

5. The second term of a compound word may be then (Ramat 1993, Adrados–Bernabé–Mendoza 1995-1998):

i) A noun (Gk. *akró-polis* 'high city, citadel')

ii) An adjective (Gk. *theo-eíkelos* 'similar to the gods') or

iii) A noun adapted to the adjectival inflection (Gk. *arguró-toxos* 'silver arc')

NOTE. Sometimes a suffix is added (*cf.* Gk. *en-neá-boios* 'of nine cows'), and the compound noun may have a different gender than the second term (*cf.* Lat. *triuium* 'cross roads', from *trēs* and *uia*).

6. The first term is a pure stem, without distinction of word class, gender or number. It may be an adverb, a numeral (Gk. *trí-llistos* 'supplicated three times', *polú-llistos* 'very supplicated') or a pronoun (*cf.* O.Ind. *tat-puruṣa* 'that man'), as well as a nominal-verbal stem with nominal (Gk. *andra-phónos* 'who kills a man'), adjetival (Gk. *akró-polis*), or verbal function (Gk. *arkhé-kakos* 'who begins the evil'), and also an adjective proper (Gk. *polú-tropos* 'of many resources').

7. Usually, the first term has zero-grade, *cf.* O.Ind. *ṇr-hán*, Gk. *polú-tropos*, Lat. *aui-(caps)*, etc. Common exceptions are stems in ***-e/os***, as Gk. *sakés-palos* 'who shakes the shield' (Gk. *sákos* 'shield'), and some suffixes which are substituted by a lengthening in **-i**, *cf.* Gk. *kudi-áneira* 'who glorifies men' (Gk. *kudrós*), Av. *bərəzi-čaxra-* 'of high wheels' (Av. *bərəzant-*).

In thematic stems, however, the thematic ***-e/o*** appears always, as an ***o*** if noun or adjective (Gk. *akró-polis*), as an ***e*** if verb (Gk. *arkhé-kakos*).

8. The first term usually defines the second, the contrary is rare; the main compound types are:

A. Formed by verbs, *cf.* O.Ind. *ṇr-hán*, Gk. *andra-phónos* (Gk. *andro-* is newer) Lat. *auceps*, O.Sla. *medv-ědĭ* 'honey-eater', *bear*, and also with the second term defining the first, as Gk. *arkhé-kakos*.

B. Nominal determiners (first term defines the second), with first term noun (*cf.* Gk. *mētro-pátōr* 'mother's father', Goth. *þiudan-gardi* 'kingdom'), adjective (*cf.* Gk. *akró-polis*, O.Sla. *dobro-godŭ* 'good time', O.Ir. *find-airgit* 'white plant', Lat. *angi-portus* 'narrow pass'), or numeral (*cf.* Lat. *tri-uium*, from *uia*, Gk. *ámaza* 'chariot frame', from *ázōn*).

C. Adjectival determiners (*tatpuruṣa-* for Indian grammarians), with first term noun (*cf.* Gk. *theo-eíkelos*, Goth. *gasti-gods* 'good for the guests'), adverb (*cf.* O.Ind. *ájñātas*, Gk. *ágnotos* 'unknown', *phroudos* 'who is on its way', from *pró* and *odós*).

D. Possessive compounds (*bahu-vrihi-* 'which has a lot of rice', for Indian grammarians), as in Eng. *barefoot*, '(who goes) with bare feet', with the first term Noun (*cf.* Gk. *arguró-tozos*, O.Sla. *črŭno-vladŭ*, 'of black hair'), adjective (*cf.* Lat. *magn-animus*, 'of great spirit'), adverb (*cf.* O.Ind. *durmanā́s*, GK. *dus-menḗs*, 'wicked').

9. The accent could also distinguish determiners from possessives, as in O.Ind. *rāja-putrás* 'a king's son', from O.Ind. *rajá-putras* 'who has a son as king, king's father', see below.

SYNTHETICS

Synthetics consist of a nominal element preceding a verbal, in their unmarked forms, as in Skt. *agnídh-* 'priest'. As in this compound, the relation of the nominal element to the verbal is that of *target*.

The particular relationship of nominal and verbal elements was determined by the lexical properties of the verb; accordingly, the primary relationship for most PIE verbs was that of *target*. But other nominal categories could also be used with verbs.

Kinds of relationships (Lehmann 1974):

1) The *receptor* relationship, as Skt. *deva-héḍana* 'god-angering', in *mā́ karma devahéḍanam* (lit. not we-do god-angering) 'we will not do anything angering the gods'.

2) The *instrument* or *means* relationship; as Skt. *ádri-jūta* 'stone-speeded', in *rátho ha vām ṛtajā́ ádrijūtaḥ pári dyā́vāprthivī́ yāti sadyáḥ* (lit. chariot Ptc. your born-at-right-time speeded-by-stones about heaven-earth goes in-one-day) 'Your chariot, created at the right time, speeded by stones, goes around heaven and earth in one day'.

3) The *time* relationship; as *ṛta-jā́* 'truly-born', in the example above.

4) The *source* relationship, as Skt. *aṅho-múc* 'distress-delivering', in *bháreshv índraṃ suhávaṃ havāmahe 'ṅhomúcaṃ sukṛ́tam* (lit. in-battles Indra well-called we-call-on freeing-from-trouble doing-well) 'In battles we call on Indra, whom it is well to call, who frees from troubles, who does well'.

5) The *place* relationship, as Skt. *dru-ṣád* 'tree-sitting', in *vér ná druṣác camvòr ā́sadad dhárih* (lit. bird like sitting-in-tree bowls he-has-sat fallow) 'Like a bird sitting in a tree the fallow one has sat down in two bowls'.

6) The *manner* relationship; as, Skt. *īśāna-kŕt* 'ruler-acting', in *ádhā yó víśvā bhúvanābhí majmánā īśānakŕt právayā abhy ávardhata* (lit. here who all worlds-above with-strenght acting-like-a-ruler with-youthful-strength above he-grew) 'Who grew beyond all worlds with his strength, acting like a ruler, having youthful strength'.

These compounds exhibit the various relationships of nominal constituents with verbal elements, as in Skt. *tvā́-datta* '(by-)you-given', in *vidmā́ hí yás te adrivas tvā́-dattaḥ* (lit. we-know Ptc. which your having-the-stones given-by-you) 'For we know your [wealth] given by you, you of the pressing-stones'.

Synthetics attested in the Rigveda accordingly illustrate all the nominal relationships determinable from sentences. Synthetics are frequently comparable to relative constructions, as in the following sentence: *ā́gnír agāmi bhā́rato vṛtrahā́ purucétanaḥ* (lit. to-Agni he-was-approached the-Bharatan Vrtra-killer by-many-seen) 'Agni, the god of the Bharatas, was approached, he who killed Vṛtra, who is seen by many'.

Besides the large number of synthetics of the NV pattern, others are attested with the pattern VN. These are largely names and epithets, such as *púṣṭi-gu*, a name meaning 'one who raises cattle', and *sanád-rayi* 'dispensing riches'.

BAHUVRIHIS

The second large group of PIE compounds, *Bahuvrihis*, are derived in accordance with the sentence pattern expressing possession. This pattern is well known from the Latin *mihi est* construction (Bennett 1914; Brugmann 1911): *nulli est homini perpetuom bonum* 'No man has perpetual blessings'.

NOTE. Lehmann (1974) accounts for the derivation of bahuvrihis, like Lat. *magnanimus* 'great-hearted', assuming that an equational sentence with a noun phrase as subject and a noun in the receptor category indicating possession is embedded with an equivalent noun, as in 'great spirit is to man' = 'the man has great spirit'.

On deletion of the equivalent NP (*homini*) in the embedded sentence, a bahuvrihi compound *magnanimus* 'greathearted' is generated. This pattern of compounding ceased to be primary and productive when the dialects developed verbal patterns for expressing possession, such as Lat. *habeo* 'I have'.

Bahuvrihis may be adjectival in use, or nominal, as in the vocative use of *sūnari* 'having good strength' (made up of *su* 'good' and **xner-* '(magical) strength') in Skt. *víśvasya hí prā́ṇanaṃ jī́vanaṁ tvé, ví yid uchási sūnari* (of-all Ptc. breath life in-you Ptc. when you-shine having-good-strength) 'For the breath and life of everything is in you, when you light up the skies, you who have good strength'. The Greek cognate may illustrate the adjectival use: *phéron d' euḗnora khalkón* (they-bore Ptc. powerful bronze) 'They carried on board the bronze of good strength'. The bahuvrihis are accordingly similar to synthetics in being comparable to relative clauses (Lehmann 1974).

NOTE. Although the bahuvrihis were no longer primary and productive in the later dialects, their pattern remained remarkably persistent, as we may note from the various *philo-* compounds in Greek, such as *philósophos* 'one who holds wisdom dear', *phíloinos* 'one who likes wine', and many more. Apart from the loss of the underlying syntactic pattern, the introduction of different accentual patterns removed the basis for bahuvrihis. As Risch pointed out, Greek *eupátōr* could either be a bahuvrihi 'having a good father' or a tatpurusha 'a noble father'. In the period before the position of the accent was determined by the quantity of final syllables, the bahuvrihi would have had the accent on the prior syllable, like *rā́ja-putra* 'having kings as sons', RV 2.27.7, in contrast with the tatpurusha *rā́ja-putrá* 'king's son', RV 10.40.3. The bahuvrihis in time, then, were far less frequent than tatpurushas, of which only a few are to be posited for Late Indo-European. An example is Gk. *propátōr 'forefather'*. If the disputed etymology of Latin *proprius 'own'* is accepted, **pro-pətrjós 'from the forefathers'*, there is evidence for assuming a PIE etymon;

Wackernagel (1905) derives Sanskrit compounds like *prá-pada* '*tip of foot*' from PIE. Yet the small number of such compounds in the early dialects indicates that they were formed in the late stage of PIE (Risch). Contrary to Pokorny's reconstruction of **pro-pətrjós* is the existence of adverb **proprītim* (<*priH-ti-) '*particularly*', found in Lucretius, which makes it difficult for the haplology to be sustained. A more plausible reconstruction is from verb **prijājō**, from **prijós**, *dear*, with an ancient meaning of '*inalienable possesion*' in Sanskrit, or just '*possesion*' in Latin (see Blanc 2004).

NOTE 2. Dvandvas, such as *índrāviṣ́ṇu* and a few other patterns, like the teens, were not highly productive in PIE, if they are to be assumed at all. Their lack of productiveness may reflect poorly developed coordination constructions in PIE (Lehmann 1969). Besides the expansion of tatpurushas and dvandvas in the dialects, we must note also the use of expanded root forms. Thematic forms of noun stems and derived forms of verbal roots are used, as in Skt. *deva-kṛta* 'made by the gods'. Such extended constituents become more and more prominent and eventually are characteristic elements of compounds, as the connecting vowel **-o-** in Greek and in early Germanic; Gk. *Apolló-dōros* 'gift of Apollo' (an *n-* stem) and Goth. *guma-kunds* 'of male sex' (also an *n-* stem). Yet the relationships between the constituents remain unchanged by such morphological innovations. The large number of tatpurushas in the dialects reflects the prominence of embedded-modifier constructions, as the earlier synthetics and bahuvrihis reflected the embedding of sentences, often to empty noun nodes. As noted above, they accordingly have given us valuable information about PIE sentence types and their internal relationships.

10.4.3. DETERMINERS IN NOMINAL PHRASES

Nouns are generally unaccompanied by modifiers. Demonstratives are infrequent; nouns which might be considered definite have no accompanying determinative marker unless they are to be stressed, in which case the demonstrative precedes. (Lehmann 1974).

The relationship between such demonstratives and accompanying nouns has been assumed to be appositional; it may be preferable to label the relationship a loose one, as of pronoun or noun plus noun, rather than adjective or article plus noun.

In Homer too the "article" is generally an anaphoric pronoun, differing from demonstratives by its lack of deictic meaning referring to location (Munro). Nominal phrases as found in Classical Greek or in later dialects are subsequent developments; the relationship between syntactic elements related by congruence, such as adjectives, or even by case, such as genitives, can often be taken as similar to an appositional relationship (Meillet 1937).

To illustrate nominal phrases, *cf.* Vedic *eṣām marútām* 'of-them of-Maruts'. The nominal phrase which may seem to consist of a demonstrative preceding a noun, *eṣām marútām*, is divided by the end of the line; accordingly *eṣām* must be interpreted as pronominal rather than adjectival.

Virtually any line of Homer might be cited to illustrate the absence of close relationships between the members of nominal phrases; *cf. Odyssey nēûs dé moi hḗd' héstēken ep' agroûnósphi póleos, en liméni Rheíthrōi hupò Nēíōi hulḗenti* 'My ship is berthed yonder in the country away from the city, in a harbor called Rheithron below Neion, which is wooded'. The nouns have no determiners even when, like *nēus*, they are definite; and the modifiers with *liméni* and *Neíoi* seem to be loosely related epithets rather than closely linked descriptive adjectives.

The conclusions about the lack of closely related nominal phrases may be supported by the status of compounds in PIE. The compounds consisting of descriptive adjectives + noun are later; the most productive are reduced verbal rather than nominal constructions. And the bahuvrihis, which indicate a descriptive relationship between the first element and the second, support the conclusion that the relationship is relatively general; *rājá-putra*, for example, means 'having sons who are kings' rather than 'having royal sons'; *gó-vapus* means 'having a shape like a cow', said of rainclouds, for which the epithet denotes the fructifying quality rather than the physical shape. (Lehmann 1974).

Accordingly, closely related nominal expressions are to be assumed only for the dialects, not for PIE. Definiteness was not indicated for nouns. The primary relationship between nominal elements, whether nouns or adjectives, was appositional.

10.4.4. APPOSITION

1. Apposition is traditionally "when paratactically joined forms are grammatically, but not in meaning, equivalent" (Lehmann 1974).

NOTE. Because of the relationship between nouns and modifiers, and also because subjects of verbs were only explicit expressions for the subjective elements in verb forms, Meillet (1937) considered apposition a basic characteristic of Indo-European syntax. Subjects were included only when a specific meaning was to be expressed.

2. A distinction is made between *appositional* and *attributive* (Delbrück); an appositional relationship between two or more words is not indicated by any formal expression, whereas an attributive relationship generally is (Lehmann 1974).

A. Thus the relationships in the following line of the Odyssey are attributive: *arnúmenos hḗn te psukhḗn kaì nóston hetaírōn* lit. 'striving-for his Ptc. life and return of-companions'. The relationship between *hḗn* and *psukhḗn* is indicated by the concordance in endings; that between *nóston* and *hetaírōn* by the genitive.

B. On the other hand the relationship between the two vocatives in the following line is appositional, because there is no mark indicating the relationship: *tôn hamóthen ge, theá, thúgater Diós, eipè kaì hēmîn* 'Tell us of these things, beginning at any point you like, goddess, daughter of Zeus'. Both vocatives can be taken independently, as can any appositional elements.

3. Asyndetic constructions which are not appositive are frequently attested, as Skt. *té vo hṛdé mánase santu yajñā́* 'These sacrifices should be in accordance with your heart, your mind'. Coordinate as well as appositive constructions could thus be without a specific coordinating marker.

4. Comparable to appositional constructions are titles, for, like appositions, the two or more nouns involved refer to one person.

NOTE. In OV languages titles are postposed in contrast with the preposing in VO languages; compare Japanese *Tanaka-san* with *Mr. Middlefield*. The title *'king'* with *Varuna* and similarly in the Odyssey, *Poseidáōni ánakti*, when *ánaks* is used as a title. But, as Lehmann himself admits, even in the early texts, titles often precede names, in keeping with the change toward a VO structure (Lehmann 1974).

5. Appositions normally follow, when nouns and noun groups are contiguous, as in the frequent descriptive epithets of Homer: *Tòn d' ēmeíbet' épeita theá, glaukôpis Athḗnē, 'Him then answered the goddess, owl-eyed Athene'*.

To indicate a marked relationship, however, they may precede (Schwyzer 1950). But the early PIE position is clear from the cognates: Skt. *dyaus pitā*, Gk. *Zeû páter*, Lat. *Jūpiter*.

10.5. MODIFIED FORMS OF PIE SIMPLE SENTENCES

10.5.1. COORDINATION

1. While coordination is prominent in the earliest texts, it is generally implicit.

The oldest surviving texts consist largely of paratactic sentences, often with no connecting particles; *cf.* Lat. *ueni, uidi, uici* 'I came, I saw, I won'; Gk. *ḗiomen, hōs ekéleues, anà drumá .../ heúromen en bḗssēisi tetugména dṓmata kalá* lit. 'we-went as you-commanded, through the-jungle.../we-found in the-valley a-polished palace beautiful'; Hitt. *adueni akueni nu* ^{URU}*ḫattusa iyannaḫe* 'we-eat, we-drink Ptc. from-Hatusa I-go'.

2. New sentences may be introduced with particles, or relationships may be indicated with pronominal elements; but these are fewer than in subsequent texts.

Similar patterns of paratactic sentences are found in Hittite, with no overt marker of coordination or of subordination. According to Friedrich (1960) "purpose and result" clauses are not found in Hittite; coordinate sentences are simply arranged side by side with the particle *nu*, as in the Hittite Laws. Conditional relationships too are found in Hittite with no indication of subordination, *v.i.* §10.5.3.

The arrangement of sentences in sequence is a typical pattern of PIE syntax, whether for hypotactic or for paratactic relationships.

3. Expressions for coordination were used largely for elements within clauses and sentences. When used to link sentences, conjunctions were often accompanied by initial particles indicating the beginning of a new clause and also indicating a variety of possible relationships with neighbouring clauses (Lehmann 1974).

NOTE. Sentence-connecting particles are, however, infrequent in Vedic and relatively infrequent in the earliest Hittite texts; Lehmann (1974) concludes that formal markers of sentence coordination were not mandatory in PIE.

COPULATIVE

The normal coordinating copulative particle in most of the dialects is a reflex of PIE -**qe**.

NOTE. Hittite *-a, -i̯a* is used similarly, as in *attaš annaš a* 'father and mother' (J. Friedrich 1960). This is probably related to Toch. B *yo*.

This is postposed to the second of two conjoined elements; as, Ved. *ágna índras ca* 'o Agni and Indra'; or to both, as Skt. *devā́ś ca ásurās ca*, 'Gods and Asuras', Gk. *patḗr andrõn te theõn te* 'father of men and gods' (Beekes 1995).

Introducing another sentence, as Gothic *fram-uh þamma sokida Peilatus fraletan ina* 'And at this Pilate sought to release him'.

There is an tendency toward a polysyndetic use (Mendoza 1998); *cf.* Gk. *aieì gár toi épis te phílē pólemoi te mákhai te* (lit. always then for-you the-discord -and dear the-wars -and the-battles -and) 'Discord, wars and battles are always dear to you'.

NOTE. With the change in coordinating constructions, new particles were introduced; some of these, for example, Lat. *et*, Goth. *jah*, O.E. *and*, have a generally accepted etymology; others, like Gk. *kaí*, are obscure in etymology. Syntactically the shift in the construction rather than the source of the particles is of primary interest, though, as noted above, the introduction of new markers for the new VO patterns provides welcome lexical evidence of a shift. The syntactic shift also brought with it patterns of coordination reduction *(Ersparung)* which have been well described for some dialects (Behaghel). Such constructions are notable especially in SVO languages, in which sequences with equivalent verbs (S, V, O, Conj., S_2, V_1, O_2) delete the second occurrence of the verb , as M.H.G. *daz einer einez will und ein ander ein anderz*, '*that one one-thing wants and another another*'. Lehmann (1974)

ALTERNATIVE

The disjunctive particle PIE **-wĕ** is also postposed to the second element; Lat. *silua alta Iouis lūcus***ue** *Diānae* 'the high forest of Jupiter **or** the grove of Diana'; or to both, as Skt. *náktaṃ vā dívā vā*, '(either) during the night or during the day', or Gk. *ḕ theòs ēè gunḗ* (with change to prepositional order) 'or goddess or woman'.

NOTE. In Hittite, however, the postposed particles *-ku* ... *-ku* (<-**qe**...-**qe**) 'or', were used with alternative function, always repeated and only as nexus between sentences; for nouns there was the particle *našma*, which stood between nouns rather than after the last. This pattern of conjunction placement came to be increasingly frequent in the dialects; it indicates that the conjunction patterns of VO structure have come to be typical already by PIH.

DISJUNCTIVE

In all older IE languages it was possible to express this function of parataxis by simple repetition of negation, and that was the only possibility in Vedic.

However, a disjunctive compound conjunction **neqe** is found in Indo-Iranian, Anatolian, Italic, Celtic and Germanic. It was not a frozen lexical remain, since the older IE languages analyse the compound as **ne**+**qe**.

NOTE. A compound with the prohibitive negation **mēqe** is also found in Indo-Iranian and Greek, and with the alternative **newe** in Indo-Iranian, Anatolian, Italic and Celtic.

The compound conjunction can appear introducing only the second member of both negatives, or it can be repeated also in the first member to emphasise the parallelism of this type of construction (Mendoza 1998).

Both systems, as well as the simple negation, are attested in the oldest texts.

ADVERSATIVE

No common adversative conjunction seems to be reconstructible for PIE, although dialectally some conjunctions did succeed with this function, probably in a LIE or post-LIE period; as, **at(i)**, **ōd**, etc. (*v.s.* §8.5).

NOTE. That has been related by Bednarczuk (1980) with the postpositive character of paratactic conjunctions of the common language, what configures them as polysyndetic and capable of joining words and sentences, while the adversative function – exclusive of the sentence parataxis – demands prepositive conjunctions and necessarily monosyndetic.

In the older IE languages, the adversative function is expressed by the same postposed copulative conjunction **-qe**, being its adversative use defined by the context, by the semantic relationship between the sentences (Gonda 1954).

10.5.2. COMPLEMENTATION

1. Compound sentences may result from the embedding of nominal modifiers.

NOTE. In VO languages embedded nominal modifiers follow nouns, whereas in OV languages they precede nouns. This observation has led to an understanding of the Hittite and the reconstructed PIE relative constructions. If we follow the standard assumption that in relative constructions a second sentence containing a noun phrase equivalent to a noun phrase in the matrix sentence is embedded in that matrix sentence, we may expect that either sentence may be modified. A sentence may also be embedded with a dummy noun; the verb forms of such embedded sentences are commonly expressed with nominal forms of the verb, variously called infinitives, supines, or participles. In OV languages these, as well as relative constructions, precede the verb of the matrix sentence (Lehmann 1974).

2. An example with participles in the IE languages is Skt. *vásānaḥ* in the last lines of the following strophic hymn: *rúśad vásānaḥ sudṛśīkarūpaḥ* lit. 'brightly dressing-himself beautifully-hued'.

It may also have "a final or consequential sense", as in the following strophic hymn: *tvám indra sravitavā́ apás kaḥ* 'You, O Indra, make the waters to flow'. Also in the poetic texts such infinitives may follow the main verb, as in *ábodhi hótā yajáthāya devā́n* (lit. he-woke-up priest for-sacrificing gods) 'The priest has awakened to sacrifice to the gods' (Lehmann 1974).

NOTE. The postposed order may result from stylistic or poetic rearrangement; yet it is also a reflection of the shift to VO order, a shift which is reflected in the normal position for infinitives in the other IE dialects. In the Brahmanas still, infinitives normally stand directly before the verb, except in interrogative and negative sentences (Delbrück). On the basis of the Brahmanic order we may assume that in PIE nonfinite verbs used as complements to principal verbs preceded them in the sentence. Hittite provides examples of preposed complementary participles and infinitives to support this assumption (J. Friedrich). Participles were used particularly with *har(k)-* 'have' and *eš-* 'be', as in *uerii̯an ešta* 'was mentioned'; the pattern is used to indicate state.

INFINITIVES AND PARTICIPLES

According to Fritz (in Meier-Brügger 2003) in Proto-Indo-European, the existence of participles may safely be asserted. Additionally, infinitive constructions with final dative, accusative of direction, and the locative of destination are presumed to have existed. While infinitives are defined by syntax, the very presence of participles reveals that there were participial constructions in Proto-Indo-European. According to J.L. García Ramón (1997), "[the assertion] of a true Proto-Indo-European infinitive ending in **-sén(i)* is justified," which could be traced to a locative form, which, according to K. Stüber (2000) appears in the case of s-stem abstract nouns with the locative forms ending in **en*.

Infinitives could indicate result, with or without an object (J. Friedrich 1960): *1-aš 1-an kunanna lē šanhanzi* (lit. one one to-kill not he-tries) 'One should not try to kill another'.

Infinitives could be used to express purpose, as in the following example, which pairs an infinitive with a noun (J. Friedrich): *tuk-ma kī uttar ŠÀ-ta šii̯anna išhiull-a ešdu* (lit. to-you-however this word in-heart for-laying instruction-and it-should-be) 'But for you this word should be for taking to heart and for instruction'.

The infinitive could be loosely related to its object, as in examples cited by Friedrich, such as *apāš-ma-mu harkanna šan(a)hta* (lit. "he-however-me for-deteriorating he-sought) 'But he sought to destroy me'.

The complementary infinitive indicates the purpose of the action; as Friedrich points out, it is attached to the verb *šanhta* plus its object *mu* in a construction quite different from that in subsequent dialects.

These uses are parallelled by uses in Vedic, as may be noted in the work of Macdonell (1916), from which some examples are taken in Lehmann (1974). On the basis of such examples in Vedic and in Hittite, he assumes that infinitive constructions were used to indicate a variety of complements in PIE.

Hittite and Sanskrit also provide examples of participles functioning appositionally or as adjectives indicating state (J. Friedrich 1960): *ammuk-u̯ar-an akkantan IQ.BI* (lit. to-me-Ptc.-indicating-quotation-him dying he-described) 'He told me that one had died'.

This pattern had been noted by Delbrück (1900) for the Rigveda, with various examples, as *śiśīhí mā śiśayáṃ tvā śṛṇomi,* 'Strengthen me; I hear that you are strong'. The adjective *śiśayá* 'strengthening' is an adjective derived from the same root as *śiśīhí*. Delbrück also noted that such "appositives" are indicated in Greek by means of clauses. Greek represents for Lehmann accordingly a further stage in the development of the IE languages to a VO order. Yet Greek still maintained preposed participles having the same subject as does the principal verb, as in: *tḕn mèn idṑn gḗthēse*, lit. 'it Ptc. seeing he-rejoiced' (Lehmann 1974).

This pattern permits the use of two verbs with only one indicating mood and person; the nonfinite verb takes these categories from the finite.

Participles were thus used in the older period for a great variety of relationships, though also without indicating some of the verbal categories.

Dependent clauses are more flexible in indicating such relationships, and more precise, especially when complementary participles and infinitives follow the principal verb.

10.5.3. SUBORDINATE CLAUSES

1. As with coordination, subordination could be made without grammatical mark in the older IE languages, hence the context alone decided if it was a subordinate; as in Eng. *the man he called paid the boy* (Lehmann 1974).

So e.g. Hom. Gk. *all' áge nûn epímeinon, <u>arḗia teúkhea duō̄</u>* 'then now wait (until) <u>I dress the weapons of war</u>'; Lat. *fac noscam* 'make me know' (Delbrück 1900).

2. These sentences, with a change in person, mood, or simply eliminating the pause between both sentences, are usually considered the origin of some types of subordinates.

Especially common is this archaic type of paratactic construction in substantive subordinates, i.e. those sentences which take the role of a verbal actor (subject or object), or of a constituent of the nominal sentence. Such archaic forms are found in substantive subordinates expressing thoughts, words, desires or fears, in which these are quoted literally, without change in person, i.e. in the direct syle, proper of a stage of the language previous to the introduction of the indirect style (Rubio 1976).

3. The most extended substantive sentence in the older languages is in fact not the one introduced by conjunctions – which is considered a late development –,

but those whose subordination is introduced by non-finite forms of the verb, like participles and infinitives.

Almost all languages have infinitives and participles functioning as subject or object of the sentence, especially with verbs of will or in nominal sentences. That is found in Hittite, Greek, Latin, Germanic, Slavic, and especially frequent are participles in ***-nt*** (the oldest ones), clearly differentiated from the main clause with the common subordinate+main order.

NOTE. The order subordinate+main seems to have been obligatory in PIE. This has been linked with the lack of subordinates of purpose and result, because in these constructions iconicity demands a postposed order. Precisely conditionals – apparently the first subordinates introduced by conjunctions, see below – have a structure which is necessarily correlative, with a systematic preposed order to the subordinate.

In the attested IE languages that relative order subordinate+main was eventually inverted, which has been linked with a typological change of a language OV into a VO one. At the same time, there was a tendency to place the relative pronoun immediately after the noun to which it refers, all of which is typically found in most IE languages of a late period.

Examples of such subordinate clauses without mark include (Mendoza 1998): Hitt. *MU.KAM-za-wa-ta šer tepawešanza nu-wa BE-LI-NI INA URUḪayaša lē paiši* 'the year having been shortened, (Ptc.) Lord, do not go to Hayasa'; Gk. *kaì prín per thumõi memaṓs Tróessi mákhesthai dè tóte min trìs tósson hélen ménos* lit. 'and before even in-his-soul willing-to against-the-Trojans fight Ptc. then to-him thrice bigger took-him impetus'.

NOTE. According to Mendoza (1998), such examples are usually analysed as absolute constructions (see above §10.1.2). In Hittite, where there are no absolutes, they are interpreted as pure nominal sentences, without *copula*.

But, if the relation between both clauses is inverted, and with it their order, the result is two juxtaposed sentences, the second one (with participle) introduced by *nu* too, but with the personal verb, with an explicit *copula*: Hitt. *man I-NA URUḪayaša paun-pat nu-za MU.KAM-za-wa-ta šer tepawešanza ešta* (lit. ptc. to Hayasa I-would-have-gone ptc. the-year in-which-it-has-been-shortened is) 'I would have gone to Hayasa, but the year got shorter'.

The conclusion is that from these sentences, with the integration of such substantive subordinate constructions into the main clause, come the absolute participle constructions attested in all IE branches but for Anatolian (Holland 1986).

4. A common resource in the older IE languages was to 'transform' finite verbs into nominal sentences, due to the syntactic flexibility of participles. As, for Gk. *hoppóteros dé ke nikḗsēi ... gunaĩká te oíkad' agésthō* 'who wins ... he carries

home the woman', Gk. <u>*tõi*</u> *dé ke* <u>*nikḗsanti*</u> *phílē keklḗsēi ákoitis* '<u>by the one</u> <u>having won</u> you will be called dear wife' (Ramat 1993).

NOTE. So e.g. the performative assertion, a linguistic act of guarantee and compromise, expressed by the syntactic secondary rule of demonstrative in Ved. *ayám te asmi* 'with-that yours I-am', is transformed into a participle clause in the complex *mā́ mā́m imam táva* <u>*sántam*</u> ... *ni gārit* 'that he bolts me not', lit. '<u>being</u> here yours'. The participle reinforces a performative assertion 'With that I promise you, Atri. Do not let Svarbhānu destroy me'. This is the case of the finite verb of existence in another linguistic act, of confessional formula; as, Hitt. *ēšziy=at iyawen=at* 'It is. We did it', which is transformed into *ašān=at iyanun=at* , lit. 'This (is) absent. I did it'. From this syntactic use of Hitt. *ašant-* we can glimpse Lat. *sōns, sontis* 'guilty', the old participle present of verb 'be', *esse*. Ramat (1993).

CONDITIONAL

Of all subordinate clauses introduced by conjunctions, only conditionals seem not to be related to the relative clauses. In fact, they are the only conjunctional subordinate developed in Hittite, well attested since the older texts (introduced by *takku*), and whose conjunction is not derived from the relative (Mendoza 1998).

According to Clackson (2007), a particular marker appears to be used to introduce conditional clauses in at least three different early branches of IE: **-qe**, the connective enclitic (although it also has other functions), both at the word level and, less generally, clause level. The Sanskrit derivative of **-qe**, *ca*, is used in thirty-one passages in the Rig-Veda, the corpus of early Sanskrit hymns, to introduce subordinate conditional or temporal clauses; in all cases the clause with the clitic *ca* stands before the main clause.

Wackernagel (1942) had noticed similar, marginal, uses of the cognates of Sanskrit *ca* to introduce subordinate, and in particular conditional, clauses in Gothic, Latin and Greek. This support for a PIE use of **-qe** to introduce conditional clauses then appeared to be confirmed by Hittite, since the element *-ku* of the conditional particle *takku* 'if', can be derived from **-qe**.

RELATIVE

Indo-Europeanists have long recognised the relationship between the subordinating particles and the stem from which relative pronouns were derived in Indo-Iranian and Greek.

Thus Delbrück has pointed out in detail how the neuter accusative form of PIE **jo-** was the basis of the conjunction **jod** in its various meanings: (1) Temporal, (2) Temporal-Causal, (3) Temporal-Conditional, (4) Purpose. He also recognised the source of conjunctional use in sentences like Skt. <u>*yáj jā́yathās tád áhar*</u> *asya kā́me* *'ṅśóḥ pīyū́ ṣam apibo giriṣṭhā́m,* 'On the day you were born you drank the mountain milk out of desire for the plant' (Lehmann 1974).

Thus, subordinated clauses that are introduced by relative pronouns can perform the function of subject, object, adverbial phrase, appositional phrase, and attribute.

a) In the older IE languages, the relative clause often precedes the main clause (and with it, the antecedent). The relative pronoun or adverb is often paired with a pronominal or adverbial antecedent, yielding what are called correlative structures of the type '*(the one) who ..., he ...*', or '*in the way which ..., in that way...*' (Fortson 2004).

b) The earliest type of subordinate **jo-**, **qi-**/**qo-** clauses must have been the preposed relative constructions; Vedic *yó no dvéṣṭi, ádharah sás padīṣṭa* 'who us hates, down he will-fall'. But elements could be left-detached for topicalisation (see below §10.6.3): *púro yád asya sampinak* (lit. rocks when of-him you-destroyed) 'when you destroyed his rocks'.

NOTE. This conclusion from Vedic receives striking support from Hittite, for in it we find the same syntactic relationship between relative clauses and other subordinate clauses as is found in Vedic, Greek, and other early dialects. But the marker for both types of clauses differs. In Hittite it is based on IE **qid** rather than **jod**; thus, Hittite too uses the relative particle for indicating subordination. The remarkable parallelism between the syntactic constructions, though they have different surface markers, must be ascribed to typological reasons; we assume that Hittite as well as Indo-Aryan and Greek was developing a lexical marker to indicate subordination. As does *yad* in Vedic, Hitt. *kuit* signals a "*loose*" relationship between clauses which must be appropriately interpreted. Lehmann (1974).

As J. Friedrich has stated (1960), *kuit* never stands initially in its clause. Sentences in which it is used are then scarcely more specifically interconnected than are conjoined sentences with no specific relating word, as in examples cited by Friedrich (ibid.): *nu taškupāi nu URU-aš dapii̯anzi išdammašzi* (lit. Ptc. you-shout Ptc. city whole it-hears) 'Now cry out [so that] the whole city hears'. Like this example, both clauses in a *kuit* construction generally are introduced with *nu* (J. Friedrich 1960). We may assume that *kuit* became a subordinating particle when such connections were omitted, as in Friedrich's example. These examples illustrate that both *yád* and *kuit* introduce causal clauses, though they do not contain indications of the origin of this use.

CORRELATIVE

It is therefore generally believed that subordinates originated in relative sentences, as Vedic, Old Irish, Avestan and Old Persian illustrate. Proverbs and maxims are a particularly conservative field in all languages, and even etymologically there are two series which appear especially often in correlatives; namely, **qo-...to-**, and **jo-...to-**.

NOTE. For IE ***qo-..to-***, *cf.* Lat. *cum...tum, qualis...talis, quam...tam*, or Lith. *kàs...tàs, kòks...tàs, kaîp...taîp, kíek...tíek*, etc., and for ***jo-...to-***, Ved. *yás...sá tád, yáthā...táthā, yā́vat...tā́vat*, Gk. *oios...toios, ósos...tósos*, O.Pers. *haya* (a compound from ***so+jo***, with the same inverse compound as Lat. *tamquam*, from two correlatives), etc.

For Haudry this correlative structure is the base for subordination in all Indo-European languages. Proto-Indo-European would therefore show an intermediate syntax between parataxis and hypotaxis, as the correlative structure is between a '*loose'* syntax and a '*locked'* one.

Examples of equivalent old correlative sentences include the following (Watkins 1976, Ramat 1993): Hitt. *nu tarḫzi kuiš nu apāš KA.TAB.ANŠE ēpzi* (lit. Ptc. wins who Ptc. he reins takes) 'Who wins, (he) takes the reins [=takes charge]'; Ved. *sa yo na ujjeṣyati sa pratamaḥ somasya pāsyati* lit. 'he who Ptc. shall-win, he the-first the-soma will-drink'; Ved. *sa yo na ujjeṣyati tasya idam bhaviṣyati* 'he who Ptc. shall-win, of-him this will-be'; Gk. *hós nun orkhéstōn ... atalótata paízei tò tóde k[]n* 'who now of the dancers more sporting plays, of him (is) this [...]'; Gk. *hoppóteros dé ke nikḗsēi ... gunaĩká te oíkad' agésthō* 'who wins ... he carries home the woman'.

RESTRICTIVE AND EXPLICATIVE RELATIVE CLAUSES

Greek, Indo-Iranian, Phrygian, Slavic and Celtic have inherited a stem **jo-** but Anatolian, Latin, Sabellian and Tocharian derive their relative pronouns from a stem **qo-/qi-**. This distribution cuts across other isoglosses separating the IE languages and does not seem to reflect a dialectal difference of the parent language.

Common examples of relative clauses are (Fortson 2004): *yéna imā́ viśvā cyavanā kṛtā́ni ... sá janāsa índraḥ* '(The one) by whom all these things have been made to shake ... that, people, (is) Indra'; Gk. *hós ke theoĩs epipeíthētai, mála t' ékluon autoĩ* 'Whoever obeys the gods, they listen to him as well'.

NOTE. Fritz (in Meier-Brügger 2003) sums up the uses of the **qi-/qo-** and **jo-** relative pronouns, according to Ch. Lehmann. Clackson's (2007) description is very clear: "A crucial element of the recent work has been the difference between restrictive or defining relatives and non-restrictive (also called descriptive or appositional) relatives. Restrictive relatives delimit the head of the relative clause, but non-restrictive relatives merely add extra information about their head. Compare the following sentences:

[a] *The tea that I drank was cold.*

[b] *The tea, which I eventually drank, was cold.*

In [a] the relative defines and restricts the referent, whereas in [b] the relative gives incidental information, and is in effect a separate assertion from that of the main clause. In English, if the relative pronoun is omitted, only a restrictive interpretation is possible. Some English speakers prefer, or are taught, to use that as a relative pronoun in restrictive clauses."

The differentiation of relative clauses introduced by **qo-/qi-** and **jo-** is summarised by Clackson (2007) according to the finds in the older IE languages:

- **qo-/qi-** shows a common use for attributive-restrictive relative clauses in Hittite and Latin, and their most common order is relative-matrix; as, Lat. *pecuniam quis nancitor habeto* 'fortune, who acquire it own it', Goth. *ni weistu hwaz ih sagen thir*, 'you don't know what I say to you'.
- **jo-** is most commonly used in appositive-explicative relative clauses in Vedic Sanskrit and Homeric Greek, with a matrix-relative order of the sentence; as, Ved. *sóma yā́s te mayobhúva ūtáyah sánti dāśúṣe tā́bhir no 'vitā́ bhava* (lit. Soma which from-you benefitious aids are for-the-one-who-worships-you, with-them of-us helper be-you) 'Soma, with your aids, which are benefitious to those who worship you, help us'.

NOTE. Clackson (2007): "Should we then conclude that PIE had two separate relative pronouns, and different clause structures for restrictive and non-restrictive relatives? It is often a fault of Indo-Europeanists to over-reconstruct, and to explain every development of the daughter languages through reconstruction of a richer system in the parent language. (...) However, the reconstruction of two relative pronouns for PIE does fit the attested facts better than any of the other theories on offer."

Very characteristically, if the antecedent is a noun rather than a pronoun, it is placed within the relative clause and in the same case as the relative, sometimes repeated in the main clause. Thus instead of saying *The gods who gave us riches can take them away*, speakers of these languages would have said literally, *Which gods gave us riches, they/those gods can* take them away (Fortson 2004): Hitt. *nu=kan kāš* IM-*aš kuēz wappuwaz danza nu zik wappuaš* ᴰMAḪ *tuēl* ŠU-*TIKA dā* (lit.) 'from which riverbank this clay (has been) taken, o genius of (that) riverbank, take (it) in your hand', i.e. 'o genius of the riverbank from which this clay has been taken ...'; Old Latin *quem agrum eōs uēndere herēdemque sequī licet, is ager uectīgal nei* siet 'the field which (lit., which field) they are allowed to sell and pass to an heir, that field may not be taxable'.

NOTE. As can be seen from some of the examples so far quoted, the relative pronoun did not need to be the first member of its clause. In several of the ancient IE languages, the relative could be preceded at least by a topicalised element, just like the subordinating conjunctions.

The difference between relative clauses introduced by **qo-/qi-** and **jo-** could also be traced back to dependent vs. independent clauses respectively, instead of restrictive vs. explicative.

NOTE. The main fact supporting this would be the position of **qi-** in Hittite sentences, where it is never found at the beginning of the sentence. Hence Hittite doesn't present structures of the type '*qui gladio ferit gladio perit*'; that is the option followed in the Modern Indo-European Syntax (Fernando López-Menchero, 2012).

CIRCUMSTANCE

Lehmann (1974) assumes that the use of Skt. *yád,* Hitt. *kuit*, and other relative particles to express a causal relationship arose from subordination of clauses introduced by them to an ablative; *cf.* Skt. *ácittī yát táva dhármā yuyopimá* lit. 'unknowing that, because your law, order we-have-disturbed', *mā́ nas tásmād énaso deva rīriṣaḥ* (lit. not us because-of-that because-of-sin O-god you-harm) 'Do not harm us, god, because of that sin [that] because unknowingly we have disturbed your law'.

As such relationships with ablatives expressing cause were not specific, more precise particles or conjunctions came to be used. In Sanskrit the ablatival *yasmāt* specifies the meaning 'because'.

Further, *yadā́* and *yátra* specify the meaning 'when'. In Hittite, *mān* came to be used for temporal relationships, possibly after combined use with *kuit; kuitman* expressed a temporal relationship even in Late Hittite, corresponding to 'while, until', though *mahhan* has replaced *mān* (J. Friedrich 1960 gives further details). The conjunction *mān* itself specifies the meanings 'if' and 'although' in standard Hittite. In both Hittite and Vedic then, the "*loose*" relative-construction relationship between subordinate clauses and principal clauses is gradually replaced by special conjunctions for the various types of hypotactic relationship: causal, temporal, conditional, concessive.

Just as the causal relationship developed from an ablative modified by a relative construction, so the temporal and conditional relationship developed from a clause modifying an underlying time node.

10.6. SYNTACTIC CATEGORIES

10.6.1. PARTICLES AS SYNTACTIC MEANS OF EXPRESSION

Noninflected words of various functions were used in indicating relationships between other words in the sentence or between sentences.

1. Some were used for modifying nouns, often indicating the relationships of nouns to verbs. Although these were generally placed after nouns and accordingly were postpositions, they have often been called prepositions by reason of their function rather than their position with regard to nouns (Delbrück).

2. Others were used for modifying verbs, often specifying more precisely the meanings of verbs; these then may be called preverbs.

3. Others, commonly referred to as sentence connectives, were used primarily to indicate the relationships between clauses or sentences (Watkins 1964; Lehmann 1969).

PREPOSITIONS AND POSTPOSITIONS

Prepositions and postpositions were simply independent adverbs in PIE (as in Anatolian, Indo-Iranian and the oldest Greek), and they could appear before or after their objects, although the oldest pattern found is agreed to be postposed. Anatolian and Vedic have almost exclusively postpositions, not prepositions; as, Hitt. *šuḫḫi* *šēr* '*on the roof*', Ved. *jánām̐* *ánu* 'among men'; and also remains in Gk. *toútōn péri* 'about these things', and Lat. mēcum 'with me' (Fortson 2004).

Postpositions in the various dialects are found with specific cases, in accordance with their meanings.

Yet in the Old Hittite texts, the genitive rather than such a specific case is prominent with postpositions derived from nouns, such as *piran* '(in) front' (Neu 1970): *kuiš LUGAL-ua-aš* ***piran*** *ēšzi* (who king's front he-sits) 'whoever sits **before** the king' (Lehmann 1974).

PREVERBS

Rather than having the close relationships to nouns illustrated above, the same adverbs could instead be associated primarily with verbs, often the same particles which were used as postpositions.

Examples include (Fortson 2004) Hitt. *š=aš šarā URU-ya pait* 'and he went up to the city'; Ved. *abhí yó mahinā́ dívaṃ mitró babhū́va saprátháḥ* 'Mitra the renowned who is superior to heaven by his greatness'; O.Av. *frō mā sāstū vahištā* 'let him teach me the best things'; Gk. *edētúos eks éron hénto* 'they put aside desire for food"; O.Lat. *ob uōs sacrō* 'I entreat you' (would be *uōs obsecrō* in Classical Latin); O.Ir. *ad- cruth caín cichither* 'fair form will be seen'.

NOTE. German and Dutch are well known for having many separable affixes. In the sentence Ger. *Ich komme gut zu Hause an* the prefix *an* in the verb *ankommen* is detached. However, in the participle, as in *Er ist angekommen* 'He has arrived', it is not separated. In Dutch, compare *Hij is aangekomen* 'He has arrived', but *Ik kom morgen aan* 'I shall arrive tomorrow'.

English has many phrasal or compound verb forms that act in this way. For example, the adverb (or adverbial particle) *up* in the phrasal verb *to screw up* can appear after the subject ("*things*") in the sentence: *He is always screwing things up.*

Non-personal forms, i.e. nouns and adjectives, form a compound (*karmadharaya*) with the preposition; as O.Ind. *prasādaḥ* 'favour', Lat *subsidium, praesidium*, O.Ind. *apaciti*, Gk. *apotisis* 'reprisal', etc.

Preverbs might occupy various positions:

1. If unmarked, they are placed before the verb, as in the examples above.

2. If marked, they are placed initially in clauses (Watkins 1964); as, Av. *pairi uši vāraiiaϑβəm* 'cover (their) ears', where the preverb (*pairi*, literally 'around') has been fronted to the beginning of the clause for prominence or emphasis.

NOTE. In the course of time the preverbs in unmarked position came to be combined with their verbs, though the identity of each element is long apparent in many of the dialects. Thus, in Modern German the primary accent is still maintained on some verbal roots, and in contrast with cognate nouns the prefix carries weak stress: *ertéilen* 'distribute', *Úrteil* 'judgment'. The steps toward the combination of preverb and verbal root have been described for the dialects, for example, Greek, in which uncombined forms as well as combined forms are attested during the period of our texts.

NOTE. In the attested IE dialects:

- Preverbs which remained uncombined came to be treated as adverbs.

- Combinations of preverbs plus verbs, on the other hand, eventually came to function like unitary elements.

The two different positions of preverbs in early texts led eventually to different word classes.

SENTENCE PARTICLES

Particles were also used to relate sentences and clauses (J. Friedrich 1959):

takku	LÚ.ULÙ^{LU}-	*EL.LUM*	*QA.AZ.ZU*	našma	GÌR-*ŠU*	kuiški
if	man	free	his-hand	or	his-foot	someone

tuu̯arnizzi	nušše	20	GÍN	KUBABBAR	paai
he-breaks	Ptc.-to-him	20	shekels	silver	he-gives

'If anyone breaks the hand or foot of a freeman, then he must give him twenty shekels of silver.'

Particles like the initial word in this example indicate the kind of clause that will follow and have long been well described. The function of particles like *nu* is not, however, equally clear.

NOTE. Dillon and Götze related *nu* and the use of sentence connectives to similar particles in Old Irish (Dillon 1947). Such particles introduce many sentences in Old Irish and have led to compound verb forms in this VSO language. Delbrück had also noted their presence in Vedic (1888).

Since introductory *šu* and *ta* were more frequent than was *nu* in the older Hittite texts, scholars assumed that sentences in IE were regularly introduced by these sentence connectives. And Sturtevant proposed, as etymology for the anaphoric pronoun, combinations of **so**- and **to**- with enclitic pronouns, as in the well-known Hittite sequence *ta-at*, *cf.* IE **tod**, and so on (see Otten and Souček 1969 for the use of such particles in one text).

It is clear that sentence connectives were used in Hittite to indicate continued treatment of a given topic (Raman 1973). It is also found with Hittite relative constructions, a function which may also be ascribed to Vedic *sá* and *tád*.

Compare this syntactic use of particles *sá, nú, tú*, in Ved. *sá hovāc Gargyaḥ* lit. 'Ptc. Ptc.-said Gargyas' *tád u hovācāsuriḥ* lit. 'Ptc. Ptc. Ptc.-said-Asuri'.

NOTE. For Lehmann (1974), since this use may be accounted for through post-PIE influences, sentence connectives may have had a minor role in PIE.

Other particles, like Hitt. *takku* 'if', had their counterparts in PIE, in this case in -**qe**. This is also true for emphatic particles like Skt. *íd*; they were used after nouns as well as imperatives.

10.6.2. MARKED ORDER IN SENTENCES

1. Elements in sentences can be emphasised, by marking; the chief device for such emphasis is initial position, i.e. elements are moved leftward in a process called *fronting*.

2. In unmarked position the preverb directly precedes the verb. Changes in normal order thus provide one of the devices for conveying emphasis.

Other devices have to do with selection, notably particles which are postposed after a marked element.

3. Emphasis can also be indicated by lexical selection.

4. Presumably other modifications might also be made, as in intonation.

The various syntactic devices accordingly provided means to introduce marking in sentences.

10.6.3. TOPICALISATION WITH REFERENCE TO EMPHASIS

1. Like emphasis, topicalisation is carried out by patterns of arrangement, but the arrangement is applied to coequal elements rather than elements which are moved from their normal order.

2. Topicalisation by arrangement is well known in the study of the early IE languages, as in the initial lines of the Homeric poems. The Iliad begins with the noun *mênin* 'wrath', the Odyssey with the noun *ándra* 'man', opening both poems: *mênin áeide* 'Sing of the wrath' and *ándra moi énnepe* 'Tell me of the man'. The very arrangement of *moi* and other enclitics occupying second position in the sentence, in accordance with Wackernagel's law, indicates the use of initial placement among nominal elements for topicalisation (Lehmann 1974).

Examples (Fortson 2004) include Hitt. *ḫalziššai=wa=tta DINGIR*^{MEŠ}*-aš attaš* ^{D}*Kumarbiš* 'Kumarbi, the father of the gods, is calling you'; O.Av. *sraōtū sāsną̊ fšə̄ŋ́hiiō suiie taštō* 'Let the bondsman (?), fashioned for benefit, hear the teachings', Gk. *ménei tò theĩon doulíāi per en phrení* 'The divine (power), even when in bondage, stays in the mind', Lat. *fuimus Trōes, fuit Īlium* 'We were (but no longer are) Trojans, Troy was (but no longer is)'.

Fortson (2004): "Certain verbs, especially existential verbs (e.g., 'there is') but also verbs of speaking and imperatives, preferentially occur clause-initially across all the IE languages: Skt. *āsīd rājā nalo nāma* 'there was a king named Nala' (Mahābhārata 3.53.1), Lat. *est in cōnspectū Tenedos nōtissima fāmā īnsula* 'within sight there is a most famous island, Tenedos' (Vergil, Aeneid 2.21-22), dialectal Old Russian *estĭ gradŭ mežu nobomŭ i zemleju* 'there is a city between heaven and earth' (Novgorod birch bark fragment 10.1)."

NOTE. The fronted element was characteristic of certain situations of the discourse, like the beginning of a text, the kataphora (repetition of a cohesive device at the end of a sentence, like a pronoun catching up an antecedent) and imperatives (Ramat 1993); compare e.g. the beginning of a typical tale 'there was a king', in Skt. *āsīd rājā*, Gk. *ẽske tis ... (w)annássōn*, Lith. *bùvo karãlius*, O.Ir. *boí rí*, Russ. *žyl byl korol'*, etc.

As these passages and many others that might be cited illustrate, the basic sentence patterns could be rearranged by stylistic rules, both for emphasis and for topicalisation. In this way the relatively strict arrangement of simple sentences could be modified to bring about variety and flexibility.

3. Clause-initial position is a place of prominence for any constituent, not only for verbs; as Hitt. *irma=šmaš=kan dāḫḫun* "sickness I have taken away from you". Topicalisation was probably a syntactic process in PIE (Fortson 2004).

4. Interrogatives, as already stated, move forward to the so-called complementiser position, which can also be occupied by other elements, like relative pronouns or subordinating conjunctions. The complementiser position precedes the rest of the clausal positions proper, but this position is preceded by the topicalisation position; if the latter is filled by a topicalised element, the complementiser is no longer clause-initial (Fortson 2004).

Some examples are Hitt. *ammuqq=a kuit ḫarkun* 'And also (that) which I had", Ved. *jātám yád enam apáso ádhārayan* 'when the craftsmen held him, just born', O.Av. *naēnaēstārō yaϑənā vohunąm mahī* 'since we are non-scorners of good things', *fēstō diē sī quid prodēgeris* 'if you splurge a bit on a holiday'.

Topicalisation usually consists of one constituent or subconstituent, but it can be more complex: Ved. *áher yātā́ram* ***kám*** *apaśya indra* '***which*** *avenger of the snake you saw, o Indra*?' *ádevena mánasā* ***yó*** *riṣaṇyáti* '**who** does wrong with impious intention'.

Cf. also from the Archaic Latin of Plautus, the subordinating conjunction *sī* 'if' can be preceded by some or all the other clausal constituents save the verb: *saluos domum sī rediero* 'if I shall have returned home safe', *perfidia et peculātus ex urbe et auāritia sī exulant* 'if betrayal and embezzlement and greed are exiled from the city' (Fortson 2004).

5. According to Clackson (2007), some early IE languages show a clear distinction between the left-detached and fronted position in the sentence. If the sentence includes one of the introductory particles **nu**, **su** or **ta** (sometimes termed S-adverbs), then these normally precede the fronted element.

In these sentences, left-detached nominal phrases are picked up by anaphoric pronouns in the body of the sentence. Enclitics and sentence adverbs are positioned as if the left-detached element was absent; as, Old Irish *maisse doíne ní=s toimled* (lit. glory of-men, not=of-it he-partook) 'The glory of men, he did not partake of it'; Lat. N. Pumidius Q.f. [11 other names omitted] *heisce magistreis Venerus Iouiae muru aedificandum coirauerunt* (lit. Pumidius-nom . . . these-nom magistrates-nom Venus-gen of-Juppiter-gen wall-acc to-be-built-acc supervised) 'Numerius Pumidius son of Quintus [and 11 others], these magistrates supervised the building of a wall to belong to Venus daughter of Juppiter'.

These examples suggest that the pattern of left-detached elements at the beginning of the sentence should probably be allowed as a possible permutation in the parent language.

6. Right-detached nominal phrases are another common feature of old IE languages. Constituents are placed to the right of the verb as in Gk. *oũtin egṑ púmaton édomai metà hoĩs hetároissin* 'none will I eat last among his comrades', where the prepositional clause is to the right of the verb *édomai* 'eat'. The object has been fronted; the reflexive pronoun *hoĩs* 'his own ones' refers to the topic *oũtin* more than the grammatical subject *egṑ*, as a rule (Ramat 1993).

The so-called 'sentence amplification' or 'sentence expansion', consists in appositional phrases and other adjuncts tacked on to the end of a grammatical sentence (Clackson 2007). The first verse of the Rigveda provides an example: *agním īḷe puróhitaṃ yajñáasya devám ṛtvíjam hótāraṃ ratnadhā́tamam* (lit. Agni-acc I-praise domestic-priest-acc sacrifice-gen god-acc sacrificer-acc invoker-acc best-bestower of treasure-acc) 'I praise Agni the domestic priest, god of the sacrifice, sacrificer, invoker, best-bestower of treasure'. All of the necessary grammatical information is contained in the first two words, which could stand on their own as a complete sentence, and the sentence is then expanded by the addition of five noun phrases in apposition to the accusative *agním*.

10.6.4. WACKERNAGEL'S LAW AND THE PLACEMENT OF CLITICS

1. One of the best known features of clausal syntax of older IE languages is the tendency of unstressed clitic particles to appear second in their clause after the first stressed element, a phenomenon discovered by Jacob Wackernagel in the late nineteenth century.

Examples include (Fortson 2004) Hitt. *kiēll=a parnaš ēšḫar papratar QATAMMA pattenuddu* 'Of this house too may it likewise drive out the bloodshed (and) uncleanliness'; Mycenaean Greek *da-mo=de=mi pa-si ko-to-na-o ke-ke-me-na-o o-na-to e-ke-e* (lit. people-NOM.=conn=she-ACC. say plot-GEN. communal-GEN. use-ACC. have-INFIN.) 'But the people say that she has the use of the communal plot'; Vedic *ā́ tvā mantrāḥ kavisastā vahantu* 'Let the spells recited by the poets lead you hither'; Greek *ẽmos d' ērigéneia phánē rhododáktulos Ēṓs* 'but when early-born, rosy-fingered Dawn appeared', Lat. *tū autem in neruō iam iacēbis* 'But you will soon be lying in custody, Gothic *fram-uh þamma sokida Peilatus fraletan ina* 'And at this Pilate sought to release him'.

NOTE. Sometimes, however, one of these clitics appears as the third or fourth word in its clause. Recent research, especially by the American linguist Mark Hale, has shown that Wackernagel's Law actually involves several processes that usually, but not always, conspire to place unstressed particles in second position in the clause. His discoveries have explained the exceptions to a strict formulation of the law (Fortson 2004).

2. Three types of postpositive clitics (and clitic-positioning rules) can be distinguished (Fortson 2004):

"a. *Word-level* clitics modify or limit a single word or constituent, and are placed directly after the word or the first element of the constituent. Such clitics tend to have the function of emphasizing the word to which they are attached, or setting it in some kind of contrastive relief or focus (the clitic is boldfaced): Hitt. *nu=wa=za apun=**pat** eši* 'occupy **only** that (land)', Vedic *pracyāváyanto ácyutā **cid*** 'the ones who move **even** unmovable things'.

If the word that such a particle modifies is first in its clause, then the particle appears (coincidentally) second in its clause: Ved. *sthirā́ **cid** ánnāi dayate ví jámbhaiḥ* '**even** tough food he cuts apart with his teeth' (Rig Veda 4.7.10), Lat. hoc **quoque** maleficium 'this crime **too**'.

Such particles, when modifying a phrase, can often come second in the phrase, as in Gk. *én **ge** taĩs Thē̃bais* 'in all of Thebes **indeed**'.

NOTE. Some clitics, such as the descendants of PIE **-qe**, *and*, can act as word-level clitics as well as sentence connectors.

b. *Sentence-connective* clitics conjoin or disjoin clauses or sub-clausal constituents. Examples of these clitics are PIE **-qe**, *and*, and **-we**, *or*. They are attached to the first word of the constituent or clause being conjoined or disjoined, whether that is a single word (Ved. *ágna índras* ***ca*** 'o Agni **and** *Indra*'), a phrase (Lat. *silua alta Iouis lūcus**ue** Diānae* 'the high forest of Jupiter **or** *the grove of Diana*'), or a clause (Old Avestan *yå̄* ***zī*** *å̄ŋharə̄ yå̄scā hənṭī yå̄scā mazdā buuaiṇtī* '**indeed** (those) who are and who will be, o Mazda').

NOTE. A more complicated example is explained by Clackson (2007) from "Ved. *utá vā yó no marcáyād ánāgasaḥ* (lit. and part rel-NOM. us-ACC. harm-OPT. innocent-ACC.-Pl.) 'Or also who would harm innocent us...' There are two enclitics, the disjunctive particle *vā*, which follows the left-detached slot, and the personal pronoun *nas* following the relative pronoun, which occupies the 'front' slot (the pronoun *nas* appears as *no* by a process of sandhi).

It should be noted that the position of the particle *vā*, which has scope over the whole sentence following the left-detached element, is exactly paralleled by the behaviour of connectives and adverbs with scope over the sentence in Greek, which stand immediately after the left-detached element. Hale (1987a and 1987b) collected evidence for second-position enclitics in Indo-Iranian and showed that, in general, enclitics with scope over the sentence and connectives occurred after left-detached elements, which he refers to as the *topic* position, whereas enclitic pronouns were placed after the fronted element. Hale claims that the behaviour of these two different sets of enclitics reflects an inherited difference between the two sentence positions."

c. *Sentential* clitics are clitics whose scope is a whole clause or sentence. These include the unstressed personal pronouns as well as a variety of sentential adverbs that serve expressive functions and are often untranslatable into English. They are positioned in various ways. Some are placed after the first stressed word in a sentence and any emphatic or sentence-connective clitics associated with that word, while others (called "special clitics" in the technical literature) are positioned after a particular syntactic structural position in the clause. If the first word in a sentence is a proclitic, that is, an unstressed word that attaches phonologically to a following stressed word, the sentential clitic will of course not come directly after it, as in Gk. *eks hēméōn* ***gár*** *phāsi kák' émmenai* '**for** they say that bad things are from us', where the proclitic *eks* 'from' is not a proper phonological host for the clitic *gár*.

Sentential clitics occur not infrequently in strings or chains: Ved. ***ná*** *vā́ u etán mriyase* 'indeed you do **not** die thereby'; Gk. ***ẽ*** *rhá nú moí ti píthoio* 'may you **indeed** now trust me somewhat'. In Vedic ***utá vā*** *yó no marcáyād ánāgasaḥ* '**or also** who would do wrong to us the innocents', where the pronominal clitic *nas (no)* 'us' is in the second position before the topicalized part, while the disjunctive clitic *vā*, PIE **-wĕ**, (and *ca*, PIE **-qe**) take the second position within the topicalized part."

3. There are so-called "preferential hosts", which are fronted rather than detached, and which are not followed by enclitics in second position, which is apparently a persistent exception to Wackernagel's Law in languages like Sanskrit, Greek or Latin. Adams (1994) explained it this way:

"Unemphatic pronouns in Classical Latin prose, far from always being placed mechanically in the second position of their colon, are often attracted to particular types of hosts, namely antithetical terms, demonstratives / deictics, adjectives of quantity and size, intensifiers, negatives, temporal adverbs and imperatives. I have suggested that what these hosts have in common is their focused character, and have accordingly argued that enclitic pronouns had tendency to gravitate towards focused constituents. The prominent constituent serving as a host may be at the head of its colon, in which case the clitic will indeed be second, in apparent conformity with Wackernagel's law. But often the host is in the second or a later position, thereby entailing a place later than second for the pronoun."

According to Clackson (2007), we should also include relative and interrogative pronouns in this list of preferential hosts for enclitics. "Adams' findings for Latin also appear to apply well to cases of enclitic pronouns which do not follow Wackernagel's Law (or even Hale's modifications of it) in Vedic Sanskrit. So for example in Vedic *ágnīṣomā yó adyá vām / idáṃ vácaḥ saparyáti* (lit. Agni-and-Soma-VOC., rel-NOM. today you-two-DAT. this-ACC. speech-ACC. he-praises) 'Agni and Soma! The one who today hymns you this praise . . .' Note the placement of enclitic pronoun *vām*, which is unexplainable in terms of 'second position', but can be explained if we consider the temporal adverb *adyá* 'today' as a preferential host.

In other languages too there is evidence for breaches of Wackernagel's Law, and for the placement of pronominal enclitics after items identified by Adams as preferential hosts. Consider the Greek sentence taken from Krisch (1990) and used by him to support Hale's arguments: Gk. *autàr egṓ theós eimi, diamperès hḗ* ***se*** *phulássō* (lit. conn I-NOM. god-NOM. I-am, thoroughly who-NOM. you-ACC. I-protect) 'But I am a goddess, the one who protects **you** steadfastly'. Here the enclitic *se* follows the relative pronoun *hḗ*, which comes second in the clause after the emphatically placed adverb diamperés. The relative here can easily be seen as a preferential host, the focussed element in its clause."

NOTE. Clackson (2007) summarises the situation by establishing that while in Hittite no enclitics are allowed after left-detached elements, or delayed after fronted element, in Sanskrit, Greek and Latin sentence enclitics can stand after left-detached elements, and pronominal enclitics may be delayed, which may therefore reflect the evolution from PIH into Late Indo-European syntax.

10.7. PHRASE AND SENTENCE PROSODY

1. On the so-called "phonology-syntax interface", Fortson (2004): "Words belonging to the same constituent that start out as contiguous in the deep structure and stay contiguous throughout the derivation will tend to be grouped together as a single phonological unit, whereas words that only become contiguous through certain kinds of movement sometimes do not. (...) For example, in Greek, clitics normally receive no accent, but if two or more occur in a string, all but the last one get accented, as in *ei mḗ tís me theō̃n* 'if no one of the gods me ...'. However, in a sequence like *doulíāi per en phrení* 'even in bondage in the mind', there are two clitics in a row but the first is not accented. The reason is that *per* 'even' emphasizes *doulíāi* 'in bondage' and is phonologically attached to it, while *en* 'in' is a preposition that governs *phrení* 'the mind' and is proclitic to that word. The two resultant clitic groups [*doulíāi per*] and [*en phrení*] form two separate prosodic groups with what is called a prosodic boundary between them. (A prosodic boundary, incidentally, is not generally audible as a pause or other break). We conclude that the rule placing an accent on the first of two successive clitics applies only if the two clitics belong to the same clitic group."

2. According to Fortson (2004), noun phrases consisting of a bare noun are much more likely to enter into certain kinds of clitic groups than are noun phrases where the noun is modified by another element. In punctuated Greek inscriptions, interpuncts do not ordinarily separate a definite article from a following noun; but an interpunct is present if the article is followed by a noun modified by another element, indicating a stronger prosodic break between the two.

In Homer, there is a different behaviour of prepositional phrases vs. the positioning of the sentence-connecting conjunction *dé*, an enclitic that normally occurs second in its clause. If the clause begins with a prepositional phrase consisting simply of a preposition plus bare noun, the clitic will follow the whole phrase (e.g. *eks pántōn dé* 'and of all'...), whereas if the clause begins with a more complex phrase consisting of a preposition followed by an adjective-noun phrase, the clitic will come in between the preposition and the rest of the phrase (e.g. *dià* *dè* *khróa kalón* 'and into the fair flesh'...). Therefore, *eks pánton* is prosodically cohesive enough to function as a single word for the purposes of clitic placement, while *dià khróa kalón* is not.

A similar phenomenon is found in the Old High German of Notker Labeo: a definite article is written without an accent when preceding a simple noun phrase (e.g. *taz héiza fíur* 'the hot fire'), indicating clisis and destressing of the article, but is written with an accent when preceding more complex noun phrases (e.g *díe uuîlsalda állero búrgô* 'the fortune of all cities').

3. Through the study of rules and behaviour of poetic meters (metrics), another rule appears (Fortson 2004): "In certain Greek and Roman meters, for example, there is a rule that a sequence of two light syllables in particular verse-positions must belong to the same word. The rule, though, has an interesting exception: a word-break between the two syllables is allowed when one of them belongs to a proclitic (as in the sequence *ut opinione* 'that in [his] opinion'). This means that the prosodic group consisting of proclitic plus word was tighter than that consisting of two full-content words – tight enough to behave, for the purposes of the poetic meter, as though there were no word-division."

10.8. POETRY

1. In the oldest poetry, some common etymologically related Indo-European *formulae* have been reconstructed; as, **klewos n̥dhchitom**, *immortal fame* (*cf.* Skt. *ákṣitam śrávas*, Gk. *kléos áphthiton*, where the Skt. form is deemed older); **mega kléwos**, *big fame*, **kléwesa nerōm** (<*$klewesh_2$ $h_2$nróm*), *famous deeds of men, heroes* (*cf.* Gk. *kléa andrōn*, Ved. *śrávas nr̥ṇā́m*); **wesu klewos**, *good fame* (*cf.* Av. *vohu sravah*, O.Ir. *fo chlú*). The sun was called 'the wheel of the sun', **sā́weljosjo qeqlos**, *cf.* Skt. *sū́ryasya cakrás*, *zaranii.caxra-.*, (from PII ***súwarjasja ḳaklas***, see Lubotsky's Indo-Aryan inherited lexicon, IEED, n.d.), Gk. *hēlíou kúklos* (<PGk ***sā́weljohjo quqlos***), O.Ice. *sunnu hvél*, O.E. *sunnan hweogul*.

NOTE. Also, the concept "sun chariot" – a mythological representation of the sun riding in a chariot – is typically Indo-European, corresponding with the Indo-European expansion after the domestication of the horse and the use of wheels. Examples include the Trundholm sun chariot of the Nordic deity, *Sól*, drawn by Arvak and Alsvid (see the cover image); Greek *Helios* riding in a chariot, *Sol Invictus* depicted riding a quadriga on the reverse of a Roman coin, and Vedic *Surya* riding in a chariot drawn by seven horses.

Epithets and adjectives pertaining to the gods might also be found (Beekes 1995); as, **dōtōr weswō̆m**, *those who give goods, riches* (*cf.* Skt. *dātā́ vásūnām*, Av. *dāta vaŋhvąm*, Gk. *dōtēres eā́ōn*), from **wesus**, *riches, goods*, from the same root as **ēsús**, *good*.

Other formulae are not etymologically related, but still deemed of PIE origin; as, Skt. *pr̥thú śrávas*, Gk. *kléos eurú*, 'broad fame'; or a common name for the sun Skt. *spáśam víśvasya jágatas* 'he who spies upon the whole world' (lit. 'the moving one', or 'the living beings'), similar to Gk. *theōn skópon ēde' kai' andrōn* 'he who spies upon gods and men' (Beekes 1995, Clackson 2007).

It is possible to reconstruct formulae from a nexus of correlations, where no single language preserves the complete formula (Clackson 2007). Watkins reconstructs the formula **pālāje wīrṓs pékewaqe** (<**peh*$_2$- **wīro*- **peku*-), *protect men and livestock*, from the correspondence of (etymologically related words underlined) Skt. *trā́yantām asmín grā́me / gā́m áśvam púruṣam paśúm* lit. 'protect in-this village cow, horse, man, (and) flock-animal' Av. *ϑrāϑrāi pasuuå vīraiiå* lit. 'for protection of-cattle (and) of-men', Lat. *pāstōrēs pecuaque salua seruāssīs* lit. 'shepherds farm-animals-and may-you-preserve', Umb. *nerf arsmo uiro pequo castruo frif salua seritu* 'magistrates ordinances men cattle fields fruit safe let-him-preserve' (Clackson 2007).

2. The metrical structure of Indo-European poetic language was reconstructed by Meillet, although his attribution of the Indo-Greek system to the parent language is not widely accepted today. The oldest Indian and Greek poems were based on a prosodic structure of alternating long and short syllables [see above §2.4.]:

Beekes (1995): "At the end of the line (the cadence) this alternation was strictly regulated, whereas it was free at the beginning. Both the Indic and the Greek systems used the caesura (word-end at a fixed place in the line at a syntactically significant break); in both systems, too, a line had a fixed number of syllables, but a line could also have a variant with a syllable less (catalexis). [Meillet] saw an exact similarity between the eleven syllable line used by the Greek poetess Sappho and the *triṣṭubh* of the Rigveda (¯ long, ˘ short, *x* long or short, | caesura; *a* begins the cadence);

triṣṭubh x x x x | x ˘ ˘, ¯ ˘ ¯ x

Sappho ¯ ˘ ¯ x | ¯ ˘ ˘ ¯ ˘ ¯ x

Meillet's theory was further developed by Roman Jakobson, who believed that the oldest Slavic metric system was comparable to the one Meillet described, and derived from an Indo-European decasyllabic line. A similar continuation could be seen in a verse-tipe utilized in Old Irish."

It is probable then that the Proto-Indo-European verse consisted of a fixed number of syllables, as was the case with Avestan. Longer lines would have contained a *caesura* (division between phrases).

Beekes (1995) takes as example of PIE poetry a stanza from a hymn of Zarathustra in Gatha-Avestan (Yasna 44.4), with a phonetic transcription: The line consists of four plus seven syllables (with a caesura after the fourth syllable):

Tat θvā pr̥sā	*r̥š mai vauca, Ahura:*
Kas-nā dr̥ta	*zam ca adah nabās ca*
avapastaiš,	*kah apah urvarās ca?*
Kah vaʔatāi	*vanmabyas ca yaugi āsuu?*
Kas-nā vahauš,	*Mazdā, dāmiš manahah?*

This I ask Thee,	tell me truthfully, O Lord:
Who has upheld	the earth below and heavens [above]
from falling down	who the waters and the plants?
Who to the wind	and the clouds has yoked the swift [horses]?
Who, Wise One, is	the founder of Good Thinking?

Beekes (1995) continues: "It is probable that this kind of song is of Indo-European origin, for we find a parallel to it in the Edda (Alvíssmál 15):

Segðu mér, Alvíss,	*–ǫll of rǫc fira*
voromc dvergr, et vitir –	
hvé sú sól heitir,	*er siá alda synir,*
heimi hveriom í.	

Tell me this, Alwis	–of everything in the world
I think, dwarf, that thou knowest–	
What the sun is called,	the sun which people see,
by all creatures of the world.	

In the answer the sun is referred to, among other things, as a 'wheel', *hvél* [see above]. The Germanic verse here is stress verse, and is not related in this respect to Indo-European poetry."

10.9. NAMES OF PERSONS

4.8.1. The use of two-word compounds for personal names was common in PIE; as, **Suklewos**, *of good fame*, with cognates found in poetic diction, *cf.* Gk. *Eukleḗs*, and Skt. *Suśráva-*, or Illyr. *Vescleves-*.

NOTE. The use of two-word compound words for personal names is common in IE languages (see above §10.4.2). They are found e.g. in Ger. *Alf-red* 'elf-counsel', O.H.G. *Hlude-rīch* 'rich in glory', O.Eng. *God-gifu* 'gift of God' (Eng. *Godiva*), Gaul. *Orgeto-rix* 'king who harms', Gaul. *Dumno-rix* 'king of the world', Gaul. *Epo-pennus* 'horse's head', O.Ir. *Cin-néide* (Eng. *Kennedy*) 'ugly head', O.Ind. *Asva-ghosa* 'tamer of horses', O.Ind. *Asvá-medhas* 'who has done the horse sacrifice', O.Pers. *Xša-yāršā* (Gk. *Xérxēs*) 'ruler of heroes', O.Pers. *Arta-xšacā* 'whose reign is through truth/law', Gk. *Sō-krátēs* 'good ruler', Gk. *Mene-ptólemos* 'who faces war', Gk. *Hipp-archus* 'horse master', Gk. *Cleo-patra*, *Pátro-klos* 'from famous lineage', Gk. *Arkhé-laos* 'who governs the people', O.Sla. *Bogu-milŭ* 'loved by god', Sla. *Vladi-mir* 'peaceful ruler', from *volodi-mirom* 'possess the world'; etc. Individual names may further be modified through the use of suffixes to form hypocorisms.

4.8.2. Other area in which it is suspected the retention of ancient Proto-Indo-European personal names is the use of animal names or numerals, composed of one stem; as **Wl̥qos**, *wolf*, *cf.* O.Ir. *Olc*, O.Eng. *Wulf*, Gk. *Lukos*, Skt. *Vŕka*; or, **Qétwr̥tos**, *fourth*, *cf.* Lat. *Quārta*, Lith. *Keturai*, Russ. *Četvertoj*, Gk. *Tetartíōn*.

NOTE. The word for 'name' and possible Indo-European names can be found in Beekes (1987), Markey (1981), Pinault (1982), Schmitt (1973), and Watkins (1970).

4.8.3. Further, the syntactical indication of the father's name also dates from Proto-Indo-European, whether by adding the name of the father in the genitive, in the sense of 'son of X', or by adding a possessive adjective that is derived from the name of the father.

NOTE. An example of the former is *Hadubrand Heribrandes suno*; an example of the later is Myc. *a-re-ku-tu-ru-wo e-te-wo-ke-re-we-i-jo*, i.e. *Alektruwōn Etewoklewehijos* 'Alektruwōn, son of Etewoklewēs', or Russ. *Nikolaj Sergejevich*. Patronymics ending in *-ios* (later *-ius*) led to what is called the nomine gentile in Rome, *cf. Gaius Iulius Caesar* with *Gaius* = *praenomen* < individual name, *Iulius* = *nomen gentile* < patronymic and *Caesar* = *cognomen*.

4.8.4. When considering the giving of names to individuals, one departs generally from the basis of the free men.

Whereas the man is addressed using the individual name, a simple 'oh woman' suffices in the case of woman. "The woman is treated more as a typus, the man as an individual". Wackernagel (1969) makes clear that the same forms of address were adopted for interactions with the gods.

According to Meier-Brügger (2003), to say that the Indo-Europeans were not very different from the Romans and Greeks would not likely be too far from the mark. In Rome, women generally carried only the nomen gentile, *cf. Cornelia*, *Julia*, etc. In the case of the Greeks, most names of women are simply feminine forms of masculine names of individuals, e.g. Myc. *a-re-ka-sa-da-ra*, i.e *Aleksandrā* (corresponding to *Aleks-anōr* 'who fights off men'), Hom. *Andromákhē*, from *Andrómakhos* 'who fights with men', etc.

PART IV

TEXTS & DICTIONARY

ETYMOLOGY

By Fernando López-Menchero

APPENDIX I: INDO-EUROPEAN IN USE

I.1. KOMTLOQJOM (CONVERSATION)

Common expressions in Indo-European include:

English	**Eurōpājóm**
hello!	**alā! / gheuse!**
dear Peter:	**qeime Petre/ qīmé Petre:**
welcome	**crātós / sucm̥tós tū**
good day	**latom ēsúm**
good morning	**wēsrom ēsúm**
good afternoon / evening	**wesprom ēsúm**
good night	**noqtim ēsúm**
how are you?	**qotā wl̥ḗjesi?**
I am fine	**wl̥ējō sū**
Who are you?	**qis essi?/ qis tū?**
Whose (son) are you?	**qesjo essi?/ qesjo tū?**
what is your name?	**qota kluwḗjesi?** lit. 'how are you heard?'
what is your name?	**qid esti tebhei nōmn̥?**
my name is Peter	**kluwējō Pertos** lit. 'I am heard Peter'
my name is Peter	**meghei Petros nōmn̥**
pleased to meet you	**gaudhējō tewe gnōtim**
please	**chedhjō** lit. 'I ask you'
thanks	**méitimons / moitmom**
thanks (I give you)	**prijēsna / prósēdjom (tebhei agō)**
I thank you	**prijējō tewom**
you are welcome, sir	**esti sū, potei**
excuse me	**n̥gnōdhi**
sorry/pardon me	**parke**
I am sorry	**kesdō**
don't worry	**mē koisāje**

good bye, darling	**sḷwḗj [sḷwēje], prijótəma**
good luck	**kobom ēsúm**
yes	**dā / jāi / ne-(ghi)**
indeed	**nem-pe / ita tod**
no	**nē / nei**
alright	**tagtéī**
attention	**probhoudhos**
where is the door	**qodhei dhworis?**
here is what I asked	**kei esti jod pṛkóm**
what is this?	**qid (esti) tod?**
this is food	**pitús tod (esti)**
what time is it?	**Qā-i esti daitis?**
it is true	**wērom tod**
very good / the best	**bhódistom / bhódsṃom**
is everything alright?	**solwā sū́ (ágontor)?**
how old are you?	**qótobhos átnobhos tū?**
I am ten years old	**dekṃ gnātós esmi** lit. 'ten born I am'
do you speak European?	**bhəsoi an Eurōpājóm?**
I speak a little	**páukolom bhəmoi**
I don't understand you	**nē tewom peumi**
tell me what you think	**seqe moi qid kṇsḗjēsi**
I don't know	**nē woida**
shut up	**takḗj [takēje] / takḗjete**
sit down	**sisde** (sg.) / **sísdete** (pl.)
come here	**cemj [cəmje] kom-ke**
I'm going right now	**nū ghenghō kom**
what do you do or study?	**qóterom ghléndhesi an drā́jesi?**
are they tired?	**An/ nom/ qid ləgḗjonti?**
are they married?	**An/ nom/ qid kom jugḗr/jugrór?**
I love women	**lubhējō pelū dhḗmonāns / cenāns**

write here your address	**deikom skreibhe kei tewe**
I live in the Main Street	**Stoighei Magnéi ceiwō / trebhō**
Lucrecia and I are friends	**Lukretjā egṓqe ámeikes smes / ámeike swes**
the cat mews in the garden	**kattā ghortei mijaluti**
the dog bites the cat	**kattām mordḗjeti kwōn**
the woman walks with the cat	**kattā dhḗmonā alā́jetor**
I see the head of the cat	**kattās dr̥kō ghebhlām**
Where is the train?	**qodhei esti douknom?**
the train is here	**douknom (esti) kei**
I want to eat fish	**welmi piskim ghostum**
do you want to sleep with me?	**welsi mojo sweptum?**
yes, I wish for it	**jāi, moksi gherijāi**
no, you stink / smell bad	**nē, smérdesi / bhrḗgjesi dus**
it is hot!	**qām kalḗjeti!** lit. *how hot is it!*
it is cold!	**qām srīgḗjeti!** lit. *how cold is it!*
I go swimming to the lake everyday	**lakum eimi dhochei snātum qāqei**
can I smoke?	**moghō (an) smeughtum?**
may I smoke?	**móghnijom meghei an smeughtum (esti)? / esti moi smeughtum?**
smoking prohibited	**smeughtum wetānóm**
happy new year	**ghoilom newom atnom**
I agree with everything that you explained me yesterday in your mail	**solwei mənjō kom, jod dhghjéstenei bhéresi dewtlei peri**
I thank you for the interest that you always have to carry on	**méndhesi prijejō te, jobhi áiwesi prōd steightum awḗjēsi**

NOTE. About the sentence “*is it possible to smoke?*”, constructed with the verb **esti**, compare Lat. *est* in Ovid (*Metamorphoses* Book III, 479) *quod tangere non est*, “*as it is not possible to touch*”; also Virgil *est cernere*, “*it can be seen*”; also, for Gk. *estì(n)*, “*it is possible*”, compare Lucian (*The Parliament of the Gods*, 12) Ἔστιν, ὦ Ἑρμῆ, “*is it possible, Hermes*”.

I.2. HORATJOSJO KANMṆ (*HORATII CARMINVM*)

Liber primus – XIV. The translation tries to respect the original Asclepiad metrical pattern.

NOTE. It takes into account the information on <http://e-spacio.uned.es/fez/eserv.php?pid=bibliuned:Epos-4B3E2DFB-2CD0-30D4-D45C-87D42540B962&dsID=PDF>.

Eurōpājóm

Ō nāu, an mari ā́isonti te prōd ati
Neuwolmōs? qid agēs? Isri ghṇde stipúm
Kopnom; dṛknija nē twoi
Rēsplighstós nocós tewe
Bhod masdōs érinōs ā́bhrikotwoisotā
Ádtempnāsqe kropā́s?; todper ṇwerwonās
Moghsēnt edli kareinās
Per teutum dhúnijom chorom
Pontom? Sekla ghi nē senti tebhei sḷwa
Nē deiwons itim ámghessi gháwēsi tū
Dhanwos dā genos atlā
Loukognā́ eti pontikā́
Gentim nōmṇqe morknóm tewe sei bhledēs
Nawtās bhéidheti nē qrumnapikēbhi qid
Bhīlús. Wentowojom tod
An tū nē séqesoi, kawḗi
Prīsnim jā bhudhis oghlos cərús bhūs meghei
Nū ghoidhos prijakoisāqe ka leghwa nē
Leukā́ns énteri ghustéi
Leinois plākoní Qékladṇs

NOTE. The form **dhanwos** has been reconstructed according to the Germanic form for convenience in metrics, instead of an older common **dhanus** (found in Old Indian and Hittite).

Latin (original)	English
O navis, referent in mare te novi	O luckless bark! new waves will force you back
Fluctus: o quid agis? fortiter occupa	To sea. O, haste to make the haven yours!
Portum: nonne vides, ut	E'en now, a helpless wrack,
Nudum remigio latus,	You drift, despoil'd of oars;
Et malus celeri saucius Africo,	The Afric gale has dealt your mast a wound;
Antennaeque gemant? ac sine funibus	Your sailyards groan, nor can your keel sustain,
Vix durare carinae	Till lash'd with cables round,
Possint imperiosius	A more imperious main.
Aequor? non tibi sunt integra lintea:	Your canvass hangs in ribbons, rent and torn;
Non Di, quos iterum pressa voces malo.	No gods are left to pray to in fresh need.
Quamvis Pontica pinnus,	A pine of Pontus born
Silvae filia nobilis.	Of noble forest breed,
Jactes et genus, et nomen inutile:	You boast your name and lineage—madly blind
Nil pictis timidus navita puppibus	Can painted timbers quell a seaman's fear?
Fidit, Tu, nisi ventis	Beware! or else the wind
Debes ludibrium, cave.	Makes you its mock and jeer.
Nuper sollicitum, quae mihi taedium,	Your trouble late made sick this heart of mine,
Nunc desiderium, curaque non levis,	And still I love you, still am ill at ease.
Interfusa nitentis	O, shun the sea, where shine
Vites aequora Cycladas.	The thick-sown Cyclades!

NOTE. Translation in English by John Conington *(Horace. The Odes and Carmen Saeculare of Horace*, 1882). Taken from <http://www.perseus.tufts.edu/>.

I.3. THE NEW TESTAMENT IN INDO-EUROPEAN

The original in Greek as well as Old Latin versions have been taken into account.

I.3.1. PATER NOS (LORD'S PRAYER)

Eurōpājóm	English	Latine	Ελληνικά
Pater Nos, kémeloisi jos essi,	Our Father, who art in heaven,	Pater noster, qui es in caelis:	Πάτερ ἡμῶν ὁ ἐν τοῖς οὐρανοῖς·
Nōmn̥ sqénetoru tewe.	Hallowed be thy Name.	sanctificetur Nomen Tuum;	ἁγιασθήτω τὸ ὄνομά σου·
Regnom cémjetōd tewe.	Thy kingdom come.	adveniat Regnum Tuum;	ἐλθέτω ἡ βασιλεία σου·
Dhidhḗtoru woljā Téwijā,	Thy will be done,	fiat voluntas Tua,	γενηθήτω τὸ θέλημά σου,
ita kémelei jota pl̥táwijāi.	On earth as it is in heaven.	sicut in caelo, et in terra.	ὡς ἐν οὐρανῷ καὶ ἐπὶ γῆς·
Qāqodjūtenom bharsjom n̥seróm edjḗw dəsdhi n̥smei	Give us this day our daily bread.	Panem nostrum cotidianum da nobis hodie;	τὸν ἄρτον ἡμῶν τὸν ἐπιούσιον δὸς ἡμῖν σήμερον·
joqe dhl̥eghlāns n̥serā́ns parke,	And forgive us our trespasses,	et dimitte nobis debita nostra,	καὶ ἄφες ἡμῖν τὰ ὀφειλήματα ἡμῶν,
swāi skéletbhos párkomos.	As we forgive those who trespass against us.	Sicut et nos dimittimus debitoribus nostris;	ὡς καὶ ἡμεῖς ἀφίεμεν τοῖς ὀφειλέταις ἡμῶν·
Enim mē n̥smé péritlōi enke prōd,	And lead us not into temptation,	et ne nos inducas in tentationem;	καὶ μὴ εἰσενέγκῃς ἡμᾶς εἰς πειρασμόν,
mō úpelēd noseje nos. Estōd.	But deliver us from evil. Amen	sed libera nos a Malo. Amen	ἀλλὰ ῥῦσαι ἡμᾶς ἀπὸ τοῦ πονηροῦ. ἀμήν.

I.3.2. SLWĒJE MARIJĀ (HAIL MARY)

Eurōpājóm	English	Latine	Ελληνικά
Sļwēje Marija, crātjã plēnā́ tū,	Hail Mary, full of grace,	Ave María, gratia plena,	Θεοτόκε Παρθένε, χαῖρε, κεχαριτωμένη Μαρία,
Arjos twojo esti;	the Lord is with thee;	Dominus tecum.	ὁ Κύριος μετὰ σοῦ.
suwoqnā́ cénāsu essi,	blessed art thou among women,	Benedicta tu in mulieribus,	εὐλογημένη σὺ ἐν γυναιξί,
suwoqnosqe úderosjo-two bhreugs, Jēsus.	and blessed is the fruit of thy womb, Jesus.	et benedictus fructus ventris tui, Iesus.	εὐλογημένος ὁ καρπὸς τῆς κοιλίας σου (ὅτι Σωτῆρα ἔτεκες τῶν ψυχῶν ἡμῶν)
Noibha Marija, Déiwosjo Mātér,	Holy Mary, Mother of God,	Sancta Maria, Mater Dei,	
nosbhos ōrāje ágeswn̥tbhos,	pray for us sinners,	ora pro nobis peccatoribus,	
nūqe mr̥teisqe nos daitéī. Estōd.	now and at the hour of our death. Amen.	nunc et in hora mortis nostrae. Amen.	

I.3.2. KRÉDDHĒMI (NICENE CREED)

Eurōpājóm	English	Latine	Ελληνικά
Oinom kréddhēmi Deiwom,	We believe in one God,	Credo in unum Deo,	Πιστεύομεν εἰς ἕνα Θεὸν
Pəterm̥ sļwomóghmonm̥,	the Father Almighty,	Patrem omnipoténtem,	Πατέρα παντοκράτορα,
djḗwepļtáwīdhōtm̥,	Maker of heaven and earth,	factórem cæli et terræ,	ποιητὴν οὐρανοῦ καὶ γῆς,
dr̥knijṓm sólwosom n̥dr̥knijṓmqe dhətorm̥;	and of all things visible and invisible.	visibílium ómnium et invisibílium;	ὁρατῶν τε πάντων και ἀοράτων.
Árjomqe Jēsum Ghristóm oinom,	And in one Lord Jesus Christ,	Et in unum Dóminum Iesum Christum,	Και εἰς ἕνα κύριον Ἰησοῦν Χριστόν,

Déiwosjo Sūnúm oinogn̥tóm,	the only-begotten Son of God,	Fílium Dei unigénitum,	τὸν υἱὸν τοῦ θεοῦ τὸν μονογενῆ,
Pətrós jom gnātóm aiwōd prāi solwōd,	begotten of the Father before all worlds (æons),	et ex Patre natum ante ómnia sæcula:	τὸν ἐκ τοῦ πατρὸς γεννηθέντα πρὸ πάντων τῶν αἰώνων,
Deiwom Deiwōd, leuksmn̥ léuksmenes, wērom Deiwom wērōd Deiwōd,	Light of Light, very God of very God,	Deum de Deo, lumen de lúmine, Deum verum de Deo vero,	φῶς ἐκ φωτός, θεὸν ἀληθινὸν ἐκ θεοῦ ἀληθινοῦ,
gnātóm, nē dhətóm,	begotten, not made,	génitum non factum,	γεννηθέντα οὐ ποιηθέντα,
Pətréi kómbhoutis,	being of one substance with the Father;	consubstantiálem Patri,	ὁμοούσιον τῷ πατρί·
josōd solwa dhaktá senti;	by whom all things were made;	per quem ómnia facta sunt;	δι' οὗ τὰ πάντα ἐγένετο·
qom n̥seróm rōdhí dhghómenom kémelojos kidét,	who for us men, and for our salvation, came down from heaven,	qui propter nos hómines et propter nostram salútem descéndit de cælis;	τὸν δι' ἡμᾶς τοὺς ἀνθρώπους καὶ διὰ τὴν ἡμετέραν σωτηρίαν κατελθόντα
enim mēmsóm Noibhō Ánəmō wéwr̥tei Marijād eksí ándhesād, enim dhghomōn geneto;	and was incarnate by the Holy Ghost of the Virgin Mary, and was made man;	et incarnátus est de Spíritu Sancto ex María Vírgine et homo factus est;	ἐκ τῶν οὐρανῶν καὶ σαρκωθέντα ἐκ πνεύματος ἁγίου καὶ Μαρίας τῆς παρθένου καὶ ἐνανθρωπήσαντα,
eti krukidhētós n̥smei prōd Pontjei upo Pilatei, qn̥tet sepēlitosqe esti,	he was crucified for us under Pontius Pilate, and suffered, and was buried,	crucifíxus étiam pro nobis sub Póntio Piláto, passus et sepúltus est;	σταυρωθέντα τε ὑπὲρ ἡμῶν ἐπὶ Ποντίου Πιλάτου, καὶ παθόντα καὶ ταφέντα,

joqe ati tritjei stéstōwe diwí, skréibhmona ad kémelomqe skandwṓs, Pətros déksijāi sedḗjeti;	and the third day he rose again, according to the Scriptures, and ascended into heaven, and sitteth on the right hand of the Father;	et resurréxit tértia die secúndum Scriptúras; et ascéndit in cælum, sedet ad déxteram Patris;	καὶ ἀναστάντα τῇ τρίτῃ ἡμέρα κατὰ τὰς γραφάς, καὶ ἀνελθόντα εἰς τοὺς οὐρανοὺς, καὶ καθεζόμενον ἐκ δεξιῶν τοῦ πατρός
joqe ati kléwosē cémseti cīwóns mr̥wonsqe kómdhēnqos;	from thence he shall come again, with glory, to judge the quick and the dead;	et íterum ventúrus est cum glória iudicáre vivos et mórtuos;	καὶ πάλιν ἐρχόμενον μετὰ δόξης κρῖναι ζῶντας καὶ νεκρούς·
qesjo regnom nē antjom bhéuseti.	whose kingdom shall have no end.	cuius regni non erit finis;	οὗ τῆς βασιλείας οὐκ ἔσται τέλος.
joqe Noibhom Ánəmom, potim ḗtrodhōtm̥qe, Pətrós Sūneusqe proilóm,	And in the Holy Ghost, the Lord and Giver of life, who proceedeth from the Father,	Et in Spíritum Sanctum, Dóminum et vivificántem: qui ex Patre *Filióque* procédit;	Καὶ εἰς τὸ Πνεῦμα τὸ Ἅγιον, τὸ κύριον, (καὶ) τὸ ζωοποιόν, τὸ ἐκ τοῦ πατρὸς ἐκπορευόμενον,
qo-i Pətrē Sūnéwēqe semli áisdetor enim magtā́jetor bhətós qom próbhātn̥s terqe esti.	who with the Father and the Son together is worshiped and glorified, who spake by the prophets.	qui cum Patre et Fílio simul adorátur et conglorificátur; qui locútus est per Prophétas;	τὸ σὺν πατρὶ καὶ υἱῷ συμπροσκυνούμενον καὶ συνδοξαζόμενον, τὸ λαλῆσαν διὰ τῶν προφητῶν.
joqe oinām, noibhām, km̥tísolwām apostólejām ékklētijām.	In one holy catholic and apostolic Church;	Et in unam sanctam cathólicam et apostólicam Ecclésiam.	εἰς μίαν, ἁγίαν, καθολικὴν καὶ ἀποστολικὴν ἐκκλησίαν·
Oinom bhətējāi agesupomoukōi cadhmn̥;	we acknowledge one baptism for the remission of sins;	Confíteor unum baptísma in remissiónem peccatorum	ὁμολογοῦμεν ἓν βάπτισμα εἰς ἄφεσιν ἁμαρτιῶν·

Mr̥wātibhorghom wélpomos saitlōmqe cītām cémsontm̥. Estōd	we look for the resurrection of the dead, and the life of the world to come. Amen.	et exspecto resurrectionem mortuorum et vitam ventúri sæculi. Amen.	προσδοκοῦμεν ἀνάστασιν νεκρῶν, καὶ ζωὴν τοῦ μέλλοντος αἰῶνος. Ἀμήν.

I.3.3. NOUDÓS SŪNÚS (PARABLE OF THE PRODIGAL SON)

	Eurōpājóm	English	Latine	Ελληνικά
11	**Dhghomōn enis sūnuwe eiket,**	“A certain man had two sons.	Homo quidam habuit duos filios:	Ἄνθρωπός τις εἶχεν δύο υἱούς.
12	**joqe jewísteros pətrei weuqét : Pəter, rijós dōdhi moi aitim qā-i meghei áineti, joqe rēim ibhom widhét.**	And the younger of them said to his father, ‘Father, give me the portion of goods that falls to me.’ So he divided to them his livelihood.	et dixit adolescentior ex illis patri: Pater, da mihi portionem substantiæ, quæ me contingit. Et divisit illis substantiam.	καὶ εἶπεν ὁ νεώτερος αὐτῶν τῷ πατρί, Πάτερ, δός μοι τὸ ἐπιβάλλον μέρος τῆς οὐσίας. ὁ δὲ διεῖλεν αὐτοῖς τὸν βίον.
13	**Enim nē péluwons dinons pos, solwa gr̥lós, jewísteros sūnús rew porsótenom oigheto londhom, idheiqe rēim nudét sewe ghlóidotos ceiwonts.**	And not many days after, the younger son gathered all together, journeyed to a far country, and there wasted his possessions with prodigal living.	Et non post multos dies, congregatis omnibus, adolescentior filius peregre profectus est in regionem longinquam, et ibi dissipavit substantiam suam vivendo luxuriose.	καὶ μετ' οὐ πολλὰς ἡμέρας συναγαγὼν πάντα ὁ νεώτερος υἱὸς ἀπεδήμησεν εἰς χώραν μακράν, καὶ ἐκεῖ διεσκόρπισεν τὴν οὐσίαν αὐτοῦ ζῶν ἀσώτως.
14	**Enim qām solwa cesét kom pos, dhorghsús molét ghrēdhus londhei ólnosmi, joqe egētum sope bhwije.**	But when he had spent all, there arose a severe famine in that land, and he began to be in want.	Et postquam omnia consummasset, facta est fames valida in regione illa, et ipse cœpit egere.	δαπανήσαντος δὲ αὐτοῦ πάντα ἐγένετο λιμὸς ἰσχυρὰ κατὰ τὴν χώραν ἐκείνην, καὶ αὐτὸς ἤρξατο ὑστερεῖσθαι.

15	**Itaqe cālós, qismōi jugeto kéiwijom ólnosjo londhī, imqe sontest porkons pāsei**	Then he went and joined himself to a citizen of that country, and he sent him into his fields to feed swine.	Et abiit, et adhæsit uni civium regionis illius: et misit illum in villam suam ut pasceret porcos.	καὶ πορευθεὶς ἐκολλήθη ἑνὶ τῶν πολιτῶν τῆς χώρας ἐκείνης, καὶ ἔπεμψεν αὐτὸν εἰς τοὺς ἀγροὺς αὐτοῦ βόσκειν χοίρους:
16	**Atqe úderom skəliqāis plḗnātum gheríjeto porkōs edent qans atqe neqis ismōi dōt.**	And he would gladly have filled his stomach with the pods that the swine ate, and no one gave him anything.	Et cupiebat implere ventrem suum de siliquis, quas porci manducabant: et nemo illi dabat.	καὶ ἐπεθύμει χορτασθῆναι ἐκ τῶν κερατίων ὧν ἤσθιον οἱ χοῖροι, καὶ οὐδεὶς ἐδίδου αὐτῷ.
17	**Swe poti wr̥tomnós, ēgt: qotjoi pətrós domei mísdhotes paskneis spréigonti, kei egṓ au dhəmī mr̥ijāi!**	"But when he came to himself, he said, 'How many of my father's hired servants have bread enough and to spare, and I perish with hunger!	In se autem reversus, dixit: Quanti mercenarii in domo patris mei abundant panibus, ego autem hic fame pereo!	εἰς ἑαυτὸν δὲ ἐλθὼν ἔφη, Πόσοι μίσθιοι τοῦ πατρός μου περισσεύονται ἄρτων, ἐγὼ δὲ λιμῷ ὧδε ἀπόλλυμαι.
18	**r̥tos pəterm̥ eisō mene ad, joqe ismōi seksō: Pəter, kémelom proti tewomqe antí memlai,**	I will arise and go to my father, and will say to him, "Father, I have sinned against heaven and before you,	surgam, et ibo ad patrem meum, et dicam ei: Pater, peccavi in cælum, et coram te:	ἀναστὰς πορεύσομαι πρὸς τὸν πατέρα μου καὶ ἐρῶ αὐτῷ, Πάτερ, ἥμαρτον εἰς τὸν οὐρανὸν καὶ ἐνώπιόν σου,
19	**jāmi nē deknós egṓ, sūnús téwijos kluwētum: dhəsdhi me swāi qimqim mísdhotom tewe.**	and I am no longer worthy to be called your son. Make me like one of your hired servants."'	jam non sum dignus vocari filius tuus: fac me sicut unum de mercenariis tuis.	οὐκέτι εἰμὶ ἄξιος κληθῆναι υἱός σου: ποίησόν με ὡς ἕνα τῶν μισθίων σου.

20	**Ita r̥tós pəterm̥ ludhét sewe. Eti jom qeli bhewn̥tí, em pətḗr tósjope dr̥ket, joqe əna kr̥sonts kómqēiljō krūtós esti enim kolsom petlós em bhusājét.**	"And he arose and came to his father. But when he was still a great way off, his father saw him and had compassion, and ran and fell on his neck and kissed him.	Et surgens venit ad patrem suum. Cum autem adhuc longe esset, vidit illum pater ipsius, et misericordia motus est, et accurrens cecidit super collum ejus, et osculatus est eum.	καὶ ἀναστὰς ἦλθεν πρὸς τὸν πατέρα ἑαυτοῦ. ἔτι δὲ αὐτοῦ μακρὰν ἀπέχοντος εἶδεν αὐτὸν ὁ πατὴρ αὐτοῦ καὶ ἐσπλαγχνίσθη καὶ δραμὼν ἐπέπεσεν ἐπὶ τὸν τράχηλον αὐτοῦ καὶ κατεφίλησεν αὐτόν.
21	**Wedét óisosmōi sūnús: Pəter, kémelom proti tewomqe antí memlai: jāmi nē deknós egṓ, sūnús téwijos nōmnādhjom**	And the son said to him, 'Father, I have sinned against heaven and in your sight, and am no longer worthy to be called your son.'	Dixitque ei filius: Pater, peccavi in cælum, et coram te: jam non sum dignus vocari filius tuus.	εἶπεν δὲ ὁ υἱὸς αὐτῷ, Πάτερ, ἥμαρτον εἰς τὸν οὐρανὸν καὶ ἐνώπιόν σου, οὐκέτι εἰμὶ ἄξιος κληθῆναι υἱός σου.
22	**nū mísdhatbhos bhəto pətḗr sewe; bhersi: prāmām dhrághete togām joqe tom woséjete, anom tosjo ghéseri kerpjonsqe esjo dəste pedsú:**	"But the father said to his servants, 'Bring out the best robe and put it on him, and put a ring on his hand and sandals on his feet.	Dixit autem pater ad servos suos: Cito proferte stolam primam, et induite illum, et date annulum in manum ejus, et calceamenta in pedes ejus:	εἶπεν δὲ ὁ πατὴρ πρὸς τοὺς δούλους αὐτοῦ, Ταχὺ ἐξενέγκατε στολὴν τὴν πρώτην καὶ ἐνδύσατε αὐτόν, καὶ δότε δακτύλιον εἰς τὴν χεῖρα αὐτοῦ καὶ ὑποδήματα εἰς τοὺς πόδας,
23	**kom piwónm̥qe bhérete loigom joqe chénte, joqe edēmos, joqe wl̥dām terpēmos,**	And bring the fatted calf here and kill it, and let us eat and be merry;	et adducite vitulum saginatum, et occidite, et manducemus, et epulemur:	καὶ φέρετε τὸν μόσχον τὸν σιτευτόν, θύσατε καὶ φαγόντες εὐφρανθῶμεν,

24	**jodqid kei sūnús mene dhedhuwós ēst atqe coje ati: skm̥bnós ēst, atqe wṛētōr. Enim wḷdām bhwijónt.**	for this my son was dead and is alive again; he was lost and is found.' And they began to be merry.	quia hic filius meus mortuus erat, et revixit: perierat, et inventus est. Et cœperunt epulari.	ὅτι οὗτος ὁ υἱός μου νεκρὸς ἦν καὶ ἀνέζησεν, ἦν ἀπολωλὼς καὶ εὑρέθη. καὶ ἤρξαντο εὐφραίνεσθαι.
25	**Agrei au senísteros ēst sūnús: joqe jom ludhét enim domom nedijeto, kómkantum léigṃqe kluwét.**	"Now his older son was in the field. And as he came and drew near to the house, he heard music and dancing.	Erat autem filius ejus senior in agro: et cum veniret, et appropinquaret domui, audivit symphoniam et chorum:	ην δὲ ὁ υἱὸς αὐτοῦ ὁ πρεσβύτερος ἐν ἀγρῷ: καὶ ὡς ἐρχόμενος ἤγγισεν τῇ οἰκίᾳ, ἤκουσεν συμφωνίας καὶ χορῶν,
26	**Joqe neqom móghuwom ghaulós pṛket qid ghāi-ke bhuwont**	So he called one of the servants and asked what these things meant.	et vocavit unum de servis, et interrogavit quid hæc essent.	καὶ προσκαλεσάμενος ἕνα τῶν παίδων ἐπυνθάνετο τί ἂν εἴη ταῦτα.
27	**Isqe sqet: bhrātēr tewe cēme enim piwonṃ patḗr two chone loigom, jodqid tom cīwóm solwom ghōde.**	And he said to him, 'Your brother has come, and because he has received him safe and sound, your father has killed the fatted calf.'	Isque dixit illi: Frater tuus venit, et occidit pater tuus vitulum saginatum, quia salvum illum recepit.	ὁ δὲ εἶπεν αὐτῷ ὅτι Ὁ ἀδελφός σου ἥκει, καὶ ἔθυσεν ὁ πατήρ σου τὸν μόσχον τὸν σιτευτόν, ὅτι ὑγιαίνοντα αὐτὸν ἀπέλαβεν.
28	**kṛditós autim esti, joqe nē en eitum wélwelāt. Ar patḗr ejos eksodlós, bhwijét im chestum.**	"But he was angry and would not go in. Therefore his father came out and pleaded with him.	Indignatus est autem, et nolebat introire. Pater ergo illius egressus, cœpit rogare illum.	ὠργίσθη δὲ καὶ οὐκ ἤθελεν εἰσελθεῖν. ὁ δὲ πατὴρ αὐτοῦ ἐξελθὼν παρεκάλει αὐτόν.

29	**Atqe se protiweqonts, patréi bhato sewe: edke totjons atnons sístāmi twei upo, joqe neqom dikām tewe klusóm dus, atqe neqom meghei ghaidom desta wl̥dāi ámik(bh)is senutéwijāi.**	So he answered and said to his father, 'Lo, these many years I have been serving you; I never transgressed your commandment at any time; and yet you never gave me a young goat, that I might make merry with my friends.	At ille respondens, dixit patri suo: Ecce tot annis servio tibi, et numquam mandatum tuum præterivi: et numquam dedisti mihi hædum ut cum amicis meis epularer.	ὁ δὲ ἀποκριθεὶς εἶπεν τῷ πατρὶ αὐτοῦ, Ἰδοὺ τοσαῦτα ἔτη δουλεύω σοι καὶ οὐδέποτε ἐντολήν σου παρῆλθον, καὶ ἐμοὶ οὐδέποτε ἔδωκας ἔριφον ἵνα μετὰ τῶν φίλων μου εὐφρανθῶ:
30	**Mō ita tom sūnús tewe kei, rēim loutsāis crālós cēme, ólnosmōi píwonm̥ loigom chonta.**	But as soon as this son of yours came, who has devoured your livelihood with harlots, you killed the fatted calf for him.'	Sed postquam filius tuus hic, qui devoravit substantiam suam cum meretricibus, venit, occidisti illi vitulum saginatum.	ὅτε δὲ ὁ υἱός σου οὗτος ὁ καταφαγών σου τὸν βίον μετὰ πορνῶν ἦλθεν, ἔθυσας αὐτῷ τὸν σιτευτὸν μόσχον.
31	**Atqe oiso tosmōi weuqét: suneu, tū áiwesi mojo essi, enim solwa menja téwija senti.**	"And he said to him, 'Son, you are always with me, and all that I have is yours.	At ipse dixit illi: Fili, tu semper mecum es, et omnia mea tua sunt:	ὁ δὲ εἶπεν αὐτῷ, Τέκνον, σὺ πάντοτε μετ' ἐμοῦ εἶ, καὶ πάντα τὰ ἐμὰ σά ἐστιν:
32	**Wl̥dā́m autim terptum, joqe gaudhētum opos ēst, jodqid bhrātēr tewe kei dhedhuwós ēst atqe coje ati; skm̥bnós ēst, atqe wr̥ētōr.**	It was right that we should make merry and be glad, for your brother was dead and is alive again, and was lost and is found.'"	epulari autem, et gaudere oportebat, quia frater tuus hic mortuus erat, et revixit; perierat, et inventus est.	εὐφρανθῆναι δὲ καὶ χαρῆναι ἔδει, ὅτι ὁ ἀδελφός σου οὗτος νεκρὸς ἦν καὶ ἔζησεν, καὶ ἀπολωλὼς καὶ εὑρέθη.

I.3.4. NEWOM SUWÉISTUNJOM (NEW TESTAMENT) – JŌHANĒS, 1, 1-14

	Eurōpājóm	English	Latine	Ελληνικά
1	**Pārjei Wr̥dhom bhewet, joqe Wr̥dhom Deiwei ēst ensí, joqe Deiwos Wr̥dhom ēst.**	In the beginning was the Word, and the Word was with God, and the Word was God.	in principio erat Verbum et Verbum erat apud Deum et Deus erat Verbum	Ἐν ἀρχῇ ἦν ὁ λόγος, καὶ ὁ λόγος ἦν πρὸς τὸν θεόν, καὶ θεὸς ἦν ὁ λόγος.
2	**Ensí id pārjei Deiwei ēst.**	He was in the beginning with God.	hoc erat in principio apud Deum	οὗτος ἦν ἐν ἀρχῇ πρὸς τὸν θεόν.
3	**Ī solwa gegnḗr enim id aneu neqid geneto josjo gégone.**	All things were made through Him, and without Him nothing was made that was made.	omnia per ipsum facta sunt et sine ipso factum est nihil quod factum est	πάντα δι' αὐτοῦ ἐγένετο, καὶ χωρὶς αὐτοῦ ἐγένετο οὐδὲ ἕν. ὃ γέγονεν
4	**Ismi cītā bhewet, joqe cītā ēst dhghómonom leuks.**	In Him was life, and the life was the light of men.	in ipso vita erat et vita erat lux hominum	ἐν αὐτῷ ζωὴ ἦν, καὶ ἡ ζωὴ ἦν τὸ φῶς τῶν ἀνθρώπων:
5	**Itaqe leuks skotei skéjeti, joqe oisām skotos nē turét.**	And the light shines in the darkness, and the darkness did not comprehend it	et lux in tenebris lucet et tenebrae eam non conprehenderunt	καὶ τὸ φῶς ἐν τῇ σκοτίᾳ φαίνει, καὶ ἡ σκοτία αὐτὸ οὐ κατέλαβεν.
6	**Bhūt wīrós Deiwō sesentnós Jōhanēs nṓmənē.**	There was a man sent from God, whose name was John.	fuit homo missus a Deo cui nomen erat Iohannes	Ἐγένετο ἄνθρωπος ἀπεσταλμένος παρὰ θεοῦ, ὄνομα αὐτῷ Ἰωάννης:
7	**Tristimonjōi ludhét se, leukbhi tristidhénts, ei oljoi ijo kréddhēsēnt.**	This man came for a witness, to bear witness of the Light, that all through him might believe.	hic venit in testimonium ut testimonium perhiberet de lumine ut omnes crederent per illum	οὗτος ἦλθεν εἰς μαρτυρίαν, ἵνα μαρτυρήσῃ περὶ τοῦ φωτός, ἵνα πάντες πιστεύσωσιν δι' αὐτοῦ.

8	**Nē olno leuks, immō, leukbhi tristidhēnts.**	He was not that Light, but was sent to bear witness of that Light.	non erat ille lux sed ut testimonium perhiberet de lumine	οὐκ ἦν ἐκεῖνος τὸ φῶς, ἀλλ' ἵνα μαρτυρήσῃ περὶ τοῦ φωτός.
9	**Leuks wērom ēst, solwom bhəneuti dhghomonm̥, dhoubnom kod cémjontm̥**	That was the true Light which gives light to every man coming into the world.	erat lux vera quae inluminat omnem hominem venientem in mundum	ην τὸ φῶς τὸ ἀληθινόν, ὃ φωτίζει πάντα ἄνθρωπον, ἐρχόμενον εἰς τὸν κόσμον.
10	**Dhoubnei ēst, enim ijo dhoubnom gegner, atqe nē im dhoubnom gnōt.**	He was in the world, and the world was made through Him, and the world did not know Him.	in mundo erat et mundus per ipsum factus est et mundus eum non cognovit	ἐν τῷ κόσμῳ ἦν, καὶ ὁ κόσμος δι' αὐτοῦ ἐγένετο, καὶ ὁ κόσμος αὐτὸν οὐκ ἔγνω.
11	**Somobhos ludhét, atqe im somói ghədónt nei ad.**	He came to His own, and His own did not receive Him.	in propria venit et sui eum non receperunt	εἰς τὰ ἴδια ἦλθεν, καὶ οἱ ἴδιοι αὐτὸν οὐ παρέλαβον.
12	**Jotjoi im ghədónt, moghtim tobhos gendhjōi dōt Diwoputla, esjo nōmn̥ kréddhēntbhos,**	But as many as received Him, to them He gave the right to become children of God, to those who believe in His name:	quotquot autem receperunt eum dedit eis potestatem filios Dei fieri his qui credunt in nomine eius	ὅσοι δὲ ἔλαβον αὐτόν, ἔδωκεν αὐτοῖς ἐξουσίαν τέκνα θεοῦ γενέσθαι, τοῖς πιστεύουσιν εἰς τὸ ὄνομα αὐτοῦ,
13	**joi nē ésenos, neqe mēmsī́ woljās, neqe wīrī́ woljās immō Déiwosjo gnātṓs sonti.**	who were born, not of blood, nor of the will of the flesh, nor of the will of man, but of God.	qui non ex sanguinibus neque ex voluntate carnis neque ex voluntate viri sed ex Deo nati sunt	οἳ οὐκ ἐξ αἱμάτων οὐδὲ ἐκ θελήματος σαρκὸς οὐδὲ ἐκ θελήματος ἀνδρὸς ἀλλ' ἐκ θεοῦ ἐγεννήθησαν.

14	**Joqe Wṛdhom mēmsóm wṛstóm esti, enim pḷtomóm ṇsmí dhēke ení, enim ejos qedos dṛkomes, qedos swāi oinognosjo Pətrós wērotjō crātjāqe plēnóm.**	And the Word became flesh and dwelt among us, and we beheld His glory, the glory as of the only begotten of the Father, full of grace and truth.	et Verbum caro factum est et habitavit in nobis et vidimus gloriam eius gloriam quasi unigeniti a Patre plenum gratiae et veritatis	Καὶ ὁ λόγος σὰρξ ἐγένετο καὶ ἐσκήνωσεν ἐν ἡμῖν, καὶ ἐθεασάμεθα τὴν δόξαν αὐτοῦ, δόξαν ὡς μονογενοῦς παρὰ πατρός, πλήρης χάριτος καὶ ἀληθείας.

NOTE. The form ***gégnisset*** is clearly taken from Latin; see <http://revistas.ucm.es/index.php/CFCA/article/view/CFCA7676130275A/3281>.

I.4. THE RIGVEDA IN INDO-EUROPEAN

Eurōpājóm	Sanskrit	English
Progṇpotis dā-toi pārjei ēst	Prajapatir vai idam-agre asit	In the beginning was Prajapati (the Creator),
tosjo woqs dwitjā ēst	Prajapatir vai idam-agre asit	With Him was the Vak (the Word),
Woqs dā Pérəmom Bhlaghmṇ	Vak vai Paramam Brahma	And the Vak (the Word) was verily the Supreme Brahman.

NOTE. It is possible that the *Logos* concept of Greek philosopher Philo of Alexandria (adopted in John 1) was influenced by the *Vak* of Hindu philosophy.

APPENDIX II: LATE INDO-EUROPEAN LEXICON

This lexicon is available online with regular updates and as automatic dictionary-translator at <http://indo-european.info/>, and an automatic online Proto-Indo-European dictionary-translator is available at <http://indo-european.info/dictionary-translator/>.

An English – Indo-European dictionary is found in Appendix II.1.

For detailed information on the Proto-Indo-European words, its etymology, usage, root and meaning, see the following section, Appendix II.2.

For detailed forms from descendant languages used for the reconstruction of PIE words, see Appendix II.3.

NOTE. The Appendix II.3 has not been included in this revised, reduced version of the grammar. Visit <http://indo-european.info/> for all free downloads available.

FORMAL ASPECTS

The reconstructed artifice *schwa* *ə (still widely used in modern IE linguistics, *cf.* e.g. Ringe 2006, de Vaan 2008, etc.) does not represent an actual vowel. It might represent in this reconstructed post-Late Indo-European lexicon:

1) The *schwa primum*, vocalic output of the older merged laryngeal **H*, assimilated to a different vowel in the different IEDs. That *laryngeal schwa* is omitted if it is word-initial and appears alone, as in **H_3bhruH*, or if the preceding syllable has full vocalism, as in **klamrós*, but it is written elsewhere, as in **pəter-*. See *The Loss of Laryngeals,* and *Conventions Used in This Book.*

2) The results of the so-called *Saussure effect*. See *The Loss of Laryngeals.*

3) The *schwa secundum*, reconstructed for irregular outputs of groups that included resonants, i.e. *C$^{(o)}$RV or *C$^{(o)}$R$^{(o)}$C, due to auxiliary vowels inserted in LIE times. For this alternating auxiliary vowel, a dot below is more commonly written for resonants plus vowel, i.e. CṚV. See *Phonology*, especially §2.3.

Some supposed late remains of the LIE merged laryngeal in groups including resonants, i.e. *CRHC, *CHRC, *CRHV, *CHRV, etc. are not written down by convention. A selection is made of the most common west IE evolution; as, Ita., Cel. **gnātós** (with an evolution equivalent to Gk. **gnētós**) for an older **gn̥**^{ə}**ʔtós**, *born*. See above *The Loss of Laryngeals*, and §2.1.

Middle-passive endings are written with the 1st sg. ***-ai***, ***-oi***, which correspond to NWIE ***-ar***. See above §7.2.2.

Sometimes, forms different to those found in this book are intentionally reconstructed in this lexicon, to complement each other and give an overall image of the possible reconstructions; as, **-e-** reduplicated athem. **dhédhēmi**, shown in this lexicon as **-i-** reduplicated athem. **dhídhēmi**, and non-reduplicated, them. **dhakjō**. See §7.4.2. *Class BII*.

Dubious reconstructions of stative verbs, added in this edition, (see §7.4.2, Class AIIIe vs. Class IIIo) include **awējō**, **bhəwējō**, **gāudhējō**, **ghəbhējō**, **lubhējō**; while some appear to be bivalent *-ejō-/-ējō-*: **dl̥ghĕjō**, **r̥kĕjō**, **tn̥ĕjō**.

Heteroclite as well as athematic (especially root) nouns are shown according to the general reconstruction paradigms. Some difficult choices have been made, though, if more than one form is found. See §§4.6, 4.7.

On the alternative vocalic reconstruction **a/o**, as in **mari/mori**, the Leiden school (de Vaan among others) defends a phonetic law Lat. *a* < PIE **o* (free and accompanied by certain consonants); as, *badius*, *canis*, *fax*, *lacus*, *lanius*, *manus*, *malleus*, *mare*, *uagus*, *ualua*, *uas*, *uaris*, etc. of which *badius*, *canis*, *lacus*, *mare*, and maybe *manus* have correlatives with root vowel O.Ir. *o*. However, we have some clear counterexamples; as *mora*, *mola*, *moneō*, *monīle* and maybe *focus*, *forō*. According to de Vaan, *cohors*, *dolō*, *dolus*, *domus*, *folium*, *glomus*, *hodiē*, *(h)olus*, *noceō*, *oculus*, *odor*, *onus*, *opus*, *ouis*, *podium*, *probus*, *procus*, *rota*, and *toga*

do not accomplish the phonetic conditions to be counterexamples.

II.1. ENGLISH – LATE INDO-EUROPEAN

English	Late Indo-European
a bit	**pau**
abandoned	**ermos**
abound	**spreigō**
about	**per(i), per(ti)**
above	**upsi**
absent	**apowesonts**
absolute	**pérəmos**
absolutely yes	**nāi**
abundance	**mūris**
abundant	**chonós**
abundant	**opnis**
abyss	**n̥bhudhnóm**
acarian	**koris**
accelerate	**spreudō**
accordance	**sm̥itis**
acorn	**cél̥n̥dis**
acorn	**medjom**
acquire	**kwāimi**
acquire	**potijai**
acquit	**luwō apó**
activate	**kjējō**
active	**strēnwos**
Adam's apple	**croghos**
address	**deikos**
adhere	**gleibhō**
adjust	**ārarjō**
administrate	**médneumi**
adorn	**mondō**
adorn	**peikō**
adult	**altjos**
advanced	**prokos**
advantage	**(sí)stāmi antí/prāi**
affirm	**əgjō**
afflict	**krēwō**
afflict	**ághneumi**
afflict	**ml̥qjō**
after	**pos(ti)**
afterwards	**pósteri**
again	**ati**
against	**komtrōd**
against	**proti**
aggravate	**odáugjai**
agile	**ágəlis**
agitate	**dhúneumi**
agitate	**kreutō**
agitated	**kighrós**
agitation	**dhūnis**
agnus castus	**weitēks**
agonise	**cl̥nāmi**
agreement	**koimā**
agreement	**meitrom**
air	**porā**
akin	**koinós**
alas	**troughi**
alas	**wai**
alder	**álesnos**
alder	**wernā**
alike	**jota sei**
alive	**cīwós**
all	**oljoi oljāi olja**
allergy	**dedrus**
alleyway	**smoughos**
allied	**soqjós**
allow	**tr̥knō**
allure	**doljō**
along	**práiteri**
already	**jāmi**
also	**toqe**
altar	**āsā**
always	**áiw(es)i**
ambush	**énsēdjom**
ancestor	**strutjos**
ancient	**prīskos**
and	**atqe**
and	**enim**
and	**joqe**
and	**qe**
and also	**itaqe**
and not	**neqe**
angelica	**qondhros**
angle	**qedos**
animal	**cīwotos**
animal	**smalos**
ankle	**spr̥os**
announce	**kárkarjō**
annoy	**peigō**
annoyance	**oghlos**
annoying	**mōlestos**
annoying	**trudsmós**
anorak	**kroknos**
another	**onjos**
another	**aljos**
anounce	**ml̥gājō**
ant	**mr̥meikā**
antique	**ántijos**
anyone	**qisqis qidqid**
apart	**səni**
apart	**sēd**
aperture	**ōstjom**
apparent	**windos**
appear	**mlōskō**

appearance	**widā́**
appease	**sēdājō**
appease	**litājō**
appendix	**plighā**
apple	**ábelos**
approach (to)	**pl̥namaí**
arch	**weitō**
arch	**wekō**
ardour	**aisdhom**
arise	**kenō**
arm	**armos**
arm	**bhāghus**
arm	**dóusontos**
armour	**twakos**
army	**korjos**
army	**strātos**
around	**ambhí**
arrange	**dúnāmi**
arrangement	**stāmn̥**
arrival	**ghētis**
arrive	**n̥kneumi**
arrow	**kēlom**
art	**artis**
article	**melmn̥**
articulation	**anglos**
as	**qām**
as big	**swālikos**
ash	**āsos**
ash	**kenēs**
ashtrē	**oskos**
ashtree	**bhr̥ksnos**
ashtree	**ósonos**
ask	**pr̥kskō**
asp	**apsā**
aspect	**spekjēs**
aspire	**wénāmoi**
ass	**kūlos**
assigned	**prōtós**
assort	**kjājō**
asunder	**wī**
asunder-legged	**wāros**
at	**ad**
at hand	**práighesto**
at least	**ge**
at that point	**tām**
ate	**ghosóm**
atribute	**bhagō**
attack	**nikjō**
attack	**wr̥gos**
attack	**wendhō**
attack (to be in)	**wr̥gējō**
attention	**probhoudhos**
attract	**spáneumi**
auger	**téredhrom**
augur	**kailom**
aunt	**ámetā**
aunt	**mātérterā**
autumn	**osēn**
avenge	**qínumoi**
avoid	**leinō**
awaken	**bhoudhejō**
axe	**adhos**
axe	**áksijā**
axe	**bheitlom**
axe	**sekūris**
axe	**tekslā**
axle	**aksis**
babble	**batā**
babble	**plabrājai**
babble	**lalājo**
baby	**dhēljos**
back	**awo**
back	**gurnos**
back	**retrōd**
backbone	**wr̥aghmn̥**
backward	**ápōqos**
backwards	**postrōd**
bad	**dus**
bad	**edwolōn**
bad	**elkós**
bad	**upelos**
badger	**bhrogkos**
badger	**mēlis**
bag	**bholghis**
bag	**kṓrukos**
bald	**kalwos**
ball	**ghroudos**
ball	**golā**
ball	**gugā**
ball	**orghis**
band	**seimā**
bandy-legged	**walgos**
banquet	**daps**
barbaric	**bálbalos**
barefoot	**bhosos**
bargain	**wesnejō**
bark	**baubājai**
barley	**ghórsdejom**
barley	**jewom**
barrel	**dōljom**
basin	**wl̥ghis**
basket	**kistā**

basket	**korbhis**
basket	**qasjos**
basket	**sportā**
basket	**woidlos**
bast	**lubhros**
bath	**lowtrom**
bath-tub	**célwonom**
be	**bhewmi**
be	**esmi**
be active, flourish	**wegējō**
be adequate	**plakējō**
be afraid	**timējō**
be angry	**eisāskai**
be annoying	**pigējō**
be available	**likējō**
be awake	**bheudhō**
be big	**augējō**
be bitter	**geigō**
be born	**gn̥jai**
be bright	**spl̥ndējō**
be broken	**lugējō**
be cold	**alghējō**
be cold	**srīgējō**
be concealed	**lətējō**
be curved	**wijējō**
be delayed	**stn̥tējō**
be dry	**āsējō**
be empty	**ghr̥ējō**
be expensive	**dápnāmi**
be experienced	**kaldējō**
be far	**(sí)stāmi apó**
be favourable	**bhəwējō**
be fit	**wəlējō**
be flat	**ləpējō**
be followed	**swemōr**
be furious	**sājō**
be glad	**ghərējō**
be high	**kelsō**
be hot	**kəlējō**
be interested	**mendhai**
be loaded	**gemō**
be mistaken	**treikō**
be named	**kluwējō**
be necessary	**opos esti**
be old	**senējō**
be pregnant	**kuwējō**
be proper	**dekējō**
be red	**rudhējō**
be rotten	**pūtējō**
be scratched	**kr̥sējō**
be sharp	**akējō**

be sitting	**sedējō**
be situated	**ēsmoi**
be sticked	**lipējō**
be swollen	**oidējō**
be swollen	**tumējō**
be swollen (to)	**swəlējō**
be thirsty	**tr̥sējō**
be used	**eukō**
be violent	**chr̥jō**
be violent	**jeugō**
be visible	**dr̥kjai peri**
be warm	**tepējō**
be wet	**mədējō**
be withered	**mr̥kējō**
beak	**rōstrom**
beak	**sroknā**
beam	**tegnom**
beam	**trabhis**
bean	**bhabhā**
bear	**r̥tkos**
bear	**bhermi (bherō)**
bear in mind	**mnājō**
beard	**bhardhā**
bearing	**bhr̥tis**
beast	**ghwerā**
beast	**weidr̥**
beast of burden	**jóugsmn̥tom**
beastly	**ghwērīnós**
beat	**wəleisō**
beat up	**orgājō**
beautiful	**chaisos**
beautiful	**wn̥mos**
beaver	**bhebhros**
because	**jod qid**
become accustomed	**swēdhskō**
become vigorous	**ḱikeumi**
bed	**spondhā**
bee	**bheiqlā**
beech	**bhāgos**
been	**bhūtós**
beer	**álumn̥**
beer	**kremom**
beer	**sudhjom**
before	**antí**
before	**pəros**
before	**prāi**
before dawn	**anksí**
befoul	**sterkō**
befriend (to)	**nínāmi**
beget	**gignō**

begin	**bhūjai**
begird	**jṓsneumi**
beguile	**dreughō**
behind	**apóteri**
being	**esn̥ts**
belch	**reugō**
believe	**ōimi**
believe	**kréddhēmi**
bell	**kólkolos**
belly	**tarsós**
belong	**ainō**
beloved	**kāros**
belt (for safety)	**wérunos**
bend	**klengō**
bend	**wərikjō**
bend	**wəroikos**
bend	**greugō**
bending	**nm̥tos**
beneficial	**síslāwos**
benefit	**lawō**
benefit	**lawtlom**
bent	**kambos**
bent	**pandos**
berry	**morom**
beseech	**prekō**
beset	**adghō**
besides	**perom**
besiege	**sedējō ambhí**
bestow	**ankmi**
betrothed	**sponstós**
better	**bhodjṓs**
better	**weljṓs**
between	**énteri**
beware	**kowejō**
biceps	**kiskā**
big	**crotsos**
big	**məgjos**
big	**məgnos**
big eater	**corós**
bile	**cheldi**
bilge out	**semjō**
billow	**sredhō**
bind	**nedskō**
bind	**bhendhō**
bind	**kekājō**
bind	**ligājō**
bind	**reigō**
bind	**síneumi**
biped	**dwipods**
birch	**bherāgs**
bird	**awis**
bird	**petsnós**
birth	**gentlom**
birth	**sūtus**
biscuit	**gōgā**
bit	**akmā**
bite	**denkō**
bite	**mordējō**
bitter	**bhidrós**
bitter	**choris**
black	**ātros**
black	**dhoubhús**
black	**kr̥snos**
blackbird	**meslā**
blade	**akjēs**
blame	**onējō**
blaze	**sweidō**
bleach	**kormnos**
bleat	**bebājō**
bleat	**blēkājō**
blind	**andhos**
blind	**kaikos**
blister	**kaldos**
blister	**wenseikā**
block	**stopejō**
blood	**esr̥**
blood	**krēws**
bloom	**bhlosējō**
blow	**bhesmi**
blow	**bhlāmi**
blow	**(ī́)wēmi**
blow up	**(pím)prēmi**
blue	**ghlastos**
blue	**m̥dhros**
blunt	**bhukús**
blunt	**dm̥pus**
boar	**apros**
boar	**twr̥kos**
board	**ploutos**
boast	**bhledō**
boast	**ghelbō**
boat	**plowós**
bodkin	**ēlā**
body	**kr̥pos**
boil	**bherwō**
boil	**seutō**
bold	**dhr̥sus**
boldness	**dhr̥stis**
bolt	**tormos**
bone	**ostis**
border	**krēqā**
bore	**bhorājō**

born	**gnātós**
bosom	**sinus**
both	**ambhou**
bought	**qrītóm**
boundary	**eghr̥**
boundary	**margōn**
bovine	**cowijós**
bow	**arqos**
bowels	**gudom**
bowl	**tekstā**
box	**kəpsā**
boy	**kelots**
boy	**maqos**
boy	**póweros**
bracelet	**welīks**
brain	**kerəsrom**
bramble	**dristos**
bran	**tolkos**
branch	**kankus**
branch	**osdos**
branches	**cespis**
brass	**ajos**
brassy	**ájesnos**
brave	**tregsnos**
breach	**bhernā**
bread	**bharsjom**
break	**bhrn̥gō**
break	**bhrúsnāmi**
break	**rumpō**
break off	**rewō**
break through	**wēdhājō**
break up	**lemō**
breast	**bhrusos**
breath	**anəmos**
breath	**ātmós**
breath	**spoisnā**
breathe	**ātō**
breathe	**pneusō**
breeze	**áweljā**
brew	**bhrewō**
briar	**ksentis**
bridge	**bhrēwā**
bright	**bhānús**
bright	**leukós**
brilliant	**argrós**
bring disgrace upon	**íneumi**
bring out	**dhraghō**
broad	**plātús**
brooch	**bharkos**
brooch	**dhéicodhlā**

brood	**aglā**
brook	**apnis**
brook	**reiwos**
broom	**aksteinos**
broom	**swoplom**
broth	**jeus**
brother	**bhrātēr**
brother-in-law	**daiwēr**
brotherly	**bhrā́trijos**
brother's son	**bhrātreinos**
brown	**bhrūnós**
bucket	**wedrom**
bud	**gnoubhos**
bug	**keimēx**
build	**demō**
building	**demos**
building place	**dm̥pedom**
bull	**porsis**
bull	**tauros**
bulrush	**bhrughnos**
bulrush	**joinkos**
bumblebee	**krāsrōn**
bundle	**bhaskis**
bundle	**dhrighsós**
burden	**bhermn̥**
burglar	**tājús**
burn	**aidhō**
burn	**smelō**
burn	**dhechō**
burn	**eusō**
burn	**kremājō**
burnt	**ustós**
burst	**spr̥gō**
burst in	**skekō**
bury	**dhelbhō**
bury	**ghrebhō**
bury	**sepēlijō**
bush	**bhrutēks**
bush	**dousmos**
bush	**qr̥snos**
but	**mō**
butter	**arwā**
butter	**ghertom**
butterfly	**pāpeljos**
buttock	**klounis**
buttocks	**pougā́**
buy	**qrínāmi**
buy	**selō**
buzz	**susājō**
cabbage	**kaulis**
cable	**snēwər**

cable	**winis**
cackle	**grakijō**
cackle	**kaklājō**
calculate	**deljō**
calf	**loigos**
calf	**wetlos**
call	**ghawō**
call for	**tolājō**
calm	**sēknis**
caluum caput	**gholwā́**
came	**ludhóm**
camel	**wl̥bhontis**
camp	**kastra**
can	**moghō**
cancer	**ghn̥dhus**
cannabis	**worgjom**
canopy	**skostrom**
cantus	**bhr̥ghtom**
captive	**kəptos**
car	**woghnos**
carbon	**kr̥dhōn**
caress	**ghneumi**
carrot	**mr̥kā**
carry	**portājō**
carry	**weghō**
cart	**kr̥sus**
carve	**skalpō**
carve	**skreidō**
carve	**smeidhō**
castle	**kasterlom**
castrate	**skerdō**
cat	**kattā**
catch	**kəpjō**
cattle	**ármn̥tom**
cattle	**peku**
cauldron	**qorjom**
cause	**winsō**
cause to sleep	**swōpijō**
cause to slope	**klínāmi**
caution	**wadhis**
cave	**antrom**
cave	**speqos**
cavern	**kowr̥**
cavity	**kusjom**
cedar	**bhrosdhos**
ceiling	**tegtom**
celebration	**eplom**
cellar	**gupā**
centre	**stornjā**
cereal	**dhōnā**
cereal	**jéwornjom**

cerebellum	**mosgom**
certain	**enis**
certainly	**dā**
certainly	**ghi**
certainly	**ka**
certainly	**smā**
certainly	**toi**
chaff	**akos**
chain	**katēsna**
chain	**seinus**
chair	**sedlā**
chalk	**krētā**
chamber	**kēlā**
chance	**wikis**
change	**mejō**
character	**mōs**
charge	**merkēds**
charioteer	**ərots**
chatter	**blatsājō**
cheap	**wésolis**
cheat	**meugō**
cheer	**owājō**
cheese	**kwatsos**
cheese	**tūrjós**
cherry tree	**kornos**
chest	**pegtos**
chest	**r̥klā**
chew	**gjewō**
chew	**mn̥tō**
child	**pūpos**
child	**putlom**
chin	**mn̥tom**
chin	**smekslā**
chirp	**bhrigijō**
chirp	**titijō**
choice	**wolos**
choke	**bhleusō**
choose	**wolējō**
choose	**opjō**
circle	**kirkos**
circuit	**ámbhinom**
circulate	**qelō**
citizen	**keiwis**
city	**polis**
civil	**kéiwijos**
clack	**glokijō**
clang	**klagjō**
classical	**ántitjos**
clean	**mūdnós**
clean	**powejō**
clean	**pr̥qjō**

clean	**pūtós**
clean	**pewō**
clear	**aiskrós**
clear	**bhlaidos**
clear	**skīrós**
cleave	**wágneumi**
cleave	**bhindō**
close	**klawdō**
close	**wəreumi**
close	**wr̥ijō**
close to	**pəra**
closed	**klawstós**
cloth	**westis**
cloth	**westrom**
clotted	**tm̥ktos**
cloud	**nebhos**
clown	**skoirsās**
club	**baktlom**
club	**lorgos**
club	**seikā**
club	**wísogā**
clumsy	**cr̥dos**
coal	**oncōl**
coast	**moljā**
coat	**pl̥tom**
cockroach	**blaktā**
cold	**kiklós**
cold	**ougros**
cold	**srīgos**
collapsed	**rwtós**
collar	**monīli**
collect	**karpō**
collect	**legō**
collection	**kómāglom**
collection	**qejtis**
colony	**ápowoiks**
colorant	**keimos**
colour	**kiwos**
colour	**wornos**
coloured	**pr̥qos**
colt	**kábn̥los**
colt	**kánkestos**
comb	**kesō**
comb	**pekō**
comb	**pektēn**
comb	**pektō**
combat	**chn̥tjā**
come	**cemjō**
come back	**ghighējō**
come out	**pārējō**
commission	**upóqrijom**

commit	**mn̥dōmi**
common	**kómmoinis**
communicate	**mesgō**
community	**kommoinitā́ts**
compasses	**kirknos**
compensate	**qinō**
compete	**sperdhō**
complain	**qésai**
complete	**kómplēnos**
complexed (to be)	**wn̥ghējō**
compose	**qejō**
comprehend	**tn̥ējō**
concession	**lētis**
concubine	**pareikā**
condense	**stejō**
condition	**dhēmn̥**
conducted	**elóm**
conflagration	**dáwetus**
connect	**serō**
conscience	**kómwoistis**
consider	**qeisō**
consideration	**qeistis**
consort	**komjugs**
conspiracy	**jālos**
conspirator	**jōrós**
conspire	**jáneumi**
construction	**demtis**
contain	**r̥kējō**
contend	**bhogājō**
contend	**wikjō**
content	**ghrobhos**
continuity	**tēn**
contrive	**smudhnō**
convex	**weksós**
convey	**ínekmi**
convey	**porejō**
convocation	**klāstis**
cook	**peqō**
cook	**peqtṓr**
cook	**poqós**
cooked	**peqtós**
cooking	**peqtis**
coot	**bhelēks**
copy	**áimneumi**
core	**pūrós**
corn	**niktis**
cornice	**ghrendhā**
cost of a feast	**dapnom**
couch	**stālos**
cough	**qostā**
cough	**tustijō**

coughing	**tustis**
courage	**nantis**
course	**drewā**
course	**kr̥stus**
court	**alkis**
court	**kómwoirjom**
courtyard	**dhworom**
cousin	**jentēr**
cover	**kelos**
cover	**skemō**
cover	**skeumō**
cover	**skeutō**
cover	**tegō**
covering	**skūtos**
cow	**cows**
cow	**ēghī**
cow	**lāpos**
cow	**wakkā**
crab	**karkros**
crack	**reimā**
crackle	**krépāmi**
cradle	**gretlom**
crane	**crús**
crawl	**rēpō**
crawl	**serpō**
crazy	**dhwolnos**
create	**genesājō**
create	**krēmi**
creãtor	**amsus**
creature	**teknom**
creep	**snəghjō**
crest	**kripstā**
crib	**bhondhsā**
crime	**kreimn̥**
crime	**lōbā**
criminal	**worghós**
crimpy hair	**gouros**
crook	**bhogjos**
crop	**sasjóm**
cross	**kreuks**
cross	**terō**
crossbeam	**ghlaghos**
crow	**kornīks**
crowd	**plēdhwis**
crowd	**slougos**
crown	**grendjom**
crumb	**groumos**
crumb	**smeikā**
crumble	**dhrubhjō**
crumble	**bhrijājō**
crush	**melujō**

crush	**mr̥tājō**
crush	**pinsō**
cry	**dhrensājō**
cry	**wāghijō**
cry	**wr̥kājō**
cry	**kreugō**
cry	**krigā**
cry	**reudō**
crying	**roudos**
cuckoo	**kukūlós**
cuckoo	**kukulājō**
cudge	**dolājō**
cuirass	**bhrusnjā**
cup	**kalēiks**
cup	**koupā**
curb	**bhegō**
curd cheese	**grutis**
curdled milk	**tm̥klos**
curly	**kripsos**
curtail	**sneitō**
curve	**witjom**
curve	**keubō**
curve	**qelpō**
curved	**km̥ros**
curved	**kr̥wos**
cushion	**qolkā**
custom	**swēdhus**
cut	**tomos**
cut	**kaidō**
cut	**kretō**
cut	**sékāmi**
cut	**tmāmi**
cut off	**snadhō**
cut off	**spl̥tājō**
cut off	**sr̥pjō**
cut open	**bhr̥ijō**
cut out	**drepō**
cut out	**treukō**
dace	**menis**
dad	**appās**
dad	**attās**
dad	**tātā**
dam	**roinos**
damage	**klādis**
damage	**lēumi**
damage	**pēmn̥**
damage	**wolsom**
dare	**dhr̥sō**
dark	**dherghos**
dark	**dhóncelos**
dark	**dhoncos**

dark	**dhūskos**
dark	**keiros**
dark	**ml̥nos**
dark	**morcós**
dark	**skeuros**
darkness	**recos**
darkness	**temesras**
dart	**golbhnos**
daughter	**dhugtēr**
daughter-in-law	**snusós**
dawn	**ausōsā**
dawn	**áussketi**
day	**dhochos**
day	**dinos**
day	**djēws**
day	**latom**
dead	**mr̥tos**
dead	**mr̥wos**
deaf	**bodhrós**
deaf	**dhoubhos**
dear	**leubhos**
dear	**prijós**
death	**chentis**
death	**dheunos**
death	**mr̥tis**
death	**neks**
debt	**dhl̥eghlā**
deceive	**chl̥nō**
deceive	**dhwerō**
deceive	**melsō**
decide	**skidjō**
declare	**lenghmi**
decline	**sterbhō**
decree	**dhedhmós**
deep	**dhubús**
deer	**kerwos**
defame	**kl̥wijō**
defecate	**ghedō**
defecate	**kakkājō**
defect	**smeros**
defective	**mn̥kos**
defence	**wertrom**
defend	**mághneumi**
deflect	**skl̥neumi**
deity	**deiwotāts**
delay	**morā**
delight	**wenjā**
demand	**kupjō**
demon	**dhwosos**
den	**bhōljóm**
dense	**tegús**

densifiy	**stoipejō**
depart	**oighai**
departure	**proitis**
deposit	**loghos**
depressed	**neiwós**
desert	**jēlom**
desert	**tuskjós**
deserve	**mərējō**
designate	**mātejō**
desire	**aisskā**
desire	**gherijai**
desire	**awējō**
desire	**chelō**
desire	**smegō**
desire	**wekmi**
desire	**wenō**
desire	**wn̥skā**
desire	**wn̥skō**
desire eagerly	**jn̥tō**
destitute	**awtjos**
destroy	**arejō**
destroy	**dheukō**
destroy	**nokejō**
destroy	**olējō**
destruction	**dhchitis**
detergent	**mūdlom**
determine	**rékneumi**
development	**augos**
devotion	**krōbhtus**
devour	**sleugō**
devour	**cerbhō**
devour	**crājō**
devour (to)	**swelājō**
dew	**dolghos**
diarrhea	**dhorjā**
dick	**bhn̥ghus**
die	**mərijai**
died	**walóm**
difference	**kritis**
different	**íteros**
different	**kritós**
dig	**bhodhjō**
dig	**kánāmi**
dig out	**teukō**
dim	**bhlendhos**
dimension	**mētis**
diminished	**dhebhús**
dinner	**kersnā**
dip	**wəronkis**
direct	**dhn̥ghus**
direct	**regō**

direction	**wertmn̥**
dirt	**kóqros**
dirt	**lutom**
dirt	**qoinom**
dirty	**coudhros**
dirty	**salús**
dirty	**keqō**
dis-	**rēd/re**
disabled	**mr̥kos**
discern	**skijō**
disgrace	**ghálerom**
disguise	**mengō**
dish	**pēlwis**
disk	**orbhis**
dismantle	**dhruslijō**
dispersed	**rārós**
dispossession	**spoljom**
disrupt	**dolejō**
distaff	**qolus**
distance	**apóstətis**
distribute	**nemō**
dive	**cadhō**
diverse	**wikwos**
divide	**kl̥jō**
divide	**r̥nāmi**
divide	**weidhō**
divide up	**daimoi**
do	**dhídhēmi-dhəkjō**
do harm	**ghudjō**
do harm	**kepō**
do military service	**dhreughō**
do not?	**nom nē**
docile	**gleghos**
doctor	**médodiks**
dog	**kolignos**
dog	**kwōn**
domain	**dm̥seghr̥**
dome	**krūtis**
door	**dhworis**
door	**wēr**
door-bar	**r̥kēslom**
double	**dwoplós**
doubt	**okējō**
dough	**reughmn̥**
dough	**taismos**
dove	**dhombhos**
dove	**kólumbhos**
down	**dhūmā**
down	**nī**
dowry	**dōtis**
dowry	**wedhnom**

drag	**selkō**
drag	**deukō**
drag	**traghō**
drag	**wersō**
drag away	**tenghō**
drapery	**drappos**
draw	**pípāmi**
draw tight	**stringō**
dream	**ónerjos**
dream	**swepr̥**
dream	**swopnjom**
dream	**swopnjājō**
dregs	**suljā**
dress	**westijō**
dress	**wosejō**
drink	**echmi**
drink	**ēchr̥**
drink	**pōtis**
drink	**pibō**
drinker	**pōtṓr**
drinking	**pōnom**
drip	**seilō**
drive	**enkō prō**
drizzle	**aghlóws**
drone	**bhoiqos**
droop	**lāgō**
drop	**bn̥dus**
drop	**dhrubhtis**
drop	**leibs**
drop	**spakos**
drum	**bámbalos**
drunken	**ēchr̥jos**
drunken	**tēmos**
dry	**kserós**
dry	**sisqos**
dry	**susdos**
dry	**susjō**
dry	**tr̥stos**
dry	**tr̥sus**
dry	**torsejō**
dry (to)	**ādmi**
dry skin	**sterbhnjom**
duck	**anəts**
dust	**pelwos**
duty (religious)	**dhēs**
dwell	**trebhō**
dwelling	**bhūtā́**
dwelling	**westus**
eagle	**éroros**
eagle owl	**bughōn**
ear	**ousis**

early	**ájeri**
early	**ghrēw**
earth	**dheghom**
earth	**pl̥táwijā**
earth	**tersā**
eastern	**áusteros**
easy	**reidhos**
eat	**áknāmi**
eat	**edmi**
eat	**weskai**
edge	**ōrā**
edge	**bhrenō**
eel	**ellus**
effort	**mōlos**
egg	**ṓw(ij)om**
eight	**oktōu**
eight hundred	**octōkm̥tṓs**
eight hundredth	**octōkm̥témtəmos**
eighteen	**óktōdekm̥**
eighteenth	**óktōdekəmos**
eighth	**oktowós**
eightieth	**oktṓdkm̥təṃos**
eighty	**oktṓdkm̥ta**
eject	**jəkjō**
elastic	**tm̥pus**
elbow	**ōlnā**
elder	**edhlos**
element	**skōlos**
eleven	**sémdekm̥**
eleventh	**sémdekəmos**
elm	**olmos**
elm	**woighos**
embank	**klāmi**
embroidery	**snētjā**
embryo	**geltis**
embryon	**crebhos**
employee	**dhəmos**
empty	**wāstos**
empty	**wōnós**
empty	**ausijō**
enact	**sankijō**
encircle	**gherdhō**
enclose	**twerō**
enclosure	**ghordhos**
enclosure	**kaghos**
enclosure	**odhrom**
enclosure	**wəregis**
enclosure	**wr̥tom**
encourage	**ghorejai**
end	**antjom**
end	**bendā**

end	**dhicsnis**
end	**termēn**
endeavour	**rōdhjō**
endure	**tlāmi**
enemy	**nemots**
enhance	**bheljō**
enjoy oneself	**terpō**
enjoyment	**terptis**
enliven	**wegō**
enough (to be)	**dheughō**
entrails	**sorwā**
entrails	**sternom**
entrance	**jā́nuwā**
envelope	**wélwtrom**
environment	**bhewtlom**
envy	**r̥sjā**
equal	**somós**
equipment	**kómopjom**
equipped with	**went**
erect	**ghorsejō**
ermine	**kormōn**
escape	**skeubhō**
establish	**tkeimi**
estimate	**qíqeimi**
eternal	**aiwós**
eternal	**jucis**
eternity	**áiwotāts**
even	**aiqos**
even	**eti**
even	**gladhros**
even	**étiqe**
evening	**wespros**
evident	**gnōros**
evil	**skelos**
example	**deikmn̥**
excavator	**kernos**
excellent	**bhodrós**
excellent	**wēsus**
excepted	**ektós**
exchange	**mítnāmi**
exchange	**moitos**
exchange	**mojnos**
exchange	**moitājō**
excite	**sprewō**
exclusive	**káiwelos**
excrement	**ghedmr̥-**
exhaustion	**dhətis**
expect	**welpō**
expel	**(jí)jēmi**
experience	**perijō**
expert	**suwids**

explain	**títermi**
explode	**bólboljō**
expression	**bhātis**
expression	**weqtlom**
extend	**spēmi**
extend	**tendō**
extend	**tenjō**
extend	**tensō**
extend (to)	**tonejō**
extended	**próstōrnos**
extension	**str̥nos**
external	**éksteros**
extinguish	**césneumi**
extraordinary	**n̥swodhros**
exuberant	**jn̥dros**
eye	**oqos**
eyebrow	**bhrūs**
face	**enīqā**
fact	**dhētis**
faint	**təmjai**
fair weather	**qoitrós, koitrós**
fall	**mūjō**
fall	**polnō**
fall	**kadō**
fall asleep	**dr̥mijō**
fall down	**pedjō**
fall down	**piptō**
fall into	**ghrewō**
fallow	**polkā**
false	**məljos**
family	**gentis**
famine	**nōunā**
famous	**klūtós**
fan	**bhlādhrom**
fan	**prējō**
fancy	**ləskējō**
far	**dew**
far	**porsōd**
far (from)	**qeli**
farewell	**r̥tís**
farm	**woikslā**
farmer	**agróqolās**
far-reaching	**sētús**
fart	**pesdō**
farther	**peros**
fashion	**teksō**
fasten	**pakō**
fastening	**apmn̥**
fasting	**donkrós**
fat	**lajos**
fat	**pīmós**

fat	**piwōn**
fatality	**moros**
father	**pətēr**
father-in-law	**swékuros**
fatherland	**pətrjā**
fatherly	**pətrjos**
fault	**agos**
fault	**loktos**
fault	**mendom**
fault	**woinā́**
favour	**wēr**
favourable	**bhōwijós**
fear	**pəwējō**
fear	**pr̥gjō**
fear	**āghar**
fear	**bhíbheimi**
fear	**dweimi**
fearful	**dwoiros**
feast	**westos**
feast	**wl̥dā́**
feather	**peróm**
feather	**petsnā**
feather	**plousmā**
feather	**pornós**
feeble	**térunos**
feed	**pāskō**
feel	**awisdhijō**
feel ashamed	**aichesājō**
feel burnt	**kn̥kējō**
female	**dhḗmonā**
fence	**saipis**
ferment	**jesō**
fern	**pratis**
ferret	**wéiwersā**
fetch	**oitmi**
fever	**tepnos**
field	**arwom**
field	**maghos**
fierce	**saiwos**
fierceness	**tonslis**
fifteen	**pénqedekm̥**
fifteenth	**pénqedekəmos**
fifth	**penqtos**
fiftieth	**penqédkm̥təmos**
fifty	**penqédkm̥ta**
fig	**bheikos**
fight	**katus**
fight	**streudō**
file	**sleimā**
fill	**píperkmi**
fill	**(pím)plēmi**

fill	**pl̥nāmi**
filling	**plēmn̥**
filling	**plētis**
filth	**mergis**
finch	**spingjā**
find	**(wí)wermi**
find by chance	**nn̥kskai**
find out	**windō**
finger	**cistis**
finger	**dékm̥tulos**
finger	**gnetō**
fingernail	**onchis**
finish	**cerjō**
fire	**ecnis**
fire	**pāwr̥**
firm	**omos**
first	**prāmos**
first	**prāwos**
first	**prīsmos**
first (of two)	**próteros**
fish	**piskis**
fist	**penqstis**
fist	**pougnos**
five	**penqe**
five hundred	**penqekm̥tṓs**
five hundredth	**penqekm̥témtəmos**
fix	**pastos**
fixed	**pəgtós**
flake	**bhlokos**
flame	**bhləgsmā**
flame	**bhokos**
flask	**óbrusjā**
flat	**lergos**
flat	**plākos**
flat	**plānos**
flat-footed	**plautos**
flatness	**pl̥tnos**
flatten	**stelghmi**
flax	**leinom**
flea	**puslēks**
fleabane	**dhwestus**
flee	**bhugjō**
fleece	**gnebhis**
flexible	**lugnós**
flight	**bhougā́**
flimmer	**merkō**
flimmer	**míkāmi**
flood	**pleudō**
floor	**plārom**
flour	**melwom**
flour	**mlātóm**

flourishing	**ghlustis**
flow	**ersō**
flow	**plewō**
flow	**sísermi**
flow	**sormos**
flow	**bhlewō**
flow	**mejājō**
flow	**srewō**
flow	**weisō**
flow down	**stelghō**
flower	**bhlōs**
flower	**bhlōtis**
fluoresce	**bhelō**
flush away	**rínāmi**
flutter	**spn̥dō**
fly	**muskā**
fly	**petō**
fly	**cəlājō**
foal	**kurnos**
foam	**spoimā**
foenum	**koinos**
fog	**kalgōn**
fog	**nebhlā**
foggy, to be	**wapējō**
fold	**cijā**
fold	**bheugō**
fold	**plékāmi**
follow	**seqai**
food	**pasknis**
food	**pitús**
food	**westā**
foot	**pods**
footprint	**lorgā**
footprint	**pedom**
forbid	**wétāmi**
force	**stolgos**
force	**tewos**
force	**twenghō**
force in	**treudō**
ford	**pr̥tus**
forearm	**lakertos**
forehead	**bhrówn̥tis**
foreigner	**ghostis**
foremost	**prījṓs**
forest	**nemos**
fork	**ghabhlom**
fork	**mergā**
form	**magō**
form	**pr̥ptus**
formerly	**ōlim**
fortieth	**qétwr̥dkm̥təmos**

fortification	**karkar**
fortify	**moinijai**
forty	**qétwr̥dkm̥ta**
forwards	**prō(d)**
foundation	**dhəmelós**
fountain	**awā**
fountain	**awn̥**
fountain	**dhontis**
four	**qetwores, qétesres**
four days	**qətwr̥djówijom**
four each	**qətrusnōs**
four hundred	**qetwr̥km̥tṓs**
four hundreth	**qetwr̥km̥témtm̥os**
four times	**qəturs**
four years	**qətwr̥atnjom**
fourteen	**qétwordekm̥**
fourteenth	**qétwordekəmos**
fourth	**qətwr̥tos**
fox	**wolpis**
foxglove	**spjonos**
fragment	**bhroustom**
fragrant	**swekos**
framework	**wītjā́**
fraud	**dolos**
fray	**sremsō**
free	**léudheros**
free	**nosejō**
freeze	**prunsō**
frequent	**menghos**
friend	**ámeikā**
friend	**amēiks**
fringe	**antjās**
from	**apo**
from	**ekstrōd**
from there	**imde**
from there	**totrōd**
from this side	**kina**
from upwards	**dē**
from which	**jomde**
frost	**pruswā́**
frozen snow	**kernós**
fruit	**ágrēnom**
fruit	**bhreugs**
fry	**bhagjō**
fry	**bhreigō**
frypan	**landhom**
fuck	**jebhō**
fuel	**dawtis**
fugacious	**tokwós**
full	**plēnós**
full	**plētós**

fundament	**upósēdjom**
fungus	**swombhós**
furniture	**endósēdjom**
furrow	**pr̥kā́**
furrow	**qelsō**
furrow	**solkos**
further	**ólteros**
furthest	**óltm̥os**
gall	**bistlis**
gape	**ghjājō**
garden	**ghortos**
garlic	**álujos**
garlic	**kesnus**
garment	**togā́**
garment	**wospos**
gather	**gr̥neumi**
gather	**katsājō**
gaul	**galnos**
gaze	**qekō**
gender	**genjos**
gentle	**klisrós**
germ	**genmn̥**
germinate	**gembhō**
get angry	**kr̥dijai**
get cumulated	**derghō**
get dressed	**owō**
get drunk	**pojejō**
get dry	**tersai**
get encrusted	**kreupō**
get in a space	**telpō**
get skilled	**dídn̥skō**
get tired	**kmāmi**
gift	**dōnom**
gird	**kingō**
girl	**maqā**
give	**(dí)dōmi**
give birth	**pərijō**
give joy	**sōlājai**
give one's opinion	**tongejō**
glade	**loukos**
glance	**augā́**
glare	**swelō**
glass	**pōtlom**
glide	**sleidhō**
glimmer	**bherkō**
glimmer	**ghlōmi**
globe	**globhos**
gloomy	**mauros**
glory	**klewos**
glove	**ghesris**
glow	**kandō**

glowing ash	**geulom**
glue	**gloitn̥**
gnat	**kūleks**
gnaw	**gnāmi**
gnaw	**ghrendō**
gnaw away	**trowō**
gnaw off	**gnabhjō**
go	**leitō**
go	**eimi**
go	**r̥skai**
go aside	**greubhō**
go away	**cícāmi**
go back to a good place/ state	**ninsai**
go down	**keidō**
goat	**bokkos**
goat	**dighā**
goat	**ghabhros**
goat	**kaprā**
goat	**kapros**
goatish	**ghaidīnós**
god	**deiwos**
goddess	**deiwā**
godly	**déiwijos**
gold	**ausom**
gold	**ghl̥tom**
golden	**ghl̥tnós**
good	**bhilis**
good	**dwenos**
good	**ēsús**
good	**mānos**
good	**probhwos**
goos	**ghansōr**
gorgeous	**kaljós**
grace	**ghəris**
grain	**grānóm**
grand-daughter	**neptis**
grandfather	**awos**
grandfather	**dhēdhjos**
grandmother	**anus**
grandmother	**áwijā**
grandson	**nepēts**
granny	**annā**
grant	**lēmi**
grass	**ghrāsmn̥**
grass	**ghrāsom**
grātus	**súghoris**
grave	**bhodsā**
gravel	**geisā**
greasy	**liprós**
great	**mgānts**

greater	**plējṓs**
greatest	**plēistos**
greatness	**məgistā́**
green	**ghelwos**
grey	**kasnos**
grey	**pálowos**
grey	**pl̥wós**
grey	**rāwos**
grind	**ghrewō**
grind	**melō**
groan	**onkājō**
groin	**ili**
groin	**n̥cḗn**
groom	**pusbhis**
ground	**bhudhnos**
ground	**swólejā**
ground	**telsus**
group	**gromos**
group	**kerdhos**
group	**qelos**
grow	**krēskō**
grow	**r̥dhjō**
grow fat	**peidō**
grow thin	**kerkō**
growl	**ghelijō**
grown	**augtós**
grown	**grn̥dhís**
grumble	**ghremō**
grumble	**wr̥n̥gai**
grunt	**bhremō**
grunt	**grundijō**
guardian	**sr̥wos**
guerrilla	**bhogā́**
guest	**ghóstipots**
guile	**astus**
gull	**medgós**
gullet	**cəlā**
gulp	**slr̥gjō**
gum	**gengā**
gush	**skatējō**
gush up	**bhrendhō**
hail	**grōdis**
hair	**ghaitā**
hair	**kaisrom**
hair	**kerom**
hair	**lowā**
hair	**pilos**
hair	**rewmn̥**
hair	**welnos**
hair	**wondhos**
hair (strong)	**saitā**

hairdresser	**tonstṓr**
half	**sēmi-**
hall	**werstidhlom**
ham	**persnā**
hammer	**matlā**
hammer	**moltlom**
hammer	**ordhos**
hand	**ghesr̥**
hand	**ghestos**
hand	**mn̥us**
hand	**wəronkā́**
handle	**ansā**
handle	**ghetlā**
handle	**skāpos**
hang	**lembō**
hang	**pendō**
happen	**gígisai**
hard	**kartús**
hardened	**kəletos**
harm	**skodhos**
harn	**wəreinā**
harrow	**óketā**
harsh	**drismós**
harvest	**əsnātis**
haste	**spoudā́**
hasten	**bhūsjō**
hasten	**skegō**
hatchet	**tōkslos**
hate	**odjō (ōda)**
hatred	**ōdjom**
have	**eikō**
have fever	**cerō**
have taste	**səpijō**
have wrinkle	**gr̥bējō**
haven	**kopnos**
hawk	**astris**
hawk	**ōkúpteros**
hazel	**kósolos**
hazelnut	**árusā**
head	**ghebhlā**
head	**kaput**
head	**kersr̥**
head of cereal	**speikā**
health	**kóilutāts**
healthy	**jekos**
healthy	**koilús**
heap	**kūmós**
heap	**struwis**
hear	**gheusō**
hear	**kl̥neumi**
hearing	**kleumn̥**

heart	**kr̥di / kr̥djom**
hearth	**aidhis**
hearth	**chornos**
heat	**āmi**
heat	**cheros**
heat	**olejō**
heath	**kaitom**
heave	**erō**
heaviness	**crutā**
heavy	**cr(āw)ús**
heavy	**crətos**
heavy	**tn̥ghus**
hedgehog	**eghjos**
hedgehog	**ghēr**
heed	**pāsmi**
heel	**kalkis**
heel	**persā**
he-goat	**bhugos**
hello	**alā!**
helmet	**kelmos**
helmet	**korudhs**
help	**jewō**
hen	**kerkos**
henbane	**bhélunā**
herb	**lubhjā**
herd	**gregs**
herdsman	**cówqolos**
herdsman	**kerdhjos**
here	**kei**
heron	**árdejā**
hesitate	**kenkai**
hide	**kēlājō**
hide	**keudhō**
hiding place	**kūlā**
high	**altós**
high	**bhr̥ghos**
high	**orús**
high	**úperos**
high	**úpselos**
hill	**kolnis**
hill	**montis**
himself	**se**
hinge	**kr̥dḗn**
hint	**apóteros**
hip	**koksā**
hip	**londhwos**
hip bone	**koksednīks**
his	**séwijos**
hiss	**streidō**
hit	**bhenjom**
hit	**kawdō**

hit	**kawō**
hit	**bhətjō**
hit	**bhlagō**
hit	**bhleicō**
hit	**bhutjō**
hit	**slakō**
hit	**steupō**
hold	**potējō**
hold	**seghō**
hold (to)	**jemō**
hole	**lugjā**
hollow	**dholos**
hollow	**dhónejā**
hollow	**ghéwejā**
hollow	**kowos**
hollow out	**skerbhō**
holy	**kwentos**
holy	**noibhos**
holy	**sakrós**
home god	**lāōs**
honey	**melit**
honour	**aisdai**
honour	**ghōdhos**
honour	**məgtājō**
hoof	**kopos**
hook	**ankos**
hook	**kenkos**
hook	**khamos**
hook	**onkos**
hoopoe	**ópopā**
hope	**spēs**
horn	**kr̥nu**
hornbeam	**gr̥beinos**
hornless	**kemos**
horse	**ekwos**
horse	**kabōn**
horse	**markos**
hostage	**gheislos**
hot	**kl̥tos**
house	**domos**
house	**weiks**
housemaster	**esos**
hovel	**cr̥cestjom**
how	**jota**
how	**qālis**
how	**qota**
how great	**qā́wn̥tos**
how many	**qot(j)os**
howbeit	**aw**
howl	**ululājō**
hub	**qolos**

hum	**kemjō**
human being	**dhghomōn**
humble	**wailos**
humiliate	**neidō**
hump	**gibbā**
hundred	**km̥tom**
hundredth	**km̥témtəmos**
hunger	**dhəmis**
hunger	**ghrēdhus**
hunt	**woitā**
hunt	**(wí)weimi**
hurry	**sperghō**
hurry	**speudō**
hut	**kleitis**
hut	**koutā**
I	**egō**
ice	**eisom**
ice	**gelu**
ice	**gləgjēs**
ice	**jegis**
icicle	**krustā**
icicle	**stejsjā**
ignorant	**n̥widis**
ill	**aigros**
ill-treat	**mr̥kjō**
illuminate	**bháneumi**
illuminate	**loukejō**
immediate	**udhús**
immediately	**kitōd**
immortal	**n̥mrtijos**
impair	**dhebhō**
impel	**peldō**
important	**swērús**
impregnate	**tengō**
impression	**wl̥tus**
in	**en**
in excess	**n̥dhi**
in the middle	**meti**
in the morning	**prōi**
incise	**ghelō**
incision	**bhr̥mā**
incite	**r̥ghējō**
incite	**trenkō**
incited	**orghós**
inclined	**nīqos**
include	**glembhō**
incompetent	**duswids**
increase	**augmn̥**
increase	**augō**
increscō	**augsō**
indeed	**gar**

indeed	**qidpe**
indication	**deiktis**
induce (to)	**woghejō**
infere	**densō**
inferior	**ńteros**
inflammation	**dheghwis**
inflate	**bhleidō**
inflate	**pusjō**
inform	**steumi**
inheritance	**orbhjom**
insect	**empis**
inside	**endo**
inside	**entós**
inside	**ētr̥**
insipid	**merwos**
inspect (to)	**skewō**
install	**dhídhneumi**
insult	**pējō**
intellect	**menmn̥**
intelligence	**sn̥stus**
intelligent	**glēkis**
intend	**seikō**
intend	**mn̥sjai**
interest	**dhēnos**
interior	**ennós**
internal	**énternos**
internal	**énteros**
interval	**énterom**
intestine	**énteros**
intestine	**ghoros**
intestine	**routos**
invert (to)	**wortejō**
investigate	**windō peri**
invisible	**eksoqs**
invite	**l̥tejō**
invoke	**kiklēskō**
iron	**īsarnom**
irritate	**prousijō**
island	**enslā**
ivy	**khéderos**
jar	**goulos**
jaws	**gombhos**
jaws	**gopos**
jet	**krosnos**
join	**jungō**
joint	**artus**
joint	**koubos**
joke	**ghloumos**
joke	**ghleumi**
journey	**itājō**
joy	**gaudhjom**

joyful	**ghoilos**
joyful	**rōdos**
judge	**jewesdiks**
juice	**sapos**
juice	**soukos**
jump	**rebhājō**
jump	**dhr̥numoi**
jump	**leigō**
jump out	**prewō**
juniper	**lentos**
juniper	**toksos**
just	**jéwestos**
keel	**kareinā**
keep	**bherghō**
keep	**kadhō**
key	**klāws**
kidney	**ārōn**
kidney	**neghrōn**
kill	**nékāmi**
kin	**genos**
kindle	**andhō**
kindness	**prósēdjom**
king	**regs**
kingdom	**regnom**
kingly	**regjos**
kiss	**kusis**
kiss	**sówijā**
kiss	**bhusājō**
knead	**bheurō**
knead	**debhō**
knee	**genu**
knee	**teupō**
knock	**bheldō**
knot	**nōdos**
knot	**osdcos**
know	**(gí)gnōskō (gnōwa)**
know	**woida**
knower	**gnōtṓr**
knowing	**woidwṓs**
knowledge	**gnōtis**
known	**gnōtós**
lack	**egējō**
lack	**kəsējō**
lack	**meitō**
lack	**menkō**
ladder	**skandslā**
ladle	**trowā**
lake	**ágherom**
lake	**lakus**
lamb	**acnos**
lamb	**wərēn**

lame	**klaudos**
lamp	**lapsā**
land	**agros**
land	**erwā**
land	**kampos**
land	**londhom**
land	**oudn̥**
land estate	**kāpos**
landlady	**dómūnā**
landlord	**dómūnos**
lap	**gremjom**
lapis lazuli	**kúwanos**
lapwing	**gówijā**
large fish	**sqalos**
last	**póstm̥os**
last year	**péruti**
late	**lodi**
later	**sḗtjosi**
laugh	**gélāmi**
laugh	**khákhatnos**
laugh	**wr̥isdējō**
law	**jewos**
law	**legs**
lax	**loksos**
lay	**leghos**
lay	**strāmn̥**
lay down	**loghejō**
lazy	**leghskós**
lead	**nijóm**
lead	**plúwaidhom**
lead	**wedhō**
leader	**deuks**
leader	**wəlos**
leaf	**bholjom**
leaf	**leups**
lean	**gneichō**
leap	**rebhā**
leap	**kekō**
learn	**didkskō**
leather	**korjom**
leather	**letrom**
leather bag	**wədris**
leave	**linqō**
leek	**pr̥som**
left	**laiwós**
left	**soujós**
left-handed	**skaiwós**
leg	**kanmā**
leg	**krous**
legal suit	**stlītis**
legbent	**watjos**

lend	**gherō**
lend	**loiqnom**
length	**dl̥nghotā**
leprosy	**trudskā**
less	**mínusi**
lessen	**sewājō**
let out	**munkō**
leuer	**weghtis**
level surface	**grejos**
lick	**linghō**
lie	**leghjai**
lie	**leghō**
lie	**keimoi**
lie	**kúbāmi**
lie	**leughō**
lie down	**jəkējō**
lie open	**pətējō**
life	**cītā**
life	**cīwos**
lifetime	**saitlom**
ligament	**tenos**
light	**bhāos**
light	**dr̥ktā**
light	**leghús**
light	**leuks**
light	**leuksmn̥**
light	**l̥nghros**
light up	**lukskējō**
lighting	**bhānom**
like	**iwe**
like	**lubhējō**
likewise	**itim**
lily	**leiljom**
limb	**apsos**
limb	**karōn**
lime-tree	**leipā**
lime-tree	**pteljā**
limit	**bhrēunā**
limp	**skn̥gjō**
line	**streibā**
line	**strigjā**
link	**nedō**
link	**wédhneumi**
lion	**wəlewā**
lip	**ghelnom**
lip	**ləbjom**
lip	**mēknos**
liquid	**latēks**
liquid	**serom**
liquid	**wəleiqos**
liquid (to be)	**wl̥iqējō**

list	**rēimn̥**
listen	**kleumi**
listening	**kleutis**
little	**paukos**
live	**cejwō**
lively	**cīwāks**
liver	**jeqr̥**
load	**gomos**
load	**onos**
lobster	**km̥ertos**
lock	**ghrendhos**
lock of hair	**pulgā**
lofty	**mlōdhrós**
long	**dl̥nghos**
long for	**gheidhō**
long hair	**káisr̥jēs**
longing	**chodhjā**
long-lasting	**sēros**
look	**spekjō**
look like	**prepō**
loom	**weimn̥**
lot	**koupnā**
lot	**teusmn̥**
lotus	**kémeros**
loud	**klārós**
loud	**torós**
louse	**lousēn**
love	**kāmi**
love	**stergō**
love	**wenos**
love (to)	**amājō**
love potion	**wenēsnom**
lovely	**koimos**
lower	**nérteros**
luck	**toughā́**
lung	**lənchijóm**
lung	**pleumōn**
lush	**cīrós**
lustful	**ləsnis**
luxury	**ghloidos**
lynx	**louksos**
magic	**qədnos**
magic	**soitos**
magic force	**qedos**
magician	**kowis**
magnanimous	**məgnánəmos**
magnificent	**m̥gadhós**
magpie	**peikos**
maid	**ándhesā**
maim	**skutājō**
maintain	**dl̥ghējō**

make	**qr̥eumi**
make adequate	**plākājō**
make afraid	**trosejō**
make bitter	**streubhō**
make black	**mercō**
make equal (to)	**somejō**
make fly	**potejō**
make grow	**augejō**
make grow	**wogsejō**
make hot	**dhochejō**
make money	**pelō**
make noise	**bhelō**
make noise	**strepō**
make slim	**mākājō**
make up	**dr̥kjō**
male	**r̥sēn**
male	**wersis**
mallow-plant	**ml̥wā**
man	**mánnusos**
man	**wīrós**
mane	**kripsnis**
manner	**koitús**
mantle	**sagom**
maple	**ákeris**
maple	**kleinos**
march	**cm̥tis**
march	**oimos**
mare	**ekwā**
mark	**ghronos**
mark	**gnṓmenjom**
marrow	**smerwā**
marry	**sneubhō**
marsh	**máreskos**
mass	**kōmos**
mass	**mōlis**
mass	**sloidhos**
massacre	**agrā**
mast	**masdos**
master	**potis**
matching	**dwīskos**
mate	**bhendhros**
mate	**dāmos**
mattock	**sligōn**
maxilla	**genus**
me	**me**
mead	**medhu**
meager	**petlos**
mean	**doiknejō**
means	**moghtrom**
measure	**mestis**
measure	**metrom**

measure	**modos**
measure	**mēmi**
measure	**mētijai**
measured	**mestós**
meat	**mēmsóm**
meet	**katsājai**
meet	**mimdō**
meet with point (to)	**aikō**
meeting	**komnom**
melodious	**bhendos**
melt	**tādhēskō**
melt	**tínāmi**
melt	**títāmi**
memory	**smemorjā**
mention	**mn̥tos**
mention	**cotejō**
metal	**roudhós**
midday	**médhidjōws**
middle	**medhjos**
middle (in the)	**obhi**
middling	**leswos**
might	**moghtis**
mild	**loisós**
mild	**moilos**
milk	**glaghti**
milk	**molgējō**
mill	**moleinā**
millet	**keros**
millet	**meljom**
millstone	**crā́wenus**
millstone	**molā**
mind	**mn̥tis**
miracle	**smeirātlom**
miserable	**treughos**
missing	**sn̥terí**
mist	**mighlā**
mistletoe	**wiskom**
mistress	**potnjā**
mix	**mikskejō**
mix	**krāmi**
model	**dhinghō**
modest	**nesros**
moisture	**aijus**
molder	**pujō**
moment	**mēlom**
money	**alchos**
month	**mēnsis**
moo	**mūgijō**
moon	**louksnā**
more	**məgis**

more	**mājis**
more	**plēis**
more than that	**immō**
morning	**āmros - āmrei**
morning	**ausrom**
morning	**wēsros**
mortar	**mr̥tāsjom**
moss	**muskos**
mother	**ammā**
mother	**mātḗr**
mother-in-law	**swekrús**
motley	**pr̥knos**
mould	**gheutis**
mound	**tumlós**
mount	**skandō**
mountain	**ceri**
mountain	**oros**
mountain	**pérkūnjom**
mountain-path	**kl̥dis**
mouse	**gleis**
mouse	**mūs**
mouth	**ōs**
mouthful	**bukkā**
move	**djejō**
move	**r̥neumi**
move	**meicō**
move	**mowejō**
move	**pelkō**
move away	**spr̥nō**
movement	**r̥nutis**
mow	**amsō**
much	**pelu**
mucus	**moukos**
mud	**korkos**
mud	**loimos**
mud	**mūtrom**
mud	**penom**
multitude	**lugtos**
multitude	**tūljom**
mum	**mammā**
mundane	**cécālos**
murder	**chenmi**
murmur	**dr̥drājō**
murmur	**mr̥mrājō**
muscle	**kīkus**
muscle	**meus / muskós**
must	**mudstos**
mutilate	**kersō**
mutilated	**klambós**
mutter	**muttijō**
mutual	**moitwos**

myop	**neukos**
mystery	**kelgā**
nail	**klawos**
nail	**onghlos**
nail	**pn̥gō**
naked	**nócodos**
name	**nōmn̥**
name	**práinōmn̥**
name	**werjō**
name	**kəlejō**
name	**nōmnājō**
narrow	**amghús**
narrowness	**ámghustis**
nates	**nətis**
native	**gnos**
nature	**bhewtis**
navel	**onbhlos**
near	**nedjos**
near	**proqēd**
neck	**amchḗn**
neck	**knokos**
neck	**kolsos**
neck	**mongos**
neck	**monos**
necklace	**torqis**
need	**n̥kējō**
needle	**akus**
neglect	**mersō**
neighbour	**nedus**
nest	**nisdos**
net	**grebhos**
net	**nedsā**
nettle	**nedis**
network	**gersā**
network	**krātis**
never	**neqom**
new	**new(ij)os**
newness	**newotāts**
nigh	**proqos**
night	**noqterinós**
night	**noqtis**
night bird	**streigs**
nightmare	**morā**
nine	**newn̥**
nine hundred	**newn̥km̥tṓs**
nine hundredth	**newn̥km̥témtəmos**
nineteen	**néwn̥dekm̥**
nineteenth	**néwn̥dekəmos**
ninetieth	**néwn̥dkm̥təmos**
ninety	**néwn̥dkm̥ta**
ninth	**néwn̥mos**

nipple	**spēnos**
nit	**sknidā**
no	**nē**
noble	**atlos**
noble	**məglos**
nobody	**neqis**
nod	**newō**
noise	**swonos**
noise	**tóntenos**
noisy	**bholós**
none	**nōinos**
nord	**skouros**
nose	**nāsis**
not	**ghawōd**
not	**mē**
not at all	**nei**
nothing	**neqid**
nourish	**alō**
now	**nū**
now	**num**
now	**numki**
nut	**knouks**
oak	**aigā**
oak	**perqos**
oak tree	**grōbhos**
oakum	**stoupā**
oar	**rēsmos**
oat	**awigsnā**
oath	**loughjom**
oath	**oitos**
obedience	**kleustis**
obey	**kleusō**
obliged	**moinis**
obscurity	**temos**
observe	**sr̥wājō**
observe	**tewai**
occipital	**moldhā**
occupation	**koisā**
odor	**odós**
of here	**ke**
of horses	**ekwīnós**
of rams/goats	**agīnós**
of this side	**kíteros**
offer	**poti linkō**
offshoot	**stelōn**
offspring	**gnās**
oil	**solpos**
oint	**oncō**
oint	**līnō**
ointed	**līnós**
ointment	**ghreimn̥**

ointment	**oncn̥**
old	**gerlós**
old	**senēks**
old	**wetwos**
old (to become)	**gerō**
omoplate	**skubtis**
on	**epi**
on account of	**rōdhí**
on top	**udsqe**
once	**semli**
one	**oinos**
one	**semos**
one-eyed	**kolnos**
one-year creature	**wetsós**
onion	**kaipā**
onion	**krémusom**
open	**ōsmi**
open	**wəreumi apo**
open land	**rewos**
opening	**kaghlā**
opinate	**kn̥sējō**
opinion	**dhōmós**
oppress	**amghō**
oppress	**ipjō**
or	**awti**
or	**loubhis**
or	**we**
orange	**badjos**
organize	**sepō**
orient	**woidejō**
origin	**ortus**
orphan	**orbhos**
otherwise	**awtim**
otherwise	**perti**
otter	**wədrā**
our	**n̥serós**
out	**ud**
outdoors	**rew**
outermost	**ékstəmos**
outside	**ek(sí)**
oven	**uqnós**
over	**(s)úperi**
over	**uperi**
over there	**oltrōd**
overcome	**təreumi**
owl	**káwonā**
own	**ghəbhējō**
ox	**uksén**
ox-stall	**cowstā́s**
paddle	**pl̥dājō**
page	**pəstrom**

pain	**edunā**
pain	**kormos**
paint	**pinkō**
palate	**stōmn̥**
palisade	**edhr̥**
palm	**pl̥mā**
panic	**mórmoros**
parcel	**glēws**
parent	**gentṓr**
parent	**gentrīks**
part	**aitis**
part	**pr̥tis**
part	**qestis**
particle	**bhrustóm**
partridge	**kákabā**
pass	**jāmi**
pass from one place to another	**ghēmi**
passage	**teqom**
past	**pr̥nos**
pasture	**pāstus**
path	**sentos**
patience	**kómtl̥tis**
patient	**tlātjos**
paunch	**pn̥dēks**
pause	**rowā́**
pay attention	**ghowejō**
pea	**kikēr**
peace	**paks**
peaceful	**qijētós**
peak	**sēr**
pear-tree	**gherdos**
pebble	**ghrowā́**
pee	**moighos**
peel	**gleubhō**
peg	**kippos**
penetrate	**neghō**
penis	**bhalnós**
penis	**lalu**
penis	**mūtos**
penis	**pesnis**
penis	**poutos**
penthouse	**kéliknom**
penury	**loigós**
people	**teutā**
people	**wolgos**
pepper	**píperi**
perch	**dhghusā**
perfect	**kómsqr̥tos**
perform	**sáneumi**
perhaps	**an**

perimeter	**wərbhis**
period	**áiwesos**
permissive	**ml̥dhos**
permit (to)	**leidmi**
persecute	**jeghō**
persecute	**wr̥nāmi**
perseverance	**mōdos**
perspective	**dr̥ksmos**
perspire	**spoisājō**
phantom	**lemsos**
pick	**lesō**
pickaxe	**səkesnā**
piece	**pr̥snā**
pig	**porkos**
pig	**sūs**
pig	**trogos**
piglet	**sūkós**
pike	**ceru**
pile	**ákeswos**
pile	**kolnom**
pillage	**wəleumi**
pillar	**stobhos**
pimple	**wəros**
pin down	**gangō**
pin down	**karnājō**
pinetree	**bharwos**
pinetree	**dhanus**
pink	**elwos**
pinnacle	**stertos**
pintle	**bendlā**
pious	**jāgjus**
pipe	**srwtom**
pipe	**strudsmā**
piss	**minghō**
pit	**skrobhis**
pitch	**peiks**
place	**stānom**
place	**stlokos**
place	**sinō**
place	**stānejō**
placed on top	**épiromos**
plait	**plektō**
plait	**resgō**
plane	**glabhō**
planet	**rewis**
planitiēs	**plātom**
plate	**stlāmn̥**
platform	**stātlom**
plea	**preks**
pleasant	**seljos**
pleasant	**swādús**

pleasant	**moghjos**
pleasantly	**ghornim**
pleased	**prītós**
pleasure	**prītis**
plough	**arātrom**
plough	**arājō**
plough animal	**aghjā**
plough handle	**seghdhlā**
plough handle	**steiwā**
ploughshare	**wogsmis**
pluck	**gnebhō**
plum	**sloiwom**
plump	**kratsos**
plunder	**mr̥namói**
plunder	**soru**
pod	**gherghros**
pod	**skl̥iqā**
poet	**wātis**
point	**ardis**
point	**glōghis**
poison	**woisos**
pole	**pertā**
pole	**spelgis**
policeman	**worós**
polish	**sleimājō**
pond	**stagnom**
ponder	**medai**
poodle	**lāmā**
pool	**staknom**
poor	**ormos**
poppy	**mā́kōn**
porcine	**swīnós**
porridge	**poltos**
portent	**sqeros**
portico	**antas**
portico	**pr̥gā**
portion	**bhagos**
portion	**onkos**
position	**stətus**
post	**ksūlom**
post	**mētā**
post	**sparos**
posterior	**ópitjos**
posterity	**troghos**
pot	**auqslā**
pot	**kumbhā**
potter wheel	**dhroghnom**
pouch	**makēn**
pour	**ghúgheumi**
pour	**ghundō**
power	**galnos**

powerful	**kúwr̥os**
praise	**loudis**
praise	**cerō**
pray	**chedhjō**
pray	**meldhō**
pray	**ōrājō**
prayer	**moldhos**
precarious	**dúsōpis**
preceding	**preistos**
precipitate	**krepō**
precisely	**arti**
precision	**nomr̥**
predator	**dhaunos**
prepare	**adejō**
presence	**weidos**
present	**deqsjō**
present	**práiloghos**
press	**bhríkāmi**
press	**dhenghō**
press	**premō**
press	**presō**
press tightly	**kamō**
prestige	**meidos**
prevail	**cínāmi**
previous	**kintos**
previous	**préwijos**
price	**pretjom**
prick	**kentrom**
prick	**wésnāmi**
prickle	**aknā**
prickle	**speiksnā**
prickle	**stigājō**
pride	**molpā́**
priest	**bhlaghmn̥**
priest	**sákrodhots**
principal	**promos**
proclaim	**əgsājō**
proclaim	**neumi**
procreation	**gentus**
produce	**gnājō**
produce	**gonējō**
produce of land	**dhēnom**
productive	**dhēlēiks**
profession	**kerdos**
profit	**bhéwedā**
profitable	**lawrós**
progeny	**teukmn̥**
prominence	**pr̥stis**
promise	**spondejō**
promontory	**akrom**
promontory	**prostos**

promote	**kákneumi**
pronounce	**bhəskō**
property	**rentus**
property	**selwā**
propice	**sinísteros**
propriety	**rēis**
prosper	**mājō**
protect	**alkejō**
protect	**pālājō**
protest	**glaghā́**
protrusion	**sondhos**
proud	**bhorsos**
proud	**meudos**
prove	**probhwājō**
provide	**áineumi**
provided with handle	**ansātos**
provision	**penos**
proximity	**enstar**
prune (to)	**kastrājō**
pubescent	**mərjos**
public servant	**ambhíagtos**
pulse	**ercom**
pumice	**poimēks**
punch	**pungō**
puncture	**dheicō**
punish	**membhō**
pure	**kəstos**
pure	**pūrós**
purpose	**meinom**
pus	**puwos**
push	**agō**
push	**kelō**
push away (to)	**steugō**
pushed	**agtós**
pustule	**pustlā**
put	**dhejō**
put	**stelō**
put forth	**prṓddōmi**
put in order	**tagjō**
put off	**nocējō**
put on	**mn̥tijai**
put to flight	**bhougājō**
putrid	**pūlós**
quadruped	**qətwr̥pods**
qualified	**dn̥sus**
qualify	**tādējō**
queen	**regeinā**
question	**pr̥kskā**
quick	**peimis**
quick	**twr̥tos**

quickly	**bhersi**
quiet	**sāmis**
quietness	**sāmn̥**
radiance	**loukós**
radiant	**loukētjos**
raffle	**kleutō**
rag	**kentom**
rag	**pannos**
rage	**rəbhjō**
rain	**wr̥stā**
rain	**plówijā**
raise	**tl̥nō**
ram	**agós**
ram	**erjos**
range (to)	**kerdhō**
rank	**agmn̥**
rather	**uta**
raven	**korwos**
raven	**wornos**
raw	**ōmós**
ray	**rədjom**
ray	**ragjā**
raze	**gneibhō**
razor	**ksnowātlā**
reach	**əpjō**
reach	**ikjō**
ready	**ōkinós**
realise	**pretō**
reality	**bhéwonom**
really	**bhod**
reap	**metō**
reason	**rətis**
reason	**argujō**
receive	**dekai**
receive	**tekō**
receive	**ghn̥dō**
recent	**kənjós**
recitate	**spelō**
reckon	**rēmoi**
reckon	**puwējō**
recline	**kumbō**
recognize	**gnōsmi**
recommend	**swādejō**
red	**rudhrós**
red (-haired)	**reudhos**
red ochre	**miljom**
red-deer	**elēn**
reddish	**rudhsós**
redness	**reudhos**
reduce	**míneumi**
reed	**arom**

refrain from	**parkō**
region	**pagos**
reject	**dikjō**
rejoice	**torpejō**
rejoice	**gāudhējō**
rejoice oneself	**tusjai**
relation	**ḗpijos**
relation	**mosgos**
relative	**pāsós**
relative	**sweljos**
relax	**remō**
release	**ledō**
relief	**podjom**
religion	**perístānom**
remain	**mənējō**
remain (water)	**stagō**
remaining	**loiqós**
remember	**mímnāskō (memna)**
remnant	**atiloiqos**
remoteness	**ekstar**
renew	**newājō**
renowned	**mōros**
rent	**doros**
rent	**keusō**
repair	**sr̥kijō**
repellent	**aghlós**
replication	**aimom**
reprove	**kudājō**
reputation	**kléumn̥tom**
request	**áisoskō**
require	**bhedhō**
residence	**sedos**
residence	**selom**
resin	**cetus**
resin	**peitus**
resonate	**tónāmi**
resound	**boukājō**
resound	**gewō**
respect	**aisō**
respect	**wərējai**
rest	**qijētis**
rest	**ermi**
rest	**qejēskō**
rest	**tl̥ijō**
restless	**n̥qijētós**
restrain	**kēsmi**
restrict	**strengō**
result	**temkō**
retain	**dhermi**
retaliation	**qoinā́**
retire	**spleighō**

revenge	**apóqitis**
rheum	**grammā**
rheum	**lippā**
rib	**kostā**
ribbon	**tenā**
rich	**deiwots**
riches	**ops**
ride	**reidhō**
right	**deksiwós**
right	**déksiteros**
right	**regtós**
right way	**jeunis**
righteous	**pūjós**
right-hand side	**deksis**
rigid	**sternós**
rigid (to be)	**stupējō**
ring	**anos**
ring	**krenghos**
ring out	**dhrenkō**
rise	**bhr̥ghjai**
rise	**nedhō**
rite	**admn̥**
rivalry	**neitom**
river	**dānus**
river ford	**wadhom**
road	**kelus**
roam	**wəgājai**
roar	**dhrēnos**
roar	**rugijō**
roaring	**ghromos**
rob	**sterō**
rock	**kárrēkā**
rock	**ondos**
rock	**pelsā**
rock	**roupis**
rock	**kr̥djō**
rod	**cosdhos**
rod	**litwos**
rod	**mentā**
rod	**slatā**
roebuck	**jorkos**
roe-deer	**olkis**
roll	**wolmos**
roof	**robhos**
room	**kētjā**
root	**wr̥djā**
root	**wr̥ādīks**
rope	**resgtis**
rope	**sognos**
rot	**kr̥jēs**
rot	**kr̥nāmi**

rotten	**kr̥nos**
rotten	**pūterós**
rough	**bhorcos**
rough	**brenghos**
round	**wolwós**
row	**wr̥stos**
row	**rējō**
rowan tree	**sorbhos**
rub	**pesmi**
rub	**serdhō**
rub	**melkō**
rub	**terjō**
rubbed	**trītós**
rubber	**gloidos**
rubbish	**ceudhos**
rubbish	**swordis**
rudder	**oisjā**
rude	**rudlós**
rudis	**kersis**
ruin	**réwesnā**
ruin	**rikjō**
rule	**wl̥dhējō**
ruler (in topography)	**stolbos**
rūmen	**reusmn̥**
ruminate	**reusmnājō**
rummage	**ruspājai**
rumor	**bhāmā**
rumor (to produce)	**reumi**
rump	**ghodos**
run	**bhecō**
run	**dhewō**
run	**dremō (dídrāmi)**
run	**kr̥sō**
run	**renō**
run	**retō**
run around	**dhreghō**
run away	**tekwō**
rust	**roudhstos**
rye	**wərughis**
ryegrass	**airā**
ryegrass	**dr̥wā**
sack	**coinos**
sacrifice	**sákrodhokjom**
sad	**creughos**
sad	**gorgós**
sad	**treistis**
sadness	**gorgnóm**
safe	**stiprós**
sailor	**nawāgós**
saint	**kadros**

salary	**misdhóm**
sale	**wesnom**
saliva	**saleiwā**
salt	**sal**
salt	**saldō**
sanctuary	**némētom**
sand	**samdhos**
sand/gravel	**pēnsús**
sandal	**pedlom**
satiated	**sətos**
satisfaction	**sātis**
satisfy	**sánāmi**
saucer	**pəterā́**
say	**seqō**
scabies	**skabhjēs**
scald-crow	**bhodhwos**
scale	**bhrounóm**
scammony	**akōkós**
scandal	**bhloskos**
scant	**mn̥wos**
scanty	**sneitos**
scar	**kekātrīks**
scar	**krenktis**
scarce	**ligos**
scatter	**sperjō**
scatter	**skédnāmi**
scene	**polpos**
scissors	**kastrom**
scold	**lājō**
scorch	**dáwneumi**
scrape	**gneidō**
scrape off	**greumō**
scrape out	**reubō**
scratch	**gr̥bhō**
scratch	**gredō**
scratch	**meukō**
scratch	**skabhō**
scrath out	**meidō**
scream	**waplājō**
scythe	**dhēlgs**
scythe	**sēklā**
sea	**mari**
sea	**tríjətos**
sea heaviness	**srodhos**
seabream	**atis**
seal	**swelāks**
seam	**sjewmn̥**
seaside	**leitos**
season	**jōrom**
seat	**sodjom**
second	**dwóteros**

second	**éteros**
second	**ónteros**
secret	**rounā**
secrete	**músnāmi**
secretion	**sāimn̥**
sect	**wereinā**
secure	**seghurós**
sedge	**olwā**
sedge	**sesqos**
see	**dr̥kō**
see	**oqō**
see	**welō**
see	**widējō**
seed	**sēmn̥**
seek	**sāgijō**
seem	**dokejō**
seen	**dr̥ktis**
seen	**wistós**
seesaw	**sweigō**
seize	**ghr̥bhjō**
seizing	**āmós**
self	**sewe**
sell	**pr̥nāmi**
send	**smeitō**
send	**sontejō**
send away	**īljō**
sense	**menos**
sentence	**bhānis**
separate	**seqos**
separate	**derō**
serpent	**natrīks**
servant	**ambhíqolos**
serve	**bhungai**
service	**upóstānom**
set	**staurejō**
set fire	**wərjō**
set out	**ərijai**
settle	**sōdejō**
settlement	**leghskā**
settlement	**sedmn̥**
seven	**septm̥**
seven hundred	**septm̥km̥tṓs**
seven hundredth	**septm̥km̥témtəmos**
seventeen	**septm̥dekm̥**
seventeenth	**septrm̥dekəmos**
seventh	**séptəmos**
seventieth	**séptm̥dkm̥təmos**
seventy	**séptm̥dkm̥ta**
sew	**sjewō**
sewer's awl	**sjūdhlā**
sewn	**sjūtós**

shackle	**winkijō**
shade	**skojá**
shadow	**skotos**
shadow	**unksrā**
shake	**kreitsō**
shake	**krotjājō**
shake	**qətjō**
shaker	**mn̥kstrom**
shall	**skelō**
shameful	**kaunós**
share	**erkō**
sharp	**akris**
sharp	**gigrós**
sharp	**kətos**
sharp	**pikrós**
sharpen	**(kí)kōmi**
sharpened point	**ákūmn̥**
shatter	**bhresjō**
shave	**ksnujō**
shave	**rādō**
shave	**tondejō**
sheath	**wageinā**
sheep	**owis**
sheep skin	**moisós**
shelduck	**ghandā**
shelf	**skolpos**
shell	**konkhā**
shelter	**krowos**
shepherd	**pōimōn**
sherd	**skroupos**
shield	**rebhō**
shield	**skoitom**
shift	**mejtis**
shimmer	**bhl̥gējō**
shin-bone	**skīwr̥**
shin-bone	**teibhjā**
shine	**erqō**
shine	**bhrēgō**
shine	**dhelō**
shine	**dídjāmi**
shine	**lukējō**
shine	**nitējō**
shine	**skejō**
shine (to)	**leukō**
ship	**nāws**
ship	**plówijom**
shirt	**kr̥stus**
shit	**coucis**
shit	**dherghs**
shit	**skerdā**
shit	**smerdā**

shit	**sterkos**
shiver	**trepō**
shiver	**tresō**
shoddy	**rupús**
shoe	**kr̥pjos**
shoot	**selgō**
shoot	**skeudō**
shore	**ā́peros**
short	**mr̥ghús**
shoulder	**omsos**
shoulder-blades	**pletjā**
shout	**genō**
show	**deikō**
shrew	**sworēx**
shriek	**krokijō**
shrine	**tegos**
shuttle	**kristājō**
sibling	**sm̥ópətōr**
sickle	**lewis**
sickle	**sr̥pā**
side	**splighstós**
side	**stlātos**
sieve	**kreidhrom**
sieve	**sējdhlom**
sieve	**krinō**
sieve	**sējō**
sign	**gnōtlom**
silent	**tausos**
silent (to be)	**silējō**
silent (to be)	**təkējō**
silently	**tausnim**
silver	**árgn̥tom**
similar	**sm̥lis**
simple	**meros**
simple	**sm̥plos**
simultaneously made	**oinowr̥stós**
sincere	**n̥dwojos**
sing	**kanō**
sing	**senchō**
single	**óinokos**
sink	**mergō**
sink	**senqō**
sip	**lm̥bō**
sip	**sorbhējō**
sir	**arjos**
sir	**audhos**
sister	**swesōr**
sister-in-law	**glōs**
sister's son	**swesreinos**
sit down	**sisdō**

site	**loghjom**
six	**seks / sweks**
six hundred	**sekskm̥tṓs**
six hundredth	**sekskm̥témtəmos**
sixteen	**séksdekm̥**
sixteenth	**séksdekəmos**
sixth	**sekstos**
sixtieth	**séksdkm̥təṃos**
sixty	**séksdkṃta**
skeletton	**skroutos**
skillful	**dhabhros**
skin	**kūtis**
skin	**pelnis**
skirt	**baitā**
skull	**mreghmós**
sky	**kémelom**
slack	**mlīnós**
slack	**slagós**
slanting	**loksós**
slate	**lēsanks**
slaughterer	**truks**
slave	**dōsos**
sleep	**swopnos**
sleep	**sesmi**
sleep	**swepō**
sleeper	**swelom**
slender	**kr̥klos**
slender	**makrós**
slip	**slabai**
slip	**sleibō**
slip	**sleubō**
slip in	**smúghneumi**
sloe	**dherghnos**
slop	**mouros**
slow	**ml̥sos**
slow	**tárudos**
small	**alpos**
small	**gherús**
small	**km̥bhis**
small	**paulos**
small pillar	**skolmā**
small sheep	**owikā́**
smaller	**meiwijṓs**
smell	**bhrēgjō**
smell	**odējō**
smell	**sísghrāmi**
smell good	**swekō**
smelling	**bhrēgrós**
smile	**smejō**
smith	**ghwobhros**
smog	**sneudhs**

smoke	**dhūjō**
smoke	**dhūmājō**
smoke	**dhūmós**
smoke	**dhwēwis**
smoke	**smoughos**
smoke	**smeughō**
smooth	**rastós**
smooth	**sleigō**
smooth	**slējús**
snail	**sleimāks**
snake	**anghwis**
snake	**kélodhros**
snake	**sérpenos**
snake	**snoghā**
snappy	**swerwos**
snare	**merghā**
snatch	**rəpjō**
sneeze	**str̥neumi**
snore	**srenkō**
snore	**stertō**
snout	**srunghos**
snow	**sneighs**
snow	**sníncheti**
so	**ita**
so	**mān**
so	**nom**
so	**swāi**
so many	**tot(j)oi**
so much	**tā́wn̥tos**
sob	**gheipō**
soft	**ml̥dus**
soften	**ml̥duwijō**
softened	**ml̥dsnos**
soil	**bhudhmn̥**
soldier	**neros**
solid	**dhobos**
solid	**māterós**
solidify	**greutō**
some	**edqos, -qā, -qod**
someone	**neqos**
someone	**edqis, edqid**
son	**sūnús**
song	**kanmn̥**
son-in-law	**gemros**
soon	**mogsū́**
soot	**dhūlis**
soot	**sōdjā**
sorrow	**croughnos**
soul	**etmn̥**
sound	**chonos**
sound	**dhwonos**

sound	**kl̥ngō**
sound	**swénāmi**
soup	**supā**
sour	**amrós**
sour	**sauros**
sow	**trogjā**
sow	**segō**
sow	**sisō**
sowing	**segēts**
sowing	**sēlom**
space	**ghewos**
spade	**laghā**
span	**potmos**
sparrow	**parsā**
sparrow	**sparwos**
speak	**mleumi**
speak	**bhāmoi**
speak	**tloqai**
speak	**wíweqmi**
spear	**ghaisom**
spear	**lostos**
spearshaft	**ghastā**
speckled	**bhr̥ktos**
speckled	**mr̥ktos**
speech	**əgtis**
speech	**bhāmn̥**
speechless	**muttis**
spelt	**ados**
spelt	**alēiks**
spend	**neudō**
spend the night	**awō**
spill	**seiqō**
spill	**sujō**
spin	**snēmi**
spit	**spjwtos**
spit	**spjewō**
splash	**persō**
spleen	**spelghā**
split	**dr̥nós**
split	**dr̥tis**
split	**dr̥tós**
split	**lúnāmi**
split	**delō**
split	**skerjō**
split	**skindō**
split	**skl̥jō**
split	**spleidō**
spoil	**deusō**
spokesman	**kn̥stṓr**
spoon	**leiglā**
spot	**kālis**

spray	**ros**
spread	**strātós**
spread	**str̥nō**
spread out	**pn̥tō**
spread out	**str̥nō prō**
spring	**lendhā**
spring	**mānājō**
spring	**wesr̥**
spring	**skatō**
spring	**skerō**
spring	**sl̥ijai**
sprout	**geimō**
sprout	**wisējō**
spurn	**tembhō**
square	**qəddrom**
squeak	**pipjājō**
squeeze	**wēskō**
stab	**pinjos**
stab	**tálejā**
stab	**weghmi**
stable	**stārós**
stain	**dherkō**
stain	**smitlā**
stain	**smā́neumi**
stake	**stauros**
staked	**staurós**
stalk	**kolmos**
stalk	**tibhjā**
stall	**stādhlom**
stamp on	**stembhō**
stand	**(sí)stāmi**
standing post	**stətis**
star	**stēr**
star	**steros**
star	**sweidos**
stare	**stelpō**
starling	**stornos**
start	**dherbhō**
starvation	**ghosdos**
stay	**wesō**
steadfast	**woikós**
steady	**dhr̥mos**
steal	**klepō**
steal	**tājō**
steam	**bholos**
steam up	**dhemō**
steep	**kloiwos**
steep	**r̥dhwos**
step	**cāmn̥**
step	**ghenghō**
step	**ghradjai**

sterile	**stérolis**
stick	**ghaisom**
stick	**spōnos**
stick	**steipēts**
stick	**stupos**
stick	**sworos**
stick	**ghaisējō**
stick	**glínāmi**
stick	**koljō**
stick	**limpō**
sticky	**gloijós**
still	**dom**
sting	**ákulos**
stink	**smerdō**
stir	**mendhō**
stir up	**joudhejō**
stir up	**sewō**
stock	**kreumi**
stone	**akmōn**
stone	**ləpods**
stone	**səksom**
stonework	**lāurā**
stool	**skabhnom**
stop	**stāwō**
stop	**stōwejō**
stop	**strigājō**
stop up	**teurō**
stork	**kíkōnjā**
storm	**m̥bhros**
story	**kleutrom**
straighten (to)	**storejō**
strain	**kemō**
strainer	**rēti**
strap	**telmṓn**
strap	**wəlōrom**
straw	**pálejā**
stream	**bhlewmn̥**
stream	**bhoglā**
stream	**srowmos**
street	**stoighos**
strenght	**belom**
strength	**weis**
strengthen	**dherghō**
stretched	**tn̥tos**
strew	**strewō**
strick	**dhōunis**
strike	**bhínāmi**
strike	**bhreukō**
strike	**keldō**
strike	**pln̥gō**
strike	**tundō**

strike	**wedhskō**
string	**strengom**
string	**tentrom**
strip off	**streigō**
stroll	**alājai**
strom	**srewtis**
strong	**bélowents**
strong	**krepús**
strong	**melos**
strong	**nertos**
struck	**bhītós**
study	**ghlendhō**
study	**stoudjom**
stuff	**bhr̥kjō**
stumble	**stemō**
stupid	**mlākós**
stupid	**mōrós**
stutter	**lepō**
subjugate	**jugājō**
subsequent	**pósteros**
succeed	**bheughō**
success	**kobom**
such	**tālis**
suck	**seugō**
suck	**dheimi**
suck	**mendō**
sudden	**abhnós**
suffer	**qn̥tjō**
suffer	**pətjai**
suitor	**prokós**
sulphur	**swelplos**
summer	**samos**
summer heat	**chrensós**
summit	**bhroigos**
summit	**kakúds**
summit	**kolmn̥**
summit	**okris**
sun	**sā́wel(jos)**
sunlight	**swelā**
superior	**(s)úperos**
supplementary	**wíteros**
support	**kleitrom**
support	**leghtrom**
support	**bhl̥kjō**
support	**steutō**
sure	**pəgrós**
surface	**pelom**
surname	**kómnōmn̥**
sustenance	**pādhlom**
swallow	**glujō**
swallow	**qemō**

swamp	**pl̥wods**
swan	**elōr**
sway	**kēwējō**
swear	**swərjō**
sweat	**swoidos**
sweat	**swoidājō**
sweet	**dl̥kus**
swell	**bhreusō**
swell	**pankō**
swell	**salom**
swell	**turgējō**
swelling	**bhuljā́**
swelling	**cotlós**
swelling	**keulom**
swelling	**panknos**
swelling	**paplā**
swelling	**pounā**
swift	**ōkús**
swim	**snāmi**
swindle	**swendhō**
swollen	**tūlós**
sword	**kladjos**
sword	**n̥sis**
syrup	**bhrwtom**
table	**speltā**
table	**stolos**
tablet	**klāros**
tablet	**loisā**
tail	**doklom**
tail	**dumbos**
tail	**ersā**
tail	**ersábhaljom**
tail	**pukos**
take	**emō**
take	**labhō**
take care	**swerghō**
talk	**gálgaljō**
talk	**garsijō**
tame	**kékuros**
tame	**dómāmi**
taste	**ml̥sjō**
taste	**geustis**
taste	**gusnō**
teach	**n̥neumi**
team	**lāwós**
tear	**dakru**
tear	**ləkesājō**
tear	**rōdō**
tear off	**weldō**
tearing	**ləkós**
teat	**dhēlós**

teat	**tettā**
technique	**teksnā**
tehth	**dekəmós**
tell	**jekō**
tell	**wedō**
tell off	**lā́mn̥tom**
temple	**temlom**
temple	**tenjom**
ten	**dekm̥**
tendon	**kenklom**
tendril	**olgjā**
tension (engine)	**tórkmn̥tom**
termite	**tr̥mos**
terrible	**ghouros**
thanks	**moitmos**
that	**ei**
that	**elno elnā elnod**
that	**eno enā enod**
that one	**oiso, oisā, oisod**
that, the one that	**jos (je), jā, jod**
thaw	**tādhis**
the other one	**álteros**
then	**n̥dha**
then	**tom**
then	**tom-ke**
there	**idhei**
therefore	**ar**
therefore	**tori**
thick	**dn̥sus**
thief	**bhōr**
thigh	**bhemr̥**
thigh	**morjods**
thigh	**touknā**
thigh-bone	**soqtis**
thin	**bhlakkos**
thin	**speimis**
thin	**tn̥us**
thing	**weqtis**
think	**mənjō**
think	**sn̥tējō**
thinnen	**kakō**
third	**tritjos**
thirst	**tr̥stis**
thirteen	**tréjesdekm̥**
thirteenth	**tréjesdekəmos**
thirtieth	**trídkm̥təmos**
thirty	**trídkm̥ta**
this	**ghoi-ke ghāi-ke ghod-ke**
this	**is, id**
this	**ko kā kod (eko ekā ekod)**

this	**se/sos sā/sī tod**
thorn	**sqijā**
thorn	**tr̥nā**
thousand	**sm̥gheslom**
thrash	**studējō**
threaten	**tercō**
threatening	**torcós**
three	**trejes trija tisres**
three hundred	**trikm̥tṓs**
three hundredth	**trikm̥témtəmos**
three in a go	**trisnōs**
three times	**trīs**
threefold	**triplós**
thriving	**spəros**
throat	**bhrugs**
throat	**gutr̥**
through	**trāntis**
throw	**supājō**
throw away	**celō**
thrush	**tr̥sdos**
thumb	**polnēks**
thunder	**tontrom**
thunder	**torsmn̥**
thunderbolt	**meldhjā**
thurify	**kodējō**
thus	**s(w)eike**
tick	**deghā**
tick	**rekā**
tie	**dídēmi**
tile	**tēglā**
time	**daitis**
time	**qr̥tus**
time	**tempos**
time	**wetos**
time before dawn	**ánksitjom**
tip	**bhr̥stís**
tip	**ghərtā**
tire	**l̥ncō**
tired	**cəlēnós**
to	**ana**
to	**dō**
to another place	**áljote**
today	**edjḗw**
together	**sm̥**
tomb	**sépeltrom**
tomorrow	**krāsi**
tongue	**dn̥ghwā**
tongue-tied	**balbos**
tool	**kaplos**
tooth	**dentis**
top	**kōnos**

torch	**chōks**
torch	**dáwētā**
torment	**cedhō**
torpid (to be)	**tr̥pējō**
tortoise	**ghelus**
torture	**cēlejō**
torture	**rigjō**
totality	**solwotāts**
touch	**palpājō**
touch	**tn̥gō**
tough	**raukos**
towards	**anta**
towards	**poti**
towards there	**totrēd**
towards this side	**kitrōd**
towel	**tergslom**
tower	**tursis**
tower	**mənijai**
town	**dounom**
track	**leisā**
track	**ogmos**
track	**werstis**
track	**pentō**
trail	**tekwos**
traitor	**prodətṓr**
trample	**trepō**
transport	**woghos**
transporter	**weghtṓr**
trap	**ləkjō**
trap	**ségneumi**
trap	**segnom**
travel	**ambhírēmos**
travel	**kelujō**
tread	**sporējō**
tread	**spr̥āmi**
treasure	**kusdhos**
treat	**drewō**
tree	**drewom**
tremble	**tremō**
trestle	**stoghos**
triplication	**trípl̥tis**
troop	**twr̥mā**
trouble	**kādos**
trouble	**oghlejō**
trough	**aldhōn**
trousers	**skousā**
trout	**perknā**
true	**wēros**
trunk	**stērps**
trunk	**stm̥nos**
trust	**bheidhō**

try	**kōnājai**
try to get	**r̥numái**
tube	**aulos**
tube	**rebhrus**
tuff of hair	**wl̥tis**
tunic	**ruktus**
tunnel	**bolkos**
turban	**wosis**
turfgrass	**smelgā**
turkey	**téturos**
turmoil	**túmolos**
turn	**rotājō**
turn	**wergō**
turn	**derbhō**
turn	**qerpō**
turn	**swerbhō**
turn	**torqejō**
turn	**trepō**
turn	**welwō**
turn	**wr̥stis**
turn	**wr̥tō**
turn around	**witājō**
turned aside	**pérpern̥ks**
turnip	**rāpom**
twelfth	**dwṓdekəmos**
twelve	**dwṓdekm̥**
twentieth	**dwídkm̥təmos**
twenty	**dwídkm̥tī**
twice	**dwīs**
twig	**lougos**
twin	**jemós**
twisted	**lordós**
two	**dwōu, dwāu, dwōu**
two each	**dwīsnōs**
two hundred	**dwikm̥tṓs**
two hundredth	**dwikm̥témtəmos**
type	**qoros**
udder	**ūdhr̥**
udder	**ūdhros**
uērus	**sontis**
ugly	**bhoidhos**
ugly	**bhoidos**
ugly	**tr̥pis**
un-	**n̥**
unbind	**luwō (lewō)**
unbound	**lūnós**
unbound	**lūtós**
uncle	**áwontlos**
uncle	**pətrujós**
under	**sup**
under	**upo**

underly	**n̥dherós**
understand	**peumi**
unexpected	**nekopīnós**
unfair	**n̥joustos**
union	**kómjougos**
unjustice	**n̥jousjom**
unknown	**n̥gnōtós**
unmade	**n̥dhētós**
unmuddy	**n̥sloimis**
until	**teni**
untouched	**kairós**
uppest	**(s)upmos**
upright	**ernos**
use	**bhreugtis**
use	**bhrūgjai**
usual	**nitjos**
uter	**úderos**
utterance	**wedmn̥**
valley	**klopnis**
valuation	**mēdos**
value	**wertos**
vane	**jālós**
vanish	**dhchínāmi**
variegated	**pelupoikos**
vase	**gheutlom**
vegetable	**ghelos**
vegetation	**dhl̥nā**
vehicle	**weghtlom**
veil	**wəreikā**
veil	**gheughō**
vein	**weisnā**
very	**abhro-**
very	**per(i), per(ti)**
very cold	**geldhós**
very well	**úperesū**
vessel	**bhidhós**
vessel	**kaukos**
vessel	**lestrom**
veteran	**gerwós**
victim	**wéiktomā**
victory	**seghos**
view	**dr̥ktis**
vigor	**wr̥gā**
vigorous	**súnoros**
vigour	**woikā́**
village	**woikos**
vine	**weitis**
vine-leaf	**pámponos**
violent	**twoisós**
violet	**sleiwos**
virginal	**poughos**

virtue	**dekos**
vis-à-vis	**seqi**
viscose	**cobhōn**
vision	**dr̥kos**
visitor	**setis**
vital energy	**aiwu**
vivid	**ētros**
voice	**woqs**
vomit	**wémāmi**
vow	**wochējō**
vulture	**bhāsos**
vulture	**cl̥turós**
wade	**sworā**
wake up	**bhudhjai**
wake up	**gerjō**
walk	**steighō**
walk	**wadhō**
wall	**mākesjā**
wall	**walnom**
wall	**dhoighos**
walls	**moinja**
walnut	**knuwā**
wander	**ersājō**
war	**dsā**
warm	**chormós**
warm	**teplós**
warm	**cherō**
warmth	**topnos**
warn	**monejō**
warp	**keukō**
warrior	**meilēts**
wart	**wersmn̥**
was	**bhūm**
wash	**klewō**
wash	**lowō**
wash	**neicō**
wasp	**wopsā**
watcher	**bhulkos**
water	**āps**
water	**aqā**
water	**m̥bhu**
water	**weri**
water	**wodā́**
water	**wodr̥**
water	**wopjā**
water	**prúsneumi**
water cloud	**nembhos**
watercress	**cérurom**
wave	**tusnā**
wave	**weipō**
wave	**welnā**

wave	**wn̥dā**
waving	**wiprós**
way	**itr̥**
way	**pontēs**
way	**tropos**
way	**weghjā**
we	**n̥sme**
we	**wejes / weje**
weak	**klamrós**
weak	**lēnis**
weaken	**bhleumi**
weaken	**mlājō**
weaken	**ml̥kāmi**
weakness	**bhelu**
wealth	**opnā**
weapon	**wēbēn**
weapon	**wedhr̥**
wear	**gesō**
weasel	**kérberos**
weasel	**mūstrom**
weather	**wedhrom**
weave	**krekō**
weave	**webhō**
weave	**wegō**
web	**tekstlom**
webbing	**wəréikonjom**
wedge	**kúnejos**
wedge	**tr̥mēts**
weed	**mousos**
weed	**runkō**
weed	**sərijō**
weep	**bhlēmi**
weft	**traghsmā**
weigh	**kenkō**
weight	**pondos**
welcome	**crātós**
well	**bhrewr̥**
well	**sū**
went	**sodóm**
west	**éperom**
wet	**molqos**
wet	**oucós**
wet	**wosmós**
wet	**rəgājō**
wet (be)	**ucējō**
what	**qis qid**
wheat	**bhar**
wheat	**bharseinā**
wheat	**bhreugsmn̥**
wheel	**dhroghós**
wheel	**qeqlom**

wheel	**rotā**
wheelrim	**kantos**
wheelrim	**witus**
whelp	**kuwos**
whelp	**mondós**
when	**jom**
when	**qm̥dō**
when	**qom**
whenever	**s(w)ei**
where	**qomde**
where	**qodhei**
where (rel.)	**jodhei**
wherefore	**jori**
wherefrom	**qotrōd**
whey	**misgā**
which	**qād**
which	**qóteros**
whine	**ghirrijō**
whip	**wəlepējō**
whip	**werbos**
whirl	**cr̥cots**
whirl	**twr̥bhōn**
whirl	**snerō**
whirlpool	**dhwolsā**
whisper	**swerō**
whisper	**swrswrājō**
whistle	**sweighlājō**
whistle	**sweisdō**
white	**albhos**
white	**argis**
white	**kweidos**
white-stained	**bhlōros**
whither	**qō**
whither	**qote**
whither	**qotrēd**
who, which	**qos qā(i) qod**
whoever	**jos qis, jā, qis, jod qid**
whoever	**qāqos**
whole	**solwos**
whore	**loutsā**
whore	**skortom**
why ?	**qori**
wicked	**n̥probhwos**
wide	**plākos**
wide	**urús**
widely known	**wíklutom**
widow	**wídhewā**
wife	**sm̥loghós**
wife	**uksōr**
wild	**ghwērós**
wild	**reudos**

will	**weltis**
will	**welmi**
willing	**wolós**
willow	**salēiks**
willow	**widhus**
win	**winkō**
wind	**wentos**
wind	**gergō**
wind	**wondhejō**
window	**louksā**
wine	**woinos**
wine-cask	**kl̥pros**
wing	**agslā**
wing	**peterós**
winnow	**neikō**
winter	**gheimr̥**
winter	**ghjems**
winterly	**gheimrīnós**
wintry	**ghéimentos**
wipe	**mn̥trājō**
wipe	**mr̥gneumi**
wipe	**tergō**
wire	**chislom**
wire	**weiros**
wisdom	**widjom**
wise	**gnōwos**
wise	**widris**
witch	**wikkā**
with	**km̥ti**
with	**kom**
withdraw	**anjō**
wither	**wijēskō**
without	**əneu**
withraw	**kesdō**
witness	**tristis**
wolf	**wailós**
wolf	**wl̥qos**
woman	**cenā**
woman	**morignā**
womb	**colbhos**
wonder	**smeirai**
wonderful	**smeiros**
wood	**deru**
wood	**kl̥dos**
wooden	**drumós**
woodpecker	**kikjā**
woodpecker	**peikā**
woodpiece	**skoidos**
woodworker	**tetkōn**
wool	**wl̥nā**
word	**wr̥dhom**

work	**drājō**
work	**drātis**
work	**opos**
work	**wergom**
work	**wr̥gjō**
work with a thread	**penō**
workman	**drātṓr**
world	**dhoubnom**
worm	**longhros**
worm	**ochis**
worm	**qr̥mis**
worm	**wormis**
worn	**bhoros**
worry	**mérneumi**
worse	**pedjṓs**
worship	**jagjō**
worthy	**deknos**
wound	**elkos**
wound	**wolnos**
wound	**chendō**
wound	**swr̥neumi**
wrap	**wipjō**
wrap out	**werpō**
wrapping	**wélwm̥en**
wrath	**eisā**
wring out	**légneumi**
wrinkle	**gorbos**
wrist	**dornom**
write	**skreibhō**
yarn	**glomos**
yarn	**snēmn̥**
yawn	**ghanos**
year	**atnos**
yell	**klāmājō**
yellow	**bhlōwos**
yellow	**knakos**
yes	**jāi**
yesterday	**dhghjesi**
yew	**oiwos**
yoke	**jugóm**
you	**jusmé**
you	**juwes / juwe**
you	**tū**
young	**júwenis**
young	**juwn̥kós**
young	**juwōn**
young goat	**ghaidos**
youngster	**machos**
youth	**júwn̥tā**
youth	**machotis**

II.2. LATE INDO-EUROPEAN – ENGLISH

Latin meaning and syntax (Synt.) further define the English meaning and proper usage of the LIE words, while the notes show their proper inflection. The PIH column shows the laryngeal reconstruction of the words, or the roots behind LIE vocabulary.

Late IE	Synt.	Notes	PIH	Meaning	(Latin)
əgjō	intr		H_3eg	affirm	aiō
əgsājō	tr			proclaim	proclamō
əgtis	fem			speech	contiō
əneu	ind			without	sine
əpjō	inc		H_2ep	reach	apīscor
ərijai	inc			set out	orior
ərots	mas	et		charioteer	auriga
əsnātis	fem	jo		harvest	segēs
ábelos	mas		H_2eb-(e)lo, ăbōl-	apple	malum
abhnós	adI		$H^{o}H^{i}_{3}$-bh- r̥/n̥; $H^{o}H^{io}_{3}$-bh-r̥/n̥ ; *cf.* ōkús	sudden	repentīnus
abhro-	praefix		(per-)	very	per-
acnos	mas		H_2eg(^{w}h)-no	lamb	agnus
ad	ind			at	ad
adejō	tr	AIIIo		prepare	praeparō
adghō	tr	AIIa	H_2edgh	beset	circumueniō
adhos	neus	es		axe	ascia
ādmi	tr	BIf	HeH^{i}_{2}-d-; adjō	dry (to)	siccō
admn̥	neu			rite	ritus
ados	neu	ádesos	H_2ed-os	spelt	ador
āghar	intr		perf.	fear	metuō
ágherom	neu			lake	lacus
aghjā	fem		H_2egh	plough animal	iūmentum
aghlós	adI			repellent	repellens
aghlóws	fem	(aghlewós)		drizzle	irrorātiō
ághneumi	tr	BIVb		afflict	affligō
agīnós	adII			of rams/goats	caprīnus
aglā	fem			brood	prōlēs
ágəlis	adI		H_2eg- Hli-/ ili- /Hlo-	agile	agilis
agmn̥	neu	en		rank	agmen
agō	cau		H_2eg	push	agō
agos	mas		H_2ego-	fault	noxa
agós	mas		HeH^{i}_{2}gó-, HeH^{i}_{3}gó- / $H^{o}H^{io}_{2}$g-, $H^{o}H^{io}_{3}$g-; aigs	ram	ariēs
agrā	fem			massacre	trucidatiō
ágrēnom	neu		H_2eg-r	fruit	fructus
agróqolās	mas			farmer	agricola
agros	mas		H_2egro-	land	ager
agslā	fem			wing	āla

agtós	adI			pushed	actus
aichesājō	sta			feel ashamed	pudet
aidhis	fem	ej		hearth	aedes
aidhō	intr		$H_2eH^{io}_2$-dh/ $H^oH^{io}_2$-dh	burn	ardeō
aigā	fem		H_2eigeH_2	oak	robus
aigros	adI		H_2oig-ro	ill	aeger
aijus	mas	(aijewós)		moisture	ūmor
aikō	tr	AIa	$H_3eH^{i\underline{o}}_2k$	meet with point (to)	ic(i)ō
áimneumi		BIVb		copy	imitor
aimom	neu		H_2eimo-	replication	effigĭēs
ainō	sta		$H_3eH^i_2$; dat; *cf.* ōimi	belong	pertineō
áineumi	tr	BIVb	$H_3eH^i_2$; uox media: áinumai	provide	praehibeō
aiqos	adI			even	aequus
airā	fem		H_2eireH_2	ryegrass	lolium
aisdai	tr		H_2eisd-	honour	honorō
aisdhom	neu			ardour	ardor
aiskrós	adI		H_1eisk- / H_2eisk- ? aidh-sk?	clear	clārus
aisō	tr		H_2eis-	respect	reuereor
áisoskō	tr		H_2eis(o)ske/o-; aisskō	request	quaerō
aisskā	fem			desire	desiderium
aitis	fem	jo	$H_3eH^i_2$-ti / $H_3H^i_2$-ti	part	pars
áiw(es)i	ind			always	semper
áiwesos	mas			period	aetas
aiwós	adII		H_2eiwo-	eternal	aeuus
áiwotāts	fem	jo		eternity	aetas
aiwu	neu		H_2oiwu(s)/ H_2oiwi-/H_2oiwo-/ $H_2oiwā$-	vital energy	uitālitās
ájeri	ind		$H^{\underline{o}}H^i_2eri$	early	mane
ájesnos	adII			brassy	aereus
ajos	neu	es	H_2ei-os	brass	aes
ákeris	fem	jo		maple	acer
ákeswos	mas			pile	aceruus
akējō	intr		$H^{\underline{o}}_3H^i_2k$-	be sharp	aceō
akjēs	fem		$H^{\underline{o}}_3H^i_2k$-	blade	aciēs
akmā	fem			bit	buccella
akmōn	mas	(ákmenos)	H_2ek-mon	stone	lapis
aknā	fem			prickle	agna
áknāmi	tr	BIVa		eat	edō
akōkós	mas		$H^{\underline{o}}_3H^i_2k$-$H_3oH^i_2k$-	scammony	acridium
akos	neu	es		chaff	acus
akris	adI		$H^{\underline{o}}_3(e)H^i_2k$-ri-, $H^{\underline{o}}_3(e)H^i_2k$-(e)ro-	sharp	ācer
akrom	neu		$H^{\underline{o}}_3H^i_2k$-ro-	promontory	promontorium
áksijā	fem			axe	ascia
aksis	mas	jo	H_2eg^ws-iH_2	axle	axis
aksteinos	fem			broom	genista
ákulos	mas			sting	aculeus

ákūmn̥	neu		$H^{o}_{3}H^{i}_{2}$k-uHmn̥	sharpened point	acūmen
akus	fem	ew		needle	acus
alā!	excl.			hello	heus!
alājai	intr			stroll	ambulō
albhos	adI		H_2elbho-	white	albus
alchos	mas			money	pecūnia
aldhōn	mas	en		trough	canālis pecudum
alēiks		(alikós)		spelt	alica
álesnos	fem		H_2el-esno-	alder	alnus
alghējō	sta			be cold	algeō
aljos	lois	id	H_2el-yo	another	alius
áljote	ind			to another place	aliō
alkejō	tr	AIIIo		protect	tueor
alkis	fem			court	cohors
alō	tr			nourish	alō
alpos	adI			small	paruus
álteros	adII			the other one	alter
altjos	adII		altjós	adult	adultus
altós	adI			high	altus
ắlujos	mas			garlic	ālius
álumn̥	neu		H_2elu-	beer	ceruisia
amājō	tr		HemH, *cf.* omos	love (to)	amō
ambhí	ind		H_2n̥tbhí ? > *H_2n̥tbhí	around	circum
ambhíagtos	mas		ambhíagots	public servant	agens publicus
ámbhinom	neu			circuit	circuitus
ambhíqolos	mas			servant	seruus
ambhírēmos	mas			travel	iter
ambhou	lois			both	ambō
amchḗn	mas	(amchnós)	H_2emg^{w}h-; *cf.* amghús	neck	collus
ámeikā	fem			friend	amīca
amēiks	mas	(amikós)		friend	amīcus
ámetā	fem			aunt	amita
amghō	tr		H_2emgh	oppress	angō
amghús	adI		H_2mghu-; amghus	narrow	angustus
ámghustis	fem			narrowness	angustiae
āmi	tr	BIIf	*cf.* aidhō; HeH^{i}_{2}-/HH^{i}_{2}-nu-mi	heat	calefaciō
ammā	fem			mother	mamma
āmós	mas			seizing	apprehensiō
amrós	adI		H_3mH_2-ró	sour	amārus
āmros - āmrei	mas		*cf.* āmi	morning	mane
amsō	tr		H_2emH_1	mow	dēmetō
an	ind			perhaps	forsan
anəts	mas / fem	et	H_2enH_2-t(i)-	duck	anas
ana	ind		∂na; H_2en-	to	ad
ándhesā	fem			maid	uirgō

andhō	tr		H_2end(h); *cf.* kandō	kindle	accendō
andhos	adI			blind	caecus
anglos	mas		H_2eng-lo	articulation	rotula
anjō	tr			withdraw	remoueō
ankos	mas		H_1enko-; *cf.* onkos	hook	ancus
ankmi	tr	BIf	$H_{2/3}$enk	bestow	dōnō
anksí	ind		*cf.* noqtis	before dawn	anteluciō
ánksitjom	neu			time before dawn	antelucānum
anəmos	mas		H_2enH_1(e)-mo	breath	animus
annā	fem			granny	anus
anos	mas			ring	anus
ansā	fem			handle	ansa
ansātos	adII			provided with handle	ansātus
amsus	mas		H_2emsu-	creātor	creātōr
anta	ind			towards	uersus
antas			H_2enH_2teH_2	portico	antae
antí	ind		H_1enti	before	ante
ántijos	adI			antique	antiquus
ántitjos				classical	*classicus*
antjās	fem	pl. tantum		fringe	antiae
antjom	neu			end	fīnis
antrom	neu			cave	tugurium
anus	fem		H_2enu-	grandmother	anus
ấperos	mas			shore	ripa
apmn̥	neu		apsmṇ	fastening	copula
apnis	fem	ej	H_2ep-ni	brook	amnis
apo	ind		H_2epo; apó	from	ab
apóqitis	fem			revenge	represalia
ápōqos	adI		*apoHk^{w}o-	backward	āuersus
apóstətis	fem			distance	distantia
apóteri	ind			behind	post
apóteros	adI			hint	posterus
apowesonts	adII		apēsn̥ts	absent	absens
ápowoiks	mas	(ápowoikjos)		colony	colonia
appās	mas			dad	pappa
apros	mas		Hepro-	boar	aper
āps	fem	(após)	H_2e(H)p-	water	aqua
apsā	fem		H_2epseH_2	asp	pōpulus tremula
apsos	mas			limb	membrum
aqā	fem		H_2ek^{w}eH_2	water	aqua
ar	ind			therefore	ergō
arājō	tr		H_2rH_1; H_1rjō; arjō	plough	arō
árarjō	tr			adjust	adaptō
arātrom	neu			plough	arātrum
árdejā	fem			heron	ardea
ardis	fem	ej		point	punctus
arejō	tr		H_2erH	destroy	destruō
árgn̥tom	neu		H_2rg-	silver	argentum
argis	adI		argus	white	albus
argrós	adI		H_2(e)rgró-	brilliant	splendidus

argujō	tr		H_2orgu-je/o	reason	arguō
arjos	mas			sir	dominus
ármn̥tom	neu			cattle	armentum
armos	mas		H_2erH-mo-	arm	armus
arom	neu		H_2erom	reed	harundō
ārōn	mas	(ā́renos)	H_2eH_2r-on/en-	kidney	rēnēs
arqos	mas		H_2rkwo-	bow	arcus
arti	ind			precisely	adeō
artis	fem	jo		art	ars
artus	mas			joint	artus
árusā	fem		H_2er-	hazelnut	abellāna
arwā	fem			butter	aruīna
arwom	neu		H_2erH_3w-o \ r̥/n- 'granum' \ -on/n- 'granātus'	field	aruum
āsā	fem		HeH^{i}_{2}-seH_2	altar	āra
āsējō	sta		HeH^{i}_{2}-s-ējō	be dry	areō
āsos	mas			ash	cinis
astris	mas	ej		hawk	astur
astus	mas			guile	astus
ati	ind			again	re(d)
atiloiqos	mas			remnant	reliquiae
atis	fem			seabream	sparus aurata
atlos	adI		H_2et-lo-	noble	nōbilis
atnos	mas			year	annus
ātmós	mas			breath	halitus
ātō	intr	AIIe	$H^{o}H^{w}_{2}$et-	breathe	respirō
atqe				and	ac
ātros	adI		H_1eH_2-tro	black	āter
attās	mas			dad	tata
audhos	mas			sir	dominus
augā́	fem		H_2eugeH_2	glance	fascis
augejō	cau	AIIIo	*cf.* wogsejō	make grow	augeō
augējō	sta	AIIIe		be big	magnus sum
augmn̥	neu	en		increase	augmentum
augō	intr		H_2ewg; *cf.* augsō	increase	increscō
augos	neu		áugestis	development	auctum
augsō	intr		*cf.* augō	increscō	increase
augtós	adI			grown	auctus
aulos	fem		HH^{w}_{1}l-	tube	conductus
auqslā	fem		*cf.* uqnós	pot	aula
ausijō	tr			empty	hauriō
ausom	neu		H_2euso-, H_2w-es-eH_2	gold	aurum
ausōsā	fem		ausṓs; H_2eus-oHs-eH_2	dawn	aurōra
ausrom	neu			morning	matīna
áussketi	intr			dawn	illūcescō
áusteros				eastern	orientālis
aw	ind			howbeit	autem
awā	fem			fountain	fons
awējō	tr		H_2ew	desire	desiderō

áweljā	fem			breeze	aura
awigsnā	fem		H_2ewig-sneH_2	oat	auēna
áwijā	fem			grandmother	auia
awis	fem	ej	H_2ewH_1i-	bird	auis
awisdhijō	tr		H_2ewi(s) + dheH_1	feel	sentiō
awn̥	neu	(ávenos)		fountain	fons
awo	ind		H_2ew(o)	back	retrō
awō	dur		H_2ew; *cf.* wesō <*H_2w-es-	spend the night	pernoctō
áwontlos	mas			uncle	auunculus
awos	mas		H_2euH_2o-	grandfather	auus
awti	ind			or	aut
awtim	ind			otherwise	autem
awtjos	adI		H_2eut-	destitute	destitūtus
badjos	adI			orange	badius
baitā	fem			skirt	falda
baktlom				club	baculum
bálbalos	and			barbaric	barbarus
balbos	adI			tongue-tied	balbus
bámbalos				drum	bombus
batā	fem			babble	locutiō sine sensu
baubājai	intr			bark	latrō
bebājō	intr			bleat	bēbō
belom	neu			strenght	uis
bélowents	neu			strong	robustus
bendā	fem			end	extrēmum
bendlā	mas			pintle	cnodax
bhəskō	tr			pronounce	pronuntiō
bhətjō	tr			hit	quatiō
bhəwējō	tr		bhH_2w- /bhH_3w dat.	be favourable	faueō
bhabhā	fem			bean	faba
bhāghus	mas	ew		arm	bracchium
bhagjō	tr			fry	frigō
bhagō	cau			atribute	addicō
bhagos	mas			portion	portiō
bhāgos	fem		bheH_2go-	beech	fāgus
bhalnós	mas			penis	pēnis
bhāmn̥	neu			speech	affāmen
bhāmā	fem			rumor	fāma
bhāmoi	intr		bhH_2-moi	speak	for
bháneumi	tr	BIVb		illuminate	illūminō
bhānis	fem			sentence	sententia
bhānom	neu			lighting	illuminātiō
bhānús	adI		bhānus	bright	lucidus
bhāos	neu	(bháaesos)	bheH_2os; bhāwos	light	lux
bhar	neu	(bharós)		wheat	far
bhardhā	fem			beard	barba
bharkos	mas			brooch	fibula
bharseinā	fem			wheat	farīna
bharsjom	neu			bread	pānis
bharwos	fem			pinetree	pīnus

bhaskis	mas			bundle	fascis
bhāsos	mas			vulture	ūltur
bhātis	fem		bhətis	expression	expressiō
bhebhros	mas			beaver	fīber
bhecō	intr	AIa		run	currō
bhedhō	intr	AIb		require	postulō
bhegō	cau			curb	arcuō
bheidhō	tr	AIa		trust	fīdō
bheikos	fem			fig	fīcus
bheiqlā	fem		bheiq-	bee	apēs
bheitlom	mas		non IE? Item pelekus ai. paraśu	axe	ascia
bheldō	intr	AIa		knock	battuō
bhelēks	fem			coot	fulica
bheljō	tr		H_3bhel	enhance	prosperō
bhelō	intr			fluoresce	superluceō
bhelō	intr		bhelH; *cf.* spelō	make noise	strepō
bhelu	neu			weakness	dēbilitas
bhélunā	fem			henbane	hyosciamus
bhemr̥		(bhémenos)		thigh	femur
bhendhō	tr	AIa		bind	ligō
bhendhros	mas			mate	collēga
bhendos	adI			melodious	melodicus
bhenjom				hit	contusiō
bherāgs	fem	(bhergos)	bherH_2-g	birch	betulla
bherghō	tr	AIa		keep	conseruō
bherkō	sta	AIa	*cf.* merkō	glimmer	fulgeō
bhermi (bherō)	tr	Bia	bhHr; bher	bear	bherō
bhermn̥	neu			burden	onus
bhernā	fem			breach	fissūra
bhersi	ind		bhristi ? *cf.* testis <*tristis	quickly	citō
bherwō	inc	AIa		boil	feruō
bhesmi	intr	BIa		blow	spirō
bheudhō	inc	AIa	*cf.* bhudhjai; caus. bhoudhejō	be awake	uigilō
bheughō	perf.	AIa		succeed	eueniō benē
bheugō		AIa		fold	flectō
bheurō	tr		(liquidō)	knead	commisceō
bhéwedā	fem			profit	compendium
bhewmi	dur	BIa / BIIb	bhwH_2	be	sum
bhéwonom	neu			reality	reālitās
bhewtis	fem	jo	bhūtis, bhūtís	nature	nātura
bhewtlom	neu			environment	circumiectus
bhíbheimi	tr			fear	timeō
bhidhós	mas			vessel	fiscus
bhidrós	adI			bitter	acerbus
bhilis	adI			good	bonus
bhínāmi	tr	BIVa	bhiH	strike	tundō
bhindō	cau			cleave	findō
bhītós	adI		bhiH-tó	struck	tusus
bhləgsmā	fem			flame	flamma

bhlādhrom	neu			fan	flābellum
bhlaghmn̥	neu			priest	flāmen
bhlagō	tr			hit	tundō
bhlaidos	adI			clear	candidus
bhlakkos	adI			thin	flaccus
bhlāmi	tr			blow	flō
bhledō	intr	AIa		boast	glorior
bhleicō	intr	AIa		hit	flīgō
bhleidō	intr	AIa		inflate	inflor
bhlēmi	intr			weep	fleō
bhlendhos	adI			dim	sublustris
bhleumi	tr	BIII/AIIIu	bhelujō	weaken	dēbilitō
bhleusō	tr	AIa		choke	suffocō
bhlewmn̥	neu	en	bhleugsmṇ ?	stream	flūmen
bhlewō	intr	AIa	bhleucō?; bhleuH-	flow	fluō
bhl̥gējō	sta			shimmer	fulgeō
bhl̥kjō	tr			support	fulciō
bhlokos	mas			flake	floccus
bhlōros				white-stained	candidē maculātus
bhlōs	mas	(bhlēsos)	bhleH$_3$-s-	flower	flōs
bhlosējō	sta			bloom	floreō
bhloskos	mas			scandal	scandalum
bhlōtis	fem	(bhlōtjos)	bhlH-ti	flower	flos
bhlōwos	adI		bhleH$_3$; *cf.* bhlōs	yellow	flāuus
bhn̥ghus	adI			dick	crassus
bhod	ind.			really	enim
bhodhjō	tr			dig	fodiō
bhodhwos	mas			scald-crow	coruus
bhodjṓs	adI		(comparātīuus)	better	melius
bhodrós	adI			excellent	excellens
bhodsā	fem			grave	fossa
bhogā́	fem			guerrilla	guerrilla
bhogājō	intr			contend	litigō
bhogjos	mas			crook	amnis
bhoglā	fem			stream	amnis
bhoidhos	adI		bhoiH-dhH$_1$o- <bhei 'timeō'	ugly	foedus
bhoidos	neu	es		ugly	foedus
bhoiqos	mas			drone	fūcus
bhokos				flame	focus
bholghis	mas	ej		bag	follis
bholjom	neu		bheljom	leaf	folium
bhōljóm	neu		bhōwljóm	den	cubīle
bholos	mas			steam	uapor
bholós	adI			noisy	strepitosus
bhondhsā	fem			crib	praesēpēs
bhōr	mas	bhrós		thief	fūr
bhorājō	tr			bore	forō
bhorcos	adI			rough	rudis
bhoros	mas			worn	gestāmen
bhorsos	adI			proud	superbus

bhosos	adII			barefoot	planipēs
bhoudhejō	cau	AIIIo		awaken	expergefaciō
bhougā́	fem			flight	fūga
bhougājō	cau			put to flight	fūgō
bhōwijós	adI		bheHwiyó-	favourable	propitius
bhrātēr	mas	(bhrātros)	bhreH$_2$-ter	brother	frāter
bhrātreinos	mas			brother's son	sobrīnus
bhrā́trijos	adII			brotherly	frāternus
bhrēgjō	intr		bhr̥Hg-i̯ó, pf. bhebhróHg/bhr̥Hg-	smell	fragrō
bhrēgō	intr	AIIf		shine	luceō
bhrēgrós	adI		bhrH$_1$g-ro, bhrH$_1$g-no; bhragrós	smelling	odōrus
bhreigō	tr	AIa	bhreig, bhri-né/n-g-	fry	frigō
bhremō	intr	AIa		grunt	fremō
bhrendhō	intr	AIa		gush up	exuberō
bhrenō	intr	AIa		edge	excellō
bhresjō	tr			shatter	disrumpō
bhreugs	mas	(bhrugós)		fruit	frux
bhreugsmn̥	neu	en		wheat	frūmentum
bhreugtis	fem	jo		use	ūsus
bhreukō	tr	AIa		strike	mulceō
bhrēunā	neu			limit	līmes
bhreusō	cau	AIa		swell	tumefaciō
bhrēwā	fem			bridge	pons
bhrewō	tr	AIa		brew	concoquō
bhrewr̥	neu	(bhrewn̥os)		well	puteus
bhr̥ghjai	intr	AIVc		rise	surgō
bhr̥ghos	adI		bhr̥ghú-	high	altus
bhrigijō	intr			chirp	frigō
bhrijājō	tr			crumble	friō
bhr̥ijō	cau		bhHriyō/bhHruyō	cut open	incīdō
bhríkāmi	tr			press	premō
bhr̥kjō	tr			stuff	farcio
bhr̥ksnos	fem		bhrH$_2$g-sno	ashtree	frāxinus
bhr̥ghtom	neu			cantus	ritual composition
bhr̥ktos	adI		*cf.* mr̥ktos	speckled	uarius
bhr̥mā				incision	incisiō
bhrn̥gō	tr		bhrH$_1$-g	break	frangō
bhrogkos	mas		bhroHgko-	badger	mēlēs
bhroigos	mas			summit	cacumen
bhrosdhos	fem			cedar	cedrus
bhrounóm	neu		*cf.* bhrūnós	scale	squāma
bhroustom	neu			fragment	frūstum
bhrówn̥tis	mas			forehead	frōns
bhr̥stís	fem			tip	cuspis
bhr̥tis	fem			bearing	portātiō
bhrughnos	fem			bulrush	iuncus
bhrūgjai	tr	AIVa	bhreuH-g	use	fruor
bhrugs	mas	(bhrugós)		throat	guttur

bhrūnós	adI		bhruH-no-; *cf.* bhrounó-	brown	spādix
bhrūs	fem	(bhruvós)	H_3bhruH; bhrews	eyebrow	brus
bhrúsnāmi	tr	BIVa		break	defringō
bhrusnjā	fem			cuirass	lorīca
bhrusos	mas			breast	pectus
bhrustóm	neu			particle	particula
bhrutēks	mas	(bhrutkós)	(bhrutkós)	bush	frutex
bhrwtom	neu		bhrwHtó-	syrup	dēfrutum
bhudhjai	inc	AIVa	bhundō; *cf.* bheudhō	wake up	expergiscōr
bhudhmn̥	neu	en		soil	solum
bhudhnos	mas			ground	fundus
bhugjō	dur			flee	fugiō
bhugos	mas			he-goat	caper
bhūjai	intr	AIIIu	bhH_2u-je/o	begin	incipiō
bhukús	adI		bhukus	blunt	hebes
bhuljā́	fem			swelling	tumor
bhulkos	mas			watcher	uigil
bhūm	intr	(aor. ab esmi)	bhHu-m; bhwom	was	fuī
bhungai	intr			serve	fungor
bhusājō	tr			kiss	osculō
bhūsjō	intr			hasten	percurrō
bhūtā́	fem			dwelling	mansiō
bhutjō	tr			hit	quatiō
bhūtós	adII			been	part. pf. esse
bistlis	fem			gall	bīlis
blaktā	fem			cockroach	blatta
blatsājō	intr			chatter	blaterō
blēkājō	intr			bleat	bēbō
bn̥dus	mas			drop	gutta
bodhrós	adI			deaf	surdus
bokkos	mas			goat	caper
bólboljō	intr	AIVd		explode	explōdō
bolkos	mas			tunnel	cuniculus
boukājō	intr			resound	personō
brenghos	adI			rough	raucus
bughōn	mas			eagle owl	bubō
bukkā	fem			mouthful	bucca
cəlā	fem			gullet	gula
cəlājō	intr			fly	uolō
cəlēnós	adI			tired	lassus
cadhō	intr		g^wH_2dh	dive	immergō
cāmn̥	neu			step	gradus
cécālos	adI			mundane	mundānus
cedhō	tr	AIa		torment	cruciō
cejwō	dur	AIa	g^wH_3ei-w	live	uīuō
cēlejō	cau	AIIIo		torture	tormentō
céln̥dis	fem	ej		acorn	glans
celō	tr	AIa	g^welH_2	throw away	abiciō
célwonom	neu		g^welH_1-ono-	bath-tub	lauābrum
cemjō	intr		g^wm̥jō, g^wm̥-skō; cm̥jō, cm̥skō	come	ueniō

cenā	fem		g^wnH_2; g^wēnis, g^wnā	woman	mulier
cerbhō				devour	uorō
ceri	neu	ej	g^werH-	mountain	mons
cerjō	intr	AIa		finish	finiō
cerō	tr	AIb		praise	laudō
cerō	sta			have fever	febriō
ceru	neu	ew		pike	ueru
cérurom	neu			watercress	berrum
césneumi	tr	BIVb	(s)g^wes(H_2); cesō, cesjō	extinguish	exstinguō
cespis	fem			branches	foliamen
cetus	mas			resin	bitūmen
ceudhos	neu	es		rubbish	immunditia
chaisos	adI		ghwH_2y-so	beautiful	pulcher
chedhjō	tr	AIa	chedhō	pray	rogō
cheldi	neu			bile	fel
chelō	tr	AIa	H_1ghwel	desire	desiderō
chendō	cau			wound	feriō
chenmi	tr			murder	interficiō
chentis	fem	jo	*cf.* chn̥tjā	death	nex
cherō	tr		chorejō	warm	calefaciō
cheros	neu	es		heat	calor
chislom	neu			wire	fīlum
chl̥nō	tr			deceive	fallō
chn̥tjā	fem		*cf.* chentis	combat	proelium
chodhjā	fem			longing	dēsiderium
chōks	fem	(chkos)	chōkeH_1?	torch	fax
chonos	mas			sound	sonitus
chonós	adI			abundant	abundans
choris	adI			bitter	acerbus
chormós	adI		chermos, chermós	warm	formus
chornos	mas		chr̥nos	hearth	fornus
chrensós	mas		chrensmós; *cf.* cherō	summer heat	aestus
chr̥jō	intr			be violent	furō
cícāmi	inc	BIIa	g^weH_2	go away	abeō
cijā	fem			fold	ouīle
cínāmi	intr	BIVa		prevail	praeualeō
cīrós	adI			lush	laetus
cistis	fem			finger	digitus
cītā	fem		$g^w$$H_3$itu-, $g^w$$H_3$i-ta$H_2$, $g^w$$H_3$iwotā	life	uita
cīwāks	adI			lively	uīuax
cīwos	mas		$g^w$$H_3$i-wo-	life	uita
cīwós	adI		$g^w$$H_3$i-wó-	alive	uīuus
cīwotos	mas			animal	animāl
cl̥nāmi	intr	BIVa	g^wlH	agonise	praepatior
cl̥turós	mas			vulture	uultur
cm̥tis	fem			march	itus
cobhōn	adI			viscose	conglūtīnōsus
coinos	mas			sack	saccus
colbhos	mas			womb	uterus

corós	mas			big eater	cibicida
cosdhos	mas			rod	uirga
cotejō	tr	AIIIo		mention	allūdō
cotlós	mas			swelling	tumōr
coucis	fem			shit	merda
coudhros	adI			dirty	immundus
cowijós	adII			bovine	bouīnus
cówqolos	mas			herdsman	pāstor
cows	and	cewos	g^weH_3u- / $g^w$$H_3$eu-	cow	bōs
cowstā́s		(cowstajós)	g^wou-stH_2	ox-stall	bouīle
cr(āw)ús	adI		g^wṛH_2-u/ g^wṛeH_2u/ g^wreH_2u; cṛ(āw)us	heavy	grauis
crətos	adI		g^wrH-tó	heavy	brūtus
crājō	tr		g^wrH_3	devour	uorō
cr̥dos	adI		cṛdus	clumsy	inconcinnus
crātós	adI		g^wrH_2-to	welcome	grātus
crā́wenus	mas		g^wreH_2-n /g^wreH_2-w	millstone	mola
cr̥cestjom	neu			hovel	gurgustium
cr̥cots	mas	(cṛcetós)		whirl	gurgues
crebhos	mas			embryon	foetus
creughos	adI		g^wru-Hgh	sad	maestus
croghos	mas			Adam's apple	adamī malum
crotsos	adI		g^wr̥sto-?	big	grossus
croughnos	adI			sorrow	maestitia
crús	fem	(cṛewós)		crane	grus
crutā	fem		g^wrH_2ruteH_2(t)- crutāts	heaviness	grauitās
dā	ind			certainly	certō
daimoi	tr			divide up	distribuō
daitis	fem		d(e)H_2i-ti-; d(e)H_2i-mon-	time	tempus
daiwēr	mas	(daiwrós)		brother-in-law	leuir
dakru	neu	ew	akru / dṛk-akru >drakru > dakru / skw-akru /H_2ekur - H_2ekuenos	tear	lacrima
dāmos	mas			mate	sodālis
dānus	mas			river	fluuius
dápnāmi	tr	BIVb		be expensive	carus esse
dapnom	neu			cost of a feast	impensa dapis
daps	mas	dapós		banquet	daps
dáwētā	fem			torch	taeda
dáwetus	mas			conflagration	incendium
dáwneumi	tr	BIVb	deH_2w--	scorch	accendō
dawtis	fem			fuel	cibus ignis
dē	ind			from upwards	dē
debhō	tr	AIa		knead	depsō
dedrus	mas			allergy	allergia
deghā	fem			tick	rihipicephalus
deikmn̥	neu			example	exemplum

deikō	tr	AIa		show	monstrō
deikos	mas		deiks (dikós)	address	directiō
deiktis	fem		quoque diktis	indication	indicātiō'
deiwā	fem			goddess	dea
déiwijos	adII			godly	dīuus
deiwos	mas			god	deus
deiwotāts	fem	(deiwotātjos)		deity	deitās
deiwots	adI	(déiwetos)		rich	dīues
dekəmós	adII			tehth	decimus
dekējō	intr			be proper	decet
dekm̥	ind		dekm(t)	ten	decem
dékm̥tulos	mas			finger	digitus
deknos	adI			worthy	dignus
dekai	tr	AIb		receive	accipiō
dekos	neu	es		virtue	decus
deksis	fem			right-hand side	dextera pars
deksiwós	fem			right	dexter
déksiteros	adII			right	dexter
deljō	tr	AIVc	dHl; del; *cf.* doljō	calculate	calculō
delō	tr			split	abiungō
demos	neu	es		building	aedēs
demō	tr		dem(H_2?)	build	construō
demtis	fem		dm̥tis; demr̥	construction	constructiō
denkō	tr	AIa		bite	admordeō
densō	tr	AIa		infere	dēdūcō
dentis	mas	jo	H1dont- / H1dn̥ t-	tooth	dens
deqsjō	fac			present	praesentō
derbhō	intr	AIa		turn	gyrō
derghō	intr	AIa		get cumulated	cumulō
derō	tr		derH; d(e)rjō, dr̥neHmi	separate	sēparō
deru	neu	(drewos)	derH-u; doru	wood	lignum
deukō	tr	AIa		drag	dūcō
deuks	and	(dukós)		leader	dux
deusō	tr			spoil	ruinō
dew	ind		dewH_2 dweH_2	far	procul
dhəmis	fem			hunger	famēs
dhəmelós	fem		dhH_1melo-	foundation	fundātiō
dhəmos	mas		dhH_1mo-	employee	famulus
dhətis	fem			exhaustion	exhaustiō
dhabhros	mas			skillful	habilis
dhanus	fem		dhanwos	pinetree	abiēs
dhaunos	adI			predator	praedator
dhchínāmi	inc	BIVb	(s)dhg^{wh}Hi	vanish	abeō
dhchitis	fem			destruction	dēlētiō
dhebhō	tr	AIa	(H)dhebh; dhébhneumi	impair	dēminuō
dhebhús	adI			diminished	dēminutus
dhechō	dur	AIa		burn	ardeō
dhēdhjos			dhēdhos	grandfather	auus

dhedhmós	mas			decree	consultus
dheghom	mas	(dhghmos)	dhghmós, dheghoms	earth	humus
dheghwis	fem			inflammation	inflammātiō
dheicō	tr	AIa	$dheig^w$	puncture	figō
dhéicodhlā				brooch	fibula
dheimi	tr		$dheH^i_1$	suck	sūgō
dhejō	tr	AIb		put	ponō
dhelbhō	tr	AIa		bury	inhumō
dhēlēiks	adI	(dhēlikós)		productive	fēlix
dhēlgs	fem	(dhḷgos)		scythe	falx
dhēljos	mas			baby	lactans
dhelō	intr	AIb		shine	splendeō
dhēlós	mas			teat	tetta
dhēmn̥	neu			condition	habitus
dhemō	intr	AIb		steam up	uaporō
dhḗmonā	fem		dhēlus	female	femina
dhenghō	tr	AIa		press	imprimō
dhēnom	neu			produce of land	genitūra terrae
dhēnos	neu	es		interest	faenus
dherbhō	inc	AIa		start	functionem incipiō
dherghnos	fem			sloe	prūnus spinōsa
dherghō	tr			strengthen	corroborō
dherghos	adI			dark	obscūrus
dherghs	fem	(dhṛghos)		shit	excrēmentum
dherkō	cau	AIa		stain	maculō
dhermi	tr		$dherH_2$	retain	retineō
dhēs	mas	(dhasós)	dhH_1s-	duty (religious)	sacrificātiō
dhētis	fem	jo	dhHtí-, dheHti-	fact	factum
dheughō	intr	AIa		enough (to be)	sufficiō
dheukō	cau	AIa		destroy	conterō
dheunos	neu	es	$dh(u)nH_2$	death	fūnus
dhewō	intr	AIb	$dhewH_1$	run	currō
dhghjesi	ind			yesterday	herī
dhghomōn	mas	(dhghómenos)		human being	homō
dhghusā	fem			perch	perca
dhicsnis	mas	jo		end	fīnis
dhídhēmi-dhəkjō	tr	BIIb / AIVb	$dheH^i_1$	do	faciō
dhídhneumi	tr	BIVb	*cf.* dhídhēmi	install	instaurō
dhinghō	tr	AVIa		model	fingō
dhl̥eghlā	fem		dhl̥ghos	debt	dēbitum
dhl̥nā	fem		$dhl̥H_1nā$; $dhelH_1$	vegetation	uiridia
dhn̥ghus	adI			direct	directus
dhobos	adI			solid	solidus
dhochejō	cau	AIIIo		make hot	foueō
dhochos	mas		(dh)echṛ / (dh)ochṛ	day	diēs
dhoighos	mas			wall	moenia
dholos	mas			hollow	cauitas
dhombhos	mas			dove	columba

dhōmós	mas			opinion	sententia
dhōnā	fem			cereal	cereāle
dhóncelos	adI			dark	fuscus
dhoncos	adI			dark	obscūrus
dhónejā	fem			hollow	uōla
dhontis	mas	ej		fountain	fons
dhorjā	fem			diarrhea	diarhea
dhoubhos	adI			deaf	surdus
dhoubhús	adI		dhoubhus	black	āter
dhoubnom	neu			world	mundus
dhōunis	mas			strick	fūnis
dhraghō	tr	AIIa		bring out	prōmō
dhreghō	intr	AIa		run around	circumcurrō
dhrenkō	intr			ring out	clangō
dhrēnos	mas			roar	gemitus
dhrensājō	intr			cry	drensō
dhreughō	sta	AIa		do military service	militō
dhrighsós	mas			bundle	fascis
dhr̥mos	adI			steady	firmus
dhr̥numoi	intr	BIVb	dherH_3	jump	saltō
dhroghnom	neu			potter wheel	tornus
dhroghós	fem			wheel	rota
dhr̥sō	tr	AIIh		dare	audeō
dhr̥stis	fem			boldness	audacia
dhr̥sus	adI			bold	audax
dhrubhjō	tr		dhrub(h)?	crumble	comminuō
dhrubhtis	fem	jo		drop	stilla
dhruslijō	tr		dherH_2	dismantle	dismontō
dhubús	adI		dhubus	deep	profundus
dhugtēr	fem	(dhugtrós)	dhugH_2ter	daughter	fīlia
dhūjō	eff		dhuH_2-jō; *cf.* dhúneumi, dhūmājō	smoke	fūmō
dhūlis	fem	ej	dhūlis	soot	fūligo
dhūmā	fem			down	collis sabulī
dhūmājō	eff		*cf.* dhūjō	smoke	fūmō
dhūmós	mas		dhuH_1-mo	smoke	fūmus
dhúneumi	tr	BIVb	*cf.* dhūjō	agitate	agitō
dhūnis	fem	ej		agitation	agitātiō
dhūskos	adI			dark	fuscus
dhwerō	tr	AIa	dhwer/dhru	deceive	defraudō
dhwestus	fem			fleabane	pulicāria
dhwēwis	mas	ej		smoke	uaporō
dhwolnos	adI			crazy	insānus
dhwolsā	fem			whirlpool	uertex
dhwonos	mas			sound	sonitus
dhworis	fem	ej	dhweris, dhur-	door	foris
dhworom	neu			courtyard	forum
dhwosos	mas		dhwosos/dhousos (masc.) /dhwesos -es- (neut.)	demon	diabolus
dídēmi	tr		dH_1(-je/o)	tie	ligō

dídjāmi	tr	BIIa	deiH$_2$; dínāmi	shine	splendeō
didkskō	tr			learn	dīscō
dídn̥skō	inc		didm̥skō; *cf.* dn̥sus	get skilled	perītus fīō
dighā	fem			goat	capra
dikjō	tr	AIVa		reject	reiciō
dinos	fem		dinā; *cf.* djēws	day	diēs
djejō	intr			move	moueō
djēws	mas	(djwos)	dyeH$_1$-w; *cf.* dinos	day	diēs
dl̥ghējō	intr		dat	maintain	contineō
dl̥kus	adI			sweet	dulcis
dl̥nghos	mas	cp. dleH$_1$ghijos-, sp. dleH$_1$ghistH$_2$o-	dlongho-, dlH$_1$gho-	long	longus
dl̥nghotā	fem		dḷnghostus / -ostis	length	longitudō
dm̥pedom	neu			building place	locus operum
dm̥pus	adI			blunt	hebes
dm̥seghr̥	neu	dṃseghnós		domain	dominium
dn̥ghwā	fem		dnghu-H2; dṇt-ghuH2 ?	tongue	lingua
dn̥sus	adI			thick	densus
dn̥sus	adI		dm̥sus; *cf.* dídn̥skō	qualified	perītus
dō	ind			to	ad
doiknejō	tr	AIIIo		mean	significō
dokejō	pred	AIIIo		seem	uideor
doklom	mas			tail	cauda
dolājō	tr		dolH$_1$-	cudge	dolō
dolejō	tr	AIIIo	dolH$_1$-	disrupt	dīrumpō
dolghos	mas			dew	ros
doljō	tr		dolHje/o-; *cf.* deljō	allure	pelliciō
dōljom	mas			barrel	dōlium
dolos	mas			fraud	dolus
dom	ind			still	dum
dómāmi	tr	BIIIa, AIIIo, AIVc, BIVa	demH$_2$; domejō, dəmjō, démāmi, dm̥nāmi, dmāsmi	tame	domō
(dí)dōmi	tr	BIIc	deH$^{w}_3$	give	dō
domos	fem	(domōs, dómewos)	dom(H$_2$)o-; domus	house	domus
dómūnā	fem			landlady	domina
dómūnos	mas			landlord	dominus
donkrós	adI			fasting	iēiūnus
dōnom	neu		doH$_3$-no /doH$_3$-ro	gift	dōnum
dornom	neu			wrist	manicula
doros	mas			rent	scissūra
dōsos	mas			slave	seruos
dōtis	fem	jo		dowry	dos
dounom	neu		duHno-, dūno-	town	oppidum
dousmos	mas			bush	dūmus
dóusontos	mas			arm	braccium
drājō	intr			work	laborō

drappos	mas			drapery	drappus
drātis	fem			work	labos
drātṓr	mas	jo		workman	operārius
dr̥drājō	intr			murmur	murmurō
dremō (dídrāmi)	intr		drewō	run	currō
drepō		AIa		cut out	abscindō
dreughō	cau	AIa		beguile	dēcipiō
drewā	fem			course	cursus
drewom	neu		*cf.* deru	tree	arbōs
drewō	tr	AIa		treat	consuēscō
drismós	adI			harsh	asper
dristos	mas			bramble	dūmus
dr̥kjai peri	intr.			be visible	manifestor
dr̥kjō	tr			make up	perspiciō
dr̥kō	tr			see	uideō
dr̥kos	mas			vision	faciēs
dr̥ksmos	mas			perspective	prospectus
dr̥ktā	fem			light	lūmen
dr̥ktis	fem			view	conspectus
dr̥ktis	fem	jo		seen	uisus
dr̥mijō	dur			fall asleep	obdormiscor
dr̥nós	mas		drH-nó	split	fragmentum
dr̥tis	fem			split	scissiō
dr̥tós	adI			split	scissus
drumós	adI			wooden	ligneus
dr̥wā	fem			ryegrass	lolium
dsā	fem		dsH$_2$	war	bellum
dumbos	mas			tail	caudula
dúnāmi	tr		duH$_2$	arrange	habilitō
dus	ind			bad	malē
dúsōpis	adI			precarious	precārius
duswids	adI			incompetent	inscius
dweimi	tr			fear	timeō
dwenos	adI			good	bonus
dwídkm̥təmos	adII			twentieth	uicesimus
dwídkm̥tī	num		(d)widkm̥tiH$_1$	twenty	uigintī
dwikm̥témtəmos	adII			two hundredth	ducentesimus
dwikm̥tṓs	num dec		dwikm̥tóm (ind.) + gen.	two hundred	ducentī
dwipods	adII	jo		biped	bīpēs
dwīs	lois			twice	bis
dwīskos	adI			matching	pār
dwīsnōs	lois			two each	bīnī
dwṓdekm̥	num			twelve	duodecim
dwṓdekəmos	adII			twelfth	duodecimus
dwoiros	adI		dweiros, dwīrós; dweisos?; *cf.* pūrós	fearful	dīrus
dwoplós	adII			double	duplus
dwóteros	adII			second	secundus
dwōu, dwāu, dwōu	num dec			two	duo

echmi	tr	BIa	*H_1eg^{wh}mi/ H_1g^{wh}n̥ti	drink	bibō
ēchr̥	neu	(échenos)	H_1eH_1g^{w}h- r̥/n	drink	pōtiō
ēchr̥jos	adI			drunken	ēbrius
ecnis	mas	jo	H_1eg^{w}-ni-	fire	ignis
edhlos	fem		H_1edh-lo-	elder	ebulus
edhr̥	neu	(édhenos)		palisade	uallum
edjḗw	ind			today	hodie
edmi	tr		H_1ed	eat	edō
edqis, edqid	pron			someone	ecquis
edqos, -qā, -qod	pron			some	ecquī, -quae, -quod
edunā	fem			pain	dolor
edwolōn	adI	(edwólonos)		bad	malus
egējō	sta			lack	egeō
ēghī	fem	(aghijós <*H_2°H_1ghiH_2-os)	H_2H_1eghiH_2	cow	uacca
eghjos	mas		H_1egh-yo / H_1ogh-i(H)no-	hedgehog	er
eghr̥	neu	(eghnós)		boundary	circunscriptiō
egō	pron	(mene)	egH(o)$_2$	I	egō
ei	ind			that	ut
eikō	tr		Heik; $H_?$	have	habeō
eimi	dur		H1ei	go	eō
eisā	fem			wrath	ira
eisāskai	inc			be angry	irāscor
eisom	neu			ice	gelū
ek(sí)			H_1egh-si	outside	ex
eksoqs	adI	(éksoqjos)		invisible	inuisibilis
ékstəmos	adI			outermost	extimus
ekstar	neu	(ékstaros)	ek-stH_2-r̥, *cf.* enstar	remoteness	longinquitās
éksteros	adI		tab	external	exterior
ekstrōd	ind			from	ex
ektós	ind			excepted	praeter
ekwā	fem			mare	equa
ekwīnós	adII			of horses	equīnus
ekwos	mas		H_1ekwo-	horse	equus
ēlā	fem			bodkin	cuspis
elēn	mas	(alnós)	*cf.* alkis	red-deer	alcēs
elkos	neu	es		wound	ulcus
elkós	adI			bad	malus
ellus	mas	ew		eel	anguilla
elno elnā elnod	pron		*cf.* eno enā enod	that	ille illa illud
elóm	tr	(aor. a gesō)		conducted	gessī
elōr	mas	(éleros)		swan	olor
elwos				pink	rosaceus
emō	tr			take	emō
empis	fem			insect	insectus
en	ind			in	in-
anghwis	fem	ej	H_2(e)ng^{w}hi- ; *cf.* ochis	snake	anguis
endo	ind		H_1(e)ndo(m)	inside	in

endósēdjom	neu			furniture	suppellex
enim	ind			and	et
enīqā	fem		eni-H_3k^w-eH_2	face	faciēs
enis	adII		tab	certain	quīdam
enkō prō	tr	AIa		drive	condūcō
ennós	adI			interior	interior
eno enā enod	pron		$H_{1/2}$eno-; *cf.* elno elnā elnod	that	ille illa illud
énsēdjom	neu			ambush	insidiae
enslā	fem			island	insula
enstar	neu	(énstaros)	en-stH2-r̥, *cf.* ekstar	proximity	proximitās
énteri	ind			between	inter
énternos	adI			internal	internus
énterom	neu			interval	interuallum
énteros	adI		tab	internal	interior
énteros	adI		tab	intestine	intestīnus
entós	ind			inside	intus
éperom	neu			west	occidens
epi	ind		H_1epi, H_1opi; opi	on	insuper
épijos	adII		H_1eH_1p-i-	relation	adfīnis
épiromos	adI		ópiromos	placed on top	supernus
eplom	neu		H_1ep-lo	celebration	celebrātiō
ercom	neu		H_1ergwo-	pulse	erūm
erjos	mas		H_1er-	ram	ariēs
erkō	fac		H_1rk	share	commūnicō
ermi	intr		H_1rH_1	rest	requiescō
ermos	adI		H_1rH_1-mo-	abandoned	solus
ernos	adI			upright	arrectus
erō	tr	AIa		heave	erigō
éroros	mas		er-H_3ero-	eagle	aquila
erqō	intr	AIa	H_1erk^w	shine	splendeō
ersā	fem		H_1ers-	tail	cauda
ersábhaljom	neu			tail	cauda
ersājō	sta			wander	errō
ersō	intr	AIa	H_1ers	flow	fluō
erwā	fem			land	terra
esmi	dur		H_1es	be	sum
ēsmoi	intr			be situated	sum
esn̥ts	part	(sn̥tos)	H_1esn̥t-; *cf.* sontis	being	qui est
esos	m		H_1esH-o-	housemaster	erus
esr̥	neu	(ésenos)	H_1esH_2-r	blood	sanguis
ēsús	adI		eH_1su- ?; ēsus	good	bonus
éteros	adII			second	secundus
eti	ind			even	etiam
étiqe	ind	etsqe		even	etiam
etmn̥	neu	en		soul	animus
ētr̥	mas	ētenós	H_1eH_1-tr	inside	interior
ētros	adI		ātros ?	vivid	uiuidus
eukō	tr	AIa	euk / eH^wk	be used	colō
eusō	intr		H_1eus	burn	ūrō
gálgaljō	intr			talk	garriō

galnos	mas			power	potentia
galnos	mas			gaul	gallus
gangō	intr			pin down	siffilō
gar	ind		ar ge	indeed	enim
garsijō	intr			talk	garriō
gāudhējō	intr		geH_2-$dheH_1$ / geH_2wi-$dheH_1$ / geH_2-dhH_1-sk ?	rejoice	gaudeō
gaudhjom	neu			joy	gaudium
ge	ind			at least	quīdem
geigō	sta	AIa		be bitter	acūtus sum
geimō	intr	AIa		sprout	germinō
geisā	fem			gravel	calculus
gélāmi	intr	BIIIa	$gelH_1$	laugh	rīdeō
geldhós	adI		*cf.* kiklós	very cold	gelidus
geltis	fem			embryo	fētus
gelu	neu	ew		ice	gelū
gembhō	intr	AIa		germinate	germinō
gemō	tr	AIb		be loaded	grauātus esse
gemros	mas		gemHro-	son-in-law	gener
genesājō	cau			create	generō
gengā	fem			gum	gingiua
genjos	mas		comp. -gnH_1yo-	gender	sexus
genmn̥	neu	en	$genH_1mn̥$	germ	germen
genō	intr	AIb		shout	clāmō
genos	neu	es	$genH_1os$	kin	genus
gentis	fem	jo	$genH_1ti$- / $gn̥H_1ti$-	family	familia
gentlom	neu		$genH_1tlo$-	birth	nascentia
gentṓr	mas		$genH_1tor$	parent	genitor
gentrīks	fem	(géntrijos)	$genH_1triH_2$	parent	genitrīx
gentus	mas		$genH_1tu$-	procreation	genitus
genu	neu			knee	genū
genus	neu			maxilla	maxilla
gergō	cau	AIa		wind	contorqueō
gerjō	tr		H_1ger; med. expergiscor	wake up	expergefaciō
gerlós	adI			old	senex
gerō	prog	AIa	$gerH_2$	old (to become)	sēnēscō
gersā	fem			network	gerra
gerwós	mas			veteran	ueterānus
gesō	tr		$(H_2)ges$	wear	gerō
geulom	neu			glowing ash	fauilla
geustis	fem	jo		taste	gustus
gewō	intr	AIa		resound	resonō
ghəbhējō	tr			own	possideō
ghərējō	eff		*cf.* gherijai; caus. ghorejoo	be glad	gaudeō
ghəris	fem			grace	gratia
ghabhlom	neu			fork	furca
ghabhros	mas			goat	hircus
ghaidīnós	adII			goatish	haedīnus

ghaidos	mas			young goat	haedus
ghaisējō	sta			stick	haereō
ghaisom	neu			spear	gaesum
ghaisom	neu			stick	pilum
ghaitā	fem			hair	capillum
ghálerom	neu			disgrace	labēs
ghandā	fem			shelduck	ganta
ghanos	neu	es		yawn	hiātus
ghansōr	mas	er		goos	anser
ghastā	fem			spearshaft	hasta
ghawō	tr		ghH$_2$ew / ghwH$_2$e	call	uocō
ghawōd	ind			not	haud
ghebhlā	fem			head	caput
ghedmr̥-	neu	(ghédmenos)		excrement	excrēmentum
ghedō	tr	AIb		defecate	iunificō
gheidhō	tr	AIa		long for	aueō
ghoi-ke ghāi-ke ghod-ke			tab	this	hic haec hoc
ghéimentos	adI			wintry	hiemālis
gheimr̥	neu	(ghéimenos)	gheims, *cf.* ghjems	winter	hiems
gheimrīnós	adII			winterly	hibernus
gheipō	intr	AIa		sob	hippitō
gheislos	mas		gh^{w}eistlo- ?	hostage	obses
ghelbō	intr	AIa		boast	glorior
ghelijō	intr			growl	grunniō
ghelnom	neu			lip	labrum
ghelō	intr			incise	insecō
ghelus	fem			tortoise	testudō
ghelos	neu	es	ghelH$_3$-os/es	vegetable	olus
ghelwos	mas		ghelis, ghélenos, ghəlis, ghl̥ros; ghelH$_3$i- ghelH$_3$(i)-wo-, ghelH$_3$-eno-, ghl̥H$_3$-i-, ghl̥H$_3$-ro-	green	uiridis
ghēmi	intr	BIIb	gheH$_1$	pass from one place to another	permeō
ghenghō	intr	AIa		step	uadō
ghēr	mas	(gherós)		hedgehog	ēr
gherdhō	tr	AIa		encircle	circumdō
gherdos	fem			pear-tree	pirus
gherghros	fem			pod	siliqua
gherijai	tr		gherH; *cf.* ghərējō	desire	desiderō
gherō	tr			lend	commodō
ghertom	neu			butter	butyrum
gherús				small	exiguus
ghesr̥	neu	(ghésenos)	*cf.* ghestos	hand	manus
ghesris	fem			glove	digitābulum
ghestos	neu		*cf.* ghēsṛ	hand	manus
ghētis	fem	jo		arrival	aduentus
ghetlā	fem			handle	stīua
gheughō	tr	AIa		veil	obumbrō

gheusō	tr	AIa		hear	audiō
gheutis	fem			mould	fūtis
gheutlom	neu			vase	bacārium
ghéwejā	fem			hollow	fouea
ghewos	es			space	spatium
ghi	ind			certainly	certō
ghighējō	intr			come back	redeō
ghirrijō	intr			whine	hirriō
ghjājō	inc			gape	hiō
ghjems	mas	(ghjmos)	gheims; *cf.* gheimṛ	winter	hiems
ghlaghos	mas			crossbeam	patibulum
ghlastos	adI		ghḷ(H)-sto-	blue	caeruleus
ghlendhō	tr	AIa		study	pertractō
ghleumi	intr			joke	nugor
ghloidos	mas			luxury	sumptus
ghlōmi	intr	BIIc	ghlH_3; ghlōjō	glimmer	renideō
ghloumos				joke	nuga
ghl̥tnós	adII			golden	aureus
ghl̥tom	neu		ghH_3-to	gold	aurum
ghlustis	fem			flourishing	fluorescentia
ghn̥dhus	mas			cancer	cancer
ghn̥dō	tr	AVIc		receive	accipiō
ghneumi	tr	BIIIb		caress	mulceō
ghōdhos	mas			honour	honos
ghodos	mas			rump	pūga
ghoilos	adI			joyful	alacer
gholwā́	fem		*cf.* ghelus 'testudō'	caluum caput	bald head
ghordhos	mas		*cf.* ghortos	enclosure	saeptum
ghorejai	cau	AIIIo	*cf.* ghərejō	encourage	hortor
ghornim	ind			pleasantly	libenter
ghoros	mas		gherH_1; ghərus	intestine	intestīna
ghórsdejom	neu		gher-, ghres-dhi, ghersdh	barley	hordeum
ghorsejō	cau	AIIIo		erect	horreō
ghortos	mas		*cf.* ghordhos	garden	hortus
ghosóm	tr	(aor. ab edmi)		ate	ēdī
ghóstipots	adII	jo		guest	hospes
ghostis	and	ej		foreigner	aduena
ghosdos	mas		ghostos	starvation	inedia
ghouros	adI			terrible	terrens
ghowejō	tr	AIIIo		pay attention	obseruō
ghradjai	dur		$g^{(h)}rd^{(h)}$	step	gredior
ghrāsmn̥	neu	en		grass	grāmen
ghrāsom	neu		ghreH_2-so; gres/ghres	grass	herba
ghr̥bhjō	tr	AIa	ghrebh(H_2) / ghreibh; ghreibhō	seize	captō
ghrebhō	tr	AIa		bury	inhumō
ghrēdhus	mas	ew	ghordhos	hunger	famēs
ghreimn̥	neu			ointment	unctiō
ghr̥ējō	sta			be empty	uacuus sum
ghremō	intr	AIa		grumble	fremō

ghrendhā	fem			cornice	corona
ghrendhos	neu	es	ghrōnā́	lock	cirrus
ghrendō	intr	AIa	chrendō, $g^{(w)h}rend^{(h)}$	gnaw	frendō
ghrēw	ind		ghreH_1u	early	mane
ghrewō	cau	AIa		grind	conterō
ghrewō	eff			fall into	ingruō
ghrobhos	mas			content	continentia
ghromos	mas			roaring	fremitus
ghronos	mas			mark	signum
ghroudos	mas			ball	pila
ghrowā́	fem			pebble	calculus
ghərtā	fem			tip	cuspis
ghudjō	tr			do harm	damnō
ghúgheumi	tr		gheu; ghewō	pour	fundō
ghundō	cau		gheu-d	pour	fundō
ghwerā	fem			beast	fera
ghwērīnós			ghwerīnós	beastly	ferīnus
ghwērós	adI		ghwēr; ghwer; ghwerós	wild	ferus
ghwobhros	mas			smith	faber
gibbā	fem			hump	gibba
gígisai	intr	BIIe	geis	happen	accidō
gignō	cau		genH_1	beget	gignō
gigrós	adI			sharp	acūtus
gjewō	tr	AIa		chew	mandō
gləgjēs	fem			ice	glaciēs
glabhō	tr			plane	ēfodiō
gladhros	adI			even	glaber
glaghā́	fem			protest	querēla
glaghti	neu			milk	lac
gleghos	adI			docile	infirmus
gleibhō	tr	AIa		adhere	adhaerō
gleis	mas	(glisós)		mouse	glis
glēkis	adI			intelligent	callidus
glembhō	cau	AIa		include	inclūdō
gleubhō	tr	AIa		peel	glūbō
glēws	mas	(gluwós)		parcel	fascis
glínāmi	intr	BIVa		stick	adhaerō
globhos	mas			globe	globus
glōghis	fem			point	cuspis
gloidos	mas			rubber	glūtinum
gloijós	adI			sticky	glutinoosus
gloitn̥	neu	gloitnós		glue	glūten
glokijō	intr			clack	glociō
glomos	neu	es		yarn	glomus
glōs	fem	(glēsos)	gH_2lōw	sister-in-law	glōs
glujō	tr	AIIIu		swallow	glūtiō
gnabhjō	tr	AIVb	gn∂bhjō	gnaw off	abrōdo
gnājō	tr			produce	gignō
gnāmi	tr		knH2; *cf.* kanmā, kn̥mā, knāmā	gnaw	adrōdō
gnās	m/f	(gnājós)		offspring	prōlēs

gnātós	adI		gnH_1-tó; comp. -gn̥tó-; *cf.* gignō	born	nātus
gnebhis	fem			fleece	uellus
gnebhō	tr	AIa		pluck	uellicō
gneibhō	tr	AIa		raze	rādō
gneichō	intr	AIa		lean	nītor
gneidō	tr	AIa		scrape	abrādō
gnetō	tr	AIb		finger	contrectō
gn̥jai	inc		gnH_1-eH_2-sk; gn̥jai; gnāskai	be born	nāscor
gnṓmenjom	neu			mark	indicium
gnōros	adI			evident	euidens
gnos	ad		in compositiōne	native	ingenuus
(gí)gnōskō (gnōwa)	tr	AVc	$gneH_3$	know	nōscō
gnōsmi	tr	BIe	gnēsmi	recognize	agnoscō
gnōtis	fem			knowledge	nōtiō
gnōtlom	neu			sign	signum
gnōtṓr	mas			knower	nōtor
gnōtós	adI		gnH_3tó-	known	nōtus
gnoubhos	mas			bud	geniculum
gnōwos	adI			wise	nāuus
golā	fem		*cf.* goulos	ball	globus
golbhnos	mas			dart	acūmen
gōgā	fem		*cf.* gugā	biscuit	buccellātum
gombhos	mas		*cf.* gembhō	jaws	dentes
gomos	mas			load	onus
gonējō	tr		$gonH_1$-eio/e-	produce	generō
gopos	mas			jaws	fauces
gorbos	mas			wrinkle	rūga
gorgnóm	neu			sadness	tristitia
gorgós	adI			sad	tristis
goulos	mas			jar	matula
gouros	mas			crimpy hair	turbidō
gówijā	fem		$gouH_2$-i?	lapwing	uanellus
grakijō	intr			cackle	gracillō
grammā	fem			rheum	grāmiae
grānóm	neu		grH_2-no-	grain	grānum
gr̥beinos	fem		(s)karp ?	hornbeam	carpinus betulus
gr̥bējō	sta			have wrinkle	rugātus sum
gr̥bhō	tr	AVIII		scratch	charaxō
grebhos	mas			net	rēte
gredō	tr	AIa		scratch	scabō
gregs	mas	(grēcos)	H_2greg-	herd	grex
grejos	neu	es		level surface	aequōr
gremjom	neu			lap	gremium
grendjom				crown	corōna
gretlom				cradle	cūnae
greubhō	dur	AIa		go aside	mē āuertō
greugō	intr	AIa		bend	curuō
greumō	tr	AIa		scrape off	abrādō

greutō	intr	AIa		solidify	solidificō
grn̥dhís	adI			grown	grandis
gr̥neumi	tr	BIVb, AIa	H_2ger; gercō, gerjō, g∂rjō	gather	cogō
grōbhos	fem			oak tree	quercus suber
grōdis	mas		grōdos	hail	grandō
gromos	mas		grōmos	group	congregātiō
groumos	mas			crumb	grūmus
grundijō	intr			grunt	grunniō
grutis	fem			curd cheese	lac passum
gudom				bowels	intestīnum
gugā	fem		*cf.* gōgā	ball	pila
gupā	fem			cellar	pitheūs
gurnos	mas			back	dorsum
gusnō	tr			taste	gustō
gutr̥	mas	(gútenos)		throat	guttur
idhei	ind			there	ibī
ikjō	tr		H_2yk	reach	ic(i)ō
ili	neu	(ílijos)		groin	intestīnum
īljō	tr	AVIII (lām-loja-leisō)	H_1lH_2 redupl. H_1i-H_1lH_3	send away	amandō
imde	ind			from there	inde
immō	adII			more than that	immō
ínekmi	tr	BIIe	H_1nk	convey	apportō
íneumi	tr	BIVb	Hei-neu-	bring disgrace upon	aerumnas obiciō
ipjō				oppress	opprimō
is, id	pron		tab	this	is, ea, id
īsarnom	neu			iron	ferrum
ita	ind		itH	so	ita
itājō	freq			journey	itō
itaqe	ind			and also	itaque
íteros	adII			different	differens
itim	ind			likewise	item
itr̥	neu	(itenos/H_1iténs)	itr̥, eitr̥	way	iter
iwe	ind		H_1iwe	like	ceu
jəkējō	sta			lie down	iaceō
jəkjō	tr			eject	iaciō
jagjō	tr		jH_2g-jo/e	worship	uenerō
jāgjus	adI		jeH_2g-ju-	pious	pius
jāi	ind			yes	certō
jālos	mas			conspiracy	coniurātiō
jālós	adI			vane	uānus
jāmi	intr		yH_2	pass	transeō
jāmi	ind			already	iam
jáneumi	tr	BIVb	ieH_2; iH_2neumi	conspire	coniurō
jā́nuwā	fem			entrance	iānua

jebhō	intr	Aib	H_2i̯ebh	fuck	futtuō
jeghō	tr			persecute	persequor
jegis	mas	ej		ice	glaciēs
jekō	tr	AIb		tell	narrō
jekos	adI			healthy	sānus
jēlom	neu			desert	desertum
(jí)jēmi	cau	BIIb	jeH_1	expel	expellō
jemō	tr			hold (to)	contineō
jemós	neu			twin	geminus
jentēr	mas	(jentrós)		cousin	frāter patruēlis/ amitinus
jeqr̥	neu	(-óneros)		liver	iecur
jesō	intr.	AIb	HH^i_2es-	ferment	fermentō
jeunis	fem			right way	uia recta
jeugō	intr		*cf.* jugājō	be violent	ferociō
jeus	neu	(jusós)		broth	ius
jewesdiks	adII	jo		judge	iudex
jewō	intr	AIa		help	adiuuō
jewom	neu			barley	hordeum
jéwornjom	fem			cereal	cereāle
jéwestos	adI			just	iūstus
jewos	neu	(jéwesos)		law	iūs
jn̥dros	adI			exuberant	laetus
jn̥tō	tr	AVIa		desire eagerly	aueō
jod qid	ind			because	quia
jodhei	rel			where (rel.)	ūbī
joinkos	mas			bulrush	iuncus
jom	rel			when	cum
jomde	rel			from which	unde
joqe	ind			and	et
jori	rel			wherefore	quapropter
jorkos	mas			roebuck	gazella
jōrom	neu		yeHro-	season	tempus
jōrós	mas			conspirator	conspirātor
jos (je), jā, jod	rel		tab	that, the one that	is quis
jṓsneumi	tr	BIVb	HieH^w_3-s	begird	cingō (to)
jos qis, jā, qis, jod qid	pron			whoever	quiscumque
jota	rel			how	quōmodo
jota sei	ind			alike	quasi
joudhejō	cau	AIIIo		stir up	commoueō
jóugsmn̥tom	mas			beast of burden	iūmentum
jucis	adII		H_2yu-gwiH_3	eternal	iūgis
jugājō	tr		*cf.* jeugō	subjugate	subiugō
jugóm	neu			yoke	iugum
jungō	tr		ieH^w_3-g	join	iungō
jusmé	pron		nom. acc.	you	uōs
júwenis	adII			young	iuuenis
juwes / juwe	pron		tab	you	uōs

juwn̥kós	adII		H_2iw-wH_1ṇkó-	young	iuuenis
júwn̥tā	fem			youth	iuuentus
juwōn	adI	(júwenos); sup. jéwistH_2o-	H_2iw-wHen--	young	iuuenis
kəlejō	tr	AIIIo	klH_1; kelmi / klenti <*kelH_1mi / kH_1lenti	name	nōminō
kəlējō	sta	AIIIe	klH_1-eH_1-	be hot	caleō
kəletos			kl̥Heto-; *cf.* kaldos	hardened	callōsus
kənjós	adI		*cf.* kenō	recent	recens
kəpjō	tr		kHp	catch	capiō
kəpsā	fem			box	capsa
kəptos				captive	captus
kəsējō	sta			lack	careō
kəstos	adI			pure	castus
kətos	adI		$H_3H^i_2kH_3$-to-	sharp	catus
ka	ind		kem; *cf.* kom	certainly	sīc
kábn̥los	mas			colt	equulus
kabōn	mas	(kábonos)		horse	equus
kadhō	tr			keep	praeseruō
kadō	prog			fall	cadō
kādos	neu	es		trouble	cūra
kadros	adII			saint	sanctus
kaghlā	fem			opening	caula
kaghos	mas			enclosure	claustrum
kaidō	cau			cut	caedō
kaikos	adI			blind	caecus
kailom	neu			augur	augurium
kaipā	fem			onion	caepa
kairós	adI			untouched	integer
káisr̥jēs	fem			long hair	caesariēs
kaisrom	neu			hair	capillum
kaitom	neu			heath	silua
káiwelos	neu			exclusive	exclusōrius
kákabā	fem			partridge	perdix
kakkājō	intr			defecate	cacō
kaklājō	intr			cackle	cacillō
kákneumi	tr	BIVb		promote	foueō
kakō	cau			thinnen	tenuefaciō
kakúds	fem	(kakudós)		summit	cacūmen
kaldējō	sta			be experienced	calleō
kaldos	mas		kH_2l	blister	callus
kalēiks	mas/ fem	(kalikós, kalijós)	kalīks	cup	calix
kalgōn		(kálgenos)		fog	cālīgo
kālis	fem			spot	macula
kaljós	adI			gorgeous	uenustus
kalkis	fem			heel	calx
kalwos	adI		kḷHwos	bald	caluus
kambos	adI			bent	tortus
kāmi	tr			love	amō
kamō	tr		kH2m	press tightly	comprimō

kampos	mas			land	campus
kánāmi	tr	BIIIa		dig	fodiō
kandō	tr			glow	candō
kánkestos	mas			colt	equulus
kankus	mas		kanku /kākā	branch	ramulus
kanmā	fem		knH2; kn̥H2mā, knāmā, knH2mi-; *cf.* gnāmi	leg	crus
kanmn̥	neu	(kánmenos)		song	carmen
kanō	intr			sing	canō
kantos	mas		kambtos?; *cf.* witus	wheelrim	cantus
kaplos	mas		*cf.* skāpos	tool	instrumentum
kāpos	mas			land estate	fundus
kaprā	fem			goat	capra
kapros				goat	caper
kaput	neu	(kaputós)		head	caput
kareinā	fem		Har-	keel	carīna
karkar	mas	(karkarós)		fortification	mūnītūra
kárkarjō				announce	nuntiō
karkros				crab	cancer
karnājō	tr	AIIIa		pin down	carinō
karōn	fem	en		limb	membrum
kāros	adI			beloved	cārus
karpō	tr			collect	carpō
kárrēkā	fem			rock	rūpēs
kartús	adI	comp. kretjós-	kar, kr̥-; kartus; kr̥tus	hard	dūrus
kasnos	mas			grey	cānus
kasterlom	neu			castle	castellum
kastra	neu	(kastrōm)		camp	castra
kastrājō	tr			prune (to)	castrō
kastrom	neu			scissors	forfex
katēsna	fem			chain	catēna
katsājai	intr			meet	congredior
katsājō	tr			gather	cōgō
kattā	fem			cat	fēlēs
katus	mas		kH_2etu-	fight	pugna
kaukos	mas			vessel	collectāculum
kaulis	fem			cabbage	caulis
kaunós	adI			shameful	pudendus
kawdō	tr	AIIa	keH_2w-d	hit	cūdō
kawō	tr	AIIb	keH_2w	hit	cūdō
káwonā	fem			owl	noctua
ko kā kod (eko ekā ekod)	pron			this	hic hae hoc
ke	ind		ki	of here	hic
kei	ind			here	hic
keidō	intr	AIa		go down	descendō
keimēx	mas			bug	cīmex
keimoi	inc			lie	iaceō
keimos	neu	kéimesos		colorant	colorans

keiros	adI			dark	obscūrus
kéiwijos	adII			civil	cīuīlis
keiwis	and	ej	keiwos	citizen	cīuis
kekājō	tr			bind	nectō
kekātrīks	fem	(kekātrikós, kekātrijós)		scar	cicatrix
kekō	intr		(s)k$H_{1/2}$ek, (s)ke$H_{1/2}$k; skekō *cf.*	leap	saltō
kékuros	adI			tame	cicur
kēlā	fem			chamber	cella
kēlājō	cau		desid. kikl̥H_1s-e/o	hide	cēlō
keldō	tr		kelH_2-d-	strike	percellō
kelgā	fem			mystery	mysterium
kéliknom	neu			penthouse	cēnaculum
kelmos	mas			helmet	galea
kelō	tr		kelH_1; kl̥nō	push	impellō
kélodhros	mas			snake	coluber
kēlom	neu			arrow	sagitta
kelos	neu	es		cover	coopertūra
kelots	mas	(kéletos)		boy	ephebus
kelsō	intr	AIa	kelH_3, kl̥neH_3-	be high	excellō
kelujō	intr			travel	iter facere
kelus	fem			road	uia
kémelom	neu			sky	caelum
kémeros	fem			lotus	lotus
(kí)kōmi	tr	BIIc	$H_3H^i_2$keH_3	sharpen	exacuō
kemjō	tr			hum	cantillō
kemō	intr	AIb		strain	adnītor
kemos	adII			hornless	incornis
kenēs	fem	(kensós)	*kon(H)I- /*ken(H)i-	ash	cinis
kenkai	intr			hesitate	uacillō
kenklom				tendon	tendō
kenkō	inc	AIa		weigh	pendō
kenkos	mas			hook	hamus
kenō	intr		kn̥jō; *cf.* kn̥jós	arise	oborior
kentom	mas			rag	pannus
kentrom	neu			prick	centrum
kepō	tr			do harm	infensō
keqō	tr	AIa		dirty	mancillō
kerəsrom	neu		kerH_2-s-ro-	brain	cerebrum
kérberos	mas			weasel	mustela
kerdhjos	mas			herdsman	pāstor
kerdhō	tr	AIa		range (to)	ordinō
kerdhos	mas			group	grex
kerdos	neu	es		profession	ars
kerkō	inc	AIa		grow thin	tenuescō
kerkos	fem			hen	gallīna
kernos	mas			excavator	pāla
kernós	mas			frozen snow	nix gelāta
kerom	neu			hair	caesariēs
keros	neu	es	ker$H_{1/3}$os-	millet	milium

kersis	adI			rudis	harsh
kersnā	fem			dinner	cēna
kersō	tr	AIa		mutilate	mutilō
kersr̥	neu	(kersenós)	kersr̥ , kersn̥, kerH1os	head	caput
kerwos	mas		kerH$_2$wo-	deer	ceruus
kesdō	intr			withraw	cēdō
kēsmi	tr		ke(k)Hs-mi	restrain	reprimō
kesnus	mas			garlic	ālius
kesō	tr			comb	pectō
kētjā	fem			room	cubiculum
keubō	cau	AIa		curve	curuō
keudhō		AIa		hide	abdī
keukō	dur		*cf.* kakúds	warp	inflectō
keulom	neu			swelling	turgentia
keusō	tr		keusH	rent	locō
kēwējō	intr		keH$_1$w-	sway	oscillō
khákhatnos	mas			laugh	cachinnus
khamos	mas			hook	hāmus
khéderos	fem			ivy	hedera
kighrós	mas			agitated	agitātus
kikēr	mas	(kikrós)		pea	cicer
ḱíkeumi	intr	BIIIb		become vigorous	uigescō
kikjā	fem			woodpecker	pīca
kiklēskō	tr	(kiklēwa)		invoke	inuocō
kiklós	adI		kelH; *cf.* geldhós	cold	frīgidus
kíkōnjā	fem			stork	ciconia
kīkus	mas	(kī'kewos)		muscle	mūsculus
kina	ind			from this side	hinc
kingō	tr			gird	cingō
kintos	adII			previous	praecēdens
kippos	mas			peg	cippus
kirknos	mas			compasses	circinus
kirkos	mas			circle	circus
kiskā	fem			biceps	biceps
kistā	fem			basket	cista
kíteros	adI			of this side	citer
kitōd	ind			immediately	citō
kitrōd	ind			towards this side	citrō
kiwos	mas			colour	colōr
kjājō	tr		kieH$_2$	assort	diribeō
kjējō	cau			activate	ciō
klādis	mas		*cf.* kl̥dos	damage	clādēs
kladjos	mas			sword	gladius
klagjō	intr			clang	clangō
klāmājō	intr			yell	clamō
klambós	adI			mutilated	mutilus
klāmi	tr			embank	aggerō
klamrós	adI		klmH$_2$-ro	weak	dēbilis
klāros	mas			tablet	tabella

klārós	adI		klH$_1$-ró	loud	resonus
klāstis	fem		klH$_1$-dhH$_1$-ti	convocation	conuocātiō
klaudos	adI			lame	claudus
klawdō	tr			close	claudō
klawos	mas			nail	clāuus
klāws	fem	(klāwós)		key	clāuis
klawstós	adI			closed	clausus
kl̥dis	fem		kəlnis?; *cf.* kəldos	mountain-path	callis
kl̥dos	mas		*cf.* klādis	wood	lignum
kleinos	fem			maple	acer
kleitis	fem			hut	casa
kleitrom	neu			support	firmāmentum
klengō	tr	AIa		bend	plicō
klepō	tr	AIa		steal	clepō
kleumi	neu		kluH	listen	audiō
kleumn̥	neu			hearing	audītus
kléumn̥tom	neu			reputation	reputātiō
kleusō	tr	AIa		obey	oboediō
kleustis	fem		klustís	obedience	oboedientia
kleutis	fem	jo	quoque klutis	listening	audientia
kleutō	tr	AIa		raffle	sortior
kleutrom	neu			story	historia
klewō	tr	AIa		wash	purgō
klewos	neu	es		glory	gloria
klínāmi	cau	aor. kleim	kli-H$_2$; klinjō	cause to slope	clinō
klisrós	adI			gentle	gentilis
kl̥jō	tr		(s)kel	divide	diuidō
kl̥neumi	tr	BIVb*	kleuH <*kl̥-ne-uHmi	hear	audiō
kl̥ngō	intr	AIIc	klH$_1$-g	sound	clangō
kloiwos	adI		kloinos	steep	clīuus
klopnis	fem	jo		valley	uallis
klounis	fem	jo		buttock	clūnis
kl̥pros	mas			wine-cask	cupa
kl̥tos	adI			hot	calidus
klūtós	adI		kluH-tó	famous	audītus
kluwējō	sta			be named	clueō
kl̥wijō	tr			defame	difāmō
kmāmi	prog		kmH$_2$	get tired	dēfetiscor
km̥bhis	adI		km̥bhnós	small	paruus
km̥ertos	mas			lobster	langusta
km̥ros				curved	camur
km̥ti	dh°r		*cf.* kom	with	cum
km̥témtəmos	adII			hundredth	centesimus
km̥tom	num			hundred	centum
knakos	adI		knH$_2$-ko	yellow	glaesus
kn̥kējō	cau	AIIIo	cau. konkejō	feel burnt	combustiōnem sentīre
knokos	mas			neck	ceruix
knouks	fem	(kneukos)		nut	nux
kn̥sējō	tr			opinate	censeō
kn̥stṓr	mas		kenstṓr	spokesman	orātor

knuwā	fem			walnut	nux
kobom	neu			success	euentus
kodējō	tr			thurify	turificō
koilús	adI		koilus	healthy	sānus
kóilutāts	fem	jo		health	ualētūdō
koimā	fem			agreement	pacta
koimos	adI			lovely	cārus
koinos	mas			foenum	hay
koinós	adII		koi(H)-no	akin	cognātus
koisā	fem			occupation	cūra
koitús	mas	(koitewós)		manner	modus
koksā	fem		kokso-	hip	coxa
koksednīks	fem	(koksednikós, koksedniyós)	-edniH$_2$	hip bone	coxendīx
kolignos	mas			dog	canis
koljō	tr			stick	adhaerō
kólkolos	mas			bell	campana
kolmn̥	neu	en		summit	culmen
kolmos	mas		kolH$_2$-mo-	stalk	calamus
kolnis	fem	ej	kolH-ni-, kl̥H-ni-, kolH-wi, kolH-wo	hill	collis
kolnom	neu			pile	sublīca
kolnos	adII			one-eyed	unioculis
kolsos	mas		nōn qolsos quoniam gmc. nōn *hw incipit	neck	collum
kólumbhos	mas			dove	columba
kom	ind		*cf.* km̥ti; *cf.* ka	with	cum
kómāglom	neu		kómagdhlom	collection	collectiō
kómjougos	mas			union	coniunctiō
komjugs	epi	komjugós		consort	coniux
kómmoinis	adII			common	commūnis
kommoinitáts	fem	jo		community	commūnitas
komnom	neu			meeting	congregātiō
kómnōmn̥	neu			surname	cognōmen
kómopjom	neu			equipment	armāmenta
kōmos	mas			mass	globus
kómplēnos	adII			complete	complētus
kómsqr̥tos	adI			perfect	perfectus
kómtl̥tis	fem			patience	patientia
komtrōd	ind			against	contrā
kómwoirjom	neu			court	curia
kómwoistis	fem			conscience	conscientia
kōnājai	inc			try	cōnōr
konkhā	fem			shell	concha
kōnos	mas		H$_3$H$^{i}_2$k-eH$_3$-no-	top	turbēn
kopos	mas		kopHo-	hoof	ungula
kopnos	mas			haven	portus
kóqros	mas			dirt	immunditia
korbhis	mas	(kórbhejos)		basket	corbis
koris	fem			acarian	acarus
korjom	neu			leather	corium
korjos	neu			army	exercitus

korkos	adI			mud	caenum
kormnos	mas			bleach	aqua lixiuiae
kormōn	mas	(kórmenos)		ermine	mustēla erminea
kormos	mas			pain	dolor
kornīks	fem	(kornikós, kornijós)		crow	cornīx
kornos	fem			cherry tree	cornus
korudhs	fem	(kórudhos)	*cf.* kr̥nu	helmet	cassis
kṓrukos	mas			bag	saccus
korwos	adI		korw-, korweH_2	raven	raucus
kósolos	fem			hazel	corilus
kostā	fem		H_3osteH_2	rib	costa
koubos	mas			joint	artus
koupā	fem		kūpā	cup	cūpa
koupnā	fem		koupnom, koupā, koupos	lot	cōpia
koutā	fem		*cf.* kotos	hut	mapālia
kowejō	tr	AIIIo	*cf.* skewō	beware	caueō
kowis	epi			magician	magus
kowos	adI			hollow	cauus
kowr̥	neu	(kówenos)	kuH_2-r	cavern	cauerna
krāmi	tr	Bib / BIVa	krH2 / kr̥neH2	mix	permisceō
krāsi	ind		*cf.* ausrom	tomorrow	cras
krāsrōn	mas	en		bumblebee	crābrō
krātis	fem	ej	krH_2tis	network	crātis
kratsos				plump	crassus
kr̥dḗn		kr̥dnos		hinge	cardō
kr̥dhōn	mas	(kr̥dhenós)		carbon	carbō
kr̥di / kr̥djom	neu	(kr̥dejós / kr̥djī)		heart	cor
kr̥dijai	prog			get angry	stomachor
kr̥djō	intr		krH-d	rock	trepidō
kr̥stus	fem			shirt	camisia
kréddhēmi	tr		krd + dhH_1/dhH_3	believe	crēdō
kreidhrom	neu			sieve	crībrum
kreimn̥	neu			crime	crīmen
kreitsō	intr	AIa		shake	agitor
krekō		AIa		weave	texō
kremājō	cau			burn	cremō
krēmi	tr		kerH_1; *cf.* krēskō; kerH_3 uescor?	create	creō
kremom	neu			beer	ceruisia
krémusom	neu			onion	caepa
krenghos	mas			ring	anus
krenktis	fem			scar	cicātrix
krépāmi	intr			crackle	crepō
krepō	intr	AIa		precipitate	praecipitor
krepús	adI			strong	fortis
krēqā	fem		krīqā ? *cf.* krinō	border	limēs
krēskō	prog		kr̥H_1ske/o-; *cf.* krēmi	grow	crēscō
krētā	fem			chalk	crēta

kretō	tr	AIa		cut	exsecō
kreugō	intr	AIa		cry	gemō
kreuks	fem	(krukós)		cross	crux
kreumi	tr		kru-H	stock	dēpositō
kreupō	inc	AIa		get encrusted	incrustor
kreutō	tr	AIa		agitate	permoueō
krēwō	tr	AIIf		afflict	adflīgō
krēws	neu	(kruwós)	kr(e)uH_2-; krew(o)s-, kruwós-	blood	cruor
krigā	fem			cry	clamor
krinō	tr		kre(H_1)i	sieve	crinō
kripsnis	fem	jo		mane	crīnis
kripsos	adI			curly	crispus
kripstā	fem			crest	crista
kristājō	cau			shuttle	agitō
kritis	fem			difference	differentia
kritós	adI			different	distinctus
kr̥jēs	fem			rot	cariēs
kr̥klos	adI			slender	gracilis
kr̥nāmi	tr		krH_1	rot	corrumpō
kr̥nos	adI			rotten	corruptus
kr̥nu	neu	kr̥newós		horn	cornū
krōbhtus	mas			devotion	dēuotiō
krokijō	intr			shriek	crociō
kroknos	mas			anorak	peplum
krosnos	mas			jet	saliens
krotjājō	tr			shake	agitō
krous	neu	(kreusos)		leg	crūs
krowos	mas			shelter	refugium
kr̥pjos	mas		krH_2pjo-; krāpjo-	shoe	calceus
kr̥pos	neu	es	k^{w}r̥pos ?	body	corpus
kr̥sējō	sta			be scratched	carreō
kr̥snos				black	āter
kr̥sō	tr	AIIh		run	currō
kr̥stus	mas			course	cursus
kr̥sus	mas			cart	currus
krustā	fem			icicle	crustula
krūtis	fem		krūtís	dome	cupula
kr̥wos	adI			curved	curuus
ksentis	fem		*cf.* ksnujō	briar	sentis
kserós	adI		ksērós	dry	siccus
ksnujō	tr		ksuwō, ksujō, ksējō, ksənjō, ksnowājō, ksnutējō	shave	abrādō
ksnowātlā	fem			razor	nouācula
ksūlom	fem			post	columna
kúbāmi	sta			lie	cubō
kudājō	intr			reprove	orbiurgō
kukulājō	intr			cuckoo	cucu facere
kukūlós	mas			cuckoo	cucūlus
kūlā	fem			hiding place	latebra
kūleks	mas	(kūlkós)		gnat	cūlex

kūlos	mas			ass	cūlus
kumbhā	fem			pot	catīnus
kumbō	intr			recline	accumbō
kūmós	mas		kuH$_1$-mo	heap	cumulus
kúnejos	mas			wedge	cuneus
kupjō	tr			demand	exigō
kurnos	mas			foal	pulllus
kusdhos	mas			treasure	thesaurus
kusis	mas			kiss	basium
kusjom	neu		kūsjom	cavity	cauea
kūtis	fem	ej	kHuti-; kūtís	skin	cutis
kúwanos	mas		kūnos	lapis lazuli	lapis lazuli
kuwējō	sta			be pregnant	grauidus sum
kuwos	mas			whelp	catulus
kúwr̥os	adI			powerful	potens
kwāimi	tr			acquire	acquīro
kwatsos	mas			cheese	caseus
kweidos	mas			white	candidus
kwentos	adII		skwentos	holy	sacer
kwōn	mas	(kwnos)		dog	canis
ləbjom	neu			lip	labrum
ləkesājō	cau			tear	lacerō
ləkjō				trap	laciō
ləkós	mas			tearing	lacerātiō
lənchijóm	neu			lung	pulmō
ləpējō	sta			be flat	plānus sum
ləpods	mas	(l∂pedós)		stone	lapis
ləskējō	sta		lH$_2$sk-	fancy	lascīuiō
ləsnis	adI		lH$_2$s-nis	lustful	lascīuus
lətējō	sta			be concealed	lateō
labhō	tr			take	emō
laghā	fem			spade	pāla
lāgō	intr	AIIe	(s)leH2g; *cf.* lṇgwō	droop	ēlanguescō
laiwós	adII			left	laeuus
lājō	tr			scold	obiurgō
lajos	neu	es		fat	adeps
lakertos	mas			forearm	lacertus
lakus	mas	ew		lake	lacus
lalājo	intr			babble	blaterō
lalu	ind			penis	pēnis
lāmā	fem			poodle	lāma
lā́mn̥tom	neu			tell off	obiurgātiō
landhom	neu			frypan	sartagō
lāōs	mas	(lā́esos)		home god	lār
lāpos	mas			cow	bōs
lapsā	fem			lamp	lampās
latēks	mas	latkos		liquid	latex
latom	mas			day	dies
lāurā	fem			stonework	opus saxeum
lawō	tr		leH$_2$u; abl.	benefit	fruor
lāwós	mas		leH$_2$wó-	team	squadra

lawrós	adI		lǝwHros	profitable	lucrifícābilis
lawtlom	neu			benefit	lucrum
ledō	tr		lH_1d	release	āmittō
leghjai	inc.			lie	accumbō
leghō	sta			lie	occubō
leghos	neu	es		lay	fulcrum
leghskā	fem			settlement	sēdēs
leghskós	adI			lazy	pīger
leghtrom	mas			support	destina
leghús	adI		*cf.* lǝnghros; leghus	light	leuis
légneumi	tr	BIVb		wring out	ēguttō
legō	tr			collect	legō
legs	fem	(lēgos)		law	lēx
leibs	mas	(libós)		drop	gutta
leidmi	tr			permit (to)	permittō
leiglā	fem		leigdhlā	spoon	ligula
leigō	intr	AIa	H_1lei-g	jump	saliō
leiljom	neu			lily	liilium
leinō	tr	AIa		avoid	uitō
leinom	neu			flax	līnum
leipā	fem			lime-tree	tilia
leisā	fem			track	līra
leitō	intr	AIa		go	eō
leitos	neu	léitesos		seaside	litus
lembō	tr	AIa		hang	suspendō
lēmi	tr	BIc	leH_1	grant	indulgeō
lemō	tr		H_3lem	break up	abrumpō
lemsos	mas			phantom	phasma
lendhā	fem			spring	fons
lēnis				weak	lēnis
lentos	fem			juniper	picea
lepō	intr			stutter	balbutiō
lenghmi		BIe		declare	dēclārō
lergos	adI			flat	plānus
lēsanks	fem	(lēsankós)	lēwanks ?	slate	ardesia
lesō	tr			pick	carpō
lestrom	neu			vessel	vās
leswos	adI			middling	sublestus
lētis	fem			concession	indulgentia
letrom	neu		CELT. *pletro- ?, *cf.* lat. pellis	leather	corium
leubhos	adI			dear	cārus
léudheros	adI		H_1leudh	free	liber
leughō	intr	AIa		lie	mentior
leukō	intr			shine (to)	luceō
leukós	adI			bright	lucens
leuks	fem	(lukós)		light	lux
leuksmn̥	neu	en		light	lūmen
lēumi	tr	BIg	leH_1u	damage	afflictō
leups	mas	(lupós)		leaf	folium
lewis	mas			sickle	falcula

ligājō	tr			bind	ligō
ligos	adI		H_3ligo-	scarce	rarus
likējō	tr			be available	praestō sum
limpō	sta			stick	haereō
linghō	tr			lick	lingō
līnō	tr		liH; linādmi	oint	linō
līnós	adI			ointed	litus
linqō	tr			leave	linquō
lipējō	sta			be sticked	adhaereō
lippā	fem			rheum	lippa
liprós	adI		lipH_2ró	greasy	adipōsus
litājō				appease	litō
litwos	mas			rod	lituus
lm̥bō	tr			sip	lambō
ln̥cō	cau	AVIc	(s)leH_2g; ln̥gō; *cf.* lāgō	tire	fatigō
ln̥ghros	adI		*cf.* leghús	light	leuis
lōbā	fem			crime	dēlictus
lodi	neu			late	tarde
loghejō	cau			lay down	dēpōnō
loghjom	neu			site	situs
loghos	mas			deposit	dēpositus
loigos	mas			calf	uitulus
loigós	mas		H_3loigo-; *cf.* ligos	penury	lack
loimos	mas		(s)H_2loimo-; sloimos	mud	līmus
loiqnom	neu		loiqnos (es-)	lend	commodātus
loiqós	adII			remaining	reliquus
loisā	fem			tablet	līra
loisós	adI			mild	mitis
loksos	mas			lax	salmō
loksós	adI			slanting	obliquus
loktos	mas		loktus	fault	culpa
londhom	neu			land	regiō
londhwos	mas			hip	lumbus
longhros	mas			worm	lombrīcus
lordós	adI			twisted	tortus
lorgā	fem			footprint	uestigium
lorgos	mas			club	uirga
lostos	mas			spear	hasta
loubhis	ind			or	uel
loudis	mas	ej		praise	laus
loughjom	neu			oath	sacramentum
lougos	mas			twig	rāmulus
loukejō	cau	AIIIo		illuminate	ilūminō
loukētjos	adI			radiant	splendidus
loukos	mas			glade	saltus
loukós	mas			radiance	splendor
louksā	fem			window	fenestra
louksnā	fem			moon	lūna
louksos	mas			lynx	lynx
lousēn	fem	(lusnós)		louse	pedis

loutsā	fem			whore	merētrix
lowā	fem			hair	coma
lowō	tr		lH_3w	wash	lauō
lowtrom	neu			bath	lābrum
l̥tejō	tr	AIIIo	H_2ltoi-, H_2lti-	invite	inuītō
lubhējō	tr			like	libet (mihi)
lubhjā	fem			herb	herba
lubhros	mas			bast	liber
ludhóm	intr	(aor. a cemjō)		came	uēnī
lugējō	sta			be broken	fractus sum
lugjā	fem			hole	ōrificium
lugnós	adI			flexible	flexibilis
lugtos	mas			multitude	cōpiae
lukējō	sta			shine	luceō
lukskējō	tr			light up	incendō
lúnāmi	tr		leH_2; leH_2u-	split	rumpō
lūnós	adI		lūtós	unbound	solūtus
lutom	neu		l(H)u-to-	dirt	lutum
lūtós	adI			unbound	solūtus
luwō (lewō)	tr		lewH	unbind	luō
luwō apó	tr			acquit	absoluō
mədējō	sta			be wet	madeō
məgjos	adI			big	magnus
məglos	adI			noble	nōbilis
məgnánəmos	adI			magnanimous	magnanimus
məgnos	adI	*cf.* məgjṓs; sup. mégistH_2o-	mH_1-gH_2 / mH_1-g-nó / mH_1-g-ló / mH_1-g-jó	big	magnus
məgis	ind		*cf.* mājis	more	magis
məgistā́	fem		məgistjom	greatness	maiestās
məgtājō	tr		*cf.* məgnos	honour	mactō
məljos	adI			false	falsus
mənējō	sta			remain	maneō
mənijai	omc			tower	ēmineō
mənjō	sta		mnH_2; mənjai	think	cōgitō
mərējō	sta			deserve	mereō
mərijai	intr			die	morior
mərjos	mas			pubescent	pūbes
machos	mas		maghu-, moghu?	youngster	iuuenis
machotis	fem			youth	iuuentūs
mághneumi	tr	BIVb		defend	dēfendō
maghos	mas			field	pratum
magō	tr		mH_2g	form	configurō
mājis	adv		*cf.* məgis	more	magis
mājō	prog			prosper	mātūrō
mākājō	cau			make slim	maciō
makēn	mas		(maknós)	pouch	crumēna
mākesjā				wall	mūrus
mā́kōn	mas	mā́kenos		poppy	papauer
makrós	adI			slender	macer
mammā	fem			mum	mamma

mān	ind		meH$_2$n	so	etenim
mānājō	intr			spring	mānō
mánnusos	mas			man	homō
mānos	adI			good	bonus
maqā	fem			girl	puella
maqos	mas			boy	ephebus
máreskos	mas			marsh	mariscus
margōn	mas	margenós		boundary	margō
mari	neu	ej	mori?	sea	mare
markos	mas			horse	equus
masdos	neu			mast	mālus
mātejō	tr			designate	dēsignō
mātḗr	fem	(mātrós)	meH$_2$-ter-	mother	māter
māterós	mas		dmāterós?	solid	solidus
mātérterā	fem			aunt	mātertera
matlā	fem			hammer	malleus
mauros	adI			gloomy	fuscus
m̥bhros	mas		*cf.* nebhos	storm	imber
m̥bhu	neu		*cf.* nebhos	water	aqua
m̥dhros	adI			blue	caeruleus
m̥gadhós	adI		m̥gH$_2$-dhH$_1$o-	magnificent	magnificus
me	pron		H$_1$me; aton.	me	mē
mē	ind			not	nē
medai	intr		mH$_1$d; cōgit.	ponder	medeor
medgós	mas			gull	mergus
médhidjōws	mas			midday	meridiēs
medhjos	adII			middle	medius
medhu	neu	ew		mead	mel
medjom	neu			acorn	glans
médneumi	tr	BIVb	meH$_1$d / mH$_1$d	administrate	administrō
médodiks	epic		med- / mēd- *cf.* regs	doctor	medicus
mēdos	neu			valuation	aestimātiō
meicō	intr	AIa	H$_1$mei-g^w; -g^w rārus	move	mutō
meidō	tr	AIa	mei /meit /meid	scrath out	desculpō
meidos	neu			prestige	auctoritās
meilēts	mas	(meiltós)		warrior	milēs
meinom	neu			purpose	propositiō
meitō	sta	AIa		lack	dēsum
meitrom	neu		mitros	agreement	contractus
meiwijṓs	adI			smaller	minor
mejājō	intr		mínāmi	flow	meō
mejō	tr	AIa	H$_2$mei; uox media intr.	change	mūtō
mejtis	fem	jo	quoque mjtis	shift	permutātiō
mēknos	mas			lip	labrum
meldhjā				thunderbolt	fulmen
meldhō	intr			pray	precor
mēlis	fem	ej		badger	mēlēs
melit	neu	mélitos		honey	mel
meljom	neu			millet	milium
melkō	tr	AIa		rub	mulceō

melmn̥	neu			article	articulus
melō	tr	AIb	melH_2	grind	molō
mēlom	neu		meH_1-lo-	moment	mōmentum
melos	adI			strong	robustus
melsō	tr	AIa	*cf.* mƏljos	deceive	mentior
melujō	tr			crush	conterō
melwom	neu			flour	farīna
membhō	tr	AIa		punish	puniō
mēmi	tr			measure	metior
mēmsóm	neu		memsóm	meat	carō
mendhai	intr		cogit.	be interested	interest
mendhō	tr	AIa		stir	uersō
mendō	tr			suck	sūgō
mendom	neu			fault	mendum
menghos	adI			frequent	frequens
mengō	tr	AIa		disguise	uestiō
menis	mas			dace	phoxinus
menkō	intr			lack	desum
menmn̥	neu	en		intellect	intellectus
menos	neu	es		sense	sensus
mēnsis	mas	ej	meH_1ns-, mH_1nt-; nom. rad. meH_1nōs gen. m(e)H_1nsés	month	mēnsis
mentā	fem			rod	uirga
mercō	tr	AIa		make black	nigrō
mergā	fem			fork	furca
merghā	fem			snare	laqueus
mergis	fem			filth	situs
mergō	cau	AIa	merg/mezg	sink	mergō
merkēds	fem	(merkƏdós)		charge	naulus
merkō			*cf.* bherkō	flimmer	fulgeō
mérneumi	tr	BIVb		worry	turbō
meros	adI		merHo-	simple	merus
mersō	tr		mr̥snāmi	neglect	neglegō
merwos				insipid	insipidus
mesgō	tr	AIa		communicate	communicō
meslā	fem			blackbird	merula
mestis	fem		memstis ?	measure	mensūra
mestós	adII		memstós?	measured	mensus
mētā	fem			post	mēta
meti	ind			in the middle	in mediā parte
mētijai	tr			measure	mētior
mētis	fem		meH_1-ti-	dimension	dīmensiō
metō	tr	AIb		reap	metō
metrom	neu	mētrom 2º comp.		measure	mensūra
meudos	adI			proud	superbus
meugō	intr	AIa		cheat	dēlūdō
meukō	tr	AIa		scratch	ērōdō
meus / muskós	neu	(mūsós)		muscle	mūs
mgānts	adI		mg(e)H_2(e)nt-	great	ingens
mighlā	fem			mist	uapor

míkāmi	dur			flimmer	micō
mikskejō	cau	AIIIo	meik/meik-sk-	mix	misceō
miljom	neu			red ochre	minium
mimdō	inc			meet	accurrō
mímnāskō (memna)	intr	AVc	cogit.	remember	memini
míneumi	cau	BIVb	eff. mínāmi	reduce	minuō
minghō	intr		H_3meigh-; mighjō	piss	mingō
mínusi	ind			less	minus
misdhóm	neu			salary	sālārium
misgā	fem		miks-	whey	sērum lactis
mítnāmi	tr	BIVa	meitH_2; uox media intr.	exchange	permūtū
mlājō	cau			weaken	dēbilitō
mlākós	adI		ml-H_2-kó	stupid	stultus
mlātóm	neu		mlH_2-tó	flour	farīna
mḷdhos	adI		ml(H_2)-dh-	permissive	permissīiuus
ml̥dsnos	adI			softened	ēmollītus
ml̥dus	adI		ml-du; tab	soft	mollis
ml̥duwijō	tr			soften	molliō
mleumi	tr	BIIIb	mleuH	speak	loquor
ml̥gājō	tr			anounce	nuntiō
mlīnós	adI			slack	ēneruis
ml̥kāmi	intr	BIIIa		weaken	ēlanguescō
ml̥nos	adI		melH_2-; mḷnejós	dark	mulleus
ml̥sjō	tr			taste	dēgustō
mlōdhrós	adI			lofty	excelsus
mlōskō	intr		mlH_3	appear	appareō
ml̥qjō	tr		*cf.* mr̥kjō	afflict	afflictō
ml̥sos	mas			slow	lentus
ml̥wā	fem		mḷH-weH2	mallow-plant	malua
mnājō	tr			bear in mind	in mente habeō
mn̥dōmi	tr			commit	mandō
mn̥kos	adI		*cf.* mənwos	defective	mancus
mn̥kstrom	neu			shaker	mixtarium
mn̥sjai	neu			intend	intendō
mn̥tijai	tr			put on	mentior
mn̥tis	fem	jo	mentis	mind	mens
mn̥tō	tr		mH_2t; mtH_2	chew	mandō
mn̥tom	neu			chin	mentum
mn̥tos	mas			mention	mentiō
mn̥trājō	tr			wipe	abrādō
mn̥us	fem	(mənewós)		hand	manus
mn̥wos	adI		*cf.* mənkos	scant	insignificans
mō	ind			but	sed
mōdos	mas		moH_3do-	perseverance	constantia
modos	neu	es		measure	modus
moghjos	adI			pleasant	amoenus
moghō	tr	AIId	mH_3gh	can	possum
moghtis	fem	jo		might	potestās
moghtrom	neu			means	remedium
moighos	mas			pee	uriina

moilos	adI		miH_1-	mild	comēs
moinijai	tr			fortify	mūniō
moinis	adI			obliged	mūnis
moinja	neu			walls	moenia
moisós	mas			sheep skin	pellis ouīna
moitājō	tr			exchange	mūtō
moitmos	mas		méitimos	thanks	grātes
moitos	mas			exchange	permūtātiū
moitwos	adII			mutual	mutuus
mojnos	mas			exchange	commūtātiō
mogsū́	ind		mogsí, moksí	soon	mox
molā	fem		$molH_1(e)H_2$	millstone	mola
moljā	fem			coast	lītus
moldhā	fem			occipital	occipitium
moldhos	mas			prayer	prex
moleinā	fem			mill	molīna
mōlestos	adI			annoying	mōlestus
molgējō	tr			milk	mulgeō
mōlis	fem	ej		mass	mōlēs
mōlos	neu	es		effort	mōlimen
molpā́	fem			pride	superbia
molqos	adI			wet	madidus
moltlom	neu		molH-tlo/-to/-lo	hammer	malleus
mondō	tr			adorn	ornō
mondós	mas			whelp	cattulus
monejō	cau	AIIIo		warn	moneō
mongos	fem			neck	collus
monīli	neu		monH-	collar	monīle
monos	mas			neck	ceruix
montis	mas	ej		hill	mons
morā	fem			delay	mora
morā	fem			nightmare	somnus terrorificus
morcós				dark	obscūrus
mordējō	tr			bite	mordeō
morignā	fem			woman	mulier
morjods	mas	ed		thigh	poples
mórmoros	mas			panic	horror
morom	neu			berry	mōrum
moros	fem		*cf.* mr̥tis	fatality	infortūnium
mōros	adI		mōros /mēros *cf.* yōrom /yērom	renowned	nōbilis
mōrós	adI			stupid	mōrus
mōs	mas	(mosós)		character	ingenium
mosgom	neu			cerebellum	cerebellum
mosgos	mas			relation	uinculum
moukos	mas			mucus	mūcus
mouros	mas		mounos	slop	illuuiēs
mousos	fem			weed	alga
mowejō	cau	AIIIo	$m(i)euH_1/m(i)eH_1u$; *cf.* Muujoo?	move	moueō
mreghmós	mas			skull	caluaria

mr̥ghús	mas			short	breuis
mr̥gneumi	tr	BIVb	H_3merg; mr̥negmi	wipe	tergō
mr̥kā				carrot	carota
mr̥kējō	sta	AIIIe	H_2mr-k	be withered	marceō
mr̥kjō	tr		*cf.* mr̥kos; cau. morkejō; *cf.* ml̥qjō	ill-treat	afflictō
mr̥kos	adI		*cf.* morkejō	disabled	murcus
mr̥ktos	adI		*cf.* bhr̥ktos	speckled	uarius
mr̥meikā	fem			ant	formīca
mr̥mrājō				murmur	murmurō
mr̥namói	tr		-nH_2moi	plunder	exspoliō
mr̥tājō	tr			crush	conterō
mr̥tāsjom	neu			mortar	mortārium
mr̥tis	fem	jo	*cf.*moros	death	mors
mr̥tos	adII			dead	mortuus
mr̥wos	adII			dead	mortuus
mūdlom	neu			detergent	dētersīuum
mūdnós				clean	mundus
mudstos	mas			must	mustus
mūgijō	intr			moo	mugiō
mūjō	intr		H_2meuH; *cf.* mowejō?	fall	cadō
munkō	tr	AVIa		let out	dīmittō
mūris	mas			abundance	cōpia
mūs	neu	(mūsós)	muH-s-; mews	mouse	mūs
muskā	fem			fly	musca
muskos	mas			moss	muscus
músnāmi	tr	BIVa	meuH; mune$H_{2/3}$-mi; meu$H_{2/3}$-s-	secrete	abdō
mūstrom	neu			weasel	mustēla
mūtos	mas		*mu$H_{1/3}$	penis	pēnis
mūtrom	neu			mud	lutum
muttijō	sta			mutter	muttiō
muttis	adI		mūtós	speechless	mutus
n̥	ind			un-	in-
nətis	fem			nates	natis
nāi	ind			absolutely yes	equidem
nantis	fem			courage	audacia
nāsis	fem	ej	neH_2s-i	nose	nārēs
natrīks	fem	(natrikós, natrijós)		serpent	natrix
nawāgós	epic			sailor	nauta
nāws	fem	(nāwós)	neH_2w-	ship	nāuis
n̥bhudhnóm	neu			abyss	abyssus
n̥cḗn	fem		H_1ngw	groin	inguen
n̥dha	ind		H_1ndh-	then	deinde
n̥dherós	adI		tab	underly	inferior
n̥dhētós	adII			unmade	infectus
n̥dhi	ind			in excess	magis etiam
n̥dwojos	adI			sincere	sincērus
nē	ind			no	nē

nebhlā	fem			fog	nebula
nebhos	nes	es	*cf.* nembhos	cloud	nūbes
nedhō			H_2nedh	rise	surgō
nedis	fem	ej		nettle	urtīca
nedjos	adI		nHed-yo-	near	propinquus
nedō	tr	AIb	nHd	link	nōdō
nedsā	fem			net	nassa
nedskō	tr	Ava	nHd-skō	bind	nectō
nedus	epi			neighbour	uicinus
neghō	tr	AIa		penetrate	penetrō
neghrōn	mas	en		kidney	rēnis
nei	ind			not at all	nequaquam
neicō	tr			wash	lauō
neidō	tr	AIa	H_3nei-d	humiliate	humiliō
neikō	tr	AIa		winnow	uentilō
neitom	neu			rivalry	inimicitia
neiwós	adI			depressed	dēpressus
nékāmi	tr			kill	necō
nekopīnós	mas			unexpected	necopiinus
neks	mas	(n̥kos)		death	nex
nembhos	mas			water cloud	nimbus
némētom	neu		nemH-	sanctuary	sanctuārium
nemō	tr		n-em(H)	distribute	distribuō
nemos	neu	es		forest	nemus
nemots	epic.	(németos)	nemH-	enemy	inimīcus
nepēts	mas	(népotos)	H_2nep-ōt-	grandson	nepos
neptis	fem	jo	H_2neptiH$_{1/2}$; neptī	grand-daughter	neptis
neqe	ind			and not	neque
neqid	pron.			nothing	nihil
neqis				nobody	nemō
neqom	ind			never	nunquam
neqos	pron.			someone	quisquis
neros	mas		H_2ner(o)-	soldier	milēs
nérteros	adII			lower	inferus
nertos	adI			strong	robustus
nesros	adI		neHs-ro	modest	modestus
neudō	tr	AIa		spend	impendō
neukos	adI			myop	myops
neumi	tr	BIIIb	neuH	proclaim	praeconor
new(ij)os	adI			new	nouus
newājō	tr			renew	nouō
newn̥	num		H_1newn	nine	nouem
néwn̥dekm̥	num			nineteen	undeuigintī
néwn̥dekəmos	adII			nineteenth	undeuicesimus
néwn̥dkm̥təmos	adII			ninetieth	nōnāgēsimus
néwn̥dkm̥ta	num		(H_1)neundkm̥t-/(H_1)neundkont-	ninety	nōnāgintā
newn̥km̥témtəmos	adII			nine hundredth	nongentesimus
newn̥km̥tṓs	num dec		newn̥km̥tóm (ind.) + gen.	nine hundred	nongentī

néwn̥mos	adII		néwm̥tos	ninth	nouenus (nōnus)
newō	intr	AIa		nod	nuō
newotāts	fem	(newotātjos)		newness	nouitās
n̥gnōtós	adI			unknown	ignōtus
n̥neumi	tr	BIVb	H$_3$n-neu; n̥skō	teach	doceō
nī	ind			down	sub
nijóm		(aor. a bherō)		lead	dūxī
nikjō			H$_3$nei-k	attack	adorior
niktis	fem			corn	grānum
nínāmi	tr	BIIa, BIVa	H$_3$nH$_2$; [illegible]nāmi	befriend (to)	faueō
ninsai		AVIa	*cf.* nosejō	go back to a good place/state	recurrō
nīqos	adII			inclined	prōnus
nisdos	mas			nest	nīdus
nitējō	sta		*nei-	shine	niteō
nı́teros	adI		tab	inferior	inferior
nitjos	adI			usual	usitātus
n̥jousjom	neu			unjustice	iuiuria
n̥joustos	adI			unfair	iniustus
n̥kējō	tr	AIIIe		need	necesse est
n̥kneumi	tr	BIVb	H$_2$nk; *cf.* nṇkskai; pf. H$_2$eH$_2$nó(n)kH$_2$e = ānoka	arrive	perueniō
n̥mrtijos	adII		ṇmṛtó-	immortal	immortālis
nm̥tos	mas			bending	plecāmentum
nn̥kskai	tr	AVc	H$_2$n-H$_2$nk-sk- ; *cf.* ṇkneumi	find by chance	nanciscor
nocējō	cau			put off	exuō
nócodos	adII		nog^{w}od(h)o- /nog^{w}oto /nog^{w}no-	naked	nūdus
nōdos	mas			knot	nōdus
noibhos	adII			holy	sanctus
nōinos	pron		nōinlos	none	nullus
nokejō	cau	AIIIo		destroy	deleō
nom	ind		*cf.* num	so	num
nom nē	ind			do not?	nonne
nōmn̥	neu	en	H$_3$neH$^u{}_3$-mn, H$_3$nH$^u{}_3$-mn,	name	nōmen
nōmnājō	tr			name	nōminō
nomr̥	neu	nómenos	nomH-	precision	subtilitās
noqterinós	adII			night	nocturnus
noqtis	neu	jo	dhnoct-? *cf.* dhoncos	night	nox
nosejō	cau	AIIIo	*cf.* ninsai	free	recipiō
nōunā	fem		noH$_2$u-	famine	esuriēs
n̥probhwos	adI			wicked	improbus
n̥qijētós	adI			restless	inquiētus
n̥serós	adII			our	noster
n̥sis	mas	jo	H$_2$n̥si / H$_2$n̥sr̥	sword	ensis
n̥sloimis	adII			unmuddy	illīmis
n̥sme	pron		nom. acc.	we	nōs

n̥swodhros	adI			extraordinary	rārus
nū	ind			now	nunc
num	ind			now	num
numki	ind		ki num	now	nunc
n̥widis	adI			ignorant	ignārus
obhi	ind			middle (in the)	ob
óbrusjā	fem			flask	obrussa
ochis	mas		H$_1$ogh^{w}is; *cf.* anghwis	worm	lombrīcus
odáugjai	intr			aggravate	exulceror
odējō	tr			smell	olō
odhrom	neu			enclosure	claustrum
odjō (ōda)	tr		H$_3$d	hate	ōdi
ōdjom	neu			hatred	ōdium
odós	mas	es		odor	odor
oghlejō	cau	AIIIo		trouble	inquietō
oghlos	mas			annoyance	molestia
ogmos	mas		H$_2$og-mo	track	orbita
oidējō	sta		H$_3$eid	be swollen	tumeō
oighai	intr			depart	proficiscor
ōimi	tr	BIIf	H$_{2/3}$eH$_3$i; *cf.* oitos,, ainō	believe	crēdō
oimos	mas			march	itus
óinokos	adII			single	ūnicus
oinos	num dec		H$_1$oi-no-	one	ūnus
oinowr̥stós	adII			simultaneously made	in eōdem tempore factus
oisjā	fem		H$_3$iH$_2$s-?	rudder	tēmō
oiso, oisā, oisod	adII			that one	iste
oitmi	tr	BIf	H$_3$oit-	fetch	appetō
oitos	mas		*cf.* ōimi, ainō	oath	sacrāmentum
oiwos	fem		H$_3$eiwo-	yew	taxus
okējō	sta			doubt	dubitō
óketā	fem			harrow	occa
ōkinós	adI			ready	compositus
okris	fem		H$^{o}_{3}$eH$^{i}_{2}$k-ri-	summit	apex
óktōdekm̥	num			eighteen	duōdeuigintī
óktōdekəmos	adII			eighteenth	duōdeuicesimus
octōkm̥témtəmos	adII			eight hundredth	octingentesimus
octōkm̥tő́s	num dec		octōkm̥tóm (ind.) + gen.	eight hundred	octingentī
oktōu	num	(āi oi)	H$_1$oktō(u)	eight	octo
oktowós	adII			eighth	octāuus
oktṓdkm̥təm̥os	adII			eightieth	octogesimus
oktṓdkm̥ta	num		oktōdkm̥t-/oktōdkont-	eighty	octōgintā
ōkúpteros	mas		H$_3$ku-/eH$_3$ku- + -ptero-/-petro-	hawk	accipiter

ōkús	adI		HeH_3-k-u-; ōkus; *cf.* abhnós	swift	rapidus
olejō	cau	AIIIo	H_2ol- / HeH^i_2 ?	heat	adoleō
olējō	cau	AIIIe	H_3elH_1	destroy	aboleō
olgjā	fem			tendril	cincinnus
ōlim	ind			formerly	ōlim
oljoi oljāi olja	pron	pl.		all	omnes
olkis	mas / fem	ej	l̥kis; *cf.* elēn	roe-deer	alcēs
olmos	fem		H_1(o)lmo-	elm	ulmus
ōlnā	fem		H_3olH_1-neH_2	elbow	ulnā
ólteros	adI			further	ulterus
óltm̥os	sup.			furthest	ultimus
oltrōd	ind			over there	ultrā
olwā	fem			sedge	ulua
omos	adI		H_3emH_3o-	firm	firmus
ōmós	adI		eH_3mH_2	raw	crūdus
omsos	mas		H_1omH-so	shoulder	umerus
onbhlos	mas		H_3nbh-	navel	umbilicus
onchis	mas	ej	H_3n(o)g^{wh}-i	fingernail	unguis
oncn̥	neu	(óncenos)	H_3eng^{w}n̥	ointment	unguen
oncō	tr	AVIII	H_3eng^{w}	oint	unguō
oncōl	mas	(n̥clós)	H_1ong^{w}-ōl, *cf.* ecnis	coal	carbō
ondos	neu	óndesos		rock	saxum
onējō	tr		H_3enH_2	blame	culpō
ónerjos	mas		Honr̥/-n- Honerio-	dream	somnus
onghlos	mas			nail	clāuus
onjos	adII			another	alius
onkājō	intr			groan	uncō
onkos	mas		*cf.* ankos	hook	uncus
onkos	mas			portion	portiō
onos	neu	es	H_3en-os-	load	onus
ónteros	adII			second	secundus
ópitjos	adII		$H_{1/2}$opitjo-: *cf.* epi/apo?	posterior	posterior
opjō	tr			choose	ēligō
opnā	fem		opnos (es-)	wealth	substantia
opnis	adI			abundant	abundans
ópopā	fem			hoopoe	upupa
opos	neu	(ópesos)	H_3ep-os-; H_3ep-r-/ H_3ep-n-	work	opus
opos esti	intr			be necessary	opportet
ops	mas	(ēpos)		riches	ops
oqō	tr			see	uideō
oqos	mas		H_3okwo-	eye	oculus
ōrā	fem			edge	ōra
ōrājō	tr			pray	ōrō
orbhis	mas		H_3erbhi-; *cf.* orghis	disk	orbis
orbhjom	neu			inheritance	hērēditās
orbhos	adII		H_3erbho-	orphan	orbus
ordhos	mas		pordhos ? *cf.* gr. perqw	hammer	malleus

orgājō	tr		H_3erg	beat up	contundō
orghis	fem	ej	H_3erghi-; *cf.* orbhis, r̥ghējō	ball	pila
orghós	tr		H_1orghó-	incited	sollicitātus,
ormos	adI			poor	pauper
oros	neu	es		mountain	mons
ortus	mas	wo-	H_3ertu-	origin	orīgō
orús	adI		H_3eru-; H_3ersi-	high	altus
ōs	neu	(sos)	H_3eH^w_3s- (Bernabé) H_1eH_3s- (Melchert) H_3eH_1s- (Vaan)	mouth	ōs
osdcos	mas			knot	nodus
osdos	mas		H_2osdo-	branch	rāmus
osēn	mas	(osnós)	H_3esH_3r̥ / H_3esH_3en	autumn	autumnus
oskos	fem		H_3es-ko- /-kā	ashtrē	frāxinus
ósonos	fem		H_3es-no-	ashtree	ornus
ostis	mas	ej	H_3estHi-; H_3estHṛ- / H_3estHṇ -	bone	os
ōsmi	tr	BIf	H_3eH^w_3s-	open	aperiō
ōstjom	neu			aperture	ōstium
oudn̥	neu	(óudesos)	H_1ud	land	terra
ougros	adI			cold	frigidus
ousis	fem		$H^{o}_3H^w_3$s-, H_3oH^w_3s-, H_3eH^w_3s-, $H_3H_3^{wo}$s-	ear	auris
ṓw(ij)om	neu		H_1oH_2w-yo	egg	ōuum
owājō	tr			cheer	ouō
owikā́	fem			small sheep	ouicula
owis	fem		H_3ewi-	sheep	ouis
owō	inc	AIId	H_3ew	get dressed	induō
pəgtós	adI		pH_1g-to	fixed	pactus
pəgrós	adI		pH_1g-ro pH1g-no	sure	constans
pəra	ind			close to	iuxta
pərijō	tr		perH_3	give birth	pariō
pəros	ind			before	prae
pəstrom	neu			page	pagina
pətējō	sta		ptH_1 /pH_1t	lie open	pateō
pətēr	mas	(p∂tros)	pH_2-ter; tab	father	pater
pəterā́	fem			saucer	patera
pətjai	tr			suffer	patior
pətrjā	fem			fatherland	patria
pətrjos	adII			fatherly	paternus
pətrujós	mas			uncle	patruus
pəwējō	sta			fear	paueō
pādhlom	neu		peH_2-dhlo/tlo-	sustenance	pābulum
pagos	mas			region	pagus
pakō	tr	AIIa	peH_2k; *cf.* pn̥gō	fasten	uinciō
paks	fem	(pākos)		peace	pax
pālājō	tr			protect	protegō
pálejā	fem			straw	palea
pálowos	adI			grey	pallidus
palpājō	tr			touch	tangō
pámponos	mas			vine-leaf	pampinus

pandos	mas			bent	pandus
panknos				swelling	pannus
pankō	intr			swell	tumescō
pannos	mas			rag	pannus
pāpeljos	mas			butterfly	pāpiliō
paplā	fem			swelling	papula
pareikā	fem			concubine	paelex
pārējō	intr			come out	pāreō
parkō	tr	AIIb		refrain from	parcō
parsā	fem			sparrow	parra
pasknis	mas	ej		food	pābulum
pāskō	tr		peH$_2$-sk; *cf.* pāsmi	feed	pāscō
pāsmi	intr	BIe	peH$_2$-sk; *cf.* pāskō; dat	heed	attendō
pāsós	mas			relative	familiāris
pastos	adI			fix	fixus
pāstus	mas			pasture	pastus
pau	ind			a bit	paucum
paukos	adI			little	paucus
paulos	adI		pauros	small	paruus
pāwr̥	neu	(pwnós)	peH$_2$w-r-	fire	ignis
pedjō	intr	AIVc		fall down	cadō
pedjṓs	adI II			worse	dēterius
pedlom	neu			sandal	sandalia
pedom	neu		pedóm ?	footprint	peda
pegtos	neu	es		chest	pectus
peidō	prog	AIa		grow fat	pinguescō
peigō	tr	AIa	peikō; *cf.* pikrós	annoy	molestō
peikā	fem			woodpecker	pīca
peikō	tr	AIa		adorn	ornō
peikos	mas			magpie	pīcus
peiks	fem	(pikós)		pitch	pix
peimis	adI			quick	celer
peitus	mas		peiHtu-	resin	resīna
pējō	tr	AIa		insult	insultō
pekō	tr			comb	pectō
pektēn	mas	(pektnós)		comb	pecten
pektō	tr	AIa		comb	pectō
peku	neu	(pékewos)		cattle	pecu
peldō	tr	AIa	pelH$_2$; *cf.* pl̥namaí	impel	pellō
pelkō	tr	AIa		move	intermoueō
pelnis	fem	jo		skin	pellis
pelō	tr	AIb		make money	lucror
pelom	neu		polos	surface	superficiēs
pelsā	fem			rock	rūpēs
pelu	ind		pelH$_1$u	much	multum
pelupoikos	adI			variegated	uarius
pēlwis	fem			dish	peluis
pelwos	neu	es	pl̥Hwo-, polHwo-, pl̥Hwi-	dust	puluis
pēmn̥	neu			damage	dētrimentum
pendō	tr			hang	pendō

penō	tr			work with a thread	cum fīlō laborō
penom	neu			mud	lutum
penos	neu	es		provision	prouisiō
penqe	num			five	quinque
pénqedekm̥	num			fifteen	quindecim
pénqedekəmos	adII			fifteenth	quindecimus
penqédkm̥təmos	adII			fiftieth	quinquāgēsimus
penqédkm̥ta	num		penkwedkm̥t- /penkwedkont-	fifty	quinquaginta
penqekm̥témtəmos	adII			five hundredth	quingentesimus
penqekm̥tṓs	num dec		penqekm̥tóm (ind.) + gen.	five hundred	quingentī
penqstis	fem	jo		fist	pugnus
penqtos	adII			fifth	quintus
pēnsús	mas			sand/gravel	saburra
pentō	tr	AIa		track	indāgō
peqō	tr	AIa		cook	coquō
peqtis	fem			cooking	coctiō
peqtṓr	mas			cook	coctor
peqtós	adI			cooked	coctus
pérəmos	adII		perəmós	absolute	absolūtus
per(i), per(ti)	ind			about	per
per(i), per(ti)	ind			very	ualdē
perijō	tr			experience	experiōr
perístānom	neu			religion	religiō
perknā	fem		*cf.* pr̥qos	trout	tructa
pérkūnjom	neu		perw-r̥ /en	mountain	mons
perom	ind		*cf.* peros	besides	praeterea
peróm	neu			feather	plūma
peros	ind		*cf.* perom	farther	prorsum
pérpern̥ks	ind			turned aside	perperām
perqos	fem			oak	quercus
persā	fem		pers(n)eH$_2$	heel	calx
persnā	fem			ham	perna
persō	intr	AIa		splash	respergō
pertā	fem			pole	pertica
perti	ind			otherwise	altrinsecus
péruti	ind			last year	anno praeterito
pesdō	intr			fart	pedō
pesmi	tr		pes	rub	fricō
pesnis	mas	jo		penis	pēnis
peterós	mas			wing	āla
petlos	adI		pétH$_2$los	meager	petilus
petō	intr		pet; petH$_{1/2/3}$ secundārium	fly	aduolō
petsnā	fem			feather	penna
petsnós	mas			bird	uolucrēs
peumi	tr	BIIIb		understand	intellegō
pewō	tr	AIa	pwH	clean	purgō
pibō	tr		peH$^{i}_{3}$	drink	bibō

pigējō	sta			be annoying	molestus (esse)
pikrós	adI		*cf.* peigō	sharp	picans
pilos	mas			hair	pilus
pīmós	adI			fat	crassus
(pím)prēmi	tr	BIIb	prH_1	blow up	conflō
pinkō	tr			paint	pingō
pinjos	neu			stab	baculum
pinsō	tr			crush	pinsō
pípāmi	tr		peH_2; *cf.* spáneumi	draw	trahō
píperi	neu	ej		pepper	piper
píperkmi	tr			fill	expleō
pipjājō	intr			squeak	pipiō
piptō	tr	(pepta)	petH	fall down	praecipitor
piskis	mas	ej		fish	piscis
pitús	mas			food	cibus
piwōn	adI		(fem. píweryā)	fat	pinguis
plabrājai	intr			babble	garriō
plākājō	cau	AIIIa	*cf.* sedējō/sēdājō	make adequate	congruere facere
plakējō	sta	AIIIe	*cf.* sedējō/sēdājō	be adequate	congruō
plākos	adI			flat	plānus
plākos	adI			wide	latus
plānos	adI		plH_2-no	flat	plānus
plārom	neu			floor	contabulātiō
plātom	neu			planitiēs	campus
plātús	adI		pl̥H_2-tu; plātus	broad	latus
plautos	adI			flat-footed	plautus
pl̥dājō	intr			paddle	plaudō
plēdhwis	fem	ej		crowd	multitūdō
plēis	ind	plōis	pleH_1-is / ploH_1-is	more	plūs
plēistos	adII	sup		greatest	plūrimus
plējṓs	adII	comp		greater	maior
plékāmi	tr			fold	plicō
plektō	tr	AIa		plait	plectō
(pím)plēmi	tr	BIIb	plH1; cf pl̥nāmi	fill	pleō
plēmn̥	neu			filling	plētūra
plēnós	adI		plH_1-nó	full	plēnus
plētis	fem			filling	plētūra
pletjā	fem	coll.		shoulder-blades	scapulae
plētós	adI		plH_2-to	full	plēnus
pleudō	tr	AIa	pleu-d	flood	inundō
pleumōn	mas	en		lung	pulmō
plewō	intr	AIa		flow	fluō
plighā	fem			appendix	appendix
pl̥mā	fem		plH_2meH_2	palm	palma
pl̥namaí	intr	BIVa	pelH_2; *cf.* peldō	approach (to)	appropinquō
pl̥nāmi	inc	BIVa	plH_1; plḗnāmi, pl̥nēmi; *cf.* pímplēmi	fill	pleō
pl̥ngō	tr	AVIc	plH_2-g	strike	plangō
plousmā	fem			feather	plūma
ploutos	mas			board	tabula

plówijā	fem			rain	pluuia
plówijom	neu		*cf.* plowós	ship	nāuis
plowós	mas		*cf.* plówijom	boat	ratis
pl̥wós	adI		pel(H)-, pḷ(H)-; pol(H)wós	grey	albogiluus
pl̥táwijā	fem		pḷtH2wiH2	earth	terra
pl̥tnos	mas		plH$_2$t-H$_2$no; *cf.* plātús	flatness	planitiēs
pl̥tom				coat	sagum
plúwaidhom	neu			lead	plumbum
pl̥wods	mas	(pḷwedos)		swamp	palus
pn̥dēks	mas	(pṇdkos)		paunch	pantex
pneusō	intr	AIa		breathe	anhelō
pn̥gō	tr	AVIb	pH$_2$g; cf pakō	nail	pangō
pn̥tō	tr		ptH$_1$ /pH$_1$t	spread out	pandō
podjom	neu			relief	podium
pods	mas	(pedos)		foot	pēs
poimēks	mas	poimkós		pumice	pūmex
pōimōn	mas	en	poH$_2$i-mōn	shepherd	pāstor
pojejō	cau	AIIIo		get drunk	inebriō
polis	fem	(pólejos)	(t)pḷH-i-	city	urbs
polkā				fallow	ueruactum
polnēks	mas	(polṇkós)		thumb	pollēx
polnō	intr		pH$_3$l	fall	cadō
polpos	mas			scene	pulpitus
poltos	mas		pelH-	porridge	puls
pondos	neu	es		weight	pondus
pōnom	neu			drinking	pōtus
pontēs	mas	(pn̥tos)	ponteH$_1$s (pn̥tH$_1$es)?; pen-(s)toH$_2$?	way	uia
poqós	mas			cook	coquus
porā	fem		prH$_1$	air	aer
porejō	cau	AIIIo	cau	convey	asportō
porkos	mas			pig	porcus
pornós	mas		*cf.* pratis 'filix'	feather	plūma
porsis	mas			bull	bouuculus
porsōd	ind			far	procul
portājō	tr			carry	portō
pos(ti)	ind			after	post
pósteri	ind			afterwards	postea
pósteros	adI		tab	subsequent	posterus
póstm̥os	sup.		tab	last	porstrēmus
postrōd	ind			backwards	retrō
potejō	cau			make fly	uolāre faciō
potējō	tr			hold	possideō
poti	ind		Hpoti	towards	uersus
poti linkō	tr		poti linekmi	offer	offerō
potijai	inc		abl	acquire	potior
potis	mas	ej		master	dominus
pōtis	fem	jo		drink	pōtiō
pōtlom	neu			glass	pōculum
potmos	mas			span	lātitūdo

potnjā	fem			mistress	domina
pōtṓr	mas			drinker	pōtor
pougá	fem			buttocks	pūga
poughos	adI			virginal	uirginālis
pougnos	mas			fist	pugnus
pounā	fem			swelling	turgentia
poutos	mas			penis	pēnis
powejō	cau	AIIIo		clean	purgō
póweros	mas			boy	puer
prāi	ind		prH$_1$i	before	prae
práighesto	ind			at hand	praestō
práiloghos	adII			present	praesens
práinōmn̥	neu	en		name	praenōmen
práiteri	ind			along	praeter
prāmos	sup		prH$_2$-mo-	first	prīmus
pratis	fem	ej	*cf.* pornós 'plūma'	fern	filix
prāwos	adII			first	prīmus
preistos	adI			preceding	anterior
prējō	intr			fan	flabellō
prekō	tr		aliquid ab aliquō; *cf.* pr̥kskō	beseech	precor
preks	fem	(prēkos)		plea	prex
premō	tr	AVIII		press	premō
prepō	intr	AIa		look like	uideor
presō	tr	AVIII		press	premō
pretjom	neu			price	pretium
pretō	tr	AIb		realise	percipiō
préwijos	adI	es		previous	anterior
prewō	dur	AIa	preugō	jump out	exsiliō
pr̥gā	fem			portico	porticus
prijós	adI			dear	cārus
prījṓs	adII	(prījesos)		foremost	prīmus
prīskos	adI		*preisk^{w}ú ?	ancient	priscus
prīsmos	sup.			first	prīmus
prītis	fem		priH-ti	pleasure	delectātiō
prītós	adI		priH-to	pleased	delectātus
pr̥gjō	tr	AIVa		fear	timeō
pr̥ká	fem			furrow	sulcus
pr̥knos	adI			motley	uarius
pr̥kskā	fem			question	quaestiō
pr̥kskō	tr		*cf.* prekō	ask	poscō
pr̥nāmi	tr	BIVa	prH$_2$	sell	uendō
pr̥nos	adI		pr̥H-nó, perH-nó	past	praeteritus
prō(d)	ind		pro	forwards	prō
probhoudhos	mas			attention	attentiō
probhwājō	tr			prove	probō
probhwos	adI		probhú-	good	bonus
prodətṓr	adII			traitor	próditor
prṓddōmi	tr			put forth	prodō
prōi	ind			in the morning	mane
proitis	fem			departure	profectiō

prokós	mas			suitor	procus
prokos	adI			advanced	prouectus
promos	sup			principal	prīmus
proqēd	ind			near	prope
proqos	adI			nigh	propinquus
prósēdjom	neu			kindness	beneficium
próstōrnos	adI			extended	extensus
prostos	mas			promontory	tumulus
próteros	adII			first (of two)	prīmus (a duobus)
proti	ind			against	contrā
prōtós	neu		prH_3-tó	assigned	attribūtus
prousijō	intr			irritate	irritō
pr̥ptus	mas	(pṛptewós)		form	forma
pr̥qjō	tr			clean	purgō
pr̥qos	adI		*cf.* perknā	coloured	uarius
pr̥snā	fem		prH_3sneH_2	piece	fragmentum
pr̥som	neu			leek	porrum
pr̥stis	mas			prominence	prominentia
pr̥tis	fem		prH_3ti-	part	pars
pr̥tus	mas	(pṛtwos)		ford	portus
prunsō	tr			freeze	gelō
prúsneumi	tr	BIVb		water	rigō
pruswā́	fem			frost	pruīna
pteljā	fem			lime-tree	tilia
pujō	inc		puH	molder	putēscō
pūjós	adI		*cf.* pūtós	righteous	pius
pukos	mas			tail	cauda
pulgā	fem			lock of hair	crīnis
pūlós	adI		*cf.* pūterós	putrid	puter
pungō	tr		peug / peuk	punch	pungō
pūpos	mas			child	pūpus
pūrós	adI		powros; *cf.* dweiros/dwīrós, skeiros/skīrós	pure	pūrus
pūrós	mas		puHro-	core	nucleus
pusbhis	mas		H_3pu-s-bhi	groom	pubēs
pusjō	tr			inflate	inflō
puslēks	mas	pusḷkós		flea	pūlēx
pustlā	fem			pustule	pustula
pūtējō	sta			be rotten	pūteō
pūterós	adI		*cf.* pūlós	rotten	puter
putlom	neu			child	infans
pūtós	adI		*cf.* pūjós	clean	putus
puwējō	tr			reckon	computō
puwos	neu	es	puH	pus	pūs
qəddrom	neu			square	quadrum
qədnos	adI			magic	magicus
qətjō	tr			shake	quatiō
qəturs	ind			four times	quater
qətrusnōs	adII			four each	quaternī
qətwr̥atnjom	neu			four years	quadriennium

qətwr̥djówijom	neu			four days	quadriduum
qətwr̥pods	adII	jo		quadruped	quadrupēs
qətwr̥tos	adII			fourth	quartus
qād	ind			which	quā
qālis	adII			how	quālis
qām	ind		k^weH_2m	as	quam
qāqos	pron			whoever	quisque
qasjos	mas			basket	cista
qā́wn̥tos	pron			how great	quantus
qe	ind		(encl.)	and	que
qedos	mas			angle	angulus
qedos	neu			magic force	magia
qeisō	tr		kʷei-s/kʷei-t	consider	considerō
qeistis	fem	AIa	quoque kwistis	consideration	considerātiō
qejēskō	intr		qiH_1	rest	quiēscō
qejō	tr			compose	compōnō
qejtis	fem		quoque qjtis	collection	collectiō
qekō	tr	AIa		gaze	prospectō
qeli	ind			far (from)	procul
qelō	dur	AIa	k^welH_2	circulate	uersor
qelos	neu			group	caterua
qelpō	tr	AIa		curve	incuruō
qelsō	tr			furrow	sulcō
qemō	tr			swallow	uorō
qeqlom	neu		qeqlóm, q∂qlos	wheel	rota
qerpō	inc	AIa		turn	reuertor
qésai	intr			complain	queror
qestis	fem			part	pars
qétwordekm̥	num			fourteen	quattuordecim
qétwordekəmos	adII			fourteenth	quattuordecimus
qetwores, qétesres	num dec		ktʷH3r-; tab; quoque q∂tw∂res, fem. qétsores	four	quattuor
qétwr̥dkm̥təmos	adII			fortieth	quadragēsimus
qétwr̥dkm̥ta	num		kwetwr̥dkm̥t- / kwetwr̥dkont-	forty	quadrāgintā
qetwr̥km̥témtm̥os	adII			four hundreth	quadrigentesimus
qetwr̥km̥tṓs	num dec		qetwr̥km̥tóm (ind.) + gen.	four hundred	quadringentī
qidpe	ind			indeed	quippe
qijētis	fem			rest	quiēs
qijētós	adI			peaceful	quiētus
qinō	tr	AVIe		compensate	compensō
qínumoi	tr			avenge	uindicō
qíqeimi	tr	BIId		estimate	aestimō
qis qid	int		tab	what	qui quae quod
qisqis qidqid	pron			anyone	quisquis quidquid
qm̥dō	int			when	quandō
qn̥tjō	tr			suffer	patior

qō	ind		qoH_2(e); qōi?	whither	quō
qodhei	int			where	ubī
qoinā́	fem			retaliation	ulciscātiō
qoinom	mas			dirt	excrēmentum
qoitrós, koitrós	adI			fair weather	serēnus
qolkā	fem			cushion	culcita
qolos	mas			hub	axis
qolus	fem	(ew)	qelus	distaff	colus
qom	ind			when	cum
qomde	ind			where	unde
qondhros	fem			angelica	angelica
qori	ind			why ?	cūr
qorjom	neu			cauldron	catīnus
qoros	mas			type	indolēs
qos qā(i) qod	rel		tab	who, which	quī quae quod
qostā	fem			cough	tussis
qot(j)os	int			how many	quot
qota	int			how	ut
qote	int			whither	quō
qóteros	pron			which	uter
qotrēd	ind			whither	quō
qotrōd	ind			wherefrom	unde
qr̥eumi	tr	BIIIb	k^wrH; qerjō	make	faciō
qrínāmi	tr		k^wrei-H_2	buy	emō
qrītóm	adII			bought	emptus
qr̥mis	mas	(qr̥mejós)		worm	uermis
qr̥snos	mas			bush	arbustus
qr̥tus	mas	(qr̥tewós)	*cf.* krwtis	time	uix
rəbhjō	intr			rage	rabō
rədjom	neu		rtH	ray	radium
rəgājō	tr			wet	rigō
rəpjō	tr			snatch	rapiō
rətis	fem	(r∂tjos)		reason	ratiō
rādō	rac		H(w)rH_2d	shave	rādō
ragjā	fem			ray	raia
rāpom	neu			turnip	rāpum
rārós	adI			dispersed	rārus
rastós	adI			smooth	glaber
raukos	adI			tough	rudis
rāwos	adI			grey	rāuus
r̥dhjō	intr			grow	crēscō
r̥dhwos	adI		Hrdh-wo-	steep	arduus
rebhā	fem			leap	saltus
rebhājō	intr			jump	saltō
rebhō	tr	AIa		shield	tegō
rebhrus	mas			tube	conductus
recos	mas		(H_1e)regwo- ; pl.	darkness	tenebrae
rēd/re	ind			dis-	re(d)
regeinā	fem		rēgnī	queen	regīna
regjos	adII			kingly	regius
regnom	neu		regjom	kingdom	regnum

regō	tr		H_3reg	direct	regō
regs	mas	(rēgos)		king	rex
regtós	mas			right	rectus
reidhō	tr	AIa		ride	equitō
reidhos	adI			easy	facilis
reigō	tr	AIa		bind	alligō
reimā	fem		reiwā	crack	rīma
rēimn̥	neu	en	rīmo-, rīmā-	list	seriēs
rēis	fem	(rijós <*H_2r̥H_1jós)	*H_2reH_1-i-	propriety	rēs
reiwos	mas		reiH_2-; *cf.* rínāmi	brook	rīuus
rējō	intr	AVIII	H_1rH	row	rēmō
rekā				tick	ricinus
rékneumi	tr	BIVb		determine	determinō
remō	intr	AIb	H_1rem	relax	requiescō
rēmoi	neu		H_2rH_1	reckon	reor
renō	intr	AIb	renH	run	currō
rentus	mas			property	possessiō
rēpō	intr			crawl	rēpō
resgō	tr	AIa		plait	plectō
resgtis	fem			rope	restis
rēsmos	mas		H_1reH_1-smo / (-t-smo ?)	oar	rēmus
rēti	neu			strainer	colum
retō	intr	AIb	retH_2	run	currō
retrōd	ind			back	retrō
reubō	intr	AIa		scrape out	abrādō
reudhos	adI			red (-haired)	rūfus
reudhos	neu	es	H_1reudhos/es	redness	rubōr
reudō	intr	AIa	reud(H); reudō / reudmi	cry	rūdō
reudos	adI			wild	rudis
reughmn̥	neu			dough	pasta
reugō	intr	AIa	H_1reu-g	belch	ructō
reumi			H_3reuH	rumor (to produce)	rūmorem faciō
reusmn̥	neu			rūmen	rūmen
reusmnājō	intr			ruminate	rūminō
rew	ind			outdoors	forās
réwesnā	fem			ruin	ruina
rewis	mas		Hrew	planet	planēta
rewmn̥	neu			hair	capillum
rewō	inc / tr	AIa	H_3rw / rwH_3	break off	dēfringō
rewos	neu	(réwesos)	rews, rows; *cf.* jewos, weis	open land	rūs
r̥ghējō	tr		*cf.* orghis	incite	sollicitō
rigjō	tr			torture	tormentō
rikjō	tr			ruin	ruinō
rínāmi	tr	BIVa	H_3reiH; *cf.* reiwos	flush away	ēgerō
r̥kējō	sta tr	AIIIe	H_2rk	contain	arceō
r̥kēslom	neu			door-bar	repagula

r̥klā	fem		r̥ktlā	chest	arcula
r̥nāmi	tr	BIVa	H_1erH_2	divide	dīuidō
r̥neumi	tr	BIVb	H_3r	move	cieō
r̥numái	tr	BIVb		try to get	capessō
r̥nutis	fem	jo		movement	mōmentum
robhos	mas		H_3robho-	roof	tectus
rōdhí	ind	(gen.)		on account of	causā
rōdhjō	tr			endeavour	conitor
rōdō	tr		H(w)rH_2d	tear	rōdō
rōdos	adI			joyful	alacer
roinos	mas			dam	agger
ros	mas	(rēsos)		spray	ros
rōstrom	neu		rōd-trom	beak	rōstrum
rotā	fem		rotH-eH_2	wheel	rota
rotājō	intr		rōteH_2-je/o-	turn	rotō
roudhós	neu	es	H_1roudhó-	metal	metallum
roudhstos	mas		r(o)udh-to?	rust	rōbīgō
roudos	mas			crying	plōrātus
rounā	fem		ruH-nā; rūnā	secret	secrētum
roupis	fem			rock	rūpēs
routos	mas			intestine	intestīnum
rowā́	fem		H_1erH_1-	pause	cessātiō
r̥sēn	mas	(r̥snos)	H_1r̥sen; *cf.* wersis	male	mās
r̥sjā	fem		H_2r-	envy	inuidia
r̥skai	intr		H_1r	go	eō
r̥tís	fem	jo		farewell	abitiō
r̥tkos	mas		H_2rt-ko-	bear	ursus
rudhējō	sta			be red	rubeō
rudhrós	adI		H_1ru-dhro-	red	ruber
rudhsós	adI			reddish	rubeus
rudlós	adI			rude	rudis
rugijō	intr		H_3reuH / H_3reug / H_3reuk	roar	rugiō
ruktus	mas			tunic	tunica
rumpō	tr			break	rumpō
runkō	tr	AVIa	H_3ruk	weed	runcō
rupús	adI		rupus	shoddy	insincērus
ruspājai	tr			rummage	rūspor
rwtós	adI		H_3rw-to	collapsed	rutus
s(w)ei	neu			whenever	sī
s(w)eike	ind			thus	sīc
səkesnā	fem			pickaxe	sacēna
səksom	neu			stone	saxum
səni	ind		snHi	apart	separātim
səpijō	tr			have taste	sapiō
sərijō	tr			weed	sarriō
sətos	tr		s$H_2$to-	satiated	satiātus
sāgijō	tr		seH_2g	seek	sāgiō
sagom	neu			mantle	sagum
sāimn̥	neu		seH_2i-mn	secretion	secrētiō
saipis	mas			fence	saepēs

saitā	fem			hair (strong)	saeta
saitlom	neu			lifetime	saeculum
saiwos	adI			fierce	saeuus
sājō	sta			be furious	saeuiō
sákrodhokjom	neu			sacrifice	sacrificium
sákrodhots	mas	et		priest	sacerdos
sakrós	adI		seH_2k- / sH_2k-	holy	sacer
sal	neu	(salós, sálejos)	sali	salt	sal
saldō	cau			salt	sallō
salēiks	fem	(salikós, salijós)	salīks	willow	salix
saleiwā	fem			saliva	salīua
salom	neu			swell	salum
salús	adI		salus	dirty	immundus
sāmn̥	neu			quietness	quiēs
samdhos	mas			sand	sabulum
sāmis	adI			quiet	quiētus
samos	mas		sm̥os, sm̥ā	summer	aestas
sánāmi	tr	BIVb	sH_2; sH_2neumi; sātijō (*cf.* westijō)	satisfy	satisfaciō
sáneumi	tr	BIVb	snH	perform	efficiō
sankijō	tr			enact	granciō
sapos	fem			juice	succus
sasjóm	neu			crop	messis
sātis	fem			satisfaction	satiās
sauros	adI		sūrós	sour	acerbus
sā́wel(jos)			seH_2w-l̥/n̥; sw-r̥/n̥	sun	sōl
se	pron	(sewe)	tab	himself	se
se/sos sā/sī tod	pron		tab	this	iste ista istud
sēd	ind			apart	sē
sēdājō	cau			appease	sēdō
sedējō	sta			be sitting	sedeō
sedējō ambhí	sta			besiege	circumsedeō
sedlā	fem			chair	sella
sedmn̥	neu			settlement	conditus
sedos	neu	es		residence	sēdēs
segēts	fem	(segtós)		sowing	satiō
seghdhlā	fem		sghedhlā, seghedhlā	plough handle	buris
seghō	tr	AIa		hold	retineō
seghos	mas			victory	uictoria
seghurós	adI			secure	firmus
ségneumi	tr	BIVb		trap	capiō
segnom	neu			trap	pedica
segō	tr	AIb		sow	serō
seikā	fem			club	fustis
seikō	tr			intend	intendō
seiqō	tr			spill	effundō
seilō	intr	AIa		drip	exstillō
seimā	fem		seiH-meH_2	band	uitta
seinus	mas		seiH-nu-	chain	catēna
sējdhlom	neu			sieve	cōlum

sējō	tr	AVIII	sH$_1$y	sieve	cōlō
sékāmi	tr		sekH$_2$; *cf.* skijō	cut	secō
sēklā	fem		sektlā	scythe	sēcula
sēknis	adI			calm	calmōsus
seks / sweks	num		ksweks ?	six	sex
séksdekm̥	num		swéksdekm̥	sixteen	sēdecim
séksdekəmos	adII		swéksdekəmos	sixteenth	sēdecimus
séksdkm̥təm̥os	adII		swels-	sixtieth	sexāgēsimus
séksdkm̥ta	num			sixty	sexāginta
sekskm̥témtəmos	adII			six hundredth	sescentesimus
sekskm̥tṓs	num		sekskm̥tóm (ind.) + gen.; sweks-	six hundred	sexceritī
sekstos	adII			sixth	sextus
sekūris	fem			axe	secūris
selgō	tr	AIa		shoot	disparō
seljos	adI			pleasant	amoenus
selkō	intr	AIa	HeH$^{w}{}_{3}$lk / s-HH$^{w}{}_{3}$elk	drag	sulcō
selō	tr	AIb		buy	emō
selom	neu		solos, solā, solis	residence	domicilium
sēlom	neu			sowing	sementis
selwā	fem			property	possessiō
sémdekm̥	num		óindekm̥	eleven	undecim
sémdekəmos	adII		óindekəmos	eleventh	undecimus
sēmi-	adII			half	medius
semjō	tr		aquam a naue	bilge out	excupāre
semli	ind			once	semel
sēmn̥	neu	sḗmenos		seed	sēmen
semos	mas		semo- / sm̥o-	one	ūnus
senchō	intr			sing	canō
senējō	sta			be old	seneō
senēks	mas	(senós)	senos; senH$_1$, senH$_2$	old	senex
senqō	inc	AIa		sink	mergō
sentos	neu	es		path	sēmita
sepēlijō	tr			bury	sepeliō
sépeltrom	neu			tomb	sepulcrum
sepō	tr			organize	apparō
séptəmos	adII			seventh	septimus
septm̥	num			seven	septem
septm̥dekm̥	num			seventeen	septemdecirn
septrm̥dekəmos	adII			seventeenth	septemdecirnus
séptm̥dkm̥təmos	adII			seventieth	septuagesimus
séptm̥dkm̥ta	num		septm̥dkm̥t- /septm̥dkont-	seventy	septuaginta
septm̥km̥témtəmos	adII			seven hundredth	septingentesimus
septm̥km̥tṓs	num dec		septm̥km̥tóm (ind.) + gen.	seven hundred	septingeritī
seqai	dur			follow	sequor
seqi	ind			vis-à-vis	aduersum
seqō	tr			say	dīcō
seqos	adI			separate	separātus

sēr	mas	(sros)		peak	culmen
serdhō	tr			rub	fricō
serō	tr	AIa		connect	serō
serom	neu			liquid	serum
sēros	adI			long-lasting	sērus
sérpenos	mas			snake	serpens
serpō	intr	AIa		crawl	serpō
sesmi				sleep	dormiō
sesqos	fem			sedge	spartum
setis	epic.			visitor	uisitātor
sētús	adI		sHi-tu, *cf.* sisō; sitús	far-reaching	sparsus
sétjosi	ind			later	posterius
seugō	tr	AIa		suck	sūgō
seutō	sta	AIa		boil	ferueō
sewājō	prog			lessen	minuō
sewe	igenes.			self	sui
séwijos	adII			his	suus
sewō	tr		seuH	stir up	permoueō
silējō	intr		sHi-	silent (to be)	sileō
síneumi	tr	BIVb	syH(w)	bind	ligō
sinísteros	adI			propice	idōneus
sinō	tr			place	sinō
sinus	mas	ew		bosom	sinus
sisdō	intr			sit down	sīdō
sísermi	intr	BIIe		flow	fluō
sísghrāmi	tr			smell	olfaciō
síslāwos	adI			beneficial	benignus
sisō	tr		sH^i_1	sow	serō
sisqos	adI			dry	siccus
skīrós	adI		skeiros?; *cf.* dwoiros/dwīrós, powros/pūrós	clear	clārus
sjewmn̥	neu		sjuHm∂n	seam	sūtūra
sjewō	tr	AIa	syHw	sew	suō
sjūdhlā	fem		syHw -(dh)leH$_2$	sewer's awl	sūbula
sjūtós	adI			sewn	sūtus
skabhjēs	fem			scabies	scabiēs
skabhnom	neu			stool	scamnus
skabhō	tr			scratch	scabō
skaiwós	adI			left-handed	scaeuus
skalpō	tr			carve	scalpō
skandō	dur			mount	scandō
skandslā	fem			ladder	scāla
skāpos	mas			handle	manubrium
skatējō	dur			gush	scateō
skatō	inc			spring	scatō
skédnāmi	tr	BIVa	skedH$_2$; *cf.* skindō	scatter	dispergō
skegō	intr			hasten	festīnō
skejō	sta	AIa		shine	luceō
skekō	intr	AIa	*cf.* kekō; (s)kH$_{1/2}$ek, (s)keH$_{1/2}$k;	burst in	irrumpō

skelō	tr	AIa		shall	debeō
skelos	neu	es		evil	scelus
skemō	tr			cover	uelō
skerbhō	tr	AIa		hollow out	excauō
skerdā	fem		(s)keHr(-deH$_2$) \Hr/Hn	shit	merda
skerdō		AIa		castrate	castrō
skerjō	tr			split	scindō
skerō	intr			spring	exsultō
skeubhō	inc	AIa		escape	effugiō
skeudō	tr	AIa		shoot	ēmittō
skeumō	tr	AIa		cover	obruō
skeuros	adI			dark	obscūrus
skeutō	tr	AIa	s-kuH-t	cover	operiō
skewō	tr	AIa	H$_2$kw-; *cf.* koweyō	inspect (to)	inspiciō
skidjō	tr			decide	dēcernō
skijō	tr		skH$_2$-(i)je/o-; *cf.* sékāmi	discern	discernō
skindō	tr		*cf.* skédnāmi	split	scindō
skīwr̥	neu	(skīwn̥ós)	(s)kiHu-	shin-bone	tībia
skl̥iqā	fem			pod	siliqua
skl̥jō	tr		(s)kel	split	scindō
skl̥neumi		BIVb		deflect	deflectō
skn̥gjō	intr			limp	claudicō
sknidā	fem			nit	ouum
skodhos	mas			harm	damnum
skoidos	mas			woodpiece	lignum
skoirsās	adII			clown	scurrā
skoitom	neu		skoito-s, skeito-m	shield	scūtum
skojá	fem			shade	umbra
skolmā	fem			small pillar	columella
skōlos	mas			element	ēlementum
skolpos	mas			shelf	pluteus
skortom	neu			whore	scortum
skostrom	neu			canopy	umbraculum
skotos	mas			shadow	umbra
skouros	mas			nord	septentriō
skousā	fem			trousers	pantalōnus
skreibhō	tr	AIa		write	scribō
skreidō	tr	AIa		carve	caelō
skrobhis	fem			pit	scrobis
skroupos	mas			sherd	scrūpus
skroutos	mas			skeletton	larua
skubtis	fem			omoplate	scapulae
skutājō	tr			maim	truncō
skūtos	mas		skuH-to	covering	operīmentum
slabai	intr			slip	labor
slagós	adI		slH$_2$gó-	slack	laxus
slakō	tr			hit	offendō
slatā	fem			rod	ferula
sleibō		AIa		slip	prolabor
sleidhō	intr	AIa		glide	surrēpō

sleigō		AIa		smooth	explanō
sleimā	fem		sleH1i-meH2	file	līma
sleimājō	tr			polish	līmō
sleimāks	mas	jo		snail	cochlea
sleiwos	adI			violet	liueus
slējús	adI		sleH1i-u-, slējus	smooth	lēuis
sleubō	inc	AIa		slip	prolabor
sleugō	tr	AIa		devour	uorō
sligōn	mas	en		mattock	ligō
sl̥ijai	inc			spring	saliō
sloidhos	mas			mass	massa
sloiwom	neu			plum	prunum
slougos	mas			crowd	multitūdō
sl̥rgjō	tr			gulp	lurcō
sm̥	ind			together	cunctim
smā	ind			certainly	certō
smalos	mas		smH1-lo, smeH1-lo	animal	animal
smegō	tr	AIa		desire	cupiō
smeidhō	tr	AIa		carve	caelō
smeikā	neu			crumb	mīca
smeirai	tr			wonder	admīror
smeirātlom	neu			miracle	mirāculum
smeiros	adI			wonderful	mīrus
smeitō	tr	AIa		send	mittō
smejō	intr	AIa		smile	arrideō
smekslā	fem		smokru- /smokur- smokuenos	chin	mentum
smelgā	fem			turfgrass	agrostis
smelō	dur	AIa		burn	urō
smemorjā	fem			memory	memoria
smā́neumi	inc	BIVb	s-m(i)H-(d); sméneumi	stain	maculō
smerdā	fem			shit	merda
smerdō	intr	AIa		stink	foeteō
smeros	neu	es		defect	mendum
smerwā	fem			marrow	medulla
smeughō	intr	AIa		smoke	fūmō
sm̥gheslom	neu			thousand	mille
sm̥itis	fem		sm̥oitis	accordance	concursus
smitlā	fem		sm(i)H2-	stain	macula
sm̥lis	adI			similar	similis
sm̥loghós	fem			wife	uxor
sm̥ópətōr	epi	sm̥óp∂tros		sibling	fraterculans
smoughos	mas			alleyway	angustiae
smoughos	mas			smoke	fūmus
sm̥plos	adI			simple	simplex
smudhnō	intr	AVId	acc. uel cōgit.	contrive	machinor
smúghneumi	tr	BIVb		slip in	irrēpō
snəghjō	intr			creep	rēpō
snadhō	tr			cut off	amputō
snāmi	intr	Bib	snH2	swim	nō
sneighs	fem	(snighwós)		snow	nix

sneitō	tr	AIa		curtail	dēminuō
sneitos	adI			scanty	exiguus
snēmi	tr		(s)-nH_1; sneH_1-ye/o-	spin	neō
snēmn̥	neu			yarn	nēmen
snerō	intr	AIa		whirl	contorqueō
snētjā	fem		snēti-, snētu-	embroidery	intextus
sneubhō	tr	AIa		marry	nūbō
sneudhs	fem	(snudhós)	(aerea)	smog	turbulentia
snēwər	neu		*sneH_1w-r̥/n̥ -	cable	mitra
sníncheti	sta			snow	ninguit
snoghā				snake	serpens
sn̥stus				intelligence	sensus
sn̥tējō				think	cōgitō
sn̥terí	ind			missing	absente
snusós	fem			daughter-in-law	norus
sōdejō	cau	AIIIo	sodejō	settle	instituō
sōdjā	mas			soot	fūlīgō
sodjom	neu			seat	solium
sodóm	intr	(aor.ab eimi)		went	iī
sognos	mas			rope	retinaculum
soitos	mas		soiH(w)-to	magic	uenēficium
sōlājai	tr		selH_2	give joy	sōlor
solkos	mas		s-HH$^{w}{}_3$olko-	furrow	sulcus
solpos	mas			oil	oleum
solwos	pron	sol̥H2-wo, sl̥H2-wo		whole	tōtus
solwotāts	fem	(solwotātjos)		totality	integritās
somejō	tr	AIIIo		make equal (to)	aequō
somós	adII		somHó-; sm̥os	equal	aequus
sondhos	mas		son-dhH_1o	protrusion	excrescentia
sontejō	cau	AIIIo		send	mittō
sontis	adI		*cf.* esn̥ts; sontjós	uērus	sons
soru	neu			plunder	spolium
soqjós	mas			allied	socius
soqtis	fem	jo	sok^{w}tH-i	thigh-bone	femur
sormos	mas		sorā	flow	fluxus
sorbhējō	tr			sip	sorbeō
sorbhos	fem			rowan tree	sorbus
sorwā	fem			entrails	uiscus
soujós	adII			left	sinister
soukos	mas		swoqós	juice	sūcus
sówijā	fem			kiss	sauia
spəros	adI		spH_1-ro	thriving	prosperus
spakos	mas			drop	gutta
spáneumi	tr	BIVb	speH_2; speH_2neumi; *cf.* pípāmi	attract	attrahō
sparos	mas			post	sparus
sparwos	mas			sparrow	parra
speikā	fem			head of cereal	spīca

speiksnā	fem			prickle	spīna
speimis	adI			thin	tenuis
spekjēs	fem			aspect	speciēs
spekjō	tr			look	speciō
spelghā	fem			spleen	lien
spelgis	mas			pole	asser
spelō	intr		*cf.* bhelō	recitate	recitō
speltā			*cf.* pelnis	table	tabula
spēmi	prog		$speH_1$	extend	extendī
spēnos	mas		psteHn ??	nipple	tetta
speqos	mas			cave	specus
sperdhō	tr	AIa		compete	certō
sperghō	intr	AIa		hurry	festīnō
sperjō	tr			scatter	spargō
spēs	fem	(spos <*spH_1os)	$speH_1$, $speH_1os$	hope	spes
speudō	tr			hurry	accelerō
spingjā	fem			finch	passer
spjewō	intr	AIa		spit	spuō
spjonos	fem			foxglove	digitālis purpurea
spjwtos	adI			spit	sputus
spleidō	tr	AIa		split	secō
spleighō	intr	AIa		retire	sēcēdō
splighstós	mas			side	latus
spl̥ndējō	sta			be bright	splendeō
spl̥tājō	tr	AIa		cut off	separō
spn̥dō	intr		s-pH_1d	flutter	coruscō
spoimā	fem			foam	spūma
spoisājō	intr			perspire	spirō
spoisnā	fem			breath	halitus
spoljom	neu			dispossession	spolium
spondejō	tr	AIIIo		promise	spondeō
spondhā	fem			bed	lectus
spōnos	mas			stick	uirga
sponstós	mas			betrothed	sponsus
sporējō	cau	AIIIe	$sporH_1$eje/o	tread	calcō
sportā	fem			basket	sporta
spoudā́	tr			haste	coactus
spr̥āmi				tread	calcō
spreigō	sta	AIa		abound	abundō
spreudō	intr	AIa		accelerate	accelerō
sprewō	tr	AIa		excite	excitō
spr̥gō	tr	AIIh	spH_2r-g	burst	displōdō
spr̥nō	cau		$sperH_1$	move away	spernō
spr̥os	mas			ankle	talus
sqalos	mas			large fish	squalus
sqeros	neu	es		portent	prodigium
sqijā	fem			thorn	spīna
sredhō	intr		sredh / sret	billow	aestuō
sremsō	intr	AIa		fray	diffilor
srenkō	intr	AIa		snore	sternuō

srewō	intr	AIa		flow	fluō
srewtis	fem		quoque srwtis	strom	fluxus
srīgējō	sta			be cold	frigeō
srīgos	neu	es		cold	frīgus
sr̥kijō	tr			repair	sarciō
srodhos	mas			sea heaviness	aestūs maritimī
sroknā	fem			beak	rostrum
srowmos	mas		srowos, srewmn̥	stream	cursus
srunghos	mas			snout	proboscis
srwtom	neu			pipe	fistula
sr̥pā	fem			sickle	falcicula
sr̥pjō	tr			cut off	putō
sr̥wājō	tr			observe	seruō
sr̥wos	mas		*r̥ sicut twr̥kos et non er sicut kerwos*	guardian	custōs
stətis	fem		steH$_2$ti- / stH$_2$ti-; stātis	standing post	statiō
stətus	mas			position	status
stādhlom	neu			stall	stābulum
stagnom	neu			pond	lacus
stagō	sta			remain (water)	remaneō
staknom	neu			pool	stagnum
stālos	mas			couch	solium
(sí)stāmi	intr	BIIa	steH$_2$; stístāmi	stand	stō
(sí)stāmi antí/prāi	sta			advantage	praestō
(sí)stāmi apó	intr			be far	distō
stāmn̥	neu		steH$_2$-mn̥ / stoH$_2$-mo-	arrangement	institūtiō
stānejō	tr	AIIIo		place	condō
stānom	neu			place	locus
stārós	adI		stərós	stable	stābilis
stātlom	neu			platform	catasta
staurejō	tr	AIIIo		set	instaurō
stauros	mas		stoH$_2$u-ro	stake	adminiculum
staurós	adI		stūrós	staked	adminiculātus
stāwō	tr	AIa		stop	dētineō
steighō	intr	AIa		walk	ambulō
steipēts	fem	(steiptós)		stick	stīpēs
steiwā	fem			plough handle	stīua
stejō	inc	AIa		condense	spissō
stejsjā	fem			icicle	stīria
stelghmi	tr	BIa	(s)tel-gh; *cf.* stelō	flatten	pauiō
stelghō	intr	AIa		flow down	dēfluō
stelō	tr			put	pōnō
stelōn		(stélenos)	*cf.* tálejā	offshoot	stolō
stelpō	intr	AIa		stare	intueor
stembhō	tr	AIa	*cf.* tembhō	stamp on	conculcō
stemō	intr			stumble	titubō
sterbhnjom	neu			dry skin	pellis sicca

sterbhō	intr	AIa		decline	decadō
stergō	tr	AIa		love	amō
sterkō	tr	AIa, BIa	sterkmi	befoul	coinquinō
sterkos	neu	es		shit	stercus
stēr	mas	(stros)	H_2ster-; steros, sterlā	star	stella
sternom	neu			entrails	intestina
sternós	adI		sterH_1-nó/ sterH_1-yó	rigid	rigidus
sterō	tr	AIa		rob	fūror
stérolis	adI			sterile	sterilis
steros	mas		H_2ster-	star	stella
stērps	mas	(str̥pos)		trunk	stirps
stertō	intr	AIa		snore	stertō
stertos	mas			pinnacle	pinaculus
steugō	tr	AIa	(s)H_2teu-g	push away (to)	abigō
steumi	tr			inform	ēnuntiō
steupō	tr	AIa		hit	quatiō
steutō	tr	AIa		support	sustineō
stigājō	tr			prickle	instigō
stiprós	adI			safe	secūrus
stlāmn̥	neu			plate	lamina
stlātos	mas		s-tlH_2-to	side	latus
stlītis	fem	ej	(s)H_2lei-t/s	legal suit	līs
stlokos	mas			place	locus
stm̥nos	mas			trunk	truncus
stn̥tējō	sta			be delayed	moror
stobhos	mas			pillar	sublicā
stoghos	mas			trestle	uara
stoighos	mas			street	uia
stoipejō	cau	AIIIo		densifiy	stīpō
stolbos	mas			ruler (in topography)	uirga
stolgos	mas			force	uis
stolos	mas		stōlos; stel > stolo-; steH_2 + lo > stōlo-	table	mensa
stōmn̥	neu	es		palate	palātum
stopejō	tr			block	interclūdō
storejō	cau	AIIIo		straighten (to)	corrigō
stornjā	fem			centre	centrum
stornos	mas		(H_2)st(o)r-no-	starling	sturnus
stoudjom	neu			study	studium
stoupā	fem			oakum	stūpā
stōwejō	cau	AIIIo	sto$H^w{}_2$-eje/o	stop	dētineō
strāmn̥	neu			lay	strām∂n
strātos	mas			army	exercitus
strātós	adI		strH_2-tó	spread	strātus
streibā	fem			line	linea
streidō	dur	AIa	streid / streig	hiss	stridō
streigō	tr	AIa		strip off	stringō
streigs	fem	(strigós)		night bird	strīx
strengō		AIa		restrict	obstringō

strengom				string	corda
strēnwos	adI			active	strēnuus
strepō	intr	AIa		make noise	strepō
streubhō	tr	AIa		make bitter	acerbō
streudō	dur	AIa		fight	certō
strewō	tr	AIa	str-w	strew	sternō
strigājō	intr			stop	strigō
strigjā	fem			line	stria
stringō	tr	AVIa		draw tight	stringō
stṛneumi	intr	BIVb	pster	sneeze	sternuō
stṛnō	tr		s-trH$_3$	spread	sternō
stṛnō prō	tr			spread out	prosternō
stṛnos	mas			extension	strātus
strudsmā	fem			pipe	canna
strutjos	mas			ancestor	abauus
struwis	fem	ej		heap	struēs
studējō	sta			thrash	studeō
stupējō	sta			rigid (to be)	stupeō
stupos	mas			stick	pālus
sū	lois		H$_1$su-(H)	well	benē
sudhjom	mas			beer	zythum
súghoris	adI	ej	súgh∂ris	grātus	gracious
sujō	tr			spill	effundō
sūkós	mas			piglet	porcellus
suljā	fem			dregs	colluuiēs
súnoros	mas			vigorous	uiridis
sūnús	mas	ew		son	fīlius
sup	ind			under	sub
supā	fem			soup	ius
supājō	tr			throw	iaciō
(s)úperi	ind		tab	over	super
(s)úperos	adI		tab	superior	superior
(s)upmos	sup.			uppest	summus
sūs	mas	(suwós)	suH-; sews	pig	sūs
susājō	intr			buzz	susurrō
susdos	mas		H$_2$sus- / H$_2$suso / H$_2$susk$^{(w)}$o-/ H$_2$susdo-/H$_2$souso-	dry	siccus
susjō	tr		H$_2$sus-	dry	siccō
sūtus	mas			birth	partus
suwids	adI			expert	doctus
swəlējō	tr		swḷHeH$_1$, inc. sw∂lēskō, caus. swolējō	be swollen (to)	tumeō
swərjō	tr		*cf.* swerō	swear	iurō
swādejō	cau	AIIIo		recommend	suādeō
swādús	adI		sweH$_2$d-u-; swādus	pleasant	suauis
swāi	ind			so	sīc
swālikos	adII			as big	tam magnus
swēdhskō	inc			become accustomed	suēscō
swēdhus	fem	ew		custom	mos

sweidō				blaze	flagrō
sweidos	neu	es		star	sīdus
sweighlājō	intr			whistle	sībilō
sweigō	prog	AIa		seesaw	oscillō
sweisdō		AIa		whistle	siffilō
swekō	intr	AIa		smell good	fragrō
swekos	adI			fragrant	fragrant
swékuros	mas			father-in-law	socer
swekrús	fem	ew	swekrúH$_2$	mother-in-law	socrus
swelā	fem			sunlight	aprīcum
swelājō	tr			devour (to)	uorō
swelāks	mas	(swélakos)		seal	phoca
sweljos	mas			relative	familiāris
swelō	intr	AIa		glare	splendeō
swelom	neu			sleeper	trauersa
swelplos	neu	es		sulphur	sulpur
swemōr	dur			be followed	secūtus ueniō
swénāmi	intr	BIIIa	swenH; swenō, swonājō caus./iter. <*swonHejō	sound	sonō
swendhō	prog	AIa	s-wndh	swindle	dēcrēscō
swepō	dur	AIa		sleep	dormiō
swepr̥	neu	(swépenos)		dream	somnium
swerbhō	inc	AIa	swr-bh	turn	gyrescō
swerghō	tr	AIa		take care	cūrō
swerō	intr	AIa	*cf.* swərjō	whisper	susurrō
swērús	adI		swērus	important	sērius
swerwos	adI			snappy	transpuntorius
swesōr	fem	er		sister	soror
swesreinos	mas			sister's son	sobrīnus
swīnós	adII			porcine	porcīnus
swoidājō	intr		swidjō	sweat	sūdō
swoidos	mas			sweat	sūdor
swólejā	fem			ground	solea
swombhós	mas			fungus	fungus
swonos	mas		swonós ?	noise	sonus
swōpijō	cau		swōpjō, swōpejō	cause to sleep	sōpiō
swoplom	neu			broom	euerriculum
swopnjājō	intr		cog.	dream	somniō
swopnjom	neu			dream	somnium
swopnos	mas			sleep	somnus
sworā	fem			wade	sūra
swordis	fem	ej		rubbish	sordēs
sworēx		(sworkós)		shrew	sorēx
sworos	mas			stick	pālus
swr̥neumi	tr	BIVb		wound	uulnerō
swrswrājō	intr			whisper	susurrō
təkējō	inc			silent (to be)	taceō
təmjai	intr		*tm̥H-i̯é-, tm̥H-sḱé-; pf. *te-tómH/tm̥H-	faint	concidō
təreumi	tr	BIIIb		overcome	superō

tādējō	tr			qualify	qualificō
tādhēskō	intr		*cf.* tītāmi	melt	tābēscō
tādhis	fem	ej	tH_2-dh/k/w	thaw	tābēs
tagjō	tr			put in order	ordinō
taismos	mas			dough	massa
tājō	tr			steal	fūror
tājús	mas	ew	tātis	burglar	fūr
tálejā	fem		*cf.* stelōn	stab	talea
tālis	adII			such	tālis
tām	ind			at that point	tam
tarsós	mas			belly	uenter
tárudos	adI			slow	tardus
tātā	neu			dad	pappa
tauros	mas			bull	taurus
tausnim	ind			silently	silenter
tausos	adI			silent	silens
tā́wn̥tos	pron			so much	tantus
tēglā	fem		tegdhlā	tile	tēgula
tegnom	neu			beam	tignum
tegō	tr			cover	tegō
tegos	neu	es		shrine	aedicula
tegtom	neu			ceiling	tectum
tegús	adI		tegus	dense	crēber
teibhjā	fem			shin-bone	tībia
teknom	neu			creature	crātūra
tekō	tr	AIb		receive	accipiō
tekslā	fem			axe	secūris
teksnā	fem			technique	ars
teksō	tr	AIa	tek(s)	fashion	fabricor
tekstā	fem			bowl	testa
tekstlom	neu			web	tēla
tekwos	neu	es		trail	iter
tekwō	intr	AIa	tHk-w	run away	ēcurrō
telmṓn	neu		tel-H_2-mon-	strap	infula
telpō	intr	AIa		get in a space	locus mihi est
telsus	fem	ew	telH_2o-, telH_2mōn (télH_2menos)	ground	tellus
tembhō	tr	AIa	(s)tem-b(h); *cf.* stembhō	spurn	contemnō
temesras	fem		pl.	darkness	tenebrae
temlom	neu		temH-lo /temH-no	temple	templum
temos	neu	es		obscurity	obscuritās
tēmos	mas			drunken	ēbrius
tempos	neu	es		time	tempus
tēn	mas	tenos		continuity	continuitās
tenā	fem			ribbon	taenia
tendō	tr			extend	tendō
tenghō	tr	AIa		drag away	abstrahō
tengō	tr	AIa		impregnate	tingō
teni	ind		tenos	until	tenus
tenjō	tr	AIa		extend	prolongō
tenjom	neu			temple	tempus

temkō	prog		tm̥nekmi	result	ēueniō
tenos	neu	es		ligament	ligāmen
tensō				extend	prōtēlō
tentrom	neu			string	fūnis
tepējō	sta	AIIIe		be warm	tepeō
teplós	adI			warm	tepidus
tepnos	neu	es		fever	febris
teqom	neu			passage	trāiectiō
tercō	tr	AIa		threaten	minor
téredhrom	neu		terH_1(e)tro-	auger	terebra
tergō	tr	AIa	*trig^{w}ō ? *cf.* gr. tr**i**bw	wipe	tergō
tergslom	neu			towel	mantellum
terjō	tr			rub	teirō
termēn	mas	(term̥nós)		end	terminus
terō	tr	BIVb	trH$^{w}_{1}$; tr̥neumi	cross	transeō
terpō	intr	AIa		enjoy oneself	oblector
terptis	fem	jo	quoque tr̥ptis	enjoyment	delectātiō
tersā	fem			earth	terra
tersai	intr			get dry	serescō
térunos	adI		teren	feeble	tener
tetkōn	mas	(tétkenos)		woodworker	lignārius
tettā	fem			teat	tetta
téturos	mas			turkey	pauō
teukmn̥	neu			progeny	progeniēs
teukō		AIa		dig out	effodiō
teupō	inc	AIa		knee	genuflector
teurō	tr	AIa		stop up	obtūrō
teusmn̥	neu			lot	cumulus
teutā	fem		teuteH_2	people	populus
tewai	tr			observe	tueor
tewos	neu	es		force	impetus
tibhjā	neu			stalk	tibia
timējō	tr			be afraid	metuō
tínāmi	intr		teiH_1; t[illegible]heumi tr.	melt	liquefiō
títāmi	intr		teH_2(i)-, *cf.* tādhēskō	melt	liquefiō
títermi	tr	BIIe		explain	explicō
titijō	intr			chirp	titiō
tkeimi	tr	Bid		establish	condō
tlāmi	sta		telH_2; *cf.* tl̥nō, tl̥nāmi	endure	resistō
tlātjos	adI			patient	patiens
tl̥ijō	sta			rest	requiescō
tl̥nō	tr		telH_2; tl̥nāmi; cf, tlāmi	raise	tollō
tloqai	intr			speak	loquor
tmāmi	tr		temH_1	cut	secō
tm̥klos	adI			curdled milk	lacte coagulātum
tm̥ktos	adI			clotted	concrētus
tm̥pus	adI			elastic	diffusilis
tn̥ējō	sta tr			comprehend	teneō
tn̥ghus	adI		*cf.* tenghō	heavy	grauis

tn̥gō	tr		teH$_1$g	touch	tangō
tn̥tos	adI			stretched	tentus
tn̥us	adI		tnH$_2$-u-	thin	tenuis
togā́	fem			garment	toga
toi	ind			certainly	profectō
tōkslos	mas			hatchet	bipennis
toksos	fem		tk-so, tok-so, tk^{w}so-, tok^w-so ?	juniper	iuniperus
tokwós	adI			fugacious	fugax
tolājō	tr			call for	aduocō
tolkos	mas			bran	furfur
tom	ind			then	tum
tom-ke	ind			then	tunc
tomos	mas			cut	sectiō
tónāmi	intr	BIIIa	(s)tenH$_2$/ (s)tonH$_2$ (s)tenō, (s)tonājō <(s)tonH$_2$ejō iter.	resonate	tonō
tondejō	tr	AIIIo		shave	tondeō
tonejō	tr	AIIIo		extend (to)	extendō
tongejō	tr	AIIIo		give one's opinion	opīnor
tonslis	fem			fierceness	tūlēs
tonstṓr	adII	jo		hairdresser	tonsōr
tóntenos	mas			noise	strepitus
tontrom	neu			thunder	tonitrus
topnos	mas			warmth	tepor
toqe	ind			also	quoque
torcós	adI			threatening	minax
tori	ind			therefore	propterea
tórkmn̥tom	neu			tension (engine)	tormentum
tormos	mas		torH$^w{}_1$mo-	bolt	cnōdax
torós	adI		torH$^w{}_1$o-	loud	penetrans
torpejō	cau	AIIIo		rejoice	delectō
torqejō	cau	AIIIo		turn	torqueō
torqis	fem	ej		necklace	torquēs
torsejō	cau	AIIIo		dry	torreō
torsmn̥	neu			thunder	tonitrum
tot(j)oi	adII			so many	tot
totrēd	ind			towards there	eō
totrōd	ind			from there	inde
toughā́	fem			luck	fortūna
touknā	fem			thigh	perna
trabhis	fem	ej		beam	trabs
traghō	tr			drag	trahō
traghsmā	fem			weft	trāma
trāntis	ind			through	trāns
trebhō	sta	AIa	trb(h)	dwell	habitō
tregsnos	mas			brave	audāx
treikō	sta		trei(H)k	be mistaken	errō
treistis	adI			sad	tristis

trejes trija tisres	num dec		tab. fem. quoque trísores	three	trēs
tréjesdekm̥	num		tr⍰dekm̥	thirteen	trēdecim
tréjesdekəmos	adII		trídekəmos	thirteenth	trēdecimus
tremō	dur	AIa		tremble	tremō
trenkō	tr	AIa		incite	incitō
trepō	intr	AIa		shiver	tremō
trepō	tr	AIa		trample	calcō
trepō	intr	Aia		turn	uertor
tresō	intr	AVIII		shiver	tremō
treudō	cau	AIa		force in	intrūdō
treughos	adI			miserable	miser
treukō	tr	AIa		cut out	abscindō
trídkm̥təmos	adII			thirtieth	tricesimus
trídkm̥ta	num		tridkm̥t-/tridkont-	thirty	trigintā
trikm̥témtəmos	adII			three hundredth	tricentesimus
trikm̥tṓs	num dec		trikm̥tóm (ind.) + gen.	three hundred	trecentī
tríjətos	mas			sea	mare
triplós	adII			threefold	triple
trípl̥tis	fem			triplication	triplicātiō
trīs	ind			three times	ter
trisnōs				three in a go	trīnī
tristis	adII	ej		witness	testis
tritjos	adII			third	tertius
trītós	adI		triH-tó	rubbed	trītus
tr̥mēts	fem	(tr̥mtos)		wedge	cuneus
tr̥mos	mas			termite	tarmes
tr̥nā	fem			thorn	spīna
troghos	mas			posterity	subolēs
trogjā	fem			sow	porca
trogos	mas			pig	porcus
tropos	mas			way	uia
trosejō	intr	AIIIo		make afraid	terreō
troughi	ind			alas	uae
trowā	fem			ladle	trua
trowō	tr	AIId	treuH, treH$_1$u	gnaw away	corrōdō
tr̥knō	tr	AVId	tr̥kneumi	allow	sinō
tr̥pējō	sta			torpid (to be)	torpeō
tr̥pis	adI			ugly	turpis
tr̥sdos	mas			thrush	turdus
tr̥sējō	sta		tr̥syō	be thirsty	sitiō
tr̥stis	fem			thirst	sitis
tr̥stos	adI			dry	siccus
tr̥sus	adI			dry	siccus
trudskā	fem			leprosy	leprae
trudsmós	adI			annoying	molestus
truks	epi	(trukós)		slaughterer	interfector
tū	pron	(tewe)		you	tū
tūljom	neu		tuHljo-	multitude	multitūdō
tūlós	adI			swollen	tumidus

tumējō	sta			be swollen	tumeō
tumlós	mas			mound	tumulus
túmolos	mas			turmoil	tumultus
tundō	tr			strike	tundō
turgējō	sta			swell	turgeō
tūrjós	mas			cheese	caseus
tursis	fem	ej		tower	turris
tusjai	intr			rejoice oneself	delector
tuskjós	neu	tustjós (teusqa -ōm ?)		desert	desertum
tusnā	fem			wave	unda
tustijō	intr			cough	tussiō
tustis	fem	ej		coughing	tussis
twakos	neu	es		armour	armatūra
twenghō	tr	AIa	twengh; twn̥ghjō, twn̥ghskō; twenk- <reform. twenghti-	force	compellō
twerō	tr	AIa		enclose	amplexor
twoisós	adI			violent	uiolentus
twr̥bhōn	mas	(twr̥bhnos)		whirl	turbō
twr̥kos	mas			boar	aper
twr̥mā	fem			troop	turma
twr̥tos	adI			quick	uelox
ucējō	sta		$H_1ug^w/H_1eug^w/H_1ueg^w$	wet (be)	ūmeō
oucós	adI		H_1oug^w- / H_1uog^w-	wet	ūdus
ud	neu			out	ex
úderos	mas			uter	úterus
ūdhr̥	neu	(ūdhenos)	H_1uHdh-r̥/n / $HeH^{w}{}_{1}dh$-r̥/n	udder	ūber
ūdhros	adI			udder	ūber
udhús	adI		udhus	immediate	immediātus
udsqe	ind			on top	insuper
uksḗn	and	(uksnós)	H_2uksen-	ox	bos
uksōr	fem	(úkseros)		wife	uxor
ululājō	intr			howl	ululō
unksrā	fem		unksnā	shadow	umbra
upelos	adI		H_2wp-elo	bad	malus
úperesū	ind			very well	optimē
uperi	ind		H_2u-per	over	super
úperos	adI			high	superus
upo	ind			under	sub
upóqrijom	neu			commission	interpretium
upósēdjom	neu			fundament	fundamentum
upóstānom	neu			service	seruitium
úpselos	adI		upsēlós	high	altus
upsi	ind			above	supra
uqnós	mas		*cf.* auqslā	oven	fornus
urús	adI		H_1ur-u; urus	wide	amplus
ustós	adI		H_1us-to-	burnt	ustus
uta	ind			rather	potius

wədrā	fem			otter	lutra
wədris	mas			leather bag	uter
wəgājai	intr			roam	uagor
wəleiqos	neu	es		liquid	liquor
wəleisō	tr	AIa		beat	uerberō
wəlējō	sta		(H)wlH_2; *cf.* w∂ldhēyō	be fit	ualeō
wəlepējō	sta			whip	lepeō
wəleumi	tr	BIIIb	H_2welH_1; welH_3 *cf.* weldō	pillage	diripiō
wəlewā	fem			lion	leō
wəlōrom	neu			strap	lōrum
wəlos	mas		wl̥Ho-	leader	dux
wəros	mas		w(o)rHo-; *cf.* wersmn̥	pimple	uarus
wəregis	mas			enclosure	clausūra
wəreikā	fem			veil	rīca
wərikjō	tr			bend	flectō
wəroikos	mas			bend	anfractus
wəréikonjom	neu			webbing	ricinium
wəreinā	fem		Hwr	harn	urīna
wərējai	tr			respect	uereor
wərēn	mas	(wr̥nos)	wr̥H_1en	lamb	ueruēx
wəreumi	tr	BIIIb	werjō, wṛneumi	close	claudō
wəreumi apo	tr	BIIIb	werjō apo, wṛneumi apo	open	aperiō
wərbhis	fem	ei	*cf.* werpō	perimeter	circumductus
wərjō	tr			set fire	accendō
wərughis	mas	ej		rye	sēcale cereāle
wadhis	mas	ej		caution	uas
wadhō	intr		g^wadh?	walk	uādō
wadhom	neu		gh^wdhó-	river ford	uadum
wageinā	fem			sheath	uagīna
wāghijō	intr			cry	uāgiō
wágneumi	tr	BIVb, AIVe	wag/weH_2g; wagjō, caus. wāgejō	cleave	disrumpō
wai	ind			alas	uae
wailos	mas			humble	humilis
wailós	mas			wolf	lupus
wakkā	fem			cow	uacca
walgos	adI			bandy-legged	ualgus
walnom	neu			wall	uallum
walóm	intr	(aor. a chenmi)		died	mortus est
wapējō	sta			foggy, to be	nebulosus sum
waplājō	sta			scream	clamō
wāros	mas			asunder-legged	uārus
wāstos	adI			empty	uānus
wātis	mas	ej		poet	uatēs
watjos	adI			legbent	uatius
we	encl			or	ue
wēbēn	mas	(webnós)		weapon	arma

webhō	tr		Hwebh	weave	texō
wēdhājō	tr		wēdhaH$_2$je/o-	break through	effodiō
wédhneumi	tr	BIVb		link	ligō
wedhnom	neu		wedhmnom ?	dowry	dōs
wedhō	tr		wHedh / Hwedh	lead	addūcō
wedhr̥	neu	wédhenos		weapon	arma
wedhrom	neu			weather	tempus
wedhskō	tr		wedhH$_1$	strike	caedō
wedmn̥	neu			utterance	locūtiō
wedō	tr	AIb	H$_2$wed(H)	tell	narrō
wedrom	neu			bucket	situlus
wegējō	sta	AIIIe		be active, flourish	uigeō
weghjā	fem			way	uia
weghmi	tr	Bia	H$_2$wegh-	stab	fodicō
weghō	tr			carry	uehō
weghtis	fem	jo		leuer	uectis
weghtlom	neu			vehicle	uehiculum
weghtṓr	mas			transporter	uector
wegō	cau	Aib, AIIIo	wogejō	enliven	uegeō
wegō	tr	AIb		weave	texō
weidr̥	neu	wiedr̥/wéidenos		beast	bestia
weidhō	tr	AIa	(d)wi-dhH$_1$; widhjō	divide	dīuidō
weidos	neu	es		presence	praesentia
weiks	mas/fem	(wikós)	*cf.* woikos	house	domus
wéiktomā	fem			victim	uictima
(wí)weimi	tr	BIId		hunt	uēnor
weimn̥	neu	en		loom	textrīnum
weipō	cau	AIa	*cf.* wipjō	wave	uibrō
weiros	mas		weiH$_1$ro-, wiH$_1$ró	wire	fūnis
weis	neu	(wīsós)	weiH-s/os/es	strength	uis
weisnā	fem			vein	uēna
weisō	sta	AIa		flow	fluō
weitēks	fem	(weitkós)		agnus castus	uitēx
weitis	fem	ej	wH$_1$i-ti-	vine	uītis
weitō	cau	AIa		arch	incuruō
wéiwersā	fem			ferret	uiuerra
wejes / weje	pron		wei-; tab	we	nōs
wekmi	tr			desire	desiderō
wekō	intr	AIb	wek, wenk	arch	flectō
weksós	adI			convex	conuexus
weldō	tr		(H)wel(H$_3$); *cf.* wəl̥eumi	tear off	uellō
welīks	fem	(welikós)	wl̥ēiks	bracelet	armilla
weljṓs	comp	sup. wélistos		better	melior
welmi	tr	BIa	welH$_1$	will	uolō
welnā	fem		wl̥nā	wave	unda
welnos	neu	es		hair	uellus
welō	tr	AIb		see	uideō

welpō	tr	AIa		expect	expectō
weltis	fem		wḷtis	will	uoluntās
wélwm̥en	neu			wrapping	tegmen
welwō	tr		H_1wl-w	turn	uoluō
wélwtrom	neu			envelope	inuolūcrum
wémāmi	tr			vomit	uomō
(í)wēmi	tr	BIIb	H_2weH_1	blow	exhalō
wénāmoi	tr			aspire	appetō
wendhō	intr	AIa		attack	oppugnō
wenēsnom	neu			love potion	uenēnum
wenjā	fem		wenH_1-iH_2; wenī	delight	deliciae
wenō	tr		wenH_1; desid. wiwn̥-H_1-se/o	desire	concupiscō
wenos	neu	es		love	amor
wenseikā	fem			blister	uensīca
went	suff	wentjos		equipped with	praeditus
wentos	mas		H_2weH_1-n̥to- / H_2wH_1ento-	wind	uentus
weqtis	fem			thing	rēs
weqtlom	neu			expression	dictus
wēr	neu	(wṛos)		door	forēs
wēr	mas	wēros		favour	fauor
werbos	neu	es	H_1wr-b	whip	flagellum
wereinā	fem			sect	secta
wergō	sta	AIa		turn	rotō
wergom	neu			work	labos
weri	neu		Hwr; wēr, wēri	water	aqua
werjō	tr		werH_1	name	nōminō
(wí)wermi	tr	BIIe		find	inueniō
wernā	fem			alder	betullla
wēros	adI			true	uērus
werpō	tr	AIa		wrap out	ēuoluō
wersis	mas	ej	*cf.* r̥sēn	male	mās
wersmn̥	neu	en	*cf.* wəros	wart	uerrūca
wersō	tr	AIa		drag	uerrō
werstis	fem			track	trames
werstidhlom	neu			hall	uestibulum
wertmn̥	neu			direction	directiō
wertos	mas			value	ualor
wertrom	neu			defence	dēfensiō
wérunos	mas			belt (for safety)	cinctus
weskai	neu			eat	uescor
wēskō	tr			squeeze	exprimō
wésnāmi	tr	BIVa		prick	instigō
wesnejō	tr	AIIIo		bargain	negotior
wesnom	neu			sale	uēnum
wesō	sta	AIb	H_2wes; *cf.* awō <*H_2ew-	stay	maneō
wésolis	adI			cheap	uīlis

wespros	mas		*we- 'exclūsīuum' / we-skw(e)ro- / wesp(e)ro- / wekero-	evening	uesper
wesr̥	neu	(wesenós / wesentós/)		spring	uēr
wēsros	mas			morning	matina
westā	fem			food	pulmentum
westijō	tr		wesmi; *cf.* wosējō	dress	uestiō
westis	fem	jo		cloth	uestis
westos	mas			feast	daps
westrom	neu			cloth	uestis
westus	mas		H_2wes-tu-, H_2wos-tu; wostus	dwelling	domicilium
wēsus	adI		H_1wesu-; wesu-/wēsu-/wosu-; we-H_1su?	excellent	excellens
wétāmi	tr		*we-* exclūsīuum	forbid	uetō
wetlos	mas			calf	uitulus
wetos	neu	es		time	tempus
wetsós	wes			one-year creature	annucula creātūra
wetwos	adI	es		old	uetus
wī	ind			asunder	sē
widā́	fem			appearance	appārentia
widējō	tr		weidmi ?	see	uideō
wídhewā	fem		H_1wídheweH$_2$	widow	uidua
widhus	fem			willow	salīx
widjom	fem		widjā	wisdom	scientia
widris	adI			wise	doctus
wijējō	sta		weH$_1$i	be curved	uieō
wijēskō	inc			wither	uiēscō
wikis	fem	ej		chance	uicis
wikjō	dur			contend	certō
wikkā	fem			witch	uenēfica
wíklutom	adII			widely known	satis constans
windō	tr	AVIb		find out	comperiō
windō peri	fac			investigate	inuestigō
windos	adI			apparent	appararens
winis	fem			cable	cable
winkijō	tr			shackle	uinciō
winkō	tr			win	uincō
winsō	tr	AVIa		cause	causō
wikwos	adI			diverse	multifārius
wipjō	tr		*cf.* weipō	wrap	inuoluō
wiprós	adI			waving	uibrans
wīrós	mas		wiHró-, weiHro-, woiHro-	man	uir
wisējō	sta			sprout	uireō
wiskom	neu		wikskom?	mistletoe	uiscum
wísogā	fem			club	uirga

wistós	adII			seen	uisus
witājō	intr			turn around	circumeō
wíteros	adI			supplementary	complementārius
wītjā́	fem		wHi-	framework	textus
witjom	neu			curve	curua
witus	mas		*cf.* kantos	wheelrim	cantus
wíweqmi	tr	BIIe		speak	loquor
wl̥bhontis	mas		H_1wlb(h)o-nt-	camel	camēlus
wl̥dā́	fem			feast	conuiuium
wl̥dhējō	tr		(H)wlH_2dh; *cf.* wḷēyō	rule	imperō
wl̥ghis	fem			basin	uallis
wl̥iqējō	sta			liquid (to be)	liqueō
wl̥nā	fem		$H_{2/3}$wlH_1-neH_2	wool	lāna
wl̥qos	mas			wolf	lupus
wl̥tis	fem			tuff of hair	caesariēs
wl̥tus	mas			impression	adspectus
wn̥dā	fem			wave	unda
wn̥ghējō	sta			complexed (to be)	tortus sum
wn̥mos	adI		wn̥Hmo-	beautiful	pulcher
wn̥skā	fem			desire	dēsiderium
wn̥skō	tr			desire	dēsiderō
wochējō	tr		H_1ewg^{w}h / H_1weg^{w}h	vow	uoueō
wodā́	fem			water	aqua
wodr̥	neu	(wédenos)	wedṛ	water	aqua
woghejō	cau	AIIIo		induce (to)	addūcō
woghnos	mas			car	uehiculum
woghos	mas			transport	uectiō
wogsejō	cau		*cf.* augejō	make grow	augeō
wogsmis	mas			ploughshare	uomer
woida	tr			know	sciō
woidejō	cau	AIIIo		orient	dirigō
woidlos	mas		woH_1i-	basket	uīdulus
woidwṓs	adII	(woidwesos)	fem: widwəsyā	knowing	conscius
woighos	fem			elm	ulmus
woikā́	fem			vigour	uigor
woikos	mas		*cf.* weiks	village	uīcus
woikós	adI		wikrós	steadfast	peruicax
woikslā	fem			farm	uilla
woinā́	fem			fault	culpa
woinos	mas		weinom	wine	uīnum
woisos	mas			poison	uenēnum
woitā	fem			hunt	uēnātus
wolējō	tr			choose	ēligō
wolgos	neu	es		people	uulgus
wolmos	mas			roll	spīra
wolnos	neu	es	H_2wolH_1nos, H_2wlH_1nos	wound	uulnus
wolos	mas		wōlos	choice	ēlectiō
wolós	mas			willing	uolens

wolpis	fem	ej		fox	uulpēs
wolsom	neu			damage	perniciēs
wolwós	adI		wōlós	round	rotundus
wondhejō	cau	AIIIo		wind	torqueō
wondhos			wondhsos	hair	caesariēs
wōnós	adI			empty	uānus
wopjā	fem			water	aqua
wopsā	fem		wop-seH_2	wasp	uespa
woqs	fem	(weqs)		voice	uox
worghós	mas			criminal	scelestus
worgjom	neu			cannabis	cannabis
wormis	mas			worm	uermis
wornos	mas			colour	color
wornos	fem		wornā	raven	coruus
worós	mas			policeman	tresuir
wortejō	cau	AIIIo		invert (to)	inuertō
wosejō	tr	AIIIo	*cf.* westijō	dress	uestiō
wosis	mas		H_1ws	turban	tiara
wosmós	adI			wet	madidus
wospos	mas			garment	indūmentum
wr̥aghmn̥	neu			backbone	spīna
wr̥dhom	neu		wr̥H_1-dhH_1o-	word	uerbum
wr̥djā	fem		wrH_2d-iH_2; cf wr̥ādēiks	root	rādix
wr̥gā	fem			vigor	uigor
wr̥gējō	sta			attack (to be in)	urgeō
wr̥gjō	tr/intr			work	laborō
wr̥gos			wrH-go-	attack	impetus
wr̥ijō	tr			close	claudō
wr̥isdējō	intr			laugh	rīdeō
wr̥kājō	intr			cry	urcō
wr̥nāmi	tr	BIVa		persecute	persequor
wr̥n̥gai	intr			grumble	ringor
wəronkā́	fem			hand	manus
wəronkis	fem			dip	fouea
wr̥ādīks	fem	(wr̥ādikós, wr̥ādijós)	wrH_2d-ei$H$-; *cf.*wr̥dyā	root	rādix
wr̥stā	fem		H_2wrs; worsos, worsā	rain	pluuia
wr̥stis	fem			turn	uersiō
wr̥stos	mas			row	uersus
wr̥tō	tr	AIIh		turn	uertō
wr̥tom	neu			enclosure	saepimen

APPENDIX III: IN-DEPTH ANALYSIS

III.1. ROOT NOUNS

	1	2	3	4	5	6	7
	pod	**g^{w}ou**	**leuk**	**wōq**	**nāu**	**kwon**	**mēns**
	foot	*cow*	*light*	*voice*	*ship*	*dog*	*month*
Nom.	pā́t	gaúḥ	ruk	vā́k	náuḥ	śvā́	mā́ḥ
Voc.		gauḥ	ruk	vāk	nauḥ	śvan	
Acc.	pā́dam	gā́m	rucam	vā́cam	nāvam	śvā́nam	
Ins.	padā́	gávā	rucā	vācā	nāvā́	śúnā	māsā́
Dat.	padé	gáve	ruce	vāce	nāve	śune	māse
Abl.	padáḥ	góḥ	rucaḥ	vācáḥ	nāváh	śúnaḥ	māsaḥ
Gen.	padaḥ	góḥ	rucaḥ	vācáḥ	nāváh	śúnaḥ	māsaḥ
Loc.	padi	gavi	ruci	vāci	nāvi	śuni	māsi
Nom.		gāvau	rucau	vācau	nāvau	śvānau	
Voc.		gāvau	rucau	vācau	nāvau	śvānau	
Acc.		gāvau	rucau	vācau	nāvau	śvānau	
Ins.	padbhyām	gobhyām	rugbhyām	vāgbhyām	naubhyām	śvabhyām	mābhyām | mādbhyām
Dat.	padbhyām	gobhyām	rugbhyām	vāgbhyām	naubhyām	śvabhyām	mādbhyām
Abl.	padbhyām	gobhyām	rugbhyām	vāgbhyām	naubhyām	śvabhyām	mādbhyām
Gen.	padoḥ	gavoḥ	rucoḥ	vācoḥ	nāvoḥ	śunoḥ	māsoḥ
Loc.	padoḥ	gavoḥ	rucoḥ	vācoḥ	nāvoḥ	śunoḥ	māsoḥ
Nom.		gā́vas	rucaḥ	vācaḥ	nā́vah	śvānaḥ	
Voc.		gāvaḥ	rucaḥ	vācaḥ	nāvaḥ	śvānaḥ	
Acc.	padáh	gāḥ	rucaḥ	vācaḥ	nāvaḥ	śunaḥ	mā́sah
Ins.	padbhiḥ	góbhiḥ	rugbhiḥ	vāgbhiḥ	naubhíh	śvábhiḥ	mādbhíh
Dat.	padbhyaḥ	gobhyaḥ	rugbhyaḥ	vāgbhyaḥ	naubhyaḥ	śvabhyaḥ	mādbhyaḥ
Abl.	padbhyaḥ	gobhyaḥ	rugbhyaḥ	vāgbhyaḥ	naubhyaḥ	śvabhyaḥ	mādbhyaḥ
Gen.	padām	gavām	rucām	vācām	nāvām	śunām	māsām
Loc.	patsu	goṣu	rukṣu	vākṣu	nauṣu	śvasu	māḥsu
	pēs	bōs	lux	uox	nāuis	canis	mensis
	pedis	bouis	lūcis	uōcis	nāuis	canis	mensis
Nom.	πούς	βοῦς	ἀνήρ	ὄψ	ναῦς	κύων	μήν, μείς
Gen.	ποδός	βοός	ἀνδρός	ὀπός	νεώς	κυνὸς	μηνός
Dat.	ποδί	βοΐ	ἀνδρί	ὀπί	νηΐ	κυνὶ	μηνί;
Acc.	πόδᾰ	βοῦν	ἄνδρα	ὄπα	ναῦν	κύνα	
Voc.	πούς	βοῦ	ἄνερ		ναῦ	κύον	

Nom.	πόδε	βόε			νῆε		
Gen.	ποδοῖν						
Dat.	ποδοῖν	βοοῖν			νεοῖν		
Acc.	πόδε						
Nom.	πόδες	βόες	ἄνδρες		νῆες	κύνες	
Gen.	ποδῶν	βοῶν	ἀνδρῶν		νεῶν	κυνῶν	μηνῶν
Dat.	ποσί(ν)	βουσί(ν)	ἀνδράσι(ν)		ναυσί(ν)	κυσὶ	
Acc.	πόδᾰς	βοῦς	ἄνδρας		ναῦς	κύνας	
nom. sg.	patas/patis	*guwau-					
acc. sg.	patan						
gen. sg.	patas						
dat.-loc. sg.	pati						
acc. pl.	pātuš < *pód-ms						
gen. pl.	patān < *pd-óm						
dat-loc. pl.	patā <*pdós						

	8	9	10	11	12	13	14
	suH	**mūs**<*muHs	**djeuH**	**judh**	**kerd**	**weik**	**dheghom**
	pig	*mouse*	*daylight*	*combat*	*heart*	*house*	*earth*
Nom.	sū́ḥ	mū́ṭ	dyáuḥ	yut	hā́rdi, (su)-hā́rt	viṭ	kṣám, kṣáḥ
Voc.	sū́ḥ	mū́ṭ	dyaùḥ	yut		viṭ	kṣám
Acc.	suvam	muṣam	dy'aam | divam	yudham		viśam	kṣám
Ins.	suvā	muṣā	divā́	yudhā́	hṛdā	viśā	kṣamā́, jmá
Dat.	suvai | suve	muṣe	dyave | divé	yudhe	hṛdé	viśe	kṣé
Abl.	suvāḥ | suvaḥ	muṣaḥ	dyóḥ | diváḥ	yudhaḥ	hṛdáḥ	viśaḥ	jmás, kṣmás
Gen.	suvāḥ | suvaḥ	muṣaḥ	dyóḥ | diváḥ	yudhaḥ	hṛdáḥ	viśaḥ	jmás, kṣmás
Loc.	suvi | suvām	muṣi	dyávi | diví	yudhi	hṛdí	viśi	kṣámi
Nom.	suvau	muṣau	dyāvau | divau	yudhau		viśau	kṣā́mā
Voc.	suvau	muṣau		yudhau		viśau	kṣā́mā
Acc.	suvau	muṣau	dyāvau | divau	yudhau		viśau	kṣā́mā
Ins.	sūbhyām	muḍbhyām		yudbhyām	hṛdbhyām	viḍbhyām	
Dat.	sūbhyām	muḍbhyām		yudbhyām	hṛdbhyām	viḍbhyām	

Abl.	sūbhyām	muḍbhyām		yudbhyām	hṛdbhyām	viḍbhyām	
Gen.	suvoḥ	muṣoḥ		yudhoḥ	hṛdoḥ	viśoḥ	
Loc.	suvoḥ	muṣoḥ		yudhoḥ	hṛdoḥ	viśoḥ	
Nom.	suvaḥ	muṣaḥ	dyāvaḥ | divaḥ	yudhaḥ		viśaḥ	kṣāmas
Voc.	suvaḥ	muṣaḥ	divaḥ	yudhaḥ		viśaḥ	kṣāmas
Acc.	suvaḥ	muṣaḥ	divaḥ	yudhaḥ	hṛdaḥ	viśaḥ	kṣā́s
Ins.	sūbhiḥ	muḍbhiḥ	dyúbhiḥ	yudbhiḥ	hṛdbhíḥ	viḍbhiḥ	
Dat.	sūbhyaḥ	muḍbhyaḥ	dyubhyaḥ	yudbhyaḥ	hṛdbhyaḥ	viḍbhyaḥ	
Abl.	sūbhyaḥ	muḍbhyaḥ	dyubhyaḥ	yudbhyaḥ	hṛdbhyaḥ	viḍbhyaḥ	
Gen.	sūnām | suvām	muṣām	divām	yudhām	hṛdām	viśām	
Loc.	sūṣu	muṭsu	dyuṣu	yutsu	hṛtsú	viṭsu	kṣā́su
	sūs	mūs	diēs	nox	cor	uīcus	humus
	suis	mūris	diei/Iouis	noctis	cordis	uicī	humī
Nom.	ὗς σῦς	μῦς	Ζεὺς	νύξ	κῆρ < κέαρ	οἶκος	χθών
Gen.	συός	μυός	Διὸς	νυκτός	κῆρος:		χθονὸς
Dat.			Διὶ	νυκτί	κῆρι		χθονὶ
Acc.	ὗν, σῦν	μῦν	Δία	νύκτα	κῆρ < κέαρ		χθόνα
Voc.		μῦ	Ζεῦ		κῆρ < κέαρ		
Nom.							
Gen.							
Dat.							
Acc.							
Nom.	ὕες, σύες	μύες, μῦες		νύκτες			
Gen.	ὑῶν, συῶν			νυκτῶν			
Dat.	(σ)υσί, (σ)ύεσσι	μυσί					
Acc.	ὕας, σύας	μύας		νύκτας			
nom. sg.			šiwaz	ne-ku-uz (nekuz)	ka-ra-az (karts)		tekan n., gen.
acc. sg.							
gen. sg.			šiwattaš	nekuz	kar-di-aš		taknas
dat.-loc. sg.							
acc. pl.							

gen. pl.							
dat-loc. pl.							

	15	16	17	18	19	20	21
	rēg	**ap**	**sneich**	**j(e)uHs**	**neuk**	**gheim**	**op**
	king	*water*	*snow*	*broth*	*nut*	*winter*	*wealth*
Nom.	rā́ṭ			yū́ṣ		himá-, héman	ápnas-
Voc.	rā́ṭ						
Acc.	rājam						
Ins.	rājā						
Dat.	rāje						
Abl.	rājaḥ						
Gen.	rājaḥ						
Loc.	rāji						
Nom.	rājau						
Voc.	rājau						
Acc.	rājau						
Ins.	rāḍbhyām						
Dat.	rāḍbhyām						
Abl.	rāḍbhyām						
Gen.	rājoḥ						
Loc.	rājoḥ						
Nom.	rājaḥ	āpaḥ					
Voc.	rājaḥ	āpaḥ					
Acc.	rājaḥ	apaḥ					
Ins.	rāḍbhiḥ	adbhiḥ					
Dat.	rāḍbhyaḥ	adbhyaḥ					
Abl.	rāḍbhyaḥ	adbhyaḥ					
Gen.	rājām	apām					
Loc.	rāṭsu	apsu					
	rex	rōs	nix	iūs	nux	hiems	ops
	rēgis	rōris	nivis	iūris	nucis	hiemis	opis
Nom.	χείρ		*νίψ			χειμάς, -ών	κλώψ
Gen.	χειρός						κλωπός
Dat.	χειρί						κλωπί
Acc.	χεῖρα		νίφα				κλῶπᾰ

Voc.							κλώψ
Nom.	χεῖρε						κλῶπε
Gen.							
Dat.	χεροῖν						κλωποῖν
Acc.							
Nom.	χεῖρες						κλῶπες
Gen.	χερῶν, χειρῶν ib						κλωπῶν
Dat.	χερσί, χειρσί, χείρεσι						κλωψί(ν)
Acc.	χεῖρας						κλῶπᾰς
nom. sg.	keššar (ghésr̥)					gim(a)-	happar
acc. sg.	kiššeran (ghsérom)						
gen. sg.	kiš(ša)raš (ghesrós / ghsrós)						
dat.-loc. sg.	kiš(ša)rī (ghesréi / ghsréi)						
acc. pl.							
gen. pl.							
dat-loc. pl.							

(<u>accent position verified</u>)

III.2. PRONOUNS

III.2.1. INDEFINITE PRONOUNS

IE	Lat.	Gk.	Skt.	Hitt.
solwom/ oljoi	tōtus/ omnes	ολοι	sava, viśva	hūmant-
qāqos	quisque	εκατεροσ, εκαστοσ	pratieka	kuissa
qisqis	quisquis quīlībĕt quīvis quīviscumque	τισ οσ τισ δη οσ τισ δηποτε οσ τισ ουν	kacit kaścana kopi	kuis kuis, kuis-as kuis,
qiskomqe, qisimmoqe	quiscumque	τισ αν τισ εαν	yah kaś cit yo yah yadanga	kuis imma, kuis imma kuis, kuis-as imma (kuis)
qéjespejoi	quidam	οιτινεσ	katipaya	kuis ki
qis, edqis (cf. rus. едвá)	ecquis, aliquis, quis, quispiam, aliquisquam	τισ	anyatama	
enis	quīdam	ενιοι	ekaścana	
somós	īdem (osc. ekkum)	ο αυτοσ	eka (aequus), sama, sah eva	eni, uni, anni, asi
se epse, epe, s(w)el (e)pe	ipse; arc. sapsa, sumpse	εαυτοσ	atman, svayam	apāsila (cf. hit. kinun lat. nunc)
neqis	nullus, nec quisquam	ουδεισ	na kah	UL kuiski
álteros, ónteros	alter		anyatara	(kuis)....kuis
aljos*, onjos	alius	αλλοσ	anya, itara, apara	tamai-

Eng.	Ger.	Goth.	Gael.	Russ.
all	alle, jeder	alls	u(i)le	все
every one	jeder	ainhvarjizuh ainhvaþaruh	cach, cách (gal. papon)	каждый, еже--какой 'what, which'
anyone	jeder	hvazuh hvarjizuh	duine ar bith	всякий
whoever	jeder der, wer auch immer	sahvazuh saei	cibé duine	кто бы ни
some	etliche			несколько
someone	jemand, irgendeiner, etwas	hvas, hvashun	nech, nach, duine	кто-нибудь, кой-что, етеръ
certain	ein gewisser	sums**	áirithe	некоторый
the same	der selbe	sama	an céanna;	тот же самый
himself	selbst	silba	fessin, fadessin >féin	сам, óнсий
none, nobody	niemand, keiner	(ni) hvashun	ní aon duine (gal. nepon)	никто
the other one	der andere		an ceann eile	другой, инóй (инъ)
someone else	anderer	aljis*	aile, aill, eile	

*from **aljos** cf. lat. alibi, gr. αλλυδισ, got. aljaþ, etc **cf. arm. intch <**sm̥ -kʷid* 'something'

III.2.2. DEMONSTRATIVE PRONOUNS

IE	Lat.	Gk.	Skt.	Hitt.
is, se	is (anaf.)	αυτοσ	sah, esah	apā
(e)ko, gho-i(ke), so, eto	hic<*gho-i-ke	ουτοσ	ay-am, id-am, (gen. asya -air. a + len) <* e/ei; esah (cf. lat. equidem)	kā, eda (def)
oiso, isto, eno	iste <*is-te	**οιοσ** <*oihos 'such'	enam (enclit.)	-----
el-ne	ille, ollus <el-ne/ol-nos	εκεινοσ	a-sau, u-	apā

Eng.	Ger.	Goth.	Gael.	Russ.
he	er, der	is	(h)í	он
this	dieser hier	hi-, sa(h)	sin	этот, сей.(ant)
-----	-----	-----	-----	-----
that, yonder	dieser da, jener	jains	(s)ut	тот

III.2.3. PERSONAL PRONOUNS

SINGULAR

	IE TON. *AT.*	LAT	OSC-*UMB*	PTOCEL	OIr I	OIr D	Welsh I	Welsh D	CORN	BRET
N	egṓ, egóm	ego	deest	me, mesme ?	mé, meisse	-----	mi, myvi, myvy, mivi	-----	my, me	me
A	mewom; *me*	mē (arc.mēd)	deest	*me, *mī	-----	-m-	-----	mi, vi, vyvi, vivi	-vy, -ma, -m-, f(f)	-me, -m-, ff
G	mene; *mo, mei*	meī	deest	*mewe, *mene, *meme	mui, muisse	mo (len)	meu	mi, my, vy (ecl.); -m	ow, ov; -m	ma, va; -m
D	meghei; *moi*	mihī	deest	*me, *mī, *moi	-----	-m-	-----	mi, vi, vyvi, vivi	vy, ma, -m-, f(f)	-me, -m-, ff
L	mei, moi	mē	deest	-----	-----	-----	-----	-----	-----	-----
I	mojo	-----	-----	-----	-----	-----	-----	-----	-----	-----
Ab	med	mē	*mehe*	-----	-----	-----	-----	-----	-----	-----
N	tū	tū	tiium, tiú	*tū, tustu	tú, tussu	-----	ti, tydi, tidi	-----	ty, te	te
A	tewom; *t(w)e*	tē	*tiu, tiom, tio, teio*	*tu	-----	-t-	-----	di, dy, de, dydi, dydy	-te, -ta, th-, -s	-de; -z-, -t
G	tewe; *t(w)o, t(w)ei*	tui; adj. touos, tuus	tuvai 'tuae', *tuua, tua, touer, tuer*	*towe < *tewe	tái	do (len)	teu	dy (len); -th (len)	the; -th, -t, -d	da (len), -z (len)
D	tebhei; *t(w)oi*	tibī	tfei, tíf, *tefe*	*t(w)oi	-----	-t-	-----	di, dy, de, dydi, dydy	-te, -ta, th-, -s	-de; -z-, -t
L	t(w)ei, t(w)oi	tē	deest (cf. 3ª sueso, seso)	-----	-----	-----	-----	-----	-----	-----
I	t(w)ojo	-----	-----	-----	-----	-----	-----	-----	-----	-----
Ab	ted	tē	deest	-----	-----	-----	-----	-----	-----	-----

GMC	GOT	ON	OE	OHG	LIT	PRUS	SLAV
*eka (cf. vén. .e.go)	ik	ek	ic	ih	aš	as	азъ
*mike (cf. vén. mego)	mik	mik	mec, mē	mih	mane	mien <*men	mę
*mīnō	meina	mīn	mīn	mīn	manęs	mais(e)	mene
*miza	mis	mēr	mē	mir	mâni(e), man	mennei, māim <instr.	мьnję; mi
.....	.....	.....	.....	.....	manyje	-----	мьnję
.....	.....	.....	.....	.....	manimi	-----	мъnoją
.....	.....	.....	.....	.....	-----	-----	-----
*þū	þū	þū	þū	dū, du	tu	toū, tou, thou, tu	ty
*þeke	þuk	þik	þe(c)	dih	tave	tien, tin <*ten	tę
*þīn	þeina	þīn	þīn	dīn	tavęs	twais(e)	tebe
*þeza	þus	þēr	þē	dir	tâvi(e), tau	tebbei, tebbe	tebję; ti
.....	.....	.....	.....	.....	tavyje	-----	tebję
.....	.....	.....	.....	.....	tavimi	-----	toboją
.....	.....	.....	.....	.....	-----	-----	-----

GK	ARM	SKR	AV	TOCH	ALB	HITT
εγω, εγων	es	ahám	azəm	näṣ, ñuk	unë	u:k (arc.), ammuk
εμε; με	is	m ι ͻ m, mā	(mā)	*mekwe	mua, mue	ammuk; -mu
εμου; μου <μεσο	im	máma, me	mana	ñi <*mäñi	im <I + em	ammēl
εμοι; μοι	imdz <*imij <*emeg^{h}(e)i	máhya, máhyam, me	mabya, mabyah (mai)			ammuk; -mu
———	is	máyi	-----			=dat.
———	inew	máyā	deest			.....
———	inén, indzén	mát	mat			ammēdaz
συ	du	tvám	tvəm, tūm (tard.) (tū)	A tu, B t(u)we	ti <*tū	zik
σε; σε <*twe	k'ez <*twe-	tv ι ͻ m, tvā	θąm (θvā)			tuk; -tta, -ttu
σου <*tweso	k'o	táva, te	tava (tai)		adi. y-t, ac. tën-t	tuēl
σοι; σοι <*twoi	k'ez <*tweg^{h}(e)i	túbhya, túbhyam, te	tabya, tabyah (tai)			tuk; -tta, -ttu
———	k'ez	tváyi, tvé	-----			=dat.
———	k'ew	tváyā	θvā (tardiiuum)			.....
———	k'én, k'ezén	tvát	θat			tuēdaz

PLURAL

	TON. *AT.*	LAT	O-*U*	PTOCEL	OIr I	OIr D	Welsh I	Welsh D	CORN	BRET
N	wejes, n̥smé	nōs		*(s)nīs <*(s)nēs; *snīsnīs	snisni, sníni, sisni, sinni, sní	-----	ni, nini	-----	ny	ni, ny
A	nōns <**nosms*, n̥smé; *nos*	nōs		*snōs	-----	-nn-	-----	-n-, -m, n(n)	ny, ny ny; -n-, -gan-, -gen-	ni, -n-, -on-, -hon-;-mp
G	n̥seróm; *nos*	nostrum, -ī	desunt	*aterom <*n̥serom /so n̥sme	athar, ár <*n̥s-rō-m	ar n-	einym, einom	an, yn; -n	an, agan, agen; -n, -gan, -gen	hon, hor, hol; -n, -on
D	n̥sméi, nosbhos	nōbis <*nosbhis (cf. pubēs <*pusbh-)		*snōs	-----	-nn-	-----	-n-, -m, n(n)	ny, ny ny, -n-, -gan-, -gen-	ni, -n-, -on-, -hon-;-mp
L	n̥smí, nosi			-----		-----	-----	-----	-----	-----
I	nosbhis			-----	-----	-----	-----	-----	-----	-----
Ab	n̥sméd			-----	-----	-----	-----	-----	-----	-----
N	juwes, jusmé	uōs	FAL uēs PAELIGN.-uus	*swīs <swēs; swīswīs	sib, sissi, síi	-----	chwi, chwich wi	-----	*why, wy*	hui, huy, c'houi
A	wōns <**wosms*, jusmé; *wos*	uōs		*swōs	-----	-b-	-----	-ch-, -ch	why,-s-, -gas-; --ges-; ugh	-huy, -hu, -uy. -u; -oz-, -ch
G	wesróm; *wos*	uostrum, -ī	*uestra* 'uestra'	*(s)wesrom	sethar, sethar-si, sar, fathar	far n-, for n-, bar n-	einwch, einywch	awch, ych; -ch	as, agas, ages; -gas, ges	(h)oz, (h)ouz, ho; -oz, -ouz
D	jusméi, wosbhos; *wos*	uōbis <*wosbhis	desunt	*swōs	-----	-b-	-----	-ch-, -ch	why,-s-, -gas-; --ges-; ugh	-huy, -hu, -uy. -u; -oz-, -ch
L	jusmí, wosi			-----	-----	-----	-----	-----	-----	-----
I	wosbhis			-----	-----	-----	-----	-----	-----	-----
Ab	jusméd			-----	-----	-----	-----	-----	-----	-----

GMC	GOT	ON	OE	OHG	LIT	PRUS	SLAV
*weys	weis	vēr	wē	wir	mes <*wes	mes <*wes	my <*wes
*uns	uns(is)	oss	ūs(ic)	unsih	mus	mans<*nans <nṓns; *nō	ny
*unserō	unsera	vār	ūser, ūre	unsēr	mūsų	nōuson, nōusan *-sōn.-	nasъ <*nōs-sōm
*uns	uns(is)	oss	ūs	uns	mums	noūmans *nōmṓns	namъ; ny
.....	.....	.....	.....	.....	mumyse		nasъ
.....	.....	.....	.....	.....	mumis		nami
.....	.....	.....	.....	.....	-----		-----
*yūs	jus	ēr	gē, gīe	ir	jūs	ioūs <jūs	vy
*(w)izwiz	izwis	yðr	ēow	iu	jus	wans<*vans <vṓns; *vō	vy
*izwerō	izwara	yð(u)ar	ēower	iuwēr	jūsų	ioūson, ioūsān <*-sōn-	vasъ
*(w)izwiz	izwis	yðr	ēow(ic)	iuwih	jums	ioūmans < *jōmṓns	vamъ ; ny
.....	.....	.....	.....	.....	jumyse		vasъ
.....	.....	.....	.....	.....	jumis		vami
.....	.....	.....	.....	.....	-----		-----

GK	ARM	SKR	AV	TOCH	ALB	HITT
ημεισ <nsme + es , eol. **αμμε** <nsme	mek' <*sme-	vayám	vayam	wes	na <*nŏs	wēs (arc.); anzās
ημασ	mez	asm ι ͻ n, nas	ahma	-m, -äm	ne <*nōs	anzās; -nnas
ημων	mer	asm ι ͻ kam, nas	(nah)		ne <*nōs	anzēl
ημιν	mez	asmábhyam , asmé, nas	ahmabya (nah)		ne <*nōs	anzās; -nnas
-----	mez	asm ι ͻ su, asmé	-----			=dat.
-----	mewk'	asm ι ͻ bhis	deest			.....
-----	ménj	asmát	ahmat			anzēdaz
υμεισ	duk' <*juH-s/ tuH-s	yūyám	yūžam		ju < *u	sumēs
υμασ	dzez	yuṣm ι ͻ n, vas	(vāh)	-m, -äm		sumās; -smas
ημων	dzer <*swesrom	yuṣm ι ͻ kam, vas	(vah)			sumenzan (arc.), sumēl
ημιν	dzez <*sg^{h}eg^{h}i <*sweg^{h}i	yuṣmábhya m, vas	šmabhya, yušmabya (vah)			sumēs; -smas
-----	dzez	yusm ι ͻ su, yuṣmé	-----			=dat.
-----	dzewk'	yuṣm ι ͻ bhis	šmā			.....
-----	dzénj	yuṣmát	šmat, yušmat			sumēdaz

III.3. WORD FORMATION: COMMON PIE LENGTHENINGS AND SUFFIXES

IE	Latin	Old Irish	West Gmc.	East Gmc.	Greek	Indian	Slavic
------	uox				φλεψ	vāc 'uox'	
	rex	rí			πουσ	rāt	
	lex	bó 'bos'	ko		βουσ	gáu/go	
	lux				ονυξ	ruk	
	grex					ap 'aqua'	
	mūs		mūs		μυσ	mū	mysi (ac.)
	pes						
	nux						
	trabs						
	nix						
-os			kamb 'pecten'	snaiws 'nix'	λογοσ 'uerbum'	śoka 'splendor'	snegъ 'nix'
					γομφοσ 'dens'	jambha 'dens'	zobъ 'dens'
					φοροσ		tokъ
					στοιχοσ		
					τροχοσ 'cursus'		
					οχοσ 'currus'		
-ós	procus				τομοσ 'secans'	vará 'sequitor'	
	coquus				τροχοσ 'rota'	śoká 'splendens'	
					λοιποσ 'reliquiae'	ghaná 'occisor'	
-us	genu(īnus) dens	gin (geno)	kinnus		γενυσ	hanu	
	pecus/pecu		haidus			ketú	
			faihu			paśú	
						dāru	
	domus				δομοσ	dáma	domъ
-jom/ja	ingenium	cride 'cor'			ικριον	vairya 'uirilitās'	stoletie 'saeculum'
	officium	sétig <-yā 'mulier'			σοφια 'sapientia'	saujanya 'probitās'	dolia 'pars'
	hospitium						
	gremium						
	prolubium						
	repudium						
	uaticinium						
	principium						
	dolium						
	feria						
	reliquiae						
-nos/nom	dōnum				υπνοσ 'somnus'	sthānam 'locus'	

	somnus				χοανοσ 'olla'	svapnah 'sopnus'	
	regnum				οργανον 'instrumentum'	snānam 'nātus'	
					λυχνοσ <ksn 'candēla'	dānam 'dōnum'	
						varna 'color' (uarius)	
						arambhanam 'initium'	
						rodanam	
						śasanam	
						anusthānam	
						adhyayanam	
						āsānam	
						adhyānam	
						abhidhānam	
						indhanam	
						kārnam	
						tādanam	
						grathanam	
						patanam	
						ádanam	
						darśanam	
						svā́danam	
-nā	lūna				ποινη 'pūnitiō'		tsená 'pretium'
	habēna				ηδονη 'uoluptās'		luna 'id.'
	pruina						
	ruina						
-njom	somnium	blíad(a)in <yā 'anūs'			–νιον	svápn(i)ya	sunie
	scrutinium					prāvīnya	žnanie 'scientia'
	triennium					kārtsnya 'totālitās'	upražnenie 'exercitium'
						kārpanya 'miseria'	cozarenie
							znamenie 'importantia'
							značenie 'significātiō'
							obъiavlenie 'nuntiātiō'
							prepodavanie
							čtenie 'lectiō'
							cobranie 'collectiō'
-tjom/tjā	exercitium					antastya- 'intestīna'	
	seruitium						

	initium praeputium tristitia indutiae						
-twom						pañcatvam 'quique elementa'	lekarstvo 'medicāmentum'
						gurutvam 'grāuitās'	gosteprimstvo 'hospitālitās'
							stroitelstvo 'constructiō'
							proizvodstvo 'productiō'
							znakomstvo 'scientia'
-men							
	nōmen	ainm			ονομα 'nōmen'	nāman 'nōmen'	vrěmę, 'tempus'
	agmen	léimm 'saltus'			φερμα 'onus'	bhárma/bhárīman	brěmę, 'onus'
	flūmen<gsm	céimm 'passus'			τερμα 'terminus'	preman 'affectiō '	čisme (s+mn) 'numerus'
	flāmen<gsm	béimm 'ictus'			α(F)ετμα 'halitus'	ashman 'saxum'	
					στιγμα 'plāga'	bharman 'onus'	
					τιμημα 'honor'	tarman	
	lūmen<ksm				γραμμα, γρασμα	bráhman	
					αγεμεν 'ferre'		
-mon/mēn	pulmō				αυτμην (αετμα)	brahmā́n	
					πυθμην	dharmā́	
					υμην		
					λιμην 'portus'		
					λειμων		
					ιδμων 'scius'		
					πνευμων 'pulmō'		
-mn̥tom	augmentum			hliumant 'reputātiō'		śrómatam 'reputātiō'	
	excrēmentum						
-on	tēmōn				τεκτων 'tignārius'	taksan	
	nefrōnēs				αρσην 'mas'	uksán	
	pecten				(F)αρην 'ariēs'	yúvan	
	gluten						

-mos	rēmus<tsm				καλαμοσ 'calamus'	kāma	
	fūmus				ανεμοσ 'uentus'	drumá	
					ολμοσ<λσμ 'mortārium'	dhūmá	
						trmá	
-mā	flamma<gsm				δρυμα		
	glūma				αιχμη <ksm 'cuspis'		
	plūma						
-los/lom/lā	prēlum				ομφαλοσ		
	candēla						
	fidēlia						
-kos/kā	pertica					prāśnika	
	parca					sainika	
						bhiksuka	
						balaka	
						karabhaka	
						maryaka	
						abhisoka	
-ro	stuprum				πτερον 'āla'		
					ολεθροσ 'dēlētiō'		
-er	leuir				δαηρ 'leuir'		
					φρεαρ 'puteus'		
					πι(F)αρ 'adeps'		
					ουθαρ 'ūter'		
					ημαρ 'diēs'		
					αλειφαρ 'adeps'		
	super				υπερ 'super'		
-tā	iuuenta				ολ(F)οτησ 'totālitās'	kṛtajnatā	
					βιοτη 'uīta'	devatā	
						ṛjutā	
						gurutā	
						sarvatā	
-tāt(i)					ικανοτησ	aristátāti	
					ισοτησ	ayaksmátāti	
					ιδιοτησ	gṛbhītátāti	
					μεσοτησ	jyesthátāti	
	deitās/dīvīnitās					devátāti	
	acritās					vasútāti	
	firmitās					ástatāti	
	commūnitās			gamaindaiths		dáksatāti	
			gemeinde	gamainths		śámtāti	

				managdut hais			
-ti	mens				φυσισ 'nātūra'	mati	
	pars				ζευξισ 'uinculum'	krti	
	mors				τερψισ 'oblectamentum'	bhakti	
	ars				βασισ 'grasus'	bati	
					υστερησισ 'dilātiō'	drsti	
					κινησισ 'mouimentum'	vipatti	
						bhrti	
						pankti	
-tu	portus		furt		αστυ 'urbs'	av. pərətu-š 'pons'	
	saltus					gántus	
-tūt	iuuentūs	oítiu 'iuuentūs'		mikiduÞs 'magnitūdō'			
	senectūs	sentu 'senectūs'					
	salūs	bethu 'uita'					
	uirtūs	oíntu 'ūnītās'					
		slántu 'salūs'					
		cáttu 'sanctitās'					
		nemarbtu 'immortālitās'					
-to					νοστοσ		
					φορτοσ		
					καματοσ		
					βιοτοσ (βιοτη)		
					κοιτοσ		
					ερπετον		
-tor/tēr	genitor				γενετωρ/γενετηρ	janitr	
					πευστηρ	gntr	
						krtr	
						drstr	
						dhaatr	
						raksitr	
						bóddha	
-in						bhāvin	graždanin 'ciuis, homō urbānus'
						puspadhārin	krestianin 'homō rusticus'
						medhavin	angličanin 'anglensis'

						kuśalin	parižanin 'parisiensis'
						ksayin	
-dhrom	crībrum						
-trom	arātrum				αροτρον 'arātrum'		
	rostrum				φερτρον 'faretra'		
	lūstrum				λεκτρον 'lectus'		
	tarātrum				νιπτρον 'lauabum'		
					σωστρον		
-dhlom	stābulum				χυτλον 'olla'		
	pābulum				γενεθλον		
-tlom	poculum					mántra	
	situlum					shrotra	
-os- (n)	onus	slíab 'mons'			κλεοσ 'gloria'	anas 'onus'	
	opus				νεφοσ 'nubēs'	apas 'opus'	
					ερεβοσ 'inferus'	shravas	
						candramas	
						tejas	
						chandas	
						tapas	
						nabhas	
						payas	
						manas	
						yaśas	
						raksas	
						rajas	
						vaksas	
						vayas	
						vasas	
						vedhas	
						śiras	
						saras	
-os- (m)	aurōr(a)	aurōr-a			εωσ 'aurōra'	usáa 'aurōra'	
	calor				αιδωσ 'pudicitia'		
	tepor						
	honor						
-estu <ed+tu /esti <ed+ti		inruccus 'opulentia'					cvežestь 'frescor'
		comláinso 'plēnitūdō'					
		áthius 'acerbitās'					
		diuitius 'simplicitās'					

		cosmuilius 'similitūdō'					
		cuibdius 'harmonia'					
		erdarcus 'pulchritūdō'					
		faitigus 'cautiō'					
		inderbus 'incertitūdō'					
		cutrummus 'equalitās'					
		mórálus 'moralitas'					
		comarbus 'hereditās'					
		coibnius 'familiāritās'					
astu<ad +tu / asti<ad +ti		flaithemnas 'dominium'		thiudinassus 'regnum'			gluposть 'stultitia'
		airechas 'nōbilitās'		gudjin-assus 'sacerdotium'			polnostь 'plēnitūdō'
		óclachas					podrobnostь 'indicātiō'
		muntaras 'familiāritās'					grustь 'tristitia'
		remthechtas 'antepositiō'					gordostь
		anamchairtes 'directiō spirituālis'					molodostь 'iuuentūs'
		lánamnas 'matrimonium'					starostь 'senectūs'
		testas 'testimonium'					iarostь 'exasperātiō'
		émechas 'opportunitās'					
		coitchennas 'generālitās'					

III.4. PHONETIC RECONSTRUCTION

III.4.1. CONSONANTS

NOTES: The PIE reconstruction is the traditional one, especially regarding the laryngeals, and the division into three velars (including the "palatovelars"); we have marked these traditional reconstructed phonemes with *italic type.* [1] After vowels. [2] Before a plosive (p, t, k). [3] Before an unstressed vowel (Verner's Law). [4] After a (Proto-Germanic) fricative (s, f). [5] Before a (PIE) front vowel (i, e). [6] Before or after a (PIE) u. [7] Before or after a (PIE) o, u. [8] Between vowels. [9] Before a resonant. [10] Before secondary (post-PIE) front-vowels. [11] After r, u, k, i (RUKI). [12] Before a stressed vowel. [13] At the end of a word. [14] After u, r or before r, l. [15] After n.

PIE	Skr.	Av.	OCS	Lith.	Arm.	Toch.	Hitt.	Gk.	Lat.	O.Ir	Gmc.
*p	p [p]	p [p]	p [p]	p [p]	h [h]; w [w] [1]	p [p]	p [p]	p [p]	p [p]	Ø; ch [x] [2]	*f; *β [3]; *p [4]
*t	t [t]	t [t]	t [t]	t [t]	tʻ [tʰ]	t [t]; c [c] [5]	t; z [5]	t [t]	t [t]	t [t]; th [θ] [8]	*θ; *ð [3]; *t [4]
_*k_	ś [ɕ]	s [s]	s [s]	š [ʃ]	s [s]	k; ś [ɕ] [9]	k [k]	k [k]	k [k]	c [k]; ch [x] [8]	*x; *ɣ [3]; k [4]
*k	k [k]; c [c] [5]	k [k]; c [ʧ] [5]	k [k]; č [ʧ] [5]; c [ʦ] [10]	k [k]	kʻ [kʰ]						
*kʷ							ku [kʷ]	p; t [5]; k [6]	qu [kʷ]; c [k] [7]	c [k]; ch [x] [8]	*xʷ; *ɣʷ, *w [3]; kʷ [4]
*b	b [b]	b [b]	b [b]	b [b]	p [p]	p [p]	p [p]	b [b]	b [b]	b [b]	*p
*d	d [d]	d [d]	d [d]	d [d]	t [t]	ʦ [ʦ]; ś [ɕ] [5]	t [t]	d [d]	d [d]	d [d]; dh [ð] [8]	*t
_*g_	j [ɟ]	z [z]	z [z]	ž [ʒ]	c [ʦ]	k [k]; ś [ɕ] [9]	k [k]	g [g]	g [g]	g [g]; gh [ɣ] [8]	*k
*g	g [g]; j [ɟ] [5]	g [g]; j [ʤ] [5]	g [g]; ž [ʒ] [5]; dz [ʣ] [10]	g [g]	k [k]						
*gʷ							ku [kʷ]	b [b]; d [d] [5]; g [g] [6]	u [w]; gu [gʷ] [15]	b [b]; m, bh [w] [8]	*kʷ
*bʰ	bh [bʱ]	b [b]	b [b]	b [b]	b [b]; w [w] [8]	p [p]	p [p]	ph [pʰ]	f [f]; b [8]	b [b]; m, bh [m, w][8]	*β
*dʰ	dh [dʱ]	d [d]	d [d]	d [d]	d [d]	t [t]; c [c] [5]	t [t]	th [tʰ]	f [f]; d [8]; b [b] [14]	d [d]; dh [ð] [8]	*ð
_*gʰ_	h [ɦ]	z [z]	z [z]	ž [ʒ]	j [ʣ]; z [z] [8]	k [k]; ś [ɕ] [5]	k [k]	ch [kʰ]	h [h]; h [h]/g [g] [9]	g [g]; gh [ɣ] [5]	*ɣ
*gʰ	gh [gʱ]; h [ɦ] [5]	g [g]; ǰ [ʤ] [5]	g [g]; ž [ʒ] [5]; dz [ʣ]] [10]	g [g]	g [g]; ǰ [ʤ] [5]						
*gʷʰ							ku [kʷ]	ph [pʰ]; th [tʰ] [5]; ch [kʰ] [6]	f [f]; g [g] / u [w] [8]; gu [gʷ] [15]	g [g]	*ɣʷ
*s	s [s]; ṣ [ʂ] [11]	h [h, x]; s [s] [2]; š [ʃ] [11]	s [s]; x [x] [11]	s [s]; š [ʃ] [11]	h [h]; s [s] [2]; [-] [8]	s [s]; ṣ [ʂ]	š [s]	h [h]; s [s] [2]; [-] [8]	s [s]; r [r] [8]	s [s]	*s; *z [3]

***m**	m [m]	m [m]	m [m]; ˛ [˜] [13]	m [m]; n [n] [13]	m [m]; n [n] [13]	m [m]; Ø [13]	m [m]; n [n] [13]	m [m]; n [n] [13]	m [m]	b [b]; m, bh [m, w] [8]; n [n] [13]	*m; Ø [13]
***n**	n [n]	n [n]	n [n]	n [n]	n [n]	n [n]; ñ [ɲ]	n [n]	n [n]	n [n]	n [n]	*n
***l**	r [r] (dial. l [l])	r [r]	l [l]	l [l]	l [l], ɫ [ɫ > ɣ]	l [l]	l [l]	l [l]	l [l]	l [l]	*l
***r**	r [r]	r [r]	r [r]	r [r]	r [ɹ]	r [r]	r [r]	r [r]	r [r]	r [r]	*r
***i̯**	y [j]	y [j]	j [j]	j [j]	Ø	y [j]	y [j]	z [?zd/dz > z] / h [h]; Ø [8]	i [j]; Ø [8]	Ø	*j
***u̯**	v [ʋ]	v [w]	v [v]	v [ʋ]	g [g] / w [w]	w [w]	w [w]	w > h / Ø [w > h / -]	u [w > v]	f [f]; Ø / w [w] [8]	*w

III.4.2. VOWELS AND SYLLABIC CONSONANTS

PIE	PIH	Skr.	Av.	OCS	Lith.	Arm.	Toch.	Hitt.	Gk.	Lat.	O.Ir	Gmc.
***e**	*e	a	a	e	e	e	ä	e, i	e	e	e	i; ai [ɛ][2]
	*h_1e											
***a**	(*a [3])			o	a	a	ā	ha, a	a	a	a	a
	*h_2e											
***o**	*h_3e					o, a	a, e	a	o	o	o	
	*o	a, ā [4]	a, ā [4]									
***ə**	*h_1	i	i, Ø	Ø	Ø	a, Ø	ā	a	e	a	a	a, Ø
	*h_2							h	a			
	*h_3								o			
***-**	*h_1	Ø	Ø			e (a?)	Ø	a	e (o)	Ø	Ø	Ø
	*h_2					a		ha	a			
	*h_3					a		a, ha	o			
***ē**	*ē	ā	ā	ě	ė	i	a/e?; ā? [8]	e, i	ē	ē	ī	ē
	*eh_1											
***ā**	(*ā [3])			a	o	a	a (A); o (B)	a, ah	ā > ē	ā	ā	ā
	*eh_2											
***ō**	*ō				uo	u	a/ā?; ū? [8]	a	ō	ō	ā; ū [8]	
	*eh_3											
***i**	*i	i	i	ь	i	i	ä	i	i	i	i	i
***ī**	*ih_1	ī	ī	i	y [i:]		i		ī	ī	ī	ei [i:]
	*ih_2					i or (j)a? [7]	yā		ī or (j)ā? [7]			
	*ih_3								ī or (j)ō? [7]			
***ei**	*ei	ē	ōi, aē		ei, ie [5]	i	e	ei	ī	īa, ē [6]		

	*h₁ei		[4]									
*oi	*oi			ě	ai, ie[5]	e		oi	ū	oe	ai	
	*h3ei											
*ai	(*ai [3])							ay	ai	ae		ae
	*h2ei											
*ēi	*ēi	āi; ā [8]	āi; ā(i)	i					āi > ēi	ī?		ai
*ōi	*ōi (*oei)		[8]	y; u [8]	ai; ui [8]			ai	āi > ēi	ō	u [8]	
*āi	*eh2ei			ě					āi > ēi	ae		ai
*u	*u	u	u	ъ	u	u	ä	u	u	u	u; o [1]	u; au [ɔ] [2]
*ū	*uh1	ū	ū	y	ū		u		ū	ū	ū	ū
	*uh2					u or (w)a? [7]	wā		ū or (w)ā? [7]			
	*uh3								ū or (w)ō? [7]			
*eu	*eu	ō	əu, ao	ju	iau	oy	u	u	eu	ū	ūa; ō [9]	iu
	*h1eu		[4]									
*ou	*ou			u	au		ou; o, au		ou			au
	*h3eu											
*au	(*au[3])					aw			au	au		
	*h2eu											
*ēu	*ēu	āu	āu	u	iau					ū?		au
*ōu	*ōu								ō			
*m̥	*m̥	a	a	ę	im̃; um̃[14]	am	äm	am	a	em	em am	um
*m̥̄	*mH	ā	ā		ìm;ùm [14]	ama	mā		mē,mā,mō	mā	mā	
*m̥m		am	am	ьm/ъm	im;um [14]	am			am	em	am	
*n̥	*n̥	a	a	ę	iñ;uñ [14]	an	än	an	a	en	en an	un
*n̥̄	*nH	ā	ā		ìn; ùn [14]	ana	nā		nē, nā, nō	nā	nā	
*n̥n		an	an	ьn/ъn	iñ; uñ [14]	an			an	en	an	
*l̥	*l̥	r̥	ərə	lь/lъ	il̃; ul̃ [14]	al	äl	al	la	ol	li	ul
*l̥̄	*lH	īr; ūr [13]	arə		ìl; ùl [14]	ala	lā		lē, lā, lō	lā	lā	
*l̥l		ir; ur [13]	ar	ыl/ъl	il; ul [14]	al, la			al	el	al	
*r̥	*r̥	r̥	ərə	rь/rъ	ir̃; ur̃ [14]	ar	är	ar	ra	or	ri	aur
*r̥̄	*rH	īr; ūr [13]	arə		ìr; ùr [14]	ara	rā		rē, rā, rō	rā	rā	
*r̥r		ir; ur [13]	ar	ьr/ъr	ir; ur [14]	ar			ar	ar	ar	

NOTES: [1] Before *wa*. [2] Before *r, h*. [3] The existence of PIE non-allophonic *a* is disputed. [4] In open syllables (Brugmann's law). [5] Under stress. [6] Before palatal consonants. [7] The so-called breaking is disputed (typical examples are **proti-h$_3$k^{w}o-* > Ved. *prátīkam* ~ Gk. πρόσωπον; **g^{w}ih$_3$u̯o-* > Ved. *jīvá-* ~ Arm. *keank'*, Gk. ζωός; **duh$_2$ro-* > Ved. *dūrá-* ~ Arm. *erkar*, Gk.

δηρός) [8] In a final syllable. [9] Before velars and unstressed [10] Before *ā* in the following syllable. [11] Before *i* in the following syllable. [12] In a closed syllable. [13] In the neighbourhood of labials. [14] In the neighbourhood of labiovelars.

BIBLIOGRAPHY AND FURTHER READING

This work is mainly a compilation of scholar knowledge, the output of two centuries of thorough research in comparative linguistics. It is highly recommended to consult other books on IE linguistics to learn Proto-Indo-European. Google books at <http://books.google.com/> is a great tool to read some parts of any of these works and decide whether it is interesting to buy them or not.

For this specific book we have used (among other, less important references) the following works (recommended further reading in **boldface**):

- Adrados, Francisco R., Bernabé, Alberto, Mendoza, Julia. *Manual de lingüística indoeuropea I*, Ediciones Clásicas, 1995.
- Adrados, Francisco R., Bernabé, Alberto, Mendoza, Julia. *Manual de lingüística indoeuropea II*, Ediciones Clásicas, 1996.
- Adrados, Francisco R., Bernabé, Alberto, Mendoza, Julia. *Manual de lingüística indoeuropea III*, Ediciones Clásicas, 1998.
- Baldi, Philips. *The Foundations of Latin*, Mouton de Gruyter, 2002.
- Bauer, Brigitte. *Archaic Syntax in Indo-European: The Spread of Transitivity in Latin and French*, Mouton de Gruyter, 2000.
- Anthony, David W. *The Horse, the Wheel, and Language: How Bronze-Age Riders from the Eurasian Steppes Shaped the Modern World*. Princeton University Press, 2007.
- **Beekes, Robert S. P. *Comparative Indo-European Linguistics: An Introduction*, Amsterdam: John Benjamins, 1995.**
- Benveniste, Émile. *Le vocabulaire des institutions indo-européennes*. Paris: Les Editions de Minuit, 1969.
- Bryce, Trevor. *The Kingdom of the Hittites*. Oxford: Oxford University Press, 1998.
- Buck, Carl Darling. *Comparative Grammar of Greek and Latin*, Chicago: University of Chicago Press, 1933.
- Cheung, Johnny: Etymological dictionary of the Iranian verb. Brill, 2007.
- **Clackson, James. *Indo-European Linguistics: An Introduction*. Cambridge University Press, 2007.**
- Cooper, Robert L. *Language planning and social change*. Cambridge: Cambridge University Press, 1989.
- Crépin, André. *Problèmes de grammaire historique*. Presses Universitaires de France, 1978.
- Derksen, Rick: Etymological dictionary of the Slavic inherited lexicon. Brill, 2008.

- **Fortson, Benjamin W. *Indo-European language and culture: an introduction*. Wiley-Blackwell, 2004.**
- Ganesh Gadre, Vasant. *Estructuras gramaticales de hindi y español*. Madrid: CSIC, 1996.
- Güterbock, Hans G., Hoffner, Harry A. *The Hittite Dictionary, fascicle 1, volume 3*. Chicago: The Oriental Institute of the University of Chicago, 1980.
- Güterbock, Hans G., Hoffner, Harry A. *The Hittite Dictionary, fascicle 2, volume 3*. Chicago: The Oriental Institute of the University of Chicago, 1983.
- Güterbock, Hans G., Hoffner, Harry A. *The Hittite Dictionary, fascicle 3, volume 3*. Chicago: The Oriental Institute of the University of Chicago, 1986.
- Gvozdanovic, Jadranka. *Indo-European Numerals*. Mouton de Gruyter, 1991.
- Jasanoff, Jay H. *Hittite and the Indo-European verb*. Oxford University Press, 2005.
- Kerns, J. Alexander. *A sketch of the Indo-European finite verb*. Brill, 1972.
- Kloekhorst, Alwin. Etymological dictionary of the Hittite inherited lexicon. Brill, 2008.
- Krahe, Hans. *Lingüística indoeuropea*. Madrid: CSIC, 1953.
- Kortlandt, Frederik Herman Henri: *Italo-Celtic origins and prehistoric development of the Irish language*. Rodopi, 2007.
- Lazzeroni, Romano. *La cultura indoeuropea*. Bari: Gius, Laterza & Figli, 1998.
- Lehmann, W. P. *Theoretical Bases of Indo-european Linguistics*. London: Routledge.
- Lehmann, W.P. *Proto-Indo-European Phonology*. Austin: University of Texas Press and Linguistic Society of America, 1952
- Lehmann, W.P. *A Reader in Nineteenth-Century Historical Indo-European Linguistics*. Bloomington: Indiana UP, 1967
- **Lehmann, W. P. *Proto-Indo-European Syntax*. Austin: University of Texas Press, 1974**
- Lehmann, W., Zgusta, L. Schleicher's tale after a century. In *Festschrift for Oswald Szemerényi on the Occasion of his 65th Birthday*. Amsterdam: B. Brogyanyi, 1979. p. 455–66
- Lindemann, F.O. *Introduction to the Laryngeal Theory*, Oslo: Norwegian University Press, 1987.
- Lubotsky, *Alexander, Sound law and analogy: papers in honor of Robert S.P. Beekes on the occasion of his 60th birthday*, Rodopi, 1997.
- **Mallory, J.P., Adams, D.Q. *The Oxford Introduction to Proto-Indo-European and the Proto-Indo-European World*. Oxford University Press, USA, 2006 (Reprinted 2007).**
- Mallory, J.P., Adams, D.Q. *Encyclopedia of Indo-European Culture*. Routledge, 1997.
- Martínez, Javier, de Vaan, Michiel. *Introducción al avéstico*. Madrid: Ediciones Clásicas, 2001.
- Matasović, Ranko: Etymological dictionary of proto-Celtic. Brill, 2009.

- Mayrhofer, Manfred. *Indogermanische Grammatik, i/2: Lautlehre*, Heidelberg: Winter, 1986.
- Masson, Emilia. *Les douze dieux de l'immortalité*. Paris: Les Belles Lettres, 1989.
- Meid, W. *Archäeologie und Sprachwissenschaft*. Innsbruck: Institut für Sprachwissenschaft der Universität.
- **Meier-Brügger, Michael, Fritz, Matthias, Mayrhofer, Manfred. *Indo-European Linguistics*. Berlin: Walter de Gruyter, 2003.**
- Miller, Gary. *Latin suffixal derivatives in English and their Indo-European ancestry*. USA: Oxford University Press, 2006.
- Monier-Williams, Sir Monier, *A Sanskrit-English Dictionary, Etymologically and Philologically arranged*, Oxford University Press, 1899.
- Penney, J.H.W., *Indo-European Perspectives, Studies In Honour of Anna Morpurgo Davies*, Oxford University Press, 2004.
- Ramat, Anna Giacalone, Ramat, Paolo. *Le lingue indoeuropee*. Bologna: Il Mulino, 1993.
- Renfrew, Colin. *Archaeology and language: The Puzzle of Indo-European Origins*. London: Jonathan Cape, 1987.
- Ringe, Donald, et al. *A History of English: Volume I: From Proto-Indo-European to Proto-Germanic*. USA: Oxford University Press, 2006.
- Roberts, Edward A., Pastor, Bárbara. *Diccionario etimológico indoeuropeo de la lengua española*. Madrid: Alianza, 1996.
- Renfrew, Colin. *Arqueología y Lenguaje: La cuestión de los orígenes indoeuropeos*. Barcelona: Crítica, 1990
- **Rix, Helmut, (ed.) *Lexikon der indogermanischen Verben: Die Wurzeln und ihre Primärstammbildungen*, Second Edition. Wiesbaden: Dr. Ludwig Reichert Verlag 2001.**
- Sánchez Salor, E. *Semántica y sintaxis. La oración compuesta latina*. Cáceres: Universidad de Extremadura, 1993.
- Shields, K. *A history of Indo-European Verb Morphology*. Amsterdam: Benjamins, 1992.
- **Sihler, Andrew L. *New Comparative Grammar of Greek and Latin*, Oxford: Oxford University Press, 1995.**
- Szemerényi, Oswald. *Einführung in die Vergleichende Sprachenwissenschaft*. Darmstadt: Wissenschaftliche Buchgesellschaft, 1989.
- Szemerényi, Oswald. *Introduction to Indo-European Linguistics*. Oxford: Oxford University Press, 1996.
- Tovar, Antonio. *Antiguo Eslavo Eclesiástico*. Madrid: Universidad Complutense, 1987.
- Tucker, T.G., *Etymological Dictionary of Latin*, Ares Publishers, 1976
- de Vaan, Michiel, de Vaan,Michiel Arnoud Cor: Etymological dictionary of Latin and the other Italic languages. Brill, 2008.
- Villar, F. *Los indoeuropeos y los orígenes de Europa*. Madrid: Gredos, 1991.

- Wackernagel, Jacob, Langslow, David: Lectures on syntax: with special reference to Greek, Latin, and Germanic. Oxford University Press, 2009.
- Watkins, Calvert, *The American Heritage Dictionary of Indo-European Roots,* 2nd ed., Houghton Mifflin Co., 2000.
- Watkins, Calvert, *How to Kill a Dragon: Aspects of Indo-European Poetics.* Oxford University Press, USA, 2001.
- West, M.L. *Indo-European Poetry and Myth.* Oxford University Press, 2009.
- Whitney, William Dwight. *Comparative Grammar of Greek and Latin.* Delhi: Motilal Banarsidass (reprint), 1924.

ONLINE RESOURCES

- Indo-European resources and dictionary-translator at <http://indo-european.info/>, managed by the Indo-European Language Association.
- Indo-European Language Association: <http://dnghu.org/> and language resources at <http://indo-european.eu/>.
- The Linguistics Research Center (LRC), University of Texas, at <http://www.utexas.edu/cola/centers/lrc/> offers online books, lessons, texts, etc. on Proto-Indo-European and early Indo-European dialects.
- The Indo-European Etymological Dictionary (IEED) at <http://www.indo-european.nl>, managed by the Department of Comparative Indo-European Linguistics at Leiden University, with some etymological dictionaries of Indo-European dialects.
- The Tower of Babel project at <http://starling.rinet.ru>, a lexicon project oriented to Indo-European, Eurasiatic, Nostratic and other language families, with free software and PDFs for download.
- Frederik Kortlandt's personal website offers some of his publications online at <http://www.kortlandt.nl/publications/>.
- The *Thesaurus Indogermanischer Text- und Sprachmaterialien* (TITUS), at <http://titus.uni-frankfurt.de/>.
- The Digital Library *Perseus Hopper* at <http://www.perseus.tufts.edu/>.

WIKIPEDIA

Wikipedia, the *Free Online Encyclopaedia*, and Wiktionary, are excellent sources of common knowledge. We want to thank to all contributors and to their founders. Even though the appropriate policy is to reference each work and their authors, it is impossible to trace back each excerpt to its origin. These are the articles whose excerpts are identifiable in this work – especially referring to IE dialects –, in order of appearance:

Indo-European languages <http://en.wikipedia.org/wiki/Indo-European_languages>
Kurgan hypothesis <http://en.wikipedia.org/wiki/Kurgan_hypothesis>
Haplogroup R1a <http://en.wikipedia.org/wiki/Haplogroup_R1a_(Y-DNA) >
Indo-Uralic: <http://en.wikipedia.org/wiki/Indo-Uralic_languages>
Old European Hydronymy: <http://en.wikipedia.org/wiki/Old_European_hydronymy>

Germanic languages: <http://en.wikipedia.org/wiki/Germanic_languages>
Romance languages: <http://en.wikipedia.org/wiki/Romance_languages>
Italic languages: <http://en.wikipedia.org/wiki/Italic_languages>
Celtic languages: <http://en.wikipedia.org/wiki/Celtic_languages>
Proto-Celtic: <http://en.wikipedia.org/wiki/Proto-Celtic_language>
Italo-Celtic: <http://en.wikipedia.org/wiki/Italo-Celtic>
Slavic languages: <http://en.wikipedia.org/wiki/Slavic_languages>
Baltic languages: <http://en.wikipedia.org/wiki/Baltic_languages>
Balto-Slavic languages <http://en.wikipedia.org/wiki/Balto-Slavic_languages>
Messapian language: <http://en.wikipedia.org/wiki/Messapian_language>
Venetic language: <http://en.wikipedia.org/wiki/Venetic_language>
Liburnian language: <http://en.wikipedia.org/wiki/Liburnian_language>
Lusitanian language: <http://en.wikipedia.org/wiki/Lusitanian_language>
Greek language: <http://en.wikipedia.org/wiki/Greek_language>
Proto-Greek language: <http://en.wikipedia.org/wiki/Proto-Greek_language>
Armenian language: <http://en.wikipedia.org/wiki/Armenian_language>
Indo-Iranians: <http://en.wikipedia.org/wiki/Indo-Iranians>
Proto-Indo-Iranian: <http://en.wikipedia.org/wiki/Proto-Indo-Iranian_language>
Phrygian language: <http://en.wikipedia.org/wiki/Phrygian_language>
Ancient Macedonian: <http://en.wikipedia.org/wiki/Ancient_Macedonian_language>
Anatolian languages: <http://en.wikipedia.org/wiki/Anatolian_languages>
Hittite language: <http://en.wikipedia.org/wiki/Hittite_language>
Luwian language: <http://en.wikipedia.org/wiki/Luwian_language>
PIE phonology: <http://en.wikipedia.org/wiki/Proto-Indo-European_phonology>
PIE verb: <http://en.wikipedia.org/wiki/Proto-Indo-European_verb>

IMAGES AND MAPS

This is a list of Wikipedia or Wikimedia users, whose images have been used. Links are to their personal sites or to the image in particular, depending on their expressed preferences – or to ours, if not available. Reference is usually only to the latest contributor (or derivative image), unless the core work was clearly done before him/her. In order of appearance of their images:

Malene Thyssen: <http://commons.wikimedia.org/wiki/User:Malene>
Mirzali Zazaoğlu <http://en.wikipedia.org/wiki/File:Writing_systems_worldwide.png>
Brianski: <http://en.wikipedia.org/wiki/File:IE_countries.svg>
Dbachmann: <http://en.wikipedia.org/wiki/User:Dbachmann>
Crates: <http://commons.wikimedia.org/wiki/User:Crates>
Cadenas2008: <http://en.wikipedia.org/wiki/File:R1bmap.JPG>
Briangotts: <http://en.wikipedia.org/wiki/User:Briangotts>
Hayden120: <http://commons.wikimedia.org/wiki/User:Hayden120>
ZyMOS: <http://en.wikipedia.org/wiki/User:ZyMOS>
Ewan ar Born: <http://fr.wikipedia.org/wiki/Utilisateur:Ewan_ar_Born>
Fabrice Philibert-Caillat:

<http://en.wikipedia.org/wiki/File:Dédicace_de_Segomaros_(inscription_gallo-grecque).png>

Therexbanner: <http://en.wikipedia.org/wiki/File:Slavic_World.png>

Slovenski Volk: <http://en.wikipedia.org/wiki/User:Slovenski_Volk>

MapMaster: <http://en.wikipedia.org/wiki/User:MapMaster>

Alcides Pinto: <http://commons.wikimedia.org/wiki/File:Iberia_Late_Bronze.svg>

Fut.Perf. at Sunrise: <http://en.wikipedia.org/wiki/User:Future_Perfect_at_Sunrise>

Marsyas: <http://commons.wikimedia.org/wiki/User:Marsyas>

Ivanchay/Infocan:<http://ru.wikipedia.org/wiki/%D0%A3%D1%87%D0%B0%D1%81%D1%82%D0%BD%D0%B8%D0%BA:Ivanchay>

Ivaşca Flavius: <http://en.wikipedia.org/wiki/User:Scooter20>

Megistias: <http://commons.wikimedia.org/wiki/User:Megistias>

Javier Fernandez-Vina: <http://en.wikipedia.org/wiki/User:Javierfv1212>

Hendrik Tammen: <http://commons.wikimedia.org/wiki/User:Enricopedia>

BIOGRAPHY

Carlos Quiles (Badajoz, 1981), awarded best Cumulative Grade Point Average (CGPA) in the four-year Baccalaureate (1995-1999), second in the Extraordinary Baccalaureate Awards of Extremadura (1999), studied the Bachelor of Laws (LLB), Bachelor of Economics (BEc), and Bachelor of Business Administration (BBA) degrees at the Carlos III University of Madrid (1999-2005). He studied an intensive English language proficiency level course (2000) in Cambridge, and was awarded a scholarship for the best CGPA of the Faculty of Social and Juridical Sciences (2001) to study in the Middlebury College German School intensive immersion program (Advanced Grammar, Modern Literature, Culture and Society). He spent an academic year (2001-2002) at the Humboldt University of Berlin, studying BEc and BBA, as well as DSH-Oberstufenkurs, and courses in French (French Law, History and Culture studies).

He worked as trainee for a Law and Financial Services firm (2005). He published some conventional proposals and dictionaries on Astur-Leonese and Galician-Portuguese dialects, designed dozens of websites, worked as foreign language teacher, and as database and web administrator (2004-2006). He finished the LLB and BBA degrees in Catalan at the Open University of Catalonia, while studying the Licentiate degree in Medicine and Surgery at the University of Extremadura (2007-2010), obtaining it within half the time planned for the European 6-year model. He is member of Spanish Bar, works as resident in Orthopaedic Surgery in Badajoz, and leads the centre of specialized language learning at Biblos Idiomas (<www.biblosidiomas.com>). He speaks English, French, German, and Russian, understands Arabic.

Fernando López-Menchero (Madrid, 1975), studied Civil Engineering (1993-1999) in the *Escuela Técnica Superior de Ingenieros de Caminos, Canales y Puertos de Madrid* (ETSICCP), in the *Ecole Nationale des Ponts et Chaussées* (ENPC), and in the Technical University of Munich, obtaining the double degree from ETSICCP (*cum laude*) and ENPC. He pursued studies in Latin, Greek, Indo-European Languages, culture from the Classics and Archaeology (2000-2005), obtaining the degree in Classical Studies from the Complutense University of Madrid (UCM). He obtained the MSc. in Public Administration (2008-2009) from the *Instituto Universitario de Investigación Ortega y Gasset* (attached to the UCM).

Most of his professional career has been involved in the road sector in the Spanish Ministry of *Fomento*, where he works as a head of service. He has also been a member of the concession team in the international company *Acciona* (1999-2000) and a collaborator at the Professional Association of Civil Engineers (2000-2001). He has worked in Germany

(1997-1998), France (2005-2006), Luxemburg (2006), Belgium (2008) and Poland (2011) in the framework of different international programmes. He is presently participating in the VII Bellevue Programme (2010-2011) of the Robert Bosch Foundation in Warsaw. He also loves programming, especially in Fortran and Visualbasic.

He speaks French with bilingual proficiency, speaks German, English, and Italian, and is now making enormous progress in Polish. He has been a successful candidate at the EPSO/AD/142/08/OPT1 competition as a linguistic administrator with main language Spanish, and thus holds a laureate for consideration by any European Institution via EPSO.